THE OXFORD
ILLUSTRATED DICKENS

THE
OLD CURIOSITY SHOP

THE OXFORD ILLUSTRATED DICKENS

Charles John Huffham Dickens was born on 7 February 1812 at Landport near Portsmouth, where his father was a Navy pay clerk. His family moved to London in 1815 and in 1817 to Chatham, where Dickens spent the happiest time of his boyhood. This was followed by a period of misery during which his father was imprisoned for debt in the Marshalsea and Dickens was withdrawn from school and, at the age of 12, sent to work in a blacking warehouse. These experiences deeply affected him and his future work. He returned to school, and left at 15 to become a clerk, a shorthand reporter in the law courts, and a reporter of debates in the Commons. In 1833 he began contributing articles to periodicals, which were later reprinted as *Sketches by Boz* (1836–7); these led to an approach from publishers, resulting in the creation of Mr Pickwick and the publication in monthly numbers of *The Posthumous Papers of the Pickwick Club* (1836–7). In 1836 he married Catherine Hogarth; they had ten children over the next 16 years. Dickens began to publish *Oliver Twist* in 1837 in *Bentley's Miscellany*, a periodical of which he was the first editor. *Nicholas Nickleby* followed in 1838–9. *The Old Curiosity Shop* (1840–1) and *Barnaby Rudge* (1841) were intended for *Master Humphrey's Clock*, a weekly written by Dickens, but he eventually abandoned 'Master Humphrey'.

Dickens's visit to America in 1842 resulted in *American Notes* (1842) and an American section in *Martin Chuzzlewit* (1843–4). He lost readership with the latter but regained it with 'A Christmas Carol' (1843), the first of his five *Christmas Books*. In 1844 he visited Italy, and contributed 'Pictures from Italy' (1846) to the *Daily News*, a paper he founded. *Dombey and Son* appeared in 1846–8 and *David Copperfield* in 1849–50. In 1850 Dickens began the weekly journal *Household Words*, incorporated in 1859 into *All The Year Round*, which he edited until his death. In these appeared essays later issued as *Reprinted Pieces* (1858) and *The Uncommercial Traveller* (1861), and his *Christmas Stories*. *A Child's History of England* was published in 1851–3, *Bleak House* in 1852–3, *Hard Times* in 1854, *Little Dorrit* in 1855–7, *A Tale of Two Cities* in 1859, *Great Expectations* in 1860–1, and *Our Mutual Friend* in 1864–5. In 1856 Dickens bought a country house, Gad's Hill Place, near Rochester, and in 1858 he and his wife separated. He threw himself into public readings of his works, which were greatly successful but draining. His last work, *The Mystery of Edwin Drood*, was left unfinished when he died suddenly on 9 June 1870.

THE

OLD CURIOSITY SHOP

By

CHARLES DICKENS

With Seventy-five Illustrations
by Cattermole and 'Phiz'
and an Introduction by
THE EARL OF WICKLOW

OXFORD   NEW YORK   TORONTO   MELBOURNE

OXFORD UNIVERSITY PRESS

Oxford University Press, Walton Street, Oxford OX2 6DP

Oxford New York Toronto
Delhi Bombay Calcutta Madras Karachi
Petaling Jaya Singapore Hong Kong Tokyo
Nairobi Dar es Salaam Cape Town
Melbourne Auckland

and associated companies in
Berlin Ibadan

Oxford is a trade mark of Oxford University Press

The Old Curiosity Shop was first published as a serial in the weekly parts of *Master Humphrey's Clock*, from Vol. i. 37 to Vol. ii. 217 (April 1840–February 1841), with illustrations by George Cattermole and 'Phiz' (Hablot K. Browne). It was first issued in book form in February 1841.

In the Oxford Illustrated Dickens (known before 1966 as the New Oxford Illustrated Dickens) it was first published in 1951, and reprinted in 1957, 1960, 1965, 1967, 1970, 1973, 1975, 1981, 1987, 1989, 1989, 1990, 1991, 1994.

Published in the United States by Oxford University Press, USA

This volume: ISBN 0 19 254506 X
21-volume set: ISBN 0 19 254522 1

Printed in the United States of America

INTRODUCTION

By the EARL OF WICKLOW

'THE magic reel,' wrote Charles Dickens, at the beginning of the last chapter of this book, 'which, rolling on before, has led the chronicler thus far, now slackens its pace, and stops. It lies before the goal; the pursuit is at an end.' It is the pursuit that shapes the story of this book, as far as it can be said to have a clearly marked plot, ending on the ironical note that Little Nell dies as her would-be benefactor reaches her; it is the pursuit that makes this to a large extent a tale of that at which Dickens excelled, the life of the road.

The road gives their liveliest colours to a number of his other books, especially perhaps to *David Copperfield* and *Nicholas Nickleby* and of course the *Pickwick Papers*, the road with its coaches and its conversations, its inns and its drinks by the way, its pageant and its vagrants, and here we have it at its richest; it might be true to say that as an artist of the road Dickens has only two rivals among English authors, Chaucer, in many ways a kindred spirit, and, far apart from him, Rudyard Kipling, whose picture of the Grand Trunk Road in *Kim* is surely one of the best panorama pieces that English letters have produced.

One learns with amusement that to the road Edward Fitz-Gerald would have sacrificed all the rest of *The Old Curiosity Shop*, and this in the interests of children! 'He extracted the narrative of Little Nell's travels, which he called a "Nelly-ad, or Homeric narration of the child's wanderings". The abstract was made for one of his nieces. "Children," he declared, "do not understand how merriment should intrude in a serious matter. This might make a nice child's book, cutting out Boz's sham pathos, as well as the real fun." '[1]

It is a strange fact that while the Old Curiosity Shop is the best known of all Dickens relics, a pilgrimage centre for countless American visitors, in the book it scarcely features at all; at the beginning the strange couple make their escape, the terribly good little girl and her asinine old grandfather, and this completely unworldly pair are merged into the stream of English

---

[1] *The Life of Edward FitzGerald*, by A. McKinley Terhune (Oxford University Press, 1947). The 'abstract' was published in Charles Ganz's book, *A FitzGerald Medley* (Methuen, 1933).

vagrancy, till at last they come to a halt for her to die in a remote village. All this time as they wander through England, they are strangely incongruous in their surroundings, 'innocents abroad' in the fullest sense of the words, and unlike Kipling's aged Lama, they have no crafty young Kim to manage their affairs; indeed, the ironical note of the book once more makes itself heard, for when they find a protectress in Mrs. Jarley of the Waxworks, Nell has to arrange a second escape by night, to prevent her grandfather robbing the good lady so as to obtain more money for gambling, and here the irony once more, gambling to make the fortunes of his grandchild.

Here we come up against a strange quality in almost all Dickens's earlier work, the contrast between a certain unreality and mawkishness in his good characters, and the rich splashes of colour that make up the rest, whether the lurid lights and shades that delineate the villains, or the gay brilliant groups and individual portraits of the comedians; it is as if the figures of the Pre-Raphaelites and of Brueghel or Hogarth were to find themselves on the same canvas. One thinks of Ruth Pinch and Florence Dombey and Oliver Twist on one side, and on the other the intense vitality of Fagin and Mrs. Gamp, of Pecksniff and Major Bagstock, to say nothing of that fair conqueror of old age, the Honourable Mrs. Skewton.

This is specially true of the work in hand. Out of the shop emerge a rather uninteresting pair of curiosities, a doting old man who is, one hopes, too ineffectual to be truly human, and, responsible for him, a courageous but priggish and unchildlike little girl. But what a character conditions their lives, the grand demon Quilp, even more in the style of Hieronymus Bosch than of Brueghel.

Quilp is really the central figure of the story: it is owing to him that the home at the Old Curiosity Shop is broken up, and that from then on the unfortunate couple are wandering; he it is who starts the intrigue that brings about Kit's conviction, having previously introduced us to that tarnished pair, Sampson and Sally Brass; indeed, his sinister influence can be felt all through, and one always has the alarming sense that he may appear at any time, as when he was found in the congregation at Little Bethel, to reappear a few hours later when he surprised the single gentleman at the inn. It would, I think, be no exaggeration to say that when he is drowned the mainspring seems to have gone out of the tale; little Nell only survives him for a short time, and the book comes to its peaceful close.

A modern critic might put forward a rather obvious psychological theory and say that his spitefulness was caused by his deformity, that he was an unhappy thwarted character trying to get his own back on the world, for ever in rebellion against his misfortune, and suffering from what I once heard a French writer describe as *l'esprit de nain*. This theory will, I think, be found lacking in subtlety. Quilp was by no means an unhappy character, and, though cruel, was not morose; he seemed to take a positive pleasure in his appearance, and though he revenged himself on Kit for calling him 'an uglier dwarf than could be seen anywhere for a penny', he did not fail to see the joke. In his ape-like antics and gambols he clearly enjoyed performing feats that would be impossible for the normally made man. Evil as his actions were, there was about them at all times a sort of perverted gaiety, a *corruptio optimi* that was certainly *pessima*, but by no means pessimistic. Whether he was forcing his spineless wife to draw out little Nell's secret, or plotting the downfall of the unfortunate Kit, or indulging in minor acts of spite such as forcing Sampson Brass to drink scalding-hot rum and tormenting his great mother-in-law Mrs. Jiniwin, he never loses his vitriolic humour or his unquenchable *joie de vivre*.

The end of Quilp is melodramatic, but it is none the worse for that; it would, no doubt, have suited him better to be transported to Botany Bay and to have had many adventures in Australia, returning unexpectedly to terrify his wife and mother-in-law, but I do not think that would ever have suited Dickens; he liked to finish off his villains in a melodramatic and gruesome way. One thinks of the deaths of Carker and Ralph Nickleby, of Jonas Chuzzlewit and Mr. Tulkinghorn, and of that brilliantly horrible moment when Fagin makes one last effort to cheat the hangman. There is irony as well as melodrama in Quilp's death, the irony at which Dickens was an adept; having barred out his pursuers, they are thus unable to save him from drowning when he stumbles into the river.

And so the horrid, vivid, fascinating little monster leaves the story and this world as well. He does so in a lurid light and in a passage of high descriptive power:

And there it lay, alone. The sky was red with flame, and the water that bore it there had been tinged with the sullen light as it flowed along. The place the deserted carcass had left so recently, a living man, was now a blazing ruin. There was something of the glare upon its face. The hair, stirred by the damp breeze, played in a kind of mockery of death—such a mockery as the dead man himself would have delighted in when alive—about its head, and its dress fluttered idly in the night wind.

In September 1940, exactly one hundred years after Dickens was engaged on the writing of this book, the *Luftwaffe*, in their attempt to destroy the docks, kindled in this very area a gigantic fire, and one can only imagine what a tale Dickens would have built round that event, had it happened in his time.

But if Quilp was the mainspring of the story, he was not the whole of it. There are the characters of the road, Codlin and Short, with their Punch and Judy show, and the informative Mr. Vuffin, the proprietor of a giant, who so sagely remarked that 'once make a giant common, and giants will never draw again. Look at wooden legs. If there was only one man with a wooden leg, what a property he'd be!' More important still, Mrs. Jarley of the Waxworks, whom one would gladly have met more often, with her snores and her tendency to low spirits, and her righteous indignation when the odious schoolmarm, Miss Monflathers, threatened that she would 'write to the legislative authorities and have her put in the stocks, or compelled to do penance in a white sheet'. One can indeed sympathize with Mrs. Jarley feeling 'a'most inclined to turn atheist' when she thought of it!

Excellent, too, is the description of the waxworks themselves, the murderess who became Mrs. Hannah More in order to conciliate Miss Monflathers, and Mary Queen of Scots 'in a dark wig, white shirt collar and male attire', who caused no small scandal by being the image of Lord Byron; and one is duly impressed by Mrs. Jarley's contempt for her fellow traveller, Punch, 'a low, practical vulgar wretch that people should scorn to look at'.

These are in the best tradition of Dickensian comedy, as are the Brasses, the obsequious Sampson, with his pale face and red hair, who must surely have been somehow related to Uriah Heep, and his masculine sister Sally, the only person in the world respected by Quilp; she is like some evil fairy, the *Reine des Crapauds* of the French tales, her head 'invariably ornamented with a brown gauze scarf, like the wing of the fabled vampire'. Kit Nubbles and his mother are on the other hand a disappointing pair, decent and kindly enough to be sure, but as literary creations mediocre, and as G. K. Chesterton shrewdly pointed out, blemished by a 'slight strain of "meekness" or the snobbishness of the respectable poor'.[1] Probably the most interesting thing to do with Mrs. Nubbles is Dickens's intense dislike of 'Little Bethel' and all that it stood for, an institution which had a markedly depressing effect on her life.

Dick Swiveller, on the other hand, is one of the subtlest characters that Dickens ever created, and according to his biographer, Forster, was his favourite as far as this book is concerned. Dick certainly lacks all Kit's rather wearisome virtues, a fact that must have been regretted by many a creditor, but with his love of the dramatic, both in quotation and behaviour, and his delightful love-affair with the Marchioness (one of the only genuine children ever created by Dickens), he is a character as fascinating as he is funny, a man with whom it would have been a great pleasure to share a bottle of gin, even if one paid for it all oneself. He is at his best when Mrs. Nubbles faints after Kit has been convicted, and he 'takes her (after some trouble) in one arm after the manner of the theatrical ravishers'; nor should the occasion be forgotten of how he complained to the single gentleman who had remained in bed all day:

'We cannot have single gentlemen coming into the place and sleeping like double gentlemen without paying extra . . . an equal amount of slumber was never got out of one bed, and if you want to sleep like that you must pay for a double-bedded room.'

Such are the characters; of the plot, as of all plots in his earlier work, there is less to be said, for it is simple, and a little naïve here and there; it is the thread of escape and pursuit on which the characters are strung. As with Mrs. Jarley's waxworks it is the figures themselves, rather than the role they play, who really count.

A few words as to the history of the book. It was written in the years 1840 to 1841, and in the preface to the first cheap edition (1848) Dickens tells how it came to be:

The first chapter of this tale appeared in the fourth number of Master Humphrey's Clock, when I had already been made uneasy

---

[1] *Charles Dickens*, c. viii.

by the desultory character of that work, and when, I believe, my readers had thoroughly participated in the feeling. The commencement of a story was a great satisfaction to me, and I had reason to believe that my readers participated in this feeling too. Hence, being pledged to some interruptions and some pursuit of the original design, I set cheerfully about disentangling myself from those impediments as fast as I could; and, that done, from that time until its completion the Old Curiosity Shop was written and published from week to week, in weekly parts.

The idea of the story first came to Dickens during a visit to Bath, in February 1840, when he was accompanied by his wife, Forster, and Landor, but at the time he merely intended to write a tale of a few chapters; it was not till some weeks later that the full-scale novel (if novel it can be called) came into view. The published book was a great success and did much to enhance the author's reputation, especially in America, where, it appears, the sentimental parts were specially popular. Since then, Master Humphrey's Clock has remained silent in its corner, after striking a few brief notes, but the *Old Curiosity Shop*, for those prepared to set out with the doddering old man and his grandchild, continues to be the gateway to many entertaining adventures.

1950

PREFACE

IN April, 1840, I issued the first number of a new weekly publication, price three pence, called MASTER HUMPHREY'S CLOCK. It was intended to consist, for the most part, of detached papers, but was to include one continuous story, to be resumed, from time to time, with such indefinite intervals between each period of resumption as might best accord with the exigencies and capabilities of the proposed Miscellany.

The first chapter of this tale appeared in the fourth number of MASTER HUMPHREY'S CLOCK, when I had already been made uneasy by the desultory character of that work, and when, I believe, my readers had thoroughly participated in the feeling. The commencement of a story was a great satisfaction to me, and I had reason to believe that my readers participated in this feeling too. Hence, being pledged to some interruptions and some pursuit of the original design, I set cheerfully about disentangling myself from those impediments as fast as I could; and, that done, from that time until its completion THE OLD CURIOSITY SHOP was written and published from week to week, in weekly parts.

When the story was finished, that it might be freed from the incumbrance of associations and interruptions with which it had no kind of concern, I caused the few sheets of MASTER HUMPHREY'S CLOCK, which had been printed in connexion with it, to be cancelled; and, like the unfinished tale of the windy night and the notary in 'The Sentimental Journey,' they became the property of the trunkmaker and the butterman. I was especially unwilling, I confess, to enrich those respectable trades with the opening paper of the abandoned design, in which MASTER HUMPHREY described himself and his manner of life. Though I now affect to make the confession philosophically, as referring to a bygone emotion, I am conscious that my pen winces a little even while I write these words. But it was done, and wisely done, and MASTER HUMPHREY'S CLOCK, as originally constructed, became one of the lost books of the earth—which, we all know, are far more precious than any that can be read for love or money.

In reference to the tale itself, I desire to say very little here. The many friends it won me, and the many hearts it turned to me when they were full of private sorrow, invest it with an interest, in my mind, which is not a public one, and the right-ful place of which appears to be 'a more removed ground.'

I will merely observe, therefore, that, in writing the book, I had it always in my fancy to surround the lonely figure of the child with grotesque and wild, but not impossible, companions, and to gather about her innocent face and pure intentions, associates as strange and uncongenial as the grim objects that are about her bed when her history is first foreshadowed.

MASTER HUMPHREY (before his devotion to the trunk and butter business) was originally supposed to be the narrator of the story. As it was constructed from the beginning, however, with a view to separate publication when completed, his demise has not involved the necessity of any alteration.

I have a mournful pride in one recollection associated with 'little Nell.' While she was yet upon her wanderings, not then concluded, there appeared in a literary journal, an essay of which she was the principal theme, so earnestly, so eloquently, and tenderly appreciative of her, and of all her shadowy kith and kin, that it would have been insensibility in me, if I could have read it without an unusual glow of pleasure and encour-agement. Long afterwards, and when I had come to know him well, and to see him, stout of heart, going slowly down into his grave, I knew the writer of that essay to be THOMAS HOOD.

LIST OF ILLUSTRATIONS

CHARACTERS

THE BACHELOR, *a kind old gentleman residing in the village where Nell and her grandfather live for a time.*

SAMPSON BRASS, *a villainous attorney; Quilp's legal adviser.*

MR. CHUCKSTER, *a clerk in the office of Mr. Witherden.*

THE CLERGYMAN, *a very kind pastor at the village where Nell and her grandfather stay for a time in their wanderings.*

TOM CODLIN, *a puppet-showman.*

MR. GARLAND, *a little, placid-faced, kind old gentleman.*

MR. ABEL GARLAND, *his son; articled to Mr. Witherden.*

GEORGE, *driver of Mrs. Jarley's caravan.*

LITTLE NELL'S GRANDFATHER, *proprietor of the Old Curiosity Shop.*

MR. HARRIS ('*Short Trotters,*' *more familiarly* '*Short*' *or* '*Trotters*'), *a showman.*

JERRY, *proprietor of a troop of dancing dogs.*

JOE JOWL, *a gambler.*

ISAAC LIST, *a gambler and knave.*

MR. MARTON, *an old schoolmaster who befriends Little Nell.*

CHRISTOPHER NUBBLES, ('*Kit*'), *a shambling, awkward, comical lad, employed as an errand-boy by Nell's grandfather, afterwards in the service of Mr. Garland.*

JACOB NUBBLES, *brother to the preceding.*

DANIEL QUILP, *a dwarf; a sly, cunning, ferocious man.*

TOM SCOTT, *a quaint boy employed by Quilp.*

THE OLD SEXTON, *an old man at the village where Little Nell and her grandfather find a home.*

THE SINGLE GENTLEMAN, *brother to Little Nell's grandfather; Master Humphrey, the narrator of the story.*

RICHARD SWIVELLER, *an easy, careless, somewhat dissipated young man; clerk to Sampson Brass.*

FREDERICK TRENT, *brother to Little Nell.*

MR. WITHERDEN, *a brisk and pompous notary.*

BARBARA, *a housemaid at Mrs. Garland's.*

BARBARA'S MOTHER.

SALLY BRASS, *the sister of Sampson Brass.*

MRS. GARLAND, *a little old lady, the counterpart of her husband.*

MRS. JARLEY, *proprietress of* '*Jarley's Waxwork.*'

MRS. JINIWIN, *the mother of Mrs. Quilp.*

THE MARCHIONESS, *a name given to the small servant at Sampson Brass's.*

MRS. NUBBLES, *mother to Kit; a poor, industrious, pious widow.*

MRS. BETSY QUILP, *the pretty, mild-spoken wife of Daniel Quilp.*

LITTLE NELL TRENT, *a small and delicate child, of much sweetness of disposition, who lives alone with her grandfather.*

CHAPTER I

ALTHOUGH I am an old man, night is generally my time for walking. In the summer I often leave home early in the morning, and roam about the fields and lanes all day, or even escape for days or weeks together; but, saving in the country, I seldom go out until after dark, though, Heaven be thanked, I love its light and feel the cheerfulness it sheds upon the earth, as much as any creature living.

I have fallen insensibly into this habit, both because it favours my infirmity, and because it affords me greater opportunity of speculating on the characters and occupations of those who fill the streets. The glare and hurry of broad noon are not adapted to idle pursuits like mine; a glimpse of passing faces caught by the light of a street lamp, or a shop window, is often better for my purpose than their full revelation in the daylight; and, if I must add the truth, night is kinder in this respect than day, which too often destroys an air-built castle at the moment of its completion, without the least ceremony or remorse.

That constant pacing to and fro, that never-ending restlessness, that incessant tread of feet wearing the rough stones smooth and glossy—is it not a wonder how the dwellers in narrow ways can bear to hear it! Think of a sick man, in such a place as Saint Martin's Court, listening to the footsteps, and in the midst of pain and weariness, obliged, despite himself (as though it were a task he must perform) to detect the child's step from the man's, the slipshod beggar from the booted exquisite, the lounging from the busy, the dull heel of the sauntering outcast from the quick tread of an expectant pleasure-seeker—think of the hum and noise being always present to his senses, and of the stream of life that will not stop, pouring on, on, on, through all his restless dreams, as if he were condemned to lie, dead but conscious, in a noisy churchyard, and had no hope of rest for centuries to come!

Then, the crowds for ever passing and repassing on the bridges (on those which are free of toll at least), where many stop on fine evenings looking listlessly down upon the water, with some vague idea that by-and-by it runs between green banks which grow wider and wider until at last it joins the broad vast sea—where some halt to rest from heavy loads, and think, as they look over the parapet, that to smoke and lounge away one's life, and lie sleeping in the sun upon a hot tarpaulin, in a dull, slow, sluggish barge, must be happiness unalloyed—and where some, and a very different class, pause with heavier loads than they, remembering to have heard or read in some old time that drowning was not a hard death, but of all means of suicide the easiest and best.

Covent Garden Market at sunrise too, in the spring or summer, when the fragrance of sweet flowers is in the air, overpowering even the unwholesome streams of last night's debauchery, and driving the dusky thrush, whose cage has hung outside a garret window all night long, half mad with joy! Poor bird! the only neighbouring thing at all akin to the other little captives, some of whom, shrinking from the hot hands of drunken purchasers, lie drooping on the path already, while others, soddened by close contact, await the time when they shall be watered and freshened up to please more sober company, and make old clerks who pass them on their road to business, wonder what has filled their breasts with visions of the country.

But my present purpose is not to expatiate upon my walks. The story I am about to relate, arose out of one of these rambles; and thus I have been led to speak of them by way of preface.

One night, I had roamed into the city, and was walking slowly on in my usual way, musing upon a great many things, when I was arrested by an inquiry, the purport of which did not reach me, but which seemed to be addressed to myself, and was preferred in a soft sweet voice that struck me very pleasantly. I turned hastily round, and found at my elbow a pretty little girl, who begged to be directed to a certain street at a considerable distance, and indeed in quite another quarter of the town.

'It is a very long way from here,' said I, 'my child.'

'I know that, sir,' she replied timidly. 'I am afraid it is a very long way; for I came from there, to-night.'

'Alone?' said I, in some surprise.

'Oh yes, I don't mind that, but I am a little frightened now, for I have lost my road.'

'And what made you ask it of me? Suppose I should tell you wrong.'

'I am sure you will not do that,' said the little creature,

'you are such a very old gentleman, and walk so slow your-self.'

I cannot describe how much I was impressed by this appeal, and the energy with which it was made, which brought a tear into the child's clear eye, and made her slight figure tremble as she looked up into my face.

'Come,' said I, 'I'll take you there.'

She put her hand in mine, as confidingly as if she had known me from her cradle, and we trudged away together: the little creature accommodating her pace to mine, and rather seeming to lead and take care of me than I to be protecting her. I observed that every now and then she stole a curious look at my face as if to make quite sure that I was not deceiving her, and that these glances (very sharp and keen they were too) seemed to increase her confidence at every repetition.

For my part, my curiosity and interest were, at least, equal to the child's; for child she certainly was, although I thought it probable from what I could make out that her very small and delicate frame imparted a peculiar youthfulness to her appear-ance. Though more scantily attired than she might have been, she was dressed with perfect neatness, and betrayed no marks of poverty or neglect.

'Who has sent you so far by yourself?' said I.

'Somebody who is very kind to me, sir.'

'And what have you been doing?'

'That, I must not tell,' said the child.

There was something in the manner of this reply which caused me to look at the little creature with an involuntary expression of surprise; for I wondered what kind of errand it might be, that occasioned her to be prepared for questioning. Her quick eye seemed to read my thoughts. As it met mine, she added that there was no harm in what she had been doing, but it was a great secret—a secret which she did not even know, herself.

This was said with no appearance of cunning or deceit, but with an unsuspicious frankness that bore the impress of truth. She walked on, as before: growing more familiar with me as we proceeded, and talking cheerfully by the way, but she said no more about her home, beyond remarking that we were going quite a new road and asking if it were a short one.

While we were thus engaged, I revolved in my mind a hun-dred explanations of the riddle, and rejected them every one.

I really felt ashamed to take advantage of the ingenuousness or grateful feeling of the child, for the purpose of gratifying my curiosity. I love these little people; and it is not a slight thing when they, who are so fresh from God, love us. As I had felt pleased, at first, by her confidence, I determined to deserve it, and to do credit to the nature which had prompted her to repose it in me.

There was no reason, however, why I should refrain from seeing the person who had inconsiderately sent her to so great a distance by night and alone; and, as it was not improbable that if she found herself near home she might take farewell of me and deprive me of the opportunity, I avoided the most frequented ways and took the most intricate. Thus it was not until we arrived in the street itself that she knew where we were. Clapping her hands with pleasure, and running on before me for a short distance, my little acquaintance stopped at a door, and remaining on the step till I came up, knocked at it when I joined her.

A part of this door was of glass, unprotected by any shutter; which I did not observe, at first, for all was very dark and silent within, and I was anxious (as indeed the child was also) for an answer to her summons. When she had knocked twice or thrice, there was a noise as if some person were moving inside, and at length a faint light appeared through the glass which, as it approached very slowly—the bearer having to make his way through a great many scattered articles— enabled me to see, both what kind of person it was who advanced, and what kind of place it was through which he came.

He was a little old man with long grey hair, whose face and figure, as he held the light above his head and looked before him as he approached, I could plainly see. Though much altered by age, I fancied I could recognise in his spare and slender form something of that delicate mould which I had noticed in the child. Their bright blue eyes were certainly alike, but his face was so deeply furrowed, and so very full of care, that here all resemblance ceased.

The place through which he made his way at leisure, was one of those receptacles for old and curious things which seem to crouch in odd corners of this town, and to hide their musty treasures from the public eye in jealousy and distrust. There were suits of mail standing like ghosts in armour, here and there; fantastic carvings brought from monkish cloisters; rusty weapons of various kinds; distorted figures in china, and wood, and iron, and ivory; tapestry, and strange furniture that might have been designed in dreams. The haggard aspect of the little old man was wonderfully suited to the place; he might have groped among old churches, and tombs, and deserted houses, and gathered all the spoils with his own hands. There was nothing in the whole collection but was in keeping with himself; nothing that looked older or more worn than he.

As he turned the key in the lock, he surveyed me with some astonishment, which was not diminished when he looked from me to my companion. The door being opened, the child addressed him as her grandfather, and told him the little story of our companionship.

'Why bless thee, child,' said the old man, patting her on the head, 'how couldst thou miss thy way? What if I had lost thee, Nell!'

'I would have found my way back to *you*, grandfather,' said the child boldly: 'never fear.'

The old man kissed her; then turned to me and begged me to walk in. I did so. The door was closed and locked. Preceding me with the light, he led me through the place I had already seen from without, into a small sitting-room behind, in which was another door opening into a kind of closet, where I saw a little bed that a fairy might have slept in: it looked so very small and was so prettily arranged. The child took a candle and tripped into this little room, leaving the old man and me together.

'You must be tired, sir,' said he as he placed a chair near the fire, 'how can I thank you?'

'By taking more care of your grandchild another time, my good friend,' I replied.

'More care!' said the old man in a shrill voice, 'more care of Nelly! why who ever loved a child as I love Nell?'

He said this with such evident surprise, that I was perplexed what answer to make; the more so, because coupled with something feeble and wandering in his manner, there were, in his face, marks of deep and anxious thought which convinced me that he could not be, as I had been at first inclined to suppose, in a state of dotage or imbecility.

'I don't think you consider—' I began.

'I don't consider!' cried the old man interrupting me, 'I

don't consider her! ah how little you know of the truth!
Little Nelly, little Nelly!'

It would be impossible for any man—I care not what
his form of speech might be—to express more affection than
the dealer in curiosities did, in these four words. I waited for
him to speak again, but he rested his chin upon his hand,
and shaking his head twice or thrice, fixed his eyes upon the
fire.

While we were sitting thus, in silence, the door of the closet
opened, and the child returned: her light brown hair hanging
loose about her neck, and her face flushed with the haste she
had made to rejoin us. She busied herself, immediately, in
preparing supper. While she was thus engaged I remarked
that the old man took an opportunity of observing me more
closely than he had done yet. I was surprised to see, that, all
this time, everything was done by the child, and that there
appeared to be no other persons but ourselves in the house.
I took advantage of a moment when she was absent to venture
a hint on this point, to which the old man replied that there
were few grown persons as trustworthy or as careful as she.

'It always grieves me,' I observed, roused by what I took to
be his selfishness: 'it always grieves me to contemplate the
initiation of children into the ways of life, when they are
scarcely more than infants. It checks their confidence and
simplicity—two of the best qualities that Heaven gives them—
and demands that they share our sorrows before they are
capable of entering into our enjoyments.'

'It will never check hers,' said the old man, looking steadily
at me, 'the springs are too deep. Besides, the children of the
poor know but few pleasures. Even the cheap delights of
childhood must be bought and paid for.'

'But—forgive me for saying this—you are surely not so very
poor'—said I.

'She is not my child, sir,' returned the old man. 'Her
mother was, and she was poor. I save nothing—not a penny
—though I live as you see, but'—he laid his hand upon my
arm and leant forward to whisper—'she shall be rich one of
these days, and a fine lady. Don't you think ill of me, because
I use her help. She gives it cheerfully as you see, and it would
break her heart if she knew that I suffered anybody else to do
for me what her little hands could undertake. I don't consider!' he cried with sudden querulousness, 'why, God knows

that this one child is the thought and object of my life, and yet he never prospers me—no, never!'

At this juncture, the subject of our conversation again returned, and the old man motioning to me to approach the table, broke off, and said no more.

We had scarcely begun our repast when there was a knock at the door by which I had entered; and Nell: bursting into a hearty laugh, which I was rejoiced to hear, for it was child-like and full of hilarity: said it was no doubt dear old Kit come back at last.

'Foolish Nell!' said the old man, fondling with her hair. 'She always laughs at poor Kit.'

The child laughed again more heartily than before, and I could not help smiling from pure sympathy. The little old man took up a candle and went to open the door. When he came back, Kit was at his heels.

Kit was a shock-headed shambling awkward lad with an uncommonly wide mouth, very red cheeks, a turned-up nose, and certainly the most comical expression of face I ever saw. He stopped short at the door on seeing a stranger, twirled in his hand a perfectly round old hat without any vestige of a brim, and, resting himself now on one leg, and now on the other, and changing them constantly, stood in the doorway, looking into the parlour with the most extraordinary leer I ever beheld. I entertained a grateful feeling towards the boy from that minute, for I felt that he was the comedy of the child's life.

'A long way, wasn't it, Kit?' said the little old man.

'Why then, it was a goodish stretch, master,' returned Kit.

'Did you find the house easily?'

'Why then, not over and above easy, master,' said Kit.

'Of course you have come back hungry?'

'Why then, I do consider myself rather so, master,' was the answer.

The lad had a remarkable manner of standing sideways as he spoke, and thrusting his head forward over his shoulder, as if he could not get at his voice without that accompanying action. I think he would have amused one anywhere, but the child's exquisite enjoyment of his oddity, and the relief it was to find that there was something she associated with merriment, in a place that appeared so unsuited to her, were quite irresistible. It was a great point too, that Kit himself was flattered by the sensation he created, and after several efforts to preserve his gravity, burst into a loud roar, and so stood with his mouth wide open and his eyes nearly shut, laughing violently.

The old man had again relapsed into his former abstraction and took no notice of what passed; but I remarked that when her laugh was over, the child's bright eyes were dimmed with tears, called forth by the fulness of heart with which she welcomed her uncouth favourite after the little anxiety of the night. As for Kit himself (whose laugh had been all the time one of that sort which very little would change into a cry) he carried a large slice of bread and meat, and a mug of beer, into a corner, and applied himself to disposing of them with great voracity.

'Ah!' said the old man, turning to me with a sigh as if I had spoken to him but that moment, 'you don't know what you say, when you tell me that I don't consider her.'

'You must not attach too great weight to a remark founded on first appearances, my friend,' said I.

'No,' returned the old man thoughtfully, 'no. Come hither, Nell.'

The little girl hastened from her seat, and put her arm about his neck.

'Do I love thee, Nell?' said he. 'Say; do I love thee, Nell, or no?'

The child only answered by her caresses, and laid her head upon his breast.

'Why dost thou sob?' said the grandfather, pressing her closer to him and glancing towards me. 'Is it because thou know'st I love thee, and dost not like that I should seem to doubt it by my question? Well, well—then let us say I love thee dearly.'

'Indeed, indeed you do,' replied the child with great earnestness, 'Kit knows you do.'

Kit, who in despatching his bread and meat had been swallowing two-thirds of his knife at every mouthful with the coolness of a juggler, stopped short in his operations on being thus appealed to, and bawled 'Nobody isn't such a fool as to say he doesn't,' after which he incapacitated himself for further conversation by taking a most prodigious sandwich at one bite.

'She is poor now,' said the old man, patting the child's

cheek, 'but, I say again, the time is coming when she shall be rich. It has been a long time coming, but it must come at last; a very long time, but it surely must come. It has come to other men who do nothing but waste and riot. When *will* it come to me?'

'I am very happy as I am, grandfather,' said the child.

'Tush, tush!' returned the old man, 'thou dost not know— how should'st thou!' Then he muttered again between his teeth, 'The time must come, I am very sure it must. It will be all the better for coming late;' and then he sighed and fell into his former musing state, and still holding the child between his knees appeared to be insensible to everything around him. By this time it wanted but a few minutes of midnight, and I rose to go: which recalled him to himself.

'One moment, Sir,' he said. 'Now, Kit—near midnight, boy, and you still here! Get home, get home, and be true to your time in the morning, for there's work to do. Good night! There, bid him good night, Nell, and let him be gone!'

'Good night, Kit,' said the child, her eyes lighting up with merriment and kindness.

'Good night, Miss Nell,' returned the boy.

'And thank this gentleman,' interposed the old man, 'but for whose care I might have lost my little girl to-night.'

'No, no, master,' said Kit, 'that won't do, that won't.'

'What do you mean?' cried the old man.

'*I*'d have found her, master,' said Kit, 'I'd have found her. I'd bet that I'd find her if she was above ground. I would, as quick as anybody, master! Ha ha ha!'

Once more opening his mouth and shutting his eyes, and laughing like a stentor, Kit gradually backed to the door, and roared himself out.

Free of the room, the boy was not slow in taking his departure; when he had gone, and the child was occupied in clearing the table, the old man said:

'I haven't seemed to thank you, Sir, enough for what you have done to-night, but I do thank you, humbly and heartily; and so does she; and her thanks are better worth than mine. I should be sorry that you went away and thought I was unmindful of your goodness, or careless of her—I am not indeed.'

I was sure of that, I said, from what I had seen. 'But,' I added, 'may I ask you a question?'

'Ay, Sir,' replied the old man, 'what is it?'

'This delicate child,' said I, 'with so much beauty and intelligence—has she nobody to care for her but you? Has she no other companion or adviser?'

'No,' he returned, looking anxiously in my face, 'no, and she wants no other.'

'But are you not fearful,' said I, 'that you may misunderstand a charge so tender? I am sure you mean well, but are you quite certain that you know how to execute such a trust as this? I am an old man like you, and I am actuated by an old man's concern in all that is young and promising. Do you not think that what I have seen of you and this little creature tonight, must have an interest not wholly free from pain?'

'Sir,' rejoined the old man after a moment's silence, 'I have no right to feel hurt at what you say. It is true that in many respects I am the child, and she the grown person—that you have seen already. But waking or sleeping, by night or day, in sickness or health, she is the one object of my care; and if you knew of how much care, you would look on me with different eyes, you would indeed. Ah! it's a weary life for an old man— a weary, weary, life—but there is a great end to gain, and that I keep before me.'

Seeing that he was in a state of excitement and impatience, I turned to put on an outer coat which I had thrown off, on entering the room: purposing to say no more. I was surprised to see the child standing patiently by, with a cloak upon her arm, and in her hand a hat and stick.

'Those are not mine, my dear,' said I.

'No,' returned the child quietly, 'they are grandfather's.'

'But he is not going out to-night.'

'Oh yes he is,' said the child, with a smile.

'And what becomes of you, my pretty one?'

'Me! I stay here of course. I always do.'

I looked in astonishment towards the old man; but he was, or feigned to be, busied in the arrangement of his dress. From him, I looked back to the slight gentle figure of the child. Alone! In that gloomy place all the long dreary night!

She evinced no consciousness of my surprise, but cheerfully helped the old man with his cloak, and, when he was ready, took a candle to light us out. Finding that we did not follow as she expected, she looked back with a smile and waited for us. The old man showed by his face that he plainly understood the cause of my hesitation, but he merely signed to me with an inclination of the head to pass out of the room before him, and remained silent. I had no resource but to comply.

When we reached the door, the child, setting down the candle, turned to say good night and raised her face to kiss me. Then, she ran to the old man, who folded her in his arms and bade God bless her.

'Sleep soundly, Nell,' he said in a low voice, 'and angels guard thy bed! Do not forget thy prayers, my sweet.'

'No indeed,' answered the child fervently, 'they make me feel so happy!'

'That's well; I know they do; they should,' said the old man. 'Bless thee a hundred times! Early in the morning I shall be home.'

'You'll not ring twice,' returned the child. 'The bell wakes me, even in the middle of a dream.'

With this, they separated. The child opened the door (now guarded by a shutter which I had heard the boy put up before he left the house) and with another farewell, whose clear and tender note I have recalled a thousand times, held it until we had passed out. The old man paused a moment while it was gently closed and fastened on the inside, and, satisfied that this was done, walked on at a slow pace. At the street-corner he stopped. Regarding me with a troubled countenance, he said that our ways were widely different, and that he must take his leave. I would have spoken, but summoning up more alacrity than might have been expected in one of his appearance, he hurried away. I could see, that, twice or thrice, he looked back as if to ascertain if I were still watching him, or perhaps to assure himself that I was not following, at a distance. The obscurity of the night favoured his disappearance, and his figure was soon beyond my sight.

I remained standing on the spot where he had left me: unwilling to depart, and yet unknowing why I should loiter there. I looked wistfully into the street we had lately quitted, and, after a time, directed my steps that way. I passed and repassed the house, and stopped and listened at the door; all was dark, and silent as the grave.

Yet I lingered about, and could not tear myself away: thinking of all possible harm that might happen to the child—of fires, and robberies, and even murder—and feeling as if some evil must ensue if I turned my back upon the place. The closing of a door or window in the street, brought me before the curiosity-dealer's once more. I crossed the road, and looked up at the house, to assure myself that the noise had not come from there. No, it was black, cold, and lifeless as before.

There were few passengers astir; the street was sad and dismal, and pretty well my own. A few stragglers from the theatres hurried by, and, now and then, I turned aside to avoid some noisy drunkard as he reeled homewards; but these interruptions were not frequent and soon ceased. The clocks struck one. Still I paced up and down, promising myself that every time should be the last, and breaking faith with myself on some new plea, as often as I did so.

The more I thought of what the old man had said, and of his looks and bearing, the less I could account for what I had seen and heard. I had a strong misgiving that his nightly absence was for no good purpose. I had only come to know the fact through the innocence of the child; and though the old man was by at the time and saw my undisguised surprise, he had preserved a strange mystery on the subject and offered no word of explanation. These reflections naturally recalled again, more strongly than before, his haggard face, his wandering manner, his restless anxious looks. His affection for the child might not be inconsistent with villany of the worst kind; even that very affection was, in itself, an extraordinary contradiction, or how could he leave her thus? Disposed as I was to think badly of him, I never doubted that his love for her was real. I could not admit the thought, remembering what had passed between us, and the tone of voice in which he had called her by her name.

'Stay here of course,' the child had said in answer to my question, 'I always do!' What could take him from home by night, and every night? I called up all the strange tales I had ever heard, of dark and secret deeds committed in great towns and escaping detection for a long series of years. Wild as many of these stories were, I could not find one adapted to this mystery, which only became the more impenetrable, in proportion as I sought to solve it.

Occupied with such thoughts as these, and a crowd of others all tending to the same point, I continued to pace the street for two long hours; at length, the rain began to descend heavily; and then, overpowered by fatigue though no less interested than I had been at first, I engaged the nearest coach and so got home. A cheerful fire was blazing on the hearth, the lamp burnt brightly, my clock received me with its old familiar welcome; everything was quiet, warm, and cheering, and in happy contrast to the gloom and darkness I had quitted.

I sat down in my easy-chair, and falling back upon its ample cushions, pictured to myself the child in her bed: alone, unwatched, uncared for, (save by angels,) yet sleeping peacefully. So very young, so spiritual, so slight and fairy-like a creature passing the long dull nights in such an uncongenial place! I could not dismiss it from my thoughts.

We are so much in the habit of allowing impressions to be made upon us by external objects, which should be produced by reflection alone, but which, without such visible aids, often escape us, that I am not sure I should have been so thoroughly possessed by this one subject, but for the heaps of fantastic things I had seen huddled together in the curiosity-dealer's warehouse. These, crowding on my mind, in connection with the child, and gathering round her, as it were, brought her condition palpably before me. I had her image, without any effort of imagination, surrounded and beset by everything that was foreign to its nature, and farthest removed from the sympathies of her sex and age. If these helps to my fancy had all been wanting, and I had been forced to imagine her in a common chamber, with nothing unusual or uncouth in its appearance, it is very probable that I should have been less impressed with her strange and solitary state. As it was, she seemed to exist in a kind of allegory; and, having these shapes about her, claimed my interest so strongly, that (as I have already remarked) I could not dismiss her from my recollection, do what I would.

'It would be a curious speculation,' said I, after some restless turns across and across the room, 'to imagine her in her future life, holding her solitary way among a crowd of wild grotesque companions; the only pure, fresh, youthful object in the throng. It would be curious to find——'

I checked myself here, for the theme was carrying me along with it at a great pace, and I already saw before me a region on which I was little disposed to enter. I agreed with myself that this was idle musing, and resolved to go to bed, and court forgetfulness.

But, all that night, waking or in my sleep, the same thoughts recurred, and the same images retained possession of my brain.

B

I had, ever before me, the old dark murky rooms—the gaunt suits of mail with their ghostly silent air—the faces all awry, grinning from wood and stone—the dust, and rust, and worm that lives in wood—and alone in the midst of all this lumber and decay and ugly age, the beautiful child in her gentle slumber, smiling through her light and sunny dreams.

CHAPTER II

AFTER combating, for nearly a week, the feeling which impelled me to revisit the place I had quitted under the circumstances already detailed, I yielded to it at length; and determining that this time I would present myself by the light of day, bent my steps thither early in the afternoon.

I walked past the house, and took several turns in the street, with that kind of hesitation which is natural to a man who is conscious that the visit he is about to pay is unexpected, and may not be very acceptable. However, as the door of the shop was shut, and it did not appear likely that I should be recognised by those within, if I continued merely to pass up and down before it, I soon conquered this irresolution, and found myself in the curiosity-dealer's warehouse.

The old man and another person were together in the back part, and there seemed to have been high words between them, for their voices which were raised to a very loud pitch suddenly stopped on my entering, and the old man advancing hastily towards me, said in a tremulous tone that he was very glad I had come.

'You interrupted us at a critical moment,' he said, pointing to the man whom I had found in company with him; 'this fellow will murder me one of these days. He would have done so, long ago, if he had dared.'

'Bah! You would swear away my life if you could,' returned the other, after bestowing a stare and a frown on me; 'we all know that!'

'I almost think I could,' cried the old man, turning feebly upon him. 'If oaths, or prayers, or words, could rid me of you, they should. I would be quit of you, and would be relieved if you were dead.'

'I know it,' returned the other. 'I said so, didn't I? But neither oaths, nor prayers, nor words, *will* kill me, and therefore I live, and mean to live.'

'And his mother died!' cried the old man, passionately clasping his hands and looking upward; 'and this is Heaven's justice!'

The other stood lounging with his foot upon a chair, and regarded him with a contemptuous sneer. He was a young man of one-and-twenty or thereabouts; well made, and certainly handsome, though the expression of his face was far from prepossessing, having in common with his manner and even his dress, a dissipated, insolent air which repelled one.

'Justice or no justice,' said the young fellow, 'here I am and here I shall stop till such time as I think fit to go, unless you send for assistance to put me out—which you won't do, I know. I tell you again that I want to see my sister.'

'*Your* sister!' said the old man bitterly.

'Ah! You can't change the relationship,' returned the other. 'If you could, you'd have done it long ago. I want to see my sister, that you keep cooped up here, poisoning her mind with your sly secrets and pretending an affection for her that you may work her to death, and add a few scraped shillings every week to the money you can hardly count. I want to see her; and I will.'

'Here's a moralist to talk of poisoned minds! Here's a generous spirit to scorn scraped-up shillings!' cried the old man, turning from him to me. 'A profligate, Sir, who has forfeited every claim not only upon those who have the misfortune to be of his blood, but upon society which knows nothing of him but his misdeeds. A liar too,' he added, in a lower voice as he drew closer to me, 'who knows how dear she is to me, and seeks to wound me even there, because there is a stranger by.'

'Strangers are nothing to me, grandfather,' said the young fellow, catching at the word, 'nor I to them, I hope. The best they can do, is to keep an eye to their business and leave me to mine. There's a friend of mine waiting outside, and as it seems that I may have to wait some time, I'll call him in, with your leave.'

Saying this, he stepped to the door, and looking down the street beckoned several times to some unseen person, who, to judge from the air of impatience with which these signals were accompanied, required a great quantity of persuasion to induce him to advance. At length there sauntered up, on the opposite side of the way—with a bad pretence of passing by accident—a figure conspicuous for its dirty smartness, which after a great many frowns and jerks of the head, in resistance of the invitation, ultimately crossed the road and was brought into the shop.

'There. It's Dick Swiveller,' said the young fellow, pushing him in. 'Sit down, Swiveller.'

'But is the old min agreeable?' said Mr. Swiveller in an under tone.

The Child in her Gentle Slumber

(p. 14)

'Sit down,' repeated his companion.

Mr. Swiveller complied, and looking about him with a propitiatory smile, observed that last week was a fine week for the ducks, and this week was a fine week for the dust; he also observed that whilst standing by the post at the street corner, he had observed a pig with a straw in his mouth issuing out of the tobacco-shop, from which appearance he argued that another fine week for the ducks was approaching, and that rain would certainly ensue. He furthermore took occasion to apologize for any negligence that might be perceptible in his dress, on the ground that last night he had had 'the sun very strong in his eyes;' by which expression he was understood to convey to his hearers in the most delicate manner possible, the information that he had been extremely drunk.

'But what,' said Mr. Swiveller with a sigh, 'what is the odds so long as the fire of soul is kindled at the taper of conwiviality, and the wing of friendship never moults a feather! What is the odds so long as the spirit is expanded by means of rosy wine, and the present moment is the least happiest of our existence!'

'You needn't act the chairman here,' said his friend, half aside.

'Fred!' cried Mr. Swiveller, tapping his nose, 'a word to the wise is sufficient for them—we may be good and happy without riches, Fred. Say not another syllable. I know my cue; smart is the word. Only one little whisper, Fred—*is* the old min friendly?'

'Never you mind,' replied his friend.

'Right again, quite right,' said Mr. Swiveller, 'caution is the word, and caution is the act.' With that, he winked as if in preservation of some deep secret, and folding his arms and leaning back in his chair, looked up at the ceiling with profound gravity.

It was perhaps not very unreasonable to suspect from what had already passed, that Mr. Swiveller was not quite recovered from the effects of the powerful sunlight to which he had made allusion; but if no such suspicion had been awakened by his speech, his wiry hair, dull eyes, and sallow face, would still have been strong witnesses against him. His attire was not, as he had himself hinted, remarkable for the nicest arrangement, but was in a state of disorder which strongly induced the idea that he had gone to bed in it. It consisted of a brown body-coat with a great many brass buttons up the front, and only one behind; a bright check neckerchief, a plaid waistcoat, soiled white trousers, and a very limp hat, worn with the wrong side foremost, to hide a hole in the brim. The breast of his coat was ornamented with an outside pocket from which there peeped forth the cleanest end of a very large and very ill-favoured handkerchief; his dirty wristbands were pulled down as far as possible and ostentatiously folded back over his cuffs; he displayed no gloves, and carried a yellow cane having at the top a bone hand with the semblance of a ring on its little finger and a black ball in its grasp. With all these personal advantages (to which may be added a strong savour of tobacco-smoke, and a prevailing greasiness of appearance) Mr. Swiveller leaned back in his chair with his eyes fixed on the ceiling, and occasionally pitching his voice to the needful key, obliged the company with a few bars of an intensely dismal air, and then, in the middle of a note, relapsed into his former silence.

The old man sat himself down in a chair, and, with folded hands, looked sometimes at his grandson and sometimes at his strange companion, as if he were utterly powerless and had no resource but to leave them to do as they pleased. The young man reclined against a table at no great distance from his friend, in apparent indifference to everything that had passed; and I—who felt the difficulty of any interference, notwithstanding that the old man had appealed to me, both by words and looks—made the best feint I could of being occupied in examining some of the goods that were disposed for sale, and paying very little attention to the persons before me.

The silence was not of long duration, for Mr. Swiveller, after favouring us with several melodious assurances that his heart was in the highlands, and that he wanted but his Arab steed as a preliminary to the achievement of great feats of valour and loyalty, removed his eyes from the ceiling and subsided into prose again.

'Fred,' said Mr. Swiveller stopping short as if the idea had suddenly occurred to him, and speaking in the same audible whispei as before, '*is* the old min friendly?'

'What does it matter?' returned his friend peevishly.

'No, but *is* he?' said Dick.

'Yes, of course. What do I care whether he is or not?'

Emboldened as it seemed by this reply to enter into a more

general conversation, Mr. Swiveller plainly laid himself out to captivate our attention.

He began by remarking that soda-water, though a good thing in the abstract, was apt to lie cold upon the stomach unless qualified with ginger, or a small infusion of brandy, which latter article he held to be preferable in all cases, saving for the one consideration of expense. Nobody venturing to dispute these positions, he proceeded to observe that the human hair was a great retainer of tobacco-smoke, and that the young gentlemen of Westminster and Eton, after eating vast quantities of apples to conceal any scent of cigars from their anxious friends, were usually detected in consequence of their heads possessing this remarkable property; whence he concluded that if the Royal Society would turn their attention to the circumstance, and endeavour to find in the resources of science a means of preventing such untoward revelations, they might indeed be looked upon as benefactors to mankind. These opinions being equally incontrovertible with those he had already pronounced, he went on to inform us that Jamaica rum, though unquestionably an agreeable spirit of great richness and flavour, had the drawback of remaining constantly present to the taste next day; and nobody being venturous enough to argue this point either, he increased in confidence and became yet more companionable and communicative.

'It's a devil of a thing, gentlemen,' said Mr. Swiveller, 'when relations fall out and disagree. If the wing of friendship should never moult a feather, the wing of relationship should never be clipped, but be always expanded and serene. Why should a grandson and grandfather peg away at each other with mutual wiolence when all might be bliss and concord? Why not jine hands and forget it?'

'Hold your tongue,' said his friend.

'Sir,' replied Mr. Swiveller, 'don't you interrupt the chair. Gentlemen, how does the case stand, upon the present occasion? Here is a jolly old grandfather—I say it with the utmost respect—and here is a wild young grandson. The jolly old grandfather says to the wild young grandson, "I have brought you up and educated you, Fred; I have put you in the way of getting on in life; you have bolted a little out of the course, as young fellows often do; and you shall never have another chance, nor the ghost of half a one." The wild young grandson makes answer to this and says, "You're as rich as rich can be; you have been at no uncommon expense on my account, you're saving up piles of money for my little sister that lives with you in a secret, stealthy, hugger-muggering kind of way and with no manner of enjoyment—why can't you stand a trifle for your grown-up relation?" The jolly old grand-father unto this, retorts, not only that he declines to fork out with that cheerful readiness which is always so agreeable and pleasant in a gentleman of his time of life, but that he will blow up, and call names, and make reflections whenever they meet. Then the plain question is, an't it a pity that this state of things should continue, and how much better would it be for the old gentleman to hand over a reasonable amount of tin, and make it all right and comfortable?'

Having delivered this oration with a great many waves and flourishes of the hand, Mr. Swiveller abruptly thrust the head of his cane into his mouth as if to prevent himself from im-pairing the effect of his speech by adding one other word.

'Why do you hunt and persecute me, God help me!' said the old man, turning to his grandson. 'Why do you bring your profligate companions here? How often am I to tell you that my life is one of care and self-denial, and that I am poor?'

'How often am I to tell you,' returned the other, looking coldly at him, 'that I know better?'

'You have chosen your own path,' said the old man. 'Follow it. Leave Nell and I to toil and work.'

'Nell will be a woman soon,' returned the other, 'and, bred in your faith, she'll forget her brother unless he shows himself sometimes.'

'Take care,' said the old man with sparkling eyes, 'that she does not forget you when you would have her memory keenest. Take care that the day don't come when you walk barefoot in the streets, and she rides by in a gay carriage of her own.'

'You mean when she has your money?' retorted the other. 'How like a poor man he talks!'

'And yet,' said the old man, dropping his voice and speak-ing like one who thinks aloud, 'how poor we are, and what a life it is! The cause is a young child's, guiltless of all harm or wrong, but nothing goes well with it! Hope and patience, hope and patience!'

These words were uttered in too low a tone to reach the ears of the young men. Mr. Swiveller appeared to think that they implied some mental struggle consequent upon the powerful

Mr. Swiveller seeks to gain Attention

(p. 19)

effect of his address, for he poked his friend with his cane and whispered his conviction that he had administered 'a clincher,' and that he expected a commission on the profits. Discovering his mistake after a while, he appeared to grow rather sleepy and discontented, and had more than once suggested the propriety of an immediate departure, when the door opened, and the child herself appeared.

CHAPTER III

THE child was closely followed by an elderly man of remarkably hard features and forbidding aspect, and so low in stature as to be quite a dwarf, though his head and face were large enough for the body of a giant. His black eyes were restless, sly, and cunning; his mouth and chin, bristly with the stubble of a coarse hard beard; and his complexion was one of that kind which never looks clean or wholesome. But what added most to the grotesque expression of his face, was a ghastly smile, which, appearing to be the mere result of habit and to have no connection with any mirthful or complacent feeling, constantly revealed the few discoloured fangs that were yet scattered in his mouth, and gave him the aspect of a panting dog. His dress consisted of a large high-crowned hat, a worn dark suit, a pair of capacious shoes, and a dirty white neckerchief sufficiently limp and crumpled to disclose the greater portion of his wiry throat. Such hair as he had, was of a grizzled black, cut short and straight upon his temples, and hanging in a frowzy fringe about his ears. His hands, which were of a rough coarse grain, were very dirty; his finger-nails were crooked, long, and yellow.

There was ample time to note these particulars, for besides that they were sufficiently obvious without very close observation, some moments elapsed before any one broke silence. The child advanced timidly towards her brother and put her hand in his; the dwarf (if we may call him so) glanced keenly at all present, and the curiosity-dealer, who plainly had not expected his uncouth visitor, seemed disconcerted and embarrassed.

'Ah!' said the dwarf, who with his hand stretched out above his eyes had been surveying the young man attentively, 'that should be your grandson, neighbour!'

'Say rather that he should not be, replied the old man. 'But he is.'

'And that?' said the dwarf, pointing to Dick Swiveller.

'Some friend of his, as welcome here as he,' said the old man.

'And that?' inquired the dwarf, wheeling round and pointing straight at me.

'A gentleman who was so good as to bring Nell home the other night when she lost her way, coming from your house.'

The little man turned to the child as if to chide her or express his wonder, but, as she was talking to the young man, held his peace, and bent his head to listen.

'Well, Nelly,' said the young fellow aloud. 'Do they teach you to hate me, eh?'

'No, no. For shame. Oh, no!' cried the child.

'To love me, perhaps?' pursued her brother with a sneer.

'To do neither,' she returned. 'They never speak to me about you. Indeed they never do.'

'I dare be bound for that,' he said, darting a bitter look at the grandfather. 'I dare be bound for that, Nell. Oh! I believe you there!'

'But I love you dearly, Fred,' said the child.

'No doubt!'

'I do indeed, and always will,' the child repeated with great emotion, 'but oh! if you would leave off vexing him and making him unhappy, then I could love you more.'

'I see!' said the young man, as he stooped carelessly over the child, and having kissed her, pushed her from him: 'There—get you away now you have said your lesson. You needn't whimper. We part good friends enough, if that's the matter.'

He remained silent, following her with his eyes, until she had gained her little room and closed the door; and then turning to the dwarf, said abruptly,

'Harkee, Mr.——'

'Meaning me?' returned the dwarf. 'Quilp is my name. You might remember. It's not a long one—Daniel Quilp.'

'Harkee, Mr. Quilp, then,' pursued the other. 'You have some influence with my grandfather there?'

'Some,' said Mr. Quilp emphatically.

'And are in a few of his mysteries and secrets?'

'A few,' replied Quilp, with equal dryness.

'Then let me tell him once for all, through you, that I will come into and go out of this place as often as I like, so long as he keeps Nell here; and that if he wants to be quit of me, he must first be quit of her. What have I done to be made a bugbear of, and to be shunned and dreaded as if I brought the plague? He'll tell you that I have no natural affection; and that I care no more for Nell, for her own sake, than I do for him. Let him say so. I care for the whim, then, of coming to and fro, and reminding her of my existence. I *will* see her when I please. That's my point. I came here to-day to maintain it, and I'll come here again fifty times with the same object and always with the same success. I said I would stop till I had gained it. I have done so, and now my visit's ended. Come, Dick.'

'Stop!' cried Mr. Swiveller, as his companion turned towards the door. 'Sir!'

'Sir, I am your humble servant,' said Mr. Quilp, to whom the monosyllable was addressed.

'Before I leave the gay and festive scene, and halls of dazzling light, sir,' said Mr. Swiveller, 'I will, with your permission, attempt a slight remark. I came here, sir, this day, under the impression that the old min was friendly.'

'Proceed, sir,' said Daniel Quilp; for the orator had made a sudden stop.

'Inspired by this idea and the sentiments it awakened, Sir, and feeling as a mutual friend that badgering, baiting, and bullying, was not the sort of thing calculated to expand the souls and promote the social harmony of the contending parties, I took upon myself to suggest a course which is *the* course to be adopted on the present occasion. Will you allow me to whisper half a syllable, sir?'

Without waiting for the permission he sought, Mr. Swiveller stepped up to the dwarf, and leaning on his shoulder and stooping down to get at his ear, said in a voice which was perfectly audible to all present,

'The watchword to the old min is—fork.'

'Is what?' demanded Quilp.

'Is fork, sir, fork,' replied Mr. Swiveller, slapping his pocket. 'You are awake, Sir?'

The dwarf nodded. Mr. Swiveller drew back and nodded likewise, then drew a little further back and nodded again, and so on. By these means he in time reached the door, where he gave a great cough to attract the dwarf's attention and gain an opportunity of expressing in dumb show, the closest confidence and most inviolable secrecy. Having performed the serious pantomime that was necessary for the due conveyance of these ideas, he cast himself upon his friend's track, and vanished.

'Humph!' said the dwarf with a sour look and a shrug of his shoulders, 'so much for dear relations. Thank God I acknowledge none! Nor need you either,' he added, turning to the old man, 'if you were not as weak as a reed, and nearly as sense-less.'

'What would you have me do?' he retorted in a kind of helpless desperation. 'It is easy to talk and sneer. What would you have me do?'

'What would *I* do if I was in your case?' said the dwarf.

'Something violent, no doubt.'

'You're right there,' returned the little man, highly gratified by the compliment, for such he evidently considered it; and grinning like a devil as he rubbed his dirty hands together. 'Ask Mrs. Quilp, pretty Mrs. Quilp, obedient, timid, loving Mrs. Quilp. But that reminds me—I have left her all alone, and she will be anxious and know not a moment's peace till I return. I know she's always in that condition when I'm away, though she doesn't dare to say so, unless I lead her on and tell her she may speak freely, and I won't be angry with her. Oh! well-trained Mrs. Quilp!'

The creature appeared quite horrible, with his monstrous head and little body, as he rubbed his hands slowly round, and round, and round again—with something fantastic even in his manner of performing this slight action—and, dropping his shaggy brows and cocking his chin in the air, glanced upward with a stealthy look of exultation that an imp might have copied and appropriated to himself.

'Here,' he said, putting his hand into his breast and sidling up to the old man as he spoke; 'I brought it myself for fear of accidents, as, being in gold, it was something large and heavy for Nell to carry in her bag. She need be accustomed to such loads betimes though, neighbour, for she will carry weight when you are dead.'

'Heaven send she may! I hope so,' said the old man with something like a groan.

'Hope so!' echoed the dwarf, approaching close to his ear; 'neighbour, I would I knew in what good investment all these supplies are sunk. But you are a deep man, and keep your secret close.'

'My secret!' said the other with a haggard look. 'Yes, you're right—I—I—keep it close—very close.'

He said no more, but, taking the money, turned away with a slow uncertain step, and pressed his hand upon his head like a weary and dejected man. The dwarf watched him sharply, while he passed into the little sitting-room and locked it in an iron safe above the chimneypiece: and after musing for a short space, prepared to take his leave, observing that unless he made good haste, Mrs. Quilp would certainly be in fits on his return.

'And so, neighbour,' he added, 'I'll turn my face homewards, leaving my love for Nelly and hoping she may never lose her way again, though her doing so, *has* procured me an honour I didn't expect.' With that he bowed and leered at me, and with a keen glance around which seemed to comprehend every object within his range of vision, however small or trivial, went his way.

I had several times essayed to go myself, but the old man had always opposed it and entreated me to remain. As he renewed his entreaties on our being left alone, and adverted with many thanks to the former occasion of our being together, I willingly yielded to his persuasions, and sat down, pretending to examine some curious miniatures and a few old medals which he placed before me. It needed no great pressing to induce me to stay, for if my curiosity had been excited on the occasion of my first visit, it certainly was not diminished now.

Nell joined us before long, and bringing some needlework to the table, sat by the old man's side. It was pleasant to observe the fresh flowers in the room, the pet bird with a green bough shading his little cage, the breath of freshness and youth which seemed to rustle through the old dull house and hover round the child. It was curious, but not so pleasant, to turn from the beauty and grace of the girl, to see the stooping figure, careworn face, and jaded aspect of the old man. As he grew weaker and more feeble, what would become of this lonely little creature; poor protector as he was, say that he died— what would her fate be, then?

The old man almost answered my thoughts, as he laid his hand on hers, and spoke aloud.

'I'll be of better cheer, Nell,' he said; 'there must be good fortune in store for thee—I do not ask it for myself, but thee. Such miseries must fall on thy innocent head without it, that I cannot but believe but that, being tempted, it will come at last!'

She looked cheerfully into his face, but made no answer.

'When I think,' said he, 'of the many years—many in thy short life—that thou hast lived alone with me; of thy monotonous existence, knowing no companions of thy own age nor any childish pleasure; of the solitude in which thou hast grown to be what thou art, and in which thou hast lived apart from nearly all thy kind but one old man; I sometimes fear I have dealt hardly by thee, Nell.'

'Grandfather!' cried the child in unfeigned surprise.

'Not in intention; no, no,' said he. 'I have ever looked forward to the time that should enable thee to mix amongst the gayest and prettiest, and take thy station with the best. But I still look forward, Nell, I still look forward. And if I should be forced to leave thee, meanwhile, how have I fitted thee for struggles with the world? The poor bird yonder, is as well qualified to encounter it, and be turned adrift upon its mercies—Hark! I hear Kit outside. Go to him, Nell, go to him.'

She rose, and hurrying away, stopped, returned back, and put her arms about the old man's neck, then left him and hurried away again—but faster this time, to hide her falling tears.

'A word in your ear, sir,' said the old man in a hurried whisper. 'I have been rendered uneasy by what you said the other night, and can only plead that I have done all for the best; that it is too late to retract, if I could (though I cannot); and that I hope to triumph yet. All is for her sake. I have borne great poverty myself, and would spare her the sufferings that poverty carries with it. I would spare her the miseries that brought her mother, my own dear child, to an early grave. I would leave her—not with resources which could be easily spent or squandered away, but with what would place her beyond the reach of want for ever. You mark me, sir? She shall have no pittance, but a fortune—Hush! I can say no more than that, now or at any other time, and she is here again!'

The eagerness with which all this was poured into my ear, the trembling of the hand with which he clasped my arm, the strained and starting eyes he fixed upon me, the wild vehemence and agitation of his manner, filled me with amazement. All that I had heard and seen, and a great part of what he had said himself, led me to suppose that he was a wealthy man. I could form no comprehension of his character, unless he were one of those miserable wretches who, having made gain the sole end and object of their lives, and having succeeded in amassing great riches, are constantly tortured by the dread of poverty, and beset by fears of loss and ruin. Many things he had said, which I had been at a loss to understand, were quite reconcileable with the idea thus presented to me, and at length I concluded that beyond all doubt he was one of this unhappy race.

The opinion was not the result of hasty consideration, for which indeed there was no opportunity at that time, as the child came back directly, and soon occupied herself in preparations for giving Kit a writing lesson, of which it seemed he had a couple every week, and one regularly on that evening, to the great mirth and enjoyment both of himself and his instructress. To relate how it was a long time before his modesty could be so far prevailed upon as to admit of his sitting down in the parlour, in the presence of an unknown gentleman—how, when he did sit down, he tucked up his sleeves and squared his elbows and put his face close to the copy-book and squinted horribly at the lines—how, from the very first moment of having the pen in his hand, he began to wallow in blots, and to daub himself with ink up to the very roots of his hair—how, if he did by accident form a letter properly, he immediately smeared it out again with his arm in his preparations to make another—how, at every fresh mistake, there was a fresh burst of merriment from the child and a louder and not less hearty laugh from poor Kit himself—and how there was all the way through, notwithstanding, a gentle wish on her part to teach, and an anxious desire on his to learn—to relate all these particulars would no doubt occupy more space and time than they deserve. It will be sufficient to say that the lesson was given; that evening passed and night came on; that the old man again grew restless and impatient; that he quitted the house secretly at the same hour as before; and that the child was once more left alone within its gloomy walls.

And now, that I have carried this history so far in my own character and introduced these personages to the reader, I shall for the convenience of the narrative detach myself from its further course, and leave those who have prominent and necessary parts in it to speak and act for themselves.

CHAPTER IV

MR. and Mrs. Quilp resided on Tower Hill; and in her bower on Tower Hill Mrs. Quilp was left to pine the absence of her lord, when he quitted her on the business which he has been already seen to transact.

Mr. Quilp could scarcely be said to be of any particular trade or calling, though his pursuits were diversified and his occupations numerous. He collected the rents of whole colonies of filthy streets and alleys by the water-side, advanced money to the seamen and petty officers of merchant vessels, had a share in the ventures of divers mates of East Indiamen, smoked his smuggled cigars under the very nose of the Custom House, and made appointments on 'Change with men in glazed hats and round jackets pretty well every day. On the Surrey side of the river was a small rat-infested dreary yard called 'Quilp's Wharf,' in which were a little wooden count-ing-house burrowing all awry in the dust as if it had fallen from the clouds and ploughed into the ground; a few fragments of rusty anchors; several large iron rings; some piles of rotten wood; and two or three heaps of old sheet copper, crumpled, cracked, and battered. On Quilp's Wharf, Daniel Quilp was a ship-breaker, yet to judge from these appearances he must either have been a ship-breaker on a very small scale, or have broken his ships up very small indeed. Neither did the place present any extraordinary aspect of life or activity, as its only human occupant was an amphibious boy in a canvas suit, whose sole change of occupation was from sitting on the head of a pile and throwing stones into the mud when the tide was out, to standing with his hands in his pockets gazing listlessly on the motion and on the bustle of the river at high-water.

The dwarf's lodging on Tower Hill comprised, besides the needful accommodation for himself and Mrs. Quilp, a small sleeping-closet for that lady's mother, who resided with the couple and waged perpetual war with Daniel; of whom, not-withstanding, she stood in no slight dread. Indeed, the ugly creature contrived by some means or other—whether by his ugliness or his ferocity or his natural cunning is no great matter—to impress with a wholesome fear of his anger, most of those with whom he was brought into daily contact and communication. Over nobody had he such complete ascendency as Mrs. Quilp herself—a pretty little, mild-spoken, blue-eyed woman, who having allied herself in wedlock to the dwarf in one of those strange infatuations of which examples are by no means scarce, performed a sound practical penance for her folly, every day of her life.

It has been said that Mrs. Quilp was pining in her bower. In her bower she was, but not alone, for besides the old lady her mother of whom mention has recently been made, there were present some half-dozen ladies of the neighbourhood who had happened by a strange accident (and also by a little under-standing among themselves) to drop in one after another, just about tea-time. This being a season favourable to conversation, and the room being a cool, shady, lazy kind of place, with some plants at the open window shutting out the dust, and interposing pleasantly enough between the tea-table within and the old Tower without, it is no wonder that the ladies felt an inclination to talk and linger, especially when there are taken into account the additional inducements of fresh butter, new bread, shrimps, and water-cresses.

Now, the ladies being together under these circumstances, it was extremely natural that the discourse should turn upon the propensity of mankind to tyrannise over the weaker sex, and the duty that devolved upon the weaker sex to resist that tyranny and assert their rights and dignity. It was natural for four reasons: firstly, because Mrs. Quilp being a young woman and notoriously under the dominion of her husband ought to be excited to rebel; secondly, because Mrs. Quilp's parent was known to be laudably shrewish in her disposition and inclined to resist male authority; thirdly, because each visitor wished to show for herself how superior she was in this respect to the generality of her sex; and fourthly, because the company being accustomed to scandalise each other in pairs, were deprived of their usual subject of conversation now that they were all assembled in close friendship, and had consequently no better employment than to attack the common enemy.

Moved by these considerations, a stout lady opened the proceedings by inquiring, with an air of great concern and sympathy, how Mr. Quilp was; whereunto Mr. Quilp's wife's mother replied sharply, 'Oh! he was well enough—nothing much was ever the matter with him—and ill weeds were sure to thrive.' All the ladies then sighed in concert, shook their heads gravely, and looked at Mrs. Quilp as at a martyr.

'Ah!' said the spokeswoman, 'I wish you'd give her a little of your advice, Mrs. Jiniwin'—Mrs. Quilp had been a Miss Jiniwin it should be observed—'nobody knows better than you, ma'am, what us women owe to ourselves.'

'Owe indeed, ma'am!' replied Mrs. Jiniwin. 'When my poor husband, her dear father, was alive, if he had ever ventur'd a cross word to *me*, I'd have——' the good old lady did not finish the sentence, but she twisted off the head of a shrimp with a vindictiveness which seemed to imply that the action was in some degree a substitute for words. In this light it was clearly understood by the other party, who immediately replied with great approbation, 'You quite enter into my feelings, ma'am, and it's jist what I'd do myself.'

'But you have no call to do it,' said Mrs. Jiniwin. 'Luckily for you, you have no more occasion to do it than I had.'

'No woman need have, if she was true to herself,' rejoined the stout lady.

'Do you hear that, Betsy?' said Mrs. Jiniwin, in a warning voice. 'How often have I said the very same words to you, and almost gone down on my knees when I spoke 'em!'

Poor Mrs. Quilp, who had looked in a state of helplessness from one face of condolence to another, coloured, smiled, and shook her head doubtfully. This was the signal for a general clamour, which beginning in a low murmur gradually swelled into a great noise in which everybody spoke at once, and all said that she being a young woman had no right to set up her opinions against the experiences of those who knew so much better; that it was very wrong of her not to take the advice of people who had nothing at heart but her good; that it was next door to being downright ungrateful to conduct herself in that manner; that if she had no respect for herself she ought to have some for other women, all of whom she compromised by her meekness; and that if she had no respect for other women, the time would come when other women would have no respect for her; and she would be very sorry for that, they could tell her. Having dealt out these admonitions, the ladies fell to a more powerful assault than they had yet made upon the mixed tea, new bread, fresh butter, shrimps, and water-cresses, and said that their vexation was so great to see her going on like that, that they could hardly bring themselves to eat a single morsel.

'It's all very fine to talk,' said Mrs. Quilp with much simplicity, 'but I know that if I was to die to-morrow, Quilp could marry anybody he pleased—now that he could, I know!'

There was quite a scream of indignation at this idea. Marry whom he pleased! They would like to see him dare to think of marrying any of them; they would like to see the faintest approach to such a thing. One lady (a widow) was quite certain she should stab him if he hinted at it.

'Very well,' said Mrs. Quilp, nodding her head, 'as I said just now, it's very easy to talk, but I say again that I know—that I'm sure—Quilp has such a way with him when he likes, that the best-looking woman here couldn't refuse him if I was dead, and she was free, and he chose to make love to her. Come!'

Everybody bridled up at this remark, as much as to say 'I know you mean me. Let him try—that's all.' And yet for some hidden reason they were all angry with the widow, and each lady whispered in her neighbour's ear that it was very plain the said widow thought herself the person referred to, and what a puss she was!

'Mother knows,' said Mrs. Quilp, 'that what I say is quite correct, for she often said so before we were married. Didn't you say so, mother?'

This inquiry involved the respected lady in rather a delicate position, for she certainly had been an active party in making her daughter Mrs. Quilp, and, besides, it was not supporting the family credit to encourage the idea that she had married a man whom nobody else would have. On the other hand, to exaggerate the captivating qualities of her son-in-law would be to weaken the cause of revolt, in which all her energies were deeply engaged. Beset by these opposing considerations, Mrs. Jiniwin admitted the powers of insinuation, but denied the right to govern, and with a timely compliment to the stout lady brought back the discussion to the point from which it had strayed.

'Oh! It's a sensible and proper thing indeed, what Mrs. George has said!' exclaimed the old lady. 'If women are only true to themselves!—But Betsy isn't, and more's the shame and pity.'

'Before I'd let a man order me about as Quilp orders her,' said Mrs. George; 'before I'd consent to stand in awe of a man as she does of him, I'd—I'd kill myself, and write a letter first to say he did it!'

This remark being loudly commended and approved of, another lady (from the Minories) put in her word:

'Mr. Quilp may be a very nice man,' said this lady, 'and I suppose there's no doubt he is, because Mrs. Quilp says he is, and Mrs. Jiniwin says he is, and they ought to know, or nobody does. But still he is not quite a—what one calls a handsome man, nor quite a young man neither, which might be a little excuse for him if anything could be; whereas his wife is young, and is good-looking, and is a woman—which is the great thing after all.'

This last clause being delivered with extraordinary pathos, elicited a corresponding murmur from the hearers, stimulated by which the lady went on to remark that if such a husband was cross and unreasonable with such a wife, then—

'If he is!' interposed the mother, putting down her tea-cup and brushing the crumbs out of her lap, preparatory to making a solemn declaration. 'If he is! He is the greatest tyrant that ever lived, she daren't call her soul her own, he makes her tremble with a word and even with a look, he frightens her to death, and she hasn't the spirit to give him a word back, no, not a single word.'

Notwithstanding that the fact had been notorious beforehand to all the tea-drinkers, and had been discussed and expatiated on at every tea-drinking in the neighbourhood for the last twelve months, this official communication was no sooner made than they all began to talk at once and to vie with each other in vehemence and volubility. Mrs. George remarked that people would talk, that people had often said this to her before, that Mrs. Simmons then and there present had told her so twenty times, that she had always said, 'No, Henrietta Simmons, unless I see it with my own eyes and hear it with my own ears, I never will believe it.' Mrs. Simmons corroborated this testimony and added strong evidence of her own. The lady from the Minories recounted a successful course of treatment under which she had placed her own husband, who from manifesting one month after marriage unequivocal symptoms of the tiger, had by this means become subdued into a perfect lamb. Another lady recounted her own personal struggle and final triumph, in the course whereof she had found it necessary to call in her mother and two aunts, and to weep incessantly night and day for six weeks. A third, who in the general confusion could secure no other listener, fastened herself upon a young woman still unmarried who happened to be amongst them, and conjured her as she valued her own peace of mind and happiness to profit by this solemn occasion, to take example from the weakness of Mrs. Quilp, and from that time forth to direct her whole thoughts to taming and subduing the rebellious spirit of man. The noise was at its height, and half the company had elevated their voices into a perfect shriek in order to drown the voices of the other half, when Mrs. Jiniwin was seen to change colour and shake her forefinger stealthily, as if exhorting them to silence. Then, and not until then, Daniel Quilp himself, the cause and occasion of all this clamour, was observed to be in the room, looking on and listening with profound attention.

'Go on, ladies, go on,' said Daniel. 'Mrs. Quilp, pray ask the ladies to stop to supper, and have a couple of lobsters and something light and palatable.'

'I—I didn't ask them to tea, Quilp,' stammered his wife. 'It's quite an accident.'

'So much the better, Mrs. Quilp: these accidental parties are always the pleasantest,' said the dwarf, rubbing his hands so hard that he seemed to be engaged in manufacturing, of the dirt with which they were encrusted, little charges for popguns. 'What! Not going, ladies! You are not going, surely!'

His fair enemies tossed their heads slightly as they sought their respective bonnets and shawls, but left all verbal contention to Mrs. Jiniwin, who finding herself in the position of champion, made a faint struggle to sustain the character.

'And why *not* stop to supper, Quilp,' said the old lady, 'if my daughter had a mind?'

'To be sure,' rejoined Daniel. 'Why not?'

'There's nothing dishonest or wrong in a supper, I hope?' said Mrs. Jiniwin.

'Surely not,' returned the dwarf. 'Why should there be? Nor anything unwholesome either, unless there's lobster salad or prawns, which I'm told are not good for digestion.'

'And you wouldn't like *your* wife to be attacked with that, or anything else that would make her uneasy, would you?' said Mrs. Jiniwin.

'Not for a score of worlds,' replied the dwarf with a grin. 'Not even to have a score of mothers-in-law at the same time— and what a blessing that would be!'

'My daughter's your wife, Mr. Quilp, certainly,' said the old lady with a giggle, meant for satirical and to imply that he needed to be reminded of the fact: 'your wedded wife.'

'So she is, certainly. So she is,' observed the dwarf.

'And she has a right to do as she likes, I hope, Quilp,' said the old lady trembling, partly with anger and partly with a secret fear of her impish son-in-law.

'Hope she has!' he replied. 'Oh! Don't you know she has? Don't you know she has, Mrs. Jiniwin?'

'I know she ought to have, Quilp, and would have, if she was of my way of thinking.'

'Why an't you of your mother's way of thinking, my dear?' said the dwarf, turning round and addressing his wife, 'why don't you always imitate your mother, my dear? She's the ornament of her sex—your father said so every day of his life, I am sure he did.'

'Her father was a blessed creetur, Quilp, and worth twenty thousand of some people,' said Mrs. Jiniwin; 'twenty hundred million thousand.'

'I should like to have known him,' remarked the dwarf. 'I dare say he was a blessed creature then; but I'm sure he is now. It was a happy release. I believe he had suffered a long time?'

The old lady gave a gasp, but nothing came of it; Quilp resumed, with the same malice in his eye and the same sarcastic politeness on his tongue.

'You look ill, Mrs. Jiniwin; I know you have been exciting yourself too much—talking perhaps, for it is your weakness. Go to bed. Do go to bed.'

'I shall go when I please, Quilp, and not before.'

'But please to go now. Do please to go now,' said the dwarf.

The old woman looked angrily at him, but retreated as he advanced, and falling back before him suffered him to shut the door upon her and bolt her out among the guests, who were by this time crowding down stairs. Being left alone with his wife, who sat trembling in a corner with her eyes fixed upon the ground, the little man planted himself before her, at some distance, and folding his arms looked steadily at her for a long time without speaking.

'Oh you nice creature!' were the words with which he broke silence; smacking his lips as if this were no figure of speech, and she were actually a sweetmeat. 'Oh you precious darling! oh you de-licious charmer!'

Mrs. Quilp sobbed; and knowing the nature of her pleasant lord, appeared quite as much alarmed by these compliments, as she would have been by the most extreme demonstrations of violence.

'She's such,' said the dwarf, with a ghastly grin,—'such a jewel, such a diamond, such a pearl, such a ruby, such a golden casket set with gems of all sorts! She's such a treasure! I'm so fond of her!'

The poor little woman shivered from head to foot; and raising her eyes to his face with an imploring look, suffered them to droop again, and sobbed once more.

'The best of her is,' said the dwarf, advancing with a sort of skip, which, what with the crookedness of his legs, the ugliness of his face, and the mockery of his manner, was perfectly goblin-like;—'the best of her is that she's so meek, and she's so mild, and she never has a will of her own, and she has such an insinuating mother!'

Uttering these latter words with a gloating maliciousness, within a hundred degrees of which no one but himself could possibly approach, Mr. Quilp planted his two hands on his knees, and straddling his legs out very wide apart, stooped slowly down, and down, and down, until, by screwing his head very much on one side, he came between his wife's eyes and the floor.

'Mrs. Quilp!'

'Yes, Quilp.'

'Am I nice to look at? Should I be the handsomest creature in the world if I had but whiskers? Am I quite a lady's man as it is?—am I, Mrs. Quilp?'

Mrs. Quilp dutifully replied, 'Yes, Quilp;' and fascinated by his gaze, remained looking timidly at him, while he treated her with a succession of such horrible grimaces, as none but himself and nightmares had the power of assuming. During the whole of this performance, which was somewhat of the longest, he preserved a dead silence, except when, by an unexpected skip or leap, he made his wife start backward with an irrepressible shriek. Then he chuckled.

'Mrs. Quilp,' he said at last.

'Yes, Quilp,' she meekly replied.

Instead of pursuing the theme he had in his mind, Quilp rose, folded his arms again, and looked at her more sternly than before, while she averted her eyes and kept them on the ground.

Quilp interrupts at Tea
(p. 34)

'Mrs. Quilp.'

'Yes, Quilp.'

'If ever you listen to these beldames again, I'll bite you.'

With this laconic threat, which he accompanied with a snarl that gave him the appearance of being particularly in earnest, Mr. Quilp bade her clear the teaboard away, and bring the rum. The spirit being set before him in a huge case-bottle, which had originally come out of some ship's locker, he ordered cold water and the box of cigars; and these being supplied, he settled himself in an arm-chair with his large head and face squeezed up against the back, and his little legs planted on the table.

'Now, Mrs. Quilp,' he said; 'I feel in a smoking humour, and shall probably blaze away all night. But sit where you are, if you please, in case I want you.'

His wife returned no other reply than the customary 'Yes, Quilp,' and the small lord of the creation took his first cigar and mixed his first glass of grog. The sun went down and the stars peeped out, the Tower turned from its own proper colours to grey and from grey to black, the room became perfectly dark and the end of the cigar a deep fiery red, but still Mr. Quilp went on smoking and drinking in the same position, and staring listlessly out of the window with the dog-like smile always on his face, save when Mrs. Quilp made some involuntary movement of restlessness or fatigue; and then it expanded into a grin of delight.

CHAPTER V

WHETHER Mr. Quilp took any sleep by snatches of a few winks at a time, or whether he sat with his eyes wide open all night long, certain it is that he kept his cigar alight, and kindled every fresh one from the ashes of that which was nearly consumed, without requiring the assistance of a candle. Nor did the striking of the clocks, hour after hour, appear to inspire him with any sense of drowsiness or any natural desire to go to rest; but rather to increase his wakefulness, which he showed, at every such indication of the progress of the night, by a suppressed cackling in his throat, and a motion of his shoulders, like one who laughs heartily, but at the same time slily and by stealth.

At length the day broke, and poor Mrs. Quilp, shivering with the cold of early morning and harassed by fatigue and want of sleep, was discovered sitting patiently on her chair, raising her eyes at intervals in mute appeal to the compassion and clemency of her lord, and gently reminding him by an occasional cough that she was still unpardoned and that her penance had been of long duration. But her dwarfish spouse still smoked his cigar and drank his rum without heeding her; and it was not until the sun had some time risen, and the activity and noise of city day were rife in the street, that he deigned to recognise her presence by any word or sign. He might not have done so even then, but for certain impatient tappings at the door which seemed to denote that some pretty hard knuckles were actively engaged upon the other side.

'Why dear me!' he said, looking round with a malicious grin, 'it's day! open the door, sweet Mrs. Quilp!'

His obedient wife withdrew the bolt, and her lady mother entered.

Now, Mrs. Jiniwin pounced into the room with great impetuosity; for, supposing her son-in-law to be still a-bed, she had come to relieve her feelings by pronouncing a strong opinion upon his general conduct and character. Seeing that he was up and dressed, and that the room appeared to have been occupied ever since she quitted it on the previous evening, she stopped short, in some embarrassment.

Nothing escaped the hawk's eye of the ugly little man, who, perfectly understanding what passed in the old lady's mind, turned uglier still in the fulness of his satisfaction, and bade her good morning, with a leer of triumph.

'Why, Betsy,' said the old woman, 'you haven't been a— you don't mean to say you've been a—'

'Sitting up all night?' said Quilp, supplying the conclusion of the sentence. 'Yes she has!'

'All night!' cried Mrs. Jiniwin.

'Aye, all night. Is the dear old lady deaf?' said Quilp, with a smile of which a frown was part. 'Who says man and wife are bad company? Ha ha! The time has flown.'

'You're a brute!' exclaimed Mrs. Jiniwin.

'Come, come,' said Quilp, wilfully misunderstanding her, of course, 'you mustn't call her names. She's married now, you know. And though she *did* beguile the time and keep me from my bed, you must not be so tenderly careful of me as to be out of humour with her. Bless you for a dear old lady. Here's your health!'

'I am *much* obliged to you,' returned the old woman, testifying by a certain restlessness in her hands a vehement desire to shake her matronly fist at her son-in-law. 'Oh! I'm very much obliged to you!'

'Grateful soul!' cried the dwarf. 'Mrs. Quilp.'

'Yes, Quilp,' said the timid sufferer.

'Help your mother to get breakfast, Mrs. Quilp. I am going to the wharf this morning—the earlier, the better, so be quick.'

Mrs. Jiniwin made a faint demonstration of rebellion by sitting down in a chair near the door and folding her arms as if in a resolute determination to do nothing. But a few whispered words from her daughter, and a kind inquiry from her son-in-law whether she felt faint, with a hint that there was abundance of cold water in the next apartment, routed these symptoms effectually, and she applied herself to the prescribed preparations with sullen diligence.

While they were in progress, Mr. Quilp withdrew to the adjoining room, and, turning back his coat-collar, proceeded to smear his countenance with a damp towel of very unwholesome appearance, which made his complexion rather more cloudy than it had been before. But, while he was thus engaged, his caution and inquisitiveness did not forsake him. With a face as sharp and cunning as ever, he often stopped, even in this short process, and stood listening for any conversation in the next room, of which he might be the theme.

C

'Ah!' he said after a short effort of attention, 'it was not the towel over my ears, I thought it wasn't. I'm a little hunchy villain and a monster, am I, Mrs. Jiniwin? Oh!'

The pleasure of this discovery called up the old dog-like smile in full force. When he had quite done with it, he shook himself in a very dog-like manner, and rejoined the ladies.

Mr. Quilp now walked up to the front of a looking-glass, and was standing there, putting on his neckerchief, when Mrs. Jiniwin, happening to be behind him, could not resist the inclination she felt to shake her fist at her tyrant son-in-law. It was the gesture of an instant, but as she did so and accompanied the action with a menacing look, she met his eye in the glass, catching her in the very act. The same glance at the mirror conveyed to her the reflection of a horribly grotesque and distorted face with the tongue lolling out: and the next instant the dwarf, turning about, with a perfectly bland and placid look, inquired in a tone of great affection,

'How are you now, my dear old darling?'

Slight and ridiculous as the incident was, it made him appear such a little fiend, and withal such a keen and knowing one, that the old woman felt too much afraid of him to utter a single word, and suffered herself to be led with extraordinary politeness to the breakfast-table. Here, he by no means diminished the impression he had just produced, for he ate hard eggs, shell and all, devoured gigantic prawns with the heads and tails on, chewed tobacco and water-cresses at the same time and with extraordinary greediness, drank boiling tea without winking, bit his fork and spoon till they bent again, and in short performed so many horrifying and uncommon acts that the women were nearly frightened out of their wits and began to doubt if he were really a human creature. At last, having gone through these proceedings and many others which were equally a part of his system, Mr. Quilp left them, reduced to a very obedient and humbled state, and betook himself to the river-side, where he took boat for the wharf on which he had bestowed his name.

It was flood tide when Daniel Quilp sat himself down in the wherry to cross to the opposite shore. A fleet of barges were coming lazily on, some sideways, some head first, some stern first; all in a wrong-headed, dogged, obstinate way, bumping up against the larger craft, running under the bows of steamboats, getting into every kind of nook and corner where they

Quilp's Wharf

Welcome to Jefferson Co PL -
Madison Main Branch!
You checked out the following items:

1. The soul of sex : cultivating
   life as an act of love
   Barcode: 39391000615524
   Due: 2017-07-06 11:59 PM
2. From a distance
   Barcode: 39391006028813
   Due: 2017-07-06 11:59 PM
3. An untamed land
   Barcode: 39391006143018
   Due: 2017-07-06 11:59 PM
4. The old curiosity shop
   Barcode: 39391000148856
   Due: 2017-07-06 11:59 PM

JFFCO-MAD 2017-06-15 14:34
You were helped by Joy

had no business, and being crunched on all sides like so many walnut shells; while each, with its pair of long sweeps struggling and splashing in the water, looked like some lumbering fish in pain. In some of the vessels at anchor all hands were busily engaged in coiling ropes, spreading out sails to dry, taking in or discharging their cargoes; in others, no life was visible but two or three tarry boys, and perhaps a barking dog running to and fro upon the deck or scrambling up to look over the side and bark the louder for the view. Coming slowly on through the forests of masts, was a great steamship, beating the water in short impatient strokes with her heavy paddles, as though she wanted room to breathe, and advancing in her huge bulk like a sea-monster among the minnows of the Thames. On either hand, were long black tiers of colliers; between them, vessels slowly working out of harbour with sails glistening in the sun, and creaking noise on board, re-echoed from a hundred quarters. The water and all upon it was in active motion, dancing and buoyant and bubbling up; while the old grey Tower and piles of building on the shore, with many a church-spire shooting up between, looked coldly on, and seemed to disdain their chafing neighbour.

Daniel Quilp, who was not much affected by a bright morning save in so far as it spared him the trouble of carrying an umbrella, caused himself to be put ashore hard by the wharf, and proceeded thither, through a narrow lane which, partaking of the amphibious character of its frequenters, had as much water as mud in its composition, and a very liberal supply of both. Arrived at his destination, the first object that presented itself to his view was a pair of very imperfectly shod feet elevated in the air with the soles upwards, which remarkable appearance was referable to the boy, who being of an eccentric spirit and having a natural taste for tumbling was now standing on his head and contemplating the aspect of the river under these uncommon circumstances. He was speedily brought on his heels by the sound of his master's voice, and as soon as his head was in its right position, Mr. Quilp, to speak expressively in the absence of a better verb, 'punched it' for him.

'Come, you let me alone,' said the boy, parrying Quilp's hand with both his elbows alternately. 'You'll get something you won't like if you don't, and so I tell you.'

'You dog,' snarled Quilp, 'I'll beat you with an iron rod,

I'll scratch you with a rusty nail, I'll pinch your eyes, if you talk to me. I will!'

With these threats he clenched his hand again, and dexterously diving in between the elbows and catching the boy's head as it dodged from side to side, gave it three or four good hard knocks. Having now carried his point and insisted on it, he left off.

'You won't do it again,' said the boy, nodding his head and drawing back, with the elbows ready in case of the worst; 'now!'

'Stand still, you dog,' said Quilp. 'I won't do it again, because I've done it as often as I want. Here. Take the key.'

'Why don't you hit one of your size?' said the boy, approaching very slowly.

'Where is there one of my size, you dog?' returned Quilp. 'Take the key, or I'll brain you with it.' Indeed he gave him a smart tap with the handle as he spoke. 'Now, open the counting-house.'

The boy sulkily complied, muttering at first, but desisting when he looked round and saw that Quilp was following him with a steady look. And here it may be remarked, that between this boy and the dwarf there existed a strange kind of mutual liking. How born or bred, or how nourished upon blows and threats on one side, and retorts and defiances on the other, is not to the purpose. Quilp would certainly suffer nobody to contradict him but the boy, and the boy would assuredly not have submitted to be so knocked about by anybody but Quilp, when he had the power to run away at any time he chose.

'Now,' said Quilp, passing into the wooden counting-house, 'you mind the wharf. Stand upon your head again, and I'll cut one of your feet off.'

The boy made no answer, but directly Quilp had shut himself in, stood on his head before the door, then walked on his hands to the back and stood on his head there, and then to the opposite side and repeated the performance. There were, indeed, four sides to the counting-house, but he avoided that one where the window was, deeming it probable that Quilp would be looking out of it. This was prudent, for in point of fact the dwarf, knowing his disposition, was lying in wait at a little distance from the sash armed with a large piece of wood, which, being rough and jagged and studded in many parts with broken nails, might possibly have hurt him.

It was a dirty little box, this counting-house, with nothing in it but an old rickety desk and two stools, a hat-peg, an ancient almanack, an inkstand with no ink and the stump of one pen, and an eight-day clock which hadn't gone for eighteen years at least, and of which the minute hand had been twisted off for a toothpick. Daniel Quilp pulled his hat over his brows, climbed on to the desk (which had a flat top), and stretching his short length upon it went to sleep with the ease of an old practitioner; intending, no doubt, to compensate himself for the deprivation of last night's rest, by a long and sound nap.

Sound it might have been, but long it was not, for he had not been asleep a quarter of an hour when the boy opened the door and thrust in his head, which was like a bundle of badly-picked oakum. Quilp was a light sleeper and started up directly.

'Here's somebody for you,' said the boy.

'Who?'

'I don't know.'

'Ask!' said Quilp, seizing the trifle of wood before-mentioned and throwing it at him with such dexterity that it was well the boy disappeared before it reached the spot on which he had stood. 'Ask, you dog.'

Not caring to venture within range of such missiles again, the boy discreetly sent, in his stead, the first cause of the interruption, who now presented herself at the door.

'What, Nelly!' cried Quilp.

'Yes,' said the child, hesitating whether to enter or retreat, for the dwarf just roused, with his dishevelled hair hanging all about him, and a yellow handkerchief over his head, was something fearful to behold; 'it's only me, sir.'

'Come in,' said Quilp, without getting off the desk. 'Come in. Stay. Just look out into the yard, and see whether there's a boy standing on his head.'

'No, sir,' replied Nell. 'He's on his feet.'

'You're sure he is?' said Quilp. 'Well. Now come in and shut the door. What's your message, Nelly?'

The child handed him a letter; Mr. Quilp, without changing his position otherwise than to turn over a little more on his side and rest his chin on his hand, proceeded to make himself acquainted with its contents.

CHAPTER VI

LITTLE NELL stood timidly by, with her eyes raised to the countenance of Mr. Quilp, as he read the letter, plainly showing by her looks that while she entertained some fear and distrust of the little man, she was much inclined to laugh at his uncouth appearance and grotesque attitude. And yet, there was visible on the part of the child a painful anxiety for his reply, and a consciousness of his power to render it disagreeable or distressing, which was strongly at variance with this impulse and restrained it more effectually than she could possibly have done by any efforts of her own.

That Mr. Quilp was himself perplexed, and that in no small degree, by the contents of the letter, was sufficiently obvious. Before he had got through the first two or three lines he began to open his eyes very wide and to frown most horribly, the next two or three caused him to scratch his head in an uncommonly vicious manner, and when he came to the conclusion he gave a long dismal whistle indicative of surprise and dismay. After folding and laying it down beside him, he bit the nails of all his ten fingers with extreme voracity; and taking it up sharply, read it again. The second perusal was to all appearance as unsatisfactory as the first, and plunged him into a profound reverie from which he awakened to another assault upon his nails and a long stare at the child, who with her eyes turned towards the ground awaited his further pleasure.

'Halloa here!' he said at length, in a voice, and with a suddenness, which made the child start as though a gun had been fired off at her ear. 'Nelly!'

'Yes, sir.'

'Do you know what's inside this letter, Nell?'

'No, sir!'

'Are you sure, quite sure, quite certain, upon your soul?'

'Quite sure, sir.'

'Do you wish you may die if you do know, hey?' said the dwarf.

'Indeed I don't know,' returned the child.

'Well!' muttered Quilp as he marked her earnest look. 'I believe you. Humph! Gone already! Gone in four-and-twenty hours. What the devil has he done with it? That's the mystery!'

This reflection set him scratching his head, and biting his nails, once more. While he was thus employed his features gradually relaxed into what was with him a cheerful smile, but which in any other man would have been a ghastly grin of pain; and when the child looked up again she found that he was regarding her with extraordinary favour and complacency.

'You look very pretty to-day, Nelly, charmingly pretty. Are you tired, Nelly?'

'No, sir. I'm in a hurry to get back, for he will be anxious while I am away.'

'There's no hurry, little Nell, no hurry at all,' said Quilp. 'How should you like to be my number two, Nelly?'

'To be what, sir?'

'My number two, Nelly; my second; my Mrs. Quilp,' said the dwarf.

The child looked frightened, but seemed not to understand him, which Mr. Quilp observing, hastened to explain his meaning more distinctly.

'To be Mrs. Quilp the second, when Mrs. Quilp the first is dead, sweet Nell,' said Quilp, wrinkling up his eyes and luring her towards him with his bent forefinger, 'to be my wife, my little cherry-cheeked, red-lipped wife. Say that Mrs. Quilp lives five years, or only four, you'll be just the proper age for me. Ha ha! Be a good girl, Nelly, a very good girl, and see if one of these days you don't come to be Mrs. Quilp of Tower Hill.'

So far from being sustained and stimulated by this delightful prospect, the child shrunk from him, and trembled. Mr. Quilp, either because frightening anybody afforded him a constitutional delight, or because it was pleasant to contemplate the death of Mrs. Quilp number one, and the elevation of Mrs. Quilp number two to her post and title, or because he was determined for purposes of his own to be agreeable and good-humoured at that particular time, only laughed and feigned to take no heed of her alarm.

'You shall come with me to Tower Hill, and see Mrs. Quilp, that is, directly,' said the dwarf. 'She's very fond of you, Nell, though not so fond as I am. You shall come home with me.'

'I must go back indeed,' said the child. 'He told me to return directly I had the answer.'

'But you haven't it, Nelly,' retorted the dwarf, 'and won't have it, and can't have it, until I have been home, so you see that to do your errand, you must go with me. Reach me yonder hat, my dear, and we'll go directly.' With that, Mr. Quilp suffered himself to roll gradually off the desk until his short legs touched the ground, when he got upon them and led the way from the counting-house to the wharf outside, where the first objects that presented themselves were the boy who had stood on his head and another young gentleman of about his own stature, rolling in the mud together, locked in a tight embrace, and cuffing each other with mutual heartiness.

'It's Kit!' cried Nelly, clasping her hands, 'poor Kit who came with me! oh pray stop them, Mr. Quilp!'

'I'll stop 'em,' cried Quilp, diving into the little counting-house and returning with a thick stick, 'I'll stop 'em. Now, my boys, fight away. I'll fight you both. I'll take both of you, both together, both together!'

With which defiances the dwarf flourished his cudgel, and dancing round the combatants and treading upon them and skipping over them, in a kind of frenzy, laid about him, now on one and now on the other, in a most desperate manner, always aiming at their heads and dealing such blows as none but the veriest little savage would have inflicted. This being warmer work than they had calculated upon, speedily cooled the courage of the belligerents, who scrambled to their feet and called for quarter.

'I'll beat you to a pulp, you dogs,' said Quilp, vainly endeavouring to get near either of them for a parting blow. 'I'll bruise you till you're copper-coloured, I'll break your faces till you haven't a profile between you, I will.'

'Come, you drop that stick or it'll be worse for you,' said his boy, dodging round him and watching an opportunity to rush in: 'you drop that stick.'

'Come a little nearer, and I'll drop it on your skull, you dog,' said Quilp with gleaming eyes: 'a little nearer; nearer yet.'

But the boy declined the invitation until his master was apparently a little off his guard, when he darted in and seizing the weapon tried to wrest it from his grasp. Quilp, who was as strong as a lion, easily kept his hold until the boy was tugging at it with his utmost power, when he suddenly let it go and sent him reeling backwards, so that he fell violently upon his head. The success of this manœuvre tickled Mr. Quilp beyond description, and he laughed and stamped upon the ground as at a most irresistible jest.

'Never mind,' said the boy, nodding his head and rubbing it at the same time; 'you see if ever I offer to strike anybody again because they say you're a uglier dwarf than can be seen anywheres for a penny, that's all.'

'Do you mean to say, I'm not, you dog?' returned Quilp.

'No!' retorted the boy.

'Then what do you fight on my wharf for, you villain?' said Quilp.

'Because he said so,' replied the boy, pointing to Kit, 'not because you an't.'

'Then why did he say,' bawled Kit, 'that Miss Nelly was ugly, and that she and my master was obliged to do whatever his master liked? Why did he say that?'

'He said what he did because he's a fool, and you said what you did because you're very wise and clever—almost too clever to live, unless you're very careful of yourself, Kit,' said Quilp with great suavity in his manner, but still more of quiet malice about his eyes and mouth. 'Here's sixpence for you, Kit. Always speak the truth. At all times, Kit, speak the truth. Lock the counting-house, you dog, and bring me the key.'

The other boy, to whom this order was addressed, did as he was told, and was rewarded for his partisanship in behalf of his master, by a dexterous rap on the nose with the key, which brought the water into his eyes. Then, Mr. Quilp departed, with the child and Kit in a boat, and the boy revenged himself by dancing on his head at intervals on the extreme verge of the wharf, during the whole time they crossed the river.

There was only Mrs. Quilp at home, and she, little expecting the return of her lord, was just composing herself for a refreshing slumber when the sound of his footsteps roused her. She had barely time to seem to be occupied in some needlework, when he entered, accompanied by the child; having left Kit down stairs.

'Here's Nelly Trent, dear Mrs. Quilp,' said her husband. 'A glass of wine, my dear, and a biscuit, for she has had a long walk. She'll sit with you, my soul, while I write a letter.'

Mrs. Quilp looked tremblingly in her spouse's face to know what this unusual courtesy might portend, and obedient to the summons she saw in his gesture, followed him into the next room.

'Mind what I say to you,' whispered Quilp. 'See if you can get out of her anything about her grandfather, or what they do, or how they live, or what he tells her. I've my reasons for knowing, if I can. You women talk more freely to one another than you do to us, and you have a soft, mild way with you that'll win upon her. Do you hear?'

'Yes, Quilp.'

'Go, then. What's the matter now?'

'Dear Quilp,' faltered his wife, 'I love the child—if you *could* do without making me deceive her——'

The dwarf muttering a terrible oath looked round as if for some weapon with which to inflict condign punishment upon his disobedient wife. The submissive little woman hurriedly entreated him not to be angry, and promised to do as he bade her.

'Do you hear me?' whispered Quilp, nipping and pinching her arm; 'worm yourself into her secrets; I know you can. I'm listening, recollect. If you're not sharp enough I'll creak the door, and woe betide you if I have to creak it much. Go!'

Mrs. Quilp departed according to order. Her amiable husband, ensconcing himself behind the partly opened door, and applying his ear close to it, began to listen with a face of great craftiness and attention.

Poor Mrs. Quilp was thinking, however, in what manner to begin or what kind of inquiries she could make; it was not until the door, creaking in a very urgent manner, warned her to proceed without further consideration, that the sound of her voice was heard.

'How very often you have come backwards and forwards lately to Mr. Quilp, my dear.'

'I have said so to grandfather, a hundred times,' returned Nell innocently.

'And what has he said to that?'

'Only sighed, and dropped his head, and seemed so sad and wretched that if you could have seen him I am sure you must have cried; you could not have helped it more than I, I know. How that door creaks!'

'It often does,' returned Mrs. Quilp with an uneasy glance towards it. 'But your grandfather—he used not to be so wretched?'

'Oh no!' said the child eagerly, 'so different! we were once so happy and he so cheerful and contented! You cannot think what a sad change has fallen on us, since.'

'I am very, very sorry, to hear you speak like this, my dear!' said Mrs. Quilp. And she spoke the truth.

Little Nell is anxious

(p. 44)

'Thank you,' returned the child, kissing her cheek, 'you are always kind to me, and it is a pleasure to talk to you. I can speak to no one else about him, but poor Kit. I am very happy, still I ought to feel happier perhaps than I do, but you cannot think how it grieves me sometimes to see him alter so.'

'He'll alter again, Nelly,' said Mrs. Quilp, 'and be what he was before.'

'Oh if God would only let that come about!' said the child with streaming eyes; 'but it is a long time now, since he first began to—I thought I saw that door moving!'

'It's the wind,' said Mrs. Quilp, faintly. 'Began to—?'

'To be so thoughtful and dejected, and to forget our old way of spending the time in the long evenings,' said the child. 'I used to read to him by the fireside, and he sat listening, and when I stopped and we began to talk, he told me about my mother, and how she once looked and spoke just like me when she was a little child. Then, he used to take me on his knee, and try to make me understand that she was not lying in her grave, but had flown to a beautiful country beyond the sky, where nothing died or ever grew old—we were very happy once!'

'Nelly, Nelly!'—said the poor woman, 'I can't bear to see one as young as you, so sorrowful. Pray don't cry.'

'I do so very seldom,' said Nell, 'but I have kept this to myself a long time, and I am not quite well, I think, for the tears come into my eyes and I cannot keep them back. I don't mind telling you my grief, for I know you will not tell it to any one again.'

Mrs. Quilp turned away her head and made no answer.

'Then,' said the child, 'we often walked in the fields and among the green trees, and when we came home at night, we liked it better for being tired, and said what a happy place it was. And if it was dark and rather dull, we used to say, what did it matter to us, for it only made us remember our last walk with greater pleasure, and look forward to our next one. But, now, we never have these walks, and though it is the same house, it is darker and much more gloomy than it used to be. Indeed!'

She paused here, but though the door creaked more than once, Mrs. Quilp said nothing.

'Mind you don't suppose,' said the child earnestly, 'that grandfather is less kind to me than he was. I think he loves me better every day, and is kinder and more affectionate than he was the day before. You do not know how fond he is of me!'

'I am sure he loves you dearly,' said Mrs. Quilp.

'Indeed, indeed he does!' cried Nell, 'as dearly as I love him. But I have not told you the greatest change of all, and this you must never breathe again to any one. He has no sleep or rest, but that which he takes by day in his easy chair; for, every night and nearly all night long, he is away from home.'

'Nelly?'

'Hush!' said the child, laying her finger on her lip and looking round. 'When he comes home in the morning, which is generally just before day, I let him in. Last night he was very late, and it was quite light. I saw that his face was deadly pale, that his eyes were bloodshot, and that his legs trembled as he walked. When I had gone to bed again, I heard him groan. I got up and ran back to him, and heard him say, before he knew that I was there, that he could not bear his life much longer, and if it was not for the child, would wish to die. What shall I do? Oh! what shall I do?'

The fountains of her heart were opened; the child, overpowered by the weight of her sorrows and anxieties, by the first confidence she had ever shown, and the sympathy with which her little tale had been received, hid her face in the arms of her helpless friend, and burst into a passion of tears.

In a few moments Mr. Quilp returned, and expressed the utmost surprise to find her in this condition, which he did very naturally and with admirable effect; for that kind of acting had been rendered familiar to him by long practice, and he was quite at home in it.

'She's tired, you see, Mrs. Quilp,' said the dwarf, squinting in a hideous manner to imply that his wife was to follow his lead. 'It's a long way from her home to the wharf, and then she was alarmed to see a couple of young scoundrels fighting, and was timorous on the water besides. All this together, has been too much for her. Poor Nell!'

Mr. Quilp unintentionally adopted the very best means he could have devised for the recovery of his young visitor, by patting her on the head. Such an application from any other hand might not have produced a remarkable effect, but the child shrunk so quickly from his touch and felt such an instinctive desire to get out of his reach, that she rose directly and declared herself ready to return.

'But you'd better wait, and dine with Mrs. Quilp and me.' said the dwarf.

'I have been away too long, sir, already,' returned Nell, drying her eyes.

'Well,' said Mr. Quilp, 'if you will go, you will, Nelly. Here's the note. It's only to say that I shall see him to-morrow, or may-be next day, and that I couldn't do that little business for him this morning. Good-bye, Nelly. Here, you sir; take care of her, d'ye hear?'

Kit, who appeared at the summons, deigned to make no reply to so needless an injunction, and after staring at Quilp in a threatening manner as if he doubted whether he might not have been the cause of Nelly shedding tears, and felt more than half disposed to revenge the fact upon him on the mere suspicion, turned about and followed his young mistress, who had by this time taken her leave of Mrs. Quilp and departed.

'You're a keen questioner, an't you, Mrs. Quilp?' said the dwarf, turning upon her as soon as they were left alone.

'What more could I do?' returned his wife mildly.

'What more could you do?' sneered Quilp, 'couldn't you have done something less? couldn't you have done what you had to do, without appearing in your favourite part of the crocodile, you minx?'

'I am very sorry for the child, Quilp,' said his wife. 'Surely I've done enough. I've led her on to tell her secret when she supposed we were alone; and you were by, God forgive me.'

'You led her on! You did a great deal truly!' said Quilp. 'What did I tell you about making me creak the door? It's lucky for you that from what she let fall, I've got the clue I want, for if I hadn't, I'd have visited the failure upon you.'

Mrs. Quilp being fully persuaded of this, made no reply. Her husband added with some exultation,

'But you may thank your fortunate stars—the same stars that made you Mrs. Quilp—you may thank them that I'm upon the old gentleman's track, and have got a new light. So let me hear no more about this matter, now, or at any other time, and don't get anything too nice for dinner, for I shan't be home to it.'

So saying, Mr. Quilp put his hat on and took himself off, and Mrs. Quilp, who was afflicted beyond measure by the recollection of the part she had just acted, shut herself up in her chamber, and smothering her head in the bedclothes bemoaned her fault more bitterly than many less tender-hearted persons would have mourned a much greater offence; for, in the majority of cases, conscience is an elastic and very flexible article, which will bear a deal of stretching and adapt itself to a great variety of circumstances. Some people by prudent management and leaving it off piece by piece, like a flannel waistcoat in warm weather, even contrive, in time, to dispense with it altogether; but there be others who can assume the garment and throw it off at pleasure; and this, being the greatest and most convenient improvement, is the one most in vogue.

CHAPTER VII

'FRED,' said Mr. Swiveller, 'remember the once popular melody of "Begone dull care;" fan the sinking flame of hilarity with the wing of friendship; and pass the rosy wine!'

Mr. Richard Swiveller's apartments were in the neighbourhood of Drury Lane, and in addition to this conveniency of situation had the advantage of being over a tobacconist's shop, so that he was enabled to procure a refreshing sneeze at any time by merely stepping out on the staircase, and was saved the trouble and expense of maintaining a snuffbox. It was in these apartments that Mr. Swiveller made use of the expressions above recorded, for the consolation and encouragement of his desponding friend; and it may not be uninteresting or improper to remark that even these brief observations partook in a double sense of the figurative and poetical character of Mr. Swiveller's mind, as the rosy wine was in fact represented by one glass of cold gin-and-water, which was replenished, as occasion required, from a bottle and jug upon the table, and was passed from one to another, in a scarcity of tumblers which, as Mr. Swiveller's was a bachelor's establishment, may be acknowledged without a blush. By a like pleasant fiction his single chamber was always mentioned in the plural number. In its disengaged times, the tobacconist had announced it in his window as 'apartments' for a single gentleman, and Mr. Swiveller, following up the hint, never failed to speak of it as his rooms, his lodgings, or his chambers: conveying to his hearers a notion of indefinite space, and leaving their imaginations to wander through long suites of lofty halls, at pleasure.

In this flight of fancy, Mr. Swiveller was assisted by a deceptive piece of furniture, in reality a bedstead, but in semblance a bookcase, which occupied a prominent situation in his chamber and seemed to defy suspicion and challenge inquiry. There is no doubt that, by day, Mr. Swiveller firmly believed this secret convenience to be a bookcase and nothing more; that he closed his eyes to the bed, resolutely denied the existence of the blankets, and spurned the bolster from his thoughts. No word of its real use, no hint of its nightly service, no allusion to its peculiar properties, had ever passed between him and his most intimate friends. Implicit faith in the deception was the first article of his creed. To be the friend of

Swiveller you must reject all circumstantial evidence, all reason, observation, and experience, and repose a blind belief in the bookcase. It was his pet weakness, and he cherished it.

'Fred!' said Mr. Swiveller, finding that his former adjuration had been productive of no effect. 'Pass the rosy!'

Young Trent, with an impatient gesture, pushed the glass towards him, and fell again into the moody attitude from which he had been unwillingly roused.

'I'll give you, Fred,' said his friend, stirring the mixture, 'a little sentiment appropriate to the occasion. Here's May the——'

'Pshaw!' interposed the other. 'You worry me to death with your chattering. You can be merry under any circumstances.'

'Why, Mr. Trent,' returned Dick, 'there is a proverb which talks about being merry and wise. There are some people who can be merry and can't be wise, and some who can be wise (or think they can) and can't be merry. I'm one of the first sort. If the proverb's a good 'un, I suppose it's better to keep to half of it than none; at all events I'd rather be merry and not wise, than be like you—neither one nor t'other.'

'Bah!' muttered his friend, peevishly.

'With all my heart,' said Mr. Swiveller. 'In the polite circles I believe this sort of thing isn't usually said to a gentleman in his own apartments, but never mind that. Make yourself at home.' Adding to this retort an observation to the effect that his friend appeared to be rather 'cranky' in point of temper, Richard Swiveller finished the rosy and applied himself to the composition of another glassful, in which, after tasting it with great relish, he proposed a toast to an imaginary company.

'Gentlemen, I'll give you, if you please, Success to the ancient family of the Swivellers, and good luck to Mr. Richard in particular—Mr. Richard, gentlemen,' said Dick with great emphasis, 'who spends all his money on his friends and is *Bah!'d* for his pains. Hear, hear!'

'Dick!' said the other, returning to his seat after having paced the room twice or thrice, 'will you talk seriously for two minutes, if I show you a way to make your fortune with very little trouble?'

'You've shown me so many,' returned Dick; 'and nothing has come of any one of 'em but empty pockets—'

'You'll tell a different story of this one, before a very long time is over,' said his companion, drawing his chair to the table. 'You saw my sister Nell?'

'What about her?' returned Dick.

'She has a pretty face, has she not?'

'Why, certainly,' replied Dick, 'I must say for her, that there's not any very strong family likeness between her and you.'

'Has she a pretty face?' repeated his friend impatiently.

'Yes,' said Dick, 'she has a pretty face, a very pretty face. What of that?'

'I'll tell you,' returned his friend. 'It's very plain that the old man and I will remain at daggers-drawn to the end of our lives, and that I have nothing to expect from him. You see that, I suppose?'

'A bat might see that, with the sun shining,' said Dick.

'It's equally plain that the money which the old flint—rot him—first taught me to expect that I should share with her at his death, will all be hers, is it not?'

'I should say it was,' replied Dick; 'unless the way in which I put the case to him, made an impression. It may have done so. It was powerful, Fred. "Here is a jolly old grandfather"— that was strong, I thought—very friendly and natural. Did it strike you in that way?'

'It didn't strike *him*,' returned the other, 'so we needn't discuss it. Now look here. Nell is nearly fourteen.'

'Fine girl of her age, but small,' observed Richard Swiveller parenthetically.

'If I am to go on, be quiet for one minute,' returned Trent, fretting at the very slight interest the other appeared to take in the conversation. 'Now I'm coming to the point.'

'That's right,' said Dick.

'The girl has strong affections, and brought up as she has been, may, at her age, be easily influenced and persuaded. If I take her in hand, I will be bound by a very little coaxing and threatening to bend her to my will. Not to beat about the bush (for the advantages of the scheme would take a week to tell), what's to prevent your marrying her?'

Richard Swiveller, who had been looking over the rim of the tumbler while his companion addressed the foregoing remarks to him with great energy and earnestness of manner, no sooner heard these words than he evinced the utmost consternation, and with difficulty ejaculated the monosyllable,

'What?'

'I say, what's to prevent,' repeated the other, with a steadiness of manner, of the effect of which upon his companion he was well assured by long experience, 'what's to prevent your marrying her?'

'And she "nearly fourteen"!' cried Dick.

'I don't mean marrying her now'—returned the brother angrily; 'say in two years' time, in three, in four. Does the old man look like a long-liver?'

'He don't look like it,' said Dick, shaking his head, 'but these old people—there's no trusting 'em, Fred. There's an aunt of mine down in Dorsetshire that was going to die when I was eight years old, and hasn't kept her word yet. They're so aggravating, so unprincipled, so spiteful—unless there's apoplexy in the family, Fred, you can't calculate upon 'em, and even then they deceive you just as often as not.'

'Look at the worst side of the question then,' said Trent as steadily as before, and keeping his eyes upon his friend. 'Suppose he lives.'

'To be sure,' said Dick. 'There's the rub.'

'I say,' resumed his friend, 'suppose he lives, and I persuaded, or if the word sounds more feasible, forced, Nell to a secret marriage with you. What do you think would come of that?'

'A family and an annual income of nothing, to keep 'em on,' said Richard Swiveller after some reflection.

'I tell you,' returned the other with an increased earnestness, which, whether it were real or assumed, had the same effect on his companion, 'that he lives for her, that his whole energies and thoughts are bound up in her, that he would no more disinherit her for an act of disobedience than he would take me into his favour again for any act of obedience or virtue that I could possibly be guilty of. He could not do it. You or any other man with eyes in his head may see that, if he chooses.'

'It seems improbable certainly,' said Dick, musing.

'It seems improbable because it is improbable,' his friend returned. 'If you would furnish him with an additional inducement to forgive you, let there be an irreconcileable breach, a most deadly quarrel, between you and me—let there be a pretence of such a thing, I mean, of course—and he'll do so fast enough. As to Nell, constant dropping will wear away a stone; you know you may trust to me as far as she is concerned. So, whether he lives or dies, what does it come to? That you become the sole inheritor of the wealth of this rich

A Cool Proposal

(*p. 55*)

old hunks; that you and I spend it together; and that you get,
into the bargain, a beautiful young wife.'

'I suppose there's no doubt about his being rich'—said Dick.

'Doubt! Did you hear what he let fall the other day when
we were there? Doubt! What will you doubt next, Dick?'

It would be tedious to pursue the conversation through all its
artful windings, or to develop the gradual approaches by which
the heart of Richard Swiveller was gained. It is sufficient to
know that vanity, interest, poverty, and every spendthrift
consideration urged him to look upon the proposal with favour,
and that where all other inducements were wanting, the
habitual carelessness of his disposition stepped in and still
weighed down the scale on the same side. To these impulses
must be added the complete ascendency which his friend had
long been accustomed to exercise over him—an ascendency
exerted in the beginning sorely at the expense of the unfortunate Dick's purse and prospects, but still maintained without
the slightest relaxation, notwithstanding that Dick suffered for
all his friend's vices and was, in nine cases out of ten, looked
upon as his designing tempter when he was indeed nothing but
his thoughtless light-headed tool.

The motives on the other side were something deeper than
any which Richard Swiveller entertained or understood, but
these being left to their own development, require no present
elucidation. The negotiation was concluded very pleasantly,
and Mr. Swiveller was in the act of stating in flowery terms
that he had no insurmountable objection to marrying anybody
plentifully endowed with money or moveables, who could be
induced to take him, when he was interrupted in his observations by a knock at the door, and the consequent necessity of
crying 'Come in.'

The door was opened, but nothing came in except a soapy
arm and a strong gush of tobacco. The gush of tobacco came
from the shop down stairs, and the soapy arm proceeded from
the body of a servant girl, who being then and there engaged
in cleaning the stairs had just drawn it out of a warm pail to
take in a letter, which letter she now held in her hand; pro-
claiming aloud, with that quick perception of surnames
peculiar to her class, that it was for Mister Snivelling.

Dick looked rather pale and foolish when he glanced at the
direction, and still more so when he came to look at the inside;
observing that this was one of the inconveniences of being a

lady's man, and that it was very easy to talk as they had been talking, but he had quite forgotten her.

'*Her*. Who?' demanded Trent.

'Sophy Wackles,' said Dick.

'Who's she?'

'She's all my fancy painted her, sir, that's what she is,' said Mr. Swiveller, taking a long pull at 'the rosy' and looking gravely at his friend. 'She is lovely, she's divine. You know her.'

'I remember,' said his companion carelessly. 'What of her?'

'Why, sir,' returned Dick, 'between Miss Sophia Wackles and the humble individual who has now the honour to address you, warm and tender sentiments have been engendered—sentiments of the most honourable and inspiring kind. The Goddess Diana, sir, that calls aloud for the chase, is not more particular in her behaviour than Sophia Wackles; I can tell you that.'

'Am I to believe there's anything real in what you say?' demanded his friend; 'you don't mean to say that any love-making has been going on?'

'Love-making, yes. Promising, no,' said Dick. 'There can be no action for breach, that's one comfort. I've never committed myself in writing, Fred.'

'And what's in the letter pray?'

'A reminder, Fred, for to-night—a small party of twenty—making two hundred light fantastic toes in all, supposing every lady and gentleman to have the proper complement. I must go, if it's only to begin breaking off the affair—I'll do it, don't you be afraid. I should like to know whether she left this, herself. If she did, unconscious of any bar to her happiness, it's affecting, Fred.'

To solve this question, Mr. Swiveller summoned the handmaid and ascertained that Miss Sophy Wackles had indeed left the letter with her own hands; and that she had come accompanied, for decorum's sake, no doubt, by a younger Miss Wackles; and that on learning that Mr. Swiveller was at home and being requested to walk up stairs, she was extremely shocked and professed that she would rather die. Mr. Swiveller heard this account with a degree of admiration not altogether consistent with the project in which he had just concurred, but his friend attached very little importance to his behaviour in this respect, probably because he knew that he had influence sufficient to control Richard Swiveller's proceedings in this or any other matter, whenever he deemed it necessary, for the advancement of his own purposes, to exert it.

CHAPTER VIII

BUSINESS disposed of, Mr. Swiveller was inwardly reminded of its being nigh dinner-time, and to the intent that his health might not be endangered by longer abstinence, dispatched a message to the nearest eating-house requiring an immediate supply of boiled beef and greens for two. With this demand, however, the eating-house (having experience of its customer) declined to comply, churlishly sending back for answer that if Mr. Swiveller stood in need of beef perhaps he would be so obliging as to come there and eat it, bringing with him, as grace before meat, the amount of a certain small account which had been long outstanding. Not at all intimidated by this rebuff, but rather sharpened in wits and appetite, Mr. Swiveller forwarded the same message to another and more distant eating-house, adding to it by way of rider that the gentleman was induced to send so far, not only by the great fame and popularity its beef had acquired, but in consequence of the extreme toughness of the beef retailed at the obdurate cook's shop, which rendered it quite unfit not merely for gentlemanly food but for any human consumption. The good effect of this politic course was demonstrated by the speedy arrival of a small pewter pyramid, curiously constructed of platters and covers, whereof the boiled-beef-plates formed the base, and a foaming quart-pot the apex; the structure being resolved into its component parts afforded all things requisite and necessary for a hearty meal, to which Mr. Swiveller and his friend applied themselves with great keenness and enjoyment.

'May the present moment,' said Dick, sticking his fork into a large carbuncular potato, 'be the worst of our lives! I like this plan of sending 'em with the peel on; there's a charm in drawing a potato from its native element (if I may so express it) to which the rich and powerful are strangers. Ah! "Man wants but little here below, nor wants that little long!" How true that is!—after dinner.'

'I hope the eating-house keeper will want but little and that *he* may not want that little long,' returned his companion; 'but I suspect you've no means of paying for this!'

'I shall be passing presently, and I'll call,' said Dick, winking his eye significantly. 'The waiter's quite helpless. The goods are gone, Fred, and there's an end of it.'

In point of fact, it would seem that the waiter felt this wholesome truth, for when he returned for the empty plates and dishes and was informed by Mr. Swiveller with dignified carelessness that he would call and settle when he should be passing presently, he displayed some perturbation of spirit, and muttered a few remarks about 'payment on delivery,' and 'no trust,' and other unpleasant subjects, but was fain to content himself with inquiring at what hour it was likely the gentleman would call, in order that being personally responsible for the beef, greens, and sundries, he might take care to be in the way at the time. Mr. Swiveller, after mentally calculating his engagements to a nicety, replied that he should look in at from two minutes before six to seven minutes past; and the man disappearing with this feeble consolation, Richard Swiveller took a greasy memorandum-book from his pocket and made an entry therein.

'Is that a reminder, in case you should forget to call?' said Trent with a sneer.

'Not exactly, Fred,' replied the imperturbable Richard, continuing to write with a business-like air. 'I enter in this little book the names of the streets that I can't go down while the shops are open. This dinner to-day closes Long Acre. I bought a pair of boots in Great Queen Street last week, and made that no thoroughfare too. There's only one avenue to the Strand left open now, and I shall have to stop up that to-night with a pair of gloves. The roads are closing so fast in every direction, that in about a month's time, unless my aunt sends me a remittance, I shall have to go three or four miles out of town to get over the way.'

'There's no fear of her failing, in the end?' said Trent.

'Why, I hope not,' returned Mr. Swiveller, 'but the average number of letters it takes to soften her is six, and this time we have got as far as eight without any effect at all. I'll write another to-morrow morning. I mean to blot it a good deal and shake some water over it out of the pepper-castor, to make it look penitent. "I'm in such a state of mind that I hardly know what I write"—blot—"if you could see me at this minute shedding tears for my past misconduct"—pepper-castor—"my hand trembles when I think"—blot again—if that don't produce the effect, it's all over.'

By this time Mr. Swiveller had finished his entry, and he now replaced his pencil in its little sheath and closed the book, in a perfectly grave and serious frame of mind. His friend discovered that it was time for him to fulfil some other engagement, and Richard Swiveller was accordingly left alone, in company with the rosy wine and his own meditations touching Miss Sophy Wackles.

'It's rather sudden,' said Dick, shaking his head with a look of infinite wisdom, and running on (as he was accustomed to do) with scraps of verse as if they were only prose in a hurry; 'when the heart of a man is depressed with fears, the mist is dispelled when Miss Wackles appears: she's a very nice girl. She's like the red red rose that's newly sprung in June—there's no denying that—she's also like a melody that's sweetly played in tune. It's really very sudden. Not that there's any need, on account of Fred's little sister, to turn cool directly, but it's better not to go too far. If I begin to cool at all I must begin at once, I see that. There's the chance of an action for breach, that's one reason. There's the chance of Sophy's getting another husband, that's another. There's the chance of—no, there's no chance of that, but it's as well to be on the safe side.'

This undeveloped consideration was the possibility, which Richard Swiveller sought to conceal even from himself, of his not being proof against the charms of Miss Wackles, and in some unguarded moment, by linking his fortunes to hers for ever, of putting it out of his own power to further the notable scheme to which he had so readily become a party. For all these reasons, he decided to pick a quarrel with Miss Wackles without delay, and casting about for a pretext, determined in favour of groundless jealousy. Having made up his mind on this important point, he circulated the glass (from his right hand to his left, and back again) pretty freely, to enable him to act his part with the greater discretion, and then, after making some slight improvements in his toilet, bent his steps towards the spot hallowed by the fair object of his meditations.

This spot was at Chelsea, for there Miss Sophia Wackles resided with her widowed mother and two sisters, in conjunction with whom she maintained a very small day-school for young ladies of proportionate dimensions; a circumstance which was made known to the neighbourhood by an oval board over the front first-floor window, whereon appeared, in circumambient flourishes, the words 'Ladies' Seminary;' and which was further published and proclaimed at intervals between the hours of half-past nine and ten in the morning, by a straggling and solitary young lady of tender years standing on the scraper on the tips of her toes and making futile attempts to reach the knocker with a spelling-book. The several duties of instruction in this establishment were thus discharged. English grammar, composition, geography, and the use of the dumb-bells, by Miss Melissa Wackles; writing, arithmetic, dancing, music, and general fascination, by Miss Sophy Wackles; the art of needlework, marking, and samplery, by Miss Jane Wackles; corporal punishment, fasting, and other tortures and terrors, by Mrs. Wackles. Miss Melissa Wackles was the eldest daughter, Miss Sophy the next, and Miss Jane the youngest. Miss Melissa might have seen five-and-thirty summers or thereabouts, and verged on the autumnal; Miss Sophy was a fresh, good-humoured, buxom girl of twenty; and Miss Jane numbered scarcely sixteen years. Mrs. Wackles was an excellent, but rather venomous old lady of three-score.

To this Ladies' Seminary then, Richard Swiveller hied, with designs obnoxious to the peace of the fair Sophia, who, arrayed in virgin white, embellished by no ornament but one blushing rose, received him on his arrival, in the midst of very elegant, not to say brilliant preparations; such as the embellishment of the room with the little flower-pots which always stood on the window-sill outside, save in windy weather when they blew into the area; the choice attire of the day-scholars who were allowed to grace the festival; the unwonted curls of Miss Jane Wackles who had kept her head during the whole of the preceding day screwed up tight in a yellow play-bill; and the solemn gentility and stately bearing of the old lady and her eldest daughter, which struck Mr. Swiveller as being uncommon but made no further impression upon him.

The truth is—and, as there is no accounting for tastes, even a taste so strange as this may be recorded without being looked upon as a wilful and malicious invention—the truth is, that neither Mrs. Wackles nor her eldest daughter had at any time greatly favoured the pretensions of Mr. Swiveller: they being accustomed to make slight mention of him as 'a gay young man' and to sigh and shake their heads ominously, whenever his name was mentioned. Mr. Swiveller's conduct in respect to Miss Sophy having been of that vague and dilatory kind which is usually looked upon as betokening no fixed matrimonial intentions, the young lady herself began in course of time to deem it highly desirable, that it should be brought to an issue one way or other. Hence, she had at last consented to play off, against Richard Swiveller, a stricken market-gardener known to be ready with his offer on the smallest encouragement, and hence—as this occasion had been specially assigned for the purpose—that great anxiety on her part for Richard Swiveller's presence which had occasioned her to leave the note he has been seen to receive. 'If he has any expectations at all or any means of keeping a wife well,' said Mrs. Wackles to her eldest daughter, 'he'll state 'em to us now or never.'—'If he really cares about me,' thought Miss Sophy, 'he must tell me so, to-night.'

But all these sayings and doings and thinkings being unknown to Mr. Swiveller, affected him not in the least; he was debating in his mind how he could best turn jealous, and wishing that Sophy were, for that occasion only, far less pretty than she was, or that she were her own sister, which would have served his turn as well, when the company came, and among them the market-gardener, whose name was Cheggs. But Mr. Cheggs came not alone or unsupported, for he prudently brought along with him his sister, Miss Cheggs, who making straight to Miss Sophy and taking her by both hands, and kissing her on both cheeks, hoped in an audible whisper that they had not come too early.

'Too early? No!' replied Sophy.

'Oh, my dear,' rejoined Miss Cheggs in the same whisper as before, 'I've been so tormented, so worried, that it's a mercy we were not here at four o'clock in the afternoon. Alick has been in *such* a state of impatience to come! You'd hardly believe that he was dressed before dinner-time and has been looking at the clock and teasing me ever since. It's all your fault, you naughty thing.'

Miss Sophy blushed, and Mr. Cheggs (who was bashful before ladies) blushed too, and Miss Sophy's mother and sisters, to prevent Mr. Cheggs from blushing more, lavished civilities and attentions upon him, and left Richard Swiveller to take care of himself. Here was the very thing he wanted; here was good cause, reason, and foundation, for pretending to be angry; but having this cause, reason, and foundation, which he had come expressly to seek, not expecting to find, Richard Swiveller was angry in sound earnest, and wondered what the devil Cheggs meant by his impudence.

However, Mr. Swiveller had Miss Sophy's hand for the first quadrille (country-dances being low, were utterly proscribed),

and so gained an advantage over his rival, who sat despond-
ingly in a corner and contemplated the glorious figure of the
young lady as she moved through the mazy dance. Nor was
this the only start Mr. Swiveller had of the market-gardener;
for, determining to show the family what quality of man they
trifled with, and influenced perhaps by his late libations, he
performed such feats of agility and such spins and twirls as
filled the company with astonishment, and in particular
caused a very long gentleman who was dancing with a very
short scholar, to stand quite transfixed by wonder and admiration. Even Mrs. Wackles forgot for the moment to snub three
small young ladies who were inclined to be happy, and could
not repress a rising thought that to have such a dancer as that
in the family would be a pride indeed.

At this momentous crisis, Miss Cheggs proved herself a
vigorous and useful ally; for, not confining herself to expressing by scornful smiles a contempt for Mr. Swiveller's accomplishments, she took every opportunity of whispering into Miss
Sophy's ear expressions of condolence and sympathy on her
being worried by such a ridiculous creature, declaring that she
was frightened to death lest Alick should fall upon him, and
beat him, in the fulness of his wrath, and entreating Miss
Sophy to observe how the eyes of the said Alick gleamed with
love and fury; passions, it may be observed, which being too
much for his eyes rushed into his nose also, and suffused it
with a crimson glow.

'You must dance with Miss Cheggs,' said Miss Sophy to
Dick Swiveller, after she had herself danced twice with Mr.
Cheggs and made great show of encouraging his advances.
'She's such a nice girl—and her brother's quite delightful.'

'Quite delightful is he?' muttered Dick. 'Quite delighted too,
I should say, from the manner in which he's looking this way.'

Here Miss Jane (previously instructed for the purpose)
interposed her many curls and whispered her sister to observe
how jealous Mr. Cheggs was.

'Jealous! Like his impudence!' said Richard Swiveller.

'His impudence, Mr. Swiveller!' said Miss Jane, tossing her
head. 'Take care he don't hear you, sir, or you may be sorry for it.'

'Oh pray, Jane——' said Miss Sophy.

'Nonsense!' replied her sister. 'Why shouldn't Mr. Cheggs
be jealous if he likes? I like that, certainly. Mr. Cheggs has as
good a right to be jealous as anybody else has, and perhaps he

Mr. Cheggs's Jealousy

(p. 61)

may have a better right soon if he hasn't already. You know best about that, Sophy!'

Though this was a concerted plot between Miss Sophy and her sister, originating in humane intentions and having for its object the inducing Mr. Swiveller to declare himself in time, it failed in its effect; for Miss Jane being one of those young ladies who are prematurely shrill and shrewish, gave such undue importance to her part that Mr. Swiveller retired in dudgeon, resigning his mistress to Mr. Cheggs and conveying a defiance into his looks which that gentleman indignantly returned.

'Did you speak to me, sir?' said Mr. Cheggs, following him into a corner.—'Have the kindness to smile, sir, in order that we may not be suspected.—Did you speak to me, sir?'

Mr. Swiveller looked with a supercilious smile at Mr. Cheggs's toes, then raised his eyes from them to his ankle, from that to his shin, from that to his knee, and so on very gradually, keeping up his right leg, until he reached his waistcoat, when he raised his eyes from button to button until he reached his chin, and travelling straight up the middle of his nose came at last to his eyes, when he said abruptly,

'No, sir, I didn't.'

'Hem!' said Mr. Cheggs, glancing over his shoulder, 'have the goodness to smile again, sir. Perhaps you wished to speak to me, sir.'

'No, sir, I didn't do that, either.'

'Perhaps you may have nothing to say to me *now*, sir,' said Mr. Cheggs fiercely.

At these words, Richard Swiveller withdrew his eyes from Mr. Cheggs's face, and travelling down the middle of his nose, and down his waistcoat, and down his right leg, reached his toes again, and carefully surveyed them; this done, he crossed over, and coming up the other leg, and thence approaching by the waistcoat as before, said when he had got to his eyes, 'No, sir, I haven't.'

'Oh indeed, sir!' said Mr. Cheggs. 'I'm glad to hear it. You know where I'm to be found, I suppose, sir, in case you *should* have anything to say to me?'

'I can easily inquire, sir, when I want to know.'

'There's nothing more we need say, I believe, sir?'

'Nothing more, sir.' With that they closed the tremendous dialogue by frowning mutually. Mr. Cheggs hastened to tender his hand to Miss Sophy, and Mr. Swiveller sat himself down in a corner in a very moody state.

Hard by this corner, Mrs. Wackles and Miss Wackles were seated, looking on at the dance; and unto Mrs. and Miss Wackles, Miss Cheggs occasionally darted when her partner was occupied with his share of the figure, and made some remark or other which was gall and wormwood to Richard Swiveller's soul. Looking into the eyes of Mrs. and Miss Wackles for encouragement, and sitting very upright and uncomfortable on a couple of hard stools, were two of the day-scholars; and when Miss Wackles smiled, and Mrs. Wackles smiled, the two little girls on the stools sought to curry favour by smiling likewise, in gracious acknowledgment of which attention the old lady frowned them down instantly, and said that if they dared to be guilty of such an impertinence again, they should be sent under convoy to their respective homes. This threat caused one of the young ladies, she being of a weak and trembling temperament, to shed tears, and for this offence they were both filed off immediately, with a dreadful promptitude that struck terror into the souls of all the pupils.

'I've got such news for you,' said Miss Cheggs, approaching once more. 'Alick has been saying such things to Sophy. Upon my word, you know, it's quite serious and in earnest, that's clear.'

'What's he been saying, my dear?' demanded Mrs. Wackles.

'All manner of things,' replied Miss Cheggs, 'you can't think how out he has been speaking!'

Richard Swiveller considered it advisable to hear no more, but taking advantage of a pause in the dancing, and the approach of Mr. Cheggs to pay his court to the old lady, swaggered with an extremely careful assumption of extreme carelessness towards the door, passing on the way Miss Jane Wackles, who in all the glory of her curls was holding a flirtation (as good practice when no better was to be had) with a feeble old gentleman who lodged in the parlour. Near the door sat Miss Sophy, still fluttered and confused by the attentions of Mr. Cheggs, and by her side Richard Swiveller lingered for a moment to exchange a few parting words.

'My boat is on the shore and my bark is on the sea, but before I pass this door I will say farewell to thee,' murmured Dick, looking gloomily upon her.

'Are you going?' said Miss Sophy, whose heart sunk within her at the result of her stratagem, but who affected a light indifference notwithstanding.

'Am I going?' echoed Dick bitterly. 'Yes, I am. What then?'

'Nothing, except that it's very early,' said Miss Sophy; 'but you are your own master of course.'

'I would that I had been my own mistress too,' said Dick, 'before I had ever entertained a thought of you. Miss Wackles, I believed you true, and I was blest in so believing, but now I mourn that e'er I knew, a girl so fair yet so deceiving.'

Miss Sophy bit her lip and affected to look with great interest after Mr. Cheggs, who was quaffing lemonade in the distance.

'I came here,' said Dick, rather oblivious of the purpose with which he had really come, 'with my bosom expanded, my heart dilated, and my sentiments of a corresponding description. I go away with feelings that may be conceived, but cannot be described: feeling within myself the desolating truth that my best affections have experienced, this night, a stifler!'

'I am sure I don't know what you mean, Mr. Swiveller,' said Miss Sophy with downcast eyes. 'I'm very sorry if——'

'Sorry, ma'am!' said Dick, 'sorry in the possession of a Cheggs! But I wish you a very good night; concluding with this slight remark, that there is a young lady growing up at this present moment for me, who has not only great personal attractions but great wealth, and who has requested her next of kin to propose for my hand, which, having a regard for some members of her family, I have consented to promise. It's a gratifying circumstance which you'll be glad to hear, that a young and lovely girl is growing into a woman expressly on my account, and is now saving up for me. I thought I'd mention it. I have now merely to apologise for trespassing so long upon your attention. Good night!'

'There's one good thing springs out of all this,' said Richard Swiveller to himself when he had reached home and was hanging over the candle with the extinguisher in his hand, 'which is, that I now go heart and soul, neck and heels, with Fred in all his scheme about little Nelly, and right glad he'll be to find me so strong upon it. He shall know all about that to-morrow, and in the mean time, as it's rather late, I'll try and get a wink or two of the balmy.'

'The balmy' came almost as soon as it was courted. In a very few minutes Mr. Swiveller was fast asleep, dreaming that he had married Nelly Trent and come into the property, and that his first act of power was to lay waste the market-garden of Mr. Cheggs and turn it into a brick-field.

CHAPTER IX

THE child, in her confidence with Mrs. Quilp, had but feebly described the sadness and sorrow of her thoughts, or the heaviness of the cloud which overhung her home, and cast dark shadows on its hearth. Besides that it was very difficult to impart to any person not intimately acquainted with the life she led, an adequate sense of its gloom and loneliness, a constant fear of in some way committing or injuring the old man to whom she was so tenderly attached, had restrained her, even in the midst of her heart's overflowing, and made her timid of allusion to the main cause of her anxiety and distress.

For, it was not the monotonous days unchequered by variety and uncheered by pleasant companionship, it was not the dark dreary evenings or the long solitary nights, it was not the absence of every slight and easy pleasure for which young hearts beat high, or the knowing nothing of childhood but its weakness and its easily wounded spirit, that had wrung such tears from Nell. To see the old man struck down beneath the pressure of some hidden grief, to mark his wavering and un-settled state, to be agitated at times with a dreadful fear that his mind was wandering, and to trace in his words and looks the dawning of despondent madness; to watch and wait and listen for confirmation of these things day after day, and to feel and know that, come what might, they were alone in the world with no one to help or advise or care about them—these were causes of depression and anxiety that might have sat heavily on an older breast with many influences at work to cheer and gladden it, but how heavily on the mind of a young child to whom they were ever present, and who was constantly surrounded by all that could keep such thoughts in restless action!

And yet, to the old man's vision, Nell was still the same. When he could, for a moment, disengage his mind from the phantom that haunted and brooded on it always, there was his young companion with the same smile for him, the same earnest words, the same merry laugh, the same love and care that, sinking deep into his soul, seemed to have been present to him through his whole life. And so he went on, content to read the book of her heart from the page first presented to him, little dreaming of the story that lay hidden in its other leaves, and murmuring within himself that at least the child was happy.

She had been once. She had gone singing through the dim rooms, and moving with gay and lightsome step among their dusty treasures, making them older by her young life, and sterner and more grim by her gay and cheerful presence. But, now, the chambers were cold and gloomy, and when she left her own little room to while away the tedious hours, and sat in one of them, she was still and motionless as their inanimate occupants, and had no heart to startle the echoes—hoarse from their long silence—with her voice.

In one of these rooms, was a window looking into the street, where the child sat, many and many a long evening, and often far into the night, alone and thoughtful. None are so anxious as those who watch and wait; at these times, mournful fancies came flocking on her mind, in crowds.

She would take her station here, at dusk, and watch the people as they passed up and down the street, or appeared at the windows of the opposite houses; wondering whether those rooms were as lonesome as that in which she sat, and whether those people felt it company to see her sitting there, as she did only to see them look out and draw in their heads again. There was a crooked stack of chimneys on one of the roofs, in which, by often looking at them, she had fancied ugly faces that were frowning over at her and trying to peer into the room; and she felt glad when it grew too dark to make them out, though she was sorry too, when the man came to light the lamps in the street—for it made it late, and very dull inside. Then, she would draw in her head to look round the room and see that everything was in its place and hadn't moved; and looking out into the street again, would perhaps see a man passing with a coffin on his back, and two or three others silently following him to a house where somebody lay dead; which made her shudder and think of such things until they suggested afresh the old man's altered face and manner, and a new train of fears and speculations. If he were to die— if sudden illness had happened to him, and he were never to come home again, alive—if, one night, he should come home, and kiss and bless her as usual, and after she had gone to bed and had fallen asleep and was perhaps dreaming pleasantly, and smiling in her sleep, he should kill himself and his blood come creeping, creeping, on the ground to her own bed-room door! These thoughts were too terrible to dwell upon, and again she would have recourse to the street, now trodden by fewer feet, and darker and more silent than before. The shops were closing fast, and lights began to shine from the upper windows, as the neighbours went to bed. By degrees, these dwindled away and disappeared, or were replaced, here and there, by a feeble rush-candle which was to burn all night. Still, there was one late shop at no great distance which sent forth a ruddy glare upon the pavement even yet, and looked bright and companionable. But, in a little time, this closed, the light was extinguished, and all was gloomy and quiet, except when some stray footsteps sounded on the pavement, or a neighbour, out later than his wont, knocked lustily at his house-door to rouse the sleeping inmates.

When the night had worn away thus far (and seldom now until it had) the child would close the window, and steal softly down stairs, thinking as she went that if one of those hideous faces below, which often mingled with her dreams, were to meet her by the way, rendering itself visible by some strange light of its own, how terrified she would be. But these fears vanished before a well-trimmed lamp and the familiar aspect of her own room. After praying fervently, and with many bursting tears, for the old man, and the restoration of his peace of mind and the happiness they had once enjoyed, she would lay her head upon the pillow and sob herself to sleep: often starting up again, before the daylight came, to listen for the bell, and respond to the imaginary summons which had roused her from her slumber.

One night, the third after Nelly's interview with Mrs. Quilp, the old man, who had been weak and ill all day, said he should not leave home The child's eyes sparkled at the intelligence, but her joy subsided when they reverted to his worn and sickly face.

'Two days,' he said, 'two whole, clear, days have passed, and there is no reply. What *did* he tell thee, Nell?'

'Exactly what I told you, dear grandfather, indeed.'

'True,' said the old man, faintly. 'Yes. But tell me again, Nell. My head fails me. What was it that he told thee? Nothing more than that he would see me to-morrow or next day? That was in the note.'

'Nothing more,' said the child. 'Shall I go to him again to-morrow, dear grandfather? Very early? I will be there and back, before breakfast.'

The old man shook his head, and sighing mournfully, drew her towards him.

''Twould be of no use, my dear, no earthly use. But if he deserts me, Nell, at this moment—if he deserts me now, when I should, with his assistance, be recompensed for all the time and money I have lost, and all the agony of mind I have undergone, which makes me what you see, I am ruined, and—worse, far worse than that—have ruined thee, for whom I ventured all. If we are beggars—!'

'What if we are?' said the child boldly. 'Let us be beggars, and be happy.'

'Beggars—and happy!' said the old man. 'Poor child!'

'Dear grandfather,' cried the girl with an energy which shone in her flushed face, trembling voice, and impassioned gesture, 'I am not a child in that, I think; but even if I am, oh hear me pray that we may beg, or work in open roads or fields, to earn a scanty living, rather than live as we do now.'

'Nelly!' said the old man.

'Yes, yes, rather than live as we do now,' the child repeated, more earnestly than before. 'If you are sorrowful, let me know why and be sorrowful too; if you waste away and are paler and weaker every day, let me be your nurse and try to comfort you. If you are poor, let us be poor together; but let me be with you, do let me be with you; do not let me see such change and not know why, or I shall break my heart and die. Dear grandfather, let us leave this sad place to-morrow, and beg our way from door to door.'

The old man covered his face with his hands, and hid it in the pillow of the couch on which he lay.

'Let us be beggars,' said the child, passing an arm round his neck, 'I have no fear but we shall have enough, I am sure we shall. Let us walk through country places, and sleep in fields and under trees, and never think of money again, or anything that can make you sad, but rest at nights, and have the sun and wind upon our faces in the day, and thank God together! Let us never set foot in dark rooms or melancholy houses, any more, but wander up and down wherever we like to go; and when you are tired, you shall stop to rest in the pleasantest place that we can find, and I will go and beg for both.'

The child's voice was lost in sobs as she dropped upon the old man's neck; nor did she weep alone.

These were not words for other tears, nor was it a scene for other eyes. And yet other ears and eyes were there and greedily taking in all that passed, and moreover they were the ears and eyes of no less a person than Mr. Daniel Quilp, who, having entered unseen when the child first placed herself at the old man's side, refrained—actuated, no doubt, by motives of the purest delicacy—from interrupting the conversation, and stood looking on with his accustomed grin. Standing, however, being a tiresome attitude to a gentleman already fatigued with walking, and the dwarf being one of that kind of persons who usually make themselves at home, he soon cast his eyes upon a chair, into which he skipped with uncommon agility, and perching himself on the back with his feet upon the seat, was thus enabled to look on and listen with greater comfort to himself, besides gratifying at the same time that taste for doing something fantastic and monkey-like, which on all occasions had strong possession of him. Here, then, he sat, one leg cocked carelessly over the other, his chin resting on the palm of his hand, his head turned a little on one side, and his ugly features twisted into a complacent grimace. And in this position the old man, happening in course of time to look that way, at length chanced to see him: to his unbounded astonishment.

The child uttered a suppressed shriek on beholding this agreeable figure; in their first surprise both she and the old man, not knowing what to say, and half doubting its reality, looked shrinkingly at it. Not at all disconcerted by this reception, Daniel Quilp preserved the same attitude, merely nodding twice or thrice with great condescension. At length, the old man pronounced his name, and inquired how he came there.

'Through the door,' said Quilp, pointing over his shoulder with his thumb. 'I'm not quite small enough to get through keyholes. I wish I was. I want to have some talk with you, particularly, and in private. With nobody present, neighbour. Good-bye, little Nelly.'

Nell looked at the old man, who nodded to her to retire, and kissed her cheek.

'Ah!' said the dwarf, smacking his lips, 'what a nice kiss that was—just upon the rosy part. What a capital kiss!'

Nell was none the slower in going away, for this remark. Quilp looked after her with an admiring leer, and when she had closed the door, fell to complimenting the old man upon her charms.

Little Nell as Comforter

'Such a fresh, blooming, modest little bud, neighbour,' said Quilp, nursing his short leg, and making his eyes twinkle very much; 'such a chubby, rosy, cosy, little Nell!'

The old man answered by a forced smile, and was plainly struggling with a feeling of the keenest and most exquisite impatience. It was not lost upon Quilp, who delighted in torturing him, or indeed anybody else, when he could.

'She's so,' said Quilp, speaking very slowly, and feigning to be quite absorbed in the subject, 'so small, so compact, so beautifully modelled, so fair, with such blue veins and such a transparent skin, and such little feet, and such winning ways—but bless me, you're nervous! Why, neighbour, what's the matter? I swear to you,' continued the dwarf, dismounting from the chair and sitting down in it, with a careful slowness of gesture very different from the rapidity with which he had sprung up unheard, 'I swear to you that I had no idea old blood ran so fast or kept so warm. I thought it was sluggish in its course, and cool, quite cool. I am pretty sure it ought to be. Yours must be out of order, neighbour.'

'I believe it is,' groaned the old man, clasping his head with both hands. 'There's burning fever here, and something now and then to which I fear to give a name.'

The dwarf said never a word, but watched his companion as he paced restlessly up and down the room, and presently returned to his seat. Here he remained, with his head bowed upon his breast for some time, and then suddenly raising it, said,

'Once, and once for all, have you brought me any money?'

'No!' returned Quilp.

'Then,' said the old man, clenching his hands desperately, and looking upward, 'the child and I are lost!'

'Neighbour,' said Quilp, glancing sternly at him, and beating his hand twice or thrice upon the table to attract his wandering attention, 'let me be plain with you, and play a fairer game than when you held all the cards, and I saw but the backs and nothing more. You have no secret from me now.'

The old man looked up, trembling.

'You are surprised,' said Quilp. 'Well, perhaps that's natural. You have no secret from me now, I say; no, not one. For now, I know, that all those sums of money, that all those loans, advances, and supplies that you have had from me, have found their way to—shall I say the word?'

'Aye!' replied the old man, 'say it, if you will.'

'To the gaming-table,' rejoined Quilp, 'your nightly haunt. This was the precious scheme to make your fortune, was it; this was the secret certain source of wealth in which I was to have sunk my money (if I had been the fool you took me for); this was your inexhaustible mine of gold, your El Dorado, eh?'

'Yes,' cried the old man, turning upon him with gleaming eyes, 'it was. It is. It will be, till I die.'

'That I should have been blinded,' said Quilp, looking contemptuously at him, 'by a mere shallow gambler!'

'I am no gambler,' cried the old man fiercely. 'I call Heaven to witness that I never played for gain of mine, or love of play; that at every piece I staked, I whispered to myself that orphan's name and called on Heaven to bless the venture;— which it never did. Whom did it prosper? Who were those with whom I played? Men who lived by plunder, profligacy, and riot; squandering their gold in doing ill, and propagating vice and evil. My winnings would have been from them, my winnings would have been bestowed to the last farthing on a young sinless child whose life they would have sweetened and made happy. What would they have contracted? The means of corruption, wretchedness, and misery. Who would not have hoped in such a cause? Tell me that! Who would not have hoped as I did?'

'When did you first begin this mad career?' asked Quilp, his taunting inclination subdued, for a moment, by the old man's grief and wildness.

'When did I first begin?' he rejoined, passing his hand across his brow. 'When *was* it, that I first began? When should it be, but when I began to think how little I had saved, how long a time it took to save at all, how short a time I might have at my age to live, and how she would be left to the rough mercies of the world, with barely enough to keep her from the sorrows that wait on poverty; then it was, that I began to think about it.'

'After you first came to me to get your precious grandson packed off to sea?' said Quilp.

'Shortly after that,' replied the old man. 'I thought of it a long time, and had it in my sleep for months. Then I began. I found no pleasure in it, I expected none. What has it ever brought me but anxious days and sleepless nights; but loss of health and peace of mind, and gain of feebleness and sorrow!'

'You lost what money you had laid by, first, and then came

to me. While I thought you were making your fortune (as you said you were) you were making yourself a beggar, eh? Dear me! And so it comes to pass that I hold every security you could scrape together, and a bill of sale upon the—upon the stock and property,' said Quilp, standing up and looking about him, as if to assure himself that none of it had been taken away. 'But did you never win?'

'Never!' groaned the old man. 'Never won back my loss!'

'I thought,' sneered the dwarf, 'that if a man played long enough he was sure to win at last, or, at the worst, not to come off a loser.'

'And so he is,' cried the old man, suddenly rousing himself from his state of despondency, and lashed into the most violent excitement, 'so he is; I have felt that from the first, I have always known it, I've seen it, I never felt it half so strongly as I feel it now. Quilp, I have dreamed, three nights, of winning the same large sum, I never could dream that dream before, though I have often tried. Do not desert me, now I have this chance. I have no resource but you, give me some help, let me try this one last hope.'

The dwarf shrugged his shoulders and shook his head.

'See, Quilp, good tender-hearted Quilp,' said the old man, drawing some scraps of paper from his pocket with a trembling hand, and clasping the dwarf's arm, 'only see here. Look at these figures, the result of long calculation, and painful and hard experience. I *must* win. I only want a little help once more, a few pounds, but two score pounds, dear Quilp.'

'The last advance was seventy,' said the dwarf; 'and it went in one night.'

'I know it did,' answered the old man, 'but that was the very worst fortune of all, and the time had not come then. Quilp, consider, consider,' the old man cried, trembling so much the while, that the papers in his hand fluttered as if they were shaken by the wind, 'that orphan child! If I were alone, I could die with gladness—perhaps even anticipate that doom which is dealt out so unequally: coming, as it does, on the proud and happy in their strength, and shunning the needy and afflicted, and all who court it in their despair—but what I have done, has been for her. Help me for her sake, I implore you; not for mine; for hers!'

'I'm sorry I've got an appointment in the city,' said Quilp, looking at his watch with perfect self-possession, 'or I should have been very glad to have spent half an hour with you while you composed yourself, very glad.'

'Nay, Quilp, good Quilp,' gasped the old man, catching at his skirts, 'you and I have talked together, more than once, of her poor mother's story. The fear of her coming to poverty has perhaps been bred in me by that. Do not be hard upon me, but take that into account. You are a great gainer by me. Oh spare me the money for this one last hope!'

'I couldn't do it really,' said Quilp with unusual politeness, 'though I tell you what—and this is a circumstance worth bearing in mind as showing how the sharpest among us may be taken in sometimes—I was so deceived by the penurious way in which you lived, alone with Nelly—'

'All done to save money for tempting fortune, and to make her triumph greater,' cried the old man.

'Yes yes, I understand that now,' said Quilp; 'but I was going to say, I was so deceived by that, your miserly way, the reputation you had among those who knew you of being rich, and your repeated assurances that you would make of my advances treble and quadruple the interest you paid me, that I'd have advanced you, even now, what you want, on your simple note of hand, if I hadn't unexpectedly become acquainted with your secret way of life.'

'Who is it,' retorted the old man desperately, 'that, notwith-standing all my caution, told you? Come. Let me know the name—the person.'

The crafty dwarf, bethinking himself that his giving up the child would lead to the disclosure of the artifice he had employed, which, as nothing was to be gained by it, it was well to conceal, stopped short in his answer and said, 'Now, who do you think?'

'It was Kit, it must have been the boy; he played the spy, and you tampered with him?' said the old man.

'How came you to think of him?' said the dwarf in a tone of great commiseration. 'Yes, it was Kit. Poor Kit!'

So saying, he nodded in a friendly manner, and took his leave: stopping when he had passed the outer door a little distance, and grinning with extraordinary delight.

'Poor Kit!' muttered Quilp. 'I think it was Kit who said I was an uglier dwarf than could be seen anywhere for a penny, wasn't it? Ha ha ha! Poor Kit!'

And with that he went his way, still chuckling as he went.

CHAPTER X

DANIEL QUILP neither entered nor left the old man's house, unobserved. In the shadow of an archway nearly opposite, leading to one of the many passages which diverged from the main street, there lingered one, who, having taken up his position when the twilight first came on, still maintained it with undiminished patience, and leaning against the wall with the manner of a person who had a long time to wait, and being well used to it was quite resigned, scarcely changed his attitude for the hour together.

This patient lounger attracted little attention from any of those who passed, and bestowed as little upon them. His eyes were constantly directed towards one object; the window at which the child was accustomed to sit. If he withdrew them for a moment, it was only to glance at a clock in some neighbouring shop, and then to strain his sight once more in the old quarter with increased earnestness and attention.

It has been remarked that this personage evinced no weariness in his place of concealment; nor did he, long as his waiting was. But as the time went on, he manifested some anxiety and surprise, glancing at the clock more frequently and at the window less hopefully than before. At length, the clock was hidden from his sight by some envious shutters, then the church steeples proclaimed eleven at night, then the quarter past, and then the conviction seemed to obtrude itself on his mind that it was of no use tarrying there any longer.

That the conviction was an unwelcome one, and that he was by no means willing to yield to it, was apparent from his reluctance to quit the spot; from the tardy steps with which he often left it, still looking over his shoulder at the same window; and from the precipitation with which he as often returned, when a fancied noise or the changing and imperfect light induced him to suppose it had been softly raised. At length, he gave the matter up, as hopeless for that night, and suddenly breaking into a run as though to force himself away, scampered off at his utmost speed, nor once ventured to look behind him lest he should be tempted back again.

Without relaxing his pace, or stopping to take breath, this mysterious individual dashed on through a great many alleys and narrow ways until he at length arrived in a square paved court, when he subsided into a walk, and making for a small house from the window of which a light was shining, lifted the latch of the door and passed in.

'Bless us!' cried a woman turning sharply round, 'who's that? Oh! It's you, Kit!'

'Yes, mother, it's me.'

'Why, how tired you look, my dear!'

'Old master an't gone out to-night,' said Kit; 'and so she hasn't been at the window at all.' With which words, he sat down by the fire and looked very mournful and discontented.

The room in which Kit sat himself down, in this condition, was an extremely poor and homely place, but with that air of comfort about it, nevertheless, which—or the spot must be a wretched one indeed—cleanliness and order can always impart in some degree. Late as the Dutch clock showed it to be, the poor woman was still hard at work at an ironing-table; a young child lay sleeping in a cradle near the fire; and another, a sturdy boy of two or three years old, very wide awake, with a very tight night-cap on his head, and a night-gown very much too small for him on his body, was sitting bolt upright in a clothes-basket, staring over the rim with his great round eyes, and looking as if he had thoroughly made up his mind never to go to sleep any more; which, as he had already declined to take his natural rest and had been brought out of bed in consequence, opened a cheerful prospect for his relations and friends. It was rather a queer-looking family: Kit, his mother, and the children, being all strongly alike.

Kit was disposed to be out of temper, as the best of us are too often—but he looked at the youngest child who was sleeping soundly, and from him to his other brother in the clothes-basket, and from him to their mother, who had been at work without complaint since morning, and thought it would be a better and kinder thing to be good-humoured. So he rocked the cradle with his foot; made a face at the rebel in the clothes-basket, which put him in high good-humour directly; and stoutly determined to be talkative and make himself agreeable.

'Ah, mother!' said Kit, taking out his clasp-knife and falling upon a great piece of bread and meat which she had had ready for him, hours before, 'what a one you are! There an't many such as you, *I* know.'

'I hope there are many a great deal better, Kit,' said Mrs.

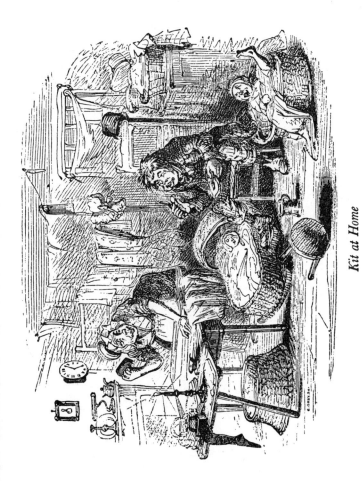

Kit at Home

Nubbles; 'and that there are, or ought to be, accordin' to what the parson at chapel says.'

'Much *he* knows about it,' returned Kit contemptuously. 'Wait till he's a widder and works like you do, and gets as little, and does as much, and keeps his spirit up the same, and then I'll ask him what's o'clock and trust him for being right to half a second.'

'Well,' said Mrs. Nubbles, evading the point, 'your beer's down there by the fender, Kit.'

'I see,' replied her son, taking up the porter pot, 'my love to you, mother. And the parson's health too if you like. I don't bear him any malice, not I!'

'Did you tell me, just now, that your master hadn't gone out to-night?' inquired Mrs. Nubbles.

'Yes,' said Kit, 'worse luck!'

'You should say better luck, I think,' returned his mother, 'because Miss Nelly won't have been left alone.'

'Ah!' said Kit, 'I forgot that. I said worse luck, because I've been watching ever since eight o'clock, and seen nothing of her.'

'I wonder what she'd say,' cried his mother, stopping in her work and looking round, 'if she knew that every night, when she—poor thing—is sitting alone at that window, you are watching in the open street for fear any harm should come to her, and that you never leave the place or come home to your bed though you're ever so tired, till such time as you think she's safe in hers.'

'Never mind what she'd say,' replied Kit, with something like a blush on his uncouth face; 'she'll never know nothing, and consequently, she'll never say nothing.'

Mrs. Nubbles ironed away in silence for a minute or two, and coming to the fireplace for another iron, glanced stealthily at Kit while she rubbed it on a board and dusted it with a duster, but said nothing until she had returned to her table again: when, holding the iron at an alarmingly short distance from her cheek, to test its temperature, and looking round with a smile, she observed:

'I know what some people would say, Kit—'

'Nonsense,' interposed Kit with a perfect apprehension of what was to follow.

'No, but they would indeed. Some people would say that you'd fallen in love with her, I know they would.'

To this, Kit only replied by bashfully bidding his mother

'get out,' and forming sundry strange figures with his legs and arms, accompanied by sympathetic contortions of his face. Not deriving from these means the relief which he sought, he bit off an immense mouthful from the bread and meat, and took a quick drink of the porter; by which artificial aids he choked himself and effected a diversion of the subject.

'Speaking seriously though, Kit,' said his mother, taking up the theme afresh, after a time, 'for of course I was only in joke just now, it's very good and thoughtful, and like you, to do this, and never let anybody know it, though some day I hope she may come to know it, for I'm sure she would be very grateful to you and feel it very much. It's a cruel thing to keep the dear child shut up there. I don't wonder that the old gentleman wants to keep it from you.'

'He don't think it's cruel, bless you,' said Kit, 'and don't mean it to be so, or he wouldn't do it—I do consider, mother, that he wouldn't do it for all the gold and silver in the world. No, no, that he wouldn't. I know him better than that.'

'Then what does he do it for, and why does he keep it so close from you?' said Mrs. Nubbles.

'That I don't know,' returned her son. 'If he hadn't tried to keep it so close though, I should never have found it out, for it was his getting me away at night and sending me off so much earlier than he used to, that first made me curious to know what was going on. Hark! what's that?'

'It's only somebody outside.'

'It's somebody crossing over here,' said Kit, standing up to listen, 'and coming very fast too. He can't have gone out after I left, and the house caught fire, mother!'

The boy stood, for a moment, really bereft, by the apprehension he had conjured up, of the power to move. The footsteps drew nearer, the door was opened with a hasty hand, and the child herself, pale and breathless, and hastily wrapped in a few disordered garments, hurried into the room.

'Miss Nelly! What is the matter?' cried mother and son together.

'I must not stay a moment,' she returned, 'grandfather has been taken very ill. I found him in a fit upon the floor—'

'I'll run for a doctor'—said Kit, seizing his brimless hat. 'I'll be there directly, I'll—'

'No, no,' cried Nell, 'there is one there, you're not wanted, you—you—must never come near us any more!'

'What!' roared Kit.

'Never again,' said the child. 'Don't ask me why, for I don't know. Pray don't ask me why, pray don't be sorry, pray don't be vexed with me! I have nothing to do with it indeed!'

Kit looked at her with his eyes stretched wide; and opened and shut his mouth a great many times; but couldn't get out one word.

'He complains and raves of you,' said the child. 'I don't know what you have done, but I hope it's nothing very bad.'

'*I* done!' roared Kit.

'He cries that you're the cause of all his misery,' returned the child with tearful eyes; 'he screamed and called for you; they say you must not come near him or he will die. You must not return to us any more. I came to tell you. I thought it would be better that I should come than somebody quite strange. Oh, Kit, what *have* you done? You, in whom I trusted so much, and who were almost the only friend I had!'

The unfortunate Kit looked at his young mistress harder and harder, and with eyes growing wider and wider, but was perfectly motionless and silent.

'I have brought his money for the week,' said the child, looking to the woman and laying it on the table—'and—and—a little more, for he was always good and kind to me. I hope he will be sorry and do well somewhere else, and not take this to heart too much. It grieves me very much to part with him like this, but there is no help. It must be done. Good night!'

With the tears streaming down her face, and her slight figure trembling with the agitation of the scene she had left, the shock she had received, the errand she had just discharged, and a thousand painful and affectionate feelings, the child hastened to the door, and disappeared as rapidly as she had come.

The poor woman, who had no cause to doubt her son, but every reason for relying on his honesty and truth, was staggered, notwithstanding, by his not having advanced one word in his defence. Visions of gallantry, knavery, robbery; and of the nightly absences from home for which he had accounted so strangely, having been occasioned by some unlawful pursuit; flocked into her brain and rendered her afraid to question him. She rocked herself upon a chair, wringing her hands and weeping bitterly, but Kit made no attempt to comfort her and remained quite bewildered. The baby in the cradle woke up and cried; the boy in the clothes-basket fell over on his back with the basket upon him, and was seen no more; the mother wept louder yet and rocked faster; but Kit, insensible to all the din and tumult, remained in a state of utter stupefaction.

CHAPTER XI

QUIET and solitude were destined to hold uninterrupted rule
no longer, beneath the roof that sheltered the child. Next
morning, the old man was in a raging fever accompanied with
delirium; and sinking under the influence of this disorder he
lay for many weeks in imminent peril of his life. There was
watching enough, now, but it was the watching of strangers
who made a greedy trade of it, and who, in the intervals of their
attendance upon the sick man huddled together with a ghastly
good-fellowship, and ate and drank and made merry; for
disease and death were their ordinary household gods.

Yet, in all the hurry and crowding of such a time, the child
was more alone than she had ever been before; alone in spirit,
alone in her devotion to him who was wasting away upon his
burning bed; alone in her unfeigned sorrow, and her un-
purchased sympathy. Day after day, and night after night,
found her still by the pillow of the unconscious sufferer, still
anticipating his every want, still listening to those repetitions
of her name and those anxieties and cares for her, which were
ever uppermost among his feverish wanderings.

The house was no longer theirs. Even the sick chamber
seemed to be retained on the uncertain tenure of Mr. Quilp's
favour. The old man's illness had not lasted many days when
he took formal possession of the premises and all upon them,
in virtue of certain legal powers to that effect, which few understood and none presumed to call in question. This important
step secured, with the assistance of a man of law whom he
brought with him for the purpose, the dwarf proceeded to
establish himself and his coadjutor in the house, as an assertion
of his claim against all comers; and then set about making his
quarters comfortable, after his own fashion.

To this end, Mr. Quilp encamped in the back parlour,
having first put an effectual stop to any further business by
shutting up the shop. Having looked out, from among the
old furniture, the handsomest and most commodious chair he
could possibly find (which he reserved for his own use) and an
especially hideous and uncomfortable one (which he consider-
ately appropriated to the accommodation of his friend), he
caused them to be carried into this room, and took up his
position in great state. The apartment was very far removed

from the old man's chamber, but Mr. Quilp deemed it prudent, as a precaution against infection from fever, and a means of wholesome fumigation, not only to smoke, himself, without cessation, but to insist upon it that his legal friend did the like. Moreover, he sent an express to the wharf for the tumbling boy, who arriving with all despatch, was enjoined to sit himself down in another chair just inside the door, continually to smoke a great pipe which the dwarf had provided for the purpose, and to take it from his lips under any pretence whatever, were it only for one minute at a time, if he dared. These arrangements completed, Mr. Quilp looked round him with chuckling satisfaction, and remarked that he called that comfort.

The legal gentleman, whose melodious name was Brass, might have called it comfort also but for two drawbacks: one was, that he could by no exertion sit easy in his chair, the seat of which was very hard, angular, slippery, and sloping; the other, that tobacco-smoke always caused him great internal discomposure and annoyance. But as he was quite a creature of Mr. Quilp's and had a thousand reasons for conciliating his good opinion, he tried to smile, and nodded his acquiescence with the best grace he could assume.

This Brass was an attorney of no very good repute, from Bevis Marks in the city of London; he was a tall, meagre man, with a nose like a wen, a protruding forehead, retreating eyes, and hair of a deep red. He wore a long black surtout reaching nearly to his ankles, short black trousers, high shoes, and cotton stockings of a bluish grey. He had a cringing manner, but a very harsh voice; and his blandest smiles were so extremely forbidding, that to have had his company under the least repulsive circumstances, one would have wished him to be out of temper that he might only scowl.

Quilp looked at his legal adviser, and seeing that he was winking very much in the anguish of his pipe, that he sometimes shuddered when he happened to inhale its full flavour, and that he constantly fanned the smoke from him, was quite overjoyed and rubbed his hands with glee.

'Smoke away, you dog,' said Quilp, turning to the boy, 'fill your pipe again and smoke it fast, down to the last whiff, or I'll put the sealing-waxed end of it in the fire and rub it red hot upon your tongue.'

Luckily the boy was case-hardened, and would have smoked

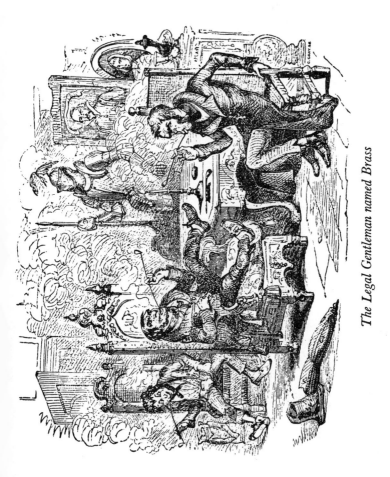

The Legal Gentleman named Brass

a small lime-kiln if anybody had treated him with it. Wherefore, he only muttered a brief defiance of his master, and did as he was ordered.

'Is it good, Brass, is it nice, is it fragrant, do you feel like the Grand Turk?' said Quilp.

Mr. Brass thought that if he did, the Grand Turk's feelings were by no means to be envied, but said it was famous, and he had no doubt he felt very like that Potentate.

'This is the way to keep off fever,' said Quilp, 'this is the way to keep off every calamity of life! We'll never leave off, all the time we stop here—smoke away, you dog, or you shall swallow the pipe!'

'Shall we stop here long, Mr. Quilp?' inquired his legal friend, when the dwarf had given his boy this gentle admonition.

'We must stop, I suppose, till the old gentleman up stairs is dead,' returned Quilp.

'He he he!' laughed Mr. Brass, 'oh! very good!'

'Smoke away!' cried Quilp. 'Never stop! you can talk as you smoke. Don't lose time.'

'He he he!' cried Brass faintly, as he again applied himself to the odious pipe. 'But if he should get better, Mr. Quilp?'

'Then we shall stop till he does, and no longer,' returned the dwarf.

'How kind it is of you, sir, to wait 'till then!' said Brass. 'Some people, sir, would have sold or removed the goods—oh dear, the very instant the law allowed 'em. Some people, sir, would have been all flintiness and granite. Some people, sir, would have—'

'Some people would have spared themselves the jabbering of such a parrot as you,' interposed the dwarf.

'He he he!' cried Brass. 'You have *such* spirits!'

The smoking sentinel at the door interposed in this place and without taking his pipe from his lips, growled,

'Here's the gal a comin' down.'

'The what, you dog?' said Quilp.

'The gal,' returned the boy. 'Are you deaf?'

'Oh!' said Quilp, drawing in his breath with great relish as if he were taking soup, 'you and I will have such a settling presently; there's such a scratching and bruising in store for you, my dear young friend! Aha! Nelly! How is he now, my duck of diamonds?'

'He's very bad,' replied the weeping child.

'What a pretty little Nell!' cried Quilp.

'Oh beautiful, sir, beautiful indeed,' said Brass. 'Quite charming!'

'Has she come to sit upon Quilp's knee,' said the dwarf, in what he meant to be a soothing tone, 'or is she going to bed in her own little room inside here? Which is poor Nelly going to do?'

'What a remarkably pleasant way he has with children!' muttered Brass, as if in confidence between himself and the ceiling; 'upon my word it's quite a treat to hear him.'

'I'm not going to stay at all,' faltered Nell. 'I want a few things out of that room, and then I—I—won't come down here any more.'

'And a very nice little room it is!' said the dwarf, looking into it as the child entered. 'Quite a bower! You're sure you're not going to use it; you're sure you're not coming back, Nelly?'

'No,' replied the child, hurrying away, with the few articles of dress she had come to remove; 'never again! Never again.'

'She's very sensitive,' said Quilp, looking after her. 'Very sensitive; that's a pity. The bedstead is much about my size. I think I shall make it *my* little room.'

Mr. Brass encouraging this idea, as he would have encouraged any other emanating from the same source, the dwarf walked in to try the effect. This he did, by throwing himself on his back upon the bed with his pipe in his mouth, and then kicking up his legs and smoking violently. Mr. Brass applauding this picture very much, and the bed being soft and comfortable, Mr. Quilp determined to use it, both as a sleeping place by night and as a kind of Divan by day; and in order that it might be converted to the latter purpose at once, remained where he was, and smoked his pipe out. The legal gentleman being by this time rather giddy and perplexed in his ideas (for this was one of the operations of the tobacco on his nervous system), took the opportunity of slinking away into the open air, where, in course of time, he recovered sufficiently to return with a countenance of tolerable composure. He was soon led on by the malicious dwarf to smoke himself into a relapse, and in that state stumbled upon a settee where he slept till morning.

Such were Mr. Quilp's first proceedings on entering upon his new property. He was, for some days, restrained by business from performing any particular pranks, as his time was pretty well occupied between taking, with the assistance of Mr. Brass, a minute inventory of all the goods in the place, and going abroad upon his other concerns which happily engaged him for several hours at a time. His avarice and caution being, now, thoroughly awakened, however, he was never absent from the house one night; and his eagerness for some termination, good or bad, to the old man's disorder, increasing rapidly, as the time passed by, soon began to vent itself in open murmurs and exclamations of impatience.

Nell shrunk timidly from all the dwarf's advances towards conversation, and fled from the very sound of his voice; nor were the lawyer's smiles less terrible to her than Quilp's grimaces. She lived in such continual dread and apprehension of meeting one or other of them on the stairs or in the passages if she stirred from her grandfather's chamber, that she seldom left it, for a moment, until late at night, when the silence encouraged her to venture forth and breathe the purer air of some empty room.

One night, she had stolen to her usual window, and was sitting there very sorrowfully—for the old man had been worse that day—when she thought she heard her name pronounced by a voice in the street. Looking down, she recognised Kit, whose endeavours to attract her attention had roused her from her sad reflections.

'Miss Nell!' said the boy in a low voice.

'Yes,' replied the child, doubtful whether she ought to hold any communication with the supposed culprit, but inclining to her old favourite still; 'what do you want?'

'I have wanted to say a word to you, for a long time,' the boy replied, 'but the people below have driven me away and wouldn't let me see you. You don't believe—I hope you don't really believe—that I deserve to be cast off as I have been; do you, miss?'

'I must believe it,' returned the child. 'Or why would grandfather have been so angry with you?'

'I don't know,' replied Kit. 'I'm sure I never deserved it from him, no, nor from you. I can say that, with a true and honest heart, any way. And then to be driven from the door, when I only came to ask how old master was—!'

'They never told me that,' said the child. 'I didn't know it indeed. I wouldn't have had them do it for the world.'

'Thank'ee, miss,' returned Kit, 'it's comfortable to hear you say that. I said I never would believe that it was your doing.'

'That was right!' said the child eagerly.

'Miss Nell,' cried the boy, coming under the window, and speaking in a lower tone, 'there are new masters down stairs. It's a change for you.'

'It is indeed,' replied the child.

'And so it will be for him when he gets better,' said the boy, pointing towards the sick room.

'—If he ever does,' added the child, unable to restrain her tears.

'Oh, he'll do that, he'll do that,' said Kit, 'I'm sure he will. You mustn't be cast down, Miss Nell. Now don't be, pray!'

These words of encouragement and consolation were few and roughly said, but they affected the child and made her, for the moment, weep the more.

'He'll be sure to get better now,' said the boy anxiously, 'if you don't give way to low spirits and turn ill yourself, which would make him worse and throw him back, just as he was recovering. When he does, say a good word—say a kind word for me, Miss Nell!'

'They tell me I must not even mention your name to him for a long, long time,' rejoined the child. 'I dare not; and even if I might, what good would a kind word do you, Kit? We shall be very poor. We shall scarcely have bread to eat.'

'It's not that I may be taken back,' said the boy, 'that I ask the favour of you. It isn't for the sake of food and wages that I've been waiting about, so long, in hopes to see you. Don't think that I'd come in a time of trouble to talk of such things as them.'

The child looked gratefully and kindly at him, but waited that he might speak again.

'No, it's not that,' said Kit hesitating, 'it's something very different from that. I haven't got much sense I know, but if he could be brought to believe that I'd been a faithful servant to him, doing the best I could, and never meaning harm, perhaps he mightn't—'

Here Kit faltered so long that the child entreated him to speak out, and quickly, for it was very late, and time to shut the window.

'Perhaps he mightn't think it over venturesome of me to say—well then, to say this,' cried Kit with sudden boldness.

'This home is gone from you and him. Mother and I have got a poor one, but that's better than this with all these people here; and why not come there, till he's had time to look about, and find a better!'

The child did not speak. Kit, in the relief of having made his proposition, found his tongue loosened, and spoke out in its favour with his utmost eloquence.

'You think,' said the boy, 'that it's very small and inconvenient. So it is, but it's very clean. Perhaps you think it would be noisy, but there's not a quieter court than ours in all the town. Don't be afraid of the children; the baby hardly ever cries, and the other one is very good—besides, *I*'d mind 'em. They wouldn't vex you much, I'm sure. Do try, Miss Nell, do try. The little front room up stairs is very pleasant. You can see a piece of the church-clock, through the chimneys, and almost tell the time; mother says it would be just the thing for you, and so it would, and you'd have her to wait upon you both, and me to run of errands. We don't mean money, bless you; you're not to think of that! Will you try him, Miss Nell? Only say you'll try him. Do try to make old master come, and ask him first what I have done. Will you only promise that, Miss Nell?'

Before the child could reply to this earnest solicitation, the street-door opened, and Mr. Brass thrusting out his night-capped head called in a surly voice, 'Who's there?' Kit immediately glided away, and Nell, closing the window softly, drew back into the room.

Before Mr. Brass had repeated his inquiry many times, Mr. Quilp, also embellished with a night-cap, emerged from the same door and looked carefully up and down the street, and up at all the windows of the house, from the opposite side. Finding that there was nobody in sight, he presently returned into the house with his legal friend, protesting (as the child heard from the staircase), that there was a league and plot against him; that he was in danger of being robbed and plundered by a band of conspirators who prowled about the house at all seasons; and that he would delay no longer, but take immediate steps for disposing of the property and returning to his own peaceful roof. Having growled forth these, and a great many other threats of the same nature, he coiled himself once more in the child's little bed, and Nell crept softly up the stairs.

It was natural enough that her short and unfinished dialogue

E

with Kit should leave a strong impression on her mind, and influence her dreams that night and her recollections for a long, long time. Surrounded by unfeeling creditors, and mercenary attendants upon the sick, and meeting in the height of her anxiety and sorrow with little regard or sympathy even from the women about her, it is not surprising that the affectionate heart of the child should have been touched to the quick by one kind and generous spirit, however uncouth the temple in which it dwelt. Thank Heaven that the temples of such spirits are not made with hands, and that they may be even more worthily hung with poor patchwork than with purple and fine linen!

CHAPTER XII

AT length, the crisis of the old man's disorder was past, and he began to mend. By very slow and feeble degrees his consciousness came back; but the mind was weakened and its functions were impaired. He was patient, and quiet; often sat brooding, but not despondently, for a long space; was easily amused, even by a sunbeam on the wall or ceiling; made no complaint that the days were long, or the nights tedious; and appeared indeed to have lost all count of time, and every sense of care or weariness. He would sit, for hours together, with Nell's small hand in his, playing with the fingers and stopping sometimes to smooth her hair or kiss her brow; and, when he saw that tears were glistening in her eyes, would look, amazed, about him for the cause, and forget his wonder even while he looked.

The child and he rode out: the old man propped up with pillows, and the child beside him. They were hand in hand as usual. The noise and motion in the streets fatigued his brain at first, but he was not surprised, or curious, or pleased, or irritated. He was asked if he remembered this, or that, 'O yes,' he said, 'quite well—why not?' Sometimes he turned his head, and looked, with earnest gaze and outstretched neck, after some stranger in the crowd, until he disappeared from sight; but, to the question why he did this, he answered not a word.

He was sitting in his easy chair one day, and Nell upon a stool beside him, when a man outside the door inquired if he might enter. 'Yes,' he said without emotion, 'it was Quilp, he knew. Quilp was master there. Of course he might come in.' And so he did.

'I'm glad to see you well again at last, neighbour,' said the dwarf, sitting down opposite to him. 'You're quite strong now?'

'Yes,' said the old man feebly, 'yes.'

'I don't want to hurry you, you know, neighbour,' said the dwarf, raising his voice, for the old man's senses were duller than they had been; 'but, as soon as you *can* arrange your future proceedings, the better.'

'Surely,' said the old man. 'The better for all parties.'

'You see,' pursued Quilp after a short pause, 'the goods being once removed, this house would be uncomfortable; uninhabitable in fact.'

'You say true,' returned the old man. 'Poor Nell too, what would *she* do?'

'Exactly,' bawled the dwarf, nodding his head; 'that's very well observed. Then will you consider about it, neighbour?'

'I will, certainly,' replied the old man. 'We shall not stop here.'

'So I supposed,' said the dwarf. 'I have sold the things. They have not yielded quite as much as they might have done, but pretty well—pretty well. To-day's Tuesday. When shall they be moved? There's no hurry—shall we say this afternoon?'

'Say Friday morning,' returned the old man.

'Very good,' said the dwarf. 'So be it,—with the understanding that I can't go beyond that day, neighbour, on any account.'

'Good,' returned the old man. 'I shall remember it.'

Mr. Quilp seemed rather puzzled by the strange, even spiritless way in which all this was said; but as the old man nodded his head and repeated 'on Friday morning. I shall remember it,' he had no excuse for dwelling on the subject any further, and so took a friendly leave with many expressions of good-will and many compliments to his friend on his looking so remarkably well; and went below stairs to report progress to Mr. Brass.

All that day, and all the next, the old man remained in this state. He wandered up and down the house and into and out of the various rooms, as if with some vague intent of bidding them adieu, but he referred neither by direct allusions nor in any other manner to the interview of the morning or the necessity of finding some other shelter. An indistinct idea he had, that the child was desolate and in want of help; for he often drew her to his bosom and bade her be of good cheer, saying that they would not desert each other; but he seemed unable to contemplate their real position more distinctly, and was still the listless, passionless creature, that suffering of mind and body had left him.

We call this a state of childishness, but it is the same poor hollow mockery of it, that death is of sleep. Where, in the dull eyes of doating men, are the laughing light and life of childhood, the gaiety that has known no check, the frankness that has felt no chill, the hope that has never withered, the joys that fade in blossoming? Where, in the sharp lineaments of rigid and unsightly death, is the calm beauty of slumber, telling of rest for the waking hours that are past, and gentle hopes and loves for those which are to come? Lay death and sleep down, side by side, and say who shall find the two akin. Send forth the child and childish man together, and blush for the pride that libels our own old happy state, and gives its title to an ugly and distorted image.

Thursday arrived, and there was no alteration in the old man. But, a change came upon him that evening, as he and the child sat silently together.

In a small dull yard below his window, there was a tree— green and flourishing enough, for such a place—and as the air stirred among its leaves, it threw a rippling shadow on the white wall. The old man sat watching the shadows as they trembled in this patch of light, until the sun went down; and when it was night, and the moon was slowly rising, he still sat in the same spot.

To one who had been tossing on a restless bed so long, even these few green leaves and this tranquil light, although it languished among chimneys and housetops, were pleasant things. They suggested quiet places afar off, and rest, and peace.

The child thought, more than once, that he was moved: and had forborne to speak. But, now, he shed tears—tears that it lightened her aching heart to see—and making as though he would fall upon his knees, besought her to forgive him.

'Forgive you—what?' said Nell, interposing to prevent his purpose. 'Oh, grandfather, what should *I* forgive?'

'All that is past, all that has come upon thee, Nell, all that was done in that uneasy dream,' returned the old man.

'Do not talk so,' said the child. 'Pray do not. Let us speak of something else.'

'Yes, yes, we will,' he rejoined. 'And it shall be of what we talked of long ago—many months—months is it, or weeks, or days? which is it, Nell?'

'I do not understand you,' said the child.

'It has come back upon me to-day, it has all come back since we have been sitting here. I bless thee for it, Nell!'

'For what, dear grandfather?'

'For what you said when we were first made beggars, Nell. Let us speak softly. Hush! for if they knew our purpose down-stairs, they would cry that I was mad and take thee from me.

We will not stop here, another day. We will go far away from here.'

'Yes, let us go,' said the child earnestly. 'Let us be gone from this place, and never turn back or think of it again. Let us wander barefoot through the world, rather than linger here.'

'We will,' answered the old man, 'we will travel afoot through the fields and woods, and by the side of rivers, and trust ourselves to God in the places where He dwells. It is far better to lie down at night beneath an open sky like that yonder —see how bright it is!—than to rest in close rooms which are always full of care and weary dreams. Thou and I together, Nell, may be cheerful and happy yet, and learn to forget this time, as if it had never been.'

'We will be happy,' cried the child. 'We never can be here.'

'No, we never can again—never again—that's truly said,' rejoined the old man. 'Let us steal away to-morrow morning —early and softly, that we may not be seen or heard—and leave no trace or track for them to follow by. Poor Nell! Thy cheek is pale, and thy eyes are heavy with watching and weeping for me—I know—for me; but thou wilt be well again, and merry too, when we are far away. To-morrow morning, dear, we'll turn our faces from this scene of sorrow, and be as free and happy as the birds.'

And then, the old man clasped his hands above her head, and said, in a few broken words, that from that time forth they would wander up and down together, and never part more until Death took one or other of the twain.

The child's heart beat high with hope and confidence. She had no thought of hunger, or cold, or thirst, or suffering. She saw in this, but a return of the simple pleasures they had once enjoyed, a relief from the gloomy solitude in which she had lived, an escape from the heartless people by whom she had been surrounded in her late time of trial, the restoration of the old man's health and peace, and a life of tranquil happiness. Sun, and stream, and meadow, and summer days, shone brightly in her view, and there was no dark tint in all the sparkling picture.

The old man had slept, for some hours, soundly in his bed, and she was yet busily engaged in preparing for their flight. There were a few articles of clothing for herself to carry, and a few for him; old garments, such as became their fallen fortunes, laid out to wear; and a staff to support his feeble steps, put ready for his use. But this was not all her task; for now she must visit the old rooms for the last time.

And how different the parting with them was, from any she had expected, and most of all from that which she had oftenest pictured to herself! How could she ever have thought of bidding them farewell in triumph, when the recollection of the many hours she had passed among them rose to her swelling heart, and made her feel the wish a cruelty: lonely and sad though many of those hours had been! She sat down at the window where she had spent so many evenings—darker far than this—and every thought of hope or cheerfulness that had occurred to her in that place came vividly upon her mind, and blotted out all its dull and mournful associations in an instant.

Her own little room too, where she had so often knelt down and prayed at night—prayed for the time which she hoped was dawning now—the little room where she had slept so peacefully, and dreamed such pleasant dreams! It was hard not to be able to glance round it once more, and to be forced to leave it without one kind look or grateful tear. There were some trifles there—poor useless things—that she would have liked to take away; but that was impossible.

This brought to mind her bird, her poor bird, who hung there yet. She wept bitterly for the loss of this little creature—until the idea occurred to her—she did not know how, or why, it came into her head—that it might, by some means, fall into the hands of Kit who would keep it for her sake, and think, perhaps, that she had left it behind in the hope that he might have it, and as an assurance that she was grateful to him. She was calmed and comforted by the thought, and went to rest with a lighter heart.

From many dreams of rambling through light and sunny places, but with some vague object unattained which ran indistinctly through them all, she awoke to find that it was yet night, and that the stars were shining brightly in the sky. At length, the day began to glimmer, and the stars to grow pale and dim. As soon as she was sure of this, she arose, and dressed herself for the journey.

The old man was yet asleep, and as she was unwilling to disturb him, she left him to slumber on, until the sun rose. He was anxious that they should leave the house without a minute's loss of time, and was soon ready.

The child then took him by the hand, and they trod lightly

and cautiously down the stairs, trembling whenever a board creaked, and often stopping to listen. The old man had forgotten a kind of wallet which contained the light burden he had to carry; and the going back a few steps to fetch it, seemed an interminable delay.

At last, they reached the passage on the ground floor, where the snoring of Mr. Quilp and his legal friend sounded more terrible in their ears than the roars of lions. The bolts of the door were rusty, and difficult to unfasten without noise. When they were all drawn back, it was found to be locked, and worst of all, the key was gone. Then the child remembered, for the first time, one of the nurses having told her that Quilp always locked both the house-doors at night, and kept the keys on the table in his bedroom.

It was not without great fear and trepidation, that little Nell slipped off her shoes and gliding through the store-room of old curiosities, where Mr. Brass—the ugliest piece of goods in all the stock—lay sleeping on a mattress, passed into her own little chamber.

Here she stood, for a few moments, quite transfixed with terror at the sight of Mr. Quilp, who was hanging so far out of bed that he almost seemed to be standing on his head, and who, either from the uneasiness of this posture, or in one of his agreeable habits, was gasping and growling with his mouth wide open, and the whites (or rather the dirty yellows) of his eyes distinctly visible. It was no time, however, to ask whether anything ailed him; so, possessing herself of the key after one hasty glance about the room, and repassing the prostrate Mr. Brass, she rejoined the old man in safety. They got the door open without noise, and passing into the street, stood still.

'Which way?' said the child.

The old man looked, irresolutely and helplessly, first at her, then to the right and left, then at her again, and shook his head. It was plain that she was thenceforth his guide and leader. The child felt it, but had no doubts or misgiving, and putting her hand in his, led him gently away.

It was the beginning of a day in June; the deep blue sky unsullied by a cloud, and teeming with brilliant light. The streets were, as yet, nearly free from passengers, the houses and shops were closed, and the healthy air of morning fell like breath from angels, on the sleeping town.

The old man and the child passed on through the glad

silence, elate with hope and pleasure. They were alone together, once again; every object was bright and fresh; nothing
reminded them, otherwise than by contrast, of the monotony
and constraint they had left behind; church towers and
steeples, frowning and dark at other times, now shone in the
sun; each humble nook and corner rejoiced in light; and the
sky, dimmed only by excessive distance, shed its placid smile on
everything beneath.

Forth from the city, while it yet slumbered, went the two
poor adventurers, wandering they knew not whither.

CHAPTER XIII

DANIEL QUILP of Tower Hill, and Sampson Brass of Bevis Marks in the city of London, Gentleman, one of her Majesty's attorneys of the Courts of King's Bench and Common Pleas at Westminster and a solicitor of the High Court of Chancery, slumbered on, unconscious and unsuspicious of any mischance, until a knocking at the street door, often repeated and gradually mounting up from a modest single rap to a perfect battery of knocks, fired in long discharges with a very short interval between, caused the said Daniel Quilp to struggle into a horizontal position, and to stare at the ceiling with a drowsy indifference, betokening that he heard the noise and rather wondered at the same, and couldn't be at the trouble of bestowing any further thought upon the subject.

As the knocking, however, instead of accommodating itself to his lazy state, increased in vigour and became more importunate, as if in earnest remonstrance against his falling asleep again, now that he had once opened his eyes, Daniel Quilp began by degrees to comprehend the possibility of there being somebody at the door; and thus he gradually came to recollect that it was Friday morning, and he had ordered Mrs. Quilp to be in waiting upon him at an early hour.

Mr. Brass, after writhing about, in a great many strange attitudes, and often twisting his face and eyes into an expression like that which is usually produced by eating gooseberries very early in the season, was by this time awake also. Seeing that Mr. Quilp invested himself in his every-day garments, he hastened to do the like, putting on his shoes before his stockings, and thrusting his legs into his coat-sleeves, and making such other small mistakes in his toilet as are not uncommon to those who dress in a hurry, and labour under the agitation of having been suddenly roused.

While the attorney was thus engaged, the dwarf was groping under the table, muttering desperate imprecations on himself, and mankind in general, and all inanimate objects to boot, which suggested to Mr. Brass the question, 'what's the matter?'

'The key,' said the dwarf, looking viciously at him, 'the door-key,—that's the matter. D'ye know anything of it?'

'How should I know anything of it, sir?' returned Mr. Brass.

'How should you?' repeated Quilp with a sneer. 'You're a nice lawyer, an't you? Ugh, you idiot!'

Not caring to represent to the dwarf in his present humour, that the loss of a key by another person could scarcely be said to affect his (Brass's) legal knowledge in any material degree, Mr. Brass humbly suggested that it must have been forgotten over night, and was, doubtless, at that moment in its native keyhole. Notwithstanding that Mr. Quilp had a strong conviction to the contrary, founded on his recollection of having carefully taken it out, he was fain to admit that this was possible, and therefore went grumbling to the door, where, sure enough, he found it.

Now, just as Mr. Quilp laid his hand upon the lock, and saw with great astonishment that the fastenings were undone, the knocking came again with most irritating violence, and the daylight which had been shining through the keyhole was intercepted on the outside by a human eye. The dwarf was very much exasperated, and wanting somebody to wreak his ill-humour upon, determined to dart out suddenly, and favour Mrs. Quilp with a gentle acknowledgment of her attention in making that hideous uproar.

With this view, he drew back the lock very silently and softly, and opening the door all at once, pounced out upon the person on the other side, who had at that moment raised the knocker for another application, and at whom the dwarf ran head first: throwing out his hands and feet together, and biting the air in the fulness of his malice.

So far, however, from rushing upon somebody who offered no resistance and implored his mercy, Mr. Quilp was no sooner in the arms of the individual whom he had taken for his wife than he found himself complimented with two staggering blows on the head, and two more, of the same quality, in the chest; and closing with his assailant, such a shower of buffets rained down upon his person as sufficed to convince him that he was in skilful and experienced hands. Nothing daunted by this reception, he clung tight to his opponent, and bit and hammered away with such good-will and heartiness, that it was at least a couple of minutes before he was dislodged. Then, and not until then, Daniel Quilp found himself, all flushed and dishevelled, in the middle of the street, with Mr. Richard Swiveller performing a kind of dance round him and requiring to know 'whether he wanted any more?'

'There's plenty more of it at the same shop,' said Mr. Swiveller, by turns advancing and retreating in a threatening attitude, 'a large and extensive assortment always on hand—country orders executed with promptitude and despatch—will you have a little more, sir?—don't say no, if you'd rather not.'

'I thought it was somebody else,' said Quilp, rubbing his shoulders; 'why didn't you say who you were?'

'Why didn't you say who *you* were,' returned Dick, 'instead of flying out of the house like a Bedlamite?'

'It was you that—that knocked,' said the dwarf, getting up with a short groan, 'was it?'

'Yes, I am the man,' replied Dick. 'That lady had begun when I came, but she knocked too soft, so I relieved her.' As he said this, he pointed towards Mrs. Quilp, who stood trembling at a little distance.

'Humph!' muttered the dwarf, darting an angry look at his wife, 'I thought it was your fault! And you, sir,—don't you know there has been somebody ill here, that you knock as if you'd beat the door down?'

'Damme!' answered Dick, 'that's why I did it. I thought there was somebody dead here.'

'You came for some purpose, I suppose,' said Quilp. 'What is it you want?'

'I want to know how the old gentleman is,' rejoined Mr. Swiveller, 'and to hear from Nell herself, with whom I should like to have a little talk. I'm a friend of the family, sir,—at least I'm the friend of one of the family, and that's the same thing.'

'You'd better walk in then,' said the dwarf. 'Go on, sir, go on. Now, Mrs. Quilp—after you, ma'am.'

Mrs. Quilp hesitated, but Mr. Quilp insisted. And it was not a contest of politeness, or by any means a matter of form, for she knew very well that her husband wished to enter the house in this order, that he might have a favourable opportunity of inflicting a few pinches on her arms, which were seldom free from impressions of his fingers in black and blue colours. Mr. Swiveller, who was not in the secret, was a little surprised to hear a suppressed scream, and, looking round, to see Mrs. Quilp following him with a sudden jerk; but he did not remark on these appearances, and soon forgot them.

'Now, Mrs. Quilp,' said the dwarf when they had entered the shop, 'go you up stairs, if you please, to Nelly's room, and tell her that she's wanted.'

The Pilgrimage begins
(p. 96)

'You seem to make yourself at home here,' said Dick, who was unacquainted with Mr. Quilp's authority.

'I *am* at home, young gentleman,' returned the dwarf.

Dick was pondering what these words might mean, and still more what the presence of Mr. Brass might mean, when Mrs. Quilp came hurrying down stairs, declaring that the rooms above were empty.

'Empty, you fool?' said the dwarf.

'I give you my word, Quilp,' answered his trembling wife, 'that I have been into every room and there's not a soul in any of them.'

'And that,' said Mr. Brass, clapping his hands once, with an emphasis, 'explains the mystery of the key!'

Quilp looked frowningly at him, and frowningly at his wife, and frowningly at Richard Swiveller; but, receiving no enlightenment from any of them, hurried up stairs, whence he soon hurried down again, confirming the report which had been already made.

'It's a strange way of going,' he said, glancing at Swiveller: 'very strange not to communicate with me who am such a close and intimate friend of his! Ah! he'll write to me no doubt, or he'll bid Nelly write—yes, yes, that's what he'll do. Nelly's very fond of me. Pretty Nell!'

Mr. Swiveller looked, as he was, all open-mouthed astonishment. Still glancing furtively at him, Quilp turned to Mr. Brass and observed, with assumed carelessness, that this need not interfere with the removal of the goods.

'For indeed,' he added, 'we knew that they'd go away to-day, but not that they'd go so early, or so quietly. But they have their reasons, they have their reasons.'

'Where in the devil's name are they gone?' said the wondering Dick.

Quilp shook his head, and pursed up his lips, in a manner which implied that he knew very well, but was not at liberty to say.

'And what,' said Dick, looking at the confusion about him, 'what do you mean by moving the goods?'

'That I have bought 'em, Sir,' rejoined Quilp. 'Eh? What then?'

'Has the sly old fox made his fortune then, and gone to live in a tranquil cot in a pleasant spot with a distant view of the changing sea?' said Dick, in great bewilderment.

'Keeping his place of retirement very close, that he may not be visited too often by affectionate grandsons and their devoted friends, eh?' added the dwarf, rubbing his hands hard; '*I* say nothing, but is that your meaning?'

Richard Swiveller was utterly aghast at this unexpected alteration of circumstances, which threatened the complete overthrow of the project in which he bore so conspicuous a part, and seemed to nip his prospects in the bud. Having only received from Frederick Trent, late on the previous night, information of the old man's illness, he had come upon a visit of condolence and inquiry to Nell, prepared with the first instalment of that long train of fascinations which was to fire her heart at last. And here, when he had been thinking of all kinds of graceful and insinuating approaches, and meditating on the fearful retaliation which was slowly working against Sophy Wackles—here were Nell, the old man, and all the money gone, melted away, decamped he knew not whither, as if with a foreknowledge of the scheme and a resolution to defeat it in the very outset, before a step was taken.

In his secret heart, Daniel Quilp was both surprised and troubled by the flight which had been made. It had not escaped his keen eye that some indispensable articles of clothing were gone with the fugitives, and knowing the old man's weak state of mind, he marvelled what that course of proceeding might be in which he had so readily procured the concurrence of the child. It must not be supposed (or it would be a gross injustice to Mr. Quilp) that he was tortured by any disinterested anxiety on behalf of either. His uneasiness arose from a misgiving that the old man had some secret store of money which he had not suspected; and the idea of its escaping his clutches, overwhelmed him with mortification and self-reproach.

In this frame of mind, it was some consolation to him to find that Richard Swiveller was, for different reasons, evidently irritated and disappointed by the same cause. It was plain, thought the dwarf, that he had come there, on behalf of his friend, to cajole or frighten the old man out of some small fraction of that wealth of which they supposed him to have an abundance. Therefore, it was a relief to vex his heart with a picture of the riches the old man hoarded, and to expatiate on his cunning in removing himself even beyond the reach of importunity.

'Well,' said Dick, with a blank look, 'I suppose it's of no use my staying here.'

'Not the least in the world,' rejoined the dwarf.

'You'll mention that I called, perhaps?' said Dick.

Mr. Quilp nodded, and said he certainly would, the very first time he saw them.

'And say,' added Mr. Swiveller, 'say, sir, that I was wafted here upon the pinions of concord; that I came to remove, with the rake of friendship, the seeds of mutual wiolence and heart-burning, and to sow in their place, the germs of social harmony. Will you have the goodness to charge yourself with that commission, sir?'

'Certainly!' rejoined Quilp.

'Will you be kind enough to add to it, sir,' said Dick, producing a very small limp card, 'that *that* is my address, and that I am to be found at home every morning? Two distinct knocks, sir, will produce the slavey at any time. My particular friends, sir, are accustomed to sneeze when the door is opened, to give her to understand that they *are* my friends and have no interested motives in asking if I'm at home. I beg your pardon; will you allow me to look at that card again?'

'Oh! by all means,' rejoined Quilp.

'By a slight and not unnatural mistake, sir,' said Dick, substituting another in its stead, 'I had handed you the pass-ticket of a select convivial circle called the Glorious Apollers, of which I have the honour to be Perpetual Grand. *That* is the proper document, sir. Good morning.'

Quilp bade him good day; the Perpetual Grand Master of the Glorious Apollers, elevating his hat in honour of Mrs. Quilp, dropped it carelessly on the side of his head again, and disappeared with a flourish.

By this time, certain vans had arrived for the conveyance of the goods, and divers strong men in caps were balancing chests of drawers and other trifles of that nature upon their heads, and performing muscular feats which heightened their complexions considerably. Not to be behindhand in the bustle, Mr. Quilp went to work with surprising vigour; hustling and driving the people about, like an evil spirit; setting Mrs. Quilp upon all kinds of arduous and impracticable tasks; carrying great weights up and down, with no apparent effort; kicking the boy from the wharf, whenever he could get near him; and inflicting, with his loads, a great many sly bumps and blows on the shoulders of Mr. Brass, as he stood upon the door-steps to answer all the inquiries of curious neighbours: which was his department. His presence and example diffused such alacrity among the persons employed, that, in a few hours, the house was emptied of everything, but pieces of matting, empty porter-pots, and scattered fragments of straw.

Seated, like an African chief, on one of these pieces of matting, the dwarf was regaling himself in the parlour, with bread and cheese and beer, when he observed without appearing to do so, that a boy was prying in at the outer door. Assured that it was Kit, though he saw little more than his nose, Mr. Quilp hailed him by his name; whereupon Kit came in and demanded what he wanted.

'Come here, you sir,' said the dwarf. 'Well, so your old master and young mistress have gone?'

'Where?' rejoined Kit, looking round.

'Do you mean to say you don't know where?' answered Quilp sharply. 'Where have they gone, eh?'

'I don't know,' said Kit.

'Come,' retorted Quilp, 'let's have no more of this! Do you mean to say that you don't know they went away by stealth, as soon as it was light this morning?'

'No,' said the boy, in evident surprise.

'You don't know that?' cried Quilp. 'Don't I know that you were hanging about the house the other night, like a thief, eh? Weren't you told then?'

'No,' replied the boy.

'You were not?' said Quilp. 'What were you told then; what were you talking about?'

Kit, who knew no particular reason why he should keep the matter secret now, related the purpose for which he had come on that occasion, and the proposal he had made.

'Oh!' said the dwarf after a little consideration. 'Then, I think they'll come to you yet.'

'Do you think they will?' cried Kit eagerly.

'Aye, I think they will,' returned the dwarf. 'Now, when they do, let me know; d'ye hear? Let me know, and I'll give you something. I want to do 'em a kindness, and I can't do 'em a kindness unless I know where they are. You hear what I say?'

Kit might have returned some answer which would not have been agreeable to his irascible questioner, if the boy from the wharf, who had been skulking about the room in search of anything that might have been left about by accident, had not happened to cry, 'Here's a bird! What's to be done with this?'

'Wring its neck,' rejoined Quilp.

'Oh no, don't do that,' said Kit, stepping forward. 'Give it to me.'

'Oh yes, I dare say,' cried the other boy. 'Come! You let the cage alone, and let me wring its neck, will you? He said I was to do it. You let the cage alone, will you?'

'Give it here, give it to me, you dogs,' roared Quilp. 'Fight for it, you dogs, or I'll wring its neck myself!'

Without further persuasion, the two boys fell upon each other, tooth and nail, while Quilp, holding up the cage in one hand, and chopping the ground with his knife in an ecstasy, urged them on by his taunts and cries to fight more fiercely. They were a pretty equal match, and rolled about together, exchanging blows which were by no means child's play, until at length Kit, planting a well-directed hit in his adversary's chest, disengaged himself, sprung nimbly up, and snatching the cage from Quilp's hands made off with his prize.

He did not stop once, until he reached home, where his bleeding face occasioned great consternation, and caused the elder child to howl dreadfully.

'Goodness gracious, Kit, what is the matter, what have you been doing?' cried Mrs. Nubbles.

'Never you mind, mother,' answered her son, wiping his face on the jack-towel behind the door. 'I'm not hurt, don't you be afraid for me. I've been a fightin' for a bird and won him, that's all. Hold your noise, little Jacob. I never see such a naughty boy in all my days!'

'You have been a fighting for a bird!' exclaimed his mother.

'Ah! Fightin' for a bird!' replied Kit, 'and here he is—Miss Nelly's bird, mother, that they was agoin' to wring the neck of! I stopped that though—ha ha ha! They wouldn't wring his neck and me by, no no. It wouldn't do, mother, it wouldn't do at all. Ha ha ha!'

Kit laughing so heartily, with his swollen and bruised face looking out of the towel, made little Jacob laugh, and then his mother laughed, and then the baby crowed and kicked with great glee, and then they all laughed in concert: partly because of Kit's triumph, and partly because they were very fond of each other. When this fit was over, Kit exhibited the bird to both children, as a great and precious rarity—it was only a poor linnet—and looking about the wall for an old nail, made a scaffolding of a chair and table and twisted it out with great exultation.

'Let me see,' said the boy, 'I think I'll hang him in the winder, because it's more light and cheerful, and he can see the sky there, if he looks up very much. He's such a one to sing, I can tell you!'

So, the scaffolding was made again, and Kit, climbing up with the poker for a hammer, knocked in the nail and hung up the cage, to the immeasurable delight of the whole family. When it had been adjusted and straightened a great many times, and he had walked backwards into the fireplace in his admiration of it, the arrangement was pronounced to be perfect.

'And now, mother,' said the boy, 'before I rest any more, I'll go out and see if I can find a horse to hold, and then I can buy some birdseed, and a bit of something nice for you, into the bargain.'

Mr. Swiveller's Pugilistic Skill

(p. 99)

CHAPTER XIV

A S it was very easy for Kit to persuade himself that the old house was in his way, his way being anywhere, he tried to look upon his passing it once more as a matter of imperative and disagreeable necessity, quite apart from any desire of his own, to which he could not choose but yield. It is not uncommon for people who are much better fed and taught than Christopher Nubbles had ever been, to make duties of their inclinations in matters of more doubtful propriety, and to take great credit for the self-denial with which they gratify themselves.

There was no need of any caution this time, and no fear of being detained by having to play out a return match with Daniel Quilp's boy. The place was entirely deserted, and looked as dusty and dingy as if it had been so for months. A rusty padlock was fastened on the door, ends of discoloured blinds and curtains flapped drearily against the half-opened upper windows, and the crooked holes cut in the closed shutters below, were black with the darkness of the inside. Some of the glass in the window he had so often watched, had been broken in the rough hurry of the morning, and that room looked more deserted and dull than any. A group of idle urchins had taken possession of the doorsteps; some were plying the knocker and listening with delighted dread to the hollow sounds it spread through the dismantled house; others were clustered about the keyhole, watching half in jest and half in earnest for 'the ghost,' which an hour's gloom, added to the mystery that hung about the late inhabitants, had already raised. Standing all alone in the midst of the business and bustle of the street, the house looked a picture of cold desolation; and Kit, who remembered the cheerful fire that used to burn there on a winter's night and the no less cheerful laugh that made the small room ring, turned quite mournfully away.

It must be especially observed in justice to poor Kit that he was by no means of a sentimental turn, and perhaps had never heard that adjective in all his life. He was only a soft-hearted grateful fellow, and had nothing genteel or polite about him; consequently, instead of going home again, in his grief, to kick the children and abuse his mother (for, when your finely strung people are out of sorts, they must have everybody else unhappy likewise), he turned his thoughts to the vulgar expedient of making them more comfortable if he could.

Bless us, what a number of gentlemen on horseback there were riding up and down, and how few of them wanted their horses held! A good city speculator or a parliamentary commissioner could have told to a fraction, from the crowds that were cantering about, what sum of money was realised in London, in the course of a year, by holding horses alone. And undoubtedly it would have been a very large one, if only a twentieth part of the gentlemen without grooms had had occasion to alight; but they had not; and it is often an ill-natured circumstance like this, which spoils the most ingenious estimate in the world.

Kit walked about, now with quick steps and now with slow; now lingering as some rider slackened his horse's pace and looked about him; and now darting at full speed up a bye-street as he caught a glimpse of some distant horseman going lazily up the shady side of the road, and promising to stop, at every door. But on they all went, one after another, and there was not a penny stirring. 'I wonder,' thought the boy, 'if one of these gentlemen knew there was nothing in the cupboard at home, whether he'd stop on purpose, and make believe that he wanted to call somewhere, that I might earn a trifle?'

He was quite tired out with pacing the streets, to say nothing of repeated disappointments, and was sitting down upon a step to rest, when there approached towards him a little clattering jingling four-wheeled chaise, drawn by a little obstinate-looking rough-coated pony, and driven by a little fat placid-faced old gentleman. Beside the little old gentleman sat a little old lady, plump and placid like himself, and the pony was coming along at his own pace and doing exactly as he pleased with the whole concern. If the old gentleman remonstrated by shaking the reins, the pony replied by shaking his head. It was plain that the utmost the pony would consent to do, was to go in his own way up any street that the old gentleman particularly wished to traverse, but that it was an understanding between them that he must do this after his own fashion or not at all.

As they passed where he sat, Kit looked so wistfully at the little turn-out, that the old gentleman looked at him. Kit rising and putting his hand to his hat, the old gentleman intimated to the pony that he wished to stop, to which proposal the pony (who seldom objected to that part of his duty) graciously acceded.

'I beg your pardon, sir,' said Kit. 'I'm sorry you stopped, sir. I only meant did you want your horse minded.'

'I'm going to get down in the next street,' returned the old gentleman. 'If you like to come on after us, you may have the job.'

Kit thanked him, and joyfully obeyed. The pony ran off at a sharp angle to inspect a lamp-post on the opposite side of the way, and then went off at a tangent to another lamp-post on the other side. Having satisfied himself that they were of the same pattern and materials, he came to a stop apparently absorbed in meditation.

'Will you go on, sir,' said the old gentleman, gravely, 'or are we to wait here for you 'till it's too late for our appointment?'

The pony remained immoveable.

'Oh you naughty Whisker,' said the old lady. 'Fie upon you! I'm ashamed of such conduct.'

The pony appeared to be touched by this appeal to his feelings, for he trotted on directly, though in a sulky manner, and stopped no more until he came to a door whereon was a brass plate with the words 'Witherden—Notary.' Here the old gentleman got out and helped out the old lady, and then took from under the seat a nosegay resembling in shape and dimensions a full-sized warming-pan with the handle cut short off. This, the old lady carried into the house with a staid and stately air, and the old gentleman (who had a club-foot) followed close upon her.

They went, as it was easy to tell from the sound of their voices, into the front parlour, which seemed to be a kind of office. The day being very warm and the street a quiet one, the windows were wide open; and it was easy to hear through the Venetian blinds all that passed inside.

At first there was a great shaking of hands and shuffling of feet, succeeded by the presentation of the nosegay; for a voice, supposed by the listener to be that of Mr. Witherden, the Notary, was heard to exclaim a great many times, 'oh, delicious!' 'oh, fragrant, indeed!' and a nose, also supposed to be the property of that gentleman, was heard to inhale the scent with a snuffle of exceeding pleasure.

'I brought it in honour of the occasion, sir,' said the old lady.

'Ah! an occasion indeed, ma'am; an occasion which does honour to me, ma'am, honour to me,' rejoined Mr. Witherden, the Notary. 'I have had many a gentleman articled to me, ma'am, many a one. Some of them are now rolling in riches, unmindful of their old companion and friend, ma'am, others are in the habit of calling upon me to this day and saying, "Mr. Witherden, some of the pleasantest hours I ever spent in my life were spent in this office—were spent, sir, upon this very stool;" but there was never one among the number, ma'am, attached as I have been to many of them, of whom I augured such bright things as I do of your only son.'

'Oh dear!' said the old lady. 'How happy you do make us when you tell us that, to be sure!'

'I tell you, ma'am,' said Mr. Witherden, 'what I think as an honest man, which, as the poet observes, is the noblest work of God. I agree with the poet in every particular, ma'am. The mountainous Alps on the one hand, or a humming-bird on the other, is nothing, in point of workmanship, to an honest man— or woman—or woman.'

'Anything that Mr. Witherden can say of me,' observed a small quiet voice, 'I can say, with interest, of him, I am sure.'

'It's a happy circumstance, a truly happy circumstance,' said the Notary, 'to happen too upon his eight-and-twentieth birthday, and I hope I know how to appreciate it. I trust, Mr. Garland, my dear sir, that we may mutually congratulate each other upon this auspicious occasion.'

To this the old gentleman replied that he felt assured they might. There appeared to be another shaking of hands in consequence, and when it was over, the old gentleman said that, though he said it who should not, he believed no son had ever been a greater comfort to his parents than Abel Garland had been to his.

'Marrying as his mother and I did, late in life, sir, after waiting for a great many years, until we were well enough off— coming together when we were no longer young, and then being blessed with one child who has always been dutiful and affectionate—why, it's a source of great happiness to us both, sir.'

'Of course it is, I have no doubt of it,' returned the Notary in a sympathising voice. 'It's the contemplation of this sort of thing, that makes me deplore my fate in being a bachelor. There was a young lady once, sir, the daughter of an outfitting warehouse of the first respectability—but that's a weakness. Chuckster, bring in Mr. Abel's articles.'

'You see, Mr. Witherden,' said the old lady, 'that Abel has not been brought up like the run of young men. He has always had a pleasure in our society, and always been with us. Abel has never been absent from us, for a day; has he, my dear?'

'Never, my dear,' returned the old gentleman, 'except when he went to Margate one Saturday with Mr. Tomkinley that had been a teacher at that school he went to, and came back upon the Monday; but he was very ill after that, you remember, my dear; it was quite a dissipation.'

'He was not used to it, you know,' said the old lady, 'and he couldn't bear it, that's the truth. Besides he had no comfort in being there without us, and had nobody to talk to or enjoy himself with.'

'That was it, you know,' interposed the same small quiet voice that had spoken once before. 'I was quite abroad, mother, quite desolate, and to think that the sea was between us—oh, I never shall forget what I felt when I first thought that the sea was between us!'

'Very natural under the circumstances,' observed the Notary. 'Mr. Abel's feelings did credit to his nature, and credit to your nature, ma'am, and his father's nature, and human nature. I trace the same current now, flowing through all his quiet and unobtrusive proceedings.—I am about to sign my name, you observe, at the foot of the articles which Mr. Chuckster will witness; and placing my finger upon this blue wafer with the vandyked corners, I am constrained to remark in a distinct tone of voice—don't be alarmed, ma'am, it is merely a form of law— that I deliver this, as my act and deed. Mr. Abel will place his name against the other wafer, repeating the same cabalistic words, and the business is over. Ha ha ha! You see how easily these things are done!'

There was a short silence, apparently, while Mr. Abel went through the prescribed form, and then the shaking of hands and shuffling of feet were renewed, and shortly afterwards there was a clinking of wine-glasses and a great talkativeness on the part of everybody. In about a quarter of an hour Mr. Chuckster (with a pen behind his ear and his face inflamed with wine) appeared at the door, and condescending to address Kit by the jocose appellation of 'Young Snob,' informed him that the visitors were coming out.

Out they came forthwith; Mr. Witherden, who was short, chubby, fresh-coloured, brisk, and pompous, leading the old lady with extreme politeness, and the father and son following them, arm in arm. Mr. Abel, who had a quaint old-fashioned air about him, looked nearly of the same age as his father, and bore a wonderful resemblance to him in face and figure, though wanting something of his full, round cheerfulness, and substituting in its place, a timid reserve. In all other respects, in the neatness of the dress, and even in the club-foot, he and the old gentleman were precisely alike.

Having seen the old lady safely in her seat, and assisted in the arrangement of her cloak and a small basket which formed an indispensable portion of her equipage, Mr. Abel got into a little box behind which had evidently been made for his express accommodation, and smiled at everybody present by turns, beginning with his mother and ending with the pony. There was then a great to-do to make the pony hold up his head that the bearing-rein might be fastened; at last even this was effected; and the old gentleman, taking his seat and the reins, put his hand in his pocket to find a sixpence for Kit.

He had no sixpences, neither had the old lady, nor Mr. Abel, nor the Notary, nor Mr. Chuckster. The old gentleman thought a shilling too much, but there was no shop in the street to get change at, so he gave it to the boy.

'There,' he said jokingly, 'I'm coming here again next Monday at the same time, and mind you're here, my lad, to work it out.'

'Thank you, sir,' said Kit. 'I'll be sure to be here.'

He was quite serious, but they all laughed heartily at his saying so, especially Mr. Chuckster, who roared outright and appeared to relish the joke amazingly. As the pony, with a presentiment that he was going home, or a determination that he would not go anywhere else (which was the same thing), trotted away pretty nimbly, Kit had no time to justify himself, and went his way also. Having expended his treasure in such purchases as he knew would be most acceptable at home, not forgetting some seed for the wonderful bird, he hastened back as fast as he could, so elated with his success and great good-fortune, that he more than half expected Nell and the old man would have arrived before him.

Kit makes an Appointment

OFTEN, while they were yet pacing the silent streets of the town on the morning of their departure, the child trembled with a mingled sensation of hope and fear as in some far-off figure imperfectly seen in the clear distance, her fancy traced a likeness to honest Kit. But although she would gladly have given him her hand and thanked him for what he had said at their last meeting, it was always a relief to find, when they came nearer to each other, that the person who approached was not he, but a stranger; for even if she had not dreaded the effect which the sight of him might have wrought upon her fellow-traveller, she felt that to bid farewell to anybody now, and most of all to him who had been so faithful and so true, was more than she could bear. It was enough to leave dumb things behind, and objects that were insensible both to her love and sorrow. To have parted from her only other friend upon the threshold of that wild journey, would have wrung her heart indeed.

Why is it that we can better bear to part in spirit than in body, and while we have the fortitude to act farewell have not the nerve to say it? On the eve of long voyages or an absence of many years, friends who are tenderly attached will separate with the usual look, the usual pressure of the hand, planning one final interview for the morrow, while each well knows that it is but a poor feint to save the pain of uttering that one word, and that the meeting will never be. Should possibilities be worse to bear than certainties? We do not shun our dying friends; the not having distinctly taken leave of one among them, whom we left in all kindness and affection, will often embitter the whole remainder of a life.

The town was glad with morning light; places that had shown ugly and distrustful all night long, now wore a smile; and sparkling sunbeams dancing on chamber windows, and twinkling through blind and curtain before sleepers' eyes, shed light even into dreams, and chased away the shadows of the night. Birds in hot rooms, covered up close and dark, felt it was morning, and chafed and grew restless in their little cells; bright-eyed mice crept back to their tiny homes and nestled timidly together; the sleek house-cat, forgetful of her prey, sat winking at the rays of sun starting through keyhole and cranny in the door, and longed for her stealthy run and warm sleek bask outside. The nobler beasts confined in dens, stood motionless behind their bars, and gazed on fluttering boughs, and sunshine peeping through some little window, with eyes in which old forests gleamed—then trod impatiently the track their prisoned feet had worn—and stopped and gazed again. Men in their dungeons stretched their cramp cold limbs and cursed the stone that no bright sun could warm. The flowers that sleep by night, opened their gentle eyes and turned them to the day. The light, creation's mind, was everywhere, and all things owned its power.

The two pilgrims, often pressing each other's hands, or exchanging a smile or cheerful look, pursued their way in silence. Bright and happy as it was, there was something solemn in the long, deserted streets, from which, like bodies without souls, all habitual character and expression had departed, leaving but one dead uniform repose, that made them all alike. All was so still at that early hour, that the few pale people whom they met seemed as much unsuited to the scene, as the sickly lamp which had been here and there left burning, was powerless and faint in the full glory of the sun.

Before they had penetrated very far into the labyrinth of men's abodes which yet lay between them and the outskirts, this aspect began to melt away, and noise and bustle to usurp its place. Some straggling carts and coaches rumbling by, first broke the charm, then others came, then others yet more active, then a crowd. The wonder was, at first, to see a tradesman's room window open, but it was a rare thing to see one closed; then, smoke rose slowly from the chimneys, and sashes were thrown up to let in air, and doors were opened, and servant girls, looking lazily in all directions but their brooms, scattered brown clouds of dust into the eyes of shrinking passengers, or listened disconsolately to milkmen who spoke of country fairs, and told of waggons in the mews, with awnings and all things complete, and gallant swains to boot, which another hour would see upon their journey.

This quarter passed, they came upon the haunts of commerce and great traffic, where many people were resorting, and business was already rife. The old man looked about him with a startled and bewildered gaze, for these were places that he hoped to shun. He pressed his finger on his lip, and drew the child along by narrow courts and winding ways, nor did he seem at ease until they had left it far behind, often casting a backward look towards it, murmuring that ruin and self-murder were crouching in every street, and would follow if they scented them; and that they could not fly too fast.

Again this quarter passed, they came upon a straggling neighbourhood, where the mean houses parcelled off in rooms, and windows patched with rags and paper, told of the populous poverty that sheltered there. The shops sold goods that only poverty could buy, and sellers and buyers were pinched and griped alike. Here were poor streets where faded gentility essayed with scanty space and shipwrecked means to make its last feeble stand, but tax-gatherer and creditor came there as elsewhere, and the poverty that yet faintly struggled was hardly less squalid and manifest than that which had long ago submitted and given up the game.

This was a wide, wide track—for the humble followers of the camp of wealth pitch their tents round about it for many a mile—but its character was still the same. Damp rotten houses, many to let, many yet building, many half-built and mouldering away—lodgings, where it would be hard to tell which needed pity most, those who let or those who came to take—children, scantily fed and clothed, spread over every street, and sprawling in the dust—scolding mothers, stamping their slip-shod feet with noisy threats upon the pavement—shabby fathers, hurrying with dispirited looks to the occupation which brought them 'daily bread' and little more—mangling-women, washerwomen, cobblers, tailors, chandlers, driving their trades in parlours and kitchens and back rooms and garrets, and some-times all of them under the same roof—brick-fields skirting gardens paled with staves of old casks, or timber pillaged from houses burnt down, and blackened and blistered by the flames —mounds of dockweed, nettles, coarse grass and oyster shells, heaped in rank confusion—small dissenting chapels to teach, with no lack of illustration, the miseries of Earth, and plenty of new churches, erected with a little superfluous wealth, to show the way to Heaven.

At length these streets becoming more straggling yet, dwindled and dwindled away, until there were only small garden patches bordering the road, with many a summer-house innocent of paint and built of old timber or some fragments of a boat, green as the tough cabbage-stalks that grew about it, and grottoed at the seams with toad-stools and

F

tight-sticking snails. To these succeeded pert cottages, two and two with plots of ground in front, laid out in angular beds with stiff box borders and narrow paths between, where footstep never strayed to make the gravel rough. Then came the public-house, freshly painted in green and white, with tea-gardens and a bowling green, spurning its old neighbour with the horse-trough where the waggons stopped; then, fields; and then, some houses, one by one, of goodly size with lawns, some even with a lodge where dwelt a porter and his wife. Then, came a turnpike; then fields again with trees and hay-stacks; then, a hill; and on the top of that, the traveller might stop, and—looking back at old Saint Paul's looming through the smoke, its cross peeping above the cloud (if the day were clear), and glittering in the sun; and casting his eyes upon the Babel out of which it grew until he traced it down to the furthest outposts of the invading army of bricks and mortar whose station lay for the present nearly at his feet—might feel at last that he was clear of London.

Near such a spot as this, and in a pleasant field, the old man and his little guide (if guide she were, who knew not whither they were bound) sat down to rest. She had had the precaution to furnish her basket with some slices of bread and meat, and here they made their frugal breakfast.

The freshness of the day, the singing of the birds, the beauty of the waving grass, the deep green leaves, the wild flowers, and the thousand exquisite scents and sounds that floated in the air, —deep joys to most of us, but most of all to those whose life is in a crowd or who live solitarily in great cities as in the bucket of a human well,—sunk into their breasts and made them very glad. The child had repeated her artless prayers once that morning, more earnestly perhaps than she had ever done in all her life, but as she felt all this they rose to her lips again. The old man took off his hat—he had no memory for the words—but he said amen, and that they were very good.

There had been an old copy of the Pilgrim's Progress, with strange plates, upon a shelf at home, over which she had often pored whole evenings, wondering whether it was true in every word, and where those distant countries with the curious names might be. As she looked back upon the place they had left, one part of it came strongly on her mind.

'Dear grandfather,' she said, 'only that this place is prettier and a great deal better than the real one, if that in the book is

A Rest by the Way

like it, I feel as if we were both Christian, and laid down on this grass all the cares and troubles we brought with us; never to take them up again.'

'No—never to return—never to return'—replied the old man, waving his hand towards the city. 'Thou and I are free of it now, Nell. They shall never lure us back.'

'Are you tired?' said the child, 'are you sure you don't feel ill from this long walk?'

'I shall never feel ill again, now that we are once away,' was his reply. 'Let us be stirring, Nell. We must be further away— a long, long way further. We are too near to stop, and be at rest. Come!'

There was a pool of clear water in the field, in which the child laved her hands and face, and cooled her feet before setting forth to walk again. She would have the old man refresh himself in this way too, and making him sit down upon the grass, cast the water on him with her hands, and dried it with her simple dress.

'I can do nothing for myself, my darling,' said the grand-father; 'I don't know how it is, I could once, but the time's gone. Don't leave me, Nell; say that thou'lt not leave me. I loved thee all the while, indeed I did. If I lose thee too, my dear, I must die!'

He laid his head upon her shoulder and moaned piteously. The time had been, and a very few days before, when the child could not have restrained her tears and must have wept with him. But now she soothed him with gentle and tender words, smiled at his thinking they could ever part, and rallied him cheerfully upon the jest. He was soon calmed and fell asleep, singing to himself in a low voice, like a little child.

He awoke refreshed, and they continued their journey. The road was pleasant, lying between beautiful pastures and fields of corn, about which, poised high in the clear blue sky, the lark trilled out her happy song. The air came laden with the frag-rance it caught upon its way, and the bees, upborne upon its scented breath, hummed forth their drowsy satisfaction as they floated by.

They were now in the open country; the houses were very few and scattered at long intervals, often miles apart. Occasionally they came upon a cluster of poor cottages, some with a chair or low board put across the open door to keep the scrambling children from the road, others shut up close while all the family

were working in the fields. These were often the commencement of a little village: and after an interval came a wheel-
wright's shed or perhaps a blacksmith's forge; then a thriving
farm with sleepy cows lying about the yard, and horses peering
over the low wall and scampering away when harnessed horses
passed upon the road, as though in triumph at their freedom.
There were dull pigs too, turning up the ground in search of
dainty food, and grunting their monotonous grumblings as
they prowled about, or crossed each other in their quest;
plump pigeons skimming round the roof or strutting on the
eaves; and ducks and geese, far more graceful in their own
conceit, waddling awkwardly about the edges of the pond or
sailing glibly on its surface. The farm-yard passed, then came
the little inn; the humbler beer-shop; and the village tradesman's; then the lawyer's and the parson's, at whose dread
names the beer-shop trembled; the church then peeped out
modestly from a clump of trees; then there were a few more
cottages; then the cage, and pound, and not unfrequently,
on a bank by the way-side, a deep old dusty well. Then
came the trim-hedged fields on either hand, and the open
road again.

They walked all day, and slept that night at a small cottage
where beds were let to travellers. Next morning they were
afoot again, and though jaded at first, and very tired, recovered
before long and proceeded briskly forward.

They often stopped to rest, but only for a short space at a
time, and still kept on, having had but slight refreshment since
the morning. It was nearly five o'clock in the afternoon, when
drawing near another cluster of labourers' huts, the child
looked wistfully in each, doubtful at which to ask for permission to rest awhile, and buy a draught of milk.

It was not easy to determine, for she was timid and fearful
of being repulsed. Here was a crying child, and there a noisy
wife. In this, the people seemed too poor; in that, too many.
At length she stopped at one where the family were seated
round the table—chiefly because there was an old man sitting
in a cushioned chair beside the hearth, and she thought he was
a grandfather and would feel for hers.

There were besides, the cottager and his wife, and three
young sturdy children, brown as berries. The request was no
sooner preferred than granted. The eldest boy ran out to
fetch some milk, the second dragged two stools towards the

door, and the youngest crept to his mother's gown, and looked at the strangers from beneath his sunburnt hand.

'God save you, master,' said the old cottager in a thin piping voice; 'are you travelling far?'

'Yes, sir, a long way'—replied the child; for her grandfather appealed to her.

'From London?' inquired the old man.

The child said yes.

Ah! He had been in London many a time—used to go there often once, with waggons. It was nigh two-and-thirty year since he had been there last, and he did hear say there were great changes. Like enough! He had changed, himself, since then. Two-and-thirty year was a long time and eighty-four a great age, though there was some he had known that had lived to very hard upon a hundred—and not so hearty as he, neither—no, nothing like it.

'Sit thee down, master, in the elbow chair,' said the old man, knocking his stick upon the brick floor, and trying to do so sharply. 'Take a pinch out o' that box; I don't take much myself, for it comes dear, but I find it wakes me up sometimes, and ye're but a boy to me. I should have a son pretty nigh as old as you if he'd lived, but they listed him for a so'ger—he come back home though, for all he had but one poor leg. He always said he'd be buried near the sun-dial he used to climb upon when he was a baby, did my poor boy, and his words come true—you can see the place with your own eyes; we've kept the turf up, ever since.'

He shook his head, and looking at his daughter with watery eyes, said she needn't be afraid that he was going to talk about that, any more. He didn't wish to trouble nobody, and if he had troubled anybody by what he said, he asked pardon, that was all.

The milk arrived, and the child producing her little basket, and selecting its best fragments for her grandfather, they made a hearty meal. The furniture of the room was very homely of course—a few rough chairs and a table, a corner cupboard with their little stock of crockery and delf, a gaudy tea-tray, representing a lady in bright red, walking out with a very blue parasol, a few common, coloured scripture subjects in frames upon the wall and chimney, an old dwarf clothes-press and an eight-day clock, with a few bright saucepans and a kettle, comprised the whole. But everything was clean and neat, and as the child glanced round, she felt a tranquil air of comfort and content to which she had long been unaccustomed.

'How far is it to any town or village?' she asked of the husband.

'A matter of good five mile, my dear,' was the reply, 'but you're not going on to-night?'

'Yes, yes, Nell,' said the old man hastily, urging her too by signs. 'Further on, further on, darling, further away if we walk 'till midnight.'

'There's a good barn hard by, master,' said the man, 'or there's travellers' lodging, I know, at the Plow an' Harrer. Excuse me, but you do seem a little tired, and unless you're very anxious to get on—'

'Yes, yes, we are,' returned the old man fretfully. 'Further away, dear Nell, pray further away.'

'We must go on, indeed,' said the child, yielding to his restless wish. 'We thank you very much, but we cannot stop so soon. I'm quite ready, grandfather.'

But the woman had observed, from the young wanderer's gait, that one of her little feet was blistered and sore, and being a woman and a mother too, she would not suffer her to go until she had washed the place and applied some simple remedy, which she did so carefully and with such a gentle hand—rough-grained and hard though it was, with work—that the child's heart was too full to admit of her saying more than a fervent 'God bless you!' nor could she look back nor trust herself to speak, until they had left the cottage some distance behind. When she turned her head, she saw that the whole family, even the old grandfather, were standing in the road watching them as they went, and so, with many waves of the hand, and cheering nods, and on one side at least not without tears, they parted company.

They trudged forward, more slowly and painfully than they had done yet, for another mile or thereabouts, when they heard the sound of wheels behind them, and looking round observed an empty cart approaching pretty briskly. The driver on coming up to them stopped his horse and looked earnestly at Nell.

'Didn't you stop to rest at a cottage yonder?' he said.

'Yes, sir,' replied the child.

'Ah! They asked me to look out for you,' said the man. 'I'm going your way. Give me your hand—jump up, master.'

This was a great relief, for they were very much fatigued and could scarcely crawl along. To them the jolting cart was a luxurious carriage, and the ride the most delicious in the world. Nell had scarcely settled herself on a little heap of straw in one corner, when she fell asleep, for the first time that day.

She was awakened by the stopping of the cart, which was about to turn up a bye-lane. The driver kindly got down to help her out, and pointing to some trees at a very short distance before them, said that the town lay there, and that they had better take the path which they would see leading through the churchyard. Accordingly, towards this spot they directed their weary steps.

CHAPTER XVI

THE sun was setting when they reached the wicket-gate at which the path began, and, as the rain falls upon the just and unjust alike, it shed its warm tint even upon the resting-places of the dead, and bade them be of good hope for its rising on the morrow. The church was old and grey, with ivy clinging to the walls, and round the porch. Shunning the tombs, it crept about the mounds, beneath which slept poor humble men: twining for them the first wreaths they had ever won, but wreaths less liable to wither and far more lasting in their kind, than some which were graven deep in stone and marble, and told in pompous terms of virtues meekly hidden for many a year, and only revealed at last to executors and mourning legatees.

The clergyman's horse, stumbling with a dull blunt sound among the graves, was cropping the grass; at once deriving orthodox consolation from the dead parishioners, and enforcing last Sunday's text that this was what all flesh came to; a lean ass who had sought to expound it also, without being qualified and ordained, was pricking his ears in an empty pound hard by, and looking with hungry eyes upon his priestly neighbour.

The old man and the child quitted the gravel path, and strayed among the tombs; for there the ground was soft, and easy to their tired feet. As they passed behind the church, they heard voices near at hand, and presently came on those who had spoken.

They were two men who were seated in easy attitudes upon the grass, and so busily engaged as to be at first unconscious of intruders. It was not difficult to divine that they were of a class of itinerant showmen—exhibitors of the freaks of Punch —for, perched cross-legged upon a tombstone behind them, was a figure of that hero himself, his nose and chin as hooked and his face as beaming as usual. Perhaps his imperturbable character was never more strikingly developed, for he preserved his usual equable smile notwithstanding that his body was dangling in a most uncomfortable position, all loose and limp and shapeless, while his long peaked cap, unequally balanced against his exceedingly slight legs, threatened every instant to bring him toppling down.

In part scattered upon the ground at the feet of the two men,

Punch in the Churchyard

and in part jumbled together in a long flat box, were the other persons of the Drama. The hero's wife and one child, the hobby-horse, the doctor, the foreign gentleman who not being familiar with the language is unable in the representation to express his ideas otherwise than by the utterance of the word 'Shallabalah' three distinct times, the radical neighbour who will by no means admit that a tin bell is an organ, the executioner, and the devil, were all here. Their owners had evidently come to that spot to make some needful repairs in the stage arrangements, for one of them was engaged in binding together a small gallows with thread, while the other was intent upon fixing a new black wig, with the aid of a small hammer and some tacks, upon the head of the radical neighbour, who had been beaten bald.

They raised their eyes when the old man and his young companion were close upon them, and pausing in their work, returned their looks of curiosity. One of them, the actual exhibitor no doubt, was a little merry-faced man with a twinkling eye and a red nose, who seemed to have unconsciously imbibed something of his hero's character. The other —that was he who took the money—had rather a careful and cautious look, which was perhaps inseparable from his occupation also.

The merry man was the first to greet the strangers with a nod; and following the old man's eyes, he observed that perhaps that was the first time he had ever seen a Punch off the stage. (Punch, it may be remarked, seemed to be pointing with the tip of his cap to a most flourishing epitaph, and to be chuckling over it with all his heart.)

'Why do you come here to do this?' said the old man, sitting down beside them, and looking at the figures with extreme delight.

'Why you see,' rejoined the little man, 'we're putting up for to-night at the public-house yonder, and it wouldn't do to let 'em see the present company undergoing repair.'

'No!' cried the old man, making signs to Nell to listen, 'why not, eh? why not?'

'Because it would destroy all the delusion, and take away all the interest, wouldn't it?' replied the little man. 'Would you care a ha'penny for the Lord Chancellor if you know'd him in private and without his wig?—certainly not.'

'Good!' said the old man, venturing to touch one of the

puppets, and drawing away his hand with a shrill laugh. 'Are you going to show 'em to-night? are you?'

'That is the intention, governor,' replied the other, 'and unless I'm much mistaken, Tommy Codlin is a calculating at this minute what we've lost through your coming upon us. Cheer up, Tommy, it can't be much.'

The little man accompanied these latter words with a wink, expressive of the estimate he had formed of the travellers' finances.

To this Mr. Codlin, who had a surly, grumbling manner, replied, as he twitched Punch off the tombstone and flung him into the box,

'I don't care if we haven't lost a farden, but you're too free. If you stood in front of the curtain and see the public's faces as I do, you'd know human natur' better.'

'Ah! it's been the spoiling of you, Tommy, your taking to that branch,' rejoined his companion. 'When you played the ghost in the reg'lar drama in the fairs, you believed in every-thing—except ghosts. But now you're a universal mistruster. I never see a man so changed.'

'Never mind,' said Mr. Codlin, with the air of a discon-tented philosopher. 'I know better now, and p'raps I'm sorry for it.'

Turning over the figures in the box like one who knew and despised them, Mr. Codlin drew one forth and held it up for the inspection of his friend:

'Look here; here's all this Judy's clothes falling to pieces again. You haven't got a needle and thread, I suppose?'

The little man shook his head, and scratched it ruefully as he contemplated this severe indisposition of a principal per-former. Seeing that they were at a loss, the child said timidly:

'I have a needle, sir, in my basket, and thread too. Will you let me try to mend it for you? I think I could do it neater than you could.'

Even Mr. Codlin had nothing to urge against a proposal so seasonable. Nelly, kneeling down beside the box, was soon busily engaged in her task, and accomplishing it to a miracle.

While she was thus engaged, the merry little man looked at her with an interest which did not appear to be diminished when he glanced at her helpless companion. When she had finished her work he thanked her, and inquired whither they were travelling.

'N—no further to-night, I think,' said the child, looking towards her grandfather.

'If you're wanting a place to stop at,' the man remarked, 'I should advise you to take up at the same house with us. That's it. The long, low, white house there. It's very cheap.'

The old man, notwithstanding his fatigue, would have remained in the churchyard all night if his new acquaintances had remained there too. As he yielded to this suggestion a ready and rapturous assent, they all rose and walked away together; he keeping close to the box of puppets in which he was quite absorbed, the merry little man carrying it slung over his arm by a strap attached to it for the purpose, Nelly having hold of her grandfather's hand, and Mr. Codlin sauntering slowly behind, casting up at the church tower and neighbouring trees such looks as he was accustomed in town-practice to direct to drawing-room and nursery windows, when seeking for a profitable spot on which to plant the show.

The public-house was kept by a fat old landlord and landlady who made no objection to receiving their new guests, but praised Nelly's beauty and were at once prepossessed in her behalf. There was no other company in the kitchen but the two showmen, and the child felt very thankful that they had fallen upon such good quarters. The landlady was very much astonished to learn that they had come all the way from London, and appeared to have no little curiosity touching their farther destination. The child parried her inquiries as well as she could, and with no great trouble, for finding that they appeared to give her pain, the old lady desisted.

'These two gentlemen have ordered supper in an hour's time,' she said, taking her into the bar; 'and your best plan will be to sup with them. Meanwhile you shall have a little taste of something that'll do you good, for I'm sure you must want it after all you've gone through to-day. Now, don't look after the old gentleman, because when you've drank that, he shall have some too.'

As nothing could induce the child to leave him alone, however, or to touch anything in which he was not the first and greatest sharer, the old lady was obliged to help him first. When they had been thus refreshed, the whole house hurried away into an empty stable where the show stood, and where, by the light of a few flaring candles stuck round a hoop which hung by a line from the ceiling, it was to be forthwith exhibited.

And now Mr. Thomas Codlin, the misanthrope, after blowing away at the Pan's pipes until he was intensely wretched, took his station on one side of the checked drapery which concealed the mover of the figures, and putting his hands in his pockets prepared to reply to all questions and remarks of Punch, and to make a dismal feint of being his most intimate private friend, of believing in him to the fullest and most unlimited extent, of knowing that he enjoyed day and night a merry and glorious existence in that temple, and that he was at all times and under every circumstance the same intelligent and joyful person that the spectators then beheld him. All this Mr. Codlin did with the air of a man who had made up his mind for the worst and was quite resigned; his eye slowly wandering about during the briskest repartee to observe the effect upon the audience, and particularly the impression made upon the landlord and landlady, which might be productive of very important results in connexion with the supper.

Upon this head, however, he had no cause for any anxiety, for the whole performance was applauded to the echo, and voluntary contributions were showered in with a liberality which testified yet more strongly to the general delight. Among the laughter none was more loud and frequent than the old man's. Nell's was unheard, for she, poor child, with her head drooping on his shoulder, had fallen asleep, and slept too soundly to be roused by any of his efforts to awaken her to a participation in his glee.

The supper was very good, but she was too tired to eat, and yet would not leave the old man until she had kissed him in his bed. He, happily insensible to every care and anxiety, sat listening with a vacant smile and admiring face to all that his new friends said; and it was not until they retired yawning to their room, that he followed the child up stairs.

It was but a loft partitioned into two compartments, where they were to rest, but they were well pleased with their lodging and had hoped for none so good. The old man was uneasy when he had lain down, and begged that Nell would come and sit at his bedside as she had done for so many nights. She hastened to him, and sat there till he slept.

There was a little window, hardly more than a chink in the wall, in her room, and when she left him, she opened it, quite wondering at the silence. The sight of the old church and the graves about it in the moonlight, and the dark trees whispering among themselves, made her more thoughtful than before. She closed the window again, and sitting down upon the bed, thought of the life that was before them.

She had a little money, but it was very little, and when that was gone, they must begin to beg. There was one piece of gold among it, and an emergency might come when its worth to them would be increased a hundredfold. It would be best to hide this coin, and never produce it unless their case was absolutely desperate, and no other resource was left them.

Her resolution taken, she sewed the piece of gold into her dress, and going to bed with a lighter heart sunk into a deep slumber.

CHAPTER XVII

ANOTHER bright day shining in through the small casement, and claiming fellowship with the kindred eyes of
the child, awoke her. At sight of the strange room and its
unaccustomed objects she started up in alarm, wondering how
she had been moved from the familiar chamber in which she
seemed to have fallen asleep last night, and whither she had
been conveyed. But, another glance around called to her
mind all that had lately passed, and she sprung from her bed,
hoping and trustful.

It was yet early, and the old man being still asleep, she
walked out into the churchyard, brushing the dew from the
long grass with her feet, and often turning aside into places
where it grew longer than in others, that she might not tread
upon the graves. She felt a curious kind of pleasure in lingering
among these houses of the dead, and read the inscriptions on the
tombs of the good people (a great number of good people were
buried there), passing on from one to another with increasing
interest.

It was a very quiet place, as such a place should be, save for
the cawing of the rooks who had built their nests among the
branches of some tall old trees, and were calling to one another,
high up in the air. First, one sleek bird, hovering near his
ragged house as it swung and dangled in the wind, uttered his
hoarse cry, quite by chance as it would seem, and in a sober
tone as though he were but talking to himself. Another
answered, and he called again, but louder than before; then
another spoke and then another; and each time the first,
aggravated by contradiction, insisted on his case more strongly.
Other voices, silent till now, struck in from boughs lower down
and higher up and midway, and to the right and left, and from
the tree-tops; and others, arriving hastily from the grey church
turrets and old belfry window, joined the clamour which rose
and fell, and swelled and dropped again, and still went on; and
all this noisy contention amidst a skimming to and fro, and
lighting on fresh branches, and frequent change of place, which
satirised the old restlessness of those who lay so still beneath the
moss and turf below, and the strife in which they had worn
away their lives.

Frequently raising her eyes to the trees whence these sounds came down, and feeling as though they made the place more quiet than perfect silence would have done, the child loitered from grave to grave, now stopping to replace with careful hands the bramble which had started from some green mound it helped to keep in shape, and now peeping through one of the low latticed· windows into the church, with its worm-eaten books upon the desks, and baize of whitened-green mouldering from the pew sides and leaving the naked wood to view. There were the seats where the poor old people sat, worn spare, and yellow like themselves; the rugged font where children had their names, the homely altar where they knelt in after life, the plain black trestles that bore their weight on their last visit to the cool old shady church. Everything told of long use and quiet slow decay; the very bell-rope in the porch was frayed into a fringe, and hoary with old age.

She was looking at a humble stone which told of a young man who had died at twenty-three years old, fifty-five years ago, when she heard a faltering step approaching, and looking round saw a feeble woman bent with the weight of years, who tottered to the foot of that same grave and asked her to read the writing on the stone. The old woman thanked her when she had done, saying that she had had the words by heart for many a long, long year, but could not see them now.

'Were you his mother?' said the child.

'I was his wife, my dear.'

She the wife of a young man of three-and-twenty! Ah, true! It was fifty-five years ago.

'You wonder to hear me say that,' remarked the old woman, shaking her head. 'You're not the first. Older folk than you have wondered at the same thing before now. Yes, I was his wife. Death doesn't change us more than life, my dear.'

'Do you come here often?' asked the child.

'I sit here very often in the summer-time,' she answered. 'I used to come here once to cry and mourn, but that was a weary while ago, bless God!'

'I pluck the daisies as they grow, and take them home,' said the old woman after a short silence. 'I like no flowers so well as these, and haven't for five-and-fifty years. It's a long time, and I'm getting very old!'

Then growing garrulous upon a theme which was new to one listener though it were but a child, she told her how she had wept and moaned and prayed to die herself, when this happened; and how when she first came to that place, a young creature strong in love and grief, she had hoped that her heart was breaking as it seemed to be. But that time passed by, and although she continued to be sad when she came there, still she could bear to come, and so went on until it was pain no longer, but a solemn pleasure, and a duty she had learned to like. And now that five-and-fifty years were gone, she spoke of the dead man as if he had been her son or grandson, with a kind of pity for his youth, growing out of her own old age, and an exalting of his strength and manly beauty as compared with her own weakness and decay; and yet she spoke about him as her husband too, and thinking of herself in connexion with him, as she used to be and not as she was now, talked of their meeting in another world, as if he were dead but yesterday, and she, separated from her former self, were thinking of the happiness of that comely girl who seemed to have died with him.

The child left her gathering the flowers that grew upon the grave, and thoughtfully retraced her steps.

The old man was by this time up and dressed. Mr. Codlin, still doomed to contemplate the harsh realities of existence, was packing among his linen the candle-ends which had been saved from the previous night's performance: while his companion received the compliments of all the loungers in the stable-yard, who, unable to separate him from the master-mind of Punch, set him down as next in importance to that merry outlaw, and loved him scarcely less. When he had sufficiently acknowledged his popularity he came in to breakfast, at which meal they all sat down together.

'And where are you going to-day?' said the little man, addressing himself to Nell.

'Indeed I hardly know,—we have not determined yet,' replied the child.

'We're going on to the races,' said the little man. 'If that's your way and you like to have us for company, let us travel together. If you prefer going alone, only say the word and you'll find that we shan't trouble you.'

'We'll go with you,' said the old man. 'Nell,—with them, with them.'

The child considered for a moment, and reflecting that she must shortly beg, and could scarcely hope to do so at a better place than where crowds of rich ladies and gentlemen were assembled together for purposes of enjoyment and festivity,

determined to accompany these men so far. She therefore
thanked the little man for his offer, and said, glancing
timidly towards his friend, that if there was no objection to
their accompanying them as far as the race town—

'Objection!' said the little man. 'Now be gracious for once,
Tommy, and say that you'd rather they went with us. I know
you would. Be gracious, Tommy.'

'Trotters,' said Mr. Codlin, who talked very slowly and eat
very greedily, as is not uncommon with philosophers and
misanthropes; 'you're too free.'

'Why what harm can it do?' urged the other.

'No harm at all in this particular case, perhaps,' replied Mr.
Codlin; 'but the principle's a dangerous one, and you're too
free I tell you.'

'Well, are they to go with us or not?'

'Yes, they are,' said Mr. Codlin; 'but you might have made
a favour of it, mightn't you?'

The real name of the little man was Harris, but it had
gradually merged into the less euphonious one of Trotters,
which, with the prefatory adjective, Short, had been conferred
upon him by reason of the small size of his legs. Short Trotters,
however, being a compound name, inconvenient of use in
friendly dialogue, the gentleman on whom it had been bestowed was known among his intimates either as 'Short,' or
'Trotters,' and was seldom accosted at full length as Short
Trotters, except in formal conversations and on occasions of
ceremony.

Short, then, or Trotters, as the reader pleases, returned unto
the remonstrance of his friend Mr. Thomas Codlin a jocose
answer calculated to turn aside his discontent; and applying
himself with great relish to the cold boiled beef, the tea, and
bread and butter, strongly impressed upon his companions that
they should do the like. Mr. Codlin indeed required no such
persuasion, as he had already eat as much as he could possibly
carry and was now moistening his clay with strong ale, whereof
he took deep draughts with a silent relish and invited nobody
to partake,—thus again strongly indicating his misanthropical
turn of mind.

Breakfast being at length over, Mr. Codlin called the bill,
and charging the ale to the company generally (a practice also
savouring of misanthropy) divided the sum-total into two fair
and equal parts, assigning one moiety to himself and friend, and

the other to Nelly and her grandfather. These being duly discharged and all things ready for their departure, they took farewell of the landlord and landlady and resumed their journey.

And here Mr. Codlin's false position in society and the effect it wrought upon his wounded spirit, were strongly illustrated; for whereas he had been last night accosted by Mr. Punch as 'master,' and had by inference left the audience to understand that he maintained that individual for his own luxurious entertainment and delight, here he was, now, painfully walking beneath the burden of that same Punch's temple, and bearing it bodily upon his shoulders on a sultry day and along a dusty road. In place of enlivening his patron with a constant fire of wit or the cheerful rattle of his quarter-staff on the heads of his relations and acquaintance, here was that beaming Punch utterly devoid of spine, all slack and drooping in a dark box, with his legs doubled up round his neck, and not one of his social qualities remaining.

Mr. Codlin trudged heavily on, exchanging a word or two at intervals with Short, and stopping to rest and growl occasionally. Short led the way; with the flat box, the private luggage (which was not extensive) tied up in a bundle, and a brazen trumpet slung from his shoulder-blade. Nell and her grandfather walked next him on either hand, and Thomas Codlin brought up the rear.

When they came to any town or village, or even to a detached house of good appearance, Short blew a blast upon the brazen trumpet and carolled a fragment of a song in that hilarious tone common to Punches and their consorts. If people hurried to the windows, Mr. Codlin pitched the temple, and hastily unfurling the drapery and concealing Short therewith, flourished hysterically on the pipes and performed an air. Then the entertainment began as soon as might be; Mr. Codlin having the responsibility of deciding on its length and of protracting or expediting the time for the hero's final triumph over the enemy of mankind, according as he judged that the after-crop of halfpence would be plentiful or scant. When it had been gathered in to the last farthing, he resumed his load and on they went again.

Sometimes they played out the toll across a bridge or ferry, and once exhibited by particular desire at a turnpike, where the collector, being drunk in his solitude, paid down a shilling

Grinder's Lot

to have it to himself. There was one small place of rich promise in which their hopes were blighted, for a favourite character in the play having gold-lace upon his coat and being a meddling wooden-headed fellow was held to be a libel on the beadle, for which reason the authorities enforced a quick retreat; but they were generally well received, and seldom left a town without a troop of ragged children shouting at their heels.

They made a long day's journey, despite these interruptions, and were yet upon the road when the moon was shining in the sky. Short beguiled the time with songs and jests, and made the best of everything that happened. Mr. Codlin, on the other hand, cursed his fate, and all the hollow things of earth (but Punch especially), and limped along with the theatre on his back, a prey to the bitterest chagrin.

They had stopped to rest beneath a finger-post where four roads met, and Mr. Codlin in his deep misanthropy had let down the drapery and seated himself in the bottom of the show, invisible to mortal eyes and disdainful of the company of his fellow-creatures, when two monstrous shadows were seen stalking towards them from a turning in the road by which they had come. The child was at first quite terrified by the sight of these gaunt giants—for such they looked as they advanced with lofty strides beneath the shadow of the trees— but Short, telling her there was nothing to fear, blew a blast upon the trumpet, which was answered by a cheerful shout.

'It's Grinder's lot, an't it?' cried Mr. Short in a loud key.

'Yes,' replied a couple of shrill voices.

'Come on then,' said Short. 'Let's have a look at you. I thought it was you.'

Thus invited, 'Grinder's lot' approached with redoubled speed and soon came up with the little party.

Mr. Grinder's company, familiarly termed a lot, consisted of a young gentleman and a young lady on stilts, and Mr. Grinder himself, who used his natural legs for pedestrian purposes and carried at his back a drum. The public costume of the young people was of the Highland kind, but the night being damp and cold, the young gentleman wore over his kilt a man's pea jacket reaching to his ankles, and a glazed hat; the young lady too was muffled in an old cloth pelisse and had a handkerchief tied about her head. Their Scotch bonnets, ornamented with plumes of jet black feathers, Mr. Grinder carried on his instrument.

'Bound for the races, I see,' said Grinder, coming up out of breath. 'So are we. How are you, Short?' With that they shook hands in a very friendly manner. The young people being too high up for the ordinary salutations, saluted Short after their own fashion. The young gentleman twisted up his right stilt and patted him on the shoulder, and the young lady rattled her tambourine.

'Practice?' said Short, pointing to the stilts.

'No,' returned Grinder. 'It comes either to walkin' in 'em or carryin' of 'em, and they like walkin' in 'em best. It's wery pleasant for the prospects. Which road are you takin'? We go the nighest.'

'Why, the fact is,' said Short, 'that we are going the longest way, because then we could stop for the night, a mile and a half on. But three or four mile gained to-night is so many saved to-morrow, and if you keep on, I think our best way is to do the same.'

'Where's your partner?' inquired Grinder.

'Here he is,' cried Mr. Thomas Codlin, presenting his head and face in the proscenium of the stage, and exhibiting an expression of countenance not often seen there; 'and he'll see *his* partner boiled alive before he'll go on to-night. That's what *he* says.'

'Well, don't say such things as them, in a spear which is dewoted to something pleasanter,' urged Short. 'Respect associations, Tommy, even if you do cut up rough.'

'Rough or smooth,' said Mr. Codlin, beating his hand on the little footboard where Punch, when suddenly struck with the symmetry of his legs and their capacity for silk stockings, is accustomed to exhibit them to popular admiration, 'rough or smooth, I won't go further than the mile and a half to-night. I put up at the Jolly Sandboys and nowhere else. If you like to come there, come there. If you like to go on by yourself, go on by yourself, and do without me if you can.'

So saying, Mr. Codlin disappeared from the scene and immediately presented himself outside the theatre, took it on his shoulders at a jerk, and made off with most remarkable agility.

Any further controversy being now out of the question, Short was fain to part with Mr. Grinder and his pupils and to follow his morose companion. After lingering at the finger-post for a few minutes to see the stilts frisking away in the moonlight and the bearer of the drum toiling slowly after them, he blew a few notes upon the trumpet as a parting salute, and hastened with all speed to follow Mr. Codlin. With this view he gave his unoccupied hand to Nell, and bidding her be of good cheer as they would soon be at the end of their journey for that night, and stimulating the old man with a similar assurance, led them at a pretty swift pace towards their destination, which he was the less unwilling to make for, as the moon was now overcast and the clouds were threatening rain.

CHAPTER XVIII

THE Jolly Sandboys was a small road-side inn of pretty ancient date, with a sign, representing three Sandboys increasing their jollity with as many jugs of ale and bags of gold, creaking and swinging on its post on the opposite side of the road. As the travellers had observed that day many indications of their drawing nearer and nearer to the race town, such as gipsy camps, carts laden with gambling booths and their appurtenances, itinerant showmen of various kinds, and beggars and trampers of every degree, all wending their way in the same direction, Mr. Codlin was fearful of finding the accommodations forestalled; this fear increasing as he diminished the distance between himself and the hostelry, he quickened his pace, and notwithstanding the burden he had to carry, maintained a round trot until he reached the threshold. Here he had the gratification of finding that his fears were without foundation, for the landlord was leaning against the doorpost looking lazily at the rain, which had by this time begun to descend heavily, and no tinkling of cracked bell, nor boisterous shout, nor noisy chorus, gave note of company within.

'All alone?' said Mr. Codlin, putting down his burden and wiping his forehead.

'All alone as yet,' rejoined the landlord, glancing at the sky, 'but we shall have more company to-night I expect. Here, one of you boys, carry that show into the barn. Make haste in out of the wet, Tom; when it came on to rain I told 'em to make the fire up, and there's a glorious blaze in the kitchen, I can tell you.'

Mr. Codlin followed with a willing mind, and soon found that the landlord had not commended his preparations without good reason. A mighty fire was blazing on the hearth and roaring up the wide chimney with a cheerful sound, which a large iron cauldron, bubbling and simmering in the heat, lent its pleasant aid to swell. There was a deep red ruddy blush upon the room, and when the landlord stirred the fire, sending the flames skipping and leaping up—when he took off the lid of the iron pot and there rushed out a savoury smell, while the bubbling sound grew deeper and more rich, and an unctuous steam came floating out, hanging in a delicious mist above their heads —when he did this, Mr. Codlin's heart was touched. He sat down in the chimney-corner and smiled.

At the Jolly Sandboys

(p. 196)

Mr. Codlin sat smiling in the chimney-corner, eyeing the landlord as with a roguish look he held the cover in his hand, and, feigning that his doing so was needful to the welfare of the cookery, suffered the delightful steam to tickle the nostrils of his guest. The glow of the fire was upon the landlord's bald head, and upon his twinkling eye, and upon his watering mouth, and upon his pimpled face, and upon his round fat figure. Mr. Codlin drew his sleeve across his lips, and said in a murmuring voice, 'What is it?'

'It's a stew of tripe,' said the landlord, smacking his lips, 'and cow-heel,' smacking them again, 'and bacon,' smacking them once more, 'and steak,' smacking them for the fourth time, 'and peas, cauliflowers, new potatoes, and sparrow-grass, all working up together in one delicious gravy.' Having come to the climax, he smacked his lips a great many times, and taking a long hearty sniff of the fragrance that was hovering about, put on the cover again with the air of one whose toils on earth were over.

'At what time will it be ready?' asked Mr. Codlin faintly.

'It'll be done to a turn,' said the landlord, looking up to the clock—and the very clock had a colour in its fat white face, and looked a clock for Jolly Sandboys to consult—'it'll be done to a turn at twenty-two minutes before eleven.'

'Then,' said Mr. Codlin, 'fetch me a pint of warm ale, and don't let nobody bring into the room even so much as a biscuit till the time arrives.'

Nodding his approval of this decisive and manly course of procedure, the landlord retired to draw the beer, and presently returning with it, applied himself to warm the same in a small tin vessel shaped funnel-wise, for the convenience of sticking it far down in the fire and getting at the bright places. This was soon done, and he handed it over to Mr. Codlin with that creamy froth upon the surface which is one of the happy circumstances attendant on mulled malt.

Greatly softened by this soothing beverage, Mr. Codlin now bethought him of his companions, and acquainted mine host of the Sandboys that their arrival might be shortly looked for. The rain was rattling against the windows and pouring down in torrents, and such was Mr. Codlin's extreme amiability of mind, that he more than once expressed his earnest hope that they would not be so foolish as to get wet.

At length they arrived, drenched with the rain and

presenting a most miserable appearance, notwithstanding that Short had sheltered the child as well as he could under the skirts of his own coat, and they were nearly breathless from the haste they had made. But their steps were no sooner heard upon the road than the landlord, who had been at the outer door anxiously watching for their coming, rushed into the kitchen and took the cover off. The effect was electrical. They all came in with smiling faces though the wet was dripping from their clothes upon the floor, and Short's first remark was, 'What a delicious smell!'

It is not very difficult to forget rain and mud by the side of a cheerful fire, and in a bright room. They were furnished with slippers and such dry garments as the house or their own bundles afforded, and ensconcing themselves, as Mr. Codlin had already done, in the warm chimney-corner, soon forgot their late troubles or only remembered them as enhancing the delights of the present time. Overpowered by the warmth and comfort and the fatigue they had undergone, Nelly and the old man had not long taken their seats here, when they fell asleep.

'Who are they?' whispered the landlord.

Short shook his head, and wished he knew himself.

'Don't *you* know?' asked the host, turning to Mr. Codlin.

'Not I,' he replied. 'They're no good, I suppose.'

'They're no harm,' said Short. 'Depend upon that. I tell you what—it's plain that the old man an't in his right mind—'

'If you haven't got anything newer than that to say,' growled Mr. Codlin, glancing at the clock, 'you'd better let us fix our minds upon the supper, and not disturb us.'

'Hear me out, won't you?' retorted his friend. 'It's very plain to me, besides, that they're not used to this way of life. Don't tell me that that handsome child has been in the habit of prowling about as she's done these last two or three days. I know better.'

'Well, who *does* tell you she has?' growled Mr. Codlin, again glancing at the clock and from it to the cauldron; 'can't you think of anything more suitable to present circumstances than saying things and then contradicting 'em?'

'I wish somebody would give you your supper,' returned Short, 'for there'll be no peace till you've got it. Have you seen how anxious the old man is to get on—always wanting to be furder away—furder away. Have you seen that?'

'Ah! what then?' muttered Thomas Codlin.

'This, then,' said Short. 'He has given his friends the slip.
Mind what I say,—he has given his friends the slip, and persuaded this delicate young creetur all along of her fondness for
him to be his guide and travelling companion—where to, he
knows no more than the man in the moon. Now I'm not a
going to stand that.'

'*You're* not a going to stand that!' cried Mr. Codlin, glancing
at the clock again and pulling his hair with both hands in a kind
of frenzy, but whether occasioned by his companion's observation or the tardy pace of Time, it was difficult to determine.
'Here's a world to live in!'

'I,' repeated Short emphatically and slowly, 'am not a-going
to stand it. I am not a going to see this fair young child a
falling into bad hands, and getting among people that she's no
more fit for, than they are to get among angels as their ordinary
chums. Therefore when they dewelope an intention of parting
company from us, I shall take measures for detaining of 'em, and
restoring 'em to their friends, who I dare say have had their
disconsolation pasted up on every wall in London by this time.'

'Short,' said Mr. Codlin, who with his head upon his hands,
and his elbows on his knees, had been shaking himself impatiently from side to side up to this point and occasionally
stamping on the ground, but who now looked up with eager
eyes; 'it's possible that there may be uncommon good sense in
what you've said. If there is, and there should be a reward,
Short, remember that we're partners in everything!'

His companion had only time to nod a brief assent to this
position, for the child awoke at the instant. They had drawn
close together during the previous whispering, and now
hastily separated and were rather awkwardly endeavouring to
exchange some casual remarks in their usual tone, when strange
footsteps were heard without, and fresh company entered.

These were no other than four very dismal dogs, who came
pattering in one after the other, headed by an old bandy dog
of particularly mournful aspect, who stopping when the last of
his followers had got as far as the door, erected himself upon
his hind legs and looked round at his companions, who immediately stood upon their hind legs, in a grave and melancholy
row. Nor was this the only remarkable circumstance about
these dogs, for each of them wore a kind of little coat of some
gaudy colour trimmed with tarnished spangles, and one of them
had a cap upon his head, tied very carefully under his chin,

G

which had fallen down upon his nose and completely obscured one eye; add to this, that the gaudy coats were all wet through and discoloured with rain, and that the wearers were splashed and dirty, and some idea may be formed of the unusual appearance of these new visitors to the Jolly Sandboys.

Neither Short nor the landlord nor Thomas Codlin, however, was in the least surprised, merely remarking that these were Jerry's dogs and that Jerry could not be far behind. So there the dogs stood, patiently winking and gaping and looking extremely hard at the boiling pot, until Jerry himself appeared, when they all dropped down at once and walked about the room in their natural manner. This posture it must be confessed did not much improve their appearance, as their own personal tails and their coat tails—both capital things in their way—did not agree together.

Jerry, the manager of these dancing dogs, was a tall black-whiskered man in a velveteen coat, who seemed well known to the landlord and his guests and accosted them with great cordiality. Disencumbering himself of a barrel organ which he placed upon a chair, and retaining in his hand a small whip wherewith to awe his company of comedians, he came up to the fire to dry himself, and entered into conversation.

'Your people don't usually travel in character, do they?' said Short, pointing to the dresses of the dogs. 'It must come expensive if they do?'

'No,' replied Jerry, 'no, it's not the custom with us. But we've been playing a little on the road to-day, and we come out with a new wardrobe at the races, so I didn't think it worth while to stop to undress. Down, Pedro!'

This was addressed to the dog with the cap on, who being a new member of the company, and not quite certain of his duty, kept his unobscured eye anxiously on his master, and was perpetually starting upon his hind legs when there was no occasion, and falling down again.

'I've got a animal here,' said Jerry, putting his hand into the capacious pocket of his coat, and diving into one corner as if he were feeling for a small orange or an apple or some such article, 'a animal here, wot I think you know something of, Short.'

'Ah!' cried Short, 'let's have a look at him.'

'Here he is,' said Jerry, producing a little terrier from his pocket. 'He was once a Toby of yours, warn't he?'

In some versions of the great drama of Punch there is a small dog—a modern innovation—supposed to be the private property of that gentleman, whose name is always Toby. This Toby has been stolen in youth from another gentleman, and fraudulently sold to the confiding hero, who having no guile himself has no suspicion that it lurks in others; but Toby, entertaining a grateful recollection of his old master, and scorning to attach himself to any new patrons, not only refuses to smoke a pipe at the bidding of Punch, but to mark his old fidelity more strongly, seizes him by the nose and wrings the same with violence, at which instance of canine attachment the spectators are deeply affected. This was the character which the little terrier in question had once sustained; if there had been any doubt upon the subject he would speedily have resolved it by his conduct; for not only did he, on seeing Short, give the strongest tokens of recognition, but catching sight of the flat box he barked so furiously at the pasteboard nose which he knew was inside, that his master was obliged to gather him up and put him into his pocket again, to the great relief of the whole company.

The landlord now busied himself in laying the cloth, in which process Mr. Codlin obligingly assisted by setting forth his own knife and fork in the most convenient place and establishing himself behind them. When everything was ready, the landlord took off the cover for the last time, and then indeed there burst forth such a goodly promise of supper, that if he had offered to put it on again or had hinted at postponement, he would certainly have been sacrificed on his own hearth.

However, he did nothing of the kind, but instead thereof assisted a stout servant girl in turning the contents of the cauldron into a large tureen; a proceeding which the dogs, proof against various hot splashes which fell upon their noses, watched with terrible eagerness. At length the dish was lifted on the table, and mugs of ale having been previously set round, little Nell ventured to say grace, and supper began.

At this juncture the poor dogs were standing on their hind legs quite surprisingly; the child, having pity on them, was about to cast some morsels of food to them before she tasted it herself, hungry though she was, when their master interposed.

'No, my dear, no, not an atom from anybody's hand but mine if you please. That dog,' said Jerry, pointing out the old leader of the troop, and speaking in a terrible voice, 'lost a halfpenny to-day. *He* goes without his supper.'

The unfortunate creature dropped upon his fore-legs directly, wagged his tail, and looked imploringly at his master.

'You must be more careful, sir,' said Jerry, walking coolly to the chair where he had placed the organ, and setting the stop. 'Come here. Now, sir, you play away at that, while we have supper, and leave off if you dare.'

The dog immediately began to grind most mournful music. His master having shown him the whip resumed his seat and called up the others, who, at his directions, formed in a row, standing upright as a file of soldiers.

'Now, gentlemen,' said Jerry, looking at them attentively. 'The dog whose name's called, eats. The dogs whose names an't called, keep quiet. Carlo!'

The lucky individual whose name was called, snapped up the morsel thrown towards him, but none of the others moved a muscle. In this manner they were fed at the discretion of their master. Meanwhile the dog in disgrace ground hard at the organ, sometimes in quick time, sometimes in slow, but never leaving off for an instant. When the knives and forks rattled very much, or any of his fellows got an unusually large piece of fat, he accompanied the music with a short howl, but he immediately checked it on his master looking round, and applied himself with increased diligence to the Old Hundredth.

The Giants waiting on the Dwarfs

(*p. 144*)

CHAPTER XIX

SUPPER was not yet over, when there arrived at the Jolly Sandboys two more travellers bound for the same haven as the rest, who had been walking in the rain for some hours, and came in shining and heavy with water. One of these was the proprietor of a giant, and a little lady without legs or arms, who had jogged forward in a van; the other, a silent gentleman who earned his living by showing tricks upon the cards, and who had rather deranged the natural expression of his countenance by putting small leaden lozenges into his eyes and bringing them out at his mouth, which was one of his professional accomplishments. The name of the first of these new-comers was Vuffin; the other, probably, as a pleasant satire upon his ugliness, was called Sweet William. To render them as comfortable as he could, the landlord bestirred himself nimbly, and in a very short time both gentlemen were perfectly at their ease.

'How's the Giant?' said Short, when they all sat smoking round the fire.

'Rather weak upon his legs,' returned Mr. Vuffin. 'I begin to be afraid he's going at the knees.'

'That's a bad look-out,' said Short.

'Aye! Bad indeed,' returned Mr. Vuffin, contemplating the fire with a sigh. 'Once get a giant shaky on his legs, and the public care no more about him than they do for a dead cabbage-stalk.'

'What becomes of the old giants?' said Short, turning to him again after a little reflection.

'They're usually kept in caravans to wait upon the dwarfs,' said Mr. Vuffin.

'The maintaining of 'em must come expensive, when they can't be shown, eh?' remarked Short, eyeing him doubtfully.

'It's better that, than letting 'em go upon the parish or about the streets,' said Mr. Vuffin. 'Once make a giant common and giants will never draw again. Look at wooden legs. If there was only one man with a wooden leg what a property *he*'d be!'

'So he would!' observed the landlord and Short both together. 'That's very true.'

'Instead of which,' pursued Mr. Vuffin, 'if you was to advertise Shakspeare played entirely by wooden legs, it's my belief you wouldn't draw a sixpence.'

'I don't suppose you would,' said Short. And the landlord said so too.

'This shows, you see,' said Mr. Vuffin, waving his pipe with an argumentative air, 'this shows the policy of keeping the used-up giants still in the carawans, where they get food and lodging for nothing, all their lives, and in general very glad they are to stop there. There was one giant—a black 'un—as left his carawan some years ago and took to carrying coach-bills about London, making himself as cheap as crossing-sweepers. He died. I make no insinuation against anybody in particular,' said Mr. Vuffin, looking solemnly round, 'but he was ruining the trade;—and he died.'

The landlord drew his breath hard, and looked at the owner of the dogs, who nodded and said gruffly that *he* remembered.

'I know you do, Jerry,' said Mr. Vuffin with profound meaning. 'I know you remember it, Jerry, and the universal opinion was, that it served him right. Why, I remember the time when old Maunders as had three-and-twenty wans—I remember the time when old Maunders had in his cottage in Spa Fields in the winter-time, when the season was over, eight male and female dwarfs setting down to dinner every day, who was waited on by eight old giants in green coats, red smalls, blue cotton stockings, and high-lows: and there was one dwarf as had grown elderly and wicious who whenever his giant wasn't quick enough to please him, used to stick pins in his legs, not being able to reach up any higher. I know that's a fact, for Maunders told it me himself.'

'What about the dwarfs when *they* get old?' inquired the landlord.

'The older a dwarf is, the better worth he is,' returned Mr. Vuffin; 'a grey-headed dwarf, well wrinkled, is beyond all suspicion. But a giant weak in the legs and not standing upright!—keep him in the carawan, but never show him, never show him, for any persuasion that can be offered.'

While Mr. Vuffin and his two friends smoked their pipes and beguiled the time with such conversation as this, the silent gentleman sat in a warm corner, swallowing, or seeming to swallow, sixpennyworth of halfpence for practice, balancing a feather upon his nose, and rehearsing other feats of dexterity of that kind, without paying any regard whatever to the company, who in their turn left him utterly unnoticed. At length the weary child prevailed upon her grandfather to retire, and they withdrew, leaving the company yet seated round the fire, and the dogs fast asleep at a humble distance.

After bidding the old man good night, Nell retired to her poor garret, but had scarcely closed the door, when it was gently tapped at. She opened it directly, and was a little startled by the sight of Mr. Thomas Codlin, whom she had left, to all appearance, fast asleep downstairs.

'What is the matter?' said the child.

'Nothing's the matter, my dear,' returned her visitor. 'I'm your friend. Perhaps you haven't thought so, but it's me that's your friend—not him.'

'Not who?' the child inquired.

'Short, my dear. I tell you what,' said Codlin, 'for all his having a kind of way with him that you'd be very apt to like, I'm the real, open-hearted man. I mayn't look it, but I am indeed.'

The child began to be alarmed, considering that the ale had taken effect upon Mr. Codlin, and that this commendation of himself was the consequence.

'Short's very well, and seems kind,' resumed the misanthrope, 'but he overdoes it. Now I don't.'

Certainly if there were any fault in Mr. Codlin's usual deportment, it was that he rather underdid his kindness to those about him, than overdid it. But the child was puzzled, and could not tell what to say.

'Take my advice,' said Codlin: 'don't ask me why, but take it. As long as you travel with us, keep as near me as you can. Don't offer to leave us—not on any account—but always stick to me and say that I'm your friend. Will you bear that in mind, my dear, and always say that it was me that was your friend?'

'Say so where,—and when?' inquired the child innocently.

'O, nowhere in particular,' replied Codlin, a little put out as it seemed by the question: 'I'm only anxious that you should think me so, and do me justice. You can't think what an interest I have in you. Why didn't you tell me your little history—that about you and the poor old gentleman? I'm the best adviser that ever was, and *so* interested in you—so much more interested than Short. I think they're breaking up down stairs; you needn't tell Short, you know, that we've had this little talk together. God bless you. Recollect the friend. Codlin's the friend, not Short. Short's very well as far as he goes, but the real friend is Codlin—not Short.'

Eking out these professions with a number of benevolent and protecting looks and great fervour of manner, Thomas Codlin stole away on tiptoe, leaving the child in a state of extreme surprise. She was still ruminating upon his curious behaviour, when the floor of the crazy stairs and landing cracked beneath the tread of the other travellers who were passing to their beds. When they had all passed, and the sound of their footsteps had died away, one of them returned, and after a little hesitation and rustling in the passage, as if he were doubtful what door to knock at, knocked at hers.

'Yes,' said the child from within.

'It's me—Short'—a voice called through the keyhole. 'I only wanted to say that we must be off early to-morrow morning, my dear, because unless we get the start of the dogs and the conjurer, the villages won't be worth a penny. You'll be sure to be stirring early and go with us? I'll call you.'

The child answered in the affirmative, and returning his 'good night' heard him creep away. She felt some uneasiness at the anxiety of these men, increased by the recollection of their whispering together down stairs and their slight confusion when she awoke, nor was she quite free from a misgiving that they were not the fittest companions she could have stumbled on. Her uneasiness, however, was nothing, weighed against her fatigue; and she soon forgot it in sleep.

Very early next morning, Short fulfilled his promise, and knocking softly at her door, entreated that she would get up directly, as the proprietor of the dogs was still snoring, and if they lost no time they might get a good deal in advance both of him and the conjurer, who was talking in his sleep, and from what he could be heard to say, appeared to be balancing a donkey in his dreams. She started from her bed without delay, and roused the old man with so much expedition that they were both ready as soon as Short himself, to that gentleman's unspeakable gratification and relief.

After a very unceremonious and scrambling breakfast, of which the staple commodities were bacon and bread, and beer, they took leave of the landlord and issued from the door of the Jolly Sandboys. The morning was fine and warm, the ground cool to the feet after the late rain, the hedges gayer and more green, the air clear, and everything fresh and healthful. Surrounded by these influences, they walked on pleasantly enough.

They had not gone very far, when the child was again struck by the altered behaviour of Mr. Thomas Codlin, who instead of plodding on sulkily by himself as he had heretofore done, kept close to her, and when he had an opportunity of looking at her unseen by his companion, warned her by certain wry faces and jerks of the head not to put any trust in Short, but to reserve all confidences for Codlin. Neither did he confine himself to looks and gestures, for when she and her grandfather were walking on beside the aforesaid Short, and that little man was talking with his accustomed cheerfulness on a variety of indifferent subjects, Thomas Codlin testified his jealousy and distrust by following close at her heels, and occasionally admonishing her ankles with the legs of the theatre in a very abrupt and painful manner.

All these proceedings naturally made the child more watchful and suspicious, and she soon observed that whenever they halted to perform outside a village alehouse or other place, Mr. Codlin while he went through his share of the entertainments kept his eye steadily upon her and the old man, or with a show of great friendship and consideration invited the latter to lean upon his arm, and so held him tight until the representation was over and they again went forward. Even Short seemed to change in this respect, and to mingle with his good-nature something of a desire to keep them in safe custody. This increased the child's misgivings, and made her yet more anxious and uneasy.

Meanwhile, they were drawing near the town where the races were to begin next day; for, from passing numerous groups of gipsies and trampers on the road, wending their way towards it, and straggling out from every by-way and cross-country lane, they gradually fell into a stream of people, some walking by the side of covered carts, others with horses, others with donkeys, others toiling on with heavy loads upon their backs, but all tending to the same point. The public-houses by the wayside, from being empty and noiseless as those in the remoter parts had been, now sent out boisterous shouts and clouds of smoke; and, from the misty windows, clusters of broad red faces looked down upon the road. On every piece of waste or common ground, some small gambler drove his noisy trade, and bellowed to the idle passers-by to stop and try their chance; the crowd grew thicker and more noisy; gilt gingerbread in blanket-stalls exposed its glories to the dust; and often a four-horse carriage, dashing by, obscured all objects in the gritty cloud it raised, and left them, stunned and blinded, far behind.

It was dark before they reached the town itself, and long indeed the few last miles had been. Here all was tumult and confusion; the streets were filled with throngs of people—many strangers were there, it seemed, by the looks they cast about—the church-bells rang out their noisy peals, and flags streamed from windows and housetops. In the large inn-yards waiters flitted to and fro and ran against each other, horses clattered on the uneven stones, carriage steps fell rattling down, and sickening smells from many dinners came in a heavy lukewarm breath upon the sense. In the smaller public-houses, fiddles with all their might and main were squeaking out the tune to staggering feet; drunken men, oblivious of the burden of their song, joined in a senseless howl, which drowned the tinkling of the feeble bell and made them savage for their drink; vagabond groups assembled round the doors to see the stroller woman dance, and add their uproar to the shrill flageolet and deafening drum.

Through this delirious scene, the child, frightened and repelled by all she saw, led on her bewildered charge, clinging close to her conductor, and trembling lest in the press she should be separated from him and left to find her way alone. Quickening their steps to get clear of all the roar and riot, they at length passed through the town and made for the race-course, which was upon an open heath, situated on an eminence, a full mile distant from its furthest bounds.

Although there were many people here, none of the best favoured or best clad, busily erecting tents and driving stakes in the ground, and hurrying to and fro with dusty feet and many a grumbled oath—although there were tired children cradled on heaps of straw beneath the wheels of carts, crying themselves to sleep—and poor lean horses and donkeys just turned loose, grazing among the men and women, and pots and kettles, and half-lighted fires, and ends of candles flaring and wasting in the air—for all this, the child felt it an escape from the town and drew her breath more freely. After a scanty supper, the purchase of which reduced her little stock so low, that she had only a few halfpence with which to buy a breakfast on the morrow, she and the old man lay down to rest in a corner of a tent, and slept, despite the busy preparations that were going on around them all night long.

Little Nell's Anxiety

(p. 149)

And now they had come to the time when they must beg their bread. Soon after sunrise in the morning she stole out from the tent, and rambling into some fields at a short distance, plucked a few wild roses and such humble flowers, purposing to make them into little nosegays and offer them to the ladies in the carriages when the company arrived. Her thoughts were not idle while she was thus employed; when she returned and was seated beside the old man in one corner of the tent, tying her flowers together, while the two men lay dozing in another corner, she plucked him by the sleeve, and slightly glancing towards them, said, in a low voice—

'Grandfather, don't look at those I talk of, and don't seem as if I spoke of anything but what I am about. What was that, you told me before we left the old house? That if they knew what we were going to do, they would say that you were mad, and part us?'

The old man turned to her with an aspect of wild terror; but she checked him by a look, and bidding him hold some flowers while she tied them up, and so bringing her lips closer to his ear, said—

'I know that was what you told me. You needn't speak, dear. I recollect it very well. It was not likely that I should forget it. Grandfather, these men suspect that we have secretly left our friends, and mean to carry us before some gentleman and have us taken care of and sent back. If you let your hand tremble so, we can never get away from them, but if you're only quiet now, we shall do so, easily.'

'How?' muttered the old man. 'Dear Nelly, how? They will shut me up in a stone room, dark and cold, and chain me up to the wall, Nell—flog me with whips, and never let me see thee more!'

'You're trembling again,' said the child. 'Keep close to me all day. Never mind them, don't look at them, but me. I shall find a time when we can steal away. When I do, mind you come with me, and do not stop or speak a word. Hush! That's all.'

'Holloa! what are you up to, my dear?' said Mr. Codlin, raising his head, and yawning. Then observing that his companion was fast asleep, he added in an earnest whisper, 'Codlin's the friend, remember—not Short.'

'Making some nosegays,' the child replied; 'I am going to try and sell some, these three days of the races. Will you have one —as a present I mean?'

Mr. Codlin would have risen to receive it, but the child hurried towards him and placed it in his hand. He stuck it in his button-hole with an air of ineffable complacency for a misanthrope, and leering exultingly at the unconscious Short, muttered, as he laid himself down again, 'Tom Codlin's the friend, by G—!'

As the morning wore on, the tents assumed a gayer and more brilliant appearance, and long lines of carriages came rolling softly on the turf. Men who had lounged about all night in smock-frocks and leather leggings, came out in silken vests and hats and plumes, as jugglers or mountebanks; or in gorgeous liveries as soft-spoken servants at gambling booths; or in sturdy yeoman dress as decoys at unlawful games. Black-eyed gipsy girls, hooded in showy handkerchiefs, sallied forth to tell fortunes, and pale slender women with consumptive faces lingered upon the footsteps of ventriloquists and conjurers, and counted the sixpences with anxious eyes long before they were gained. As many of the children as could be kept within bounds, were stowed away, with all the other signs of dirt and poverty, among the donkeys, carts, and horses; and as many as could not be thus disposed of ran in and out in all intricate spots, crept between people's legs and carriage wheels, and came forth unharmed from under horses' hoofs. The dancing-dogs, the stilts, the little lady and the tall man, and all the other attractions, with organs out of number and bands innumerable, emerged from the holes and corners in which they had passed the night, and flourished boldly in the sun.

Along the uncleared course, Short led his party, sounding the brazen trumpet and revelling in the voice of Punch; and at his heels went Thomas Codlin, bearing the show as usual, and keeping his eye on Nelly and her grandfather, as they rather lingered in the rear. The child bore upon her arm the little basket with her flowers, and sometimes stopped, with timid and modest looks, to offer them at some gay carriage; but alas! there were many bolder beggars there, gipsies who promised husbands, and other adepts in their trade, and although some ladies smiled gently as they shook their heads, and others cried to the gentlemen beside them 'See, what a pretty face!' they let the pretty face pass on, and never thought that it looked tired or hungry.

There was but one lady who seemed to understand the child, and she was one who sat alone in a handsome carriage, while two young men in dashing clothes, who had just dismounted from it, talked and laughed loudly at a little distance, appearing to forget her, quite. There were many ladies all around, but they turned their backs, or looked another way, or at the two young men (not unfavourably at *them*), and left her to herself. She motioned away a gipsy-woman urgent to tell her fortune, saying that it was told already and had been for some years, but called the child towards her, and taking her flowers put money into her trembling hand, and bade her go home and keep at home for God's sake.

Many a time they went up and down those long, long lines, seeing everything but the horses and the race; when the bell rung to clear the course, going back to rest among the carts and donkeys, and not coming out again until the heat was over. Many a time, too, was Punch displayed in the full zenith of his humour, but all this while the eye of Thomas Codlin was upon them, and to escape without notice was impracticable.

At length, late in the day, Mr. Codlin pitched the show in a convenient spot, and the spectators were soon in the very triumph of the scene. The child, sitting down with the old man close behind it, had been thinking how strange it was that horses who were such fine honest creatures should seem to make vagabonds of all the men they drew about them, when a loud laugh at some extemporaneous witticism of Mr. Short's, having allusion to the circumstances of the day, roused her from her meditation and caused her to look around.

If they were ever to get away unseen, that was the very moment. Short was plying the quarter-staves vigorously and knocking the characters in the fury of the combat against the sides of the show, the people were looking on with laughing faces, and Mr. Codlin had relaxed into a grim smile as his roving eye detected hands going into waistcoat pockets and groping secretly for sixpences. If they were ever to get away unseen, that was the very moment. They seized it, and fled.

They made a path through booths and carriages and throngs of people, and never once stopped to look behind. The bell was ringing and the course was cleared by the time they reached the ropes, but they dashed across it insensible to the shouts and screeching that assailed them for breaking in upon its sanctity, and creeping under the brow of the hill at a quick pace, made for the open fields.

CHAPTER XX

DAY after day as he bent his steps homeward, returning from some new effort to procure employment, Kit raised his eyes to the window of the little room he had so much commended to the child, and hoped to see some indication of her presence. His own earnest wish, coupled with the assurance he had received from Quilp, filled him with the belief that she would yet arrive to claim the humble shelter he had offered, and from the death of each day's hope, another hope sprung up to live to-morrow.

'I think they must certainly come to-morrow, eh, mother?' said Kit, laying aside his hat with a weary air and sighing as he spoke. 'They have been gone a week. They surely couldn't stop away more than a week, could they now?'

The mother shook her head, and reminded him how often he had been disappointed already.

'For the matter of that,' said Kit, 'you speak true and sensible enough, as you always do, mother. Still, I do consider that a week is quite long enough for 'em to be rambling about; don't you say so?'

'Quite long enough, Kit, longer than enough, but they may not come back for all that.'

Kit was for a moment disposed to be vexed by this contradiction, and not the less so from having anticipated it in his own mind and knowing how just it was. But the impulse was only momentary, and the vexed look became a kind one before it had crossed the room.

'Then what do you think, mother, has become of 'em? You don't think they've gone to sea, anyhow?'

'Not gone for sailors, certainly,' returned the mother with a smile. 'But I can't help thinking that they have gone to some foreign country.'

'I say,' cried Kit with a rueful face, 'don't talk like that, mother.'

'I am afraid they have, and that's the truth,' she said. 'It's the talk of all the neighbours, and there are some even that know of their having been seen on board ship, and can tell you the name of the place they've gone to, which is more than I can, my dear, for it's a very hard one.'

'I don't believe it,' said Kit. 'Not a word of it. A set of idle chatterboxes, how should they know?'

'They may be wrong of course,' returned the mother, 'I can't tell about that, though I don't think it's at all unlikely that they're in the right, for the talk is that the old gentleman had put by a little money that nobody knew of, not even that ugly little man you talk to me about—what's his name—Quilp; and that he and Miss Nell have gone to live abroad where it can't be taken from them, and they will never be disturbed. That don't seem very far out of the way now, do it?'

Kit scratched his head mournfully, in reluctant admission that it did not, and clambering up to the old nail took down the cage and set himself to clean it and to feed the bird. His thoughts reverting from this occupation to the little old gentleman who had given him the shilling, he suddenly recollected that that was the very day—nay, nearly the very hour—at which the little old gentleman had said he should be at the Notary's house again. He no sooner remembered this, than he hung up the cage with great precipitation, and hastily explaining the nature of his errand, went off at full speed to the appointed place.

It was some two minutes after the time when he reached the spot, which was a considerable distance from his home, but by great good luck the little old gentleman had not yet arrived; at least there was no pony-chaise to be seen, and it was not likely that he had come and gone again in so short a space. Greatly relieved to find that he was not too late, Kit leant against a lamp-post to take breath, and waited the advent of the pony and his charge.

Sure enough, before long the pony came trotting round the corner of the street, looking as obstinate as pony might, and picking his steps as if he were spying about for the cleanest places, and would by no means dirty his feet or hurry himself inconveniently. Behind the pony sat the little old gentleman, and by the old gentleman's side sat the little old lady, carrying just such a nosegay as she had brought before.

The old gentleman, the old lady, the pony, and the chaise, came up the street in perfect unanimity, until they arrived within some half-a-dozen doors of the Notary's house, when the pony, deceived by a brass-plate beneath a tailor's knocker, came to a halt, and maintained by a sturdy silence, that that was the house they wanted.

'Now, sir, will you have the goodness to go on; this is *not* the place,' said the old gentleman.

The pony looked with great attention into a fire-plug which was near him, and appeared to be quite absorbed in contemplating it.

'Oh dear, such a naughty Whisker!' cried the old lady. 'After being so good too, and coming along so well! I am quite ashamed of him. I don't know what we are to do with him, I really don't.'

The pony having thoroughly satisfied himself as to the nature and properties of the fire-plug, looked into the air after his old enemies the flies, and as there happened to be one of them tickling his ear at that moment he shook his head and whisked his tail, after which he appeared full of thought but quite comfortable and collected. The old gentleman having exhausted his powers of persuasion, alighted to lead him; whereupon the pony, perhaps because he held this to be a sufficient concession, perhaps because he happened to catch sight of the other brass-plate, or perhaps because he was in a spiteful humour, darted off with the old lady and stopped at the right house, leaving the old gentleman to come panting on behind.

It was then that Kit presented himself at the pony's head, and touched his hat with a smile.

'Why, bless me,' cried the old gentleman, 'the lad *is* here! My dear, do you see?'

'I said I'd be here, sir,' said Kit, patting Whisker's neck. 'I hope you've had a pleasant ride, sir. He's a very nice little pony.'

'My dear,' said the old gentleman. 'This is an uncommon lad; a good lad, I'm sure.'

'I'm sure he is,' rejoined the old lady. 'A very good lad, and I am sure he is a good son.'

Kit acknowledged these expressions of confidence by touching his hat again and blushing very much. The old gentleman then handed the old lady out, and after looking at him with an approving smile, they went into the house—talking about him as they went, Kit could not help feeling. Presently Mr. Witherden, smelling very hard at the nosegay, came to the window and looked at him, and after that Mr. Abel came and looked at him, and after that the old gentleman and lady came and looked at him again, and after that they all came and looked at him together, which Kit, feeling very much embarrassed by, made a pretence of not observing. Therefore he patted the pony more and more; and this liberty the pony most handsomely permitted.

The faces had not disappeared from the window many moments, when Mr. Chuckster in his official coat, and with his hat hanging on his head just as it happened to fall from its peg, appeared upon the pavement, and telling him he was wanted inside, bade him go in and he would mind the chaise the while. In giving him this direction Mr. Chuckster remarked that he wished that he might be blessed if he could make out whether he (Kit) was 'precious raw' or 'precious deep,' but intimated by a distrustful shake of the head, that he inclined to the latter opinion.

Kit entered the office in a great tremor, for he was not used to going among strange ladies and gentlemen, and the tin boxes and bundles of dusty papers had in his eyes an awful and venerable air. Mr. Witherden too was a bustling gentleman who talked loud and fast, and all eyes were upon him, and he was very shabby.

'Well, boy,' said Mr. Witherden, 'you came to work out that shilling;—not to get another, hey?'

'No indeed, sir,' replied Kit, taking courage to look up. 'I never thought of such a thing.'

'Father alive?' said the Notary.

'Dead, sir.'

'Mother?'

'Yes, sir.'

'Married again—eh?'

Kit made answer, not without some indignation, that she was a widow with three children, and that as to her marrying again, if the gentleman knew her he wouldn't think of such a thing. At this reply Mr. Witherden buried his nose in the flowers again, and whispered behind the nosegay to the old gentleman that he believed the lad was as honest a lad as need be.

'Now,' said Mr. Garland when they had made some further inquiries of him, 'I am not going to give you anything—'

'Thank you, sir,' Kit replied; and quite seriously too, for this announcement seemed to free him from the suspicion which the Notary had hinted.

'—But,' resumed the old gentleman, 'perhaps I may want to know something more about you, so tell me where you live, and I'll put it down in my pocket-book.'

Kit told him, and the old gentleman wrote down the address with his pencil. He had scarcely done so, when there was a great uproar in the street, and the old lady hurrying to the window cried that Whisker had run away, upon which Kit darted out to the rescue, and the others followed.

It seemed that Mr. Chuckster had been standing with his hands in his pockets looking carelessly at the pony, and occasionally insulting him with such admonitions as 'Stand still,'—'Be quiet,'—'Wo-a-a,' and the like, which by a pony of spirit cannot be borne. Consequently, the pony being deterred by no considerations of duty or obedience, and not having before him the slightest fear of the human eye, had at length started off, and was at that moment rattling down the street,—Mr. Chuckster, with his hat off and a pen behind his ear, hanging on in the rear of the chaise and making futile attempts to draw it the other way, to the unspeakable admiration of all beholders. Even in running away, however, Whisker was perverse, for he had not gone very far when he suddenly stopped, and before assistance could be rendered, commenced backing at nearly as quick a pace as he had gone forward. By these means Mr. Chuckster was pushed and hustled to the office again, in a most inglorious manner, and arrived in a state of great exhaustion and discomfiture.

The old lady then stepped into her seat, and Mr. Abel (whom they had come to fetch) into his. The old gentleman, after reasoning with the pony on the extreme impropriety of his conduct, and making the best amends in his power to Mr. Chuckster, took his place also, and they drove away, waving a farewell to the Notary and his clerk, and more than once turning to nod kindly to Kit as he watched them from the road.

CHAPTER XXI

KIT turned away and very soon forgot the pony, and the chaise, and the little old lady, and the little old gentleman, and the little young gentleman to boot, in thinking what could have become of his late master and his lovely grandchild, who were the fountain-head of all his meditations. Still casting about for some plausible means of accounting for their non-appearance, and of persuading himself that they must soon return, he bent his steps towards home, intending to finish the task which the sudden recollection of his contract had interrupted, and then to sally forth once more to seek his fortune for the day.

When he came to the corner of the court in which he lived, lo and behold there was the pony again! Yes, there he was, looking more obstinate than ever; and alone in the chaise, keeping a steady watch upon his every wink, sat Mr. Abel, who, lifting up his eyes by chance and seeing Kit pass by, nodded to him as though he would have nodded his head off.

Kit wondered to see the pony again, so near his own home too, but it never occurred to him for what purpose the pony might have come there, or where the old lady and the old gentleman had gone, until he lifted the latch of the door, and walking in, found them seated in the room in conversation with his mother, at which unexpected sight he pulled off his hat and made his best bow in some confusion.

'We are here before you, you see, Christopher,' said Mr. Garland, smiling.

'Yes, sir,' said Kit; and as he said it, he looked towards his mother for an explanation of the visit.

'The gentleman's been kind enough, my dear,' said she, in reply to this mute interrogation, 'to ask me whether you were in a good place, or in any place at all, and when I told him no, you were not in any, he was so good as to say that—'

'That we wanted a good lad in our house,' said the old gentleman and the old lady both together, 'and that perhaps we might think of it, if we found everything as we would wish it to be.'

As this thinking of it, plainly meant the thinking of engaging Kit, he immediately partook of his mother's anxiety and fell into a great flutter; for the little old couple were very methodical and cautious, and asked so many questions that he began to be afraid there was no chance of his success.

'You see, my good woman,' said Mrs. Garland to Kit's mother, 'that it's necessary to be very careful and particular in such a matter as this, for we're only three in family, and are very quiet regular folks, and it would be a sad thing if we made any kind of mistake, and found things different from what we hoped and expected.'

To this, Kit's mother replied, that certainly it was quite true, and quite right, and quite proper, and Heaven forbid that she should shrink, or have cause to shrink, from any inquiry into her character or that of her son, who was a very good son though she was his mother, in which respect, she was bold to say, he took after his father, who was not only a good son to *his* mother, but the best of husbands and the best of fathers besides, which Kit could and would corroborate she knew, and so would little Jacob and the baby likewise if they were old enough, which unfortunately they were not, though as they didn't know what a loss they had had, perhaps it was a great deal better that they should be as young as they were; and so Kit's mother wound up a long story by wiping her eyes with her apron, and patting little Jacob's head, who was rocking the cradle and staring with all his might at the strange lady and gentleman.

When Kit's mother had done speaking, the old lady struck in again, and said that she was quite sure she was a very honest and very respectable person or she never would have expressed herself in that manner, and that certainly the appearance of the children and the cleanliness of the house deserved great praise and did her the utmost credit, whereat Kit's mother dropped a curtsey and became consoled. Then the good woman entered into a long and minute account of Kit's life and history from the earliest period down to that time, not omitting to make mention of his miraculous fall out of a back-parlour window when an infant of tender years, or his uncommon sufferings in a state of measles, which were illustrated by correct imitations of the plaintive manner in which he called for toast and water, day and night, and said, 'don't cry, mother, I shall soon be better;' for proof of which statements reference was made to Mrs. Green, lodger, at the cheesemonger's round the corner, and divers other ladies and gentlemen in various parts of England and Wales, (and one Mr. Brown who was supposed to be then a corporal in the East Indies, and who could of course be found with very little trouble), within whose personal knowledge the circumstances had occurred. This narration ended, Mr. Garland put some questions to Kit respecting his qualifications and general acquirements, while Mrs. Garland noticed the children, and hearing from Kit's mother certain remarkable circumstances which had attended the birth of each, related certain other remarkable circumstances which had attended the birth of her own son, Mr. Abel, from which it appeared that both Kit's mother and herself had been, above and beyond all other women of what condition or age soever, peculiarly hemmed in with perils and dangers. Lastly, inquiry was made into the nature and extent of Kit's wardrobe, and a small advance being made to improve the same, he was formally hired at an annual income of Six Pounds, over and above his board and lodging, by Mr. and Mrs. Garland, of Abel Cottage, Finchley.

It would be difficult to say which party appeared most pleased with this arrangement, the conclusion of which was hailed with nothing but pleasant looks and cheerful smiles on both sides. It was settled that Kit should repair to his new abode on the next day but one, in the morning; and finally, the little old couple, after bestowing a bright half-crown on little Jacob and another on the baby, took their leaves; being escorted as far as the street by their new attendant, who held the obdurate pony by the bridle while they took their seats, and saw them drive away with a lightened heart.

'Well, mother,' said Kit, hurrying back into the house, 'I think my fortune's about made now.'

'I should think it was indeed, Kit,' rejoined his mother. 'Six pound a year! Only think!'

'Ah!' said Kit, trying to maintain the gravity which the consideration of such a sum demanded, but grinning with delight in spite of himself. 'There's a property!'

Kit drew a long breath when he had said this, and putting his hands deep into his pockets as if there were one year's wages at least in each, looked at his mother, as though he saw through her, and down an immense perspective of sovereigns beyond.

'Please God we'll make such a lady of you for Sundays, mother! such a scholar of Jacob, such a child of the baby, such a room of the one up stairs! Six pound a year!'

'Hem!' croaked a strange voice. 'What's that about six pound a year? What about six pound a year?' And as the voice made this inquiry, Daniel Quilp walked in with Richard Swiveller at his heels.

'Who said he was to have six pound a year?' said Quilp, looking sharply round. 'Did the old man say it, or did little Nell say it? And what's he to have it for, and where are they, eh?'

The good woman was so much alarmed by the sudden apparition of this unknown piece of ugliness, that she hastily caught the baby from its cradle and retreated into the furthest corner of the room; while little Jacob, sitting upon his stool with his hands on his knees, looked full at him in a species of fascination, roaring lustily all the time. Richard Swiveller took an easy observation of the family over Mr. Quilp's head, and Quilp himself, with his hands in his pockets, smiled in an exquisite enjoyment of the commotion he occasioned.

'Don't be frightened, mistress,' said Quilp, after a pause. 'Your son knows me; I don't eat babies; I don't like 'em. It will be as well to stop that young screamer though, in case I should be tempted to do him a mischief. Holloa, sir! Will you be quiet?'

Little Jacob stemmed the course of two tears which he was squeezing out of his eyes, and instantly subsided into a silent horror.

'Mind you don't break out again, you villain,' said Quilp, looking sternly at him, 'or I'll make faces at you and throw you into fits, I will. Now you, sir, why haven't you been to me as you promised?'

'What should I come for?' retorted Kit. 'I hadn't any business with you, no more than you had with me.'

'Here, mistress,' said Quilp, turning quickly away, and appealing from Kit to his mother. 'When did his old master come or send here last? Is he here now? If not, where's he gone?'

'He has not been here at all,' she replied. 'I wish we knew where they have gone, for it would make my son a good deal easier in his mind, and me too. If you're the gentleman named Mr. Quilp, I should have thought you'd have known, and so I told him only this very day.'

'Humph!' muttered Quilp, evidently disappointed to believe that this was true. 'That's what you tell this gentleman too, is it?'

'If the gentleman comes to ask the same question, I can't tell him anything else, sir; and I only wish I could, for our own sakes,' was the reply.

Quilp glanced at Richard Swiveller, and observed that having met him on the threshold, he assumed that he had come in search of some intelligence of the fugitives. He supposed he was right?

'Yes,' said Dick, 'that was the object of the present expedition. I fancied it possible—but let us go ring fancy's knell. *I'll* begin it.'

'You seem disappointed,' observed Quilp.

'A baffler, sir, a baffler, that's all,' returned Dick. 'I have entered upon a speculation which has proved a baffler; and a Being of brightness and beauty will be offered up a sacrifice at Cheggs's altar. That's all, sir.'

The dwarf eyed Richard with a sarcastic smile, but Richard, who had been taking a rather strong lunch with a friend, observed him not, and continued to deplore his fate with mournful and despondent looks. Quilp plainly discerned that there was some secret reason for this visit and his uncommon disappointment, and, in the hope that there might be means of mischief lurking beneath it, resolved to worm it out. He had no sooner adopted this resolution, than he conveyed as much honesty into his face as it was capable of expressing, and sympathised with Mr. Swiveller exceedingly.

'I am disappointed myself,' said Quilp, 'out of mere friendly feeling for them; but you have real reasons, private reasons I have no doubt, for your disappointment, and therefore it comes heavier than mine.'

'Why, of course it does,' Dick observed, testily.

'Upon my word, I'm very sorry, very sorry. I'm rather cast down myself. As we are companions in adversity, shall we be companions in the surest way of forgetting it? If you had no particular business, now, to lead you in another direction,' urged Quilp, plucking him by the sleeve and looking slyly up into his face out of the corners of his eyes, 'there is a house by the water-side where they have some of the noblest Schiedam—reputed to be smuggled, but that's between ourselves—that can be got in all the world. The landlord knows me. There's a little summer-house overlooking the river, where we might take a glass of this delicious liquor with a whiff of the best tobacco—it's in this case, and of the rarest quality, to my certain knowledge—and be perfectly snug and happy, could we possibly contrive it; or is there any very particular engagement that peremptorily takes you another way, Mr. Swiveller, eh?'

As the dwarf spoke, Dick's face relaxed into a compliant smile, and his brows slowly unbent. By the time he had finished, Dick was looking down at Quilp in the same sly manner as Quilp was looking up at him, and there remained nothing more to be done but to set out for the house in question. This they did, straightway. The moment their backs were turned, little Jacob thawed, and resumed his crying from the point where Quilp had frozen him.

The summer-house of which Mr. Quilp had spoken was a rugged wooden box, rotten and bare to see, which overhung the river's mud, and threatened to slide down into it. The tavern to which it belonged was a crazy building, sapped and undermined by the rats, and only upheld by great bars of wood which were reared against its walls, and had propped it up so long that even they were decaying and yielding with their load, and of a windy night might be heard to creak and crack as if the whole fabric were about to come toppling down. The house stood—if anything so old and feeble could be said to stand—on a piece of waste ground, blighted with the unwholesome smoke of factory chimneys, and echoing the clank of iron wheels and rush of troubled water. Its internal accommodations amply fulfilled the promise of the outside. The rooms were low and damp, the clammy walls were pierced with chinks and holes, the rotten floors had sunk from their level, the very beams started from their places and warned the timid stranger from their neighbourhood.

To this inviting spot, entreating him to observe its beauties as they passed along, Mr. Quilp led Richard Swiveller, and on the table of the summer-house, scored deep with many a gallows and initial letter, there soon appeared a wooden keg, full of the vaunted liquor. Drawing it off into the glasses with the skill of a practised hand, and mixing it with about a third part of water, Mr. Quilp assigned to Richard Swiveller his portion, and lighting his pipe from an end of a candle in a very old and battered lantern, drew himself together upon a seat and puffed away.

'Is it good?' said Quilp, as Richard Swiveller smacked his lips, 'is it strong and fiery? Does it make you wink, and choke, and your eyes water, and your breath come short—does it?'

'Does it?' cried Dick, throwing away part of the contents of his glass, and filling it up with water, 'why, man, you don't mean to tell me that you drink such fire as this?'

'No?' rejoined Quilp. 'Not drink it? Look here. And here. And here again. Not drink it?'

As he spoke, Daniel Quilp drew off and drank three small glassfuls of the raw spirit, and then with a horrible grimace took a great many pulls at his pipe, and swallowing the smoke, discharged it in a heavy cloud from his nose. This feat accomplished he drew himself together in his former position, and laughed excessively.

'Give us a toast!' cried Quilp, rattling on the table in a dexterous manner with his fist and elbow alternately, in a kind of tune, 'a woman, a beauty. Let's have a beauty for our toast and empty our glasses to the last drop. Her name, come!'

'If you want a name,' said Dick, 'here's Sophy Wackles.'

'Sophy Wackles,' screamed the dwarf, 'Miss Sophy Wackles that is—Mrs. Richard Swiveller that shall be—that shall be—ha ha ha!'

'Ah!' said Dick, 'you might have said that a few weeks ago, but it won't do now, my buck. Immolating herself upon the shrine of Cheggs—'

'Poison Cheggs, cut Cheggs's ears off,' rejoined Quilp. 'I won't hear of Cheggs. Her name is Swiveller or nothing. I'll drink her health again, and her father's, and her mother's; and to all her sisters and brothers—the glorious family of the Wackleses—all the Wackleses in one glass—down with it to the dregs!'

'Well,' said Richard Swiveller, stopping short in the act of raising the glass to his lips and looking at the dwarf in a species of stupor as he flourished his arms and legs about: 'you're a jolly fellow, but of all the jolly fellows I ever saw or heard of, you have the queerest and most extraordinary way with you, upon my life you have.'

This candid declaration tended rather to increase than restrain Mr. Quilp's eccentricities, and Richard Swiveller, astonished to see him in such a roystering vein, and drinking not a little himself, for company,—began imperceptibly to become more companionable and confiding, so that, being judiciously led on by Mr. Quilp, he grew at last very confiding indeed. Having once got him into this mood, and knowing now the key-note to strike whenever he was at a loss,

Daniel Quilp's task was comparatively an easy one, and he was soon in possession of the whole details of the scheme contrived between the easy Dick and his more designing friend

'Stop!' said Quilp. 'That's the thing, that's the thing. It can be brought about, it shall be brought about. There's my hand upon it; I am your friend from this minute.'

'What! do you think there's still a chance?' inquired Dick, in surprise at this encouragement.

'A chance!' echoed the dwarf, 'a certainty! Sophy Wackles may become a Cheggs or anything else she likes, but not a Swiveller. Oh you lucky dog! He's richer than any Jew alive; you're a made man. I see in you now nothing but Nelly's husband, rolling in gold and silver. I'll help you. It shall be done. Mind my words, it shall be done.'

'But how?' said Dick.

'There's plenty of time,' rejoined the dwarf, 'and it shall be done. We'll sit down and talk it over again all the way through. Fill your glass while I'm gone. I shall be back directly—directly.'

With these hasty words, Daniel Quilp withdrew into a dismantled skittle-ground behind the public-house, and, throwing himself upon the ground actually screamed and rolled about in uncontrollable delight.

'Here's sport!' he cried, 'sport ready to my hand, all invented and arranged, and only to be enjoyed. It was this shallow-pated fellow who made my bones ache t'other day, was it? It was his friend and fellow-plotter, Mr. Trent, that once made eyes at Mrs. Quilp, and leered and looked, was it? After labouring for two or three years in their precious scheme, to find that they've got a beggar at last, and one of them tied for life. Ha ha ha! He shall marry Nell. He shall have her, and I'll be the first man, when the knot's tied hard and fast, to tell 'em what they've gained and what I've helped 'em to. Here will be a clearing of old scores, here will be a time to remind 'em what a capital friend I was, and how I helped them to the heiress. Ha ha ha!'

In the height of his ecstasy, Mr. Quilp had like to have met with a disagreeable check, for rolling very near a broken dog-kennel, there leapt forth a large fierce dog, who, but that his chain was of the shortest, would have given him a disagreeable salute. As it was, the dwarf remained upon his back in perfect safety, taunting the dog with hideous faces, and triumphing

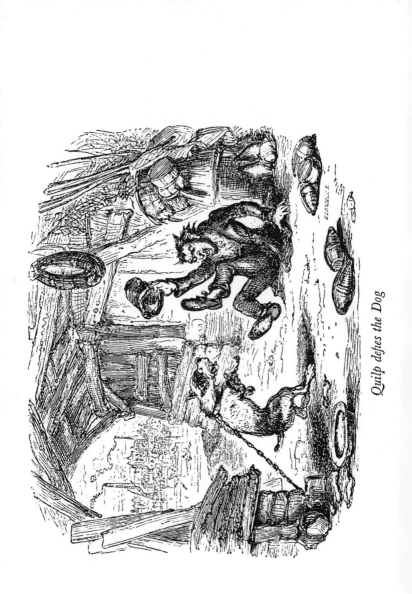

Quilp defies the Dog

over him in his inability to advance another inch, though there were not a couple of feet between them.

'Why don't you come and bite me, why don't you come and tear me to pieces, you coward?' said Quilp, hissing and worrying the animal till he was nearly mad. 'You're afraid, you bully, you're afraid, you know you are.'

The dog tore and strained at his chain with starting eyes and furious bark, but there the dwarf lay, snapping his fingers with gestures of defiance and contempt. When he had sufficiently recovered from his delight, he rose, and with his arms a-kimbo, achieved a kind of demon-dance round the kennel, just without the limits of the chain, driving the dog quite wild. Having by this means composed his spirits and put himself in a pleasant train, he returned to his unsuspicious companion, whom he found looking at the tide with exceeding gravity, and thinking of that same gold and silver which Mr. Quilp had mentioned.

CHAPTER XXII

THE remainder of that day and the whole of the next were a busy time for the Nubbles family, to whom everything connected with Kit's outfit and departure was matter of as great moment as if he had been about to penetrate into the interior of Africa, or to take a cruise round the world. It would be difficult to suppose that there ever was a box which was opened and shut so many times within four-and-twenty hours, as that which contained his wardrobe and necessaries; and certainly there never was one which to two small eyes presented such a mine of clothing, as this mighty chest with its three shirts and proportionate allowance of stockings and pocket-handkerchiefs, disclosed to the astonished vision of little Jacob. At last it was conveyed to the carrier's, at whose house at Finchley Kit was to find it next day; and the box being gone, there remained but two questions for consideration: firstly, whether the carrier would lose, or dishonestly feign to lose, the box upon the road; secondly, whether Kit's mother perfectly understood how to take care of herself in the absence of her son.

'I don't think there's hardly a chance of his really losing it, but carriers are under great temptation to pretend they lose things, no doubt,' said Mrs. Nubbles apprehensively, in reference to the first point.

'No doubt about it,' returned Kit, with a serious look; 'upon my word, mother, I don't think it was right to trust it to itself. Somebody ought to have gone with it, I'm afraid.'

'We can't help it now,' said his mother; 'but it was foolish and wrong. People oughtn't to be tempted.'

Kit inwardly resolved that he would never tempt a carrier any more, save with an empty box; and having formed this Christian determination, he turned his thoughts to the second question.

'You know you must keep up your spirits, mother, and not be lonesome because I'm not at home. I shall very often be able to look in when I come into town I dare say, and I shall send you a letter sometimes, and when the quarter comes round, I can get a holiday of course; and then see if we don't take little Jacob to the play, and let him know what oysters means.'

'I hope plays mayn't be sinful, Kit, but I'm a'most afraid,' said Mrs. Nubbles.

'I know who has been putting that in your head,' rejoined her son disconsolately; 'that's Little Bethel again. Now I say, mother, pray don't take to going there regularly, for if I was to see your good-humoured face that has always made home cheerful, turned into a grievous one, and the baby trained to look grievous too, and to call itself a young sinner (bless its heart) and a child of the devil (which is calling its dead father names); if I was to see this, and see little Jacob looking grievous likewise, I should so take it to heart that I'm sure I should go and list for a soldier, and run my head on purpose against the first cannon-ball I saw coming my way.'

'Oh, Kit, don't talk like that.'

'I would, indeed, mother, and unless you want to make me feel very wretched and uncomfortable, you'll keep that bow on your bonnet, which you'd more than half a mind to pull off last week. Can you suppose there's any harm in looking as cheerful and being as cheerful as our poor circumstances will permit? Do I see anything in the way I'm made, which calls upon me to be a snivelling, solemn, whispering chap, sneaking about as if I couldn't help it, and expressing myself in a most unpleasant snuffle? on the contrary, don't I see every reason why I shouldn't? Just hear this! Ha ha ha! An't that as nat'ral as walking, and as good for the health? Ha ha ha! An't that as nat'ral as a sheep's bleating, or a pig's grunting, or a horse's neighing, or a bird's singing? Ha ha ha! Isn't it, mother?'

There was something contagious in Kit's laugh, for his mother, who had looked grave before, first subsided into a smile, and then fell to joining in it heartily, which occasioned Kit to say that he knew it was natural, and to laugh the more. Kit and his mother, laughing together in a pretty loud key, woke the baby, who, finding that there was something very jovial and agreeable in progress, was no sooner in its mother's arms than it began to kick and laugh, most vigorously. This new illustration of his argument so tickled Kit, that he fell backward in his chair in a state of exhaustion, pointing at the baby and shaking his sides till he rocked again. After recovering twice or thrice, and as often relapsing, he wiped his eyes and said grace; and a very cheerful meal their scanty supper was.

With more kisses, and hugs, and tears, than many young

gentlemen who start upon their travels, and leave well-stocked homes behind them, would deem within the bounds of probability (if matter so low could be herein set down), Kit left the house at an early hour next morning, and set out to walk to Finchley; feeling a sufficient pride in his appearance to have warranted his excommunication from Little Bethel from that time forth, if he had ever been one of that mournful congregation.

Lest anybody should feel a curiosity to know how Kit was clad, it may be briefly remarked that he wore no livery, but was dressed in a coat of pepper-and-salt with waistcoat of canary colour, and nether garments of iron-grey; besides these glories, he shone in the lustre of a new pair of boots and an extremely stiff and shiny hat, which on being struck anywhere with the knuckles, sounded like a drum. And in this attire, rather wondering that he attracted so little attention, and attributing the circumstance to the insensibility of those who got up early, he made his way towards Abel Cottage.

Without encountering any more remarkable adventure on the road, than meeting a lad in a brimless hat, the exact counterpart of his old one, on whom he bestowed half the sixpence he possessed, Kit arrived in course of time at the carrier's house, where, to the lasting honour of human nature, he found the box in safety. Receiving from the wife of this immaculate man, a direction to Mr. Garland's, he took the box upon his shoulder and repaired thither directly.

To be sure, it was a beautiful little cottage with a thatched roof and little spires at the gable-ends, and pieces of stained glass in some of the windows, almost as large as pocket-books. On one side of the house was a little stable, just the size for the pony, with a little room over it, just the size for Kit. White curtains were fluttering, and birds in cages that looked as bright as if they were made of gold, were singing at the windows; plants were arranged on either side of the path, and clustered about the door; and the garden was bright with flowers in full bloom, which shed a sweet odour all round, and had a charming and elegant appearance. Everything within the house and without, seemed to be the perfection of neatness and order. In the garden there was not a weed to be seen, and to judge from some dapper gardening-tools, a basket, and a pair of gloves which were lying in one of the walks, old Mr. Garland had been at work in it that very morning.

Kit looked about him, and admired, and looked again, and this a great many times before he could make up his mind to turn his head another way and ring the bell. There was abundance of time to look about him again though, when he had rung it, for nobody came, so after ringing it twice or thrice he sat down upon his box, and waited.

He rung the bell a great many times, and yet nobody came. But at last, as he was sitting upon the box thinking about giants' castles, and princesses tied up to pegs by the hair of their heads, and dragons bursting out from behind gates, and other incidents of the like nature, common in story-books to youths of low degree on their first visit to strange houses, the door was gently opened, and a little servant-girl, very tidy, modest, and demure, but very pretty too, appeared.

'I suppose you're Christopher, sir,' said the servant-girl.

Kit got off the box, and said yes, he was.

'I'm afraid you've rung a good many times perhaps,' she rejoined, 'but we couldn't hear you, because we've been catching the pony.'

Kit rather wondered what this meant, but as he couldn't stop there, asking questions, he shouldered the box again and followed the girl into the hall, where through a back-door he descried Mr. Garland leading Whisker in triumph up the garden, after that self-willed pony had (as he afterwards learned) dodged the family round a small paddock in the rear, for one hour and three quarters.

The old gentleman received him very kindly and so did the old lady, whose previous good opinion of him was greatly enhanced by his wiping his boots on the mat until the soles of his feet burnt again. He was then taken into the parlour to be inspected in his new clothes; and when he had been surveyed several times, and had afforded by his appearance unlimited satisfaction, he was taken into the stable (where the pony received him with uncommon complaisance); and thence into the little chamber he had already observed, which was very clean and comfortable: and thence into the garden, in which the old gentleman told him he would be taught to employ himself, and where he told him, besides, what great things he meant to do to make him comfortable, and happy, if he found he deserved it. All these kindnesses, Kit acknowledged with various expressions of gratitude, and so many touches of the new hat, that the brim suffered considerably. When the old gentleman had said all he had to say in the way of promise and advice, and Kit had said all he had to say in the way of assurance and thankfulness, he was handed over again to the old lady, who, summoning the little servant-girl (whose name was Barbara), instructed her to take him down stairs and give him something to eat and drink, after his walk.

Down stairs, therefore, Kit went; and at the bottom of the stairs there was such a kitchen as was never before seen or heard of out of a toy-shop window, with everything in it as bright and glowing, and as precisely ordered too, as Barbara herself. And in this kitchen, Kit sat himself down at a table as white as a table-cloth, to eat cold meat, and drink small ale, and use his knife and fork the more awkwardly, because there was an unknown Barbara looking on and observing him.

It did not appear, however, that there was anything remarkably tremendous about this strange Barbara, who having lived a very quiet life, blushed very much and was quite as embarrassed and uncertain what she ought to say or do, as Kit could possibly be. When he had sat for some little time, attentive to the ticking of the sober clock, he ventured to glance curiously at the dresser, and there, among the plates and dishes, were Barbara's little work-box with a sliding lid to shut in the balls of cotton, and Barbara's prayer-book, and Barbara's hymn-book, and Barbara's Bible. Barbara's little looking-glass hung in a good light near the window, and Barbara's bonnet was on a nail behind the door. From all these mute signs and tokens of her presence, he naturally glanced at Barbara herself, who sat as mute as they, shelling peas into a dish; and just when Kit was looking at her eyelashes and wondering—quite in the simplicity of his heart—what colour her eyes might be, it perversely happened that Barbara raised her head a little to look at him, when both pair of eyes were hastily withdrawn, and Kit leant over his plate, and Barbara over her pea-shells, each in extreme confusion at having been detected by the other.

The Kitchen at Abel Cottage

MR. RICHARD SWIVELLER wending homeward from the Wilderness (for such was the appropriate name of Quilp's choice retreat), after a sinuous and corkscrew fashion, with many checks and stumbles; after stopping suddenly and staring about him, then as suddenly running forward for a few paces, and as suddenly halting again and shaking his head; doing everything with a jerk and nothing by premeditation;— Mr. Richard Swiveller wending his way homeward after this fashion, which is considered by evil-minded men to be symbolical of intoxication, and is not held by such persons to denote that state of deep wisdom and reflection in which the actor knows himself to be, began to think that possibly he had misplaced his confidence and that the dwarf might not be precisely the sort of person to whom to entrust a secret of such delicacy and importance. And being led and tempted on by this remorseful thought into a condition which the evil-minded class before referred to would term the maudlin state or stage of drunkenness, it occurred to Mr. Swiveller to cast his hat upon the ground, and moan, crying aloud that he was an unhappy orphan, and that if he had not been an unhappy orphan things had never come to this.

'Left an infant by my parents, at an early age,' said Mr. Swiveller, bewailing his hard lot, 'cast upon the world in my tenderest period, and thrown upon the mercies of a deluding dwarf, who can wonder at my weakness! Here's a miserable orphan for you. Here,' said Mr. Swiveller, raising his voice to a high pitch, and looking sleepily round, 'is a miserable orphan!'

'Then,' said somebody hard by, 'let me be a father to you.'

Mr. Swiveller swayed himself to and fro to preserve his balance, and, looking into a kind of haze which seemed to surround him, at last perceived two eyes dimly twinkling through the mist, which he observed after a short time were in the neighbourhood of a nose and mouth. Casting his eyes down towards that quarter in which, with reference to a man's face, his legs are usually to be found, he observed that the face had a body attached; and when he looked more intently he was satisfied that the person was Mr. Quilp, who indeed had been in his company all the time, but whom he had some vague idea of having left a mile or two behind.

'You have deceived an orphan, sir,' said Mr. Swiveller solemnly.

'I! I'm a second father to you,' replied Quilp.

'You my father, sir!' retorted Dick. 'Being all right myself, sir, I request to be left alone—instantly, sir.'

'What a funny fellow you are!' cried Quilp.

'Go, sir,' returned Dick, leaning against a post and waving his hand. 'Go, deceiver, go. Some day, sir, p'r'aps you'll waken, from pleasure's dream to know, the grief of orphans forsaken. Will you go, sir?'

The dwarf taking no heed of this adjuration, Mr. Swiveller advanced with the view of inflicting upon him condign chastisement. But forgetting his purpose or changing his mind before he came close to him, he seized his hand and vowed eternal friendship, declaring with an agreeable frankness that from that time forth they were brothers in everything but personal appearance. Then he told his secret over again, with the addition of being pathetic on the subject of Miss Wackles, who, he gave Mr. Quilp to understand, was the occasion of any slight incoherency he might observe in his speech at that moment, which was attributable solely to the strength of his affection and not to rosy wine or other fermented liquor. And then they went on arm-in-arm, very lovingly together.

'I'm as sharp,' said Quilp to him, at parting, 'as sharp as a ferret, and as cunning as a weasel. You bring Trent to me; assure him that I'm his friend, though I fear he a little distrusts me (I don't know why, I have not deserved it); and you've both of you made your fortunes—in perspective.'

'That's the worst of it,' returned Dick. 'These fortunes in perspective look such a long way off.'

'But they look smaller than they really are, on that account,' said Quilp, pressing his arm. 'You'll have no conception of the value of your prize until you draw close to it. Mark that.'

'D'ye think not?' said Dick.

'Aye, I do; and I am certain of what I say, that's better,' returned the dwarf. 'You bring Trent to me. Tell him I am his friend and yours—why shouldn't I be?'

'There's no reason why you shouldn't certainly,' replied Dick, 'and perhaps there are a great many why you should—at least there would be nothing strange in your wanting to be my friend, if you were a choice spirit, but then you know you're *not* a choice spirit.'

Quilp's Discovery

'I not a choice spirit?' cried Quilp.

'Devil a bit, sir,' returned Dick. 'A man of your appearance couldn't be. If you're any spirit at all, sir, you're an evil spirit. Choice spirits,' added Dick, smiting himself on the breast, 'are quite a different-looking sort of people, you may take your oath of that, sir.'

Quilp glanced at his free-spoken friend with a mingled expression of cunning and dislike, and wringing his hand almost at the same moment, declared that he was an uncommon character and had his warmest esteem. With that they parted; Mr. Swiveller to make the best of his way home and sleep himself sober; and Quilp to cogitate upon the discovery he had made, and exult in the prospect of the rich field of enjoyment and reprisal it opened to him.

It was not without great reluctance and misgiving that Mr. Swiveller, next morning, his head-racked by the fumes of the renowned Schiedam, repaired to the lodging of his friend Trent (which was in the roof of an old house in an old ghostly inn), and recounted by very slow degrees what had yesterday taken place between him and Quilp. Nor was it without great surprise and much speculation on Quilp's probable motives, nor without many bitter comments on Dick Swiveller's folly, that his friend received the tale.

'I don't defend myself, Fred,' said the penitent Richard; 'but the fellow has such a queer way with him and is such an artful dog, that first of all he set me upon thinking whether there was any harm in telling him, and while I was thinking, screwed it out of me. If you had seen him drink and smoke, as I did, you couldn't have kept anything from him. He's a Salamander you know, that's what *he* is.'

Without inquiring whether Salamanders were of necessity good confidential agents, or whether a fire-proof man was as a matter of course trustworthy, Frederick Trent threw himself into a chair, and, burying his head in his hands, endeavoured to fathom the motives which had led Quilp to insinuate himself into Richard Swiveller's confidence;—for that the disclosure was of his seeking, and had not been spontaneously revealed by Dick, was sufficiently plain from Quilp's seeking his company and enticing him away.

The dwarf had twice encountered him when he was endeavouring to obtain intelligence of the fugitives. This, perhaps, as he had not shown any previous anxiety about them, was enough to awaken suspicion in the breast of a creature so jealous and distrustful by nature, setting aside any additional impulse to curiosity that he might have derived from Dick's incautious manner. But knowing the scheme they had planned, why should he offer to assist it? This was a question more difficult of solution; but as knaves generally overreach themselves by imputing their own designs to others, the idea immediately presented itself that some circumstances of irritation between Quilp and the old man, arising out of their secret transactions and not unconnected perhaps with his sudden disappearance, now rendered the former desirous of revenging himself upon him by seeking to entrap the sole object of his love and anxiety into a connexion of which he knew he had a dread and hatred. As Frederick Trent himself, utterly regardless of his sister, had this object at heart, only second to the hope of gain, it seemed to him the more likely to be Quilp's main principle of action. Once investing the dwarf with a design of his own in abetting them, which the attainment of their purpose would serve, it was easy to believe him sincere and hearty in the cause; and as there could be no doubt of his proving a powerful and useful auxiliary, Trent determined to accept his invitation and go to his house that night, and if what he said and did confirmed him in the impression he had formed, to let him share the labour of their plan, but not the profit.

Having revolved these things in his mind and arrived at this conclusion, he communicated to Mr. Swiveller as much of his meditations as he thought proper (Dick would have been perfectly satisfied with less), and giving him the day to recover himself from his late salamandering, accompanied him at evening to Mr. Quilp's house.

Mightily glad Mr. Quilp was to see them, or mightily glad he seemed to be; and fearfully polite Mr. Quilp was to Mrs. Quilp and Mrs. Jiniwin; and very sharp was the look he cast on his wife to observe how she was affected by the recognition of young Trent. Mrs. Quilp was as innocent as her own mother of any emotion, painful or pleasant, which the sight of him awakened, but as her husband's glance made her timid and confused, and uncertain what to do or what was required of her, Mr. Quilp did not fail to assign her embarrassment to the cause he had in his mind, and while he chuckled at his penetration was secretly exasperated by his jealousy.

Nothing of this appeared, however. On the contrary, Mr. Quilp was all blandness and suavity, and presided over the case-bottle of rum with extraordinary open-heartedness.

'Why, let me see,' said Quilp. 'It must be a matter of nearly two years since we were first acquainted.'

'Nearer three, I think,' said Trent.

'Nearer three!' cried Quilp. 'How fast time flies. Does it seem as long as that to you, Mrs. Quilp?'

'Yes, I think it seems full three years, Quilp,' was the unfortunate reply.

'Oh indeed, ma'am,' thought Quilp, 'you have been pining, have you? Very good, ma'am.'

'It seems to me but yesterday that you went out to Demerara in the Mary Anne,' said Quilp; 'but yesterday, I declare. Well, I like a little wildness. I was wild myself once.'

Mr. Quilp accompanied this admission with such an awful wink, indicative of old rovings and backslidings, that Mrs. Jiniwin was indignant, and could not forbear from remarking under her breath that he might at least put off his confessions until his wife was absent; for which act of boldness and insubordination Mr. Quilp first stared her out of countenance and then drank her health ceremoniously.

'I thought you'd come back directly, Fred. I always thought that,' said Quilp, setting down his glass. 'And when the Mary Anne returned with you on board, instead of a letter to say what a contrite heart you had, and how happy you were in the situation that had been provided for you, I was amused—exceedingly amused. Ha ha ha!'

The young man smiled, but not as though the theme was the most agreeable one that could have been selected for his entertainment; and for that reason Quilp pursued it.

'I always will say,' he resumed, 'that when a rich relation having two young people—sisters or brothers, or brother and sister—dependent on him, attaches himself exclusively to one, and casts off the other, he does wrong.'

The young man made a movement of impatience, but Quilp went on as calmly as if he were discussing some abstract question in which nobody present had the slightest personal interest.

'It's very true,' said Quilp, 'that your grandfather urged repeated forgiveness, ingratitude, riot, and extravagance, and all that; but as I told him "these are common faults." "But he's a scoundrel," said he. "Granting that," said I (for the sake of argument of course), "a great many young noblemen and gentlemen are scoundrels too!" But he wouldn't be convinced.'

'I wonder at that, Mr. Quilp,' said the young man sarcastically.

'Well, so did I at the time,' returned Quilp, 'but he was always obstinate. He was in a manner a friend of mine, but he was always obstinate and wrong-headed. Little Nell is a nice girl, a charming girl, but you're her brother, Frederick. You're her brother after all; as you told him the last time you met, he can't alter that.'

'He would if he could, confound him for that and all other kindnesses,' said the young man impatiently. 'But nothing can come of this subject now, and let us have done with it in the Devil's name.'

'Agreed,' returned Quilp, 'agreed on my part readily. Why have I alluded to it? Just to show you, Frederick, that I have always stood your friend. You little knew who was your friend, and who your foe; now did you? You thought I was against you, and so there has been a coolness between us; but it was all on your side, entirely on your side. Let's shake hands again, Fred.'

With his head sunk down between his shoulders, and a hideous grin overspreading his face, the dwarf stood up and stretched his short arm across the table. After a moment's hesitation, the young man stretched out his to meet it; Quilp clutched his fingers in a grip that for the moment stopped the current of the blood within them, and pressing his other hand upon his lip and frowning towards the unsuspicious Richard, released them and sat down.

This action was not lost upon Trent, who, knowing that Richard Swiveller was a mere tool in his hands and knew no more of his designs than he thought proper to communicate, saw that the dwarf perfectly understood their relative position, and fully entered into the character of his friend. It is something to be appreciated, even in knavery. This silent homage to his superior abilities, no less than a sense of the power with which the dwarf's quick perception had already invested him, inclined the young man towards that ugly worthy, and determined him to profit by his aid.

It being now Mr. Quilp's cue to change the subject with all convenient expedition, lest Richard Swiveller in his heedlessness should reveal anything which it was inexpedient for the women to know, he proposed a game at four-handed cribbage; and partners being cut for, Mrs. Quilp fell to Frederick Trent, and Dick himself to Quilp. Mrs. Jiniwin being very fond of cards was carefully excluded by her son-in-law from any participation in the game, and had assigned to her the duty of occasionally replenishing the glasses from the case-bottle; Mr. Quilp from that moment keeping one eye constantly upon her, lest she should by any means procure a taste of the same, and thereby tantalising the wretched old lady (who was as much attached to the case-bottle as the cards) in a double degree and most ingenious manner.

But it was not to Mrs. Jiniwin alone that Mr. Quilp's attention was restricted, as several other matters required his constant vigilance. Among his various eccentric habits he had a humorous one of always cheating at cards, which rendered necessary on his part, not only a close observance of the game, and a sleight-of-hand in counting and scoring, but also involved the constant correction, by looks, and frowns, and kicks under the table, of Richard Swiveller, who being be-wildered by the rapidity with which his cards were told, and the rate at which the pegs travelled down the board, could not be prevented from sometimes expressing his surprise and incredulity. Mrs. Quilp too was the partner of young Trent, and for every look that passed between them, and every word they spoke, and every card they played, the dwarf had eyes and ears; not occupied alone with what was passing above the table, but with signals that might be exchanging beneath it, which he laid all kinds of traps to detect; besides often treading on his wife's toes to see whether she cried out or remained silent under the infliction, in which latter case it would have been quite clear that Trent had been treading on her toes before. Yet, in the midst of all these distractions, the one eye was upon the old lady always, and if she so much as stealthily advanced a tea-spoon towards a neighbouring glass (which she often did), for the purpose of abstracting but one sup of its sweet contents, Quilp's hand would overset it in the very moment of her triumph, and Quilp's mocking voice implore her to regard her precious health. And in any one of these his many cares, from first to last, Quilp never flagged nor faltered.

At length, when they had played a great many rubbers and drawn pretty freely upon the case-bottle, Mr. Quilp warned his lady to retire to rest, and that submissive wife complying, and being followed by her indignant mother, Mr. Swiveller fell asleep. The dwarf beckoning his remaining companion to the other end of the room, held a short conference with him in whispers.

'It's as well not to say more than one can help before our worthy friend,' said Quilp, making a grimace towards the slumbering Dick. 'Is it a bargain between us, Fred? Shall he marry little rosy Nell by-and-by?'

'You have some end of your own to answer, of course,' returned the other.

'Of course I have, dear Fred,' said Quilp, grinning to think how little he suspected what the real end was. 'It's retaliation perhaps; perhaps whim. I have influence, Fred, to help or oppose. Which way shall I use it? There are a pair of scales, and it goes into one.'

'Throw it into mine then,' said Trent.

'It's done, Fred,' rejoined Quilp, stretching out his clenched hand and opening it as if he had let some weight fall out. 'It's in the scale from this time, and turns it, Fred. Mind that.'

'Where have they gone?' asked Trent.

Quilp shook his head, and said that point remained to be discovered, which it might be, easily. When it was, they would begin their preliminary advances. He would visit the old man, or even Richard Swiveller might visit him, and by affecting a deep concern in his behalf, and imploring him to settle in some worthy home, lead to the child's remembering him with gratitude and favour. Once impressed to this extent, it would be easy, he said, to win her in a year or two, for she supposed the old man to be poor, as it was a part of his jealous policy (in common with many other misers) to feign to be so, to those about him.

'He has feigned it often enough to me, of late,' said Trent.

'Oh! and to me too!' replied the dwarf. 'Which is more extraordinary, as I know how rich he really is.'

'I suppose you should,' said Trent.

'I think I should indeed,' rejoined the dwarf; and in that, at least, he spoke the truth.

After a few more whispered words, they returned to the table, and the young man rousing Richard Swiveller informed him that he was waiting to depart. This was welcome news to Dick, who started up directly. After a few words of confidence in the result of their project had been exchanged, they bade the grinning Quilp good night.

Quilp crept to the window as they passed in the street below, and listened. Trent was pronouncing an encomium upon his wife, and they were both wondering by what enchantment she had been brought to marry such a misshapen wretch as he. The dwarf after watching their retreating shadows with a wider grin than his face had yet displayed, stole softly in the dark to bed.

In this hatching of their scheme, neither Trent nor Quilp had had one thought about the happiness or misery of poor innocent Nell. It would have been strange if the careless profligate, who was the butt of both, had been harassed by any such consideration; for his high opinion of his own merits and deserts rendered the project rather a laudable one than other-wise; and if he had been visited by so unwonted a guest as reflection, he would—being a brute only in the gratification of his appetites—have soothed his conscience with the plea that he did not mean to beat or kill his wife, and would therefore, after all said and done, be a very tolerable, average husband.

CHAPTER XXIV

IT was not until they were quite exhausted and could no longer maintain the pace at which they had fled from the race-ground, that the old man and the child ventured to stop, and sit down to rest upon the borders of a little wood. Here, though the course was hidden from their view, they could yet faintly distinguish the noise of distant shouts, the hum of voices, and the beating of drums. Climbing the eminence which lay between them and the spot they had left, the child could even discern the fluttering flags and white tops of booths; but no person was approaching towards them, and their resting-place was solitary and still.

Some time elapsed before she could reassure her trembling companion, or restore him to a state of moderate tranquillity. His disordered imagination represented to him a crowd of persons stealing towards them beneath the cover of the bushes, lurking in every ditch, and peeping from the boughs of every rustling tree. He was haunted by apprehensions of being led captive to some gloomy place where he would be chained and scourged, and worse than all, where Nell could never come to see him, save through iron bars and gratings in the wall. His terrors affected the child. Separation from her grandfather was the greatest evil she could dread; and feeling for the time as though, go where they would, they were to be hunted down, and could never be safe but in hiding, her heart failed her, and her courage drooped.

In one so young, and so unused to the scenes in which she had lately moved, this sinking of the spirit was not surprising. But, Nature often enshrines gallant and noble hearts in weak bosoms—oftenest, God bless her, in female breasts—and when the child, casting her tearful eyes upon the old man, remembered how weak he was, and how destitute and helpless he would be if she failed him, her heart swelled within her, and animated her with new strength and fortitude.

'We are quite safe now, and have nothing to fear indeed, dear grandfather,' she said.

'Nothing to fear!' returned the old man. 'Nothing to fear if they took me from thee! Nothing to fear if they parted us! Nobody is true to me. No, not one. Not even Nell!'

'Oh! do not say that,' replied the child, 'for if ever anybody

At the Schoolmaster's Porch

was true at heart, and earnest, I am. I am sure you know I am.'

'Then how,' said the old man, looking fearfully round, 'how can you bear to think that we are safe, when they are searching for me everywhere, and may come here, and steal upon us, even while we're talking?'

'Because I'm sure we have not been followed,' said the child. 'Judge for yourself, dear grandfather; look round, and see how quiet and still it is. We are alone together, and may ramble where we like. Not safe! Could I feel easy—did I feel at ease— when any danger threatened you?'

'True, too,' he answered, pressing her hand, but still looking anxiously about. 'What noise was that?'

'A bird,' said the child, 'flying into the wood, and leading the way for us to follow. You remember that we said we would walk in woods and fields, and by the side of rivers, and how happy we would be—you remember that? But here, while the sun shines above our heads, and everything is bright and happy, we are sitting sadly down, and losing time. See what a pleasant path; and there's the bird—the same bird—now he flies to another tree, and stays to sing. Come!'

When they rose up from the ground, and took the shady track which led them through the wood, she bounded on before, printing her tiny footsteps in the moss, which rose elastic from so light a pressure and gave it back as mirrors throw off breath; and thus she lured the old man on, with many a backward look and merry beck, now pointing stealthily to some lone bird as it perched and twittered on a branch that strayed across their path, now stopping to listen to the songs that broke the happy silence, or watch the sun as it trembled through the leaves, and stealing in among the ivied trunks of stout old trees, opened long paths of light. As they passed onward, parting the boughs that clustered in their way, the serenity which the child had first assumed, stole into her breast in earnest; the old man cast no longer fearful looks behind, but felt at ease and cheerful, for the further they passed into the deep green shade, the more they felt that the tranquil mind of God was there, and shed its peace on them.

At length the path becoming clearer and less intricate, brought them to the end of the wood, and into a public road. Taking their way along it for a short distance, they came to a lane, so shaded by the trees on either hand that they met together overhead, and arched the narrow way. A broken finger-post announced that this led to a village three miles off; and thither they resolved to bend their steps.

The miles appeared so long that they sometimes thought they must have missed their road. But at last, to their great joy, it led downwards in a steep descent, with overhanging banks over which the footpaths led; and the clustered houses of the village peeped from the woody hollow below.

It was a very small place. The men and boys were playing at cricket on the green; and as the other folks were looking on, they wandered up and down, uncertain where to seek a humble lodging. There was but one old man in the little garden before his cottage, and him they were timid of approaching, for he was the schoolmaster, and had 'School' written up over his window in black letters on a white board. He was a pale, simple-looking man, of a spare and meagre habit, and sat among his flowers and beehives, smoking his pipe, in the little porch before his door.

'Speak to him, dear,' the old man whispered.

'I am almost afraid to disturb him,' said the child timidly. 'He does not seem to see us. Perhaps if we wait a little, he may look this way.'

They waited, but the schoolmaster cast no look towards them, and still sat, thoughtful and silent, in the little porch. He had a kind face. In his plain old suit of black, he looked pale and meagre. They fancied, too, a lonely air about him and his house, but perhaps that was because the other people formed a merry company upon the green, and he seemed the only solitary man in all the place.

They were very tired, and the child would have been bold enough to address even a schoolmaster, but for something in his manner which seemed to denote that he was uneasy or distressed. As they stood hesitating at a little distance, they saw that he sat for a few minutes at a time like one in a brown study, then laid aside his pipe and took a few turns in his garden, then approached the gate and looked towards the green, then took up his pipe again with a sigh, and sat down as thoughtfully as before.

As nobody else appeared and it would soon be dark, Nell at length took courage, and when he had resumed his pipe and seat, ventured to draw near, leading her grandfather by the hand. The slight noise they made in raising the latch of the

wicket-gate, caught his attention. He looked at them kindly
but seemed disappointed too, and slightly shook his head.

Nell dropped a curtsey, and told him they were poor
travellers who sought a shelter for the night which they would
gladly pay for, so far as their means allowed. The schoolmaster
looked earnestly at her as she spoke, laid aside his pipe, and
rose up directly.

'If you could direct us anywhere, sir,' said the child, 'we
should take it very kindly.'

'You have been walking a long way,' said the schoolmaster.

'A long way, sir,' the child replied.

'You're a young traveller, my child,' he said, laying his
hand gently on her head. 'Your grandchild, friend?'

'Aye, sir,' cried the old man, 'and the stay and comfort of
my life.'

'Come in,' said the schoolmaster.

Without further preface he conducted them into his little
schoolroom, which was parlour and kitchen likewise, and told
them that they were welcome to remain under his roof till
morning. Before they had done thanking him, he spread a
coarse white cloth upon the table, with knives and platters;
and bringing out some bread and cold meat and a jug of beer,
besought them to eat and drink.

The child looked round the room as she took her seat. There
were a couple of forms, notched and cut and inked all over;
a small deal desk perched on four legs, at which no doubt the
master sat; a few dog's-eared books upon a high shelf; and beside them a motley collection of peg-tops, balls, kites, fishing-lines,
marbles, half-eaten apples, and other confiscated property of idle
urchins. Displayed on hooks upon the wall in all their terrors,
were the cane and ruler; and near them, on a small shelf of its
own, the dunce's cap, made of old newspapers and decorated
with glaring wafers of the largest size. But, the great ornaments of
the walls were certain moral sentences fairly copied in good
round text, and well-worked sums in simple addition and multi-
plication, evidently achieved by the same hand, which were
plentifully pasted all round the room: for the double purpose, as
it seemed, of bearing testimony to the excellence of the school,
and kindling a worthy emulation in the bosoms of the scholars.

'Yes,' said the old schoolmaster, observing that her attention
was caught by these latter specimens. 'That's beautiful
writing, my dear.'

'Very, sir,' replied the child modestly, 'is it yours?'

'Mine!' he returned, taking out his spectacles and putting them on, to have a better view of the triumphs so dear to his heart. '*I* couldn't write like that, now-a-days. No. They're all done by one hand; a little hand it is, not so old as yours, but a very clever one.'

As the schoolmaster said this, he saw that a small blot of ink had been thrown on one of the copies, so he took a penknife from his pocket, and going up to the wall, carefully scraped it out. When he had finished, he walked slowly backward from the writing, admiring it as one might contemplate a beautiful picture, but with something of sadness in his voice and manner which quite touched the child, though she was unacquainted with its cause.

'A little hand indeed,' said the poor schoolmaster. 'Far beyond all his companions, in his learning and his sports too, how did he ever come to be so fond of me? That I should love him is no wonder, but that he should love me—' and there the schoolmaster stopped, and took off his spectacles to wipe them, as though they had grown dim.

'I hope there is nothing the matter, sir,' said Nell anxiously.

'Not much, my dear,' returned the schoolmaster. 'I hoped to have seen him on the green to-night. He was always foremost among them. But he'll be there to-morrow.'

'Has he been ill?' asked the child, with a child's quick sympathy.

'Not very. They said he was wandering in his head yesterday, dear boy, and so they said the day before. But that's a part of that kind of disorder; it's not a bad sign—not at all a bad sign.'

The child was silent. He walked to the door, and looked wistfully out. The shadows of night were gathering, and all was still.

'If he could lean upon anybody's arm, he would come to me, I know,' he said, returning into the room. 'He always came into the garden to say good night. But perhaps his illness has only just taken a favourable turn, and it's too late for him to come out, for it's very damp and there's a heavy dew. It's much better he shouldn't come to-night.'

The schoolmaster lighted a candle, fastened the window-shutter, and closed the door. But after he had done this, and sat silent a little time, he took down his hat, and said he would go and satisfy himself, if Nell would sit up till he returned. The child readily complied, and he went out.

She sat there half-an-hour or more, feeling the place very strange and lonely, for she had prevailed upon the old man to go to bed, and there was nothing to be heard but the ticking of an old clock, and the whistling of the wind among the trees. When he returned, he took his seat in the chimney corner, but remained silent for a long time. At length he turned to her, and speaking very gently, hoped she would say a prayer that night for a sick child.

'My favourite scholar!' said the poor schoolmaster, smoking a pipe he had forgotten to light, and looking mournfully round upon the walls. 'It is a little hand to have done all that, and waste away with sickness. It is a very, very little hand!'

CHAPTER XXV

AFTER a sound night's rest in a chamber in the thatched roof, in which it seemed the sexton had for some years been a lodger, but which he had lately deserted for a wife and a cottage of his own, the child rose early in the morning and descended to the room where she had supped last night. As the schoolmaster had already left his bed and gone out, she bestirred herself to make it neat and comfortable, and had just finished its arrangement when the kind host returned.

He thanked her many times, and said that the old dame who usually did such offices for him had gone to nurse the little scholar whom he had told her of. The child asked how he was, and hoped he was better.

'No,' rejoined the schoolmaster, shaking his head sorrowfully, 'no better. They even say he is worse.'

'I am very sorry for that, sir,' said the child.

The poor schoolmaster appeared to be gratified by her earnest manner, but yet rendered more uneasy by it, for he added hastily that anxious people often magnified an evil and thought it greater than it was; 'for my part,' he said, in his quiet, patient way, 'I hope it's not so. I don't think he can be worse.'

The child asked his leave to prepare breakfast, and her grandfather coming down stairs, they all three partook of it together. While the meal was in progress, their host remarked that the old man seemed much fatigued, and evidently stood in need of rest.

'If the journey you have before you is a long one,' he said, 'and don't press you for one day, you're very welcome to pass another night here. I should really be glad if you would, friend.'

He saw that the old man looked at Nell, uncertain whether to accept or decline his offer; and added,

'I shall be glad to have your young companion with me for one day. If you can do a charity to a lone man, and rest yourself at the same time, do so. If you must proceed upon your journey, I wish you well through it, and will walk a little way with you before school begins.'

'What are we to do, Nell?' said the old man irresolutely, 'say what we're to do, dear.'

It required no great persuasion to induce the child to

answer that they had better accept the invitation and remain. She was happy to show her gratitude to the kind schoolmaster by busying herself in the performance of such household duties as his little cottage stood in need of. When these were done, she took some needlework from her basket, and sat herself down upon a stool beside the lattice, where the honeysuckle and woodbine entwined their tender stems, and stealing into the room filled it with their delicious breath. Her grandfather was basking in the sun outside, breathing the perfume of the flowers, and idly watching the clouds as they floated on before the light summer wind.

As the schoolmaster, after arranging the two forms in due order, took his seat behind his desk and made other preparations for school, the child was apprehensive that she might be in the way, and offered to withdraw to her little bedroom. But this he would not allow, and as he seemed pleased to have her there, she remained, busying herself with her work.

'Have you many scholars, sir?' she asked.

The poor schoolmaster shook his head, and said that they barely filled the two forms.

'Are the others clever, sir?' asked the child, glancing at the trophies on the wall.

'Good boys,' returned the schoolmaster, 'good boys enough, my dear, but they'll never do like that.'

A small white-headed boy with a sunburnt face appeared at the door while he was speaking, and stopping there to make a rustic bow, came in and took his seat upon one of the forms. The white-headed boy then put an open book, astonishingly dog's-eared, upon his knees, and thrusting his hands into his pockets began counting the marbles with which they were filled: displaying in the expression of his face a remarkable capacity of totally abstracting his mind from the spelling on which his eyes were fixed. Soon afterwards another white-headed little boy came straggling in, and after him a red-headed lad, and after him two more with white heads, and then one with a flaxen poll, and so on until the forms were occupied by a dozen boys or thereabouts, with heads of every colour but grey, and ranging in their ages from four years old to fourteen years or more; for the legs of the youngest were a long way from the floor when he sat upon the form, and the eldest was a heavy good-tempered foolish fellow, about half a head taller than the schoolmaster.

At the top of the first form—the post of honour in the school —was the vacant place of the little sick scholar, and at the head of the row of pegs on which those who came in hats or caps were wont to hang them up, one was left empty. No boy attempted to violate the sanctity of seat or peg, but many a one looked from the empty spaces to the schoolmaster, and whispered his idle neighbour behind his hand.

Then began the hum of conning over lessons and getting them by heart, the whispered jest and stealthy game, and all the noise and drawl of school; and in the midst of the din sat the poor schoolmaster, the very image of meekness and simplicity, vainly attempting to fix his mind upon the duties of the day, and to forget his little friend. But the tedium of his office reminded him more strongly of the willing scholar, and his thoughts were rambling from his pupils—it was plain.

None knew this better than the idlest boys, who, growing bolder with impunity, waxed louder and more daring; playing odd-or-even under the master's eye, eating apples openly and without rebuke, pinching each other in sport or malice without the least reserve, and cutting their autographs in the very legs of his desk. The puzzled dunce, who stood beside it to say his lesson out of book, looked no longer at the ceiling for forgotten words, but drew closer to the master's elbow and boldly cast his eye upon the page; the wag of the little troop squinted and made grimaces (at the smallest boy of course), holding no book before his face, and his approving audience knew no constraint in their delight. If the master did chance to rouse himself and seem alive to what was going on, the noise subsided for a moment, and no eyes met his but wore a studious and a deeply humble look; but the instant he relapsed again, it broke out afresh, and ten times louder than before.

Oh! how some of those idle fellows longed to be outside, and how they looked at the open door and window, as if they half meditated rushing violently out, plunging into the woods, and being wild boys and savages from that time forth. What rebellious thoughts of the cool river, and some shady bathing-place beneath willow trees with branches dipping in the water, kept tempting and urging that sturdy boy, who, with his shirt-collar unbuttoned and flung back as far as it could go, sat fanning his flushed face with a spelling-book, wishing himself a whale, or a tittlebat, or a fly, or anything but a boy at school on that hot, broiling day! Heat! ask that other boy, whose

The Dunce improves the Occasion

seat being nearest to the door gave him opportunities of gliding out into the garden and driving his companions to madness by dipping his face into the bucket of the well and then rolling on the grass—ask him if there were ever such a day as that, when even the bees were diving deep down into the cups of flowers and stopping there, as if they had made up their minds to retire from business and be manufacturers of honey no more. The day was made for laziness, and lying on one's back in green places, and staring at the sky till its brightness forced one to shut one's eyes and go to sleep; and was this a time to be poring over musty books in a dark room, slighted by the very sun itself? Monstrous!

Nell sat by the window occupied with her work, but attentive still to all that passed, though sometimes rather timid of the boisterous boys. The lessons over, writing-time began; and there being but one desk and that the master's, each boy sat at it in turn and laboured at his crooked copy, while the master walked about. This was a quieter time; for he would come and look over the writer's shoulder, and tell him mildly to observe how such a letter was turned in such a copy on the wall, praise such an up-stroke here and such a down-stroke there, and bid him take it for his model. Then he would stop and tell them what the sick child had said last night, and how he had longed to be among them once again; and such was the poor schoolmaster's gentle and affectionate manner, that the boys seemed quite remorseful that they had worried him so much, and were absolutely quiet; eating no apples, cutting no names, inflicting no pinches, and making no grimaces, for full two minutes afterwards.

'I think, boys,' said the schoolmaster when the clock struck twelve, 'that I shall give an extra half-holiday this afternoon.'

At this intelligence, the boys, led on and headed by the tall boy, raised a great shout, in the midst of which the master was seen to speak, but could not be heard. As he held up his hand, however, in token of his wish that they should be silent, they were considerate enough to leave off, as soon as the longest-winded among them were quite out of breath.

'You must promise me first,' said the schoolmaster, 'that you'll not be noisy, or at least, if you are, that you'll go away and be so—away out of the village I mean. I'm sure you wouldn't disturb your old playmate and companion.'

There was a general murmur (and perhaps a very sincere

I

one, for they were but boys) in the negative; and the tall boy, perhaps as sincerely as any of them, called those about him to witness that he had only shouted in a whisper.

'Then pray don't forget, there's my dear scholars,' said the schoolmaster, 'what I have asked you, and do it as a favour to me. Be as happy as you can, and don't be unmindful that you are blessed with health. Good-bye all!'

'Thank'ee, sir,' and 'good-bye, sir,' were said a great many times in a variety of voices, and the boys went out very slowly and softly. But there was the sun shining and there were the birds singing, as the sun only shines and the birds only sing on holidays and half-holidays; there were the trees waving to all free boys to climb and nestle among their leafy branches; the hay, entreating them to come and scatter it to the pure air; the green corn, gently beckoning towards wood and stream; the smooth ground, rendered smoother still by blending lights and shadows, inviting to runs and leaps, and long walks God knows whither. It was more than boy could bear, and with a joyous whoop the whole cluster took to their heels, and spread themselves about, shouting and laughing as they went.

'It's natural, thank Heaven!' said the poor schoolmaster, looking after them. 'I'm very glad they didn't mind me!'

It is difficult, however, to please everybody, as most of us would have discovered, even without the fable which bears that moral; and in the course of the afternoon several mothers and aunts of pupils looked in to express their entire disapproval of the schoolmaster's proceeding. A few confined themselves to hints, such as politely inquiring what red-letter day or saint's day the almanack said it was; a few (these were the profound village politicians) argued that it was a slight to the throne·and an affront to church and state, and savoured of revolutionary principles, to grant a half-holiday upon any lighter occasion than the birthday of the Monarch; but the majority expressed their displeasure on private grounds and in plain terms, arguing that to put the pupils on this short allowance of learning was nothing but an act of downright robbery and fraud: and one old lady, finding that she could not inflame or irritate the peaceable schoolmaster by talking to him, bounced out of his house and talked at him for half-an-hour outside his own window, to another old lady, saying that of course he would deduct this half-holiday from his weekly charge, or of course he would naturally expect to have an opposition started against him; there was no want of idle chaps in that neighbourhood (here the old lady raised her voice), and some chaps who were too idle even to be schoolmasters, might soon find that there were other chaps put over their heads, and so she would have them take care, and look pretty sharp about them. But all these taunts and vexations failed to elicit one word from the meek schoolmaster, who sat with the child by his side, —a little more dejected perhaps, but quite silent and uncomplaining.

Towards night an old woman came tottering up the garden as speedily as she could, and meeting the schoolmaster at the door, said he was to go to Dame West's directly, and had best run on before her. He and the child were on the point of going out together for a walk, and without relinquishing her hand, the schoolmaster hurried away, leaving the messenger to follow as she might. .

They stopped at a cottage-door, and the schoolmaster knocked softly at it with his hand. It was opened without loss of time. They entered a room where a little group of women were gathered about one, older than the rest, who was crying very bitterly, and sat wringing her hands and rocking herself to and fro.

'Oh, dame!' said the schoolmaster, drawing near her chair, 'is it so bad as this?'

'He's going fast,' cried the old woman; 'my grandson's dying. It's all along of you. You shouldn't see him now, but for his being so earnest on it. This is what his learning has brought him to. Oh dear, dear, dear, what can I do?'

'Do not say that I am in any fault,' urged the gentle schoolmaster. 'I am not hurt, dame. No, no. You are in great distress of mind, and don't mean what you say. I am sure you don't.'

'I do,' returned the old woman. 'I mean it all. If he hadn't been poring over his books out of fear of you, he would have been well and merry now, I know he would.'

The schoolmaster looked round upon the other women as if to entreat some one among them to say a kind word for him, but they shook their heads, and murmured to each other that they never thought there was much good in learning, and that this convinced them. Without saying a word in reply, or giving them a look of reproach, he followed the old woman who had summoned him (and who had now rejoined them) into another room, where his infant friend, half-dressed, lay stretched upon a bed.

He was a very young boy; quite a little child. His hair still hung in curls about his face, and his eyes were very bright; but their light was of Heaven, not earth. The schoolmaster took a seat beside him, and stooping over the pillow, whispered his name. The boy sprung up, stroked his face with his hand, and threw his wasted arms round his neck, crying out that he was his dear kind friend.

'I hope I always was. I meant to be, God knows,' said the poor schoolmaster.

'Who is that?' said the boy, seeing Nell. 'I am afraid to kiss her, lest I should make her ill. Ask her to shake hands with me.'

The sobbing child came closer up, and took the little languid hand in hers. Releasing his again after a time, the sick boy laid him gently down.

'You remember the garden, Harry,' whispered the schoolmaster, anxious to rouse him, for a dulness seemed gathering upon the child, 'and how pleasant it used to be in the evening time? You must make haste to visit it again, for I think the very flowers have missed you, and are less gay than they used to be. You will come soon, my dear, very soon now,—won't you?'

The boy smiled faintly—so very, very faintly—and put his hand upon his friend's grey head. He moved his lips too, but no voice came from them; no, not a sound.

In the silence that ensued, the hum of distant voices borne upon the evening air came floating through the open window. 'What's that?' said the sick child, opening his eyes.

'The boys at play upon the green.'

He took a handkerchief from his pillow, and tried to wave it above his head. But the feeble arm dropped powerless down.

'Shall I do it?' said the schoolmaster.

'Please wave it at the window,' was the faint reply. 'Tie it to the lattice. Some of them may see it there. Perhaps they'll think of me, and look this way.'

He raised his head, and glanced from the fluttering signal to his idle bat, that lay with slate and book and other boyish property upon a table in the room. And then he laid him softly down once more, and asked if the little girl were there, for he could not see her.

She stepped forward, and pressed the passive hand that lay upon the coverlet. The two old friends and companions—for such they were, though they were man and child—held each other in a long embrace, and then the little scholar turned his face towards the wall, and fell asleep.

The poor schoolmaster sat in the same place, holding the small cold hand in his, and chafing it. It was but the hand of a dead child. He felt that; and yet he chafed it still, and could not lay it down.

CHAPTER XXVI

ALMOST broken-hearted, Nell withdrew with the school-master from the bedside and returned to his cottage. In the midst of her grief and tears she was yet careful to conceal their real cause from the old man, for the dead boy had been a grandchild, and left but one aged relative to mourn his premature decay.

She stole away to bed as quickly as she could, and when she was alone, gave free vent to the sorrow with which her breast was overcharged. But the sad scene she had witnessed, was not without its lesson of content and gratitude; of content with the lot which left her health and freedom; and gratitude that she was spared to the one relative and friend she loved, and to live and move in a beautiful world, when so many young creatures—as young and full of hope as she—were stricken down and gathered to their graves. How many of the mounds in that old churchyard where she had lately strayed, grew green above the graves of children! And though she thought as a child herself, and did not perhaps sufficiently consider to what a bright and happy existence those who die young are borne, and how in death they lose the pain of seeing others die around them, bearing to the tomb some strong affection of their hearts (which makes the old die many times in one long life), still she thought wisely enough, to draw a plain and easy moral from what she had seen that night, and to store it, deep in her mind.

Her dreams were of the little scholar: not coffined and covered up, but mingling with angels, and smiling happily. The sun darting his cheerful rays into the room, awoke her; and now there remained but to take leave of the poor school-master and wander forth once more.

By the time they were ready to depart, school had begun. In the darkened room, the din of yesterday was going on again: a little sobered and softened down, perhaps, but only a very little, if at all. The schoolmaster rose from his desk and walked with them to the gate.

It was with a trembling and reluctant hand, that the child held out to him the money which the lady had given her at the races for her flowers: faltering in her thanks as she thought how small the sum was, and blushing as she offered it. But he bade her put it up, and stooping to kiss her cheek, turned back into his house.

They had not gone half-a-dozen paces when he was at the door again: the old man retraced his steps to shake hands, and the child did the same.

'Good fortune and happiness go with you!' said the poor schoolmaster. 'I am quite a solitary man now. If you ever pass this way again, you'll not forget the little village-school.'

'We shall never forget it, sir,' rejoined Nell; 'nor ever forget to be grateful to you for your kindness to us.'

'I have heard such words from the lips of children very often,' said the schoolmaster, shaking his head, and smiling thoughtfully, 'but they were soon forgotten. I had attached one young friend to me, the better friend for being young—but that's over —God bless you!'

They bade him farewell very many times, and turned away, walking slowly and often looking back, until they could see him no more. At length they had left the village far behind, and even lost sight of the smoke behind the trees. They trudged onward now, at a quicker pace, resolving to keep the main road, and go wherever it might lead them.

But main roads stretch a long, long way. With the exception of two or three inconsiderable clusters of cottages which they passed, without stopping, and one lonely roadside public-house where they had some bread and cheese, this highway had led them to nothing—late in the afternoon—and still lengthened out, far in the distance, the same dull, tedious, winding course, that they had been pursuing all day. As they had no resource, however, but to go forward, they still kept on, though at a much slower pace, being very weary and fatigued.

The afternoon had worn away into a beautiful evening, when they arrived at a point where the road made a sharp turn and struck across a common. On the border of this common, and close to the hedge which divided it from the cultivated fields, a caravan was drawn up to rest; upon which, by reason of its situation, they came so suddenly that they could not have avoided it if they would.

It was not a shabby, dingy, dusty cart, but a smart little house upon wheels, with white dimity curtains festooning the windows, and window-shutters of green picked out with panels of a staring red, in which happily-contrasted colours the whole concern shone brilliant. Neither was it a poor caravan drawn by a single donkey or emaciated horse, for a pair of horses in pretty good condition were released from the shafts and grazing on the frouzy grass. Neither was it a gipsy caravan, for at the open door (graced with a bright brass knocker) sat a Christian lady, stout and comfortable to look upon, who wore a large bonnet trembling with bows. And that it was not an unprovided or destitute caravan was clear from this lady's occupation, which was the very pleasant and refreshing one of taking tea. The tea-things, including a bottle of rather suspicious character and a cold knuckle of ham, were set forth upon a drum, covered with a white napkin; and there, as if at the most convenient round-table in all the world, sat this roving lady, taking her tea and enjoying the prospect.

It happened that at that moment the lady of the caravan had her cup (which, that everything about her might be of a stout and comfortable kind, was a breakfast cup) to her lips, and that having her eyes lifted to the sky in her enjoyment of the full flavour of the tea, not unmingled possibly with just the slightest dash or gleam of something out of the suspicious bottle—but this is mere speculation and not distinct matter of history—it happened that being thus agreeably engaged, she did not see the travellers when they first came up. It was not until she was in the act of setting down the cup, and drawing a long breath after the exertion of causing its contents to disappear, that the lady of the caravan beheld an old man and a young child walking slowly by, and glancing at her proceedings with eyes of modest but hungry admiration.

'Hey!' cried the lady of the caravan, scooping the crumbs out of her lap and swallowing the same before wiping her lips. 'Yes, to be sure—Who won the Helter-Skelter Plate, child?'

'Won what, ma'am?' asked Nell.

'The Helter-Skelter Plate at the races, child—the plate that was run for on the second day.'

'On the second day, ma'am?'

'Second day! Yes, second day,' repeated the lady with an air of impatience. 'Can't you say who won the Helter-Skelter Plate when you're asked the question civilly?'

'I don't know, ma'am.'

'Don't know!' repeated the lady of the caravan; 'why, you were there. I saw you with my own eyes.'

Nell was not a little alarmed to hear this, supposing that the lady might be intimately acquainted with the firm of Short and Codlin; but what followed tended to reassure her.

'And very sorry I was,' said the lady of the caravan, 'to see

The Lady of the Caravan

you in company with a Punch; a low, practical, wulgar wretch, that people should scorn to look at.'

'I was not there by choice,' returned the child; 'we didn't know our way, and the two men were very kind to us, and let us travel with them. Do you—do you know them, ma'am?'

'Know 'em, child!' cried the lady of the caravan in a sort of shriek. 'Know *them!* But you're young and inexperienced, and that's your excuse for asking sich a question. Do I look as if I know'd 'em, does the caravan look as if *it* know'd 'em?'

'No, ma'am, no,' said the child, fearing she had committed some grievous fault. 'I beg your pardon.'

It was granted immediately, though the lady still appeared much ruffled and discomposed by the degrading supposition. The child then explained that they had left the races on the first day, and were travelling to the next town on that road, where they purposed to spend the night. As the countenance of the stout lady began to clear up, she ventured to inquire how far it was. The reply—which the stout lady did not come to, until she had thoroughly explained that she went to the races on the first day in a gig, and as an expedition of pleasure, and that her presence there had no connexion with any matters of business or profit—was, that the town was eight miles off.

This discouraging information a little dashed the child, who could scarcely repress a tear as she glanced along the darkening road. Her grandfather made no complaint, but he sighed heavily as he leaned upon his staff, and vainly tried to pierce the dusty distance.

The lady of the caravan was in the act of gathering her tea equipage together preparatory to clearing the table, but noting the child's anxious manner she hesitated and stopped. The child curtseyed, thanked her for her information, and giving her hand to the old man had already got some fifty yards or so, away, when the lady of the caravan called to her to return.

'Come nearer, nearer still'—said she, beckoning to her to ascend the steps. 'Are you hungry, child?'

'Not very, but we are tired, and it's—it *is* a long way—'

'Well, hungry or not, you had better have some tea,' rejoined her new acquaintance. 'I suppose you are agreeable to that, old gentleman?'

The grandfather humbly pulled off his hat and thanked her. The lady of the caravan then bade him come up the steps likewise, but the drum proving an inconvenient table for two, they descended again, and sat upon the grass, where she handed down to them the tea-tray, the bread and butter, the knuckle of ham, and in short everything of which she had partaken herself, except the bottle which she had already embraced an opportunity of slipping into her pocket.

'Set 'em out near the hind wheels, child, that's the best place'—said their friend, superintending the arrangements from above. 'Now hand up the teapot for a little more hot water, and a pinch of fresh tea, and then both of you eat and drink as much as you can, and don't spare anything; that's all I ask of you.'

They might perhaps have carried out the lady's wish, if it had been less freely expressed, or even if it had not been expressed at all. But as this direction relieved them from any shadow of delicacy or uneasiness, they made a hearty meal and enjoyed it to the utmost.

While they were thus engaged, the lady of the caravan alighted on the earth, and with her hands clasped behind her, and her large bonnet trembling excessively, walked up and down in a measured tread and very stately manner, surveying the caravan from time to time with an air of calm delight, and deriving particular gratification from the red panels and the brass knocker. When she had taken this gentle exercise for some time, she sat down upon the steps and called 'George;' whereupon a man in a carter's frock, who had been so shrouded in a hedge up to this time as to see everything that passed without being seen himself, parted the twigs that concealed him, and appeared in a sitting attitude, supporting on his legs a baking-dish and a half-gallon stone bottle, and bearing in his right hand a knife, and in his left a fork.

'Yes, Missus'—said George.

'How did you find the cold pie, George?'

'It warn't amiss, mum.'

'And the beer,' said the lady of the caravan, with an appearance of being more interested in this question than the last; 'is it passable, George?'

'It's more flatterer than it might be,' George returned, 'but it an't so bad for all that.'

To set the mind of his mistress at rest, he took a sip (amounting in quantity to a pint or thereabouts) from the stone bottle, and then smacked his lips, winked his eye, and nodded his head. No doubt with the same amiable desire, he immediately resumed his knife and fork, as a practical assurance that the beer had wrought no bad effect upon his appetite.

The lady of the caravan looked on approvingly for some time, and then said,

'Have you nearly finished?'

'Wery nigh, mum.' And indeed, after scraping the dish all round with his knife and carrying the choice brown morsels to his mouth, and after taking such a scientific pull at the stone bottle that, by degrees almost imperceptible to the sight, his head went further and further back until he lay nearly at his full length upon the ground, this gentleman declared himself quite disengaged, and came forth from his retreat.

'I hope I haven't hurried you, George,' said his mistress, who appeared to have a great sympathy with his late pursuit.

'If you have,' returned the follower, wisely reserving himself for any favourable contingency that might occur, 'we must make up for it next time, that's all.'

'We are not a heavy load, George?'

'That's always what the ladies say,' replied the man, looking a long way round, as if he were appealing to Nature in general against such monstrous propositions. 'If you see a woman a driving, you'll always perceive that she never will keep her whip still; the horse can't go fast enough for her. If cattle have got their proper load, you never can persuade a woman that they'll not bear something more. What is the cause of this here?'

'Would these two travellers make much difference to the horses, if we took them with us?' asked his mistress, offering no reply to the philosophical inquiry, and pointing to Nell and the old man, who were painfully preparing to resume their journey on foot.

'They'd make a difference in course,' said George doggedly.

'Would they make much difference?' repeated his mistress. 'They can't be very heavy.'

'The weight o' the pair, mum,' said George, eyeing them with the look of a man who was calculating within half an ounce or so, 'would be a trifle under that of Oliver Cromwell.'

Nell was very much surprised that the man should be so accurately acquainted with the weight of one whom she had read of in books as having lived considerably before their time, but speedily forgot the subject in the joy of hearing that they were to go forward in the caravan, for which she thanked its lady with unaffected earnestness. She helped with great readiness and alacrity to put away the tea-things and other matters that were lying about, and, the horses being by that time harnessed, mounted into the vehicle, followed by her delighted grandfather. Their patroness then shut the door and sat herself down by her drum at an open window; and, the steps being struck by George and stowed under the carriage, away they went, with a great noise of flapping and creaking and straining, and the bright brass knocker, which nobody ever knocked at, knocking one perpetual double knock of its own accord as they jolted heavily along.

CHAPTER XXVII

WHEN they had travelled slowly forward for some short distance, Nell ventured to steal a look round the caravan and observe it more closely. One half of it—that moiety in which the comfortable proprietress was then seated—was carpeted, and so partitioned off at the further end as to accommodate a sleeping-place, constructed after the fashion of a berth on board ship, which was shaded, like the little windows, with fair white curtains, and looked comfortable enough, though by what kind of gymnastic exercise the lady of the caravan ever contrived to get into it, was an unfathomable mystery. The other half served for a kitchen, and was fitted up with a stove whose small chimney passed through the roof. It held also a closet or larder, several chests, a great pitcher of water, and a few cooking-utensils and articles of crockery. These latter necessaries hung upon the walls, which, in that portion òf the establishment devoted to the lady of the caravan, were ornamented with such gayer and lighter decorations as a triangle and a couple of well-thumbed tambourines.

The lady of the caravan sat at one window in all the pride and poetry of the musical instruments, and little Nell and her grandfather sat at the other in all the humility of the kettle and saucepans, while the machine jogged on and shifted the darkening prospect very slowly. At first the two travellers spoke little, and only in whispers, but as they grew more familiar with the place they ventured to converse with greater freedom, and talked about the country through which they were passing, and the different objects that presented themselves, until the old man fell asleep; which the lady of the caravan observing, invited Nell to come and sit beside her.

'Well, child,' she said, 'how do you like this way of travelling?'

Nell replied that she thought it was very pleasant indeed, to which the lady assented in the case of people who had their spirits. For herself, she said, she was troubled with a lowness in that respect which required a constant stimulant; though whether the aforesaid stimulant was derived from the suspicious bottle of which mention has been already made or from other sources, she did not say.

'That's the happiness of you young people,' she continued.

'You don't know what it is to be low in your feelings.
You always have your appetites too, and what a comfort
that is.'

Nell thought that she could sometimes dispense with her own
appetite very conveniently; and thought, moreover, that there
was nothing either in the lady's personal appearance or in her
manner of taking tea, to lead to the conclusion that her natural
relish for meat and drink had at all failed her. She silently
assented, however, as in duty bound, to what the lady had
said, and waited until she should speak again.

Instead of speaking, however, she sat looking at the child
for a long time in silence, and then getting up, brought
out from a corner a large roll of canvas about a yard in
width, which she laid upon the floor and spread open with
her foot until it nearly reached from one end of the caravan
to the other.

'There, child,' she said, 'read that.'

Nell walked down it, and read aloud, in enormous black
letters, the inscription, 'JARLEY'S WAX-WORK.'

'Read it again,' said the lady, complacently.

'Jarley's Wax-Work,' repeated Nell.

'That's me,' said the lady. 'I am Mrs. Jarley.'

Giving the child an encouraging look, intended to reassure
her and let her know, that, although she stood in the presence
of the original Jarley, she must not allow herself to be utterly
overwhelmed and borne down, the lady of the caravan un-
folded another scroll, whereon was the inscription, 'One
hundred figures the full size of life,' and then another scroll, on
which was written, 'The only stupendous collection of real
wax-work in the world,' and then several smaller scrolls with
such inscriptions as 'Now exhibiting within'—'The genuine and
only Jarley'—'Jarley's unrivalled collection'—'Jarley is the
delight of the Nobility and Gentry'—'The Royal Family are
the patrons of Jarley.' When she had exhibited these leviathans
of public announcement to the astonished child, she brought
forth specimens of the lesser fry in the shape of handbills, some
of which were couched in the form of parodies on popular
melodies, as 'Believe me if all Jarley's wax-work so rare'—'I saw
thy show in youthful prime'—'Over the water to Jarley;' while,
to consult all tastes, others were composed with a view to the
lighter and more facetious spirits, as a parody on the favourite
air of 'If I had a donkey,' beginning

If I know'd a donkey wot wouldn't go
To see Mrs. JARLEY's wax-work show,
Do you think I'd acknowledge him?
  Oh no no!
              Then run to Jarley's—

—besides several compositions in prose, purporting to be
dialogues between the Emperor of China and an oyster, or the
Archbishop of Canterbury and a dissenter on the subject of
church-rates, but all having the same moral, namely, that the
reader must make haste to Jarley's, and that children and
servants were admitted at half-price. When she had brought
all these testimonials of her important position in society to
bear upon her young companion, Mrs. Jarley rolled them up,
and having put them carefully away, sat down again, and looked
at the child in triumph.

'Never go into the company of a filthy Punch any more,' said
Mrs. Jarley, 'after this.'

'I never saw any wax-work, ma'am,' said Nell. 'Is it funnier
than Punch?'

'Funnier!' said Mrs. Jarley in a shrill voice. 'It is not funny
at all.'

'Oh!' said Nell, with all possible humility.

'It isn't funny at all,' repeated Mrs. Jarley. 'It's calm and—
what's that word again—critical?—no—classical, that's it—
it is calm and classical. No low beatings and knockings about,
no jokings and squeakings like your precious Punches, but
always the same, with a constantly unchanging air of coldness
and gentility; and so like life, that if wax-work only spoke
and walked about, you'd hardly know the difference. I
won't go so far as to say, that, as it is, I'ye seen wax-work quite
like life, but I've certainly seen some life that was exactly like
wax-work.'

'Is it here, ma'am?' asked Nell, whose curiosity was awakened
by this description.

'Is what here, child?'

'The wax-work, ma'am.'

'Why, bless you, child, what are you thinking of? How
could such a collection be here, where you see everything
except the inside of one little cupboard and a few boxes? It's
gone on in the other wans to the assembly-rooms, and there
it'll be exhibited the day after to-morrow. You are going to the
same town, and you'll see it I dare say. It's natural to expect

that you'll see it, and I've no doubt you will. I suppose you couldn't stop away if you was to try ever so much.'

'I shall not be in the town, I think, ma'am,' said the child.

'Not there?' cried Mrs. Jarley. 'Then where will you be?'

'I—I—don't quite know. I am not certain.'

'You don't mean to say that you're travelling about the country without knowing where you're going to?' said the lady of the caravan. 'What curious people you are! What line are you in? You looked to me at the races, child, as if you were quite out of your element, and had got there by accident.'

'We were there quite by accident,' returned Nell, confused by this abrupt questioning. 'We are poor people, ma'am, and are only wandering about. We have nothing to do;—I wish we had.'

'You amaze me more and more,' said Mrs. Jarley, after remaining for some time as mute as one of her own figures. 'Why, what do you call yourselves? Not beggars?'

'Indeed, ma'am, I don't know what else we are,' returned the child.

'Lord bless me,' said the lady of the caravan. 'I never heard of such a thing. Who'd have thought it!'

She remained so long silent after this exclamation, that Nell feared she felt her having been induced to bestow her protection and conversation upon one so poor, to be an outrage upon her dignity that nothing could repair. This persuasion was rather confirmed than otherwise by the tone in which she at length broke silence and said,

'And yet you can read. And write too, I shouldn't wonder?'

'Yes, ma'am,' said the child, fearful of giving new offence by the confession.

'Well, and what a thing that is,' returned Mrs. Jarley. 'I can't!'

Nell said 'indeed' in a tone which might imply, either that she was reasonably surprised to find the genuine and only Jarley, who was the delight of the Nobility and Gentry and the peculiar pet of the Royal Family, destitute of these familiar arts; or that she presumed so great a lady could scarcely stand in need of such ordinary accomplishments. In whatever way Mrs. Jarley received the response, it did not provoke her to further questioning, or tempt her into any more remarks at the time, for she relapsed into a thoughtful silence, and remained in that state so long that Nell withdrew to the other window and rejoined her grandfather, who was now awake.

Nell hides from Quilp

(p. 207)

At length the lady of the caravan shook off her fit of meditation, and, summoning the driver to come under the window at
which she was seated, held a long conversation with him in a
low tone of voice, as if she were asking his advice on an important point, and discussing the pros and cons of some very
weighty matter. This conference at length concluded, she
drew in her head again, and beckoned Nell to approach.

'And the old gentleman too,' said Mrs. Jarley; 'for I want to
have a word with him. Do you want a good situation for your
grand-daughter, master? If you do, I can put her in the way
of getting one. What do you say?'

'I can't leave her,' answered the old man. 'We can't
separate. What would become of me without her?'

'I should have thought you were old enough to take care of
yourself, if you ever will be,' retorted Mrs. Jarley sharply.

'But he never will be,' said the child in an earnest whisper.
'I fear he never will be again. Pray do not speak harshly to him.
We are very thankful to you,' she added aloud; 'but neither of
us could part from the other if all the wealth of the world were
halved between us.'

Mrs. Jarley was a little disconcerted by this reception of her
proposal, and looked at the old man, who tenderly took Nell's
hand and detained it in his own, as if she could have very well
dispensed with his company or even his earthly existence.
After an awkward pause, she thrust her head out of the window
again, and had another conference with the driver upon some
point on which they did not seem to agree quite so readily as on
their former topic of discussion; but they concluded at last, and
she addressed the grandfather again.

'If you're really disposed to employ yourself,' said Mrs.
Jarley, 'there would be plenty for you to do in the way of
helping to dust the figures, and take the checks, and so forth.
What I want your grand-daughter for, is to point 'em out to
the company; they would be soon learnt, and she has a way
with her that people wouldn't think unpleasant, though she
does come after me; for I've been always accustomed to go
round with visitors myself, which I should keep on doing now,
only that my spirits make a little ease absolutely necessary.
It's not a common offer, bear in mind,' said the lady, rising into
the tone and manner in which she was accustomed to address
her audiences; 'it's Jarley's wax-work, remember. The duty's
very light and genteel, the company particularly select, the

exhibition takes place in assembly-rooms, town-halls, large rooms at inns, or auction galleries. There is none of your open-air wagrancy at Jarley's, recollect; there is no tarpaulin and sawdust at Jarley's, remember. Every expectation held out in the handbills is realised to the utmost, and the whole forms an effect of imposing brilliancy hitherto unrivalled in this kingdom. Remember that the price of admission is only sixpence, and that this is an opportunity which may never occur again!'

Descending from the sublime when she had reached this point, to the details of common life, Mrs. Jarley remarked that with reference to salary she could pledge herself to no specific sum until she had sufficiently tested Nell's abilities, and narrowly watched her in the performance of her duties. But board and lodging, both for her and her grandfather, she bound herself to provide, and she furthermore passed her word that the board should always be good in quality, and in quantity plentiful.

Nell and her grandfather consulted together, and while they were so engaged, Mrs. Jarley with her hands behind her walked up and down the caravan, as she had walked after tea on the dull earth, with uncommon dignity and self-esteem. Nor will this appear so slight a circumstance as to be unworthy of mention, when it is remembered that the caravan was in uneasy motion all the time, and that none but a person of great natural stateliness and acquired grace could have forborne to stagger.

'Now, child?' cried Mrs. Jarley, coming to a halt as Nell turned towards her.

'We are very much obliged to you, ma'am,' said Nell, 'and thankfully accept your offer.'

'And you'll never be sorry for it,' returned Mrs. Jarley. 'I'm pretty sure of that. So as that's all settled, let us have a bit of supper.'

In the meanwhile, the caravan blundered on as if it too had been drinking strong beer and was drowsy, and came at last upon the paved streets of a town which were clear of passengers, and quiet, for it was by this time near midnight, and the towns-people were all abed. As it was too late an hour to repair to the exhibition room, they turned aside into a piece of waste ground that lay just within the old town-gate, and drew up there for the night, near to another caravan, which, notwithstanding that it bore on the lawful panel the great name of Jarley, and was employed besides in conveying from place to place the

wax-work which was its country's pride, was designated by a
grovelling stamp-office as a 'Common Stage Waggon,' and
numbered too—seven thousand odd hundred—as though its
precious freight were mere flour or coals!

This ill-used machine being empty (for it had deposited its
burden at the place of exhibition, and lingered here until its
services were again required) was assigned to the old man as
his sleeping-place for the night; and within its wooden walls,
Nell made him up the best bed she could, from the materials at
hand. For herself, she was to sleep in Mrs. Jarley's own
travelling-carriage, as a signal mark of that lady's favour and
confidence.

She had taken leave of her grandfather and was returning to
the other waggon, when she was tempted by the pleasant
coolness of the night to linger for a little while in the air. The
moon was shining down upon the old gateway of the town,
leaving the low archway very black and dark; and with a
mingled sensation of curiosity and fear, she slowly approached
the gate, and stood still to look up at it, wondering to see how
dark, and grim, and old, and cold, it looked.

There was an empty niche from which some old statue had
fallen or been carried away hundreds of years ago, and she was
thinking what strange people it must have looked down upon
when it stood there, and how many hard struggles might have
taken place, and how many murders might have been done,
upon that silent spot, when there suddenly emerged from the
black shade of the arch, a man. The instant he appeared, she
recognised him. Who could have failed to recognise, in that
instant, the ugly mis-shapen Quilp!

The street beyond was so narrow, and the shadow of the
houses on one side of the way so deep, that he seemed to have
risen out of the earth. But there he was. The child withdrew
into a dark corner, and saw him pass close to her. He had a
stick in his hand, and, when he had got clear of the shadow of
the gateway, he leant upon it, looked back—directly, as it
seemed, towards where she stood—and beckoned.

To her? oh no, thank God, not to her; for as she stood, in an
extremity of fear, hesitating whether to scream for help, or come
from her hiding-place and fly, before he should draw nearer,
there issued slowly forth from the arch another figure—that of
a boy—who carried on his back a trunk.

'Faster, sirrah!' cried Quilp, looking up at the old gateway, and showing in the moonlight like some monstrous image that had come down from its niche and was casting a backward glance at its old house, 'faster!'

'It's a dreadful heavy load, sir,' the boy pleaded. I've come on very fast, considering.'

'*You* have come fast, considering!' retorted Quilp; 'you creep, you dog, you crawl, you measure distance like a worm. There are the chimes now, half-past twelve.'

He stopped to listen, and then turning upon the boy with a suddenness and ferocity that made him start, asked at what hour that London coach passed the corner of the road. The boy replied, at one.

'Come on then,' said Quilp, 'or I shall be too late. Faster—do you hear me? Faster.'

The boy made all the speed he could, and Quilp led onward, constantly turning back to threaten him, and urge him to greater haste. Nell did not dare to move until they were out of sight and hearing, and then hurried to where she had left her grandfather, feeling as if the very passing of the dwarf so near him must have filled him with alarm and terror. But he was sleeping soundly, and she softly withdrew.

As she was making her way to her own bed, she determined to say nothing of this adventure, as upon whatever errand the dwarf had come (and she feared it must have been in search of them) it was clear by his inquiry about the London coach that he was on his way homeward, and as he had passed through that place, it was but reasonable to suppose that they were safer from his inquiries there, than they could be elsewhere. These reflections did not remove her own alarm, for she had been too much terrified to be easily composed, and felt as if she were hemmed in by a legion of Quilps, and the very air itself were filled with them.

The delight of the Nobility and Gentry and the patronised of Royalty had, by some process of self-abridgment known only to herself, got into her travelling bed, where she was snoring peacefully, while the large bonnet, carefully disposed upon the drum, was revealing its glories by the light of a dim lamp that swung from the roof. The child's bed was already made upon the floor, and it was a great comfort to her to hear the steps removed as soon as she had entered, and to know that all easy communication between persons outside and the brass knocker was by this means effectually prevented. Certain guttural sounds, too, which from time to time ascended through the floor of the caravan, and a rustling of straw in the same direction, apprised her that the driver was couched upon the ground beneath, and gave her an additional feeling of security.

Notwithstanding these protections, she could get none but broken sleep by fits and starts all night, for fear of Quilp, who throughout her uneasy dreams was somehow connected with the wax-work, or was wax-work himself, or was Mrs. Jarley and wax-work too, or was himself, Mrs. Jarley, wax-work, and a barrel-organ all in one, and yet not exactly any of them either. At length, towards break of day, that deep sleep came upon her which succeeds to weariness and over-watching, and which has no consciousness but one of overpowering and irresistible enjoyment.

CHAPTER XXVIII

SLEEP hung upon the eyelids of the child so long, that, when she awoke, Mrs. Jarley was already decorated with her large bonnet, and actively engaged in preparing breakfast. She received Nell's apology for being so late with perfect good humour, and said that she should not have roused her if she had slept on till noon.

'Because it does you good,' said the lady of the caravan, 'when you're tired, to sleep as long as ever you can, and get the fatigue quite off; and that's another blessing of your time of life—you can sleep so very sound.'

'Have you had a bad night, ma'am?' asked Nell.

'I seldom have anything else, child,' replied Mrs. Jarley, with the air of a martyr. 'I sometimes wonder how I bear it.'

Remembering the snores which had proceeded from that cleft in the caravan in which the proprietress of the waxwork passed the night, Nell rather thought she must have been dreaming of lying awake. However, she expressed herself very sorry to hear such a dismal account of her state of health, and shortly afterwards sat down with her grandfather and Mrs. Jarley to breakfast. The meal finished, Nell assisted to wash the cups and saucers, and put them in their proper places, and these household duties performed, Mrs. Jarley arrayed herself in an exceedingly bright shawl for the purpose of making a progress through the streets of the town.

'The wan will come on to bring the boxes,' said Mrs. Jarley, 'and you had better come in it, child. I am obliged to walk, very much against my will; but the people expect it of me, and public characters can't be their own masters and mistresses in such matters as these. How do I look, child?'

Nell returned a satisfactory reply, and Mrs. Jarley, after sticking a great many pins into various parts of her figure, and making several abortive attempts to obtain a full view of her own back, was at last satisfied with her appearance, and went forth majestically.

The caravan followed at no great distance. As it went jolting through the streets, Nell peeped from the window, curious to see in what kind of place they were, and yet fearful of encountering at every turn the dreaded face of Quilp. It was a pretty large town, with an open square which they were crawling slowly across, and in the middle of which was the Town-Hall, with a clock-tower and a weathercock. There were houses of stone, houses of red brick, houses of yellow brick, houses of lath and plaster; and houses of wood, many of them very old, with withered faces carved upon the beams, and staring down into the street. These had very little winking windows, and low-arched doors, and, in some of the narrower ways, quite overhung the pavement. The streets were very clean, very sunny, very empty, and very dull. A few idle men lounged about the two inns, and the empty market-place, and the tradesmen's doors, and some old people were dozing in chairs outside an alms-house wall; but scarcely any passengers who seemed bent on going anywhere, or to have any object in view, went by; and if perchance some straggler did, his footsteps echoed on the hot bright pavement for minutes afterwards. Nothing seemed to be going on but the clocks, and they had such drowsy faces, such heavy lazy hands, and such cracked voices that they surely must have been too slow. The very dogs were all asleep, and the flies, drunk with moist sugar in the grocer's shop, forgot their wings and briskness, and baked to death in dusty corners of the window.

Rumbling along with most unwonted noise, the caravan stopped at last at the place of exhibition, where Nell dismounted amidst an admiring group of children, who evidently supposed her to be an important item of the curiosities, and were fully impressed with the belief that her grandfather was a cunning device in wax. The chests were taken out with all convenient despatch, and taken in to be unlocked by Mrs. Jarley, who, attended by George and another man in velveteen shorts and a drab hat ornamented with turnpike tickets, were waiting to dispose their contents (consisting of red festoons and other ornamental devices in upholstery work) to the best advantage in the decoration of the room.

They all got to work without loss of time, and very busy they were. As the stupendous collection were yet concealed by cloths, lest the envious dust should injure their complexions, Nell bestirred herself to assist in the embellishment of the room, in which her grandfather also was of great service. The two men being well used to it, did a great deal in a short time; and Mrs. Jarley served out the tin-tacks from a linen pocket like a toll-collector's which she wore for the purpose, and encouraged her assistants to renewed exertion.

While they were thus employed, a tallish gentleman with a hook nose and black hair, dressed in a military surtout very short and tight in the sleeves, and which had once been frogged and braided all over, but was now sadly shorn of its garniture and quite threadbare—dressed too in ancient grey pantaloons fitting tight to the leg, and a pair of pumps in the winter of their existence—looked in at the door and smiled affably. Mrs. Jarley's back being then towards him, the military gentleman shook his forefinger as a sign that her myrmidons were not to apprise her of his presence, and stealing up close behind her, tapped her on the neck, and cried playfully 'Boh!'

'What, Mr. Slum!' cried the lady of the wax-work. 'Lor! who'd have thought of seeing you here?'

''Pon my soul and honour,' said Mr. Slum, 'that's a good remark. 'Pon my soul and honour that's a wise remark. Who *would* have thought it! George, my faithful feller, how are you?'

George received this advance with a surly indifference, observing that he was well enough for the matter of that, and hammering lustily all the time.

'I came here,' said the military gentleman, turning to Mrs. Jarley,—''pon my soul and honour I hardly know what I came here for. It would puzzle me to tell you, it would by Gad. I wanted a little inspiration, a little freshening up, a little change of ideas, and——'Pon my soul and honour,' said the military gentleman, checking himself and looking round the room, 'what a devilish classical thing this is! By Gad, it's quite Minervian!'

'It'll look well enough when it comes to be finished,' observed Mrs. Jarley.

'Well enough!' said Mr. Slum. 'Will you believe me when I say it's the delight of my life to have dabbled in poetry, when I think I've exercised my pen upon this charming theme? By the way—any orders? Is there any little thing I can do for you?'

'It comes so very expensive, sir,' replied Mrs. Jarley, 'and I really don't think it does much good.'

'Hush! No, no!' returned Mr. Slum, elevating his hand. 'No fibs. I'll not hear it. Don't say it don't do good. Don't say it. I know better!'

'I don't think it does,' said Mrs. Jarley.

'Ha, ha!' cried Mr. Slum, 'you're giving way, you're coming down. Ask the perfumers, ask the blacking-makers, ask the

hatters, ask the old lottery-office keepers—ask any man among
'em what my poetry has done for him, and mark my words, he
blesses the name of Slum. If he's an honest man, he raises his
eyes to heaven, and blesses the name of Slum—mark that!
You are acquainted with Westminster Abbey, Mrs. Jarley?'

'Yes, surely.'

'Then upon my soul and honour, ma'am, you'll find in a
certain angle of that dreary pile, called Poets' Corner, a few
smaller names than Slum,' retorted that gentleman, tapping
himself expressively on the forehead to imply that there was
some slight quantity of brain behind it. 'I've got a little trifle
here, now,' said Mr. Slum, taking off his hat which was full of
scraps of paper, 'a little trifle here, thrown off in the heat of the
moment, which I should say was exactly the thing you wanted
to set this place on fire with. It's an acrostic—the name at this
moment is Warren, but the idea's a convertible one, and a
positive inspiration for Jarley. Have the acrostic.'

'I suppose it's very dear,' said Mrs. Jarley.

'Five shillings,' returned Mr. Slum, using his pencil as a
tooth-pick. 'Cheaper than any prose.'

'I couldn't give more than three,' said Mrs. Jarley.

'—And six,' retorted Slum. 'Come. Three-and-six.'

Mrs. Jarley was not proof against the poet's insinuating
manner, and Mr. Slum entered the order in a small note-book
as a three-and-sixpenny one. Mr. Slum then withdrew to alter
the acrostic, after taking a most affectionate leave of his
patroness, and promising to return, as soon as he possibly
could, with a fair copy for the printer.

As his presence had not interfered with or interrupted the
preparations, they were now far advanced, and were completed
shortly after his departure. When the festoons were all put up
as tastily as they might be, the stupendous collection was uncovered, and there were displayed, on a raised platform some
two feet from the floor, running round the room and parted
from the rude public by a crimson rope breast high, divers
sprightly effigies of celebrated characters, singly and in groups,
clad in glittering dresses of various climes and times, and
standing more or less unsteadily upon their legs, with their
eyes very wide open, and their nostrils very much inflated, and
the muscles of their legs and arms very strongly developed, and
all their countenances expressing great surprise. All the
gentlemen were very pigeon-breasted and very blue about the

beards; and all the ladies were miraculous figures; and all the ladies and all the gentlemen were looking intensely nowhere, and staring with extraordinary earnestness at nothing.

When Nell had exhausted her first raptures at this glorious sight, Mrs. Jarley ordered the room to be cleared of all but herself and the child, and, sitting herself down in an arm-chair in the centre, formally invested Nell with a willow wand, long used by herself for pointing out the characters, and was at great pains to instruct her in her duty.

'That,' said Mrs. Jarley in her exhibition tone, as Nell touched a figure at the beginning of the platform, 'is an unfortunate Maid of Honour in the Time of Queen Elizabeth, who died from pricking her finger in consequence of working upon a Sunday. Observe the blood which is trickling from her finger; also the gold-eyed needle of the period, with which she is at work.'

All this, Nell repeated twice or thrice: pointing to the finger and the needle at the right times: and then passed on to the next.

'That, ladies and gentlemen,' said Mrs. Jarley, 'is Jasper Packlemerton of atrocious memory, who courted and married fourteen wives, and destroyed them all, by tickling the soles of their feet when they were sleeping in the consciousness of innocence and virtue. On being brought to the scaffold and asked if he was sorry for what he had done, he replied yes, he was sorry for having let 'em off so easy, and hoped all Christian husbands would pardon him the offence. Let this be a warning to all young ladies to be particular in the character of the gentlemen of their choice. Observe that his fingers are curled as if in the act of tickling, and that his face is represented with a wink, as he appeared when committing his barbarous murders.'

When Nell knew all about Mr. Packlemerton, and could say it without faltering, Mrs. Jarley passed on to the fat man, and then to the thin man, the tall man, the short man, the old lady who died of dancing at a hundred and thirty-two, the wild boy of the woods, the woman who poisoned fourteen families with pickled walnuts, and other historical characters and interesting but misguided individuals. And so well did Nell profit by her instructions, and so apt was she to remember 'hem, that by the time they had been shut up together for a ~uple of hours, she was in full possession of the history of the

Mrs. Jarley's Waxwork

whole establishment, and perfectly competent to the enlightenment of visitors.

Mrs. Jarley was not slow to express her admiration at this
happy result, and carried her young friend and pupil to inspect
the remaining arrangements within doors, by virtue of which
the passage had been already converted into a grove of green
baize hung with the inscription she had already seen (Mr.
Slum's productions), and a highly ornamented table placed at
the upper end for Mrs. Jarley herself, at which she was to
preside and take the money, in company with his Majesty
King George the Third, Mr. Grimaldi as clown, Mary Queen
of Scots, an anonymous gentleman of the Quaker persuasion,
and Mr. Pitt holding in his hand a correct model of the bill for
the imposition of the window duty. The preparations without
doors had not been neglected either; a nun of great personal
attractions was telling her beads on the little portico over
the door; and a brigand with the blackest possible head of hair,
and the clearest possible complexion, was at that moment going
round the town in a cart, consulting the miniature of a lady.

It now only remained that Mr. Slum's compositions should
be judiciously distributed; that the pathetic effusions should
find their way to all private houses and tradespeople; and that
the parody commencing 'If I know'd a donkey,' should be
confined to the taverns, and circulated only among the
lawyers' clerks and choice spirits of the place. When this had
been done, and Mrs. Jarley had waited upon the boarding-
schools in person, with a handbill composed expressly for them,
in which it was distinctly proved that wax-work refined the mind,
cultivated the taste, and enlarged the sphere of the human
understanding, that indefatigable lady sat down to dinner, and
drank out of the suspicious bottle to a flourishing campaign.

K

UNQUESTIONABLY Mrs. Jarley had an inventive genius. In the midst of the various devices for attracting visitors to the exhibition, little Nell was not forgotten. The light cart in which the Brigand usually made his perambulations being gaily dressed with flags and streamers, and the Brigand placed therein, contemplating the miniature of his beloved as usual, Nell was accommodated with a seat beside him, decorated with artificial flowers, and in this state and ceremony rode slowly through the town every morning, dispersing handbills from a basket, to the sound of drum and trumpet. The beauty of the child, coupled with her gentle and timid bearing, produced quite a sensation in the little country place. The Brigand, heretofore a source of exclusive interest in the streets, became a mere secondary consideration, and to be important only as a part of the show of which she was the chief attraction. Grown-up folks began to be interested in the bright-eyed girl, and some score of little boys fell desperately in love, and constantly left inclosures of nuts and apples, directed in small-text, at the wax-work door.

This desirable impression was not lost on Mrs. Jarley, who, lest Nell should become too cheap, soon sent the Brigand out alone again, and kept her in the exhibition room, where she described the figures every half-hour to the great satisfaction of admiring audiences. And these audiences were of a very superior description, including a great many young ladies' boarding-schools, whose favour Mrs. Jarley had been at great pains to conciliate, by altering the face and costume of Mr. Grimaldi as clown to represent Mr. Lindley Murray as he appeared when engaged in the composition of his English Grammar, and turning a murderess of great renown into Mrs. Hannah More—both of which likenesses were admitted by Miss Monflathers, who was at the head of the head Boarding and Day Establishment in the town, and who condescended to take a Private View with eight chosen young ladies, to be quite startling from their extreme correctness. Mr. Pitt in a nightcap and bedgown, and without his boots, represented the poet Cowper with perfect exactness; and Mary Queen of Scots in a dark wig, white shirt-collar, and male attire, was such a complete image of Lord Byron that the young ladies quite

Producing a Sensation

screamed when they saw it. Miss Monflathers, however, rebuked this enthusiasm, and took occasion to reprove Mrs. Jarley for not keeping her collection more select: observing that His Lordship had held certain opinions quite incompatible with wax-work honours, and adding something about a Dean and Chapter, which Mrs. Jarley did not understand.

Although her duties were sufficiently laborious, Nell found in the lady of the caravan a very kind and considerate person, who had not only a peculiar relish for being comfortable herself, but for making everybody about her comfortable also; which latter taste, it may be remarked, is, even in persons who live in much finer places than caravans, a far more rare and uncommon one than the first, and is not by any means its necessary consequence. As her popularity procured her various little fees from the visitors on which her patroness never demanded any toll, and as her grandfather too was well treated and useful, she had no cause of anxiety in connexion with the wax-work, beyond that which sprung from her recollection of Quilp, and her fears that he might return and one day suddenly encounter them.

Quilp indeed was a perpetual nightmare to the child, who was constantly haunted by a vision of his ugly face and stunted figure. She slept, for their better security, in the room where the wax-work figures were, and she never retired to this place at night but she tortured herself—she could not help it—with imagining a resemblance, in some one or other of their death-like faces, to the dwarf, and this fancy would sometimes so gain upon her that she would almost believe he had removed the figure and stood within the clothes. Then there were so many of them with their great glassy eyes—and, as they stood one behind the other all about her bed, they looked so like living creatures, and yet so unlike in their grim stillness and silence, that she had a kind of terror of them for their own sakes, and would often lie watching their dusky figures until she was obliged to rise and light a candle, or go and sit at the open window and feel a companionship in the bright stars. At these times, she would recall the old house and the window at which she used to sit alone; and then she would think of poor Kit and all his kindness, until the tears came into her eyes, and she would weep and smile together.

Often and anxiously at this silent hour, her thoughts reverted to her grandfather, and she would wonder how much

he remembered of their former life, and whether he was ever
really mindful of the change in their condition and of their
late helplessness and destitution. When they were wandering
about, she seldom thought of this, but now she could not help
considering what would become of them if he fell sick, or
her own strength were to fail her. He was very patient and
willing, happy to execute any little task, and glad to be of use;
but he was in the same listless state, with no prospect of
improvement—a mere child—a poor, thoughtless, vacant
creature—a harmless fond old man, susceptible of tender love
and regard for her, and of pleasant and painful impressions,
but alive to nothing more. It made her very sad to know that
this was so—so sad to see it that sometimes when he sat idly by,
smiling and nodding to her when she looked round, or when
he caressed some little child and carried it to and fro, as he was
fond of doing by the hour together, perplexed by its simple
questions, yet patient under his own infirmity, and seeming
almost conscious of it too, and humbled even before the mind
of an infant—so sad it made her to see him thus, that she would
burst into tears, and, withdrawing into some secret place, fall
down upon her knees, and pray that he might be restored.

But, the bitterness of her grief was not in beholding him in
this condition, when he was at least content and tranquil, nor
in her solitary meditations on his altered state, though these
were trials for a young heart. Cause for deeper and heavier
sorrow was yet to come.

One evening, a holiday night with them, Nell and her
grandfather went out to walk. They had been rather closely
confined for some days, and the weather being warm, they
strolled a long distance. Clear of the town, they took a foot-
path which struck through some pleasant fields, judging that
it would terminate in the road they quitted and enable them to
return that way. It made, however, a much wider circuit than
they had supposed, and thus they were tempted onward until
sunset, when they reached the track of which they were in
search, and stopped to rest.

It had been gradually getting overcast, and now the sky was
dark and lowering, save where the glory of the departing sun
piled up masses of gold and burning fire, decaying embers of
which gleamed here and there through the black veil, and
shone redly down upon the earth. The wind began to moan in
hollow murmurs, as the sun went down carrying glad day

elsewhere; and a train of dull clouds coming up against it, menaced thunder and lightning. Large drops of rain soon began to fall, and, as the storm clouds came sailing onward, others supplied the void they left behind and spread over all the sky. Then was heard the low rumbling of distant thunder, then the lightning quivered, and then the darkness of an hour seemed to have gathered in an instant.

Fearful of taking shelter beneath a tree or hedge, the old man and the child hurried along the high road, hoping to find some house in which they could seek a refuge from the storm, which had now burst forth in earnest, and every moment increased in violence. Drenched with the pelting rain, confused by the deafening thunder, and bewildered by the glare of the forked lightning, they would have passed a solitary house without being aware of its vicinity, had not a man, who was standing at the door, called lustily to them to enter.

'Your ears ought to be better than other folks' at any rate, if you make so little of the chance of being struck blind,' he said, retreating from the door and shading his eyes with his hands as the jagged lightning came again. 'What were you going past for, eh?' he added, as he closed the door and led the way along a passage to a room behind.

'We didn't see the house, sir, till we heard you calling,' Nell replied.

'No wonder,' said the man, 'with this lightning in one's eyes, by-the-by. You had better stand by the fire here, and dry yourselves a bit. You can call for what you like if you want anything. If you don't want anything, you are not obliged to give an order. Don't be afraid of that. This is a public-house, that's all. The Valiant Soldier is pretty well known hereabouts.'

'Is this house called the Valiant Soldier, sir?' asked Nell.

'I thought everybody knew that,' replied the landlord. 'Where have you come from, if you don't know the Valiant Soldier as well as the church catechism? This is the Valiant Soldier, by James Groves,—Jem Groves—honest Jem Groves, as is a man of unblemished moral character, and has a good dry skittle-ground. If any man has got anything to say again Jem Groves, let him say it to Jem Groves, and Jem Groves can accommodate him with a customer on any terms from four pound a side to forty.'

With these words, the speaker tapped himself on the waist-coat to intimate that he was the Jem Groves so highly eulogized;

sparred scientifically at a counterfeit Jem Groves, who was
sparring at society in general from a black frame over the
chimney-piece; and, applying a half-emptied glass of spirits and
water to his lips, drank Jem Groves's health.

The night being warm, there was a large screen drawn
across the room, for a barrier against the heat of the fire. It
seemed as if somebody on the other side of this screen had been
insinuating doubts of Mr. Groves's prowess, and had thereby
given rise to these egotistical expressions, for Mr. Groves
wound up his defiance by giving a loud knock upon it with his
knuckles and pausing for a reply from the other side.

'There an't many men,' said Mr. Groves, no answer being
returned, 'who would ventur' to cross Jem Groves under his own
roof. There's only one man, I know, that has nerve enough for
that, and that man's not a hundred mile from here neither.
But he's worth a dozen men, and I let him say of me whatever
he likes in consequence,—he knows that.'

In return for this complimentary address, a very gruff hoarse
voice bade Mr. Groves 'hold his nise and light a candle.' And
the same voice remarked that the same gentleman 'needn't
waste his breath in brag, for most people knew pretty well
what sort of stuff he was made of.'

'Nell, they're—they're playing cards,' whispered the old
man, suddenly interested. 'Don't you hear them?'

'Look sharp with that candle,' said the voice; 'it's as much
as I can do to see the pips on the cards as it is; and get this
shutter closed as quick as you can, will you? Your beer will
be the worse for to-night's thunder I expect.—Game! Seven-
and-sixpence to me, old Isaac. Hand over.'

'Do you hear, Nell, do you hear them?' whispered the old
man again, with increased earnestness, as the money chinked
upon the table.

'I haven't seen such a storm as this,' said a sharp cracked
voice of most disagreeable quality, when a tremendous peal of
thunder had died away, 'since the night when old Luke Withers
won thirteen times running on the red. We all said he had the
Devil's luck and his own, and as it was the kind of night for the
Devil to be out and busy, I suppose he *was* looking over his
shoulder, if anybody could have seen him.'

'Ah!' returned the gruff voice; 'for all old Luke's winning
through thick and thin of late years, I remember the time
when he was the unluckiest and unfortunatest of men. He never

took a dice-box in his hand, or held a card, but he was plucked, pigeoned, and cleaned out completely.'

'Do you hear what he says?' whispered the old man. 'Do you hear that, Nell?'

The child saw with astonishment and alarm that his whole appearance had undergone a complete change. His face was flushed and eager, his eyes were strained, his teeth set, his breath came short and thick, and the hand he laid upon her arm trembled so violently that she shook beneath its grasp.

'Bear witness,' he muttered, looking upward, 'that I always said it; that I knew it, dreamed of it, felt it was the truth, and that it must be so! What money have we, Nell? Come! I saw you with some money yesterday. What money have we? Give it to me.'

'No, no, let me keep it, grandfather,' said the frightened child. 'Let us go away from here. Do not mind the rain. Pray let us go.'

'Give it to me, I say,' returned the old man fiercely. 'Hush, hush, don't cry, Nell. If I spoke sharply, dear, I didn't mean it. It's for thy good. I have wronged thee, Nell, but I will right thee yet, I will indeed. Where is the money?'

'Do not take it,' said the child. 'Pray do not take it, dear. For both our sakes let me keep it, or let me throw it away—better let me throw it away, than you take it now. Let us go; do let us go.'

'Give me the money,' returned the old man, 'I must have it. There—there—that's my dear Nell. I'll right thee one day, child, I'll right thee, never fear!'

She took from her pocket a little purse. He seized it with the same rapid impatience which had characterised his speech, and hastily made his way to the other side of the screen. It was impossible to restrain him, and the trembling child followed close behind.

The landlord had placed a light upon the table, and was engaged in drawing the curtain of the window. The speakers whom they had heard were two men, who had a pack of cards and some silver money between them, while upon the screen itself the games they had played were scored in chalk. The man with the rough voice was a burly fellow of middle age, with large black whiskers, broad cheeks, a coarse wide mouth, and bull neck, which was pretty freely displayed as his shirt-collar was only confined by a loose red neckerchief. He wore his hat, which was of a brownish-white, and had beside him a thick knotted stick. The other man, whom his companion had called Isaac, was of a more slender figure—stooping, and high in the shoulders—with a very ill-favoured face, and a most sinister and villainous squint.

'Now, old gentleman,' said Isaac, looking round. 'Do you know either of us? This side of the screen is private, sir.'

'No offence, I hope,' returned the old man.

'But by G——, sir, there *is* offence,' said the other, interrupting him, 'when you intrude yourself upon a couple of gentlemen who are particularly engaged.'

'I had no intention to offend,' said the old man, looking anxiously at the cards. 'I thought that—'

'But you had no right to think, sir,' retorted the other. 'What the devil has a man at your time of life to do with thinking?'

'Now, bully boy,' said the stout man, raising his eyes from his cards for the first time, 'can't you let him speak?'

The landlord, who had apparently resolved to remain neutral until he knew which side of the question the stout man would espouse, chimed in at this place with 'Ah, to be sure, can't you let him speak, Isaac List?'

'Can't I let him speak?' sneered Isaac in reply, mimicking as nearly as he could, in his shrill voice, the tones of the landlord. 'Yes, I can let him speak, Jemmy Groves.'

'Well then, do it, will you?' said the landlord.

Mr. List's squint assumed a portentous character, which seemed to threaten a prolongation of this controversy, when his companion, who had been looking sharply at the old man, put a timely stop to it.

'Who knows,' said he, with a cunning look, 'but the gentleman may have civilly meant to ask if he might have the honour to take a hand with us!'

'I did mean it,' cried the old man. 'That is what I mean. That is what I want now!'

'I thought so,' returned the same man. 'Then who knows but the gentleman, anticipating our objection to play for love, civilly desired to play for money?'

The old man replied by shaking the little purse in his eager hand, and then throwing it down upon the table, and gathering up the cards as a miser would clutch at gold.

'Oh! That indeed—' said Isaac; 'if that's what the gentleman meant, I beg the gentleman's pardon. Is this the gentleman's little purse? A very pretty little purse. Rather a light purse,' added Isaac, throwing it into the air and catching it dexterously, 'but enough to amuse a gentleman for half an hour or so.'

'We'll make a four-handed game of it, and take in Groves,' said the stout man. 'Come, Jemmy.'

The landlord, who conducted himself like one who was well used to such little parties, approached the table and took his seat. The child, in a perfect agony, drew her grandfather aside, and implored him, even then, to come away.

'Come; and we may be so happy,' said the child.

'We *will* be happy,' replied the old man hastily. 'Let me go, Nell. The means of happiness are on the cards and the dice. We must rise from little winnings to great. There's little to be won here; but great will come in time. I shall but win back my own, and it's all for thee, my darling.'

'God help us!' cried the child. 'Oh! what hard fortune brought us here?'

'Hush!' rejoined the old man, laying his hand upon her mouth. 'Fortune will not bear chiding. We must not reproach her, or she shuns us; I have found that out.'

'Now, mister,' said the stout man. 'If you're not coming yourself, give us the cards, will you?'

'I am coming,' cried the old man. 'Sit thee down, Nell, sit thee down and look on. Be of good heart, it's all for thee—all —every penny. I don't tell them, no, no, or else they wouldn't play, dreading the chance that such a cause must give me. Look at them. See what they are and what thou art. Who doubts that we must win!'

'The gentleman has thought better of it, and isn't coming,' said Isaac, making as though he would rise from the table. 'I'm sorry the gentleman's daunted—nothing venture, nothing have —but the gentleman knows best.'

'Why I am ready. You have all been slow but me,' said the old man. 'I wonder who is more anxious to begin than I.'

As he spoke he drew a chair to the table; and the other three closing round it at the same time, the game commenced.

The child sat by, and watched its progress with a troubled mind. Regardless of the run of luck, and mindful only of the desperate passion which had its hold upon her grandfather, losses and gains were to her alike. Exulting in some brief triumph, or cast down by a defeat, there he sat so wild and restless, so feverishly and intensely anxious, so terribly eager, so ravenous for the paltry stakes, that she could have almost better borne to see him dead. And yet she was the innocent cause of all this torture, and he, gambling with such a savage thirst for gain as the most insatiable gambler never felt, had not one selfish thought!

On the contrary, the other three—knaves and gamesters by their trade—while intent upon their game, were yet as cool and quiet as if every virtue had been centred in their breasts. Sometimes one would look up to smile to another, or to snuff the feeble candle, or to glance at the lightning as it shot through the open window and fluttering curtain, or to listen to some louder peal of thunder than the rest, with a kind of momentary impatience, as if it put him out; but there they sat, with a calm indifference to everything but their cards, perfect philosophers in appearance, and with no greater show of passion or excitement than if they had been made of stone.

The storm had raged for full three hours; the lightning had grown fainter and less frequent; the thunder, from seeming to roll and break above their heads, had gradually died away into a deep hoarse distance; and still the game went on, and still the anxious child was quite forgotten.

A Game of Cards

A^T length the play came to an end, and Mr. Isaac List rose the only winner. Mat and the landlord bore their losses with professional fortitude. Isaac pocketed his gains with the air of a man who had quite made up his mind to win, all along, and was neither surprised nor pleased.

Nell's little purse was exhausted; but although it lay empty by his side, and the other players had now risen from the table, the old man sat poring over the cards, dealing them as they had been dealt before, and turning up the different hands to see what each man would have held if they had still been playing. He was quite absorbed in this occupation, when the child drew near and laid her hand upon his shoulder, telling him it was near midnight.

'See the curse of poverty, Nell,' he said, pointing to the packs he had spread out upon the table. 'If I could have gone on a little longer, only a little longer, the luck would have turned on my side. Yes, it's as plain as the marks upon the cards. See here—and there—and here again.'

'Put them away,' urged the child. 'Try to forget them.'

'Try to forget them!' he rejoined, raising his haggard face to hers, and regarding her with an incredulous stare. 'To forget them! How are we ever to grow rich if I forget them?'

The child could only shake her head.

'No, no, Nell,' said the old man, patting her cheek; 'they must not be forgotten. We must make amends for this as soon as we can. Patience—patience, and we'll right thee yet, I promise thee. Lose to-day, win to-morrow. And nothing can be won without anxiety and care—nothing. Come, I am ready.'

'Do you know what the time is?' said Mr. Groves, who was smoking with his friends. 'Past twelve o'clock—'

'—And a rainy night,' added the stout man.

'The Valiant Soldier, by James Groves. Good beds. Cheap entertainment for man and beast,' said Mr. Groves, quoting his signboard. 'Half-past twelve o'clock.'

'It's very late,' said the uneasy child. 'I wish we had gone before. What will they think of us! It will be two o'clock by the time we get back. What would it cost, sir, if we stopped here?'

'Two good beds, one-and-sixpence; supper and beer one

shilling; total two shillings and sixpence,' replied the Valiant Soldier.

Now, Nell had still the piece of gold sewn in her dress; and when she came to consider the lateness of the hour, and the somnolent habits of Mrs. Jarley, and to imagine the state of consternation in which they would certainly throw that good lady by knocking her up in the middle of the night—and when she reflected, on the other hand, that if they remained where they were, and rose early in the morning, they might get back before she awoke, and could plead the violence of the storm by which they had been overtaken, as a good apology for their absence—she decided, after a great deal of hesitation, to remain. She therefore took her grandfather aside, and telling him that she had still enough left to defray the cost of their lodging, proposed that they should stay there for the night.

'If I had had but that money before—if I had only known of it a few minutes ago!' muttered the old man.

'We will decide to stop here if you please,' said Nell, turning hastily to the landlord.

'I think that's prudent,' returned Mr. Groves. 'You shall have your suppers directly.'

Accordingly, when Mr. Groves had smoked his pipe out, knocked out the ashes, and placed it carefully in a corner of the fireplace, with the bowl downwards, he brought in the bread and cheese, and beer, with many high encomiums upon their excellence, and bade his guests fall to and make themselves at home. Nell and her grandfather ate sparingly, for both were occupied with their own reflections; the other gentlemen, for whose constitutions beer was too weak and tame a liquid, consoled themselves with spirits and tobacco.

As they would leave the house very early in the morning, the child was anxious to pay for their entertainment before they retired to bed. But as she felt the necessity of concealing her little hoard from her grandfather, and had to change the piece of gold, she took it secretly from its place of concealment, and embraced an opportunity of following the landlord when he went out of the room; and tendered it to him in the little bar.

'Will you give me the change here, if you please?' said the child.

Mr. James Groves was evidently surprised, and looked at the money, and rang it, and looked at the child, and at the money again, as though he had a mind to inquire how she

Miss Monflathers chides Nell

came by it. The coin being genuine, however, and changed at his house, he probably felt, like a wise landlord, that it was no business of his. At any rate, he counted out the change, and gave it her. The child was returning to the room where they had passed the evening, when she fancied she saw a figure just gliding in at the door. There was nothing but a long dark passage between this door and the place where she had changed the money, and, being very certain that no person had passed in or out while she stood there, the thought struck her that she had been watched.

But by whom? When she re-entered the room, she found its inmates exactly as she had left them. The stout fellow lay upon two chairs, resting his head on his hand, and the squint-ing man reposed in a similar attitude on the opposite side of the table. Between them sat her grandfather, looking intently at the winner with a kind of hungry admiration, and hanging upon his words as if he were some superior being. She was puzzled for a moment, and looked round to see if any one else were there. No. Then she asked her grandfather in a whisper whether anybody had left the room while she was absent. 'No,' he said, 'nobody.'

It must have been her fancy then; and yet it was strange, that, without anything in her previous thoughts to lead to it, she should have imagined this figure so very distinctly. She was still wondering and thinking of it, when a girl came to light her to bed.

The old man took leave of the company at the same time, and they went up stairs together. It was a great, rambling house, with dull corridors and wide staircases which the flaring candles seemed to make more gloomy. She left her grandfather in his chamber, and followed her guide to another, which was at the end of a passage, and approached by some half-dozen crazy steps. This was prepared for her. The girl lingered a little while to talk, and tell her grievances. She had not a good place, she said; the wages were low, and the work was hard. She was going to leave it in a fortnight; the child couldn't recommend her to another, she supposed? Indeed she was afraid another would be difficult to get after living there, for the house had a very indifferent character; there was far too much card-playing, and such like. She was very much mistaken if some of the people who came there oftenest were quite as honest as they might be, but she wouldn't have it known that she had said so, for the world. Then there were some rambling allusions to a rejected sweetheart, who had threatened to go a soldiering—a final promise of knocking at the door early in the morning—and 'Good night.'

The child did not feel comfortable when she was left alone. She could not help thinking of the figure stealing through the passage down stairs; and what the girl had said did not tend to reassure her. The men were very ill-looking. They might get their living by robbing and murdering travellers. Who could tell?

Reasoning herself out of these fears, or losing sight of them for a little while, there came the anxiety to which the adventures of the night gave rise. Here was the old passion awakened again in her grandfather's breast, and to what further distraction it might tempt him Heaven only knew. What fears their absence might have occasioned already! Persons might be seeking for them even then. Would they be forgiven in the morning, or turned adrift again! Oh! why had they stopped in that strange place? It would have been better, under any circumstances, to have gone on!

At last, sleep gradually stole upon her—a broken, fitful sleep, troubled by dreams of falling from high towers, and waking with a start and in great terror. A deeper slumber followed this—and then——What! That figure in the room.

A figure was there. Yes, she had drawn up the blind to admit the light when it should be dawn, and there, between the foot of the bed and the dark casement, it crouched and slunk along, groping its way with noiseless hands, and stealing round the bed. She had no voice to cry for help, no power to move, but lay still, watching it.

On it came—on, silently and stealthily, to the bed's head. The breath so near her pillow, that she shrunk back into it, lest those wandering hands should light upon her face. Back again it stole to the window—then turned its head towards her.

The dark form was a mere blot upon the lighter darkness of the room, but she saw the turning of the head, and felt and knew how the eyes looked and the ears listened. There it remained, motionless as she. At length, still keeping the face towards her, it busied its hands in something, and she heard the chink of money.

Then, on it came again, silent and stealthy as before, and replacing the garments it had taken from the bedside, dropped upon its hands and knees, and crawled away. How slowly it seemed to move, now that she could hear but not see it, creeping along the floor! It reached the door at last, and stood upon its feet. The steps creaked beneath its noiseless tread, and it was gone.

The first impulse of the child was to fly from the terror of being by herself in that room—to have somebody by—not to be alone—and then her power of speech would be restored. With no consciousness of having moved, she gained the door.

There was the dreadful shadow, pausing at the bottom of the steps.

She could not pass it; she might have done so, perhaps, in the darkness without being seized, but her blood curdled at the thought. The figure stood quite still, and so did she; not boldly, but of necessity; for going back into the room was hardly less terrible than going on.

The rain beat fast and furiously without, and ran down in plashing streams from the thatched roof. Some summer insect, with no escape into the air, flew blindly to and fro, beating its body against the walls and ceiling, and filling the silent place with murmurs. The figure moved again. The child involuntarily did the same. Once in her grandfather's room, she would be safe.

It crept along the passage until it came to the very door she longed so ardently to reach. The child, in the agony of being so near, had almost darted forward with the design of bursting into the room and closing it behind her, when the figure stopped again.

The idea flashed suddenly upon her—what if it entered there, and had a design upon the old man's life! She turned faint and sick. It did. It went in. There was a light inside. The figure was now within the chamber, and she, still dumb—quite dumb, and almost senseless—stood looking on.

The door was partly open. Not knowing what she meant to do, but meaning to preserve him or be killed herself, she staggered forward and looked in.

What sight was that which met her view!

The bed had not been lain on, but was smooth and empty. And at a table sat the old man himself; the only living creature there; his white face pinched and sharpened by the greediness which made his eyes unnaturally bright—counting the money of which his hands had robbed her.

CHAPTER XXXI

WITH steps more faltering and unsteady than those with which she had approached the room, the child withdrew from the door, and groped her way back to her own chamber. The terror she had lately felt was nothing compared with that which now oppressed her. No strange robber, no treacherous host conniving at the plunder of his guests, or stealing to their beds to kill them in their sleep, no nightly prowler, however terrible and cruel, could have awakened in her bosom half the dread which the recognition of her silent visitor inspired. The grey-headed old man gliding like a ghost into her room and acting the thief while he supposed her fast asleep, then bearing off his prize and hanging over it with the ghastly exultation she had witnessed, was worse—immeasurably worse, and far more dreadful, for the moment, to reflect upon —than anything her wildest fancy could have suggested. If he should return—there was no lock or bolt upon the door, and if, distrustful of having left some money yet behind, he should come back to seek for more—a vague awe and horror surrounded the idea of his slinking in again with stealthy tread, and turning his face toward the empty bed, while she shrank down close at his feet to avoid his touch, which was almost insupportable. She sat and listened. Hark! A footstep on the stairs, and now the door was slowly opening. It was but imagination, yet imagination had all the terrors of reality; nay, it was worse, for the reality would have come and gone, and there an end, but in imagination it was always coming, and never went away.

The feeling which beset the child was one of dim uncertain horror. She had no fear of the dear old grandfather, in whose love for her this disease of the brain had been engendered; but the man she had seen that night, wrapt in the game of chance, lurking in her room, and counting the money by the glimmering light, seemed like another creature in his shape, a monstrous distortion of his image, a something to recoil from, and be the more afraid of, because it bore a likeness to him, and kept close about her, as he did. She could scarcely connect her own affectionate companion, save by his loss, with this old man, so like yet so unlike him. She had wept to see him dull and quiet. How much greater cause she had for weeping now!

The child sat watching and thinking of these things, until the phantom in her mind so increased in gloom and terror, that she felt it would be a relief to hear the old man's voice, or, if he were asleep, even to see him, and banish some of the fears that clustered round his image. She stole down the stairs and passage again. The door was still ajar as she had left it, and the candle burning as before.

She had her own candle in her hand, prepared to say, if he were waking, that she was uneasy and could not rest, and had come to see if his were still alight. Looking into the room, she saw him lying calmly on his bed, and so took courage to enter.

Fast asleep. No passion in the face, no avarice, no anxiety, no wild desire; all gentle, tranquil, and at peace. This was not the gambler, or the shadow in her room; this was not even the worn and jaded man whose face had so often met her own in the grey morning light; this was her dear old friend, her harmless fellow-traveller, her good, kind grandfather.

She had no fear as she looked upon his slumbering features, but she had a deep and weighty sorrow, and it found its relief in tears.

'God bless him!' said the child, stooping softly to kiss his placid cheek. 'I see too well now, that they would indeed part us if they found us out, and shut him up from the light of the sun and sky. He has only me to help him. God bless us both!'

Lighting her candle, she retreated as silently as she had come, and, gaining her own room once more, sat up during the remainder of that long, long, miserable night.

At last the day turned her waning candle pale, and she fell asleep. She was quickly roused by the girl who had shown her up to bed; and, as soon as she was dressed, prepared to go down to her grandfather. But first she searched her pocket and found that her money was all gone—not a sixpence remained.

The old man was ready, and in a few seconds they were on their road. The child thought he rather avoided her eye, and appeared to expect that she would tell him of her loss. She felt she must do that, or he might suspect the truth.

'Grandfather,' she said in a tremulous voice, after they had walked about a mile in silence, 'do you think they are honest people at the house yonder?'

'Why?' returned the old man trembling. 'Do I think them honest—yes, they played honestly.'

'I'll tell you why I ask,' rejoined Nell. 'I lost some money last night—out of my bedroom I am sure. Unless it was taken by somebody in jest—only in jest, dear grandfather, which would make me laugh heartily if I could but know it—'

'Who would take money in jest?' returned the old man in a hurried manner. 'Those who take money, take it to keep. Don't talk of jest.'

'Then it was stolen out of my room, dear,' said the child, whose last hope was destroyed by the manner of this reply.

'But is there no more, Nell?' said the old man; 'no more anywhere? Was it all taken—every farthing of it—was there nothing left?'

'Nothing,' replied the child.

'We must get more,' said the old man, 'we must earn it, Nell, hoard it up, scrape it together, come by it somehow. Never mind this loss. Tell nobody of it, and perhaps we may regain it. Don't ask how;—we may regain it, and a great deal more;—but tell nobody, or trouble may come of it. And so they took it out of thy room, when thou wert asleep!' he added in a compassionate tone, very different from the secret, cunning way in which he had spoken until now. 'Poor Nell, poor little Nell!'

The child hung down her head and wept. The sympathising tone in which he spoke, was quite sincere; she was sure of that. It was not the lightest part of her sorrow to know that this was done for her.

'Not a word about it to any one but me,' said the old man, 'no, not even to me,' he added hastily, 'for it can do no good. All the losses that ever were, are not worth tears from thy eyes, darling. Why should they be, when we will win them back?'

'Let them go,' said the child, looking up. 'Let them go, once and for ever, and I would never shed another tear if every penny had been a thousand pounds.'

'Well, well,' returned the old man, checking himself as some impetuous answer rose to his lips, 'she knows no better. I ought to be thankful for it.'

'But listen to me,' said the child earnestly, 'will you listen to me?'

'Aye, aye, I'll listen,' returned the old man, still without looking at her; 'a pretty voice. It has always a sweet sound to me. It always had when it was her mother's, poor child.'

'Let me persuade you, then—oh, do let me persuade you,'

said the child, 'to think no more of gains or losses, and to try no fortune but the fortune we pursue together.'

'We pursue this aim together,' retorted her grandfather, still looking away and seeming to confer with himself. 'Whose image sanctifies the game?'

'Have we been worse off,' resumed the child, 'since you forgot those cares, and we have been travelling on together? Have we not been much better and happier without a home to shelter us, than ever we were in that unhappy house, when they were on your mind?'

'She speaks the truth,' murmured the old man in the same tone as before. 'It must not turn me, but it is the truth; no doubt it is.'

'Only remember what we have been since that bright morning when we turned our backs upon it for the last time,' said Nell, 'only remember what we have been since we have been free of all those miseries—what peaceful days and quiet nights we have had—what pleasant times we have known—what happiness we have enjoyed. If we have been tired or hungry, we have been soon refreshed, and slept the sounder for it. Think what beautiful things we have seen, and how contented we have felt. And why was this blessed change?'

He stopped her with a motion of his hand, and bade her talk to him no more just then, for he was busy. After a time he kissed her cheek, still motioning her to silence, and walked on, looking far before him, and sometimes stopping and gazing with a puckered brow upon the ground, as if he were painfully trying to collect his disordered thoughts. Once she saw tears in his eyes. When he had gone on thus for some time, he took her hand in his as he was accustomed to do, with nothing of the violence or animation of his late manner; and so, by degrees so fine that the child could not trace them, he settled down into his usual quiet way, and suffered her to lead him where she would.

When they presented themselves in the midst of the stupendous collection, they found, as Nell had anticipated, that Mrs. Jarley was not yet out of bed, and that, although she had suffered some uneasiness on their account overnight, and had indeed sat up for them until past eleven o'clock, she had retired in the persuasion, that, being overtaken by storm at some distance from home, they had sought the nearest shelter, and would not return before morning. Nell immediately applied herself with great assiduity to the decoration and preparation of the room, and had the satisfaction of completing her task, and dressing herself neatly, before the beloved of the Royal Family came down to breakfast.

'We haven't had,' said Mrs. Jarley when the meal was over, 'more than eight of Miss Monflathers's young ladies all the time we've been here, and there's twenty-six of 'em, as I was told by the cook when I asked her a question or two and put her on the free-list. We must try 'em with a parcel of new bills, and you shall take it, my dear, and see what effect that has upon 'em.'

The proposed expedition being one of paramount importance, Mrs. Jarley adjusted Nell's bonnet with her own hands, and declaring that she certainly did look very pretty, and reflected credit on the establishment, dismissed her with many commendations, and certain needful directions as to the turnings on the right which she was to take, and the turnings on the left which she was to avoid. Thus instructed, Nell had no difficulty in finding out Miss Monflathers's Boarding and Day Establishment, which was a large house, with a high wall, and a large garden-gate with a large brass plate, and a small grating through which Miss Monflathers's parlour-maid inspected all visitors before admitting them; for nothing in the shape of a man—no, not even a milkman—was suffered, without special licence, to pass that gate. Even the tax-gatherer, who was stout, and wore spectacles and a broad-brimmed hat, had the taxes handed through the grating. More obdurate than gate of adamant or brass, this gate of Miss Monflathers's frowned on all mankind. The very butcher respected it as a gate of mystery, and left off whistling when he rang the bell.

As Nell approached the awful door, it turned slowly upon its hinges with a creaking noise, and, forth from the solemn grove beyond, came a long file of young ladies, two and two, all with open books in their hands, and some with parasols likewise. And last of the goodly procession came Miss Monflathers, bearing herself a parasol of lilac silk, and supported by two smiling teachers, each mortally envious of the other, and devoted unto Miss Monflathers.

Confused by the looks and whispers of the girls, Nell stood with downcast eyes and suffered the procession to pass on, until Miss Monflathers, bringing up the rear, approached her, when she curtseyed and presented her little packet; on receipt whereof Miss Monflathers commanded that the line should halt.

'You're the wax-work child, are you not?' said Miss Monflathers.

'Yes, ma'am,' replied Nell, colouring deeply, for the young ladies had collected about her, and she was the centre on which all eyes were fixed.

'And don't you think you must be a very wicked little child,' said Miss Monflathers, who was of rather uncertain temper, and lost no opportunity of impressing moral truths upon the tender minds of the young ladies, 'to be a wax-work child at all?'

Poor Nell had never viewed her position in this light, and not knowing what to say, remained silent, blushing more deeply than before.

'Don't you know,' said Miss Monflathers, 'that it's very naughty and unfeminine, and a perversion of the properties wisely and benignantly transmitted to us, with expansive powers to be roused from their dormant state through the medium of cultivation?'

The two teachers murmured their respectful approval of this home-thrust, and looked at Nell as though they would have said that there indeed Miss Monflathers had hit her very hard. Then they smiled and glanced at Miss Monflathers, and then, their eyes meeting, they exchanged looks which plainly said that each considered herself smiler-in-ordinary to Miss Monflathers, and regarded the other as having no right to smile, and that her so doing was an act of presumption and impertinence.

'Don't you feel how naughty it is of you,' resumed Miss Monflathers, 'to be a wax-work child, when you might have the proud consciousness of assisting, to the extent of your infant powers, the manufactures of your country; of improving your mind by the constant contemplation of the steam-engine; and of earning a comfortable and independent subsistence of from two-and-ninepence to three shillings per week? Don't you know that the harder you are at work, the happier you are?'

'"How doth the little—"' murmured one of the teachers, in quotation from Doctor Watts.

'Eh?' said Miss Monflathers, turning smartly round. 'Who said that?'

Of course the teacher who had not said it, indicated the

rival who had, whom Miss Monflathers frowningly requested to hold her peace; by that means throwing the informing teacher into raptures of joy.

'The little busy bee,' said Miss Monflathers, drawing herself up, 'is applicable only to genteel children.

"In books, or work, or healthful play"

is quite right as far as they are concerned; and the work means painting on velvet, fancy needlework, or embroidery. In such cases as these,' pointing to Nell, with her parasol, 'and in the case of all poor people's children, we should read it thus:

"In work, work, work. In work alway
Let my first years be past,
That I may give for ev'ry day
Some good account at last." '

A deep hum of applause rose not only from the two teachers, but from all the pupils, who were equally astonished to hear Miss Monflathers improvising after this brilliant style; for although she had been long known as a politician, she had never appeared before as an original poet. Just then somebody happened to discover that Nell was crying, and all eyes were again turned towards her.

There were indeed tears in her eyes, and drawing out her handkerchief to brush them away, she happened to let it fall. Before she could stoop to pick it up, one young lady of about fifteen or sixteen, who had been standing a little apart from the others, as though she had no recognised place among them, sprang forward and put it in her hand. She was gliding timidly away again, when she was arrested by the governess.

'It was Miss Edwards who did that, I *know*,' said Miss Monflathers predictively. 'Now I am sure that was Miss Edwards.'

It was Miss Edwards, and everybody said it was Miss Edwards, and Miss Edwards herself admitted that it was.

'Is it not,' said Miss Monflathers, putting down her parasol to take a severer view of the offender, 'a most remarkable thing, Miss Edwards, that you have an attachment to the lower classes which always draws you to their sides; or, rather, is it not a most extraordinary thing that all I say and do will not wean you from propensities which your original station in life have unhappily rendered habitual to you, you extremely vulgar-minded girl?'

'I really intended no harm, ma'am,' said a sweet voice. 'It was a momentary impulse, indeed.'

'An impulse!' repeated Miss Monflathers scornfully. 'I wonder that you presume to speak of impulses to me'—both the teachers assented—'I am astonished'—both the teachers were astonished—'I suppose it is an impulse which induces you to take the part of every grovelling and debased person that comes in your way'—both the teachers supposed so too.

'But I would have you know, Miss Edwards,' resumed the governess in a tone of increased severity, 'that you cannot be permitted—if it be only for the sake of preserving a proper example and decorum in this establishment—that you cannot be permitted, and that you shall not be permitted, to fly in the face of your superiors in this exceedingly gross manner. If *you* have no reason to feel a becoming pride before wax-work children, there are young ladies here who have, and you must either defer to those young ladies or leave the establishment, Miss Edwards.'

This young lady, being motherless and poor, was apprenticed at the school—taught for nothing—teaching others what she learnt, for nothing—boarded for nothing—lodged for nothing—and set down and rated as something immeasurably less than nothing, by all the dwellers in the house. The servant-maids felt her inferiority, for they were better treated; free to come and go, and regarded in their stations with much more respect. The teachers were infinitely superior, for they had paid to go to school in their time, and were paid now. The pupils cared little for a companion who had no grand stories to tell about home; no friends to come with post-horses, and be received in all humility, with cake and wine, by the governess; no deferential servant to attend and bear her home for the holidays; nothing genteel to talk about, and nothing to display. But why was Miss Monflathers always vexed and irritated with the poor apprentice—how did that come to pass?

Why, the gayest feather in Miss Monflathers's cap, and the brightest glory of Miss Monflathers's school, was a baronet's daughter—the real live daughter of a real live baronet—who, by some extraordinary reversal of the Laws of Nature, was not only plain in features but dull in intellect, while the poor apprentice had both a ready wit, and a handsome face and figure. It seems incredible. Here was Miss Edwards, who only paid a small premium which had been spent long ago, every day outshining and excelling the baronet's daughter, who learned all the extras (or was taught them all) and whose half-yearly bill came to double that of any other young lady's in the school, making no account of the honour and reputation of her pupilage. Therefore, and because she was a dependant, Miss Monflathers had a great dislike to Miss Edwards, and was spiteful to her, and aggravated by her, and, when she had compassion on little Nell, verbally fell upon and maltreated her as we have already seen.

'You will not take the air to-day, Miss Edwards,' said Miss Monflathers. 'Have the goodness to retire to your own room, and not to leave it without permission.'

The poor girl was moving hastily away, when she was suddenly, in nautical phrase, 'brought to' by a subdued shriek from Miss Monflathers.

'She has passed me without any salute!' cried the governess, raising her eyes to the sky. 'She has actually passed me without the slightest acknowledgment of my presence!'

The young lady turned and curtsied. Nell could see that she raised her dark eyes to the face of her superior, and that their expression, and that of her whole attitude for the instant, was one of mute but most touching appeal against this ungenerous usage. Miss Monflathers only tossed her head in reply, and the great gate closed upon a bursting heart.

'As for you, you wicked child,' said Miss Monflathers, turning to Nell, 'tell your mistress that if she presumes to take the liberty of sending to me any more, I will write to the legislative authorities and have her put in the stocks, or compelled to do penance in a white sheet; and you may depend upon it that you shall certainly experience the treadmill if you dare to come here again. Now, ladies, on.'

The procession filed off, two and two, with the books and parasols, and Miss Monflathers, calling the baronet's daughter to walk with her and smooth her ruffled feelings, discarded the two teachers—who by this time had exchanged their smiles for looks of sympathy—and left them to bring up the rear, and hate each other a little more for being obliged to walk together.

CHAPTER XXXII

MRS. JARLEY'S wrath on first learning that she had been threatened with the indignity of Stocks and Penance, passed all description. The genuine and only Jarley exposed to public scorn, jeered by children, and flouted by beadles! The delight of the Nobility and Gentry shorn of a bonnet which a Lady Mayoress might have sighed to wear, and arrayed in a white sheet as a spectacle of mortification and humility! And Miss Monflathers, the audacious creature who presumed, even in the dimmest and remotest distance of her imagination, to conjure up the degrading picture, 'I am a'most inclined,' said Mrs. Jarley, bursting with the fulness of her anger and the weakness of her means of revenge, 'to turn atheist when I think of it!'

But instead of adopting this course of retaliation, Mrs. Jarley, on second thoughts, brought out the suspicious bottle, and ordering glasses to be set forth upon her favourite drum, and sinking into a chair behind it, called her satellites about her, and to them several times recounted, word for word, the affronts she had received. This done, she begged them in a kind of deep despair to drink; then laughed, then cried, then took a little sip herself, then laughed and cried again, and took a little more; and so, by degrees, the worthy lady went on, increasing in smiles and decreasing in tears, until at last she could not laugh enough at Miss Monflathers, who, from being an object of dire vexation, became one of sheer ridicule and absurdity.

'For which of us is best off, I wonder,' quoth Mrs. Jarley, 'she or me! It's only talking, when all is said and done, and if she talks of me in the stocks, why I can talk of her in the stocks, which is a good deal funnier if we come to that. Lord, what *does* it matter, after all!'

Having arrived at this comfortable frame of mind (to which she had been greatly assisted by certain short interjectional remarks of the philosophical George), Mrs. Jarley consoled Nell with many kind words, and requested as a personal favour that whenever she thought of Miss Monflathers, she would do nothing else but laugh at her, all the days of her life.

So ended Mrs. Jarley's wrath, which subsided long before the going down of the sun. Nell's anxieties, however, were of a deeper kind, and the checks they imposed upon her cheerfulness were not so easily removed.

That evening, as she had dreaded, her grandfather stole away, and did not come back until the night was far spent. Worn out as she was, and fatigued in mind and body, she sat up alone, counting the minutes, until he returned—penniless, broken-spirited, and wretched, but still hotly bent upon his infatuation.

'Get me money,' he said wildly, as they parted for the night. 'I must have money, Nell. It shall be paid thee back with gallant interest one day, but all the money that comes into thy hands, must be mine—not for myself, but to use for thee. Remember, Nell, to use for thee!'

What could the child do with the knowledge she had, but give him every penny that came into her hands, lest he should be tempted on to rob their benefactress? If she told the truth (so thought the child) he would be treated as a madman; if she did not supply him with money, he would supply himself; supplying him, she fed the fire that burnt him up, and put him perhaps beyond recovery. Distracted by these thoughts, borne down by the weight of the sorrow which she dared not tell, tortured by a crowd of apprehensions whenever the old man was absent, and dreading alike his stay and his return, the colour forsook her cheek, her eye grew dim, and her heart was oppressed and heavy. All her old sorrows had come back upon her, augmented by new fears and doubts; by day they were ever present to her mind; by night they hovered round her pillow, and haunted her in dreams.

It was natural that, in the midst of her affliction, she should often revert to that sweet young lady of whom she had only caught a hasty glance, but whose sympathy, expressed in one slight brief action, dwelt in her memory like the kindnesses of years. She would often think, if she had such a friend as that to whom to tell her griefs, how much lighter her heart would be—that if she were but free to hear that voice, she would be happier. Then she would wish that she were something better, that she were not quite so poor and humble, that she dared address her without fearing a repulse; and then feel that there was an immeasurable distance between them, and have no hope that the young lady thought of her any more.

It was now holiday-time at the schools, and the young ladies had gone home, and Miss Monflathers was reported to be

Mrs. Jarley at the Pay-place

(p. 243)

flourishing in London, and damaging the hearts of middle-aged gentlemen, but nobody said anything about Miss Edwards, whether she had gone home, or whether she had any home to go to, whether she was still at the school, or anything about her. But one evening, as Nell was returning from a lonely walk, she happened to pass the inn where the stage-coaches stopped, just as one drove up, and there was the beautiful girl she so well remembered, pressing forward to embrace a young child whom they were helping down from the roof.

Well, this was her sister, her little sister, much younger than Nell, whom she had not seen (so the story went afterwards) for five years, and to bring whom to that place on a short visit, she had been saving her poor means all that time. Nell felt as if her heart would break when she saw them meet. They went a little apart from the knot of people who had congregated about the coach, and fell upon each other's neck, and sobbed, and wept with joy. Their plain and simple dress, the distance which the child had come alone, their agitation and delight, and the tears they shed, would have told their history by themselves.

They became a little more composed in a short time, and went away, not so much hand in hand as clinging to each other. 'Are you sure you're happy, sister?' said the child as they passed where Nell was standing. 'Quite happy now,' she answered. 'But always?' said the child. 'Ah, sister, why do you turn away your face?'

Nell could not help following at a little distance. They went to the house of an old nurse, where the elder sister had engaged a bed-room for the child. 'I shall come to you early every morning,' she said, 'and we can be together all the day.'—'Why not at night-time too? Dear sister, would they be angry with you for *that?*'

Why were the eyes of little Nell wet, that night, with tears like those of the two sisters? Why did she bear a grateful heart because they had met, and feel it pain to think that they would shortly part? Let us not believe that any selfish reference—unconscious though it might have been—to her own trials awoke this sympathy, but thank God that the innocent joys of others can strongly move us, and that we, even in our fallen nature, have one source of pure emotion which must be prized in Heaven!

By morning's cheerful glow, but oftener still by evening's gentle light, the child, with a respect for the short and happy intercourse of these two sisters which forbade her to approach and say a thankful word, although she yearned to do so, followed them at a distance in their walks and rambles, stopping when they stopped, sitting on the grass when they sat down, rising when they went on, and feeling it a companionship and delight to be so near them. Their evening walk was by a river's side. Here, every night, the child was too, unseen by them, unthought of, unregarded; but feeling as if they were her friends, as if they had confidences and trusts together, as if her load were lightened and less hard to bear; as if they mingled their sorrows, and found mutual consolation. It was a weak fancy perhaps, the childish fancy of a young and lonely creature; but night after night, and still the sisters loitered in the same place, and still the child followed with a mild and softened heart.

She was much startled, on returning home one night, to find that Mrs. Jarley had commanded an announcement to be prepared, to the effect that the stupendous collection would only remain in its present quarters one day longer; in fulfilment of which threat (for all announcements connected with public amusements are well known to be irrevocable and most exact), the stupendous collection shut up next day.

'Are we going from this place directly, ma'am?' said Nell.

'Look here, child,' returned Mrs. Jarley. 'That'll inform you.' And so saying, Mrs. Jarley produced another announcement, wherein it was stated, that, in consequence of numerous inquiries at the wax-work door, and in consequence of crowds having been disappointed in obtaining admission, the Exhibition would be continued for one week longer, and would re-open next day.

'For now that the schools are gone, and the regular sightseers exhausted,' said Mrs. Jarley, 'we come to the General Public, and they want stimulating.'

Upon the following day at noon, Mrs. Jarley established herself behind the highly-ornamented table, attended by the distinguished effigies before mentioned, and ordered the doors to be thrown open for the readmission of a discerning and enlightened public. But the first day's operations were by no means of a successful character, inasmuch as the general public, though they manifested a lively interest in Mrs. Jarley

personally, and such of her waxen satellites as were to be seen
for nothing, were not affected by any impulses moving them
to the payment of sixpence a head. Thus, notwithstanding that
a great many people continued to stare at the entry and the
figures therein displayed; and remained there with great
perseverance, by the hour at a time, to hear the barrel-organ
played and to read the bills; and notwithstanding that they
were kind enough to recommend their friends to patronise the
exhibition in the like manner, until the doorway was regularly
blockaded by half the population of the town, who, when they
went off duty, were relieved by the other half; it was not found
that the treasury was any the richer, or that the prospects of
the establishment were at all encouraging.

In this depressed state of the classical market, Mrs. Jarley
made extraordinary efforts to stimulate the popular taste, and
whet the popular curiosity. Certain machinery in the body of
the nun on the leads over the door was cleaned up and put in
motion, so that the figure shook its head paralytically all day
long, to the great admiration of a drunken, but very Protes-
tant, barber over the way, who looked upon the said paralytic
motion as typical of the degrading effect wrought upon the
human mind by the ceremonies of the Romish Church, and
discoursed upon that theme with great eloquence and morality.
The two carters constantly passed in and out of the exhibition-
room, under various disguises, protesting aloud that the sight
was better worth the money than anything they had beheld in
all their lives, and urging the bystanders, with tears in their
eyes, not to neglect such a brilliant gratification. Mrs. Jarley
sat in the pay-place, chinking silver moneys from noon till
night, and solemnly calling upon the crowd to take notice that
the price of admission was only sixpence, and that the departure of the whole collection, on a short tour among the
Crowned Heads of Europe, was positively fixed for that day
week.

'So be in time, be in time, be in time,' said Mrs. Jarley at
the close of every such address. 'Remember that this is
Jarley's stupendous collection of upwards of One Hundred
Figures, and that it is the only collection in the world; all others
being impostors and deceptions. Be in time, be in time, be in
time!'

CHAPTER XXXIII

AS the course of this tale requires that we should become
acquainted, somewhere hereabouts, with a few particulars
connected with the domestic economy of Mr. Sampson Brass,
and as a more convenient place than the present is not likely
to occur for that purpose, the historian takes the friendly
reader by the hand, and springing with him into the air, and
cleaving the same at a greater rate than ever Don Cleophas
Leandro Perez Zambullo and his familiar travelled through
that pleasant region in company, alights with him upon the
pavement of Bevis Marks.

The intrepid aeronauts alight before a small dark house,
once the residence of Mr. Sampson Brass.

In the parlour window of this little habitation, which is so
close upon the footway that the passenger who takes the wall
brushes the dim glass with his coat-sleeve—much to its improvement, for it is very dirty—in this parlour window in the
days of its occupation by Sampson Brass, there hung, all awry
and slack, and discoloured by the sun, a curtain of faded green,
so threadbare from long service as by no means to intercept
the view of the little dark room, but rather to afford a favourable medium through which to observe it accurately. There
was not much to look at. A rickety table, with spare bundles
of papers, yellow and ragged from long carriage in the pocket,
ostentatiously displayed upon its top; a couple of stools set
face to face on opposite sides of this crazy piece of furniture; a
treacherous old chair by the fireplace, whose withered arms
had hugged full many a client and helped to squeeze him dry;
a second-hand wig-box, used as a depository for blank writs
and declarations and other small forms of law, once the sole
contents of the head which belonged to the wig which belonged
to the box, as they were now of the box itself; two or three
common books of practice; a jar of ink, a pounce-box, a
stunted hearth-broom, a carpet trodden to shreds but still
clinging with the tightness of desperation to its tacks—these,
with the yellow wainscot of the walls, the smoke-discoloured
ceiling, the dust and cobwebs, were among the most prominent
decorations of the office of Mr. Sampson Brass.

But this was mere still-life, of no greater importance than
the plate, 'BRASS, Solicitor,' upon the door, and the bill, 'First

floor to let to a single gentleman,' which was tied to the knocker. The office commonly held two examples of animated nature, more to the purpose of this history, and in whom it has a stronger interest and more particular concern. Of these, one was Mr. Brass himself, who has already appeared in these pages. The other was his clerk, assistant, housekeeper, secretary, confidential plotter, adviser, intriguer, and bill of cost increaser, Miss Brass—a kind of amazon at common law, of whom it may be desirable to offer a brief description.

Miss Sally Brass, then, was a lady of thirty-five or thereabouts, of a gaunt and bony figure, and a resolute bearing, which if it repressed the softer emotions of love, and kept admirers at a distance, certainly inspired a feeling akin to awe in the breasts of those male strangers who had the happiness to approach her. In face she bore a striking resemblance to her brother Sampson—so exact, indeed, was the likeness between them, that had it consorted with Miss Brass's maiden modesty and gentle womanhood to have assumed her brother's clothes in a frolic and sat down beside him, it would have been difficult for the oldest friend of the family to determine which was Sampson and which Sally, especially as the lady carried upon her upper lip certain reddish demonstrations, which, if the imagination had been assisted by her attire, might have been mistaken for a beard. These were, however, in all probability, nothing more than eyelashes in a wrong place, as the eyes of Miss Brass were quite free from any such natural impertinences. In complexion Miss Brass was sallow—rather a dirty sallow, so to speak—but this hue was agreeably relieved by the healthy glow which mantled in the extreme tip of her laughing nose. Her voice was exceedingly impressive—deep and rich in quality, and, once heard, not easily forgotten. Her usual dress was a green gown, in colour not unlike the curtain of the office window, made tight to the figure, and terminating at the throat, where it was fastened behind by a peculiarly large and massive button. Feeling, no doubt, that simplicity and plainness are the soul of elegance, Miss Brass wore no collar or kerchief except upon her head, which was invariably ornamented with a brown gauze scarf, like the wing of the fabled vampire, and which, twisted into any form that happened to suggest itself, formed an easy and graceful head-dress.

Such was Miss Brass in person. In mind, she was of a strong

and vigorous turn, having from her earliest youth devoted herself with uncommon ardour to the study of the law; not wasting her speculations upon its eagle flights, which are rare, but tracing it attentively through all the slippery and eel-like crawlings in which it commonly pursues its way. Nor had she, like many persons of great intellect, confined herself to theory, or stopped short where practical usefulness begins; inasmuch as she could engross, fair-copy, fill up printed forms with perfect accuracy, and, in short, transact any ordinary duty of the office down to pouncing a skin of parchment or mending a pen. It is difficult to understand how, possessed of these combined attractions, she should remain Miss Brass; but whether she had steeled her heart against mankind, or whether those who might have wooed and won her, were deterred by fears that, being learned in the law, she might have too near her fingers' ends those particular statutes which regulate what are familiarly termed actions for breach, certain it is that she was still in a state of celibacy, and still in daily occupation of her old stool opposite to that of her brother Sampson. And equally certain it is, by the way, that between these two stools a great many people had come to the ground.

One morning Mr. Sampson Brass sat upon his stool copying some legal process, and viciously digging his pen deep into the paper, as if he were writing upon the very heart of the party against whom it was directed; and Miss Sally Brass sat upon her stool making a new pen preparatory to drawing out a little bill, which was her favourite occupation; and so they sat in silence for a long time, until Miss Brass broke silence.

'Have you nearly done, Sammy?' said Miss Brass; for in her mild and feminine lips, Sampson became Sammy, and all things were softened down.

'No,' returned her brother. 'It would have been all done though, if you had helped at the right time.'

'Oh yes, indeed,' cried Miss Sally; 'you want my help, don't you?—*you*, too, that are going to keep a clerk!'

'Am I going to keep a clerk for my own pleasure, or because of my own wish, you provoking rascal?' said Mr. Brass, putting his pen in his mouth, and grinning spitefully at his sister. 'What do you taunt me about going to keep a clerk for?'

It may be observed in this place, lest the fact of Mr. Brass calling a lady, a rascal, should occasion any wonderment or surprise, that he was so habituated to having her near him in

a man's capacity, that he had gradually accustomed himself
to talk to her as though she were really a man. And this feeling
was so perfectly reciprocal, that not only did Mr. Brass often
call Miss Brass a rascal, or even put an adjective before the
rascal, but Miss Brass looked upon it as quite a matter of
course, and was as little moved as any other lady would be by
being called an angel.

'What do you taunt me, after three hours' talk last night,
with going to keep a clerk for?' repeated Mr. Brass, grinning
again with the pen in his mouth, like some nobleman's or
gentleman's crest. 'Is it my fault?'

'All I know is,' said Miss Sally, smiling drily, for she
delighted in nothing so much as irritating her brother, 'that if
every one of your clients is to force us to keep a clerk, whether
we want to or not, you had better leave off business, strike
yourself off the roll, and get taken in execution as soon as
you can.'

'Have we got any other client like him?' said Brass. 'Have
we got another client like him now—will you answer me that?'

'Do you mean in the face?' said his sister.

'Do I mean in the face?' sneered Sampson Brass, reaching
over to take up the bill-book, and fluttering its leaves rapidly.
'Look here—Daniel Quilp, Esquire—Daniel Quilp, Esquire
—Daniel Quilp, Esquire—all through. Whether should I
take a clerk that he recommends, and says, "this is the man for
you," or lose all this, eh?'

Miss Sally deigned to make no reply, but smiled again, and
went on with her work.

'But I know what it is,' resumed Brass after a short silence.
'You're afraid you won't have as long a finger in the business
as you've been used to have. Do you think I don't see through
that?'

'The business wouldn't go on very long, I expect, without
me,' returned his sister composedly. 'Don't you be a fool
and provoke me, Sammy, but mind what you're doing, and
do it.'

Sampson Brass, who was at heart in great fear of his sister,
sulkily bent over his writing again, and listened as she said:

'If I determined that the clerk ought not to come, of course
he wouldn't be allowed to come. You know that well enough,
so don't talk nonsense.'

Mr. Brass received this observation with increased meekness, merely remarking, under his breath, that he didn't like that kind of joking, and that Miss Sally would be 'a much better fellow' if she forbore to aggravate him. To this compliment Miss Sally replied, that she had a relish for the amusement, and had no intention to forego its gratification. Mr. Brass not caring, as it seemed, to pursue the subject any further, they both plied their pens at a great pace, and there the discussion ended.

While they were thus employed, the window was suddenly darkened, as by some person standing close against it. As Mr. Brass and Miss Sally looked up to ascertain the cause, the top sash was nimbly lowered from without, and Quilp thrust in his head.

'Hallo!' he said, standing on tip-toe on the window-sill, and looking down into the room. 'Is there anybody at home? Is there any of the Devil's ware here? Is Brass at a premium, eh?'

'Ha, ha, ha!' laughed the lawyer in an affected ecstasy. 'Oh, very good, sir! Oh, very good indeed! Quite eccentric! Dear me, what humour he has!'

'Is that my Sally?' croaked the dwarf, ogling the fair Miss Brass. 'Is it Justice with the bandage off her eyes, and without the sword and scales? Is it the Strong Arm of the Law? Is it the Virgin of Bevis?'

'What an amazing flow of spirits!' cried Brass. 'Upon my word, it's quite extraordinary!'

'Open the door,' said Quilp, 'I've got him here. Such a clerk for you, Brass, such a prize, such an ace of trumps. Be quick and open the door, or if there's another lawyer near and he should happen to look out of window, he'll snap him up before your eyes, he will.'

It is probable that the loss of the phœnix of clerks, even to a rival practitioner, would not have broken Mr. Brass's heart; but, pretending great alacrity, he rose from his seat, and going to the door, returned, introducing his client, who led by the hand no less a person than Mr. Richard Swiveller.

'There she is,' said Quilp, stopping short at the door, and wrinkling up his eyebrows as he looked towards Miss Sally; 'there is the woman I ought to have married—there is the beautiful Sarah—there is the female who has all the charms of her sex and none of their weaknesses. Oh, Sally, Sally!'

To this amorous address Miss Brass briefly responded 'Bother!'

A Colleague for Miss Brass

'Hard-hearted as the metal from which she takes her name,' said Quilp. 'Why don't she change it—melt down the brass, and take another name?'

'Hold your nonsense, Mr. Quilp, do,' returned Miss Sally, with a grim smile. 'I wonder you're not ashamed of yourself before a strange young man.'

'The strange young man,' said Quilp, handing Dick Swiveller forward, 'is too susceptible himself not to understand me well. This is Mr. Swiveller, my intimate friend—a gentleman of good family and great expectations, but who, having rather involved himself by youthful indiscretion, is content for a time to fill the humble station of a clerk—humble, but here most enviable. What a delicious atmosphere!'

If Mr. Quilp spoke figuratively, and meant to imply that the air breathed by Miss Sally Brass was sweetened and rarefied by that dainty creature, he had doubtless good reason for what he said. But if he spoke of the delights of the atmosphere of Mr. Brass's office in a literal sense, he had certainly a peculiar taste, as it was of a close and earthy kind, and, besides being frequently impregnated with strong whiffs of the second-hand wearing apparel exposed for sale in Duke's Place and Houndsditch, had a decided flavour of rats and mice, and a taint of mouldiness. Perhaps some doubts of its pure delight presented themselves to Mr. Swiveller, as he gave vent to one or two short abrupt sniffs, and looked incredulously at the grinning dwarf.

'Mr. Swiveller,' said Quilp, 'being pretty well accustomed to the agricultural pursuits of sowing wild oats, Miss Sally, prudently considers that half a loaf is better than no bread. To be out of harm's way he prudently thinks is something too, and therefore he accepts your brother's offer. Brass, Mr. Swiveller is yours.'

'I am very glad, sir,' said Mr. Brass, 'very glad indeed. Mr. Swiveller, sir, is fortunate enough to have your friendship. You may be very proud, sir, to have the friendship of Mr. Quilp.'

Dick murmured something about never wanting a friend or a bottle to give him, and also gasped forth his favourite allusion to the wing of friendship and its never moulting a feather; but his faculties appeared to be absorbed in the contemplation of Miss Sally Brass, at whom he stared with blank and rueful looks, which delighted the watchful dwarf beyond measure. As to the divine Miss Sally herself, she rubbed her hands as men of business do, and took a few turns up and down the office with her pen behind her ear.

'I suppose,' said the dwarf, turning briskly to his legal friend, 'that Mr. Swiveller enters upon his duties at once? It's Monday morning.'

'At once, if you please, sir, by all means,' returned Brass.

'Miss Sally will teach him law, the delightful study of the law,' said Quilp; 'she'll be his guide, his friend, his companion, his Blackstone, his Coke upon Littleton, his Young Lawyer's Best Companion.'

'He is exceedingly eloquent,' said Brass, like a man abstracted, and looking at the roofs of the opposite houses, with his hands in his pockets; 'he has an extraordinary flow of language. Beautiful, really.'

'With Miss Sally,' Quilp went on, 'and the beautiful fictions of the law, his days will pass like minutes. Those charming creations of the poet, John Doe and Richard Roe, when they first dawn upon him, will open a new world for the enlargement of his mind and the improvement of his heart.'

'Oh, beautiful, beautiful! Beau-ti-ful indeed!' cried Brass. 'It's a treat to hear him!'

'Where will Mr. Swiveller sit?' said Quilp, looking round.

'Why, we'll buy another stool, sir,' returned Brass. 'We hadn't any thoughts of having a gentleman with us, sir, until you were kind enough to suggest it, and our accommodation's not extensive. We'll look about for a second-hand stool, sir. In the meantime, if Mr. Swiveller will take my seat, and try his hand at a fair copy of this ejectment, as I shall be out pretty well all the morning——'

'Walk with me,' said Quilp. 'I have a word or two to say to you on points of business. Can you spare the time?'

'Can I spare the time to walk with *you*, sir? You're joking, sir, you're joking with me,' replied the lawyer, putting on his hat. 'I'm ready, sir, quite ready. My time must be fully occupied indeed, sir, not to leave me time to walk with you. It's not everybody, Sir, who has an opportunity of improving himself by the conversation of Mr. Quilp.'

The dwarf glanced sarcastically at his brazen friend, and, with a short dry cough, turned upon his heel to bid adieu to Miss Sally. After a very gallant parting on his side, and a very cool and gentlemanly sort of one on hers, he nodded to Dick Swiveller, and withdrew with the attorney.

Dick stood at the desk in a state of utter stupefaction, staring with all his might at the beauteous Sally, as if she had been some curious animal whose like had never lived. When the dwarf got into the street, he mounted again upon the window-sill, and looked into the office for a moment with a grinning face, as a man might peep into a cage. Dick glanced upward at him, but without any token of recognition; and long after he had disappeared, still stood gazing upon Miss Sally Brass, seeing or thinking of nothing else, and rooted to the spot.

Miss Brass being by this time deep in the bill of costs, took no notice whatever of Dick, but went scratching on, with a noisy pen, scoring down the figures with evident delight, and working like a steam-engine. There stood Dick, gazing now at the green gown, now at the brown head-dress, now at the face, and now at the rapid pen, in a state of stupid perplexity, wondering how he got into the company of that strange monster, and whether it was a dream and he would ever wake. At last he heaved a deep sigh, and began slowly pulling off his coat.

Mr. Swiveller pulled off his coat, and folded it up with great elaboration, staring at Miss Sally all the time; then put on a blue jacket with a double row of gilt buttons, which he had originally ordered for aquatic expeditions, but had brought with him that morning for office purposes; and, still keeping his eye upon her, suffered himself to drop down silently upon Mr. Brass's stool. Then he underwent a relapse, and becoming powerless again, rested his chin upon his hand, and opened his eyes so wide, that it appeared quite out of the question that he could ever close them any more.

When he had looked so long that he could see nothing, Dick took his eyes off the fair object of his amazement, turned over the leaves of the draft he was to copy, dipped his pen into the inkstand, and at last, and by slow approaches, began to write. But he had not written half-a-dozen words when, reaching over to the inkstand to take a fresh dip, he happened to raise his eyes. There was the intolerable brown head-dress—there was the green gown—there, in short, was Miss Sally Brass, arrayed in all her charms, and more tremendous than ever.

This happened so often, that Mr. Swiveller by degrees began to feel strange influences creeping over him—horrible desires to annihilate this Sally Brass—mysterious promptings to knock her head-dress off and try how she looked without it.

There was a very large ruler on the table; a large, black, shining ruler. Mr. Swiveller took it up and began to rub his nose with it.

From rubbing his nose with the ruler, to poising it in his hand and giving it an occasional flourish after the tomahawk manner, the transition was easy and natural. In some of these flourishes it went close to Miss Sally's head; the ragged edges of the head-dress fluttered with the wind it raised; advance it but an inch, and that great brown knot was on the ground: yet still the unconscious maiden worked away, and never raised her eyes.

Well, this was a great relief. It was a good thing to write doggedly and obstinately until he was desperate, and then snatch up the ruler and whirl it about the brown head-dress with the consciousness that he could have it off if he liked. It was a good thing to draw it back, and rub his nose very hard with it, if he thought Miss Sally was going to look up, and to recompense himself with more hardy flourishes when he found she was still absorbed. By these means Mr. Swiveller calmed the agitation of his feelings, until his applications to the ruler became less fierce and frequent, and he could even write as many as half-a-dozen consecutive lines without having recourse to it,—which was a great victory.

CHAPTER XXXIV

IN course of time, that is to say, after a couple of hours or so, of diligent application, Miss Brass arrived at the conclusion of her task, and recorded the fact by wiping her pen upon the green gown, and taking a pinch of snuff from a little round tin box which she carried in her pocket. Having disposed of this temperate refreshment, she arose from her stool, tied her papers into a formal packet with red tape, and taking them under her arm, marched out of the office.

Mr. Swiveller had scarcely sprung off his feet and commenced the performance of a maniac hornpipe, when he was interrupted, in the fulness of his joy at being again alone, by the opening of the door, and the reappearance of Miss Sally's head.

'I am going out,' said Miss Brass.

'Very good, ma'am,' returned Dick. 'And don't hurry yourself on my account to come back, ma'am,' he added inwardly.

'If anybody comes on office business, take their messages, and say that the gentleman who attends to that matter isn't in at present, will you?' said Miss Brass.

'I will, ma'am,' replied Dick.

'I shan't be very long,' said Miss Brass, retiring.

'I'm sorry to hear it, ma'am,' rejoined Dick when she had shut the door. 'I hope you may be unexpectedly detained, ma'am. If you could manage to be run over, ma'am, but not seriously, so much the better.'

Uttering these expressions of good-will with extreme gravity, Mr. Swiveller sat down in the client's chair and pondered; then took a few turns up and down the room and fell into the chair again.

'So I'm Brass's clerk, am I?' said Dick. 'Brass's clerk, eh? And the clerk of Brass's sister—clerk to a female Dragon. Very good, very good! What shall I be next? Shall I be a convict in a felt hat and a grey suit, trotting about a dockyard with my number neatly embroidered on my uniform, and the order of the garter on my leg, restrained from chafing my ankle by a twisted belcher handkerchief? Shall I be that? Will that do, or is it too genteel? Whatever you please, have it your own way, of course.'

As he was entirely alone, it may be presumed that, in these remarks, Mr. Swiveller addressed himself to his fate or destiny, whom, as we learn by the precedents, it is the custom of heroes to taunt in a very bitter and ironical manner when they find themselves in situations of an unpleasant nature. This is the more probable from the circumstance of Mr. Swiveller directing his observations to the ceiling, which these bodily personages are usually supposed to inhabit—except in theatrical cases, when they live in the heart of the great chandelier.

'Quilp offers me this place, which he says he can insure me,' resumed Dick after a thoughtful silence, and telling off the circumstances of his position, one by one, upon his fingers; 'Fred, who, I could have taken my affidavit, would not have heard of such a thing, backs Quilp to my astonishment, and urges me to take it also—staggerer, number one. My aunt in the country stops the supplies, and writes an affectionate note to say that she has made a new will, and left me out of it—staggerer, number two. No money; no credit; no support from Fred, who seems to turn steady all at once; notice to quit the old lodgings—staggerers, three, four, five, and six! Under an accumulation of staggerers, no man can be considered a free agent. No man knocks himself down; if his destiny knocks him down, his destiny must pick him up again. Then I'm very glad that mine has brought all this upon itself, and I shall be as careless as I can, and make myself quite at home to spite it. So go on, my buck,' said Mr. Swiveller, taking his leave of the ceiling with a significant nod, 'and let us see which of us will be tired first!'

Dismissing the subject of his downfall with these reflections, which were no doubt very profound, and are indeed not altogether unknown in certain systems of moral philosophy, Mr. Swiveller shook off his despondency and assumed the cheerful ease of an irresponsible clerk.

As a means towards his composure and self-possession, he entered into a more minute examination of the office than he had yet had time to make; looked into the wig-box, the books, and ink-bottle; untied and inspected all the papers; carved a few devices on the table with the sharp blade of Mr. Brass's penknife; and wrote his name on the inside of the wooden coal-scuttle. Having, as it were, taken formal possession of his clerkship in virtue of these proceedings, he opened the window and leaned negligently out of it until a beer-boy happened to pass, whom he commanded to set down his tray and to serve him with a pint of mild porter, which he drank upon the spot and promptly paid for, with the view of breaking ground for a system of future credit and opening a correspondence tending thereto, without loss of time. Then, three or four little boys dropped in, on legal errands from three or four attorneys of the Brass grade: whom Mr Swiveller received and dismissed with about as professional a manner, and as correct and comprehensive an understanding of their business, as would have been shown by a clown in a pantomime under similar circumstances. These things done and over, he got upon his stool again and tried his hand at drawing caricatures of Miss Brass with a pen and ink, whistling very cheerfully all the time.

He was occupied in this diversion when a coach stopped near the door, and presently afterwards there was a loud double-knock. As this was no business of Mr. Swiveller's, the person not ringing the office bell, he pursued his diversion with perfect composure, notwithstanding that he rather thought there was nobody else in the house.

In this, however, he was mistaken; for, after the knock had been repeated with increased impatience, the door was opened, and somebody with a very heavy tread went up the stairs and into the room above. Mr. Swiveller was wondering whether this might be another Miss Brass, twin sister to the Dragon, when there came a rapping of knuckles at the office door.

'Come in!' said Dick. 'Don't stand upon ceremony. The business will get rather complicated if I've many more customers. Come in!'

'Oh, please,' said a little voice very low down in the doorway, 'will you come and show the lodgings?'

Dick leant over the table, and descried a small slipshod girl in a dirty coarse apron and bib, which left nothing of her visible but her face and feet. She might as well have been dressed in a violin-case.

'Why, who are you?' said Dick.

To which the only reply was, 'Oh, please will you come and show the lodgings?'

There never was such an old-fashioned child in her looks and manner. She must have been at work from her cradle. She seemed as much afraid of Dick, as Dick was amazed at her.

'I hav'n't got anything to do with the lodgings,' said Dick. 'Tell 'em to call again.'

'Oh, but please will you come and show the lodgings?' returned the girl; 'it's eighteen shillings a week and us finding plate and linen. Boots and clothes is extra, and fires in winter-time is eightpence a day.'

'Why don't you show 'em yourself? You seem to know all about 'em,' said Dick.

'Miss Sally said I wasn't to, because people wouldn't believe the attendance was good if they saw how small I was first.'

'Well, but they'll see how small you are afterwards, won't they?' said Dick.

'Ah! But then they'll have taken 'em for a fortnight certain,' replied the child with a shrewd look; 'and people don't like moving when they're once settled.'

'This is a queer sort of thing,' muttered Dick, rising. 'What do you mean to say you are—the cook?'

'Yes, I do plain cooking,' replied the child. 'I'm housemaid too; I do all the work of the house.'

'I suppose Brass and the Dragon and I, do the dirtiest part of it,' thought Dick. And he might have thought much more, being in a doubtful and hesitating mood, but that the girl again urged her request, and certain mysterious bumping sounds on the passage and staircase seemed to give note of the applicant's impatience. Richard Swiveller, therefore, sticking a pen behind each ear, and carrying another in his mouth as a token of his great importance and devotion to business, hurried out to meet and treat with the single gentleman.

He was a little surprised to perceive that the bumping sounds were occasioned by the progress upstairs of the single gentle-man's trunk, which, being nearly twice as wide as the stair-case, and exceedingly heavy withal, it was no easy matter for the united exertions of the single gentleman and the coachman to convey up the steep ascent. But there they were, crushing each other, and pushing and pulling with all their might, and getting the trunk tight and fast in all kinds of impossible angles, and to pass them was out of the question; for which sufficient reason, Mr. Swiveller followed slowly behind, entering a new protest on every stair against the house of Mr. Sampson Brass being thus taken by storm.

To these remonstrances, the single gentleman answered not a word, but when the trunk was at last got into the bedroom,

Taken by a Single Gentleman

sat down upon it and wiped his bald head and face with his handkerchief. He was very warm, and well he might be; for, not to mention the exertion of getting the trunk up stairs, he was closely muffled in winter garments, though the thermometer had stood all day at eighty-one in the shade.

'I believe, sir,' said Richard Swiveller, taking his pen out of his mouth, 'that you desire to look at these apartments. They are very charming apartments, sir. They command an uninterrupted view of—of over the way, and they are within one minute's walk of—of the corner of the street. There is exceedingly mild-porter, sir, in the immediate vicinity, and the contingent advantages are extraordinary.'

'What's the rent?' said the single gentleman.

'One pound per week,' replied Dick, improving on the terms.

'I'll take 'em.'

'The boots and clothes are extras,' said Dick; 'and the fires in winter-time are——'

'Are all agreed to,' answered the single gentleman.

'Two weeks certain,' said Dick, 'are the——'

'Two weeks!' cried the single gentleman gruffly, eyeing him from top to toe. 'Two years. I shall live here for two years. Here. Ten pounds down. The bargain's made.'

'Why you see,' said Dick, 'my name is not Brass, and——'

'Who said it was? *My* name's not Brass. What then?'

'The name of the master of the house is,' said Dick.

'I'm glad of it,' returned the single gentleman; 'it's a good name for a lawyer. Coachman, you may go. So may you, sir.'

Mr. Swiveller was so much confounded by the single gentleman riding rough-shod over him at this rate, that he stood looking at him almost as hard as he had looked at Miss Sally. The single gentleman, however, was not in the slightest degree affected by this circumstance, but proceeded with perfect composure to unwind the shawl which was tied round his neck, and then to pull off his boots. Freed of these encumbrances, he went on to divest himself of his other clothing, which he folded up, piece by piece, and ranged in order on the trunk. Then, he pulled down the window-blinds, drew the curtains, wound up his watch, and, quite leisurely and methodically, got into bed.

'Take down the bill,' were his parting words, as he looked out from between the curtains; 'and let nobody call me till I ring the bell.'

With that the curtains closed, and he seemed to snore immediately.

'This is a most remarkable and supernatural sort of house!' said Mr. Swiveller, as he walked into the office with the bill in his hand. 'She-dragons in the business, conducting themselves like professional gentlemen; plain cooks of three feet high appearing mysteriously from under ground; strangers walking in and going to bed without leave or licence in the middle of the day! If he should be one of the miraculous fellows that turn up now and then, and has gone to sleep for two years, I shall be in a pleasant situation. It's my destiny, however, and I hope Brass may like it. I shall be sorry if he don't. But it's no business of mine—I have nothing whatever to do with it!'

CHAPTER XXXV

MR. BRASS on returning home received the report of his clerk with much complacency and satisfaction, and was particular in inquiring after the ten-pound note, which, proving on examination to be a good and lawful note of the Governor and Company of the Bank of England, increased his good-humour considerably. Indeed he so overflowed with liberality and condescension, that, in the fulness of his heart, he invited Mr. Swiveller to partake of a bowl of punch with him at that remote and indefinite period which is currently denominated 'one of these days,' and paid him many handsome compliments on the uncommon aptitude for business which his conduct on the first day of his devotion to it had so plainly evinced.

It was a maxim with Mr. Brass that the habit of paying compliments kept a man's tongue oiled without any expense; and, as that useful member ought never to grow rusty or creak in turning on its hinges in the case of a practitioner of the law, in whom it should be always glib and easy, he lost few opportunities of improving himself by the utterance of handsome speeches and eulogistic expressions. And this had passed into such a habit with him, that, if he could not be correctly said to have his tongue at his fingers' ends, he might certainly be said to have it anywhere but in his face: which being, as we have already seen, of a harsh and repulsive character, was not oiled so easily, but frowned above all the smooth speeches—one of nature's beacons, warning off those who navigated the shoals and breakers of the World, or of that dangerous strait the Law, and admonishing them to seek less treacherous harbours and try their fortune elsewhere.

While Mr. Brass by turns overwhelmed his clerk with compliments and inspected the ten-pound note, Miss Sally showed little emotion and that of no pleasurable kind, for as the tendency of her legal practice had been to fix her thoughts on small gains and gripings, and to whet and sharpen her natural wisdom, she was not a little disappointed that the single gentleman had obtained the lodgings at such an easy rate, arguing that when he was seen to have set his mind upon them, he should have been at the least charged double or treble the usual terms, and that, in exact proportion as he pressed forward, Mr. Swiveller should have hung back. But neither the opinion of Mr. Brass, nor the dissatisfaction of Miss Sally, wrought any impression upon that young gentleman, who, throwing the responsibility of this and all other acts and deeds thereafter to be done by him, upon his unlucky destiny, was quite resigned and comfortable: fully prepared for the worst, and philosophically indifferent to the best.

'Good morning, Mr. Richard,' said Brass, on the second day of Mr. Swiveller's clerkship. 'Sally found you a second-hand stool, sir, yesterday evening, in Whitechapel. She's a rare fellow at a bargain, I can tell you, Mr. Richard. You'll find that a first-rate stool, sir, take my word for it.'

'It's rather a crazy one to look at,' said Dick.

'You'll find it a most amazing stool to sit down upon, you may depend,' returned Mr. Brass. 'It was bought in the open street just opposite the hospital, and as it has been standing there a month or two, it has got rather dusty and a little brown from being in the sun, that's all.'

'I hope it hasn't got any fevers or anything of that sort in it,' said Dick, sitting himself down discontentedly, between Mr. Sampson and the chaste Sally. 'One of the legs is longer than the others.'

'Then we get a bit of timber in, sir,' retorted Brass. 'Ha, ha, ha! We get a bit of timber in, sir, and that's another advantage of my sister's going to market for us. Miss Brass, Mr. Richard, is the——'

'Will you keep quiet?' interrupted the fair subject of these remarks, looking up from her papers. 'How am I to work if you keep on chattering?'

'What an uncertain chap you are!' returned the lawyer. 'Sometimes you're all for a chat. At another time you're all for work. A man never knows what humour he'll find you in.'

'I'm in a working humour now,' said Sally, 'so don't disturb me, if you please. And don't take him,' Miss Sally pointed with the feather of her pen to Richard, 'off his business. He won't do more than he can help, I dare say.'

Mr. Brass had evidently a strong inclination to make an angry reply, but was deterred by prudent or timid considerations, as he only muttered something about aggravation and a vagabond; not associating the terms with any individual, but mentioning them as connected with some abstract ideas which happened to occur to him. They went on writing for a long time in silence after this—in such a dull silence that Mr. Swiveller (who required excitement) had several times fallen asleep, and written divers strange words in an unknown character with his eyes shut, when Miss Sally at length broke in upon the monotony of the office by pulling out the little tin box, taking a noisy pinch of snuff, and then expressing her opinion that Mr. Richard Swiveller had 'done it.'

'Done what, ma'am?' said Richard.

'Do you know,' returned Miss Brass, 'that the lodger isn't up yet—that nothing has been seen or heard of him since he went to bed yesterday afternoon?'

'Well, ma'am,' said Dick, 'I suppose he may sleep his ten pound out, in peace and quietness, if he likes.'

'Ah! I begin to think he'll never wake,' observed Miss Sally.

'It's a very remarkable circumstance,' said Brass, laying down his pen; 'really, very remarkable. Mr. Richard, you'll remember, if this gentleman should be found to have hung himself to the bed-post, or any unpleasant accident of that kind should happen—you'll remember, Mr. Richard, that this ten-pound note was given to you in part payment of two years' rent? You'll bear that in mind, Mr. Richard; you had better make a note of it, sir, in case you should ever be called upon to give evidence.'

Mr. Swiveller took a large sheet of foolscap, and with a countenance of profound gravity, began to make a very small note in one corner.

'We can never be too cautious,' said Mr. Brass. 'There is a deal of wickedness going about the world, a deal of wickedness. Did the gentleman happen to say, sir——but never mind that at present, sir; finish that little memorandum first.'

Dick did so, and handed it to Mr. Brass, who had dismounted from his stool, and was walking up and down the office.

'Oh, this is the memorandum, is it?' said Brass, running his eye over the document. 'Very good. Now, Mr. Richard, did the gentleman say anything else?'

'No.'

'Are you sure, Mr. Richard,' said Brass, solemnly, 'that the gentleman said nothing else?'

'Devil a word, sir,' replied Dick.

'Think again, sir,' said Brass; 'it's my duty, sir, in the

position in which I stand, and as an honourable member of the legal profession—the first profession in this country, sir, or in any other country, or in any of the planets that shine above us at night and are supposed to be inhabited—it's my duty, sir, as an honourable member of that profession, not to put to you a leading question in a matter of this delicacy and importance. Did the gentleman, sir, who took the first floor of you yesterday afternoon, and who brought with him a box of property—a box of property—say anything more than is set down in this memorandum?'

'Come, don't be a fool,' said Miss Sally.

Dick looked at her, and then at Brass, and then at Miss Sally again, and still said 'No.'

'Pooh, pooh! Deuce take it, Mr. Richard, how dull you are!' cried Brass, relaxing into a smile. 'Did he say anything about his property?—there!'

'That's the way to put it,' said Miss Sally, nodding to her brother.

'Did he say, for instance,' added Brass, in a kind of comfortable, cozy tone—'I don't assert that he did say so, mind; I only ask you, to refresh your memory—did he say, for instance, that he was a stranger in London—that it was not his humour or within his ability to give any references—that he felt we had a right to require them—and that, in case anything should happen to him, at any time, he particularly desired that whatever property he had upon the premises should be considered mine, as some slight recompense for the trouble and annoyance I should sustain—and were you, in short,' added Brass, still more comfortably and cozily than before, 'were you induced to accept him on my behalf, as a tenant, upon those conditions?'

'Certainly not,' replied Dick.

'Why then, Mr. Richard,' said Brass, darting at him a supercilious and reproachful look, 'it's my opinion that you've mistaken your calling, and will never make a lawyer.'

'Not if you live a thousand years,' added Miss Sally. Whereupon the brother and sister took each a noisy pinch of snuff from the little tin box, and fell into a gloomy thoughtfulness.

Nothing further passed up to Mr. Swiveller's dinner-time, which was at three o'clock, and seemed about three weeks in coming. At the first stroke of the hour, the new clerk disappeared. At the last stroke of five, he reappeared, and the office, as if by magic, became fragrant with the smell of gin and water and lemon-peel.

'Mr. Richard,' said Brass, 'this man's not up yet. Nothing will wake him, Sir. What's to be done?'

'I should let him have his sleep out,' returned Dick.

'Sleep out!' cried Brass; 'why he has been asleep now, six-and-twenty hours. We have been moving chests of drawers over his head, we have knocked double knocks at the street-door, we have made the servant-girl fall down stairs several times, (she's a light weight, and it don't hurt her much,) but nothing wakes him.'

'Perhaps a ladder,' suggested Dick, 'and getting in at the first-floor window——'

'But then there's a door between; besides, the neighbours would be up in arms,' said Brass.

'What do you say to getting on the roof of the house through the trap-door, and dropping down the chimney?' suggested Dick.

'That would be an excellent plan,' said Brass, 'if anybody would be'—and here he looked very hard at Mr. Swiveller—'would be kind, and friendly, and generous enough, to undertake it. I dare say it would not be anything like as disagreeable as one supposes.'

Dick had made the suggestion, thinking that the duty might possibly fall within Miss Sally's department. As he said nothing further, and declined taking the hint, Mr. Brass was fain to propose that they should go up stairs together, and make a last effort to awaken the sleeper by some less violent means, which, if they failed on this last trial, must positively be succeeded by stronger measures. Mr. Swiveller, assenting, armed himself with his stool and the large ruler, and repaired with his employer to the scene of action, where Miss Brass was already ringing a hand-bell with all her might, and yet without producing the smallest effect upon their mysterious lodger.

'They are his boots, Mr. Richard!' said Brass.

'Very obstinate-looking articles they are too,' quoth Richard Swiveller. And truly, they were as sturdy and bluff a pair of boots as one would wish to see; as firmly planted on the ground as if their owner's legs and feet had been in them; and seeming, with their broad soles and blunt toes, to hold possession of their place by main force.

'I can't see anything but the curtain of the bed,' said Brass, applying his eye to the keyhole of the door. 'Is he a strong man, Mr. Richard?'

'Very,' answered Dick.

'It would be an extremely unpleasant circumstance if he was to bounce out suddenly,' said Brass. 'Keep the stairs clear. I should be more than a match for him, of course, but I'm the master of the house, and the laws of hospitality must be respected.—Hallo there! Hallo, hallo!'

While Mr. Brass, with his eye curiously twisted into the keyhole, uttered these sounds as a means of attracting the lodger's attention, and while Miss Brass plied the hand-bell, Mr. Swiveller put his stool close against the wall by the side of the door, and mounting on the top and standing bolt upright, so that if the lodger did make a rush, he would most probably pass him in its onward fury, began a violent battery with the ruler upon the upper panels of the door. Captivated with his own ingenuity, and confident in the strength of his position, which he had taken up after the method of those hardy individuals who open the pit and gallery doors of theatres on crowded nights, Mr. Swiveller rained down such a shower of blows, that the noise of the bell was drowned; and the small servant, who lingered on the stairs below, ready to fly at a moment's notice, was obliged to hold her ears lest she should be rendered deaf for life.

Suddenly the door was unlocked on the inside, and flung violently open. The small servant flew to the coal-cellar; Miss Sally dived into her own bed-room; Mr. Brass, who was not remarkable for personal courage, ran into the next street, and finding that nobody followed him, armed with a poker or other offensive weapon, put his hands in his pockets, walked very slowly all at once, and whistled.

Meanwhile, Mr. Swiveller, on the top of the stool, drew himself into as flat a shape as possible against the wall, and looked, not unconcernedly, down upon the single gentleman, who appeared at the door growling and cursing in a very awful manner, and, with the boots in his hand, seemed to have an intention of hurling them down stairs on speculation. This idea, however, he abandoned. He was turning into his room again, still growling vengefully, when his eyes met those of the watchful Richard.

'Have *you* been making that horrible noise?' said the single gentleman.

Mr. Brass at the Keyhole

'I have been helping, sir,' returned Dick, keeping his eye upon him, and waving the ruler gently in his right hand, as an indication of what the single gentleman had to expect if he attempted any violence.

'How dare you then,' said the lodger, 'Eh?'

To this, Dick made no other reply than by inquiring whether the lodger held it to be consistent with the conduct and character of a gentleman to go to sleep for six-and-twenty hours at a stretch, and whether the peace of an amiable and virtuous family was to weigh as nothing in the balance.

'Is my peace nothing?' said the single gentleman.

'Is their peace nothing, sir?' returned Dick. 'I don't wish to hold out any threats, sir—indeed the law does not allow of threats, for to threaten is an indictable offence—but if ever you do that again, take care you're not sat upon by the coroner and buried in a cross-road before you wake. We have been distracted with fears that you were dead, sir,' said Dick, gently sliding to the ground, 'and the short and the long of it is, that we cannot allow single gentlemen to come into this establishment and sleep like double gentlemen without paying extra for it.'

'Indeed!' cried the lodger.

'Yes, sir, indeed,' returned Dick, yielding to his destiny and saying whatever came uppermost; 'an equal quantity of slumber was never got out of one bed and bedstead, and if you're going to sleep in that way, you must pay for a double-bedded room.'

Instead of being thrown into a greater passion by these remarks, the lodger lapsed into a broad grin and looked at Mr. Swiveller with twinkling eyes. He was a brown-faced sun-burnt man, and appeared browner and more sunburnt from having a white nightcap on. As it was clear that he was a choleric fellow in some respects, Mr. Swiveller was relieved to find him in such good humour, and, to encourage him in it, smiled himself.

The lodger, in the testiness of being so rudely roused, had pushed his nightcap very much on one side of his bald head. This gave him a rakish eccentric air which, now that he had leisure to observe it, charmed Mr. Swiveller exceedingly; therefore, by way of propitiation, he expressed his hope that the gentleman was going to get up, and further that he would never do so any more.

M

'Come here, you impudent rascal!' was the lodger's answer as he re-entered his room.

Mr. Swiveller followed him in, leaving the stool outside, but reserving the ruler in case of a surprise. He rather congratulated himself on his prudence when the single gentleman, without notice or explanation of any kind, double-locked the door.

'Can you drink anything?' was his next inquiry.

Mr. Swiveller replied that he had very recently been assuaging the pangs of thirst, but that he was still open to 'a modest quencher,' if the materials were at hand. Without another word spoken on either side, the lodger took from his great trunk, a kind of temple, shining as of polished silver, and placed it carefully on the table.

Greatly interested in his proceedings, Mr. Swiveller observed him closely. Into one little chamber of this temple, he dropped an egg; into another some coffee; into a third a compact piece of raw steak from a neat tin case; into a fourth, he poured some water. Then, with the aid of a phosphorus-box and some matches, he procured a light and applied it to a spirit-lamp which had a place of its own below the temple; then, he shut down the lids of all the little chambers; then he opened them; and then, by some wonderful and unseen agency, the steak was done, the egg was boiled, the coffee was accurately prepared, and his breakfast was ready.

'Hot water—' said the lodger, handing it to Mr. Swiveller with as much coolness as if he had a kitchen fire before him— 'extraordinary rum—sugar—and a travelling glass. Mix for yourself. And make haste.'

Dick complied, his eyes wandering all the time from the temple on the table, which seemed to do everything, to the great trunk which seemed to hold everything. The lodger took his breakfast like a man who was used to work these miracles, and thought nothing of them.

'The man of the house is a lawyer, is he not?' said the lodger.

Dick nodded. The rum was amazing.

'The woman of the house—what's she?'

'A dragon,' said Dick.

The single gentleman, perhaps because he had met with such things in his travels, or perhaps because he *was* a single gentleman, evinced no surprise, but merely inquired 'Wife or

Sister?' 'Sister,' said Dick.—'So much the better,' said the single gentleman, 'he can get rid of her when he likes.'

'I want to do as I like, young man,' he added after a short silence; 'to go to bed when I like, get up when I like, come in when I like, go out when I like,—to be asked no questions and be surrounded by no spies. In this last respect, servants are the devil. There's only one here.'

'And a very little one,' said Dick.

'And a very little one,' repeated the lodger. 'Well, the place will suit me, will it?'

'Yes,' said Dick.

'Sharks, I suppose?' said the lodger.

Dick nodded assent, and drained his glass.

'Let them know my humour,' said the single gentleman, rising. 'If they disturb me, they lose a good tenant. If they know me to be that, they know enough. If they try to know more, it's a notice to quit. It's better to understand these things at once. Good day.'

'I beg your pardon,' said Dick, halting in his passage to the door, which the lodger prepared to open. 'When he who adores thee has left but the name—'

'What do you mean?'

'But the name,' said Dick—'has left but the name—in case of letters or parcels—'

'I never have any,' returned the lodger.

'Or in case anybody should call.'

'Nobody ever calls on me.'

'If any mistake should arise from not having the name, don't say it was my fault, sir,' added Dick, still lingering.—'Oh blame not the bard—'

'I'll blame nobody,' said the lodger, with such irascibility that in a moment Dick found himself on the staircase, and the locked door between them.

Mr. Brass and Miss Sally were lurking hard by, having been, indeed, only routed from the keyhole by Mr. Swiveller's abrupt exit. As their utmost exertions had not enabled them to overhear a word of the interview, however, in consequence of a quarrel for precedence, which, though limited of necessity to pushes and pinches and such quiet pantomime, had lasted the whole time, they hurried him down to the office to hear his account of the conversation.

This Mr. Swiveller gave them—faithfully as regarded the

wishes and character of the single gentleman, and poetically as concerned the great trunk, of which he gave a description more remarkable for brilliancy of imagination than a strict adherence to truth; declaring, with many strong asseverations, that it contained a specimen of every kind of rich food and wine, known in these times, and in particular that it was of a self-acting kind and served up whatever was required, as he supposed by clock-work. He also gave them to understand that the cooking apparatus roasted a fine piece of sirloin of beef, weighing about six pounds avoirdupois, in two minutes and a quarter, as he had himself witnessed, and proved by his sense of taste; and further, that, however the effect was produced, he had distinctly seen water boil and bubble up when the single gentleman winked; from which facts he (Mr. Swiveller) was led to infer that the lodger was some great conjuror or chemist, or both, whose residence under that roof could not fail at some future day to shed a great credit and distinction on the name of Brass, and add a new interest to the history of Bevis Marks.

There was one point which Mr. Swiveller deemed it unnecessary to enlarge upon, and that was the fact of the modest quencher, which, by reason of its intrinsic strength and its coming close upon the heels of the temperate beverage he had discussed at dinner, awakened a slight degree of fever, and rendered necessary two or three other modest quenchers at the public-house in the course of the evening.

CHAPTER XXXVI

AS the single gentleman after some weeks' occupation of his lodgings, still declined to correspond, by word or gesture, either with Mr. Brass or his sister Sally, but invariably chose Richard Swiveller as his channel of communication; and as he proved himself in all respects a highly desirable inmate, paying for everything beforehand, giving very little trouble, making no noise, and keeping early hours; Mr. Richard imperceptibly rose to an important position in the family, as one who had influence over this mysterious lodger, and could negotiate with him, for good or evil, when nobody else durst approach his person.

If the truth must be told, even Mr. Swiveller's approaches to the single gentleman were of a very distant kind, and met with small encouragement; but, as he never returned from a monosyllabic conference with the unknown, without quoting such expressions as 'Swiveller, I know I can rely upon you,'— 'I have no hesitation in saying, Swiveller, that I entertain a regard for you,'—'Swiveller, you are my friend, and will stand by me I am sure,' with many other short speeches of the same familiar and confiding kind, purporting to have been addressed by the single gentleman to himself, and to form the staple of their ordinary discourse, neither Mr. Brass nor Miss Sally for a moment questioned the extent of his influence, but accorded to him their fullest and most unqualified belief.

But quite apart from, and independent of, this source of popularity, Mr. Swiveller had another, which promised to be equally enduring, and to lighten his position considerably.

He found favour in the eyes of Miss Sally Brass. Let not the light scorners of female fascination erect their ears to listen to a new tale of love which shall serve them for a jest; for Miss Brass, however accurately formed to be beloved, was not of the loving kind. That amiable virgin, having clung to the skirts of the Law from her earliest youth; having sustained herself by their aid, as it were, in her first running alone, and maintained a firm grasp upon them ever since; had passed her life in a kind of legal childhood. She had been remarkable, when a tender prattler, for an uncommon talent in counterfeiting the walk and manner of a bailiff: in which character she had learned to tap her little playfellows on the shoulder, and to carry them off to imaginary sponging-houses, with a correctness of imitation which was the surprise and delight of all who witnessed her performances, and which was only to be exceeded by her exquisite manner of putting an execution into her doll's house, and taking an exact inventory of the chairs and tables. These artless sports had naturally soothed and cheered the decline of her widowed father: a most exemplary gentleman, (called 'Old Foxey' by his friends from his extreme sagacity,) who encouraged them to the utmost, and whose chief regret, on finding that he drew near to Houndsditch churchyard, was, that his daughter could not take out an attorney's certificate and hold a place upon the roll. Filled with this affectionate and touching sorrow, he had solemnly confided her to his son Sampson as an invaluable auxiliary; and from the old gentleman's decease to the period of which we treat, Miss Sally Brass had been the prop and pillar of his business.

It is obvious that, having devoted herself from infancy to this one pursuit and study, Miss Brass could know but little of the world, otherwise than in connection with the law; and that from a lady gifted with such high tastes, proficiency in those gentler and softer arts in which women usually excel, was scarcely to be looked for. Miss Sally's accomplishments were all of a masculine and strictly legal kind. They began with the practice of an attorney and they ended with it. She was in a state of lawful innocence, so to speak. The law had been her nurse. And, as bandy-legs or such physical deformities in children are held to be the consequence of bad nursing, so, if in a mind so beautiful any moral twist or bandiness could be found, Miss Sally Brass's nurse was alone to blame.

It was on this lady, then, that Mr. Swiveller burst in full freshness as something new and hitherto undreamed of, lighting up the office with scraps of song and merriment, conjuring with inkstands and boxes of wafers, catching three oranges in one hand, balancing stools upon his chin and penknives on his nose, and constantly performing a hundred other feats with equal ingenuity; for with such unbendings did Richard, in Mr. Brass's absence, relieve the tedium of his confinement. These social qualities, which Miss Sally first discovered by accident, gradually made such an impression upon her, that she would entreat Mr. Swiveller to relax as though she were not by, which Mr. Swiveller, nothing loth, would readily consent to do. By these means a friendship sprung up between them. Mr. Swiveller gradually came to look upon her as her brother Sampson did, and as he would have looked upon any other clerk. He imparted to her the mystery of going the odd man or plain Newmarket for fruit, ginger-beer, baked potatoes, or even a modest quencher, of which Miss Brass did not scruple to partake. He would often persuade her to undertake his share of writing in addition to her own; nay, he would sometimes reward her with a hearty slap on the back, and protest that she was a devilish good fellow, a jolly dog, and so forth; all of which compliments Miss Sally would receive in entire good part and with perfect satisfaction.

One circumstance troubled Mr. Swiveller's mind very much, and that was that the small servant always remained somewhere in the bowels of the earth under Bevis Marks, and never came to the surface unless the single gentleman rang his bell, when she would answer it and immediately disappear again. She never went out, or came into the office, or had a clean face, or took off the coarse apron, or looked out of any one of the windows, or stood at the street-door for a breath of air, or had any rest or enjoyment whatever. Nobody ever came to see her, nobody spoke of her, nobody cared about her. Mr. Brass had said once, that he believed she was a 'love-child,' (which means anything but a child of love,) and that was all the information Richard Swiveller could obtain.

'It's of no use asking the dragon,' thought Dick one day, as he sat contemplating the features of Miss Sally Brass. 'I suspect if I asked any questions on that head, our alliance would be at an end. I wonder whether she *is* a dragon by-the-bye, or something in the mermaid way. She has rather a scaly appearance. But mermaids are fond of looking at themselves in the glass, which she can't be. And they have a habit of combing their hair, which she hasn't. No, she's a dragon.'

'Where are you going, old fellow?' said Dick aloud, as Miss Sally wiped her pen as usual on the green dress, and uprose from her seat.

'To dinner,' answered the dragon.

'To dinner!' thought Dick, 'that's another circumstance. I don't believe that small servant ever has anything to eat.'

'Sammy won't be home,' said Miss Brass. 'Stop 'till I come back. I sha'n't be long.'

Dick nodded, and followed Miss Brass—with his eyes to the

door, and with his ears to a little back parlour, where she and her brother took their meals.

'Now,' said Dick, walking up and down with his hands in his pockets, 'I'd give something—if I had it—to know how they use that child, and where they keep her. My mother must have been a very inquisitive woman; I have no doubt I'm marked with a note of interrogation somewhere. My feelings I smother, but thou hast been the cause of this anguish my—upon my word,' said Mr. Swiveller, checking himself and falling thoughtfully into the client's chair, 'I should like to know how they use her!'

After running on, in this way, for some time, Mr. Swiveller softly opened the office door, with the intention of darting across the street for a glass of the mild porter. At that moment he caught a parting glimpse of the brown head-dress of Miss Brass flitting down the kitchen stairs. 'And by Jove!' thought Dick, 'she's going to feed the small servant. Now or never!'

First peeping over the handrail and allowing the head-dress to disappear in the darkness below, he groped his way down, and arrived at the door of a back kitchen immediately after Miss Brass had entered the same, bearing in her hand a cold leg of mutton. It was a very dark miserable place, very low and very damp: the walls disfigured by a thousand rents and blotches. The water was trickling out of a leaky butt, and a most wretched cat was lapping up the drops with the sickly eagerness of starvation. The grate, which was a wide one, was wound and screwed up tight, so as to hold no more than a little thin sandwich of fire. Everything was locked up; the coal-cellar, the candle-box, the salt-box, the meat-safe, were all padlocked. There was nothing that a beetle could have lunched upon. The pinched and meagre aspect of the place would have killed a chameleon: he would have known, at the first mouthful, that the air was not eatable, and must have given up the ghost in despair.

The small servant stood with humility in presence of Miss Sally, and hung her head.

'Are you there?' said Miss Sally.

'Yes, ma'am,' was the answer in a weak voice.

'Go further away from the leg of mutton, or you'll be picking it, I know,' said Miss Sally.

The girl withdrew into a corner, while Miss Brass took a key from her pocket, and opening the safe, brought from it a

The Small Servant's Dinner

dreary waste of cold potatoes, looking as eatable as Stone-
henge. This she placed before the small servant, ordering her
to sit down before it, and then, taking up a great carving-knife,
made a mighty show of sharpening it upon the carving-fork.

'Do you see this?' said Miss Brass, slicing off about two
square inches of cold mutton, after all this preparation, and
holding it out on the point of the fork.

The small servant looked hard enough at it with her hungry
eyes to see every shred of it, small as it was, and answered,
'Yes.'

'Then don't you ever go and say,' retorted Miss Sally, 'that
you hadn't meat here. There, eat it up.'

This was soon done. 'Now, do you want any more?' said
Miss Sally.

The hungry creature answered with a faint 'No.' They
were evidently going through an established form.

'You've been helped once to meat,' said Miss Brass, sum-
ming up the facts; 'you have had as much as you can eat,
you're asked if you want any more, and you answer, "No!"
Then don't you ever go and say you were allowanced, mind
that.'

With those words, Miss Sally put the meat away and locked
the safe, and then drawing near to the small servant, overlooked her while she finished the potatoes.

It was plain that some extraordinary grudge was working
in Miss Brass's gentle breast, and that it was that which
impelled her, without the smallest present cause, to rap the
child with the blade of the knife, now on her hand, now on her
head, and now on her back, as if she found it quite impossible
to stand so close to her without administering a few slight
knocks. But Mr. Swiveller was not a little surprised to see his
fellow-clerk, after walking slowly backwards towards the door,
as if she were trying to withdraw herself from the room but
could not accomplish it, dart suddenly forward, and falling
on the small servant give her some hard blows with her
clenched hand. The victim cried, but in a subdued manner
as if she feared to raise her voice, and Miss Sally, comforting
herself with a pinch of snuff, ascended the stairs, just as
Richard had safely reached the office.

CHAPTER XXXVII

THE single gentleman among his other peculiarities—and he had a very plentiful stock, of which he every day furnished some new specimen—took a most extraordinary and remarkable interest in the exhibition of Punch. If the sound of a Punch's voice, at ever so remote a distance, reached Bevis Marks, the single gentleman, though in bed and asleep, would start up, and, hurrying on his clothes, make for the spot with all speed, and presently return at the head of a long procession of idlers, having in the midst the theatre and its proprietors. Straightway, the stage would be set up in front of Mr. Brass's house; the single gentleman would establish himself at the first-floor window; and the entertainment would proceed, with all its exciting accompaniments of fife and drum and shout, to the excessive consternation of all sober votaries of business in that silent thoroughfare. It might have been expected that when the play was done, both players and audience would have dispersed; but the epilogue was as bad as the play, for no sooner was the Devil dead, than the manager of the puppets and his partner were summoned by the single gentleman to his chamber, where they were regaled with strong waters from his private store, and where they held with him long conversations, the purport of which no human being could fathom. But the secret of these discussions was of little importance. It was sufficient to know that while they were proceeding, the concourse without still lingered round the house; that boys beat upon the drum with their fists, and imitated Punch with their tender voices; that the office-window was rendered opaque by flattened noses, and the keyhole of the street-door luminous with eyes; that every.time the single gentleman or either of his guests was seen at the upper window, or so much as the end of one of their noses was visible, there was a great shout of execration from the excluded mob, who remained howling and yelling, and refusing consolation, until the exhibitors were delivered up to them to be attended elsewhere. It was sufficient, in short, to know that Bevis Marks was revolutionised by these popular movements, and that peace and quietness fled from its precincts.

Nobody was rendered more indignant by these proceedings than Mr. Sampson Brass, who, as he could by no means afford to lose so profitable an inmate, deemed it prudent to pocket his lodger's affront along with his cash, and to annoy the audiences who clustered round his door by such imperfect means of retaliation as were open to him, and which were confined to the trickling down of foul water on their heads from unseen watering-pots, pelting them with fragments of tile and mortar from the roof of the house, and bribing the drivers of hackney cabriolets to come suddenly round the corner and dash in among them precipitately. It may, at first sight, be matter of surprise to the thoughtless few that Mr. Brass, being a professional gentleman, should not have legally indicted some party or parties, active in the promotion of the nuisance, but they will be good enough to remember, that as Doctors seldom take their own prescriptions, and Divines do not always practise what they preach, so Lawyers are shy of meddling with the Law on their own account: knowing it to be an edged tool of uncertain application, very expensive in the working, and rather remarkable for its properties of close shaving, than for its always shaving the right person.

'Come,' said Mr. Brass one afternoon, 'this is two days without a Punch. I'm in hopes he has run through 'em all, at last.'

'Why are you in hopes?' returned Miss Sally. 'What harm do they do?'

'Here's a pretty sort of a fellow!' cried Brass, laying down his pen in despair. 'Now here's an aggravating animal!'

'Well, what harm do they do?' retorted Sally.

'What harm!' cried Brass. 'Is it no harm to have a constant hallooing and hooting under one's very nose, distracting one from business, and making one grind one's teeth with vexation? Is it no harm to be blinded and choked up, and have the king's highway stopped with a set of screamers and roarers whose throats must be made of—of—'

'Brass,' suggested Mr. Swiveller.

'Ah! of brass,' said the lawyer, glancing at his clerk, to assure himself that he had suggested the word in good faith and without any sinister intention. 'Is that no harm?'

The lawyer stopped short in his invective, and listening for a moment, and recognising the well-known voice, rested his head upon his hand, raised his eyes to the ceiling, and muttered faintly,

'There's another!'

Up went the single gentleman's window directly.

'There's another,' repeated Brass; 'and if I could get a break and four blood horses to cut into the Marks when the crowd is at its thickest, I'd give eighteenpence and never grudge it!'

The distant squeak was heard again. The single gentleman's door burst open. He ran violently down the stairs, out into the street, and so past the window, without any hat, towards the quarter whence the sound proceeded—bent, no doubt, upon securing the strangers' services directly.

'I wish I only knew who his friends were,' muttered Sampson, filling his pockets with papers; 'if they'd just get up a pretty little Commission *de lunatico* at the Gray's Inn Coffee House, and give me the job, I'd be content to have the lodgings empty for one while, at all events.'

With which words, and knocking his hat over his eyes as if for the purpose of shutting out even a glimpse of the dreadful visitation, Mr. Brass rushed from the house and hurried away.

As Mr. Swiveller was decidedly favourable to these performances, upon the ground that looking at a Punch, or indeed looking at anything out of window, was better than working; and as he had been, for this reason, at some pains to awaken in his fellow-clerk a sense of their beauties and manifold deserts; both he and Miss Sally rose as with one accord and took up their positions at the window: upon the sill whereof, as in a post of honour, sundry young ladies and gentlemen who were employed in the dry nurture of babies, and who made a point of being present, with their young charges, on such occasions, had already established themselves as comfortably as the circumstances would allow.

The glass being dim, Mr. Swiveller, agreeably to a friendly custom which he had established between them, hitched off the brown head-dress from Miss Sally's head, and dusted it carefully therewith. By the time he had handed it back, and its beautiful wearer had put it on again (which she did with perfect composure and indifference), the lodger returned with the show and showmen at his heels, and a strong addition to the body of spectators. The exhibitor disappeared with all speed behind the drapery; and his partner, stationing himself by the side of the theatre, surveyed the audience with a remarkable expression of melancholy, which became more remarkable still when he breathed a hornpipe tune into that

An Interview with Codlin and Short

sweet musical instrument which is popularly termed a mouth-organ, without at all changing the mournful expression of the upper part of his face, though his mouth and chin were, of necessity, in lively spasms.

The drama proceeded to its close, and held the spectators enchained in the customary manner. The sensation which kindles in large assemblies, when they are relieved from a state of breathless suspense and are again free to speak and move, was yet rife, when the lodger, as usual, summoned the men up stairs.

'Both of you,' he called from the window; for only the actual exhibitor—a little fat man—prepared to obey the summons. 'I want to talk to you. Come both of you!'

'Come, Tommy,' said the little man.

'I an't a talker,' replied the other. 'Tell him so. What should I go and talk for?'

'Don't you see the gentleman's got a bottle and glass up there?' returned the little man.

'And couldn't you have said so, at first?' retorted the other with sudden alacrity. 'Now, what are you waiting for? Are you going to keep the gentleman expecting us all day? haven't you *no* manners?'

With this remonstrance, the melancholy man, who was no other than Mr. Thomas Codlin, pushed past his friend and brother in the craft, Mr. Harris, otherwise Short or Trotters, and hurried before him to the single gentleman's apartment.

'Now, my men,' said the single gentleman; 'you have done very well. What will you take? Tell that little man behind, to shut the door.'

'Shut the door, can't you?' said Mr. Codlin, turning gruffly to his friend. 'You might have knowed that the gentleman wanted the door shut, without being told, I think.'

Mr. Short obeyed, observing under his breath that his friend seemed unusually 'cranky,' and expressing a hope that there was no dairy in the neighbourhood, or his temper would certainly spoil its contents.

The gentleman pointed to a couple of chairs, and intimated by an emphatic nod of his head that he expected them to be seated. Messrs. Codlin and Short, after looking at each other with considerable doubt and indecision, at length sat down—each on the extreme edge of the chair pointed out to him—and held their hats very tight, while the single gentleman filled a couple of glasses from a bottle on the table beside him, and presented them in due form.

'You're pretty well browned by the sun, both of you,' said their entertainer. 'Have you been travelling?'

Mr. Short replied in the affirmative with a nod and a smile. Mr. Codlin added a corroborative nod and a short groan, as if he still felt the weight of the Temple on his shoulders.

'To fairs, markets, races, and so forth, I suppose?' pursued the single gentleman.

'Yes, sir,' returned Short, 'pretty nigh all over the West of England.'

'I have talked to men of your craft from North, East, and South,' returned their host, in rather a hasty manner; 'but I never lighted on any from the West before.'

'It's our reg'lar summer circuit is the West, master,' said Short; 'that's where it is. We takes the East of London in the spring and winter, and the West of England in the summer-time. Many's the hard day's walking in rain and mud, and with never a penny earned, we've had down in the West.'

'Let me fill your glass again.'

'Much obleeged to you, sir, I think I will,' said Mr. Codlin, suddenly thrusting in his own and turning Short's aside. 'I'm the sufferer, sir, in all the travelling, and in all the staying at home. In town or country, wet or dry, hot or cold, Tom Codlin suffers. But Tom Codlin isn't to complain for all that. Oh, no! Short may complain, but if Codlin grumbles by so much as a word—oh dear, down with him, down with *him* directly. It isn't *his* place to grumble. That's quite out of the question.'

'Codlin an't without his usefulness,' observed Short with an arch look, 'but he don't always keep his eyes open. He falls asleep sometimes, you know. Remember them last races, Tommy.'

'Will you never leave off aggravating a man?' said Codlin. 'It's very like I was asleep when five-and-tenpence was collected, in one round, isn't it? I was attending to my business, and couldn't have my eyes in twenty places at once, like a peacock, no more than you could. If I an't a match for an old man and a young child, you an't neither, so don't throw that out against me, for the cap fits your head quite as correct as it fits mine.'

'You may as well drop the subject, Tom,' said Short. 'It isn't particular agreeable to the gentleman, I dare say.'

'Then you shouldn't have brought it up,' returned Mr. Codlin; 'and I ask the gentleman's pardon on your account, as a giddy chap that likes to hear himself talk, and don't much care what he talks about, so that he does talk.'

Their entertainer had sat perfectly quiet in the beginning of this dispute, looking first at one man and then at the other, as if he were lying in wait for an opportunity of putting some further question, or reverting to that from which the discourse had strayed.' But, from the point where Mr. Codlin was charged with sleepiness, he had shown an increasing interest in the discussion: which now attained a very high pitch.

'You are the two men I want,' he said, 'the two men I have been looking for, and searching after! Where are that old man and that child you speak of?'

'Sir?' said Short, hesitating, and looking towards his friend.

'The old man and his grandchild who travelled with you— where are they? It will be worth your while to speak out, I assure you; much better worth your while than you believe. They left you, you say,—at those races, as I understand. They have been traced to that place, and there lost sight of. Have you no clue, can you suggest no clue, to their recovery?'

'Did I always say, Thomas,' cried Short, turning with a look of amazement to his friend, 'that there was sure to be an inquiry after them two travellers?'

'*You* said!' returned Mr. Codlin. 'Did I always say that that 'ere blessed child was the most interesting I ever see? Did I always say I loved her, and doated on her? Pretty creetur, I think I hear her now. "Codlin's my friend," she says, with a tear of gratitude a trickling down her little eye: "Codlin's my friend," she says—"not Short. Short's very well," she says; "I've no quarrel with Short; he means kind, I dare say; but Codlin," she says, "has the feelings for *my* money, though he mayn't look it."'

Repeating these words with great emotion, Mr. Codlin rubbed the bridge of his nose with his coat-sleeve, and shaking his head mournfully from side to side, left the single gentleman to infer that, from the moment when he lost sight of his dear young charge, his peace of mind and happiness had fled.

'Good Heaven!' said the single gentleman, pacing up and down the room, 'have I found these men at last, only to discover that they can give me no information or assistance! It would have been better to have lived on, in hope, from day to day, and never to have lighted on them, than to have my expectations scattered thus.'

'Stay a minute,' said Short. 'A man of the name of Jerry—you know Jerry, Thomas?'

'Oh, don't talk to me of Jerrys,' replied Mr. Codlin. 'How can I care a pinch of snuff for Jerrys, when I think of that 'ere darling child? "Codlin's my friend," she says, "dear, good, kind Codlin, as is always a devising pleasures for me! I don't object to Short," she says, "but I cotton to Codlin." Once,' said that gentleman reflectively, 'she called me Father Codlin. I thought I should have bust!'

'A man of the name of Jerry, sir,' said Short, turning from his selfish colleague to their new acquaintance, 'wot keeps a company of dancing dogs, told me, in a accidental sort of a way, that he had seen the old gentleman in connexion with a travelling wax-work, unbeknown to him. As they'd given us the slip, and nothing had come of it, and this was down in the country that he'd been seen, I took no measures about it, and asked no questions. But I can, if you like.'

'Is this man in town?' said the impatient single gentleman. 'Speak faster.'

'No he isn't, but he will be to-morrow, for he lodges in our house,' replied Mr. Short rapidly.

'Then bring him here,' said the single gentleman. 'Here's a sovereign a-piece. If I can find these people through your means, it is but a prelude to twenty more. Return to me to-morrow, and keep your own counsel on this subject—though I need hardly tell you that; for you'll do so for your own sakes. Now, give me your address, and leave me.'

The address was given, the two men departed, the crowd went with them, and the single gentleman for two mortal hours walked in uncommon agitation up and down his room, over the wondering heads of Mr. Swiveller and Miss Sally Brass.

Jerry's Dancing Dogs

CHAPTER XXXVIII

KIT—for it happens at this juncture, not only that we have breathing time to follow his fortunes, but that the necessities of these adventures so adapt themselves to our ease and inclination as to call upon us imperatively to pursue the track we most desire to take—Kit, while the matters treated of in the last fifteen chapters were yet in progress, was, as the reader may suppose, gradually familiarising himself more and more with Mr. and Mrs. Garland, Mr. Abel, the pony, and Barbara, and gradually coming to consider them one and all as his particular private friends, and Abel Cottage, Finchley, as his own proper home.

Stay—the words are written, and may go, but if they convey any notion that Kit, in the plentiful board and comfortable lodging of his new abode, began to think slightingly of the poor fare and furniture of his old dwelling, they do their office badly and commit injustice. Who so mindful of those he left at home—albeit they were but a mother and two young babies —as Kit? What boastful father in the fulness of his heart ever related such wonders of his infant prodigy, as Kit never wearied of telling Barbara in the evening time, concerning little Jacob? Was there ever such a mother as Kit's mother, on her son's showing? or was there ever such comfort in poverty as in the poverty of Kit's family, if any correct judgment might be arrived at, from his own glowing account!

And let me linger in this place, for an instant, to remark that if ever household affections and loves are graceful things, they are graceful in the poor. The ties that bind the wealthy and the proud to home may be forged on earth, but those which link the poor man to his humble hearth are of the truer metal and bear the stamp of Heaven. The man of high descent may love the halls and lands of his inheritance as a part of himself: as trophies of his birth and power; his associations with them are associations of pride and wealth and triumph; the poor man's attachment to the tenements he holds, which strangers have held before, and may to-morrow occupy again, has a worthier root, struck deep into a purer soil. His household gods are of flesh and blood, with no alloy of silver, gold, or precious stone; he has no property but in the affections of his own heart; and when they endear bare floors and walls, despite of rags and toil and scanty fare, that man has his love of home from God, and his rude hut becomes a solemn place.

Oh! if those who rule the destinies of nations would but remember this—if they would but think how hard it is for the very poor to have engendered in their hearts, that love of home from which all domestic virtues spring, when they live in dense and squalid masses where social decency is lost, or rather never found,—if they would but turn aside from the wide thorough-fares and great houses, and strive to improve the wretched dwellings in bye-ways where only Poverty may walk,—many low roofs would point more truly to the sky, than the loftiest steeple that now rears proudly up from the midst of guilt, and crime, and horrible disease, to mock them by its contrast. In hollow voices from Workhouse, Hospital, and Jail, this truth is preached from day to day, and has been proclaimed for years. It is no light matter—no outcry from the working vulgar—no mere question of the people's health and comforts that may be whistled down on Wednesday nights. In love of home, the love of country has its rise; and who are the truer patriots or the better in time of need—those who venerate the land, owning its wood, and stream, and earth, and all that they produce? or those who love their country, boasting not a foot of ground in all its wide domain!

Kit knew nothing about such questions, but he knew that his old home was a very poor place, and that his new one was very unlike it, and yet he was constantly looking back with grateful satisfaction and affectionate anxiety, and often indited square-folded letters to his mother, inclosing a shilling or eighteen-pence or such other small remittance, which Mr. Abel's liberality enabled him to make. Sometimes being in the neighbourhood, he had leisure to call upon her, and then, great was the joy and pride of Kit's mother, and extremely noisy the satisfaction of little Jacob and the baby, and cordial the congratulations of the whole court, who listened with admiring ears to the accounts of Abel Cottage, and could never be told too much of its wonders and magnificence.

Although Kit was in the very highest favour with the old lady and gentleman, and Mr. Abel, and Barbara, it is certain that no member of the family evinced such a remarkable partiality for him as the self-willed pony, who, from being the most obstinate and opinionated pony on the face of the earth, was, in his hands, the meekest and most tractable of animals.

It is true that in exact proportion as he became manageable by Kit he became utterly ungovernable by anybody else, (as if he had determined to keep him in the family at all risks and hazards,) and that, even under the guidance of his favourite, he would sometimes perform a great variety of strange freaks and capers, to the extreme discomposure of the old lady's nerves; but as Kit always represented that this was only his fun, or a way he had of showing his attachment to his employers, Mrs. Garland gradually suffered herself to be persuaded into the belief, in which she at last became so strongly confirmed, that if, in one of these ebullitions, he had overturned the chaise, she would have been quite satisfied that he did it with the very best intentions.

Besides becoming in a short time a perfect marvel in all stable matters, Kit soon made himself a very tolerable gardener, a handy fellow within doors, and an indispensable attendant on Mr. Abel, who every day gave him some new proof of his confidence and approbation. Mr. Witherden the Notary, too, regarded him with a friendly eye; and even Mr. Chuckster would sometimes condescend to give him a slight nod, or to honour him with that peculiar form of recognition which is called 'taking a sight,' or to favour him with some other salute combining pleasantry with patronage.

One morning Kit drove Mr. Abel to the Notary's office, as he sometimes did, and having set him down at the house, was about to drive off to a livery stable hard by, when this same Mr. Chuckster emerged from the office door, and cried 'Woa-a-a-a-a-a!'—dwelling upon the note a long time, for the purpose of striking terror into the pony's heart, and asserting the supremacy of man over the inferior animals.

'Pull up, Snobby,' cried Mr. Chuckster, addressing himself to Kit. 'You're wanted inside here.'

'Has Mr. Abel forgotten anything, I wonder?' said Kit as he dismounted.

'Ask no questions, Snobby,' returned Mr. Chuckster, 'but go and see. Woa-a-a then, will you? If that pony was mine, I'd break him.'

'You must be very gentle with him, if you please,' said Kit, 'or you'll find him troublesome. You'd better not keep on pulling his ears, please. I know he won't like it.'

To this remonstrance Mr. Chuckster deigned no other answer, than addressing Kit with a lofty and distant air as 'young feller,' and requesting him to cut and come again with all speed. The 'young feller' complying, Mr. Chuckster put his hands in his pockets, and tried to look as if he were not minding the pony, but happened to be lounging there by accident.

Kit scraped his shoes very carefully (for he had not yet lost his reverence for the bundles of papers and the tin boxes), and tapped at the office door, which was quickly opened by the Notary himself.

'Oh! come in, Christopher,' said Mr. Witherden.

'Is that the lad?' asked an elderly gentleman, but of a stout, bluff figure—who was in the room.

'That's the lad,' said Mr. Witherden. 'He fell in with my client, Mr. Garland, sir, at this very door. I have reason to think he is a good lad, sir, and that you may believe what he says. Let me introduce Mr. Abel Garland, sir—his young master; my articled pupil, sir, and most particular friend:— my most particular friend, sir,' repeated the Notary, drawing out his silk handkerchief and flourishing it about his face.

'Your servant, sir,' said the stranger gentleman.

'Yours, sir, I'm sure,' replied Mr. Abel mildly. 'You were wishing to speak to Christopher, sir?'

'Yes, I was. Have I your permission?'

'By all means.'

'My business is no secret; or I should rather say it need be no secret *here*,' said the stranger, observing that Mr. Abel and the Notary were preparing to retire. 'It relates to a dealer in curiosities with whom he lived, and in whom I am earnestly and warmly interested. I have been a stranger to this country, gentlemen, for very many years, and if I am deficient in form and ceremony, I hope you will forgive me.'

'No forgiveness is necessary, sir;—none whatever,' replied the Notary. And so said Mr. Abel.

'I have been making inquiries in the neighbourhood in which his old master lived,' said the stranger, 'and I learn that he was served by this lad. I have found out his mother's house, and have been directed by her to this place as the nearest in which I should be likely to find him. That's the cause of my presenting myself here this morning.'

'I am very glad of any cause, sir,' said the Notary, 'which procures me the honour of this visit.'

'Sir,' retorted the stranger, 'you speak like a mere man of the

world, and I think you something better. Therefore, pray do
not sink your real character in paying unmeaning compliments
to me.'

'Hem!' coughed the Notary. 'You're a plain speaker, sir.'

'And a plain dealer,' returned the stranger. 'It may be my
long absence and inexperience that lead me to the conclusion;
but if plain speakers are scarce in this part of the world, I
fancy plain dealers are still scarcer. If my speaking should
offend you, sir, my dealing, I hope, will make amends.'

Mr. Witherden seemed a little disconcerted by the elderly
gentleman's mode of conducting the dialogue; and as for Kit,
he looked at him in open-mouthed astonishment: wondering
what kind of language he would address to him, if he talked
in that free and easy way to a Notary. It was with no harsh-
ness, however, though with something of constitutional irrita-
bility and haste, that he turned to Kit and said:

'If you think, my lad, that I am pursuing these inquiries
with any other view than that of serving and reclaiming those
I am in search of, you do me a very great wrong, and deceive
yourself. Don't be deceived, I beg of you, but rely upon my
assurance. The fact is, gentlemen,' he added, turning again to
the Notary and his pupil, 'that I am in a very painful and
wholly unexpected position. I came to this city with a darling
object at my heart, expecting to find no obstacle or difficulty
in the way of its attainment. I find myself suddenly checked
and stopped short, in the execution of my design, by a mystery
which I cannot penetrate. Every effort I have made to penetrate it, has only served to render it darker and more obscure;
and I am afraid to stir openly in the matter, lest those whom I
anxiously pursue, should fly still farther from me. I assure you
that if you could give me any assistance, you would not be
sorry to do so, if you knew how greatly I stand in need of it,
and what a load it would relieve me from.'

There was a simplicity in this confidence which occasioned
it to find a quick response in the breast of the good-natured
Notary, who replied, in the same spirit, that the stranger had
not mistaken his desire, and that if he could be of service to
him, he would, most readily.

Kit was then put under examination and closely questioned
by the unknown gentleman, touching his old master and the
child, their lonely way of life, their retired habits, and strict
seclusion. The nightly absence of the old man, the solitary

existence of the child at those times, his illness and recovery, Quilp's possession of the house, and their sudden disappearance, were all the subjects of much questioning and answer. Finally, Kit informed the gentleman that the premises were now to let, and that a board upon the door referred all inquirers to Mr. Sampson Brass, Solicitor, of Bevis Marks, from whom he might perhaps learn some further particulars.

'Not by inquiry,' said the gentleman, shaking his head. 'I live there.'

'Live at Brass's the attorney's!' cried Mr. Witherden in some surprise: having professional knowledge of the gentleman in question.

'Aye,' was the reply. 'I entered on his lodgings t'other day, chiefly because I had seen this very board. It matters little to me where I live, and I had a desperate hope that some intelligence might be cast in my way there, which would not reach me elsewhere. Yes, I live at Brass's—more shame for me, I suppose?'

'That's a mere matter of opinion,' said the Notary, shrugging his shoulders. 'He is looked upon as rather a doubtful character.'

'Doubtful?' echoed the other. 'I am glad to hear there's any doubt about it. I supposed that had been thoroughly settled, long ago. But will you let me speak a word or two with you in private?'

Mr. Witherden consenting, they walked into that gentleman's private closet, and remained there, in close conversation, for some quarter of an hour, when they returned into the outer office. The stranger had left his hat in Mr. Witherden's room, and seemed to have established himself in this short interval on quite a friendly footing.

'I'll not detain you any longer now,' he said, putting a crown into Kit's hand, and looking towards the Notary, 'You shall hear from me again. Not a word of this, you know, except to your master and mistress.'

'Mother, sir, would be glad to know—' said Kit, faltering.

'Glad to know what?'

'Anything—so that it was no harm—about Miss Nell.'

'Would she? Well then, you may tell her if she can keep a secret. But mind, not a word of this to anybody else. Don't forget that. Be particular.'

'I'll take care, sir,' said Kit. 'Thankee, sir, and good morning.'

Now, it happened that the gentleman, in his anxiety to impress upon Kit that he was not to tell anybody what had passed between them, followed him out to the door to repeat his caution, and it further happened that at that moment the eyes of Mr. Richard Swiveller were turned in that direction, and beheld his mysterious friend and Kit together.

It was quite an accident, and the way in which it came about was this. Mr. Chuckster, being a gentleman of a cultivated taste and refined spirit, was one of that Lodge of Glorious Apollos whereof Mr. Swiveller was Perpetual Grand. Mr. Swiveller, passing through the street in the execution of some Brazen errand, and beholding one of his Glorious Brotherhood intently gazing on a pony, crossed over to give him that fraternal greeting with which Perpetual Grands are, by the very constitution of their office, bound to cheer and encourage their disciples. He had scarcely bestowed upon him his blessing, and followed it with a general remark touching the present state and prospects of the weather, when, lifting up his eyes, he beheld the single gentleman of Bevis Marks in earnest conversation with Christopher Nubbles.

'Hallo!' said Dick, 'who *is* that?'

'He called to see my Governor this morning,' replied Mr. Chuckster; 'beyond that, I don't know him from Adam.'

'At least you know his name?' said Dick.

To which Mr. Chuckster replied, with an elevation of speech becoming a Glorious Apollo, that he was 'everlastingly blessed' if he did.

'All I know, my dear feller,' said Mr. Chuckster, running his fingers through his hair, 'is, that he is the cause of my having stood here twenty minutes, for which I hate him with a mortal and undying hatred, and would pursue him to the confines of eternity if I could afford the time.'

While they were thus discoursing, the subject of their conversation (who had not appeared to recognise Mr. Richard Swiveller) re-entered the house, and Kit came down the steps and joined them; to whom Mr. Swiveller again propounded his inquiry with no better success.

'He is a very nice gentleman, sir,' said Kit, 'and that's all *I* know about him.'

Mr. Chuckster waxed wroth at this answer, and without applying the remark to any particular case, mentioned, as a general truth, that it was expedient to break the heads of

Snobs, and to tweak their noses. Without expressing his concurrence in this sentiment, Mr. Swiveller after a few moments of abstraction inquired which way Kit was driving, and, being informed, declared it was his way, and that he would trespass on him for a lift. Kit would gladly have declined the proffered honour, but as Mr. Swiveller was already established in the seat beside him, he had no means of doing so, otherwise than by a forcible ejectment, and therefore drove briskly off—so briskly indeed, as to cut short the leave-taking between Mr. Chuckster and his Grand Master, and to occasion the former gentleman some inconvenience from having his corns squeezed by the impatient pony.

As Whisker was tired of standing, and Mr. Swiveller was kind enough to stimulate him by shrill whistles, and various sporting cries, they rattled off at too sharp a pace to admit of much conversation: especially as the pony, incensed by Mr. Swiveller's admonitions, took a particular fancy for the lamp-posts and cart-wheels, and evinced a strong desire to run on the pavement and rasp himself against the brick walls. It was not, therefore, until they had arrived at the stable, and the chaise had been extricated from a very small doorway, into which the pony dragged it under the impression that he could take it along with him into his usual stall, that Mr. Swiveller found time to talk.

'It's hard work,' said Richard. 'What do you say to some beer?'

Kit at first declined, but presently consented, and they adjourned to the neighbouring bar together.

'We'll drink our friend what's-his-name,' said Dick, holding up the bright frothy pot; '—that was talking to you this morning, you know—*I* know him—a good fellow, but eccentric—very—here's what's-his-name!'

Kit pledged him.

'He lives in my house,' said Dick; 'at least in the house occupied by the firm in which I'm a sort of a—of a managing partner—a difficult fellow to get anything out of, but we like him—we like him.'

'I must be going, sir, if you please,' said Kit, moving away.

'Don't be in a hurry, Christopher,' replied his patron, 'we'll drink your mother.'

'Thank you, sir.'

'An excellent woman that mother of yours, Christopher,'

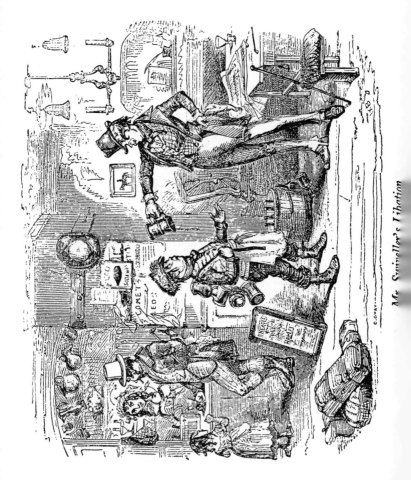

Mr. Swiveller's Libation

said Mr. Swiveller. 'Who ran to catch me when I fell, and kissed the place to make it well? My mother. A charming woman. He's a liberal sort of fellow. We must get him to do something *for* your mother. Does he know her, Christopher?'

Kit shook his head, and glancing slyly at his questioner, thanked him, and made off before he could say another word.

'Humph!' said Mr. Swiveller pondering, 'this is queer. Nothing but mysteries in connection with Brass's house. I'll keep my own counsel, however. Everybody and anybody has been in my confidence as yet, but now I think I'll set up in business for myself. Queer—very queer!'

After pondering deeply and with a face of exceeding wisdom for some time, Mr. Swiveller drank some more of the beer, and summoning a small boy who had been watching his proceedings, poured forth the few remaining drops as a libation on the gravel, and bade him carry the empty vessel to the bar with his compliments, and above all things to lead a sober and temperate life, and abstain from all intoxicating and exciting liquors. Having given him this piece of moral advice for his trouble (which, as he wisely observed, was far better than halfpence), the Perpetual Grand Master of the Glorious Apollos thrust his hands into his pockets and sauntered away; still pondering as he went.

N

ALL that day, though he waited for Mr. Abel until evening, Kit kept clear of his mother's house, determined not to anticipate the pleasures of the morrow, but to let them come in their full rush of delight; for to-morrow was the great and long-looked-for epoch in his life—to-morrow was the end of his first quarter—the day of receiving, for the first time, one fourth part of his annual income of Six Pounds in one vast sum of Thirty Shillings—to-morrow was to be a half-holiday devoted to a whirl of entertainments, and little Jacob was to know what oysters meant, and to see a play.

All manner of incidents combined in favour of the occasion: not only had Mr. and Mrs. Garland forewarned him that they intended to make no deduction for his outfit from the great amount, but to pay it him unbroken in all its gigantic grandeur; not only had the unknown gentleman increased the stock by the sum of five shillings, which was a perfect god-send and in itself a fortune; not only had these things come to pass which nobody could have calculated upon, or in their wildest dreams have hoped; but it was Barbara's quarter too—Barbara's quarter, that very day—and Barbara had a half-holiday as well as Kit, and Barbara's mother was going to make one of the party, and to take tea with Kit's mother, and cultivate her acquaintance.

To be sure Kit looked out of his window very early that morning to see which way the clouds were flying, and to be sure Barbara would have been at hers too, if she had not sat up so late over-night, starching and ironing small pieces of muslin, and crimping them into frills, and sewing them on to other pieces to form magnificent wholes for next day's wear. But they were both up very early for all that, and had small appetites for breakfast and less for dinner, and were in a state of great excitement when Barbara's mother came in, with astonishing accounts of the fineness of the weather out of doors (but with a very large umbrella notwithstanding, for people like Barbara's mother seldom make holiday without one), and when the bell rung for them to go up stairs and receive their quarter's money in gold and silver.

Well, wasn't Mr. Garland kind when he said 'Christopher, here's your money, and you have earned it well;' and wasn't

Mrs. Garland kind when she said 'Barbara, here's yours, and I'm much pleased with you;' and didn't Kit sign his name bold to his receipt, and didn't Barbara sign her name all a trembling to hers; and wasn't it beautiful to see how Mrs. Garland poured out Barbara's mother a glass of wine; and didn't Barbara's mother speak up when she said 'Here's blessing you, ma'am, as a good lady, and you, sir, as a good gentleman, and, Barbara, my love to you, and here's towards you, Mr. Christopher;' and wasn't she as long drinking it as if it had been a tumblerful; and didn't she look genteel, standing there with her gloves on; and wasn't there plenty of laughing and talking among them as they reviewed all these things upon the top of the coach; and didn't they pity the people who hadn't got a holiday!

But Kit's mother, again—wouldn't anybody have supposed she had come of a good stock and been a lady all her life! There she was, quite ready to receive them, with a display of tea-things that might have warmed the heart of a china-shop; and little Jacob and the baby in such a state of perfection that their clothes looked as good as new, though Heaven knows they were old enough! Didn't she say before they had sat down five minutes that Barbara's mother was exactly the sort of lady she expected, and didn't Barbara's mother say that Kit's mother was the very picture of what *she* had expected, and didn't Kit's mother compliment Barbara's mother on Barbara, and didn't Barbara's mother compliment Kit's mother on Kit, and wasn't Barbara herself quite fascinated with little Jacob, and did ever a child show off when he was wanted, as that child did, or make such friends as he made!

'And we are both widows too!' said Barbara's mother. 'We must have been made to know each other.'

'I haven't a doubt about it,' returned Mrs. Nubbles. 'And what a pity it is we didn't know each other sooner.'

'But then, you know, it's such a pleasure,' said Barbara's mother, 'to have it brought about by one's son and daughter, that it's fully made up for. Now, an't it?'

To this, Kit's mother yielded her full assent, and tracing things back from effects to causes, they naturally reverted to their deceased husbands, respecting whose lives, deaths, and burials, they compared notes, and discovered sundry circumstances that tallied with wonderful exactness; such as Barbara's father having been exactly four years and ten months older than Kit's father, and one of them having died on a Wednesday and the other on a Thursday, and both of them having been of a very fine make and remarkably good-looking, with other extraordinary coincidences. These recollections being of a kind calculated to cast a shadow on the brightness of the holiday, Kit diverted the conversation to general topics, and they were soon in great force again, and as merry as before. Among other things, Kit told them about his old place, and the extraordinary beauty of Nell (of whom he had talked to Barbara a thousand times already); but the last-named circumstance failed to interest his hearers to anything like the extent he had supposed, and even his mother said (looking accidentally at Barbara at the same time) that there was no doubt Miss Nell was very pretty, but she was but a child after all, and there were many young women quite as pretty as she; and Barbara mildly observed that she should think so, and that she never could help believing Mr. Christopher must be under a mistake—which Kit wondered at very much, not being able to conceive what reason she had for doubting him. Barbara's mother, too, observed that it was very common for young folks to change at about fourteen or fifteen, and whereas they had been very pretty before, to grow up quite plain; which truth she illustrated by many forcible examples, especially one of a young man, who, being a builder with great prospects, had been particular in his attentions to Barbara, but whom Barbara would have nothing to say to; which (though everything happened for the best) she almost thought was a pity. Kit said he thought so too, and so he did honestly, and he wondered what made Barbara so silent all at once, and why his mother looked at him as if he shouldn't have said it.

However, it was high time now to be thinking of the play; for which great preparation was required, in the way of shawls and bonnets, not to mention one handkerchief full of oranges and another of apples, which took some time tying up, in consequence of the fruit having a tendency to roll out at the corners. At length, everything was ready, and they went off very fast; Kit's mother carrying the baby, who was dreadfully wide-awake, and Kit holding little Jacob in one hand, and escorting Barbara with the other—a state of things which occasioned the two mothers, who walked behind, to declare that they looked quite family folks, and caused Barbara to blush and say, 'Now don't, mother!' But Kit said she had no

At Astley's

(p. 293)

call to mind what they said; and indeed she need not have had, if she had known how very far from Kit's thoughts any love-making was. Poor Barbara!

At last they got to the theatre, which was Astley's: and in some two minutes after they had reached the yet unopened door, little Jacob was squeezed flat, and the baby had received divers concussions, and Barbara's mother's umbrella had been carried several yards off and passed back to her over the shoulders of the people, and Kit had hit a man on the head with the handkerchief of apples for 'scrowdging' his parent with unnecessary violence, and there was a great uproar. But, when they were once past the pay-place and tearing away for very life with their checks in their hands, and, above all, when they were fairly in the theatre, and seated in such places that they couldn't have had better if they had picked them out, and taken them beforehand, all this was looked upon as quite a capital joke, and an essential part of the entertainment.

Dear, dear, what a place it looked, that Astley's; with all the paint, gilding, and looking-glass; the vague smell of horses suggestive of coming wonders; the curtain that hid such gorgeous mysteries; the clean white sawdust down in the circus; the company coming in and taking their places; the fiddlers looking carelessly up at them while they tuned their instruments, as if they didn't want the play to begin, and knew it all beforehand! What a glow was that, which burst upon them all, when that long, clear, brilliant row of lights came slowly up; and what the feverish excitement when the little bell rang and the music began in good earnest, with strong parts for the drums, and sweet effects for the triangles! Well might Barbara's mother say to Kit's mother that the gallery was the place to see from, and wonder it wasn't much dearer than the boxes: well might Barbara feel doubtful whether to laugh or cry, in her flutter of delight.

Then the play itself! the horses which little Jacob believed from the first to be alive, and the ladies and gentlemen of whose reality he could be by no means persuaded, having never seen or heard anything at all like them—the firing, which made Barbara wink—the forlorn lady, who made her cry—the tyrant, who made her tremble—the man who sang the song with the lady's-maid and danced the chorus, who made her laugh—the pony who reared up on his hind legs when he saw the murderer, and wouldn't hear of walking on all-fours again until he was taken into custody—the clown who ventured on such familiarities with the military man in boots—the lady who jumped over the nine-and-twenty ribbons and came down safe upon the horse's back—everything was delightful, splendid, and surprising! Little Jacob applauded till his hands were sore; Kit cried 'an-kor' at the end of everything, the three-act piece included; and Barbara's mother beat her umbrella on the floor, in her ecstasies, until it was nearly worn down to the gingham.

In the midst of all these fascinations, Barbara's thoughts seemed to have been still running on what Kit had said at tea-time; for, when they were coming out of the play, she asked him, with an hysterical simper, if Miss Nell was as handsome as the lady who jumped over the ribbons.

'As handsome as *her?*' said Kit. 'Double as handsome.'

'Oh, Christopher! I'm sure she was the beautifullest creature ever was,' said Barbara.

'Nonsense!' returned Kit. 'She was well enough, I don't deny that; but think how she was dressed and painted, and what a difference that made. Why *you* are a good deal better-looking than her, Barbara.'

'Oh, Christopher!' said Barbara, looking down.

'You are, any day,' said Kit,—'and so's your mother.' Poor Barbara!

What was all this though—even all this—to the extraordinary dissipation that ensued, when Kit, walking into an oyster-shop as bold as if he lived there, and not so much as looking at the counter or the man behind it, led his party into a box—a private box, fitted up with red curtains, white table-cloth, and cruet-stand complete—and ordered a fierce gentleman with whiskers, who acted as waiter and called him, him Christopher Nubbles, 'sir,' to bring three dozen of his largest-sized oysters, and to look sharp about it! Yes, Kit told this gentleman to look sharp, and he not only said he would look sharp, but he actually did, and presently came running back with the newest loaves, and the freshest butter, and the largest oysters, ever seen. Then said Kit to this gentleman, 'A pot of beer'—just so—and the gentleman, instead of replying, 'Sir, did you address that language to me?' only said, 'Pot o' beer, sir? Yes, sir,' and went off and fetched it, and put it on the table in a small decanter-stand, like those which blind men's dogs carry about the streets in their mouths, to catch the halfpence in; and both Kit's mother and Barbara's mother declared as he turned away that he was one of the slimmest and gracefullest young men she had ever looked upon.

Then they fell to work upon the supper in earnest; and there was Barbara, that foolish Barbara, declaring that she could not eat more than two, and wanting more pressing than you would believe before she would eat four: though her mother and Kit's mother made up for it pretty well, and ate and laughed and enjoyed themselves so thoroughly that it did Kit good to see them, and made him laugh and eat likewise from strong sympathy. But the greatest miracle of the night was little Jacob, who ate oysters as if he had been born and bred to the business—sprinkled the pepper and the vinegar with a discretion beyond his years—and afterwards built a grotto on the table with the shells. There was the baby too, who had never closed an eye all night, but had sat as good as gold, trying to force a large orange into his mouth, and gazing intently at the lights in the chandelier—there he was, sitting up in his mother's lap, staring at the gas without winking, and making indentations in his soft visage with an oyster-shell, to that degree that a heart of iron must have loved him! In short, there never was a more successful supper; and when Kit ordered in a glass of something hot to finish with, and proposed Mr. and Mrs. Garland before sending it round, there were not six happier people in all the world.

But all happiness has an end—hence the chief pleasure of its next beginning—and as it was now growing late, they agreed it was time to turn their faces homewards. So, after going a little out of their way to see Barbara and Barbara's mother safe to a friend's house where they were to pass the night, Kit and his mother left them at the door, with an early appointment for returning to Finchley next morning, and a great many plans for next quarter's enjoyment. Then, Kit took little Jacob on his back, and giving his arm to his mother, and a kiss to the baby, they all trudged merrily home together.

CHAPTER XL

FULL of that vague kind of penitence which holidays awaken next morning, Kit turned out at sunrise, and, with his faith in last night's enjoyments a little shaken by cool daylight and the return to every-day duties and occupations, went to meet Barbara and her mother at the appointed place. And being careful not to awaken any of the little household, who were yet resting from their unusual fatigues, Kit left his money on the chimney-piece, with an inscription in chalk calling his mother's attention to the circumstance, and informing her that it came from her dutiful son; and went his way, with a heart something heavier than his pockets, but free from any very great oppression notwithstanding.

Oh these holidays! why will they leave us some regret? why cannot we push them back, only a week or two in our memories, so as to put them at once at that convenient distance whence they may be regarded either with a calm indifference or a pleasant effort of recollection? why will they hang about us, like the flavour of yesterday's wine, suggestive of headaches and lassitude, and those good intentions for the future, which, under the earth, form the everlasting pavement of a large estate, and, upon it, usually endure until dinner-time or thereabouts?

Who will wonder that Barbara had a headache, or that Barbara's mother was disposed to be cross, or that she slightly underrated Astley's, and thought the clown was older than they had taken him to be last night? Kit was not surprised to hear her say so—not he. He had already had a misgiving that the inconstant actors in that dazzling vision had been doing the same thing the night before last, and would do it again that night, and the next, and for weeks and months to come, though he would not be there. Such is the difference between yesterday and to-day. We are all going to the play, or coming home from it.

However, the Sun himself is weak when he first rises, and gathers strength and courage as the day gets on. By degrees, they began to recall circumstances more and more pleasant in their nature, until, what between talking, walking, and laughing, they reached Finchley in such good heart, that Barbara's mother declared she never felt less tired or in better

Mr. Garland and Kit

(p. 297)

spirits. And so said Kit. Barbara had been silent all the way, but she said so too. Poor little Barbara! She was very quiet.

They were at home in such good time that Kit had rubbed down the pony and made him as spruce as a racehorse, before Mr. Garland came down to breakfast; which punctual and industrious conduct the old lady, and the old gentleman, and Mr. Abel, highly extolled. At his usual hour (or rather at his usual minute and second, for he was the soul of punctuality) Mr. Abel walked out, to be overtaken by the London coach, and Kit and the old gentleman went to work in the garden.

This was not the least pleasant of Kit's employments. On a fine day they were quite a family party; the old lady sitting hard by with her work-basket on a little table; the old gentleman digging, or pruning, or clipping about with a large pair of shears, or helping Kit in some way or other with great assiduity; and Whisker looking on from his paddock in placid contemplation of them all. To-day they were to trim the grape-vine, so Kit mounted half-way up a short ladder, and began to snip and hammer away, while the old gentleman, with a great interest in his proceedings, handed up the nails and shreds of cloth as he wanted them. The old lady and Whisker looked on as usual.

'Well, Christopher,' said Mr. Garland, 'and so you have made a new friend, eh?'

'I beg your pardon, sir?' returned Kit, looking down from the ladder.

'You have made a new friend, I hear from Mr. Abel,' said the old gentleman, 'at the office!'

'Oh! Yes sir, yes. He behaved very handsome, sir.'

'I'm glad to hear it,' returned the old gentleman with a smile. 'He is disposed to behave more handsomely still, though, Christopher.'

'Indeed, sir! It's very kind in him, but I don't want him to, I'm sure,' said Kit, hammering stoutly at an obdurate nail.

'He is rather anxious,' pursued the old gentleman, 'to have you in his own service—take care what you're doing, or you will fall down and hurt yourself.'

'To have me in his service, sir?' cried Kit, who had stopped short in his work and faced about on the ladder like some dexterous tumbler. 'Why, sir, I don't think he can be in earnest when he says that.'

'Oh! But he is indeed,' said Mr. Garland. 'And he has told Mr. Abel so.'

'I never heard of such a thing!' muttered Kit, looking ruefully at his master and mistress. 'I wonder at him; that I do.'

'You see, Christopher,' said Mr. Garland, 'this is a point of much importance to you, and you should understand and consider it in that light. This gentleman is able to give you more money than I—not, I hope, to carry through the various relations of master and servant, more kindness and confidence, but certainly, Christopher, to give you more money.'

'Well,' said Kit, 'after that, sir—'

'Wait a moment,' interposed Mr. Garland. 'That is not all. You were a very faithful servant to your old employers, as I understand, and should this gentleman recover them, as it is his purpose to attempt doing by every means in his power, I have no doubt that you, being in his service, would meet with your reward. Besides,' added the old gentleman with stronger emphasis, 'besides having the pleasure of being again brought into communication with those to whom you seem to be very strongly and disinterestedly attached. You must think of all this, Christopher, and not be rash or hasty in your choice.'

Kit did suffer one twinge, one momentary pang, in keeping the resolution he had already formed, when this last argument passed swiftly into his thoughts, and conjured up the realization of all his hopes and fancies. But it was gone in a minute, and he sturdily rejoined that the gentleman must look out for somebody else, as he did think he might have done at first.

'He has no right to think that I'd be led away to go to him, sir,' said Kit, turning round again after half a minute's hammering. 'Does he think I'm a fool?'

'He may, perhaps, Christopher, if you refuse his offer,' said Mr. Garland gravely.

'Then let him, sir,' retorted Kit; 'what do I care, sir, what he thinks? why should I care for his thinking, sir, when I know that I should be a fool, and worse than a fool, sir, to leave the kindest master and mistress that ever was or can be, who took me out of the streets a very poor and hungry lad indeed—poorer and hungrier perhaps than even you think for, sir—to go to him or anybody? If Miss Nell was to come back, ma'am,' added Kit, turning suddenly to his mistress, 'why that would be another thing, and perhaps if *she* wanted me, I might ask you now and then to let me work for her when all was done at home. But when she comes back, I see now that she'll be rich as old master always said she would, and being a rich young lady, what could she want of me? No, no,' added Kit, shaking his head sorrowfully, 'she'll never want me any more, and bless her, I hope she never may, though I *should* like to see her too!'

Here Kit drove a nail into the wall, very hard—much harder than was necessary—and having done so, faced about again.

'There's the pony, sir,' said Kit—'Whisker, ma'am (and he knows so well I'm talking about him that he begins to neigh directly, sir),—would he let anybody come near him but me, ma'am? Here's the garden, sir, and Mr. Abel, ma'am. Would Mr. Abel part with me, sir, or is there anybody that could be fonder of the garden, ma'am? It would break mother's heart, sir, and even little Jacob would have sense enough to cry his eyes out, ma'am, if he thought that Mr. Abel could wish to part with me so soon, after having told me, only the other day, that he hoped we might be together for years to come—'

There is no telling how long Kit might have stood upon the ladder, addressing his master and mistress by turns, and generally turning towards the wrong person, if Barbara had not at that moment come running up to say that a messenger from the office had brought a note, which, with an expression of some surprise at Kit's oratorical appearance, she put into her master's hand.

'Oh!' said the old gentleman after reading it, 'ask the messenger to walk this way.' Barbara tripping off to do as she was bid, he turned to Kit and said that they would not pursue the subject any further, and that Kit could not be more unwilling to part with them, than they would be to part with Kit; a sentiment which the old lady very generously echoed.

'At the same time, Christopher,' added Mr. Garland, glancing at the note in his hand, 'if the gentleman should want to borrow you now and then for an hour or so, or even a day or so, at a time, we must consent to lend you, and you must consent to be lent.—Oh! here is the young gentleman. How do you do, sir?'

This salutation was addressed to Mr. Chuckster, who, with his hat extremely on one side, and his hair a long way beyond it, came swaggering up the walk.

'Hope I see you well, sir,' returned that gentleman. 'Hope I see *you* well, ma'am. Charming box this, sir. Delicious country to be sure.'

'You want to take Kit back with you, I find?' observed Mr. Garland.

'I have got a chariot-cab waiting on purpose,' replied the clerk. 'A very spanking grey in that cab, sir, if you're a judge of horse-flesh.'

Declining to inspect the spanking grey, on the plea that he was but poorly acquainted with such matters, and would but imperfectly appreciate his beauties, Mr. Garland invited Mr. Chuckster to partake of a slight repast in the way of lunch. That gentleman readily consenting, certain cold viands, flanked with ale and wine, were speedily prepared for his refreshment.

At this repast, Mr. Chuckster exerted his utmost abilities to enchant his entertainers, and impress them with a conviction of the mental superiority of those who dwelt in town; with which view he led the discourse to the small scandal of the day, in which he was justly considered by his friends to shine prodigiously. Thus, he was in a condition to relate the exact circumstances of the difference between the Marquis of Mizzler and Lord Bobby, which it appeared originated in a disputed bottle of champagne, and not in a pigeon-pie, as erroneously reported in the newspapers; neither had Lord Bobby said to the Marquis of Mizzler, 'Mizzler, one of us two tells a lie, and I'm not the man,' as incorrectly stated by the same authorities; but 'Mizzler, you know where I'm to be found, and damme, sir, find me if you want me'—which, of course, entirely changed the aspect of this interesting question, and placed it in a very different light. He also acquainted them with the precise amount of the income guaranteed by the Duke of Thigsberry to Violetta Stetta of the Italian Opera, which it appeared was payable quarterly, and not half-yearly, as the public had been given to understand, and which was *ex*clusive, and not *in*clusive, (as had been monstrously stated,) of jewellery, perfumery, hair-powder for five footmen, and two daily changes of kid-gloves for a page. Having entreated the old lady and gentleman to set their minds at rest on these absorbing points, for they might rely on his statement being the correct one, Mr. Chuckster entertained them with theatrical chit-chat and the court circular; and so wound up a brilliant and fascinating conversation which he had maintained alone, and without any assistance whatever, for upwards of three-quarters of an hour.

'And now that the nag has got his wind again,' said Mr. Chuckster, rising in a graceful manner, 'I'm afraid I must cut my stick.'

Neither Mr. nor Mrs. Garland offered any opposition to his tearing himself away, (feeling, no doubt, that such a man could ill be spared from his proper sphere of action,) and therefore Mr. Chuckster and Kit were shortly afterwards upon their way to town; Kit being perched upon the box of the cabriolet beside the driver, and Mr. Chuckster seated in solitary state inside, with one of his boots sticking out at each of the front windows.

When they reached the Notary's house, Kit followed into the office, and was desired by Mr. Abel to sit down and wait, for the gentleman who wanted him had gone out, and perhaps might not return for some time. This anticipation was strictly verified, for Kit had had his dinner, and his tea, and had read all the lighter matter in the Law-List, and the Post-Office Directory, and had fallen asleep a great many times, before the gentleman whom he had seen before, came in; which he did at last in a very great hurry.

He was closeted with Mr. Witherden for some little time, and Mr. Abel had been called in to assist at the conference, before Kit, wondering very much what he was wanted for, was summoned to attend them.

'Christopher,' said the gentleman, turning to him directly he entered the room, 'I have found your old master and young mistress.'

'No, sir! Have you, though?' returned Kit, his eyes sparkling with delight. 'Where are they, sir? How are they, sir? Are they—are they near here?'

'A long way from here,' returned the gentleman, shaking his head. 'But I am going away to-night to bring them back, and I want you to go with me.'

'Me, sir?' cried Kit, full of joy and surprise.

'The place,' said the strange gentleman, turning thoughtfully to the Notary, 'indicated by this man of the dogs, is—how far from here—sixty miles?'

'From sixty to seventy.'

'Humph! If we travel post all night, we shall reach there in good time to-morrow morning. Now, the only question is, as they will not know me, and the child, God bless her, would think that any stranger pursuing them had a design upon her grandfather's liberty,—can I do better than take this lad, whom they both know and will readily remember, as an assurance to them of my friendly intentions?'

'Certainly not,' replied the Notary. 'Take Christopher by all means.'

'I beg your pardon, sir,' said Kit, who had listened to this discourse with a lengthening countenance, 'but if that's the reason, I'm afraid I should do more harm than good—Miss Nell, sir, *she* knows me, and would trust in me, I am sure; but old master—I don't know why, gentlemen; nobody does—would not bear me in his sight after he had been ill, and Miss Nell herself told me that I must not go near him or let him see me any more. I should spoil all that you were doing if I went, I'm afraid. I'd give the world to go, but you had better not take me, sir.'

'Another difficulty!' cried the impetuous gentleman. 'Was ever man so beset as I? Is there nobody else that knew them, nobody else in whom they had any confidence? Solitary as their lives were, is there no one person who would serve my purpose?'

'*Is* there, Christopher?' said the Notary.

'Not one, sir,' replied Kit. 'Yes, though—there's my mother.'

'Did they know her?' said the single gentleman.

'Know her, sir! why, she was always coming backwards and forwards. They were as kind to her as they were to me. Bless you, sir, she expected they'd come back to her house.'

'Then where the devil is the woman?' said the impatient gentleman, catching up his hat. 'Why isn't she here? Why is that woman always out of the way when she is most wanted?'

In a word, the single gentleman was bursting out of the office, bent upon laying violent hands on Kit's mother, forcing her into a post-chaise, and carrying her off, when this novel kind of abduction was with some difficulty prevented by the joint efforts of Mr. Abel and the Notary, who restrained him by dint of their remonstrances, and persuaded him to sound

Kit upon the probability of her being able and willing to undertake such a journey on so short a notice.

This occasioned some doubts on the part of Kit, and some violent demonstrations on that of the single gentleman, and a great many soothing speeches on that of the Notary and Mr. Abel. The upshot of the business was, that Kit, after weighing the matter in his mind and considering it carefully, promised, on behalf of his mother, that she should be ready within two hours from that time to undertake the expedition, and engaged to produce her in that place, in all respects equipped and prepared for the journey, before the specified period had expired.

Having given this pledge, which was rather a bold one, and not particularly easy of redemption, Kit lost no time in sallying forth, and taking measures for its immediate fulfilment.

CHAPTER XLI

KIT made his way through the crowded streets, dividing the stream of people, dashing across the busy roadways, diving into lanes and alleys, and stopping or turning aside for nothing, until he came in front of the Old Curiosity Shop, when he came to a stand; partly from habit and partly from being out of breath.

It was a gloomy autumn evening, and he thought the old place had never looked so dismal as in its dreary twilight. The windows broken, the rusty sashes rattling in their frames, the deserted house a dull barrier dividing the glaring lights and bustle of the street into two long lines, and standing in the midst, cold, dark, and empty,—presented a cheerless spectacle which mingled harshly with the bright prospects the boy had been building up for its late inmates, and came like a disappointment or misfortune. Kit would have had a good fire roaring up the empty chimneys, lights sparkling and shining through the windows, people moving briskly to and fro, voices in cheerful conversation, something in unison with the new hopes that were astir. He had not expected that the house would wear any different aspect—had known indeed that it could not—but coming upon it in the midst of eager thoughts and expectations, it checked the current in its flow, and darkened it with a mournful shadow.

Kit, however, fortunately for himself, was not learned enough or contemplative enough to be troubled with presages of evil afar off, and, having no mental spectacles to assist his vision in this respect, saw nothing but the dull house, which jarred uncomfortably upon his previous thoughts. So, almost wishing that he had not passed it, though hardly knowing why, he hurried on again, making up by his increased speed for the few moments he had lost.

'Now, if she should be out,' thought Kit, as he approached the poor dwelling of his mother, 'and I not able to find her, this impatient gentleman would be in a pretty taking. And sure enough there's no light, and the door's fast. Now, God forgive me for saying so, but if this is Little Bethel's doing, I wish Little Bethel was—was farther off,' said Kit checking himself, and knocking at the door.

A second knock brought no reply from within the house;

but caused a woman over the way to look out and inquire who that was, awanting Mrs. Nubbles.

'Me,' said Kit. 'She's at—at Little Bethel, I suppose?'—getting out the name of the obnoxious conventicle with some reluctance, and laying a spiteful emphasis upon the words.

The neighbour nodded assent.

'Then pray tell me where it is,' said Kit, 'for I have come on a pressing matter, and must fetch her out, even if she was in the pulpit.'

It was not very easy to procure a direction to the fold in question, as none of the neighbours were of the flock that resorted thither, and few knew anything more of it than the name. At last, a gossip of Mrs. Nubbles's, who had accompanied her to chapel on one or two occasions when a comfortable cup of tea had preceded her devotions, furnished the needful information, which Kit had no sooner obtained than he started off again.

Little Bethel might have been nearer, and might have been in a straighter road, though in that case the reverend gentleman who presided over its congregation would have lost his favourite allusion to the crooked ways by which it was approached, and which enabled him to liken it to Paradise itself, in contradistinction to the parish church and the broad thoroughfare leading thereunto. Kit found it, at last, after some trouble, and pausing at the door to take breath that he might enter with becoming decency, passed into the chapel.

It was not badly named in one respect, being in truth a particularly little Bethel—a Bethel of the smallest dimensions—with a small number of small pews, and a small pulpit, in which a small gentleman (by trade a Shoemaker, and by calling a Divine) was delivering in a by no means small voice, a by no means small sermon, judging of its dimensions by the condition of his audience, which, if their gross amount were but small, comprised a still smaller number of hearers, as the majority were slumbering.

Among these was Kit's mother, who, finding it matter of extreme difficulty to keep her eyes open after the fatigues of last night, and feeling their inclination to close strongly backed and seconded by the arguments of the preacher, had yielded to the drowsiness that overpowered her, and fallen asleep; though not so soundly but that she could, from time to time, utter a slight and almost inaudible groan, as if in recognition of the orator's doctrines. The baby in her arms was as fast asleep as she; and little Jacob, whose youth prevented him from recognising in this prolonged spiritual nourishment anything half as interesting as oysters, was alternately very fast asleep and very wide awake, as his inclination to slumber, or his terror of being personally alluded to in the discourse, gained the mastery over him.

'And now I'm here,' thought Kit, gliding into the nearest empty pew which was opposite his mother's, and on the other side of the little aisle, 'how am I ever to get at her, or persuade her to come out? I might as well be twenty miles off. She'll never wake till it's all over, and there goes the clock again! If he would but leave off for a minute, or if they'd only sing!'—

But there was little encouragement to believe that either event would happen for a couple of hours to come. The preacher went on telling them what he meant to convince them of before he had done, and it was clear that if he only kept to one-half of his promises and forgot the other, he was good for that time at least.

In his desperation and restlessness Kit cast his eyes about the chapel, and happening to let them fall upon a little seat in front of the clerk's desk, could scarcely believe them when they showed him—Quilp!

He rubbed them twice or thrice, but still they insisted that Quilp was there, and there indeed he was, sitting with his hands upon his knees, and his hat between them on a little wooden bracket, with the accustomed grin on his dirty face, and his eyes fixed upon the ceiling. He certainly did not glance at Kit or at his mother, and appeared utterly unconscious of their presence; still Kit could not help feeling, directly, that the attention of the sly little fiend was fastened upon them, and upon nothing else.

But, astounded as he was by the apparition of the dwarf among the Little Bethelites, and not free from a misgiving that it was the forerunner of some trouble or annoyance, he was compelled to subdue his wonder and to take active measures for the withdrawal of his parent, as the evening was now creeping on, and the matter grew serious. Therefore, the next time little Jacob woke, Kit set himself to attract his wandering attention, and this not being a very difficult task (one sneeze effected it), he signed to him to rouse his mother.

Ill-luck would have it, however, that, just then, the preacher, in a forcible exposition of one head of his discourse, leaned over upon the pulpit-desk so that very little more of him than his legs remained inside; and, while he made vehement gestures with his right hand, and held on with his left, stared, or seemed to stare, straight into little Jacob's eyes, threatening him by his strained look and attitude—so it appeared to the child—that if he so much as moved a muscle, he, the preacher, would be literally, and not figuratively, 'down upon him' that instant. In this fearful state of things, distracted by the sudden appearance of Kit, and fascinated by the eyes of the preacher, the miserable Jacob sat bolt upright, wholly incapable of motion, strongly disposed to cry but afraid to do so, and returning his pastor's gaze until his infant eyes seemed starting from their sockets.

'If I must do it openly, I must,' thought Kit. With that he walked softly out of his pew and into his mother's, and, as Mr. Swiveller would have observed if he had been present, 'collared' the baby without speaking a word.

'Hush, mother!' whispered Kit. 'Come along with me, I've got something to tell you.'

'Where am I?' said Mrs. Nubbles.

'In this blessed Little Bethel,' returned her son, peevishly.

'Blessed indeed!' cried Mrs. Nubbles, catching at the word. 'Oh, Christopher, how have I been edified this night!'

'Yes, yes, I know,' said Kit hastily; 'but come along, mother, everybody's looking at us. Don't make a noise—bring Jacob—that's right!'

'Stay, Satan, stay!' cried the preacher, as Kit was moving off.

'The gentleman says you're to stay, Christopher,' whispered his mother.

'Stay, Satan, stay!' roared the preacher again. 'Tempt not the woman that doth incline her ear to thee, but hearken to the voice of him that calleth. He hath a lamb from the fold!' cried the preacher, raising his voice still higher and pointing to the baby. 'He beareth off a lamb, a precious lamb! He goeth about, like a wolf in the night season, and inveigleth the tender lambs!'

Kit was the best-tempered fellow in the world, but considering this strong language, and being somewhat excited by the circumstances in which he was placed, he faced round to the pulpit with the baby in his arms, and replied aloud:

'No, I don't. He's my brother.'

'He's *my* brother!' cried the preacher.

'He isn't,' said Kit indignantly. 'How can you say such a thing? And don't call me names if you please; what harm have I done? I shouldn't have come to take 'em away, unless I was obliged, you may depend upon that. I wanted to do it very quiet, but you wouldn't let me. Now, you have the goodness to abuse Satan and them, as much as you like, Sir, and to let me alone if you please.'

So saying, Kit marched out of the chapel, followed by his mother and little Jacob, and found himself in the open air, with an indistinct recollection of having seen the people wake up and look surprised, and of Quilp having remained throughout the interruption, in his old attitude, without moving his eyes from the ceiling, or appearing to take the smallest notice of anything that passed.

'Oh, Kit!' said his mother, with her handkerchief to her eyes, 'what have you done? I never can go there again—never!'

'I'm glad of it, mother. What was there in the little bit of pleasure you took last night that made it necessary for you to be low-spirited and sorrowful to-night? That's the way you do. If you're happy or merry ever, you come here to say, along with that chap, that you're sorry for it. More shame for you, mother, I was going to say.'

'Hush, dear!' said Mrs. Nubbles; 'you don't mean what you say, I know, but you're talking sinfulness.'

'Don't mean it? But I do mean it!' retorted Kit. 'I don't believe, mother, that harmless cheerfulness and good humour are thought greater sins in Heaven than shirt-collars are, and I do believe that those chaps are just about as right and sensible in putting down the one as in leaving off the other—that's my belief. But I won't say anything more about it, if you'll promise not to cry, that's all; and you take the baby that's a lighter weight, and give me little Jacob; and as we go along (which we must do pretty quick) I'll give you the news I bring, which will surprise you a little, I can tell you. There—that's right. Now you look as if you'd never seen Little Bethel in all your life, as I hope you never will again; and here's the baby; and little Jacob, you get atop of my back and catch hold of me tight round the neck, and whenever a Little Bethel parson calls you a precious lamb or says your brother's one, you tell him it's the truest thing he's said for a twelvemonth, and that if he'd got a little more of the lamb himself, and less of the

Kit's Mother on a Journey

(p. 310)

mint-sauce—not being quite so sharp and sour over it—I should like him all the better. That's what you've got to say to *him*, Jacob.'

Talking on in this way, half in jest and half in earnest, and cheering up his mother, the children, and himself, by the one simple process of determining to be in a good humour, Kit led them briskly forward; and on the road home, he related what had passed at the Notary's house, and the purpose with which he had intruded on the solemnities of Little Bethel.

His mother was not a little startled on learning what service was required of her, and presently fell into a confusion of ideas, of which the most prominent were that it was a great honour and dignity to ride in a post-chaise, and that it was a moral impossibility to leave the children behind. But this objection, and a great many others, founded on certain articles of dress being at the wash, and certain other articles having no existence in the wardrobe of Mrs. Nubbles, were overcome by Kit, who opposed to each and every of them, the pleasure of recovering Nell, and the delight it would be to bring her back in triumph.

'There's only ten minutes now, mother'—said Kit when they reached home. 'There's a bandbox. Throw in what you want, and we'll be off directly.'

To tell how Kit then hustled into the box all sorts of things which could, by no remote contingency, be wanted, and how he left out everything likely to be of the smallest use; how a neighbour was persuaded to come and stop with the children, and how the children at first cried dismally, and then laughed heartily on being promised all kinds of impossible and un-heard-of toys; how Kit's mother wouldn't leave off kissing them, and how Kit couldn't make up his mind to be vexed with her for doing it; would take more time and room than you and I can spare. So, passing over all such matters, it is sufficient to say that within a few minutes after the two hours had expired, Kit and his mother arrived at the Notary's door, where a post-chaise was already waiting.

'With four horses I declare!' said Kit, quite aghast at the preparations. 'Well you *are* going to do it, mother! Here she is, sir. Here's my mother. She's quite ready, sir.'

'That's well,' returned the gentleman. 'Now, don't be in a flutter, ma'am; you'll be taken great care of. Where's the box with the new clothing and necessaries for them?'

'Here it is,' said the Notary. 'In with it, Christopher.'

'All right, sir,' replied Kit. 'Quite ready now, sir.'

'Then come along,' said the single gentleman. And thereupon he gave his arm to Kit's mother, handed her into the carriage as politely as you please, and took his seat beside her.

Up went the steps, bang went the door, round whirled the wheels, and off they rattled, with Kit's mother hanging out at one window waving a damp pocket-handkerchief and screaming out a great many messages to little Jacob and the baby, of which nobody heard a word.

Kit stood in the middle of the road, and looked after them with tears in his eyes—not brought there by the departure he witnessed, but by the return to which he looked forward. 'They went away,' he thought, 'on foot, with nobody to speak to them or say a kind word at parting, and they'll come back, drawn by four horses, with this rich gentleman for their friend, and all their troubles over! She'll forget that she taught me to write—'

Whatever Kit thought about after this, took some time to think of, for he stood gazing up the lines of shining lamps, long after the chaise had disappeared, and did not return into the house until the Notary and Mr. Abel, who had themselves lingered outside till the sound of the wheels was no longer distinguishable, had several times wondered what could possibly detain him.

CHAPTER XLII

IT behoves us to leave Kit for a while, thoughtful and expectant, and to follow the fortunes of little Nell; resuming
the thread of the narrative at the point where it was left, some
chapters back.

In one of those wanderings in the evening time, when,
following the two sisters at a humble distance, she felt, in her
sympathy with them and her recognition in their trials of
something akin to her own loneliness of spirit, a comfort and
consolation which made such moments a time of deep delight,
though the softened pleasure they yielded was of that kind
which lives and dies in tears—in one of those wanderings at
the quiet hour of twilight, when sky, and earth, and air, and
rippling water, and sound of distant bells, claimed kindred
with the emotions of the solitary child, and inspired her with
soothing thoughts, but not of a child's world or its easy joys—
in one of those rambles which had now become her only
pleasure or relief from care, light had faded into darkness and
evening deepened into night, and still the young creature
lingered in the gloom; feeling a companionship in Nature so
serene and still, when noise of tongues and glare of garish
lights would have been solitude indeed.

The sisters had gone home, and she was alone. She raised
her eyes to the bright stars, looking down so mildly from the
wide worlds of air, and, gazing on them, found new stars burst
upon her view, and more beyond, and more beyond again,
until the whole great expanse sparkled with shining spheres,
rising higher and higher in immeasurable space, eternal in
their numbers as in their changeless and incorruptible existence. She bent over the calm river, and saw them shining in
the same majestic order as when the dove beheld them gleaming through the swollen waters, upon the mountain-tops down
far below, and dead mankind, a million fathoms deep.

The child sat silently beneath a tree, hushed in her very
breath by the stillness of the night, and all its attendant
wonders. The time and place awoke reflection, and she
thought with a quiet hope—less hope, perhaps, than resignation—on the past, and present, and what was yet before her.
Between the old man and herself there had come a gradual
separation, harder to bear than any former sorrow. Every

evening, and often in the day-time too, he was absent, alone; and although she well knew where he went, and why—too well from the constant drain upon her scanty purse and from his haggard look—he evaded all inquiry, maintained a strict reserve, and even shunned her presence.

She sat meditating sorrowfully upon this change, and mingling it, as it were, with everything about her, when the distant church-clock bell struck nine. Rising at the sound, she retraced her steps, and turned thoughtfully towards the town.

She had gained a little wooden bridge, which, thrown across the stream, led into a meadow in her way, when she came suddenly upon a ruddy light, and looking forward more attentively, discerned that it proceeded from what appeared to be an encampment of gipsies, who had made a fire in one corner at no great distance from the path, and were sitting or lying round it. As she was too poor to have any fear of them, she did not alter her course, (which, indeed, she could not have done without going a long way round,) but quickened her pace a little, and kept straight on.

A movement of timid curiosity impelled her, when she approached the spot, to glance towards the fire. There was a form between it and her, the outline strongly developed against the light, which caused her to stop abruptly. Then, as if she had reasoned with herself and were assured that it could not be, or had satisfied herself that it was not that of the person she had supposed, she went on again.

But at that instant the conversation, whatever it was, which had been carried on near this fire was resumed, and the tones of the voice that spoke—she could not distinguish words—sounded as familiar to her as her own.

She turned, and looked back. The person had been seated before, but was now in a standing posture, and leaning forward on a stick on which he rested both hands. The attitude was no less familiar to her than the tone of voice had been. It *was* her grandfather.

Her first impulse was to call to him; her next to wonder who his associates could be, and for what purpose they were together. Some vague apprehension succeeded, and, yielding to the strong inclination it awakened, she drew nearer to the place; not advancing across the open field, however, but creeping towards it by the hedge.

A Parley with the Cardsharpers

In this way she advanced within a few feet of the fire, and standing among a few young trees, could both see and hear, without much danger of being observed.

There were no women or children, as she had seen in other gipsy camps they had passed in their wayfaring, and but one gipsy—a tall athletic man, who stood with his arms folded, leaning against a tree at a little distance off, looking now at the fire, and now, under his black eyelashes, at three other men who were there, with a watchful but half-concealed interest in their conversation. Of these, her grandfather was one; the others she recognised as the first card-players at the public-house on the eventful night of the storm—the man whom they had called Isaac List, and his gruff companion. One of the low, arched gipsy-tents, common to that people, was pitched hard by, but it either was, or appeared to be, empty.

'Well, are you going?' said the stout man, looking up from the ground where he was lying at his ease, into her grand-father's face. 'You were in a mighty hurry a minute ago. Go, if you like. You're your own master, I hope?'

'Don't vex him,' returned Isaac List, who was squatting like a frog on the other side of the fire, and had so screwed himself up that he seemed to be squinting all over; 'he didn't mean any offence.'

'You keep me poor, and plunder me, and make a sport and jest of me besides,' said the old man, turning from one to the other. 'Ye'll drive me mad among ye.'

The utter irresolution and feebleness of the grey-haired child, contrasted with the keen and cunning looks of those in whose hands he was, smote upon the little listener's heart. But she constrained herself to attend to all that passed, and to note each look and word.

'Confound you, what do you mean?' said the stout man, rising a little, and supporting himself on his elbow. 'Keep *you* poor! You'd keep us poor if you could, wouldn't you? That's the way with you whining, puny, pitiful players. When you lose, you're martyrs; but I don't find that when you win, you look upon the other losers in that light. As to plunder!' cried the fellow, raising his voice—'Damme, what do you mean by such ungentlemanly language as plunder, eh?'

The speaker laid himself down again at full length, and gave one or two short, angry kicks, as if in further expression of his unbounded indignation. It was quite plain that he acted the

o

bully, and his friend the peacemaker, for some particular purpose; or rather, it would have been to any one but the weak old man; for they exchanged glances quite openly, both with each other and with the gipsy, who grinned his approval of the jest until his white teeth shone again.

The old man stood helplessly among them for a little time, and then said, turning to his assailant:

'You yourself were speaking of plunder just now, you know. Don't be so violent with me. You were, were you not?'

'Not of plundering among present company! Honour among—among gentlemen, sir,' returned the other, who seemed to have been very near giving an awkward termination to the sentence.

'Don't be hard upon him, Jowl,' said Isaac List. 'He's very sorry for giving offence. There—go on with what you were saying—go on.'

'I'm a jolly old tender-hearted lamb, I am,' cried Mr. Jowl, 'to be sitting here at my time of life giving advice when I know it won't be taken, and that I shall get nothing but abuse for my pains. But that's the way I've gone through life. Experience has never put a chill upon my warm-heartedness.'

'I tell you he's very sorry, don't I?' remonstrated Isaac List, 'and that he wishes you'd go on.'

'*Does* he wish it?' said the other.

'Ay,' groaned the old man sitting down, and rocking himself to and fro. 'Go on, go on. It's in vain to fight with it; I can't do it; go on.'

'I go on then,' said Jowl, 'where I left off, when you got up so quick. If you're persuaded that it's time for luck to turn, as it certainly is, and find that you haven't means enough to try it, (and that's where it is, for you know, yourself, that you never have the funds to keep on long enough at a sitting,) help yourself to what seems put in your way on purpose. Borrow it, I say, and, when you're able, pay it back again.'

'Certainly,' Isaac List struck in, 'if this good lady as keeps the wax-works has money, and does keep it in a tin box when she goes to bed, and doesn't lock her door for fear of fire, it seems a easy thing; quite a Providence, *I* should call it—but then I've been religiously brought up.'

'You see, Isaac,' said his friend, growing more eager, and drawing himself closer to the old man, while he signed to the gipsy not to come between them; 'you see, Isaac, strangers are going in and out every hour of the day; nothing would be more likely than for one of these strangers to get under the good lady's bed, or lock himself in the cupboard; suspicion would be very wide, and would fall a long way from the mark, no doubt. I'd give him his revenge to the last farthing he brought, whatever the amount was.'

'But could you?' urged Isaac List. 'Is your bank strong enough?'

'Strong enough!' answered the other, with assumed disdain. 'Here, you sir, give me that box out of the straw!'

This was addressed to the gipsy, who crawled into the low tent on all-fours, and after some rummaging and rustling returned with a cash-box, which the man who had spoken opened with a key he wore about his person.

'Do you see this?' he said, gathering up the money in his hand and letting it drop back into the box, between his fingers, like water. 'Do you hear it? Do you know the sound of gold? There, put it back—and don't talk about banks again, Isaac, till you've got one of your own.'

Isaac List, with great apparent humility, protested that he had never doubted the credit of a gentleman so notorious for his honourable dealing as Mr. Jowl, and that he had hinted at the production of the box, not for the satisfaction of his doubts, for he could have none, but with a view to being regaled with a sight of so much wealth, which, though it might be deemed by some but an unsubstantial and visionary pleasure, was to one in his circumstances a source of extreme delight, only to be surpassed by its safe depository in his own personal pockets. Although Mr. List and Mr. Jowl addressed themselves to each other, it was remarkable that they both looked narrowly at the old man, who, with his eyes fixed upon the fire, sat brooding over it, yet listening eagerly—as it seemed from a certain involuntary motion of the head, or twitching of the face from time to time—to all they said.

'My advice,' said Jowl, lying down again with a careless air, 'is plain—I have given it, in fact. I act as a friend. Why should I help a man to the means perhaps of winning all I have, unless I considered him my friend? It's foolish, I dare say, to be so thoughtful of the welfare of other people, but that's my constitution, and I can't help it; so don't blame me, Isaac List.'

'*I* blame you!' returned the person addressed; 'not for the world, Mr. Jowl. I wish I could afford to be as liberal as you; and, as you say, he might pay it back if he won—and if he lost—'

'You're not to take that into consideration at all,' said Jowl. 'But suppose he did, (and nothing's less likely, from all I know of chances,) why, it's better to lose other people's money than one's own, I hope?'

'Ah!' cried Isaac List rapturously, 'the pleasures of winning! The delight of picking up the money—the bright, shining yellow-boys—and sweeping 'em into one's pocket! The deliciousness of having a triumph at last, and thinking that one didn't stop short and turn back, but went half-way to meet it! The——but you're not going, old gentleman?'

'I'll do it,' said the old man, who had risen and taken two or three hurried steps away, and now returned as hurriedly. 'I'll have it, every penny.'

'Why, that's brave,' cried Isaac, jumping up and slapping him on the shoulder; 'and I respect you for having so much young blood left. Ha, ha, ha! Joe Jowl's half sorry he advised you now. We've got the laugh against him. Ha, ha, ha!'

'He gives me my revenge, mind,' said the old man, pointing to him eagerly with his shrivelled hand: 'mind—he stakes coin against coin, down to the last one in the box, be there many or few. Remember that!'

'I'm witness,' returned Isaac. 'I'll see fair between you.'

'I have passed my word,' said Jowl with feigned reluctance, 'and I'll keep it. When does this match come off? I wish it was over.—To-night?'

'I must have the money first,' said the old man; 'and that I'll have to-morrow—'

'Why not to-night?' urged Jowl.

'It's late now, and I should be flushed and flurried,' said the old man. 'It must be softly done. No, to-morrow night.'

'Then to-morrow be it,' said Jowl. 'A drop of comfort here. Luck to the best man! Fill!'

The gipsy produced three tin cups, and filled them to the brim with brandy. The old man turned aside and muttered to himself before he drank. Her own name struck upon the listener's ear, coupled with some wish so fervent, that he seemed to breathe it in an agony of supplication.

'God be merciful to us!' cried the child within herself, 'and help us in this trying hour! What shall I do to save him?'

The remainder of their conversation was carried on in a lower tone of voice, and was sufficiently concise; relating merely to the execution of the project, and the best precautions for diverting suspicion. The old man then shook hands with his tempters, and withdrew.

They watched his bowed and stooping figure as it retreated slowly, and when he turned his head to look back, which he often did, waved their hands, or shouted some brief encouragement. It was not until they had seen him gradually diminish into a mere speck upon the distant road, that they turned to each other, and ventured to laugh aloud.

'So,' said Jowl, warming his hands at the fire, 'it's done at last. He wanted more persuading than I expected. It's three weeks ago, since we first put this in his head. What'll he bring, do you think?'

'Whatever he brings, it's halved between us,' returned Isaac List.

The other man nodded. 'We must make quick work of it,' he said, 'and then cut his acquaintance, or we may be suspected. Sharp's the word.'

List and the gipsy acquiesced. When they had all three amused themselves a little with their victim's infatuation, they dismissed the subject as one which had been sufficiently discussed, and began to talk in a jargon which the child did not understand. As their discourse appeared to relate to matters in which they were warmly interested, however, she deemed it the best time for escaping unobserved; and crept away with slow and cautious steps, keeping in the shadow of the hedges, or forcing a path through them or the dry ditches, until she could emerge upon the road at a point beyond their range of vision. Then she fled homeward as quickly as she could, torn and bleeding from the wounds of thorns and briars, but more lacerated in mind, and threw herself upon her bed, distracted.

The first idea that flashed upon her mind was flight, instant flight; dragging him from that place, and rather dying of want upon the roadside, than ever exposing him again, to such terrible temptations. Then, she remembered that the crime was not to be committed until next night, and there was the intermediate time for thinking, and resolving what to do. Then, she was distracted with a horrible fear that he might be committing it at that moment; with a dread of hearing shrieks and cries piercing the silence of the night; with fearful thoughts of what he might be tempted and led on to do, if he were detected in the act, and had but a woman to struggle with. It was impossible to bear such torture. She stole to the room where the money was, opened the door, and looked in. God be praised! He was not there, and she was sleeping soundly.

She went back to her own room, and tried to prepare herself for bed. But who could sleep—sleep! who could lie passively down, distracted by such terrors? They came upon her more and more strongly yet. Half undressed, and with her hair in wild disorder, she flew to the old man's bedside, clasped him by the wrist, and roused him from his sleep.

'What's this?' he cried, starting up in bed, and fixing his eyes upon her spectral face.

'I have had a dreadful dream,' said the child, with an energy that nothing but such terrors could have inspired. 'A dreadful, horrible dream. I have had it once before. It is a dream of grey-haired men like you, in darkened rooms by night, robbing sleepers of their gold. Up, up!' The old man shook in every joint, and folded his hands like one who prays.

'Not to me,' said the child, 'not to me—to Heaven, to save us from such deeds! This dream is too real. I cannot sleep, I cannot stay here, I cannot leave you alone under the roof where such dreams come. Up! We must fly.'

He looked at her as if she were a spirit—she might have been for all the look of earth she had—and trembled more and more.

'There is no time to lose; I will not lose one minute,' said the child. 'Up! and away with me!'

'To-night?' murmured the old man.

'Yes, to-night,' replied the child. 'To-morrow night will be too late. The dream will have come again. Nothing but flight can save us. Up!'

The old man rose from his bed: his forehead bedewed with the cold sweat of fear; and, bending before the child as if she had been an angel messenger sent to lead him where she would, made ready to follow her. She took him by the hand and led him on. As they passed the door of the room he had proposed to rob, she shuddered and looked up into his face. What a white face was that, and with what a look did he meet hers!

She took him to her own chamber, and, still holding him by the hand as if she feared to lose him for an instant, gathered together the little stock she had, and hung her basket on her arm. The old man took his wallet from her hands and strapped it on his shoulders—his staff, too, she had brought away—and then she led him forth.

Through the strait streets, and narrow crooked outskirts, their trembling feet passed quickly. Up the steep hill too, crowned by the old grey castle, they toiled with rapid steps, and had not once looked behind.

But as they drew nearer the ruined walls, the moon rose in all her gentle glory, and, from their venerable age, garlanded with ivy, moss, and waving grass, the child looked back upon the sleeping town, deep in the valley's shade: and on the far-off river with its winding track of light: and on the distant hills; and as she did so, she clasped the hand she held, less firmly, and bursting into tears, fell upon the old man's neck.

CHAPTER XLIII

HER momentary weakness past, the child again summoned the resolution which had until now sustained her, and, endeavouring to keep steadily in her view the one idea that they were flying from disgrace and crime, and that her grandfather's preservation must depend solely on her firmness, unaided by one word of advice or any helping hand, urged him onward and looked back no more.

While he, subdued and abashed, seemed to crouch before her, and to shrink and cower down, as if in the presence of some superior creature, the child herself was sensible of a new feeling within her, which elevated her nature, and inspired her with an energy and confidence she had never known. There was no divided responsibility now; the whole burden of their two lives had fallen upon her, and henceforth she must think and act for both. 'I have saved him,' she thought. 'In all dangers and distresses, I will remember that.'

At any other time, the recollection of having deserted the friend who had shown them so much homely kindness, without a word of justification—the thought that they were guilty, in appearance, of treachery and ingratitude—even the having parted from the two sisters—would have filled her with sorrow and regret. But now, all other considerations were lost in the new uncertainties and anxieties of their wild and wandering life; and the very desperation of their condition roused and stimulated her.

In the pale moonlight, which lent a wanness of its own to the delicate face where thoughtful care already mingled with the winning grace and loveliness of youth, the too bright eye, the spiritual head, the lips that pressed each other with such high resolve and courage of the heart, the slight figure firm in its bearing and yet so very weak, told their silent tale; but told it only to the wind that rustled by, which, taking up its burden, carried, perhaps to some mother's pillow, faint dreams of childhood fading in its bloom, and resting in the sleep that knows no waking.

The night crept on apace, the moon went down, the stars grew pale and dim, and morning, cold as they, slowly approached. Then, from behind a distant hill, the noble sun rose up, driving the mists in phantom shapes before it, and

Flight by Water

(p. 322)

clearing the earth of their ghostly forms till darkness came again. When it had climbed higher into the sky, and there was warmth in its cheerful beams, they laid them down to sleep, upon a bank, hard by some water.

But Nell retained her grasp upon the old man's arm, and long after he was slumbering soundly, watched him with untiring eyes. Fatigue stole over her at last; her grasp relaxed, tightened, relaxed again, and they slept side by side.

A confused sound of voices, mingling with her dreams, awoke her. A man of very uncouth and rough appearance was standing over them, and two of his companions were looking on, from a long heavy boat which had come close to the bank while they were sleeping. The boat had neither oar nor sail, but was towed by a couple of horses, who, with the rope to which they were harnessed slack and dripping in the water, were resting on the path.

'Holloa!' said the man roughly. 'What's the matter here?'

'We were only asleep, sir,' said Nell. 'We have been walking all night.'

'A pair of queer travellers to be walking all night,' observed the man who had first accosted them. 'One of you is a trifle too old for that sort of work, and the other a trifle too young. Where are you going?'

Nell faltered, and pointed at hazard towards the West, upon which the man inquired if she meant a certain town which he named. Nell, to avoid more questioning, said 'Yes, that was the place.'

'Where have you come from?' was the next question; and this being an easier one to answer, Nell mentioned the name of the village in which their friend the schoolmaster dwelt, as being less likely to be known to the men or to provoke further inquiry.

'I thought somebody had been robbing and ill-using you, might be,' said the man. 'That's all. Good day.'

Returning his salute and feeling greatly relieved by his departure, Nell looked after him as he mounted one of the horses, and the boat went on. It had not gone very far, when it stopped again, and she saw the men beckoning to her.

'Did you call to me?' said Nell, running up to them.

'You may go with us if you like,' replied one of those in the boat. 'We're going to the same place.'

The child hesitated for a moment. Thinking, as she had

thought with great trepidation more than once before, that the men whom she had seen with her grandfather might, perhaps, in their eagerness for the booty, follow them, and, regaining their influence over him, set hers at nought; and that if they went with these men, all traces of them must surely be lost at that spot; determined to accept the offer. The boat came close to the bank again, and before she had had any more time for consideration, she and her grandfather were on board, and gliding smoothly down the canal.

The sun shone pleasantly on the bright water, which was sometimes shaded by trees, and sometimes open to a wide extent of country, intersected by running streams, and rich with wooded hills, cultivated land, and sheltered farms. Now and then, a village with its modest spire, thatched roofs, and gable-ends, would peep out from among the trees; and, more than once, a distant town, with great church towers looming through its smoke, and high factories or workshops rising above the mass of houses, would come in view, and, by the length of time it lingered in the distance, show them how slowly they travelled. Their way lay, for the most part, through the low grounds, and open plains; and except these distant places, and occasionally some men working in the fields, or lounging on the bridges under which they passed, to see them creep along, nothing encroached on their monotonous and secluded track.

Nell was rather disheartened, when they stopped at a kind of wharf late in the afternoon, to learn from one of the men that they would not reach their place of destination until next day, and that, if she had no provision with her, she had better buy it there. She had but a few pence, having already bargained with them for some bread, but even of these it was necessary to be very careful, as they were on their way to an utterly strange place, with no resource whatever. A small loaf and a morsel of cheese, therefore, were all she could afford, and with these she took her place in the boat again, and, after half an hour's delay during which the men were drinking at the public-house, proceeded on the journey.

They brought some beer and spirits into the boat with them, and what with drinking freely before, and again now, were soon in a fair way of being quarrelsome and intoxicated. Avoiding the small cabin, therefore, which was very dark and filthy, and to which they often invited both her and her grandfather,

Nell sat in the open air with the old man by her side: listening
to their boisterous hosts with a palpitating heart, and almost
wishing herself safe on shore again though she should have to
walk all night.

They were, in truth, very rugged, noisy fellows, and quite
brutal among themselves, though civil enough to their two
passengers. Thus, when a quarrel arose between the man who
was steering and his friend in the cabin, upon the question
who had first suggested the propriety of offering Nell some
beer, and when the quarrel led to a scuffle in which they beat
each other fearfully, to her inexpressible terror, neither visited
his displeasure upon her, but each contented himself with
venting it on his adversary, on whom, in addition to blows,
he bestowed a variety of compliments, which, happily for the
child, were conveyed in terms, to her quite unintelligible.
The difference was finally adjusted, by the man who had come
out of the cabin knocking the other into it head first, and taking
the helm into his own hands, without evincing the least
discomposure himself, or causing any in his friend, who, being
of a tolerably strong constitution and perfectly inured to such
trifles, went to sleep as he was, with his heels upwards, and
in a couple of minutes or so was snoring comfortably.

By this time it was night again, and though the child felt
cold, being but poorly clad, her anxious thoughts were far
removed from her own suffering or uneasiness, and busily
engaged in endeavouring to devise some scheme for their joint
subsistence. The same spirit which had supported her on the
previous night, upheld and sustained her now. Her grandfather lay sleeping safely at her side, and the crime to which his
madness urged him, was not committed. That was her comfort.

How every circumstance of her short, eventful life, came
thronging into her mind, as they travelled on! Slight incidents,
never thought of or remembered until now; faces, seen once
and ever since forgotten; words, scarcely heeded at the time;
scenes, of a year ago and those of yesterday, mixing up and
linking themselves together; familiar places shaping themselves
out in the darkness from things which, when approached, were,
of all others, the most remote and most unlike them; sometimes, a strange confusion in her mind relative to the occasion
of her being there, and the place to which she was going, and
the people she was with; and imagination suggesting remarks
and questions which sounded so plainly in her ears, that she

would start, and turn, and be almost tempted to reply;—all the fancies and contradictions common in watching and excitement and restless change of place, beset the child.

She happened, while she was thus engaged, to encounter the face of the man on deck, in whom the sentimental stage of drunkenness had now succeeded to the boisterous, and who, taking from his mouth a short pipe, quilted over with string for its longer preservation, requested that she would oblige him with a song.

'You've got a very pretty voice, a very soft eye, and a very strong memory,' said this gentleman; 'the voice and eye I've got evidence for, and the memory's an opinion of my own. And I'm never wrong. Let me hear a song this minute.'

'I don't think I know one, sir,' returned Nell.

'You know forty-seven songs,' said the man, with a gravity which admitted of no altercation on the subject. 'Forty-seven's your number. Let me hear one of 'em—the best. Give me a song this minute.'

Not knowing what might be the consequences of irritating her friend, and trembling with the fear of doing so, poor Nell sang him some little ditty which she had learned in happier times, and which was so agreeable to his ear, that on its conclusion he in the same peremptory manner requested to be favoured with another, to which he was so obliging as to roar a chorus to no particular tune, and with no words at all, but which amply made up in its amazing energy for its deficiency in other respects. The noise of this vocal performance awakened the other man, who, staggering upon deck and shaking his late opponent by the hand, swore that singing was his pride and joy and chief delight, and that he desired no better entertainment. With a third call, more imperative than either of the two former, Nell felt obliged to comply, and this time a chorus was maintained not only by the two men together, but also by the third man on horseback, who being by his position debarred from a nearer participation in the revels of the night, roared when his companions roared, and rent the very air. In this way, with little cessation, and singing the same songs again and again, the tired and exhausted child kept them in good humour all that night; and many a cottager, who was roused from his soundest sleep by the discordant chorus as it floated away upon the wind, hid his head beneath the bed-clothes and trembled at the sounds.

Watching the Furnace Fire

(p. 331)

At length the morning dawned. It was no sooner light than it began to rain heavily. As the child could not endure the intolerable vapours of the cabin, they covered her, in return for her exertions, with some pieces of sail-cloth and ends of tarpaulin, which sufficed to keep her tolerably dry and to shelter her grandfather besides. As the day advanced the rain increased. At noon it poured down more hopelessly and heavily than ever, without the faintest promise of abatement.

They had, for some time, been gradually approaching the place for which they were bound. The water had become thicker and dirtier; other barges, coming from it, passed them frequently; the paths of coal-ash and huts of staring brick, marked the vicinity of some great manufacturing town; while scattered streets and houses, and smoke from distant furnaces, indicated that they were already in the outskirts. Now, the clustered roofs, and piles of buildings, trembling with the working of engines, and dimly resounding with their shrieks and throbbings; the tall chimneys vomiting forth a black vapour, which hung in a dense ill-favoured cloud above the housetops and filled the air with gloom; the clank of hammers beating upon iron, the roar of busy streets and noisy crowds, gradually augmenting until all the various sounds blended into one and none was distinguishable for itself, announced the termination of their journey.

The boat floated into the wharf to which it belonged. The men were occupied directly. The child and her grandfather, after waiting in vain to thank them, or ask them whither they should go, passed through a dirty lane into a crowded street, and stood, amid its din and tumult, and in the pouring rain, as strange, bewildered, and confused, as if they had lived a thousand years before, and were raised from the dead and placed there by a miracle.

CHAPTER XLIV

THE throng of people hurried by, in two opposite streams, with no symptom of cessation or exhaustion; intent upon their own affairs; and undisturbed in their business specula- tions, by the roar of carts and waggons laden with clashing wares, the slipping of horses' feet upon the wet and greasy pavement, the rattling of the rain on windows and umbrella- tops, the jostling of the more impatient passengers, and all the noise and tumult of a crowded street in the high tide of its occupation: while the two poor strangers, stunned and be- wildered by the hurry they beheld but had no part in, looked mournfully on; feeling, amidst the crowd, a solitude which has no parallel but in the thirst of the shipwrecked mariner, who, tost to and fro upon the billows of a mighty ocean, his red eyes blinded by looking on the water which hems him in on every side, has not one drop to cool his burning tongue.

They withdrew into a low archway for shelter from the rain, and watched the faces of those who passed, to find in one among them a ray of encouragement or hope. Some frowned, some smiled, some muttered to themselves, some made slight gestures, as if anticipating the conversation in which they would shortly be engaged, some wore the cunning look of bargaining and plotting, some were anxious and eager, some slow and dull; in some countenances, were written gain; in others, loss. It was like being in the confidence of all these people to stand quietly there, looking into their faces as they flitted past. In busy places, where each man has an object of his own, and feels assured that every other man has his, his character and purpose are written broadly in his face. In the public walks and lounges of a town, people go to see and to be seen, and there the same expression, with little variety, is repeated a hundred times. The working-day faces come nearer to the truth, and let it out more plainly.

Falling into that kind of abstraction which such a solitude awakens, the child continued to gaze upon the passing crowd with a wondering interest, amounting almost to a temporary forgetfulness of her own condition. But cold, wet, hunger, want of rest, and lack of any place in which to lay her aching head, soon brought her thoughts back to the point whence they had strayed. No one passed who seemed to notice them, or to whom she durst appeal. After some time, they left their place of refuge from the weather, and mingled with the concourse.

Evening came on. They were still wandering up and down, with fewer people about them, but with the same sense of solitude in their own breasts, and the same indifference from all around. The lights in the streets and shops made them feel yet more desolate, for with their help, night and darkness seemed to come on faster. Shivering with the cold and damp, ill in body, and sick to death at heart, the child needed her utmost firmness and resolution even to creep along.

Why had they ever come to this noisy town, when there were peaceful country places, in which, at least, they might have hungered and thirsted, with less suffering than in its squalid strife? They were but an atom, here, in a mountain-heap of misery, the very sight of which increased their hopelessness and suffering.

The child had not only to endure the accumulated hardships of their destitute condition, but to bear the reproaches of her grandfather, who began to murmur at having been led away from their late abode, and demand that they should return to it. Being now penniless, and no relief or prospect of relief appearing, they retraced their steps through the deserted streets, and went back to the wharf, hoping to find the boat in which they had come, and to be allowed to sleep on board that night. But here again they were disappointed, for the gate was closed, and some fierce dogs, barking at their approach, obliged them to retreat.

'We must sleep in the open air to-night, dear,' said the child in a weak voice, as they turned away from this last repulse; 'and to-morrow we will beg our way to some quiet part of the country, and try to earn our bread in very humble work.'

'Why did you bring me here?' returned the old man fiercely. 'I cannot bear these close eternal streets. We came from a quiet part. Why did you force me to leave it?'

'Because I must have that dream I told you of, no more,' said the child, with a momentary firmness that lost itself in tears; 'and we must live among poor people, or it will come again. Dear grandfather, you are old and weak, I know; but look at me. I never will complain if you will not, but I have some suffering indeed.'

'Ah! poor, houseless, wandering, motherless child!' cried

the old man, clasping his hands and gazing as if for the first time upon her anxious face, her travel-stained dress, and bruised and swollen feet; 'has all my agony of care brought her to this at last? Was I a happy man once, and have I lost happiness and all I had, for this?'

'If we were in the country now,' said the child, with assumed cheerfulness, as they walked on looking about them for a shelter, 'we should find some good old tree, stretching out his green arms as if he loved us, and nodding and rustling as if he would have us fall asleep, thinking of him while he watched. Please God, we shall be there soon—to-morrow or next day at the farthest—and in the meantime let us think, dear, that it was a good thing we came here; for we are lost in the crowd and hurry of this place, and if any cruel people should pursue us, they could surely never trace us further. There's comfort in that. And here's a deep old doorway—very dark, but quite dry, and warm too, for the wind don't blow in here— What's that?'

Uttering a half shriek, she recoiled from a black figure which came suddenly out of the dark recess in which they were about to take refuge, and stood still, looking at them.

'Speak again,' it said; 'do I know the voice?'

'No,' replied the child timidly; 'we are strangers, and having no money for a night's lodging, were going to rest here.'

There was a feeble lamp at no great distance; the only one in the place, which was a kind of square yard, but sufficient to show how poor and mean it was. To this, the figure beckoned them; at the same time drawing within its rays, as if to show that it had no desire to conceal itself or take them at an advantage.

The form was that of a man, miserably clad and begrimed with smoke, which, perhaps by its contrast with the natural colour of his skin, made him look paler than he really was. That he was naturally of a very wan and pallid aspect, however, his hollow cheeks, sharp features, and sunken eyes, no less than a certain look of patient endurance, sufficiently testified. His voice was harsh by nature, but not brutal; and though his face, besides possessing the characteristics already mentioned, was overshadowed by a quantity of long dark hair, its expression was neither ferocious nor bad.

'How came you to think of resting there?' he said. 'Or how,' he added, looking more attentively at the child, 'do you come to want a place of rest at this time of night?'

'Our misfortunes,' the grandfather answered, 'are the cause.'

'Do you know,' said the man, looking still more earnestly at Nell, 'how wet she is, and that the damp streets are not a place for her?'

'I know it well, God help me,' he replied. 'What can I do?'

The man looked at Nell again, and gently touched her garments, from which the rain was running off in little streams. 'I can give you warmth,' he said, after a pause; 'nothing else. Such lodging as I have, is in that house,' pointing to the doorway from which he had emerged, 'but she is safer and better there than here. The fire is in a rough place, but you can pass the night beside it safely, if you'll trust yourselves to me. You see that red light yonder?'

They raised their eyes, and saw a lurid glare hanging in the dark sky; the dull reflection of some distant fire.

'It's not far,' said the man. 'Shall I take you there? You were going to sleep upon cold bricks; I can give you a bed of warm ashes—nothing better.'

Without waiting for any further reply than he saw in their looks, he took Nell in his arms, and bade the old man follow.

Carrying her as tenderly, and as easily too, as if she had been an infant, and showing himself both swift and sure of foot, he led the way through what appeared to be the poorest and most wretched quarter of the town; and turning aside to avoid the overflowing kennels or running waterspouts, but holding his course, regardless of such obstructions, and making his way straight through them. They had proceeded thus, in silence, for some quarter of an hour, and had lost sight of the glare to which he had pointed, in the dark and narrow ways by which they had come, when it suddenly burst upon them again, streaming up from the high chimney of a building close before them.

'This is the place,' he said, pausing at a door to put Nell down and take her hand. 'Don't be afraid. There's nobody here will harm you.'

It needed a strong confidence in this assurance to induce them to enter, and what they saw inside did not diminish their apprehension and alarm. In a large and lofty building, supported by pillars of iron, with great black apertures in the upper walls, open to the external air; echoing to the roof with the beating of hammers and roar of furnaces, mingled with the hissing of red-hot metal plunged in water, and a hundred strange unearthly noises never heard elsewhere; in this gloomy place, moving like demons among the flame and smoke, dimly and fitfully seen, flushed and tormented by the burning fires, and wielding great weapons, a faulty blow from any one of which must have crushed some workman's skull, a number of men laboured like giants. Others, reposing upon heaps of coals or ashes, with their faces turned to the black vault above, slept or rested from their toil. Others again, opening the white-hot furnace-doors, cast fuel on the flames, which came rushing and roaring forth to meet it, and licked it up like oil. Others drew forth, with clashing noise, upon the ground, great sheets of glowing steel, emitting an insupportable heat, and a dull deep light like that which reddens in the eyes of savage beasts.

Through these bewildering sights and deafening sounds, their conductor led them to where, in a dark portion of the building, one furnace burnt by night and day—so, at least, they gathered from the motion of his lips, for as yet they could only see him speak: not hear him. The man who had been watching this fire, and whose task was ended for the present, gladly withdrew, and left them with their friend, who, spreading Nell's little cloak upon a heap of ashes, and showing her where she could hang her outer clothes to dry, signed to her and the old man to lie down and sleep. For himself, he took his station on a rugged mat before the furnace-door, and resting his chin upon his hands, watched the flame as it shone through the iron chinks, and the white ashes as they fell into their bright hot grave below.

The warmth of her bed, hard and humble as it was, combined with the great fatigue she had undergone, soon caused the tumult of the place to fall with a gentler sound upon the child's tired ears, and was not long in lulling her to sleep. The old man was stretched beside her, and with her hand upon his neck she lay and dreamed.

It was yet night when she awoke, nor did she know how long, or for how short a time, she had slept. But she found herself protected, both from any cold air that might find its way into the building, and from the scorching heat, by some of the workmen's clothes; and glancing at their friend saw that he sat in exactly the same attitude, looking with a fixed earnestness of attention towards the fire, and keeping so very still that he did not even seem to breathe. She lay in the state between sleeping and waking, looking so long at his motionless figure that at length she almost feared he had died as he sat there; and softly rising and drawing close to him, ventured to whisper in his ear.

He moved, and glancing from her to the place she had lately occupied, as if to assure himself that it was really the child so near him, looked inquiringly into her face.

'I feared you were ill,' she said. 'The other men are all in motion, and you are so very quiet.'

'They leave me to myself,' he replied. 'They know my humour. They laugh at me, but don't harm me in it. See yonder there—that's *my* friend.'

'The fire?' said the child.

'It has been alive as long as I have,' the man made answer. 'We talk and think together all night long.'

The child glanced quickly at him in her surprise, but he had turned his eyes in their former direction, and was musing as before.

'It's like a book to me,' he said—'the only book I ever learned to read; and many an old story it tells me. It's music, for I should know its voice among a thousand, and there are other voices in its roar. It has its pictures too. You don't know how many strange faces and different scenes I trace in the red-hot coals. It's my memory, that fire, and shows me all my life.'

The child, bending down to listen to his words, could not help remarking with what brightened eyes he continued to speak and muse.

'Yes,' he said, with a faint smile, 'it was the same when I was quite a baby, and crawled about it, till I fell asleep. My father watched it then.'

'Had you no mother?' asked the child.

'No, she was dead. Women work hard in these parts. She worked herself to death they told me, and, as they said so then, the fire has gone on saying the same thing ever since. I suppose it was true. I have always believed it.'

'Were you brought up here, then?' said the child.

'Summer and winter,' he replied. 'Secretly at first, but when they found it out, they let him keep me here. So the fire nursed me—the same fire. It has never gone out.'

'You are fond of it?' said the child.

'Of course I am. He died before it. I saw him fall down—just there, where those ashes are burning now—and wondered, I remember, why it didn't help him.'

'Have you been here ever since?' asked the child.

'Ever since I came to watch it; but there was a while between, and a very cold dreary while it was. It burned all the time though, and roared and leaped when I came back, as it used to do in our play days. You may guess, from looking at me, what kind of child I was, but for all the difference between us I *was* a child, and when I saw you in the street to-night, you put me in mind of myself, as I was after he died, and made me wish to bring you to the fire. I thought of those old times again, when I saw you sleeping by it. You should be sleeping now. Lie down again, poor child, lie down again!'

With that, he led her to her rude couch, and covering her with the clothes with which she had found herself enveloped when she woke, returned to his seat, whence he moved no more unless to feed the furnace, but remained motionless as a statue. The child continued to watch him for a little time, but soon yielded to the drowsiness that came upon her, and, in the dark strange place and on the heap of ashes, slept as peacefully as if the room had been a palace chamber, and the bed, a bed of down.

When she awoke again, broad day was shining through the lofty openings in the walls, and, stealing in slanting rays but midway down, seemed to make the building darker than it had been at night. The clang and tumult were still going on, and the remorseless fires were burning fiercely as before; for few changes of night and day brought rest or quiet there.

Her friend parted his breakfast—a scanty mess of coffee and some coarse bread—with the child and her grandfather, and inquired whither they were going. She told him that they sought some distant country place remote from towns or even other villages, and with a faltering tongue inquired what road they would do best to take.

'I know little of the country,' he said, shaking his head, 'for such as I, pass all our lives before our furnace doors, and seldom go forth to breathe. But there *are* such places yonder.'

'And far from here?' said Nell.

'Aye, surely. How could they be near us, and be green and fresh? The road lies, too, through miles and miles, all lighted up by fires like ours—a strange black road, and one that would frighten you by night.'

'We are here and must go on,' said the child boldly; for she saw that the old man listened with anxious ears to this account.

'Rough people—paths never made for little feet like yours—a dismal blighted way—is there no turning back, my child?'

'There is none,' cried Nell, pressing forward. 'If you can direct us, do. If not, pray do not seek to turn us from our purpose. Indeed you do not know the danger that we shun, and how right and true we are in flying from it, or you would not try to stop us, I am sure you would not.'

'God forbid, if it is so!' said their uncouth protector, glancing from the eager child to her grandfather, who hung his head and bent his eyes upon the ground. 'I'll direct you from the door, the best I can. I wish I could do more.'

He showed them, then, by which road they must leave the town, and what course they should hold when they had gained it. He lingered so long on these instructions, that the child, with a fervent blessing, tore herself away, and stayed to hear no more.

But, before they had reached the corner of the lane, the man came running after them, and, pressing her hand, left something in it—two old, battered, smoke-encrusted penny pieces. Who knows but they shone as brightly in the eyes of angels, as golden gifts that have been chronicled on tombs?

And thus they separated; the child to lead her sacred charge farther from guilt and shame; the labourer to attach a fresh interest to the spot where his guests had slept, and read new histories in his furnace fire.

CHAPTER XLV

IN all their journeying, they had never longed so ardently, they had never so pined and wearied, for the freedom of pure air and open country, as now. No, not even on that memorable morning, when, deserting their old home, they abandoned themselves to the mercies of a strange world, and left all the dumb and senseless things they had known and loved, behind—not even then, had they so yearned for the fresh solitudes of wood, hillside, and field, as now, when the noise and dirt and vapour of the great manufacturing town, reeking with lean misery and hungry wretchedness, hemmed them in on every side, and seemed to shut out hope, and render escape impossible.

'Two days and nights!' thought the child. 'He said two days and nights we should have to spend among such scenes as these. Oh! if we live to reach the country once again, if we get clear of these dreadful places, though it is only to lie down and die, with what a grateful heart I shall thank God for so much mercy!'

With thoughts like this, and with some vague design of travelling to a great distance among streams and mountains, where only very poor and simple people lived, and where they might maintain themselves by very humble helping work in farms, free from such terrors as that from which they fled,—the child, with no resource but the poor man's gift, and no encouragement but that which flowed from her own heart, and its sense of the truth and right of what she did, nerved herself to this last journey and boldly pursued her task.

'We shall be very slow to-day, dear,' she said, as they toiled painfully through the streets; 'my feet are sore, and I have pains in all my limbs from the wet of yesterday. I saw that he looked at us and thought of that, when he said how long we should be upon the road.'

'It was a dreary way he told us of,' returned her grandfather, piteously. 'Is there no other road? Will you not let me go some other way than this?'

'Places lie beyond these,' said the child, firmly, 'where we may live in peace, and be tempted to do no harm. We will take the road that promises to have that end, and we would not turn out of it, if it were a hundred times worse than our fears lead us to expect. We would not, dear, would we?'

'No,' replied the old man, wavering in his voice, no less than in his manner. 'No. Let us go on. I am ready. I am quite ready, Nell.'

The child walked with more difficulty than she had led her companion to expect, for the pains that racked her joints were of no common severity, and every exertion increased them. But they wrung from her no complaint, or look of suffering; and, though the two travellers proceeded very slowly, they did proceed. Clearing the town in course of time, they began to feel that they were fairly on their way.

A long suburb of red-brick houses,—some with patches of garden-ground, where coal-dust and factory smoke darkened the shrinking leaves and coarse rank flowers, and where the struggling vegetation sickened and sank under the hot breath of kiln and furnace, making them by its presence seem yet more blighting and unwholesome than in the town itself,—a long, flat, straggling suburb passed, they came, by slow degrees, upon a cheerless region, where not a blade of grass was seen to grow, where not a bud put forth its promise in the spring, where nothing green could live but on the surface of the stagnant pools, which here and there lay idly sweltering by the black roadside.

Advancing more and more into the shadow of this mournful place, its dark depressing influence stole upon their spirits, and filled them with a dismal gloom. On every side, and far as the eye could see into the heavy distance, tall chimneys, crowding on each other, and presenting that endless repetition of the same dull, ugly, form, which is the horror of oppressive dreams, poured out their plague of smoke, obscured the light, and made foul the melancholy air. On mounds of ashes by the wayside, sheltered only by a few rough boards, or rotten penthouse roofs, strange engines spun and writhed like tortured creatures; clanking their iron chains, shrieking in their rapid whirl from time to time as though in torment unendurable, and making the ground tremble with their agonies. Dismantled houses here and there appeared, tottering to the earth, propped up by fragments of others that had fallen down, unroofed, windowless, blackened, desolate, but yet inhabited. Men, women, children, wan in their looks and ragged in attire, tended the engines, fed their tributary fire, begged upon the road, or scowled half-naked from the doorless houses. Then, came more of the wrathful monsters, whose like they almost seemed to be in their wildness and their untamed air, screeching and turning round and round again; and still, before, behind, and to the right and left, was the same interminable perspective of brick towers, never ceasing in their black vomit, blasting all things living or inanimate, shutting out the face of day, and closing in on all these horrors with a dense dark cloud.

But, night-time in this dreadful spot!—night, when the smoke was changed to fire; when every chimney spirted up its flame; and places, that had been dark vaults all day, now shone red-hot, with figures moving to and fro within their blazing jaws, and calling to one another with hoarse cries—night, when the noise of every strange machine was aggravated by the darkness; when the people near them looked wilder and more savage; when bands of unemployed labourers paraded the roads, or clustered by torch-light round their leaders, who told them, in stern language, of their wrongs, and urged them on to frightful cries and threats; when maddened men, armed with sword and firebrand, spurning the tears and prayers of women who would restrain them, rushed forth on errands of terror and destruction, to work no ruin half so surely as their own—night, when carts came rumbling by, filled with rude coffins (for contagious disease and death had been busy with the living crops); when orphans cried, and distracted women shrieked and followed in their wake—night, when some called for bread, and some for drink to drown their cares, and some with tears, and some with staggering feet, and some with bloodshot eyes, went brooding home—night, which, unlike the night that Heaven sends on earth, brought with it no peace, nor quiet, nor signs of blessed sleep—who shall tell the terrors of the night to the young wandering child!

And yet she lay down, with nothing between her and the sky; and, with no fear for herself, for she was past it now, put up a prayer for the poor old man. So very weak and spent, she felt, so very calm and unresisting, that she had no thought of any wants of her own, but prayed that God would raise up some friend for *him*. She tried to recall the way they had come, and to look in the direction where the fire by which they had slept last night was burning. She had forgotten to ask the name of the poor man, their friend, and when she had remembered him in her prayers, it seemed ungrateful not to turn one look towards the spot where he was watching.

A Procession of the Unemployed

A penny loaf was all they had had that day. It was very little, but even hunger was forgotten in the strange tranquillity that crept over her senses. She lay down, very gently, and, with a quiet smile upon her face, fell into a slumber. It was not like sleep—and yet it must have been, or why those pleasant dreams of the little scholar all night long!

Morning came. Much weaker, diminished powers even of sight and hearing, and yet the child made no complaint—perhaps would have made none, even if she had not had that inducement to be silent, travelling by her side. She felt a hopelessness of their ever being extricated together from that forlorn place; a dull conviction that she was very ill, perhaps dying; but no fear or anxiety.

A loathing of food that she was not conscious of until they expended their last penny in the purchase of another loaf, prevented her partaking even of this poor repast. Her grandfather ate greedily, which she was glad to see.

Their way lay through the same scenes as yesterday, with no variety or improvement. There was the same thick air, difficult to breathe; the same blighted ground, the same hopeless prospect, the same misery and distress. Objects appeared more dim, the noise less, the path more rugged and uneven, for sometimes she stumbled, and became roused, as it were, in the effort to prevent herself from falling. Poor child! the cause was in her tottering feet.

Towards the afternoon, her grandfather complained bitterly of hunger. She approached one of the wretched hovels by the wayside, and knocked with her hand upon the door.

'What would you have here?' said a gaunt man, opening it.

'Charity. A morsel of bread.'

'Do you see that?' returned the man hoarsely, pointing to a kind of bundle on the ground. 'That's a dead child. I and five hundred other men were thrown out of work, three months ago. That is my third dead child, and last. Do you think *I* have charity to bestow, or a morsel of bread to spare?'

The child recoiled from the door, and it closed upon her. Impelled by strong necessity, she knocked at another: a neighbouring one, which, yielding to the slight pressure of her hand, flew open.

It seemed that a couple of poor families lived in this hovel, for two women, each among children of her own, occupied different portions of the room. In the centre, stood a grave gentleman in black who appeared to have just entered, and who held by the arm a boy.

'Here, woman,' he said, 'here's your deaf and dumb son. You may thank me for restoring him to you. He was brought before me, this morning, charged with theft; and with any other boy it would have gone hard, I assure you. But, as I had compassion on his infirmities, and thought he might have learnt no better, I have managed to bring him back to you. Take more care of him for the future.'

'And won't you give me back *my* son?' said the other woman, hastily rising and confronting him. 'Won't you give me back *my* son, sir, who was transported for the same offence?'

'Was *he* deaf and dumb, woman?' asked the gentleman sternly.

'Was he not, sir?'

'You know he was not.'

'He was,' cried the woman. 'He was deaf, dumb, and blind, to all that was good and right, from his cradle. Her boy may have learnt no better! where did mine learn better? where could he? who was there to teach him better, or where was it to be learnt?'

'Peace, woman,' said the gentleman, 'your boy was in possession of all his senses.'

'He was,' cried the mother; 'and he was the more easy to be led astray because he had them. If you save this boy because he may not know right from wrong, why did you not save mine who was never taught the difference? You gentlemen have as good a right to punish her boy, that God has kept in ignorance of sound and speech, as you have to punish mine, that you kept in ignorance yourselves. How many of the girls and boys—ah, men and women too—that are brought before you and you don't pity, are deaf and dumb in their minds, and go wrong in that state, and are punished in that state, body and soul, while you gentlemen are quarrelling among yourselves whether they ought to learn this or that?—Be a just man, sir, and give me back my son.'

'You are desperate,' said the gentleman, taking out his snuff-box, 'and I am sorry for you.'

'I *am* desperate,' returned the woman, 'and you have made me so. Give me back my son, to work for these helpless children. Be a just man, sir, and, as you have had mercy upon this boy, give me back my son!'

The child had seen and heard enough to know that this was not a place at which to ask for alms. She led the old man softly from the door, and they pursued their journey.

With less and less of hope or strength, as they went on, but with an undiminished resolution not to betray by any word or sign her sinking state, so long as she had energy to move, the child, throughout the remainder of that hard day, compelled herself to proceed: not even stopping to rest as frequently as usual, to compensate in some measure for the tardy pace at which she was obliged to walk. Evening was drawing on, but had not closed in, when—still travelling among the same dismal objects—they came to a busy town.

Faint and spiritless as they were, its streets were insupportable. After humbly asking for relief at some few doors, and being repulsed, they agreed to make their way out of it as speedily as they could, and try if the inmates of any lone house beyond, would have more pity on their exhausted state.

They were dragging themselves along through the last street, and the child felt that the time was close at hand when her enfeebled powers would bear no more. There appeared before them, at this juncture, going in the same direction as themselves, a traveller on foot, who, with a portmanteau strapped to his back, leaned upon a stout stick as he walked, and read from a book which he held in his other hand.

It was not an easy matter to come up with him, and beseech his aid, for he walked fast, and was a little distance in advance. At length, he stopped, to look more attentively at some passage in his book. Animated with a ray of hope, the child shot on before her grandfather, and, going close to the stranger without rousing him by the sound of her footsteps, began, in a few faint words, to implore his help.

He turned his head. The child clapped her hands together, uttered a wild shriek, and fell senseless at his feet.

P

IT was the poor schoolmaster. No other than the poor schoolmaster. Scarcely less moved and surprised by the sight of the child than she had been on recognising him, he stood, for a moment, silent and confounded by this unexpected apparition, without even the presence of mind to raise her from the ground.

But, quickly recovering his self-possession, he threw down his stick and book, and dropping on one knee beside her, endeavoured, by such simple means as occurred to him, to restore her to herself; while her grandfather, standing idly by, wrung his hands, and implored her with many endearing expressions to speak to him, were it only a word.

'She is quite exhausted,' said the schoolmaster, glancing upward into his face. 'You have taxed her powers too far, friend.'

'She is perishing of want,' rejoined the old man. 'I never thought how weak and ill she was, till now.'

Casting a look upon him, half-reproachful and half-compassionate, the schoolmaster took the child in his arms, and, bidding the old man gather up her little basket and follow him directly, bore her away at his utmost speed.

There was a small inn within sight, to which, it would seem, he had been directing his steps when so unexpectedly overtaken. Towards this place he hurried with his unconscious burden, and rushing into the kitchen, and calling upon the company there assembled to make way for God's' sake, deposited it on a chair before the fire.

The company, who rose in confusion on the schoolmaster's entrance, did as people usually do under such circumstances. Everybody called for his or her favourite remedy, which nobody brought; each cried for more air, at the same time carefully excluding what air there was, by closing round the object of sympathy; and all wondered why somebody else didn't do what it never appeared to occur to them might be done by themselves.

The landlady, however, who possessed more readiness and activity than any of them, and who had withal a quicker perception of the merits of the case, soon came running in, with a little hot brandy and water, followed by her servant-girl, carrying vinegar, hartshorn, smelling-salts, and such other

Nell in a Faint
(*p. 340*)

restoratives; which, being duly administered, recovered the child so far as to enable her to thank them in a faint voice, and to extend her hand to the poor schoolmaster, who stood, with an anxious face, hard by. Without suffering her to speak another word, or so much as to stir a finger any more, the women straightway carried her off to bed; and, having covered her up warm, bathed her cold feet, and wrapped them in flannel, they despatched a messenger for the doctor.

The doctor, who was a red-nosed gentleman with a great bunch of seals dangling below a waistcoat of ribbed black satin, arrived with all speed, and taking his seat by the bedside of poor Nell, drew out his watch, and felt her pulse. Then he looked at her tongue, then he felt her pulse again, and while he did so, he eyed the half-emptied wineglass as if in profound abstraction.

'I should give her—' said the doctor at length, 'a teaspoonful, every now and then, of hot brandy and water.'

'Why, that's exactly what we've done, sir!' said the delighted landlady.

'I should also,' observed the doctor, who had passed the foot-bath on the stairs, 'I should also,' said the doctor, in the voice of an oracle, 'put her feet in hot water, and wrap them up in flannel. I should likewise,' said the doctor with increased solemnity, 'give her something light for supper—the wing of a roasted fowl now—'

'Why, goodness gracious me, sir, it's cooking at the kitchen fire this instant!' cried the landlady. And so indeed it was, for the schoolmaster had ordered it to be put on, and it was getting on so well that the doctor might have smelt it if he had tried; perhaps he did.

'You may then,' said the doctor, rising gravely, 'give her a glass of hot mulled port wine, if she likes wine—'

'And a toast, sir?' suggested the landlady.

'Ay,' said the doctor, in the tone of a man who makes a dignified concession. 'And a toast—of bread. But be very particular to make it of bread, if you please, ma'am.'

With which parting injunction, slowly and portentously delivered, the doctor departed, leaving the whole house in admiration of that wisdom which tallied so closely with their own. Everybody said he was a very shrewd doctor indeed, and knew perfectly what people's constitutions were; which there appears some reason to suppose he did.

While her supper was preparing, the child fell into a refreshing sleep, from which they were obliged to rouse her when it was ready. As she evinced extraordinary uneasiness on learning that her grandfather was below stairs, and as she was greatly troubled at the thought of their being apart, he took his supper with her. Finding her still very restless on this head, they made him up a bed in an inner room, to which he presently retired. The key of this chamber happened by good fortune to be on that side of the door which was in Nell's room; she turned it on him when the landlady had withdrawn, and crept to bed again with a thankful heart.

The schoolmaster sat for a long time smoking his pipe by the kitchen fire, which was now deserted, thinking, with a very happy face, on the fortunate chance which had brought him so opportunely to the child's assistance, and parrying, as well as in his simple way he could, the inquisitive cross-examination of the landlady, who had a great curiosity to be made acquainted with every particular of Nell's life and history. The poor schoolmaster was so open-hearted, and so little versed in the most ordinary cunning or deceit, that she could not have failed to succeed in the first five minutes, but that he happened to be unacquainted with what she wished to know; and so he told her. The landlady, by no means satisfied with this assurance, which she considered an ingenious evasion of the question, rejoined that he had his reasons of course. Heaven forbid that she should wish to pry into the affairs of her customers, which indeed were no business of hers, who had so many of her own. She had merely asked a civil question, and to be sure she knew it would meet with a civil answer. She was quite satisfied—quite. She had rather perhaps that he would have said at once that he didn't choose to be communicative, because that would have been plain and intelligible. However, she had no right to be offended, of course. He was the best judge, and had a perfect right to say what he pleased; nobody could dispute that for a moment. Oh dear, no!

'I assure you, my good lady,' said the mild schoolmaster, 'that I have told you the plain truth. As I hope to be saved, I have told you the truth.'

'Why then, I do believe you are in earnest,' rejoined the landlady, with ready good-humour, 'and I'm very sorry I have teased you. But curiosity you know is the curse of our sex, and that's the fact.'

The landlord scratched his head, as if he thought the curse sometimes involved the other sex likewise; but he was prevented from making any remark to that effect, if he had it in contemplation to do so, by the schoolmaster's rejoinder.

'You should question me for half-a-dozen hours at a sitting, and welcome, and I would answer you patiently for the kindness of heart you have shown to-night, if I could,' he said. 'As it is, please to take care of her in the morning, and let me know early how she is; and to understand that I am paymaster for the three.'

So, parting with them on most friendly terms (not the less cordial perhaps for this last direction), the schoolmaster went to his bed, and the host and hostess to theirs.

The report in the morning was, that the child was better, but was extremely weak, and would at least require a day's rest, and careful nursing, before she could proceed upon her journey. The schoolmaster received this communication with perfect cheerfulness, observing that he had a day to spare—two days for that matter—and could very well afford to wait. As the patient was to sit up in the evening, he appointed to visit her in her room at a certain hour, and rambling out with his book, did not return until the hour arrived.

Nell could not help weeping when they were left alone; whereat, and at sight of her pale face and wasted figure, the simple schoolmaster shed a few tears himself, at the same time showing in very energetic language how foolish it was to do so, and how very easily it could be avoided, if one tried.

'It makes me unhappy even in the midst of all this kindness,' said the child, 'to think that we should be a burden upon you. How can I ever thank you? If I had not met you so far from home, I must have died, and he would have been left alone.'

'We'll not talk about dying,' said the schoolmaster; 'and as to burdens, I have made my fortune since you slept at my cottage.'

'Indeed!' cried the child joyfully.

'Oh yes,' returned her friend. 'I have been appointed clerk and schoolmaster to a village a long way from here—and a long way from the old one as you may suppose—at five-and-thirty pounds a year. Five-and-thirty pounds!'

'I am very glad,' said the child—'so very, very glad.'

'I am on my way there now,' resumed the schoolmaster.

'They allowed me the stage-coach hire—outside stage-coach hire all the way. Bless you, they grudge me nothing. But as the time at which I am expected there, left me ample leisure, I determined to walk instead. How glad I am, to think I did so!'

'How glad should we be!'

'Yes, yes,' said the schoolmaster, moving restlessly in his chair, 'certainly, that's very true. But you—where are you going, where are you coming from, what have you been doing since you left me, what had you been doing before? Now, tell me—do tell me. I know very little of the world, and perhaps you are better fitted to advise me in its affairs than I am qualified to give advice to you; but I am very sincere, and I have a reason (you have not forgotten it) for loving you. I have felt since that time as if my love for him who died, had been transferred to you who stood beside his bed. If this,' he added, looking upwards, 'is the beautiful creation that springs from ashes, let its peace prosper with me, as I deal tenderly and compassionately by this young child!'

The plain, frank kindness of the honest schoolmaster, the affectionate earnestness of his speech and manner, the truth which was stamped upon his every word and look, gave the child a confidence in him, which the utmost arts of treachery and dissimulation could never have awakened in her breast. She told him all—that they had no friend or relative—that she had fled with the old man, to save him from a madhouse and all the miseries he dreaded—that she was flying now, to save him from himself—and that she sought an asylum in some remote and primitive place, where the temptation before which he fell would never enter, and her late sorrows and distresses could have no place.

The schoolmaster heard her with astonishment. 'This child!'—he thought—'has this child heroically persevered under all doubts and dangers, struggled with poverty and suffering, upheld and sustained by strong affection and the consciousness of rectitude alone! And yet the world is full of such heroism. Have I yet to learn that the hardest and best-borne trials are those which are never chronicled in any earthly record, and are suffered every day! And should I be surprised to hear the story of this child!'

What more he thought or said, matters not. It was concluded that Nell and her grandfather should accompany him to the village whither he was bound, and that he should endeavour to find them some humble occupation by which they could subsist. 'We shall be sure to succeed,' said the schoolmaster, heartily. 'The cause is too good a one to fail.'

They arranged to proceed upon their journey next evening, as a stage-waggon, which travelled for some distance on the same road as they must take, would stop at the inn to change horses, and the driver for a small gratuity would give Nell a place inside. A bargain was soon struck when the waggon came; and in due time it rolled away; with the child comfortably bestowed among the softer packages, her grandfather and the schoolmaster walking on beside the driver, and the landlady and all the good folks of the inn screaming out their good wishes and farewells.

What a soothing, luxurious, drowsy way of travelling, to lie inside that slowly-moving mountain, listening to the tinkling of the horses' bells, the occasional smacking of the carter's whip, the smooth rolling of the great broad wheels, the rattle of the harness, the cheery good-nights of passing travellers jogging past on little short-stepped horses—all made pleasantly indistinct by the thick awning, which seemed made for lazy listening under, till one fell asleep! The very going to sleep, still with an indistinct idea, as the head jogged to and fro upon the pillow, of moving onward with no trouble or fatigue, and hearing all these sounds like dreamy music, lulling to the senses—and the slow waking up, and finding one's self staring out through the breezy curtain half-opened in the front, far up into the cold bright sky with its countless stars, and downward at the driver's lantern dancing on like its namesake Jack of the swamps and marshes, and sideways at the dark grim trees, and forward at the long bare road rising up, up, up, until it stopped abruptly at a sharp high ridge as if there were no more road, and all beyond was sky—and the stopping at the inn to bait, and being helped out, and going into a room with fire and candles, and winking very much, and being agreeably reminded that the night was cold, and anxious for very comfort's sake to think it colder than it was! —What a delicious journey was that journey in the waggon!

Then the going on again—so fresh at first, and shortly afterwards so sleepy. The waking from a sound nap as the mail came dashing past like a highway comet, with gleaming lamps and rattling hoofs, and visions of a guard behind, standing up to keep his feet warm, and of a gentleman in a fur cap opening his eyes and looking wild and stupefied—the stopping at the turnpike where the man was gone to bed, and knocking at the door until he answered with a smothered shout from under the bed-clothes in the little room above, where the faint light was burning, and presently came down, night-capped and shivering, to throw the gate wide open, and wish all waggons off the road except by day. The cold sharp interval between night and morning—the distant streak of light widening and spreading, and turning from grey to white, and from white to yellow, and from yellow to burning red—the presence of day, with all its cheerfulness and life—men and horses at the plough—birds in the trees and hedges, and boys in solitary fields, frightening them away with rattles. The coming to a town—people busy in the markets; light carts and chaises round the tavern yard; tradesmen standing at their doors; men running horses up and down the street for sale; pigs plunging and grunting in the dirty distance, getting off with long strings at their legs, running into clean chemists' shops and being dislodged with brooms by 'prentices: the night-coach changing horses—the passengers cheerless, cold, ugly, and discontented, with three months' growth of hair in one night—the coachman fresh as from a bandbox, and exquisitely beautiful by contrast:—so much bustle, so many things in motion, such a variety of incidents—when was there a journey with so many delights as that journey in the waggon?

Sometimes walking for a mile or two while her grandfather rode inside, and sometimes even prevailing upon the school-master to take her place and lie down to rest, Nell travelled on very happily until they came to a large town, where the waggon stopped, and where they spent a night. They passed a large church; and in the streets were a number·of old houses, built of a kind of earth or plaster, crossed and recrossed in a great many directions with black beams, which gave them a remarkable and very ancient look. The doors, too, were arched and low, some with oaken portals and quaint benches, where the former inhabitants had sat on summer evenings. The windows were latticed in little diamond panes, that seemed to wink and blink upon the passengers as if they were dim of sight. They had long since got clear of the smoke and furnaces, except in one or two solitary instances, where a factory planted among fields withered the space about it, like a burning mountain. When they had passed through this town, they entered again upon the country, and began to draw near their place of destination.

It was not so near, however, but that they spent another night upon the road; not that their doing so was quite an act of necessity, but that the schoolmaster, when they approached within a few miles of his village, had a fidgety sense of his dignity as the new clerk, and was unwilling to make his entry in dusty shoes, and travel-disordered dress. It was a fine, clear, autumn morning, when they came upon the scene of his promotion, and stopped to contemplate its beauties.

'See—here's the church!' cried the delighted schoolmaster in a low voice; 'and that old building close beside it, is the school-house, I'll be sworn. Five-and-thirty pounds a year in this beautiful place!'

They admired everything—the old grey porch, the mullioned windows, the venerable gravestones dotting the green churchyard, the ancient tower, the very weathercock; the brown thatched roofs of cottage, barn, and homestead, peeping from among the trees; the stream that rippled by the distant watermill; the blue Welsh mountains far away. It was for such a spot the child had wearied in the dense, dark, miserable haunts of labour. Upon her bed of ashes, and amidst the squalid horrors through which they had forced their way, visions of such scenes—beautiful indeed, but not more beautiful than this sweet reality—had been always present to her mind. They had seemed to melt into a dim and airy distance, as the prospect of ever beholding them again grew fainter; but, as they receded, she had loved and panted for them more.

'I must leave you somewhere for a few minutes,' said the schoolmaster, at length breaking the silence into which they had fallen in their gladness. 'I have a letter to present, and inquiries to make, you know. Where shall I take you? To the little inn yonder?'

'Let us wait here,' rejoined Nell. 'The gate is open. We will sit in the church porch till you come back.'

'A good place too,' said the schoolmaster, leading the way towards it, disencumbering himself of his portmanteau, and placing it on the stone seat. 'Be sure that I come back with good news, and am not long gone!'

So, the happy schoolmaster put on a bran-new pair of

gloves which he had carried in a little parcel in his pocket all the way, and hurried off, full of ardour and excitement.

The child watched him from the porch until the intervening foliage hid him from her view, and then stepped softly out into the old churchyard—so solemn and quiet that every rustle of her dress upon the fallen leaves, which strewed the path and made her footsteps noiseless, seemed an invasion of its silence. It was a very aged, ghostly place; the church had been built many hundreds of years ago, and had once had a convent or monastery attached; for arches in ruins, remains of oriel windows, and fragments of blackened walls, were yet standing; while other portions of the old building, which had crumbled away and fallen down, were mingled with the churchyard earth and overgrown with grass, as if they too claimed a burying-place and sought to mix their ashes with the dust of men. Hard by these gravestones of dead years, and forming a part of the ruin which some pains had been taken to render habitable in modern times, were two small dwellings with sunken windows and oaken doors, fast hastening to decay, empty and desolate.

Upon these tenements, the attention of the child became exclusively riveted. She knew not why. The church, the ruin, the antiquated graves, had equal claims at least upon a stranger's thoughts, but from the moment when her eyes first rested on these two dwellings, she could turn to nothing else. Even when she had made the circuit of the enclosure, and, returning to the porch, sat pensively waiting for their friend, she took her station where she could still look upon them, and felt as if fascinated towards that spot.

A very Aged, Ghostly Place
(p. 348)

CHAPTER XLVII

KIT'S mother and the single gentleman—upon whose track it is expedient to follow with hurried steps, lest this history should be chargeable with inconstancy, and the offence of leaving its characters in situations of uncertainty and doubt— Kit's mother and the single gentleman, speeding onward in the post-chaise-and-four whose departure from the Notary's door we have already witnessed, soon left the town behind them, and struck fire from the flints of the broad highway.

The good woman, being not a little embarrassed by the novelty of her situation, and certain maternal apprehensions that perhaps by this time little Jacob, or the baby, or both, had fallen into the fire, or tumbled down stairs, or had been squeezed behind doors, or had scalded their windpipes in endeavouring to allay their thirst at the spouts of tea-kettles, preserved an uneasy silence; and meeting from the window the eyes of turnpike-men, omnibus-drivers, and others, felt in the new dignity of her position like a mourner at a funeral, who, not being greatly afflicted by the loss of the departed, recognizes his every-day acquaintance from the window of the mourning coach, but is constrained to preserve a decent solemnity, and the appearance of being indifferent to all external objects.

To have been indifferent to the companionship of the single gentleman would have been tantamount to being gifted with nerves of steel. Never did chaise inclose, or horses draw, such a restless gentleman as he. He never sat in the same position for two minutes together, but was perpetually tossing his arms and legs about, pulling up the sashes and letting them violently down, or thrusting his head out of one window to draw it in again and thrust it out of another. He carried in his pocket, too, a fire-box of mysterious and unknown construction; and as sure as ever Kit's mother closed her eyes, so surely—whisk, rattle, fizz—there was the single gentleman consulting his watch by a flame of fire, and letting the sparks fall down among the straw as if there were no such thing as a possibility of himself and Kit's mother being roasted alive before the boys could stop their horses. Whenever they halted to change, there he was—out of the carriage without letting down the steps, bursting about the inn-yard like a lighted cracker, pulling out his watch by lamplight and forgetting to look at it before he put it up again, and in short committing so many extravagances that Kit's mother was quite afraid of him. Then, when the horses were to, in he came like a Harlequin, and before they had gone a mile, out came the watch and the fire-box together, and Kit's mother was wide awake again, with no hope of a wink of sleep for that stage.

'Are you comfortable?' the single gentleman would say after one of these exploits, turning sharply round.

'Quite, sir, thank you.'

'Are you sure? An't you cold?'

'It is a little chilly, sir,' Kit's mother would reply.

'I knew it!' cried the single gentleman, letting down one of the front glasses. 'She wants some brandy and water! Of course she does. How could I forget it? Hallo! Stop at the next inn, and call out for a glass of hot brandy and water.'

It was in vain for Kit's mother to protest that she stood in need of nothing of the kind. The single gentleman was inexorable; and whenever he had exhausted all other modes and fashions of restlessness, it invariably occurred to him that Kit's mother wanted brandy and water.

In this way they travelled on until near midnight, when they stopped to supper, for which meal the single gentleman ordered everything eatable that the house contained; and because Kit's mother didn't eat everything at once, and eat it all, he took it into his head that she must be ill.

'You're faint,' said the single gentleman, who did nothing himself but walk about the room. 'I see what's the matter with you, ma'am. You're faint.'

'Thank you, sir, I'm not indeed.'

'I know you are. I'm sure of it. I drag this poor woman from the bosom of her family at a minute's notice, and she goes on getting fainter and fainter before my eyes. I'm a pretty fellow! How many children have you got, ma'am?'

'Two, sir, besides Kit.'

'Boys, ma'am?'

'Yes, sir.'

'Are they christened?'

'Only half baptised as yet, sir.'

'I'm godfather to both of 'em. Remember that, if you please, ma'am. You had better have some mulled wine.'

'I couldn't touch a drop indeed, sir.'

'You must,' said the single gentleman. 'I see you want it. I ought to have thought of it before.'

Immediately flying to the bell, and calling for mulled wine as impetuously as if it had been wanted for instant use in the recovery of some person apparently drowned, the single gentleman made Kit's mother swallow a bumper of it at such a high temperature that the tears ran down her face, and then hustled her off to the chaise again, where—not impossibly from the effects of this agreeable sedative—she soon became insensible to his restlessness, and fell fast asleep. Nor were the happy effects of this prescription of a transitory nature, as, notwithstanding that the distance was greater, and the journey longer, than the single gentleman had anticipated, she did not awake until it was broad day, and they were clattering over the pavement of a town.

'This is the place!' cried her companion, letting down all the glasses. 'Drive to the wax-work!'

The boy on the wheeler touched his hat, and setting spurs to his horse, to the end that they might go in brilliantly, all four broke into a smart canter, and dashed through the streets with a noise that brought the good folks wondering to their doors and windows, and drowned the sober voices of the town-clocks as they chimed out half-past eight. They drove up to a door round which a crowd of persons were collected, and there stopped.

'What's this?' said the single gentleman, thrusting out his head. 'Is anything the matter here?'

'A wedding, sir, a wedding!' cried several voices. 'Hurrah!'

The single gentleman, rather bewildered by finding himself the centre of this noisy throng, alighted with the assistance of one of the postillions, and handed out Kit's mother, at sight of whom the populace cried out, 'Here's another wedding!' and roared and leaped for joy.

'The world has gone mad, I think,' said the single gentleman, pressing through the concourse with his supposed bride. 'Stand back here, will you, and let me knock.'

Anything that makes a noise is satisfactory to a crowd. A score of dirty hands were raised directly to knock for him, and seldom has a knocker of equal powers been made to produce more deafening sounds than this particular engine on the occasion in question. Having rendered these voluntary services, the throng modestly retired a little, preferring that the single gentleman should bear their consequences alone.

'Now, sir, what do you want?' said a man with a large white bow at his button-hole, opening the door, and confronting him with a very stoical aspect.

'Who has been married here, my friend?' said the single gentleman.

'I have.'

'You! and to whom in the devil's name?'

'What right have you to ask?' returned the bridegroom, eyeing him from top to toe.

'What right?' cried the single gentleman, drawing the arm of Kit's mother more tightly through his own, for that good woman evidently had it in contemplation to run away. 'A right you little dream of. Mind, good people, if this fellow has been marrying a minor—tut, tut, that can't be. Where is the child you have here, my good fellow? You call her Nell. Where is she?'

As he propounded this question, which Kit's mother echoed, somebody in a room near at hand, uttered a great shriek, and a stout lady in a white dress came running to the door, and supported herself upon the bridegroom's arm.

'Where is she?' cried this lady. 'What news have you brought me? What has become of her?'

The single gentleman started back, and gazed upon the face of the late Mrs. Jarley (that morning wedded to the philosophic George, to the eternal wrath and despair of Mr. Slum the poet), with looks of conflicting apprehension, disappointment, and incredulity. At length he stammered out,

'I ask *you* where she is? What do you mean?'

'Oh sir!' cried the bride. 'If you have come here to do her any good, why weren't you here a week ago?'

'She is not—not dead?' said the person to whom she addressed herself, turning very pale.

'No, not so bad as that.'

'I thank God!' cried the single gentleman feebly. 'Let me come in.'

They drew back to admit him, and when he had entered, closed the door.

'You see in me, good people,' he said, turning to the newly-married couple, 'one to whom life itself is not dearer than the two persons whom I seek. They would not know me. My features are strange to them, but if they or either of them are here, take this good woman with you, and let them see her first, for her they both know. If you deny them from any mistaken regard or fear for them, judge of my intentions by their recognition of this person as their old humble friend.'

'I always said it!' cried the bride, 'I knew she was not a common child! Alas, sir! we have no power to help you, for all that we could do, has been tried in vain.'

With that, they related to him, without disguise or concealment, all that they knew of Nell and her grandfather, from their first meeting with them, down to the time of their sudden disappearance; adding (which was quite true) that they had made every possible effort to trace them, but without success; having been at first in great alarm for their safety, as well as on account of the suspicions to which they themselves might one day be exposed in consequence of their abrupt departure. They dwelt upon the old man's imbecility of mind, upon the uneasiness the child had always testified when he was absent, upon the company he had been supposed to keep, and upon the increased depression which had gradually crept over her and changed her both in health and spirits. Whether she had missed the old man in the night, and, knowing or conjecturing whither he had bent his steps, had gone in pursuit, or whether they had left the house together, they had no means of determining. Certain they considered it, that there was but slender prospect left of hearing of them again, and that whether their flight originated with the old man, or with the child, there was now no hope of their return.

To all this, the single gentleman listened with the air of a man quite borne down by grief and disappointment. He shed tears when they spoke of the grandfather, and appeared in deep affliction.

Not to protract this portion of our narrative, and to make short work of a long story, let it be briefly written that before the interview came to a close, the single gentleman deemed he had sufficient evidence of having been told the truth, and that he endeavoured to force upon the bride and bridegroom an acknowledgment of their kindness to the unfriended child, which, however, they steadily declined accepting. In the end, the happy couple jolted away in the caravan to spend their honeymoon in a country excursion; and the single gentleman and Kit's mother stood ruefully before their carriage-door.

'Where shall we drive you, sir?' said the post-boy.

'You may drive me,' said the single gentleman, 'to the—'

He was not going to add 'inn', but he added it for the sake of Kit's mother; and to the inn they went.

Rumours had already got abroad that the little girl who used to show the wax-work, was the child of great people who had been stolen from her parents in infancy, and had only just been traced. Opinion was divided whether she was the daughter of a prince, a duke, an earl, a viscount, or a baron, but all agreed upon the main fact, and that the single gentleman was her father; and all bent forward to catch a glimpse, though it were only of the tip of his noble nose, as he rode away, desponding, in his four-horse chaise.

What would he have given to know, and what sorrow would have been saved if he had only known, that at that moment both child and grandfather were seated in the old church porch, patiently awaiting the schoolmaster's return?

A Gracious Invitation

(p. 355)

CHAPTER XLVIII

POPULAR rumour concerning the single gentleman and his errand, travelling from mouth to mouth, and waxing stronger in the marvellous as it was bandied about,—for your popular rumour, unlike the rolling stone of the proverb, is one which gathers a deal of moss in its wanderings up and down,—occasioned his dismounting at the inn-door to be looked upon as an exciting and attractive spectacle, which could scarcely be enough admired; and drew together a large concourse of idlers, who having recently been, as it were, thrown out of employment by the closing of the wax-work and the completion of the nuptial ceremonies, considered his arrival as little else than a special providence, and hailed it with demonstrations of the liveliest joy.

Not at all participating in the general sensation, but wearing the depressed and wearied look of one who sought to meditate on his disappointment in silence and privacy, the single gentleman alighted, and handed out Kit's mother with a gloomy politeness which impressed the lookers-on extremely. That done, he gave her his arm and escorted her into the house, while several active waiters ran on before as a skirmishing party, to clear the way and to show the room which was ready for their reception.

'Any room will do,' said the single gentleman. 'Let it be near at hand, that's all.'

'Close here, sir, if you please to walk this way.'

'Would the gentleman like this room?' said a voice, as a little out-of-the-way door at the foot of the well staircase flew briskly open and a head popped out. 'He's quite welcome to it. He's as welcome as flowers in May, or coals at Christmas. *Would* you like this room, sir? Honour me by walking in. Do me the favour, pray.'

'Goodness gracious me!' cried Kit's mother, falling back in extreme surprise, 'only think of this!'

She had some reason to be astonished, for the person who proffered the gracious invitation was no other than Daniel Quilp. The little door out of which he had thrust his head was close to the inn larder; and there he stood, bowing with grotesque politeness; as much at his ease as if the door were that of his own house; blighting all the legs of mutton and cold roast fowls by his close companionship, and looking like the evil genius of the cellars come from underground upon some work of mischief.

'Would you do me the honour?' said Quilp.

'I prefer being alone,' replied the single gentleman.

'Oh!' said Quilp. And with that, he darted in again with one jerk and clapped the little door to, like a figure in a Dutch clock when the hour strikes.

'Why it was only last night, sir,' whispered Kit's mother, 'that I left him in Little Bethel.'

'Indeed!' said her fellow-passenger. 'When did that person come here, waiter?'

'Come down by the night-coach, this morning, sir.'

'Humph! And when is he going?'

'Can't say, sir, really. When the chambermaid asked him just now if he should want a bed, sir, he first made faces at her, and then wanted to kiss her.'

'Beg him to walk this way,' said the single gentleman. 'I should be glad to exchange a word with him, tell him. Beg him to come at once, do you hear?'

The man stared on receiving these instructions, for the single gentleman had not only displayed as much astonishment as Kit's mother at sight of the dwarf, but, standing in no fear of him, had been at less pains to conceal his dislike and repugnance. He departed on his errand, however, and immediately returned, ushering in its object.

'Your servant, sir,' said the dwarf. 'I encountered your messenger half-way. I thought you'd allow me to pay my compliments to you. I hope you're well. I hope you're very well.'

There was a short pause, while the dwarf, with half-shut eyes and puckered face, stood waiting for an answer. Receiving none, he turned towards his more familiar acquaintance.

'Christopher's mother!' he cried. 'Such a dear lady, such a worthy woman, so blest in her honest son! How is Christopher's mother? Have change of air and scene improved her? Her little family too, and Christopher? Do they thrive? Do they flourish? Are they growing into worthy citizens, eh?'

Making his voice ascend in the scale with every succeeding question, Mr. Quilp finished in a shrill squeak, and subsided into the panting look which was customary with him, and which, whether it were assumed or natural, had equally the effect of banishing all expression from his face, and rendering it, as far as it afforded any index to his mood or meaning, a perfect blank.

'Mr. Quilp,' said the single gentleman.

The dwarf put his hand to his great flapped ear, and counterfeited the closest attention.

'We two have met before—'

'Surely,' cried Quilp, nodding his head. 'Oh surely, sir. Such an honour and pleasure—it's both, Christopher's mother, it's both—is not to be forgotten so soon. By no means!'

'You may remember that the day I arrived in London, and found the house to which I drove, empty and deserted, I was directed by some of the neighbours to you, and waited upon you without stopping for rest or refreshment?'

'How precipitate that was, and yet what an earnest and vigorous measure!' said Quilp, conferring with himself, in imitation of his friend Mr. Sampson Brass.

'I found,' said the single gentleman, 'you most unaccountably in possession of everything that had so recently belonged to another man, and that other man, who up to the time of your entering upon his property had been looked upon as affluent, reduced to sudden beggary, and driven from house and home.'

'We had warrant for what we did, my good sir,' rejoined Quilp, 'we had our warrant. Don't say driven either. He went of his own accord—vanished in the night, sir.'

'No matter,' said the single gentleman angrily. 'He was gone.'

'Yes, he was gone,' said Quilp, with the same exasperating composure. 'No doubt he was gone. The only question was, where. And it's a question still.'

'Now, what am I to think,' said the single gentleman, sternly regarding him, 'of you, who, plainly indisposed to give me any information then—nay, obviously holding back, and sheltering yourself with all kinds of cunning, trickery, and evasion,—are dogging my footsteps now?'

'I dogging!' cried Quilp.

'Why, are you not?' returned his questioner, fretted into a state of the utmost irritation. 'Were you not a few hours since, sixty miles off, and in the chapel to which this good woman goes to say her prayers?'

'She was there too, I think!' said Quilp, still perfectly unmoved. 'I might say, if I was inclined to be rude, how do I

know but you are dogging *my* footsteps? Yes, I was at chapel.
What then? I've read in books that pilgrims were used to go to
chapel before they went on journeys, to put up petitions for
their safe return. Wise men! journeys are very perilous—
especially outside the coach. Wheels come off, horses take
fright, coachmen drive too fast, coaches overturn. I always go
to chapel before I start on journeys. It's the last thing I do on
such occasions, indeed.'

That Quilp lied most heartily in this speech, it needed no
very great penetration to discover, although for anything that
he suffered to appear in his face, voice, or manner, he might
have been clinging to the truth with the quiet constancy of a
martyr.

'In the name of all that's calculated to drive one crazy, man,'
said the unfortunate single gentleman, 'have you not, for some
reason of your own, taken upon yourself my errand? don't you
know with what object I have come here, and if you do know,
can you throw no light upon it?'

'You think I'm a conjuror, sir,' replied Quilp, shrugging up
his shoulders. 'If I was, I should tell my own fortune—and
make it.'

'Ah! we have said all we need say, I see,' returned the other,
throwing himself impatiently upon a sofa. 'Pray leave us, if
you please.'

'Willingly,' returned Quilp. 'Most willingly. Christopher's
mother, my good soul, farewell. A pleasant journey—*back*, sir.
Ahem!'

With these parting words, and with a grin upon his features
altogether indescribable, but which seemed to be compounded
of every monstrous grimace of which men or monkeys are
capable, the dwarf slowly retreated and closed the door behind
him.

'Oho!' he said when he had regained his own room, and sat
himself down in a chair with his arms akimbo. 'Oho! Are you
there, my friend? In-deed!'

Chuckling as though in very great glee, and recompensing
himself for the restraint he had lately put upon his countenance
by twisting it into all imaginable varieties of ugliness, Mr.
Quilp, rocking himself to and fro in his chair and nursing his
left leg at the same time, fell into certain meditations, of which
it may be necessary to relate the substance.

First, he reviewed the circumstances which had led to his

repairing to that spot, which were briefly these. Dropping in at Mr. Sampson Brass's office on the previous evening, in the absence of that gentleman and his learned sister, he had lighted upon Mr. Swiveller, who chanced at the moment to be sprinkling a glass of warm gin and water on the dust of the law, and to be moistening his clay, as the phrase goes, rather copiously. But as clay in the abstract, when too much moistened, becomes of a weak and uncertain consistency, breaking down in unexpected places, retaining impressions but faintly, and preserving no strength or steadiness of character, so Mr. Swiveller's clay, having imbibed a considerable quantity of moisture, was in a very loose and slippery state, insomuch that the various ideas impressed upon it were fast losing their distinctive character, and running into each other. It is not uncommon for human clay in this condition to value itself above all things upon its great prudence and sagacity; and Mr. Swiveller, especially, prizing himself upon these qualities, took occasion to remark that he had made strange discoveries in connection with the single gentleman who lodged above, which he had determined to keep within his own bosom, and which neither tortures nor cajolery should ever induce him to reveal. Of this determination Mr. Quilp expressed his high approval, and setting himself in the same breath to goad Mr. Swiveller on to further hints, soon made out that the single gentleman had been seen in communication with Kit, and that this was the secret which was never to be disclosed.

Possessed of this piece of information, Mr. Quilp directly supposed that the single gentleman above stairs must be the same individual who had waited on him, and having assured himself by further inquiries that this surmise was correct, had no difficulty in arriving at the conclusion that the intent and object of his correspondence with Kit was the recovery of his old client and the child. Burning with curiosity to know what proceedings were afoot, he resolved to pounce upon Kit's mother as the person least able to resist his arts, and consequently the most likely to be entrapped into such revelations as he sought; so taking an abrupt leave of Mr. Swiveller, he hurried to her house. The good woman being from home, he made inquiries of a neighbour, as Kit himself did soon afterwards, and being directed to the chapel betook himself there, in order to waylay her, at the conclusion of the service.

He had not sat in the chapel more than a quarter of an hour, and with his eyes piously fixed upon the ceiling was chuckling inwardly over the joke of his being there at all, when Kit himself appeared. Watchful as a lynx, one glance showed the dwarf that he had come on business. Absorbed in appearance, as we have seen, and feigning a profound abstraction, he noted every circumstance of his behaviour, and when he withdrew with his family, shot out after him. In fine, he traced them to the Notary's house; learnt the destination of the carriage from one of the postillions; and knowing that a fast night-coach started for the same place, at the very hour which was on the point of striking, from a street hard by, darted round to the coach-office without more ado, and took his seat upon the roof. After passing and repassing the carriage on the road, and being passed and repassed by it sundry times in the course of the night, according as their stoppages were longer or shorter, or their rate of travelling varied, they reached the town almost together. Quilp kept the chaise in sight, mingled with the crowd, learnt the single gentleman's errand, and its failure, and having possessed himself of all that it was material to know, hurried off, reached the inn before him, had the interview just now-detailed, and shut himself up in the little room in which he hastily reviewed all these occurrences.

'You are there, are you, my friend?' he repeated, greedily biting his nails. 'I am suspected and thrown aside, and Kit's the confidential agent, is he? I shall have to dispose of him, I fear. If we had come up with them this morning,' he continued, after a thoughtful pause, 'I was ready to prove a pretty good claim. I could have made my profit. But for these canting hypocrites, the lad and his mother, I could get this fiery gentleman as comfortable into my net as our old friend—our mutual friend, ha! ha!—and chubby, rosy Nell. At the worst, it's a golden opportunity, not to be lost. Let us find them first, and I'll find means of draining you of some of your superfluous cash, sir, while there are prison bars, and bolts, and locks, to keep your friend or kinsman safely. I hate your virtuous people!' said the dwarf, throwing off a bumper of brandy, and smacking his lips, 'ah! I hate 'em every one!'

This was not a mere empty vaunt, but a deliberate avowal of his real sentiments; for Mr. Quilp, who loved nobody, had by little and little come to hate everybody nearly or remotely connected with his ruined client:—the old man himself, because he had been able to deceive him and elude his vigilance —the child, because she was the object of Mrs. Quilp's commiseration and constant self-reproach—the single gentleman, because of his unconcealed aversion to himself—Kit and his mother, most mortally, for the reasons shown. Above and beyond that general feeling of opposition to them, which would have been inseparable from his ravenous desire to enrich himself by these altered circumstances, Daniel Quilp hated them every one.

In this amiable mood, Mr. Quilp enlivened himself and his hatreds with more brandy, and then, changing his quarters, withdrew to an obscure alehouse, under cover of which seclusion he instituted all possible inquiries that might lead to the discovery of the old man and his grandchild. But all was in vain. Not the slightest trace or clue could be obtained. They had left the town by night; no one had seen them go; no one had met them on the road; the driver of no coach, cart, or waggon, had seen any travellers answering their description; nobody had fallen in with them, or heard of them. Convinced at last that for the present all such attempts were hopeless, he appointed two or three scouts, with promises of large rewards in case of their forwarding him any intelligence, and returned to London by next day's coach.

It was some gratification to Mr. Quilp to find, as he took his place upon the roof, that Kit's mother was alone inside; from which circumstance he derived in the course of the journey much cheerfulness of spirit, inasmuch as her solitary condition enabled him to terrify her with many extraordinary annoyances; such as hanging over the side of the coach at the risk of his life, and staring in with his great goggle eyes, which seemed in hers the more horrible from his face being upside down; dodging her in this way from one window to another; getting nimbly down whenever they changed horses and thrusting his head in at the window with a dismal squint: which ingenious tortures had such an effect upon Mrs. Nubbles, that she was quite unable for the time to resist the belief that Mr. Quilp did in his own person represent and embody that Evil Power, who was so vigorously attacked at Little Bethel, and who, by reason of her backslidings in respect of Astley's and oysters, was now frolicsome and rampant.

Kit, having been apprised by letter of his mother's intended return, was waiting for her at the coach-office; and great was his surprise when he saw, leering over the coachman's shoulder like some familiar demon, invisible to all eyes but his, the well-known face of Quilp.

'How are you, Christopher?' croaked the dwarf from the coach-top. 'All right, Christopher. Mother's inside.'

'Why, how did he come here, mother?' whispered Kit.

'I don't know how he came or why, my dear,' rejoined Mrs. Nubbles, dismounting with her son's assistance, 'but he has been a terrifying of me out of my seven senses all this blessed day.'

'He has?' cried Kit.

'You wouldn't believe it, that you wouldn't,' replied his mother, 'but don't say a word to him, for I really don't believe he's human. Hush! Don't turn round as if I was talking of him, but he's a squinting at me now in the full blaze of the coach-lamp, quite awful!'

In spite of his mother's injunction, Kit turned sharply round to look. Mr. Quilp was serenely gazing at the stars, quite absorbed in celestial contemplation.

'Oh, he's the artfullest creetur!' cried Mrs. Nubbles. 'But come away. Don't speak to him for the world.'

'Yes I will, mother. What nonsense. I say, sir—'

Mr. Quilp affected to start, and looked smilingly round.

'You let my mother alone, will you?' said Kit. 'How dare you tease a poor lone woman like her, making her miserable and melancholy as if she hadn't got enough to make her so, without you. An't you ashamed of yourself, you little monster?'

'Monster!' said Quilp inwardly with a smile. 'Ugliest dwarf that could be seen anywhere for a penny—monster—ah!'

'You show her any of your impudence again,' resumed Kit, shouldering the bandbox, 'and I tell you what, Mr. Quilp, I won't bear with you any more. You have no right to do it; I'm sure we never interfered with you. This isn't the first time; and if ever you worry or frighten her again, you'll oblige me (though I should be very sorry to do it, on account of your size) to beat you.'

Quilp said not a word in reply, but walking so close to Kit as to bring his eyes within two or three inches of his face, looked fixedly at him, retreated a little distance without averting his gaze, approached again, again withdrew, and so on for half-a-dozen times, like a head in a phantasmagoria. Kit stood his ground as if in expectation of an immediate assault, but finding that nothing came of these gestures, snapped his fingers and walked away; his mother dragging him off as fast as she could, and, even in the midst of his news of little Jacob and the baby, looking anxiously over her shoulder to see if Quilp were following.

CHAPTER XLIX

KIT'S mother might have spared herself the trouble of looking back so often, for nothing was further from Mr. Quilp's thoughts than any intention of pursuing her and her son, or renewing the quarrel with which they had parted. He went his way, whistling from time to time some fragments of a tune; and with a face quite tranquil and composed, jogged pleasantly towards home; entertaining himself as he went with visions of the fears and terrors of Mrs. Quilp, who, having received no intelligence of him for three whole days and two nights, and having had no previous notice of his absence, was doubtless by that time in a state of distraction, and constantly fainting away with anxiety and grief.

This facetious probability was so congenial to the dwarf's humour, and so exquisitely amusing to him, that he laughed as he went along until the tears ran down his cheeks; and more than once, when he found himself in a bye street, vented his delight in a shrill scream, which greatly terrifying any lonely passenger, who happened to be walking on before him expecting nothing so little, increased his mirth, and made him remarkably cheerful and light-hearted.

In this happy flow of spirits, Mr. Quilp reached Tower Hill, when, gazing up at the window of his own sitting-room, he thought he descried more light than is usual in a house of mourning. Drawing nearer, and listening attentively, he could hear several voices in earnest conversation, among which he could distinguish, not only those of his wife and mother-in-law, but the tongues of men.

'Ha!' cried the jealous dwarf. 'What's this? Do they entertain visitors while I'm away?'

A smothered cough from above, was the reply. He felt in his pockets for his latch-key, but had forgotten it. There was no resource but to knock at the door.

'A light in the passage,' said Quilp, peeping through the keyhole. 'A very soft knock; and, by your leave, my lady, I may yet steal upon you unawares. Soho!'

A very low and gentle rap received no answer from within. But after a second application to the knocker, no louder than the first, the door was softly opened by the boy from the wharf, whom Quilp instantly gagged with one hand, and dragged into the street with the other.

'You'll throttle me, master,' whispered the boy. 'Let go, will you?'

'Who's up stairs, you dog?' retorted Quilp in the same tone. 'Tell me. And don't speak above your breath, or I'll choke you in good earnest.'

The boy could only point to the window, and reply with a stifled giggle, expressive of such intense enjoyment, that Quilp clutched him by the throat and might have carried his threat into execution, or at least have made very good progress towards that end, but for the boy's nimbly extricating himself from his grasp, and fortifying himself behind the nearest post, at which, after some fruitless attempts to catch him by the hair of the head, his master was obliged to come to a parley.

'Will you answer me?' said Quilp. 'What's going on, above?'

'You won't let one speak,' replied the boy. 'They—ha, ha, ha!—they think you're—you're dead. Ha ha ha!'

'Dead!' cried Quilp, relaxing into a grim laugh himself. 'No. Do they? Do they really, you dog?'

'They think you're—you're drowned,' replied the boy, who in his malicious nature had a strong infusion of his master. 'You was last seen on the brink of the wharf, and they think you tumbled over. Ha ha!'

The prospect of playing the spy under such delicious circumstances, and of disappointing them all by walking in alive, gave more delight to Quilp than the greatest stroke of good fortune could possibly have inspired him with. He was no less tickled than his hopeful assistant, and they both stood for some seconds, grinning and gasping and wagging their heads at each other, on either side of the post, like an unmatchable pair of Chinese idols.

'Not a word,' said Quilp, making towards the door on tiptoe. 'Not a sound, not so much as a creaking board, or a stumble against a cobweb. Drowned, eh, Mrs. Quilp! Drowned!'

So saying, he blew out the candle, kicked off his shoes, and groped his way up stairs; leaving his delighted young friend in an ecstasy of summersets on the pavement.

The bedroom-door on the staircase being unlocked, Mr. Quilp slipped in, and planted himself behind the door of communication between that chamber and the sitting-room, which standing ajar to render both more airy, and having a

Q

very convenient chink (of which he had often availed himself for purposes of espial, and had indeed enlarged with his pocket-knife), enabled him not only to hear, but to see distinctly, what was passing.

Applying his eye to this convenient place, he descried Mr. Brass seated at the table with pen, ink, and paper, and the case-bottle of rum—his own case-bottle, and his own particular Jamaica—convenient to his hand; with hot water, fragrant lemons, white lump sugar, and all things fitting; from which choice materials, Sampson, by no means insensible to their claims upon his attention, had compounded a mighty glass of punch reeking hot; which he was at that very moment stirring up with a teaspoon, and contemplating with looks in which a faint assumption of sentimental regret, struggled but weakly with a bland and comfortable joy. At the same table, with both her elbows upon it, was Mrs. Jiniwin; no longer sipping other people's punch feloniously with teaspoons, but taking deep draughts from a jorum of her own; while her daughter—not exactly with ashes on her head, or sackcloth on her back, but preserving a very decent and becoming appearance of sorrow nevertheless—was reclining in an easy chair, and soothing her grief with a smaller allowance of the same glib liquid. There were also present, a couple of water-side men, bearing between them certain machines called drags; even these fellows were accommodated with a stiff glass apiece; and as they drank with a great relish, and were naturally of a red-nosed, pimple-faced, convivial look, their presence rather increased than detracted from that decided appearance of comfort, which was the great characteristic of the party.

'If I could poison that dear old lady's rum and water,' murmured Quilp, 'I'd die happy.'

'Ah!' said Mr. Brass, breaking the silence, and raising his eyes to the ceiling with a sigh, 'who knows but he may be looking down upon us now! Who knows but he may be surveying of us from—from somewheres or another, and contemplating us with a watchful eye! Oh Lor!'

Here Mr. Brass stopped to drink half his punch, and then resumed; looking at the other half, as he spoke, with a dejected smile.

'I can almost fancy,' said the lawyer, shaking his head, 'that I see his eye glistening down at the very bottom of my liquor. When shall we look upon his like again? Never, never! One

minute we are here'—holding his tumbler before his eyes—
'the next we are there'—gulping down its contents, and striking
himself emphatically a little below the chest—'in the silent
tomb. To think that I should be drinking his very rum! It
seems like a dream.'

With the view, no doubt, of testing the reality of his position,
Mr. Brass pushed his tumbler as he spoke towards Mrs.
Jiniwin for the purpose of being replenished; and turned
towards the attendant mariners.

'The search has been quite unsuccessful then?'

'Quite, master. But I should say that if he turns up anywhere, he'll come ashore somewhere about Grinidge to-
morrow, at ebb tide, eh, mate?'

The other gentleman assented, observing that he was
expected at the Hospital, and that several pensioners would be
ready to receive him whenever he arrived.

'Then we have nothing for it but resignation,' said Mr.
Brass; 'nothing but resignation, and expectation. It would be
a comfort to have his body; it would be a dreary comfort.'

'Oh, beyond a doubt,' assented Mrs. Jiniwin hastily; 'if we
once had that, we should be quite sure.'

'With regard to the descriptive advertisement,' said Sampson
Brass, taking up his pen. 'It is a melancholy pleasure to recall
his traits. Respecting his legs now—?'

'Crooked, certainly,' said Mrs. Jiniwin.

'Do you think they *were* crooked?' said Brass, in an insinuating tone. 'I think I see them now coming up the street very
wide apart, in nankeen pantaloons a little shrunk and without
straps. Ah! what a vale of tears we live in. Do we say crooked?'

'I think they were a little so,' observed Mrs. Quilp with a sob.

'Legs crooked,' said Brass, writing as he spoke. 'Large head,
short body, legs crooked—'

'Very crooked,' suggested Mrs. Jiniwin.

'We'll not say very crooked, ma'am,' said Brass piously.
'Let us not bear hard upon the weaknesses of the deceased. He
is gone, ma'am, to where his legs will never come in question.—
We will content ourselves with crooked, Mrs. Jiniwin.'

'I thought you wanted the truth,' said the old lady. 'That's
all.'

'Bless your eyes, how I love you,' muttered Quilp. 'There
she goes again. Nothing but punch!'

'This is an occupation,' said the lawyer, laying down his pen and emptying his glass, 'which seems to bring him before my eyes like the Ghost of Hamlet's father, in the very clothes that he wore on work-a-days. His coat, his waistcoat, his shoes and stockings, his trousers, his hat, his wit and humour, his pathos and his umbrella, all come before me like visions of my youth. His linen!' said Mr. Brass, smiling fondly at the wall, 'his linen which was always of a particular colour, for such was his whim and fancy—how plain I see his linen now!'

'You had better go on, sir,' said Mrs. Jiniwin impatiently.

'True, ma'am, true,' cried Mr. Brass. 'Our faculties must not freeze with grief. I'll trouble you for a little more of that, ma'am. A question now arises, with relation to his nose.'

'Flat,' said Mrs. Jiniwin.

'Aquiline!' cried Quilp, thrusting in his head, and striking the feature with his fist. 'Aquiline, you hag. Do you see it? Do you call this flat? Do you? Eh?'

'Oh capital, capital!' shouted Brass, from the mere force of habit. 'Excellent! How very good he is! He's a most remarkable man—so extremely whimsical! Such an amazing power of taking people by surprise!'

Quilp paid no regard whatever to these compliments, nor to the dubious and frightened look into which the lawyer gradually subsided, nor to the shrieks of his wife and mother-in-law, nor to the latter's running from the room, nor to the former's fainting away. Keeping his eye fixed on Sampson Brass, he walked up to the table, and beginning with his glass, drank off the contents, and went regularly round until he had emptied the other two, when he seized the case-bottle, and hugging it under his arm, surveyed him with a most extraordinary leer.

'Not yet, Sampson,' said Quilp. 'Not just yet!'

'Oh very good indeed!' cried Brass, recovering his spirits a little. 'Ha ha ha! Oh exceedingly good! There's not another man alive who could carry it off like that. A most difficult position to carry off. But he has such a flow of good-humour, such an amazing flow!'

'Good night,' said the dwarf, nodding expressively.

'Good night, sir, good night,' cried the lawyer, retreating backwards towards the door. 'This is a joyful occasion indeed, extremely joyful. Ha ha ha! oh very rich, very rich indeed, remarkably so!'

Waiting until Mr. Brass's ejaculations died away in the

distance (for he continued to pour them out, all the way
down stairs), Quilp advanced towards the two men, who yet
lingered in a kind of stupid amazement.

'Have you been dragging the river all day, gentlemen?'
said the dwarf, holding the door open with great politeness.

'And yesterday too, master.'

'Dear me, you've had a deal of trouble. Pray consider
everything yours that you find upon the—upon the body.
Good night!'

The men looked at each other, but had evidently no inclination to argue the point just then, and shuffled out of the room.
The speedy clearance effected, Quilp locked the doors; and
still embracing the case-bottle with shrugged-up shoulders and
folded arms, stood looking at his insensible wife like a dismounted nightmare.

CHAPTER L

MATRIMONIAL differences are usually discussed by the parties concerned in the form of dialogue, in which the lady bears at least her full half share. Those of Mr. and Mrs. Quilp, however, were an exception to the general rule; the remarks which they occasioned being limited to a long soliloquy on the part of the gentleman, with perhaps a few deprecatory observations from the lady, not extending beyond a trembling monosyllable uttered at long intervals, and in a very submissive and humble tone. On the present occasion, Mrs. Quilp did not for a long time venture even on this gentle defence, but when she had recovered from her fainting-fit, sat in a tearful silence, meekly listening to the reproaches of her lord and master.

Of these Mr. Quilp delivered himself with the utmost animation and rapidity, and with so many distortions of limb and feature, that even his wife, although tolerably well accustomed to his proficiency in these respects, was well-nigh beside herself with alarm. But the Jamaica rum, and the joy of having occasioned a heavy disappointment, by degrees cooled Mr. Quilp's wrath; which from being at savage heat, dropped slowly to the bantering or chuckling point, at which it steadily remained.

'So you thought I was dead and gone, did you?' said Quilp. 'You thought you were a widow, eh? Ha, ha, ha, you jade!'

'Indeed, Quilp,' returned his wife. 'I'm very sorry——'

'Who doubts it?' cried the dwarf. 'You very sorry? to be sure you are. Who doubts that you're *very* sorry?'

'I don't mean sorry that you have come home again alive and well,' said his wife, 'but sorry that I should have been led into such a belief. I am glad to see you, Quilp; indeed I am.'

In truth Mrs. Quilp did seem a great deal more glad to behold her lord than might have been expected, and did evince a degree of interest in his safety which, all things considered, was rather unaccountable. Upon Quilp, however, this circumstance made no impression, farther than as it moved him to snap his fingers close to his wife's eyes, with divers grins of triumph and derision.

'How could you go away so long, without saying a word to me or letting me hear of you or know anything about you?'

asked the poor little woman, sobbing. 'How could you be so cruel, Quilp?'

'How could I be so cruel? cruel!' cried the dwarf. 'Because I was in the humour. I'm in the humour now. I shall be cruel when I like. I'm going away again.'

'Not again!'

'Yes, again. I'm going away now. I'm off directly. I mean to go and live wherever the fancy seizes me—at the wharf—at the counting-house—and be a jolly bachelor. You were a widow in anticipation. Damme,' screamed the dwarf, 'I'll be a bachelor in earnest.'

'You can't be serious, Quilp,' sobbed his wife.

'I tell you,' said the dwarf, exulting in his project, 'that I'll be a bachelor, a devil-may-care bachelor; and I'll have my bachelor's hall at the counting-house, and at such times come near it if you dare. And mind too that I don't pounce in upon you at unseasonable hours again, for I'll be a spy upon you, and come and go like a mole or a weasel. Tom Scott—where's Tom Scott?'

'Here I am, master,' cried the voice of the boy, as Quilp threw up the window.

'Wait there, you dog,' returned the dwarf, 'to carry a bachelor's portmanteau. Pack it up, Mrs. Quilp. Knock up the dear old lady to help; knock her up. Halloa there! Halloa!'

With these exclamations, Mr. Quilp caught up the poker, and hurrying to the door of the good lady's sleeping-closet, beat upon it therewith until she awoke in inexpressible terror, thinking that her amiable son-in-law surely intended to murder her in justification of the legs she had slandered. Impressed with this idea, she was no sooner fairly awake than she screamed violently, and would have quickly precipitated herself out of the window and through a neighbouring skylight, if her daughter had not hastened in to undeceive her, and implore her assistance. Somewhat reassured by her account of the service she was required to render, Mrs. Jiniwin made her appearance in a flannel dressing-gown; and both mother and daughter, trembling with terror and cold—for the night was now far advanced—obeyed Mr. Quilp's directions in submissive silence. Prolonging his preparations as much as possible, for their greater comfort, that eccentric gentleman superintended the packing of his wardrobe, and having added to it with his own hands, a plate, knife and fork, spoon, teacup and saucer, and other small household matters of that nature, strapped up the portmanteau, took it on his shoulders, and actually marched off without another word, and with the case-bottle (which he had never once put down) still tightly clasped under his arm. Consigning his heavier burden to the care of Tom Scott when he reached the street, taking a dram from the bottle for his own encouragement, and giving the boy a rap on the head with it as a small taste for himself, Quilp very deliberately led the way to the wharf, and reached it at between three and four o'clock in the morning.

'Snug!' said Quilp, when he had groped his way to the wooden counting-house, and opened the door with a key he carried about with him. 'Beautifully snug! Call me at eight, you dog.'

With no more formal leave-taking or explanation, he clutched the portmanteau, shut the door on his attendant, and climbing on the desk, and rolling himself up as round as a hedgehog, in an old boat-cloak, fell fast asleep.

Being roused in the morning at the appointed time, and roused with difficulty, after his late fatigues, Quilp instructed Tom Scott to make a fire in the yard of sundry pieces of old timber, and to prepare some coffee for breakfast; for the better furnishing of which repast he entrusted him with certain small moneys, to be expended in the purchase of hot rolls, butter, sugar, Yarmouth bloaters, and other articles of housekeeping; so that in a few minutes a savoury meal was smoking on the board. With this substantial comfort, the dwarf regaled himself to his heart's content; and being highly satisfied with this free and gipsy mode of life (which he had often meditated, as offering, whenever he chose to avail himself of it, an agreeable freedom from the restraints of matrimony, and a choice means of keeping Mrs. Quilp and her mother in a state of incessant agitation and suspense), bestirred himself to improve his retreat, and render it more commodious and comfortable.

With this view, he issued forth to a place hard by, where sea-stores were sold, purchased a second-hand hammock, and had it slung in seamanlike fashion from the ceiling of the counting-house. He also caused to be erected, in the same mouldy cabin, an old ship's stove with a rusty funnel to carry the smoke through the roof; and these arrangements completed, surveyed them with ineffable delight.

'I've got a country-house like Robinson Crusoe,' said the

A Descriptive Advertisement
(p. 367)

dwarf, ogling the accommodations; 'a solitary, sequestered, desolate-island sort of spot, where I can be quite alone when I have business on hand, and be secure from all spies and listeners. Nobody near me here, but rats, and they are fine stealthy secret fellows. I shall be as merry as a grig among these gentry. I'll look out for one like Christopher, and poison him—ha, ha, ha! Business though—business—we must be mindful of business in the midst of pleasure, and the time has flown this morning, I declare.'

Enjoining Tom Scott to await his return, and not to stand upon his head, or throw a summerset, or so much as walk upon his hands meanwhile, on pain of lingering torments, the dwarf threw himself into a boat, and crossing to the other side of the river, and then speeding away on foot, reached Mr. Swiveller's usual house of entertainment in Bevis Marks, just as that gentleman sat down alone to dinner in its dusky parlour.

'Dick'—said the dwarf, thrusting his head in at the door, 'my pet, my pupil, the apple of my eye, hey, hey!'

'Oh you're there, are you?' returned Mr. Swiveller; '*how* are you?'

'How's Dick?' retorted Quilp. 'How's the cream of clerk-ship, eh?'

'Why, rather sour, sir,' replied Mr. Swiveller. 'Beginning to border upon cheesiness, in fact.'

'What's the matter?' said the dwarf, advancing. 'Has Sally proved unkind? "Of all the girls that are so smart, there's none like—" eh, Dick?'

'Certainly not,' replied Mr. Swiveller, eating his dinner with great gravity, 'none like her. She's the sphynx of private life is Sally B.'

'You're out of spirits,' said Quilp, drawing up a chair 'What's the matter?'

'The law don't agree with me,' returned Dick. 'It isn't moist enough, and there's too much confinement. I have been thinking of running away.'

'Bah!' said the dwarf. 'Where would you run to, Dick?'

'I don't know,' returned Mr. Swiveller. 'Towards Highgate, I suppose. Perhaps the bells might strike up "Turn again, Swiveller, Lord Mayor of London." Whittington's name was Dick. I wish cats were scarcer.'

Quilp looked at his companion with his eyes screwed up into a comical expression of curiosity, and patiently awaited his further explanation; upon which, however, Mr. Swiveller appeared in no hurry to enter, as he ate a very long dinner in profound silence, finally pushed away his plate, threw himself back into his chair, folded his arms, and stared ruefully at the fire, in which some ends of cigars were smoking on their own account, and sending up a fragrant odour.

'Perhaps you'd like a bit of cake'—said Dick, at last turning to the dwarf. 'You're quite welcome to it. You ought to be, for it's of your making.'

'What do you mean?' said Quilp.

Mr. Swiveller replied by taking from his pocket a small and very greasy parcel, slowly unfolding it, and displaying a little slab of plum-cake extremely indigestible in appearance, and bordered with a paste of white sugar an inch and a half deep.

'What should you say this was?' demanded Mr. Swiveller.

'It looks like a bride-cake,' replied the dwarf, grinning.

'And whose should you say it was?' inquired Mr. Swiveller, rubbing the pastry against his nose with a dreadful calmness. 'Whose?'

'Not—'

'Yes,' said Dick, 'the same. You needn't mention her name. There's no such name now. Her name is Cheggs now, Sophy Cheggs. Yet loved I as man never loved that hadn't wooden legs, and my heart, my heart is breaking for the love of Sophy Cheggs.'

With this extemporary adaptation of a popular ballad to the distressing circumstances of his own case, Mr. Swiveller folded up the parcel again, beat it very flat between the palms of his hands, thrust it into his breast, buttoned his coat over it, and folded his arms upon the whole.

'Now, I hope you're satisfied, sir,' said Dick; 'and I hope Fred's satisfied. You went partners in the mischief, and I hope you like it. This is the triumph I was to have, is it? It's like the old country-dance of that name, where there are two gentlemen to one lady, and one has her, and the other hasn't, but comes limping up behind to make out the figure. But it's Destiny, and mine's a crusher!'

Disguising his secret joy in Mr. Swiveller's defeat, Daniel Quilp adopted the surest means of soothing him, by ringing the bell, and ordering in a supply of rosy wine (that is to say, of its usual representative), which he put about with great alacrity, calling upon Mr. Swiveller to pledge him in various toasts derisive of Cheggs, and eulogistic of the happiness of single men. Such was their impression on Mr. Swiveller, coupled with the reflection that no man could oppose his destiny, that in a very short space of time his spirits rose surprisingly, and he was enabled to give the dwarf an account of the receipt of the cake, which, it appeared, had been brought to Bevis Marks by the two surviving Miss Wackleses in person, and delivered at the office door with much giggling and joyfulness.

'Ha!' said Quilp. 'It will be our turn to giggle soon. And that reminds me—you spoke of young Trent—where is he?'

Mr. Swiveller explained that his respectable friend had recently accepted a responsible situation in a locomotive gaming-house, and was at that time absent on a professional tour among the adventurous spirits of Great Britain.

'That's unfortunate,' said the dwarf, 'for I came, in fact, to ask you about him. A thought has occurred to me, Dick; your friend over the way—'

'Which friend?'

'In the first floor.'

'Yes?'

'Your friend in the first floor, Dick, may know him.'

'No, he don't,' said Mr. Swiveller, shaking his head.

'Don't! No, because he has never seen him,' rejoined Quilp; 'but if we were to bring them together, who knows, Dick, but Fred, properly introduced, would serve his turn almost as well as little Nell or her grandfather—who knows but it might make the young fellow's fortune, and, through him, yours, eh?'

'Why, the fact is, you see,' said Mr. Swiveller, 'that they *have been* brought together.'

'Have been!' cried the dwarf, looking suspiciously at his companion. 'Through whose means?'

'Through mine,' said Dick, slightly confused. 'Didn't I mention it to you the last time you called over yonder?'

'You know you didn't,' returned the dwarf.

'I believe you're right,' said Dick. 'No. I didn't, I recollect. Oh yes, I brought 'em together that very day. It was Fred's suggestion.'

'And what came of it?'

'Why, instead of my friend's bursting into tears when he knew who Fred was, embracing him kindly, and telling him that he was his grandfather, or his grandmother in disguise (which we fully expected), he flew into a tremendous passion; called him all manner of names; said it was in a great measure his fault that little Nell and the old gentleman had ever been brought to poverty; didn't hint at our taking anything to drink; and—and in short rather turned us out of the room than otherwise.'

'That's strange,' said the dwarf, musing.

'So we remarked to each other at the time,' returned Dick coolly, 'but quite true.'

Quilp was plainly staggered by this intelligence, over which he brooded for some time in moody silence, often raising his eyes to Mr. Swiveller's face, and sharply scanning its expression. As he could read in it, however, no additional information or anything to lead him to believe he had spoken falsely; and as Mr. Swiveller, left to his own meditations, sighed deeply, and was evidently growing maudlin on the subject of Mrs. Cheggs; the dwarf soon broke up the conference and took his departure, leaving the bereaved one to his melancholy ruminations.

'Have been brought together, eh?' said the dwarf as he walked the streets alone. 'My friend has stolen a march upon me. It led him to nothing, and therefore is no great matter, save in the intention. I'm glad he has lost his mistress. Ha ha! The blockhead mustn't leave the law at present. I'm sure of him where he is, whenever I want him for my own purposes, and, besides, he's a good unconscious spy on Brass, and tells, in his cups, all that he sees and hears. You're useful to me, Dick, and cost nothing but a little treating now and then. I am not sure that it may not be worth while, before long, to take credit with the stranger, Dick, by discovering your designs upon the child; but for the present we'll remain the best friends in the world, with your good leave.'

Pursuing these thoughts, and gasping as he went along, after his own peculiar fashion, Mr. Quilp once more crossed the Thames, and shut himself up in his Bachelor's Hall, which, by reason of its newly-erected chimney depositing the smoke inside the room and carrying none of it off, was not quite so agreeable as more fastidious people might have desired. Such inconveniences, however, instead of disgusting the dwarf with his new abode, rather suited his humour; so, after dining luxuriously from the public-house, he lighted his pipe, and smoked against the chimney until nothing of him was visible

Mrs. Quilp visits Bachelor's Hall

through the mist but a pair of red and highly inflamed eyes, with sometimes a dim vision of his head and face, as, in a violent fit of coughing, he slightly stirred the smoke and scattered the heavy wreaths by which they were obscured. In the midst of this atmosphere, which must infallibly have smothered any other man, Mr. Quilp passed the evening with great cheerfulness; solacing himself all the time with the pipe and the casebottle; and occasionally entertaining himself with a melodious howl, intended for a song, but bearing not the faintest resemblance to any scrap of any piece of music, vocal or instrumental, ever invented by man. Thus he amused himself until nearly midnight, when he turned into his hammock with the utmost satisfaction.

The first sound that met his ears in the morning—as he half opened his eyes, and, finding himself so unusually near the ceiling, entertained a drowsy idea that he must have been transformed into a fly or bluebottle in the course of the night,— was that of a stifled sobbing and weeping in the room. Peeping cautiously over the side of his hammock, he descried Mrs. Quilp, to whom, after contemplating her for some time in silence, he communicated a violent start by suddenly yelling out—

'Halloa!'

'Oh, Quilp!' cried his poor little wife, looking up. 'How you frightened me!'

'I meant to, you jade,' returned the dwarf. 'What do you want here? I'm dead, an't I?'

'Oh, please come home, do come home,' said Mrs. Quilp, sobbing; 'we'll never do so any more, Quilp, and after all it was only a mistake that grew out of our anxiety.'

'Out of your anxiety,' grinned the dwarf. 'Yes, I know that —out of your anxiety for my death. I shall come home when I please, I tell you. I shall come home when I please, and go when I please. I'll be a Will o' the Wisp, now here, now there, dancing about you always, starting up when you least expect me, and keeping you in a constant state of restlessness and irritation. Will you begone?'

Mrs. Quilp durst only make a gesture of entreaty.

'I tell you no,' cried the dwarf. 'No. If you dare to come here again unless you're sent for, I'll keep watch-dogs in the yard that'll growl and bite—I'll have man-traps, cunningly altered and improved for catching women—I'll have spring guns, that shall explode when you tread upon the wires, and blow you into little pieces. Will you go?'

'Do forgive me. Do come back,' said his wife, earnestly.

'No-o-o-o-o!' roared Quilp. 'Not till my own good time, and then I'll return again as often as I choose, and be accountable to nobody for my goings or comings. You see the door there. Will you go?'

Mr. Quilp delivered this last command in such a very energetic voice, and moreover accompanied it with such a sudden gesture, indicative of an intention to spring out of his hammock, and, nightcapped as he was, bear his wife home again through the public streets, that she sped away like an arrow. Her worthy lord stretched his neck and eyes until she had crossed the yard, and then, not at all sorry to have had this opportunity of carrying his point, and asserting the sanctity of his castle, fell into an immoderate fit of laughter, and laid himself down to sleep again.

CHAPTER LI

THE bland and open-hearted proprietor of Bachelor's Hall slept on amidst the congenial accompaniments of rain, mud, dirt, damp, fog, and rats, until late in the day; when, summoning his valet Tom Scott to assist him to rise, and to prepare breakfast, he quitted his couch, and made his toilet. This duty performed, and his repast ended, he again betook himself to Bevis Marks.

This visit was not intended for Mr. Swiveller, but for his friend and employer Mr. Sampson Brass. Both gentlemen, however, were from home, nor was the life and light of law, Miss Sally, at her post either. The fact of their joint desertion of the office was made known to all comers by a scrap of paper in the handwriting of Mr. Swiveller, which was attached to the bell-handle, and which, giving the reader no clue to the time of day when it was first posted, furnished him with the rather vague and unsatisfactory information that that gentleman would 'return in an hour.'

'There's a servant, I suppose,' said the dwarf, knocking at the house-door. 'She'll do.'

After a sufficiently long interval, the door was opened, and a small voice immediately accosted him with, 'Oh please will you leave a card or message?'

'Eh?' said the dwarf, looking down (it was something quite new to him) upon the small servant.

To this, the child, conducting her conversation as upon the occasion of her first interview with Mr. Swiveller, again replied, 'Oh please will you leave a card or message?'

'I'll write a note,' said the dwarf, pushing past her into the office; 'and mind your master has it directly he comes home.' So Mr. Quilp climbed up to the top of a tall stool to write the note, and the small servant, carefully tutored for such emergencies, looked on with her eyes wide open, ready, if he so much as abstracted a wafer, to rush into the street and give the alarm to the police.

As Mr. Quilp folded his note (which was soon written: being a very short one) he encountered the gaze of the small servant. He looked at her, long and earnestly.

'How are you?' said the dwarf, moistening a wafer with horrible grimaces.

The small servant, perhaps frightened by his looks, returned no audible reply; but it appeared from the motion of her lips that she was inwardly repeating the same form of expression concerning the note or message.

'Do they use you ill here? is your mistress a Tartar?' said Quilp with a chuckle.

In reply to the last interrogation, the small servant, with a look of infinite cunning mingled with fear, screwed up her mouth very tight and round, and nodded violently.

Whether there was anything in the peculiar slyness of her action which fascinated Mr. Quilp, or anything in the expression of her features at the moment which attracted his attention for some other reason; or whether it merely occurred to him as a pleasant whim to stare the small servant out of countenance; certain it is, that he planted his elbows square and firmly on the desk, and squeezing up his cheeks with his hands, looked at her fixedly.

'Where do you come from?' he said after a long pause, stroking his chin.

'I don't know.'

'What's your name?'

'Nothing.'

'Nonsense!' retorted Quilp. 'What does your mistress call you when she wants you?'

'A little devil,' said the child.

She added in the same breath, as if fearful of any further questioning, 'But please will you leave a card or message?'

These unusual answers might naturally have provoked some more inquiries. Quilp, however, without uttering another word, withdrew his eyes from the small servant, stroked his chin more thoughtfully than before, and then, bending over the note as if to direct it with scrupulous and hairbreadth nicety, looked at her, covertly but very narrowly, from under his bushy eyebrows. The result of this secret survey was, that he shaded his face with his hands, and laughed slyly and noiselessly, until every vein in it was swollen almost to bursting. Pulling his hat over his brow to conceal his mirth and its effects, he tossed the letter to the child, and hastily withdrew.

Once in the street, moved by some secret impulse, he laughed, and held his sides, and laughed again, and tried to peer through the dusty area railings as if to catch another glimpse of the child, until he was quite tired out. At last, he travelled back to the Wilderness, which was within rifle-shot of his bachelor retreat, and ordered tea in the wooden summer-house that afternoon for three persons; an invitation to Miss Sally Brass and her brother to partake of that entertainment at that place, having been the object both of his journey and his note.

It was not precisely the kind of weather in which people usually take tea in summer-houses, far less in summer-houses in an advanced state of decay, and overlooking the slimy banks of a great river at low water. Nevertheless, it was in this choice retreat that Mr. Quilp ordered a cold collation to be prepared, and it was beneath its cracked and leaky roof that he, in due course of time, received Mr. Sampson and his sister Sally.

'You're fond of the beauties of nature,' said Quilp with a grin. 'Is this charming, Brass? Is it unusual, unsophisticated, primitive?'

'It's delightful indeed, sir,' replied the lawyer.

'Cool?' said Quilp.

'N-not particularly so, I think, sir,' rejoined Brass, with his teeth chattering in his head.

'Perhaps a little damp and ague-ish?' said Quilp.

'Just damp enough to be cheerful, sir,' rejoined Brass. 'Nothing more, sir, nothing more.'

'And Sally?' said the delighted dwarf. 'Does *she* like it?'

'She'll like it better,' returned that strong-minded lady, 'when she has tea; so let us have it, and don't bother.'

'Sweet Sally!' cried Quilp, extending his arms as if about to embrace her. 'Gentle, charming, overwhelming Sally.'

'He's a very remarkable man indeed!' soliloquised Mr. Brass. 'He's quite a Troubadour, you know; quite a Troubadour!'

These complimentary expressions were uttered in a somewhat absent and distracted manner; for the unfortunate lawyer, besides having a bad cold in his head, had got wet in coming, and would have willingly borne some pecuniary sacrifice if he could have shifted his present raw quarters to a warm room, and dried himself at a fire. Quilp, however,—who, beyond the gratification of his demon whims, owed Sampson some acknowledgment of the part he had played in the mourning scene of which he had been a hidden witness, marked these symptoms of uneasiness with a delight past all expression, and derived from them a secret joy which the costliest banquet could never have afforded him.

It is worthy of remark, too, as illustrating a little feature in the character of Miss Sally Brass, that, although on her own account she would have borne the discomforts of the Wilderness with a very ill grace, and would probably, indeed, have walked off before the tea appeared, she no sooner beheld the latent uneasiness and misery of her brother than she developed a grim satisfaction, and began to enjoy herself after her own manner. Though the wet came stealing through the roof and trickling down upon their heads, Miss Brass uttered no complaint, but presided over the tea equipage with imperturbable composure. While Mr. Quilp, in his uproarious hospitality, seated himself upon an empty beer-barrel, vaunted the place as the most beautiful and comfortable in the three kingdoms, and elevating his glass, drank to their next merry-meeting in that jovial spot; and Mr. Brass, with the rain plashing down into his teacup, made a dismal attempt to pluck up his spirits and appear at his ease; and Tom Scott, who was in waiting at the door under an old umbrella, exulted in his agonies, and bade fair to split his sides with laughing; while all this was passing, Miss Sally Brass, unmindful of the wet which dripped down upon her own feminine person and fair apparel, sat placidly behind the tea-board erect and grizzly, contemplating the unhappiness of her brother with a mind at ease, and content, in her amiable disregard of self, to sit there all night, witnessing the torments which his avaricious and grovelling nature compelled him to endure and forbade him to resent. And this, it must be observed, or the illustration would be incomplete, although in a business point of view she had the strongest sympathy with Mr. Sampson, and would have been beyond measure indignant if he had thwarted their client in any one respect.

In the height of his boisterous merriment, Mr. Quilp, having on some pretence dismissed his attendant sprite for the moment, resumed his usual manner all at once, dismounted from his cask, and laid his hand upon the lawyer's sleeve.

'A word,' said the dwarf, 'before we go farther. Sally, hark'ee for a minute.'

Miss Sally drew closer, as if accustomed to business conferences with their host which were the better for not having air.

'Business,' said the dwarf, glancing from brother to sister. 'Very private business. Lay your heads together when you're by yourselves.'

'Certainly, Sir,' returned Brass, taking out his pocket-book and pencil. 'I'll take down the heads if you please, sir. Remarkable documents,' added the lawyer, raising his eyes to the ceiling, 'most remarkable documents. He states his points so clearly that it's a treat to have 'em! I don't know any act of parliament that's equal to him in clearness.'

'I shall deprive you of a treat,' said Quilp. 'Put up your book. We don't want any documents. So. There's a lad named Kit—'

Miss Sally nodded, implying that she knew of him.

'Kit!' said Mr. Sampson.—'Kit! Ha! I've heard the name before, but I don't exactly call to mind—I don't exactly—'

'You're as slow as a tortoise, and more thick-headed than a rhinoceros,' returned his obliging client with an impatient gesture.

'He's extremely pleasant!' cried the obsequious Sampson. 'His acquaintance with Natural History too is surprising. Quite a Buffoon, quite!'

There is no doubt that Mr. Brass intended some compliment or other; and it has been argued with show of reason that he would have said Buffon, but made use of a superfluous vowel. Be this as it may, Quilp gave him no time for correction, as he performed that office himself by more than tapping him on the head with the handle of his umbrella.

'Don't let's have any wrangling,' said Miss Sally, staying his hand. 'I've showed you that I know him, and that's enough.'

'She's always foremost!' said the dwarf, patting her on the back and looking contemptuously at Sampson. 'I don't like Kit, Sally.'

'Nor I,' rejoined Miss Brass.

'Nor I,' said Sampson.

'Why, that's right!' cried Quilp. 'Half our work is done already. This Kit is one of your honest people; one of your fair characters; a prowling prying hound; a hypocrite; a double-faced, white-livered, sneaking spy; a crouching cur to those that feed and coax him, and a barking yelping dog to all besides.'

'Fearfully eloquent!' cried Brass with a sneeze. 'Quite appalling!'

'Come to the point,' said Miss Sally, 'and don't talk so much.'

'Right again!' exclaimed Quilp, with another contemptuous look at Sampson, 'always foremost! I say, Sally, he is a yelping, insolent dog to all besides, and most of all, to me. In short, I owe him a grudge.'

'That's enough, sir,' said Sampson.

'No, it's not enough, sir,' sneered Quilp; 'will you hear me out? Besides that I owe him a grudge on that account, he thwarts me at this minute, and stands between me and an end which might otherwise prove a golden one to us all. Apart from that, I repeat that he crosses my humour, and I hate him. Now, you know the lad, and can guess the rest. Devise your own means of putting him out of my way, and execute them. Shall it be done?'

'It shall, sir,' said Sampson.

'Then give me your hand,' retorted Quilp. 'Sally, girl, yours. I rely as much, or more, on you than him. Tom Scott comes back. Lantern, pipes, more grog, and a jolly night of it!'

No other word was spoken, no other look exchanged, which had the slightest reference to this, the real occasion of their meeting. The trio were well accustomed to act together, and were linked to each other by ties of mutual interest and advantage, and nothing more was needed. Resuming his boisterous manner with the same ease with which he had thrown it off, Quilp was in an instant the same uproarious, reckless little savage he had been a few seconds before. It was ten o'clock at night before the amiable Sally supported her beloved and loving brother from the Wilderness, by which time he needed the utmost support her tender frame could render; his walk being from some unknown reason anything but steady, and his legs constantly doubling up in unexpected places.

Overpowered, notwithstanding his late prolonged slumbers, by the fatigues of the last few days, the dwarf lost no time in creeping to his dainty house, and was soon dreaming in his hammock. Leaving him to visions, in which perhaps the quiet figures we quitted in the old church porch were not without their share, be it our task to rejoin them as they sat and watched.

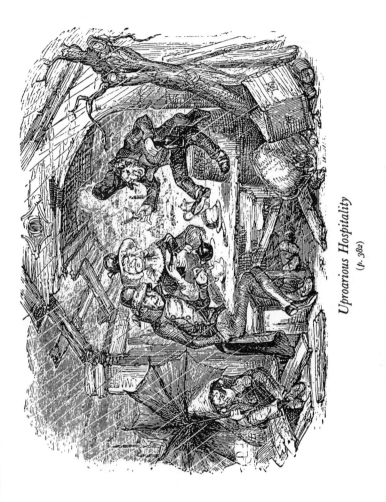

Uproarious Hospitality

(p. 382)

CHAPTER LII

AFTER a long time, the schoolmaster appeared at the wicket-gate of the churchyard, and hurried towards them, jingling in his hand, as he came along, a bundle of rusty keys. He was quite breathless with pleasure and haste when he reached the porch, and at first could only point towards the old building which the child had been contemplating so earnestly.

'You see those two old houses,' he said at last.

'Yes, surely,' replied Nell. 'I have been looking at them nearly all the time you have been away.'

'And you would have looked at them more curiously yet, if you could have guessed what I have to tell you,' said her friend. 'One of those houses is mine.'

Without saying any more, or giving the child time to reply, the schoolmaster took her hand, and, his honest face quite radiant with exultation, led her to the place of which he spoke.

They stopped before its low arched door. After trying several of the keys in vain, the schoolmaster found one to fit the huge lock, which turned back, creaking, and admitted them into the house.

The room into which they entered was a vaulted chamber once nobly ornamented by cunning architects, and still retaining, in its beautiful groined roof and rich stone tracery, choice remnants of its ancient splendour. Foliage carved in the stone, and emulating the mastery of Nature's hand, yet remained to tell how many times the leaves outside had come and gone, while it lived on unchanged. The broken figures supporting the burden of the chimney-piece, though mutilated, were still distinguishable for what they had been—far different from the dust without—and showed sadly by the empty hearth, like creatures who had outlived their kind, and mourned their own too slow decay.

In some old time—for even change was old in that old place —a wooden partition had been constructed in one part of the chamber to form a sleeping-closet, into which the light was admitted at the same period by a rude window, or rather niche, cut in the solid wall. This screen, together with two seats in the broad chimney, had at some forgotten date been part of the church or convent; for the oak, hastily appropriated to its present purpose, had been little altered from its former shape, and presented to the eye a pile of fragments of rich carving from old monkish stalls.

An open door leading to a small room or cell, dim with the light that came through leaves of ivy, completed the interior of this portion of the ruin. It was not quite destitute of furniture. A few strange chairs, whose arms and legs looked as though they had dwindled away with age; a table, the very spectre of its race; a great old chest that had once held records in the church, with other quaintly-fashioned domestic necessaries, and store of firewood for the winter, were scattered around, and gave evident tokens of its occupation as a dwelling-place at no very distant time.

The child looked around her, with that solemn feeling with which we contemplate the work of ages that have become but drops of water in the great ocean of eternity. The old man had followed them, but they were all three hushed for a space, and drew their breath softly, as if they feared to break the silence even by so slight a sound.

'It is a very beautiful place!' said the child, in a low voice.

'I almost feared you thought otherwise,' returned the schoolmaster. 'You shivered when we first came in, as if you felt it cold or gloomy.'

'It was not that,' said Nell, glancing round with a slight shudder. 'Indeed I cannot tell you what it was, but when I saw the outside, from the church porch, the same feeling came over me. It is its being so old and grey perhaps.'

'A peaceful place to live in, don't you think so?' said her friend.

'Oh yes,' rejoined the child, clasping her hands earnestly. 'A quiet, happy place—a place to live and learn to die in!' She would have said more, but that the energy of her thoughts caused her voice to falter, and come in trembling whispers from her lips.

'A place to live, and learn to live, and gather health of mind and body in,' said the schoolmaster; 'for this old house is yours.'

'Ours!' cried the child.

'Ay,' returned the schoolmaster gaily, 'for many a merry year to come, I hope. I shall be a close neighbour—only next door—but this house is yours.'

Having now disburdened himself of his great surprise, the schoolmaster sat down, and drawing Nell to his side, told her how he had learnt that that ancient tenement had been occupied for a very long time by an old person, nearly a hundred years of age, who kept the keys of the church, opened and closed it for the services, and showed it to strangers; how she had died not many weeks ago, and nobody had yet been found to fill the office; how, learning all this in an interview with the sexton, who was confined to his bed by rheumatism, he had been bold to make mention of his fellow-travellers, which had been so favourably received by that high authority, that he had taken courage, acting on his advice, to propound the matter to the clergyman. In a word, the result of his exertions was, that Nell and her grandfather were to be carried before the last-named gentleman next day; and, his approval of their conduct and appearance reserved as a matter of form, that they were already appointed to the vacant post.

'There's a small allowance of money,' said the school-master. 'It is not much, but still enough to live upon in this retired spot. By clubbing our funds together, we shall do bravely; no fear of that.'

'Heaven bless and prosper you!' sobbed the child.

'Amen, my dear,' returned her friend cheerfully; 'and all of us, as it will, and has, in leading us through sorrow and trouble to this tranquil life. But we must look at *my* house now. Come!'

They repaired to the other tenement; tried the rusty keys as before; at length found the right one; and opened the worm-eaten door. It led into a chamber, vaulted and old, like that from which they had come, but not so spacious, and having only one other little room attached. It was not difficult to divine that the other house was of right the schoolmaster's, and that he had chosen for himself the least commodious, in his care and regard for them. Like the adjoining habitation, it held such old articles of furniture as were absolutely necessary, and had its stack of firewood.

To make these dwellings as habitable and full of comfort as they could, was now their pleasant care. In a short time, each had its cheerful fire glowing and crackling on the hearth, and reddening the pale old wall with a hale and healthy blush. Nell, busily plying her needle, repaired the tattered window-hangings, drew together the rents that time had worn in the threadbare scraps of carpet, and made them whole and decent. The schoolmaster swept and smoothed the ground before the door, trimmed the long grass, trained the ivy and creeping plants which hung their drooping heads in melancholy neglect;

and gave to the outer walls a cheery air of home. The old man, sometimes by his side and sometimes with the child, lent his aid to both, went here and there on little patient services, and was happy. Neighbours, too, as they came from work, proffered their help; or sent their children with such small presents or loans as the strangers needed most. It was a busy day; and night came on, and found them wondering that there was yet so much to do, and that it should be dark so soon.

They took their supper together, in the house which may be henceforth called the child's; and, when they had finished their meal, drew round the fire, and almost in whispers—their hearts were too quiet and glad for loud expression—discussed their future plans. Before they separated, the schoolmaster read some prayers aloud; and then, full of gratitude and happiness, they parted for the night.

At that silent hour, when her grandfather was sleeping peacefully in his bed, and every sound was hushed, the child lingered before the dying embers, and thought of her past fortunes as if they had been a dream and she only now awoke. The glare of the sinking flame, reflected in the oaken panels whose carved tops were dimly seen in the dusky roof—the aged walls, where strange shadows came and went with every flickering of the fire—the solemn presence, within, of that decay which falls on senseless things the most enduring in their nature: and, without, and round about on every side, of Death —filled her with deep and thoughtful feelings, but with none of terror or alarm. A change had been gradually stealing over her, in the time of her loneliness and sorrow. With failing strength and heightening resolution, there had sprung up a purified and altered mind; there had grown in her bosom blessed thoughts and hopes, which are the portion of few but the weak and drooping. There were none to see the frail, perishable figure, as it glided from the fire and leaned pensively at the open casement; none but the stars, to look into the up-turned face and read its history. The old church bell rang out the hour with a mournful sound, as if it had grown sad from so much communing with the dead and unheeded warning to the living; the fallen leaves rustled; the grass stirred upon the graves; all else was still and sleeping.

Some of those dreamless sleepers lay close within the shadow of the church—touching the wall, as if they clung to it for comfort and protection. Others had chosen to lie beneath the

Nell's New Home
(*p. 385*)

changing shade of trees; others by the path, that footsteps might come near them; others, among the graves of little children. Some had desired to rest beneath the very ground they had trodden in their daily walks; some, where the setting sun might shine upon their beds; some, where its light would fall upon them when it rose. Perhaps not one of the imprisoned souls had been able quite to separate itself in living thought from its old companion. If any had, it had still felt for it a love like that which captives have been known to bear towards the cell in which they have been long confined, and, even at parting, hung upon its narrow bounds affectionately.

It was long before the child closed the window, and approached her bed. Again something of the same sensation as before—an involuntary chill—a momentary feeling akin to fear—but vanishing directly, and leaving no alarm behind. Again, too, dreams of the little scholar; of the roof opening, and a column of bright faces, rising far away into the sky, as she had seen in some old scriptural picture once, and looking down on her, asleep. It was a sweet and happy dream. The quiet spot, outside, seemed to remain the same, saving that there was music in the air, and a sound of angel's wings. After a time the sisters came there, hand in hand, and stood among the graves. And then the dream grew dim, and faded.

With the brightness and joy of morning, came the renewal of yesterday's labours, the revival of its pleasant thoughts, the restoration of its energies, cheerfulness, and hope. They worked gaily in ordering and arranging their houses until noon, and then went to visit the clergyman.

He was a simple-hearted old gentleman, of a shrinking, subdued spirit, accustomed to retirement, and very little acquainted with the world, which he had left many years before to come and settle in that place. His wife had died in the house in which he still lived, and he had long since lost sight of any earthly cares or hopes beyond it.

He received them very kindly, and at once showed an interest in Nell; asking her name, and age, her birthplace, the circumstances which had led her there, and so forth. The schoolmaster had already told her story. They had no other friends or home to leave, he said, and had come to share his fortunes. He loved the child as though she were his own.

'Well, well,' said the clergyman. 'Let it be as you desire. She is very young.'

R

'Old in adversity and trial, sir,' replied the schoolmaster.

'God help her. Let her rest, and forget them,' said the old gentleman. 'But an old church is a dull and gloomy place for one so young as you, my child.'

'Oh no, sir,' returned Nell. 'I have no such thoughts, indeed.'

'I would rather see her dancing on the green at nights,' said the old gentleman, laying his hand upon her head, and smiling sadly, 'than have her sitting in the shadow of our mouldering arches. You must look to this, and see that her heart does not grow heavy among these solemn ruins. Your request is granted, friend.'

After more kind words, they withdrew, and repaired to the child's house; where they were yet in conversation on their happy fortune, when another friend appeared.

This was a little old gentleman, who lived in the parsonage-house, and had resided there (so they learnt soon afterwards) ever since the death of the clergyman's wife, which had happened fifteen years before. He had been his college friend and always his close companion; in the first shock of his grief he had come to console and comfort him; and from that time they had never parted company. The little old gentleman was the active spirit of the place, the adjuster of all differences, the promoter of all merry-makings, the dispenser of his friend's bounty, and of no small charity of his own besides; the universal mediator, comforter, and friend. None of the simple villagers had cared to ask his name, or, when they knew it, to store it in their memory. Perhaps from some vague rumour of his college honours which had been whispered abroad on his first arrival, perhaps because he was an unmarried, unencumbered gentleman, he had been called the bachelor. The name pleased him, or suited him as well as any other, and the Bachelor he had ever since remained. And the bachelor it was, it may be added, who with his own hands had laid in the stock of fuel which the wanderers had found in their new habitation.

The bachelor, then—to call him by his usual appellation—lifted the latch, showed his little round mild face for a moment at the door, and stepped into the room like one who was no stranger to it.

'You are Mr. Marton, the new schoolmaster?' he said, greeting Nell's kind friend.

'I am, sir.'

'You come well recommended, and I am glad to see you. I should have been in the way yesterday, expecting you, but I rode across the country to carry a message from a sick mother to her daughter in service some miles off, and have but just now returned. This is our young church-keeper? You are not the less welcome, friend, for her sake, or for this old man's; nor the worse teacher for having learnt humanity.'

'She has been ill, sir, very lately,' said the schoolmaster, in answer to the look with which their visitor regarded Nell when he had kissed her cheek.

'Yes, yes. I know she has,' he rejoined. 'There have been suffering and heartache here.'

'Indeed there have, sir.'

The little old gentleman glanced at the grandfather, and back again at the child, whose hand he took tenderly in his, and held.

'You will be happier here,' he said; 'we will try, at least, to make you so. You have made great improvements here already. Are they the work of your hands?'

'Yes, sir.'

'We may make some others—not better in themselves, but with better means perhaps,' said the bachelor. 'Let us see now, let us see.'

Nell accompanied him into the other little rooms, and over both the houses, in which he found various small comforts wanting, which he engaged to supply from a certain collection of odds and ends he had at home, and which must have been a very miscellaneous and extensive one, as it comprehended the most opposite articles imaginable. They all came, however, and came without loss of time; for the little old gentleman, disappearing for some five or ten minutes, presently returned, laden with old shelves, rugs, blankets, and other household gear, and followed by a boy bearing a similar load. These being cast on the floor in a promiscuous heap, yielded a quantity of occupation in arranging, erecting, and putting away; the superintendence of which task evidently afforded the old gentleman extreme delight, and engaged him for some time with great briskness and activity. When nothing more was left to be done, he charged the boy to run off and bring his schoolmates to be marshalled before their new master, and solemnly reviewed.

'As good a set of fellows, Marton, as you'd wish to see,' he said, turning to the schoolmaster when the boy was gone; 'but I don't let 'em know I think so. That wouldn't do, at all.'

The messenger soon returned at the head of a long row of urchins, great and small, who, being confronted by the bachelor at the house door, fell into various convulsions of politeness; clutching their hats and caps, squeezing them into the smallest possible dimensions, and making all manner of bows and scrapes, which the little old gentleman contemplated with excessive satisfaction, and expressed his approval of by a great many nods and smiles. Indeed, his approbation of the boys was by no means so scrupulously disguised as he had led the schoolmaster to suppose, inasmuch as it broke out in sundry loud whispers and confidential remarks which were perfectly audible to them every one.

'This first boy, schoolmaster,' said the bachelor, 'is John Owen; a lad of good parts, sir, and frank, honest temper; but too thoughtless, too playful, too light-headed by far. That boy, my good sir, would break his neck with pleasure, and deprive his parents of their chief comfort—and between ourselves, when you come to see him at hare and hounds, taking the fence and ditch by the finger-post, and sliding down the face of the little quarry, you'll never forget it. It's beautiful!'

John Owen having been thus rebuked, and being in perfect possession of the speech aside, the bachelor singled out another boy.

'Now, look at that lad, sir,' said the bachelor. 'You see that fellow? Richard Evans his name is, sir. An amazing boy to learn, blessed with a good memory, and a ready understanding, and moreover with a good voice and ear for psalm-singing, in which he is the best among us. Yet, sir, that boy will come to a bad end; he'll never die in his bed; he's always falling asleep in sermon-time—and to tell you the truth, Mr. Marton, I always did the same at his age, and feel quite certain that it was natural to my constitution and I couldn't help it.'

This hopeful pupil edified by the above terrible reproval, the bachelor turned to another.

'But if we talk of examples to be shunned,' said he, 'if we come to boys that should be a warning and a beacon to all their fellows, here's the one, and I hope you won't spare him. This is the lad, sir; this one with the blue eyes and light hair. This is a swimmer, sir, this fellow—a diver, Lord save us! This is a boy, sir, who had a fancy for plunging into eighteen feet of water, with his clothes on, and bringing up a blind man's dog, who was being drowned by the weight of his chain and collar, while his master stood wringing his hands upon the bank, bewailing the loss of his guide and friend. I sent the boy two guineas anonymously, sir,' added the bachelor, in his peculiar whisper, 'directly I heard of it; but never mention it on any account, for he hasn't the least idea that it came from me.'

Having disposed of this culprit, the bachelor turned to another, and from him to another, and so on through the whole array, laying, for their wholesome restriction within due bounds, the same cutting emphasis on such of their propensities as were dearest to his heart and were unquestionably referable to his own precept and example. Thoroughly persuaded, in the end, that he had made them miserable by his severity, he dismissed them with a small present, and an admonition to walk quietly home, without any leapings, scufflings, or turnings out of the way; which injunction, he informed the schoolmaster in the same audible confidence, he did not think he could have obeyed when he was a boy, had his life depended on it.

Hailing these little tokens of the bachelor's disposition as so many assurances of his own welcome course from that time, the schoolmaster parted from him with a light heart and joyous spirits, and deemed himself one of the happiest men on earth. The windows of the two old houses were ruddy again, that night, with the reflection of the cheerful fires that burnt within; and the bachelor and his friend, pausing to look upon them as they returned from their evening walk, spoke softly together of the beautiful child, and looked round upon the churchyard with a sigh.

CHAPTER LIII

NELL was stirring early in the morning, and having discharged her household tasks, and put everything in order for the good schoolmaster (though sorely against his will, for he would have spared her the pains), took down, from its nail by the fireside, a little bundle of keys with which the bachelor had formally invested her on the previous day, and went out alone to visit the old church.

The sky was serene and bright, the air clear, perfumed with the fresh scent of newly fallen leaves, and grateful to every sense. The neighbouring stream sparkled, and rolled onward with a tuneful sound; the dew glistened on the green mounds, like tears shed by Good Spirits over the dead.

Some young children sported among the tombs, and hid from each other, with laughing faces. They had an infant with them, and had laid it down asleep upon a child's grave, in a little bed of leaves. It was a new grave—the resting-place, perhaps, of some little creature, who, meek and patient in its illness, had often sat and watched them, and now seemed, to their minds, scarcely changed.

She drew near and asked one of them whose grave it was. The child answered that that was not its name; it was a garden —his brother's. It was greener, he said, than all the other gardens, and the birds loved it better because he had been used to feed them. When he had done speaking, he looked at her with a smile, and kneeling down and nestling for a moment with his cheek against the turf, bounded merrily away.

She passed the church, gazing upward at its old tower, went through the wicket gate, and so into the village. The old sexton, leaning on a crutch, was taking the air at his cottage door, and gave her good morrow.

'You are better?' said the child, stopping to speak to him.

'Ay surely,' returned the old man. 'I'm thankful to say, much better.'

'You will be quite well soon.'

'With Heaven's leave, and a little patience. But come in, come in!'

The old man limped on before, and warning her of the downward step, which he achieved himself with no small difficulty, led the way into his little cottage.

'It is but one room, you see. There is another up above, but the stair has got harder to climb o' late years, and I never use it. I'm thinking of taking to it again, next summer, though.'

The child wondered how a grey-headed man like him—one of his trade too—could talk of time so easily. He saw her eyes wandering to the tools that hung upon the wall, and smiled.

'I warrant now,' he said, 'that you think all those are used in making graves.'

'Indeed, I wondered that you wanted so many.'

'And well you might. I am a gardener. I dig the ground, and plant things that are to live and grow. My works don't all moulder away, and rot in the earth. You see that spade in the centre?'

'The very old one—so notched and worn? Yes.'

'That's the sexton's spade, and it's a well-used one, as you see. We're healthy people here, but it has done a power of work. If it could speak now, that spade, it would tell you of many an unexpected job that it and I have done together; but I forget 'em, for my memory's a poor one.—That's nothing new,' he added hastily. 'It always was.'

'There are flowers and shrubs to speak to your other work,' said the child.

'Oh yes. And tall trees. But they are not so separate from the sexton's labours as you think.'

'No!'

'Not in my mind, and recollection—such as it is,' said the old man. 'Indeed they often help it. For say that I planted such a tree for such a man. There it stands, to remind me that he died. When I look at its broad shadow, and remember what it was in his time, it helps me to the age of my other work, and I can tell you pretty nearly when I made his grave.'

'But it may remind you of one who is still alive,' said the child.

'Of twenty that are dead, in connexion with that one who lives, then,' rejoined the old man; 'wife, husband, parents, brothers, sisters, children, friends—a score at least. So it happens that the sexton's spade gets worn and battered. I shall need a new one—next summer.'

The child looked quickly towards him, thinking that he jested with his age and infirmity: but the unconscious sexton was quite in earnest.

'Ah!' he said, after a brief silence. 'People never learn.

They never learn. It's only we who turn up the ground, where nothing grows and everything decays, who think of such things as these—who think of them properly, I mean. You have been into the church?'

'I am going there now,' the child replied.

'There's an old well there,' said the sexton, 'right underneath the belfry; a deep, dark, echoing well. Forty year ago, you had only to let down the bucket till the first knot in the rope was free of the windlass, and you heard it splashing in the cold dull water. By little and little the water fell away, so that in ten year after that, a second knot was made, and you must unwind so much rope, or the bucket swung light and empty at the end. In ten years' time, the water fell again, and a third knot was made. In ten years more, the well dried up; and now, if you lower the bucket till your arms are tired, and let out nearly all the cord, you'll hear it, of a sudden, clanking and rattling on the ground below; with a sound of being so deep and so far down, that your heart leaps into your mouth, and you start away as if you were falling in.'

'A dreadful place to come on in the dark!' exclaimed the child, who had followed the old man's looks and words until she seemed to stand upon its brink.

'What is it but a grave!' said the sexton. 'What else! And which of our old folks, knowing all this, thought, as the spring subsided, of their own failing strength, and lessening life? Not one!'

'Are you very old yourself?' asked the child, involuntarily.

'I shall be seventy-nine—next summer.'

'You still work when you are well?'

'Work! To be sure. You shall see my gardens hereabout. Look at the window there. I made, and have kept, that plot of ground entirely with my own hands. By this time next year I shall hardly see the sky, the boughs will have grown so thick. I have my winter work at night besides.'

He opened, as he spoke, a cupboard close to where he sat, and produced some miniature boxes, carved in a homely manner and made of old wood.

'Some gentlefolks who are fond of ancient days, and what belongs to them,' he said, 'like to buy these keepsakes from our church and ruins. Sometimes, I make them of scraps of oak that turn up here and there; sometimes of bits of coffins which the vaults have long preserved. See here—this is a little chest of the last kind, clasped at the edges with fragments of brass plates that had writing on 'em once, though it would be hard to read it now. I haven't many by me at this time of year, but these shelves will be full—next summer.'

The child admired and praised his work, and shortly afterwards departed; thinking, as she went, how strange it was, that this old man, drawing from his pursuits, and everything around him, one stern moral, never contemplated its application to himself; and, while he dwelt upon the uncertainty of human life, seemed both in word and deed to deem himself immortal. But her musings did not stop here, for she was wise enough to think that by a good and merciful adjustment this must be human nature, and that the old sexton, with his plans for next summer, was but a type of all mankind.

Full of these meditations, she reached the church. It was easy to find the key belonging to the outer door, for each was labelled on a scrap of yellow parchment. Its very turning in the lock awoke a hollow sound, and when she entered with a faltering step, the echoes that it raised in closing, made her start.

If the peace of the simple village had moved the child more strongly, because of the dark and troubled ways that lay beyond, and through which she had journeyed with such failing feet, what was the deep impression of finding herself alone in that solemn building, where the very light, coming through sunken windows, seemed old and grey, and the air, redolent of earth and mould, seemed laden with decay, purified by time of all its grosser particles, and sighing through arch and aisle, and clustered pillars, like the breath of ages gone! Here was the broken pavement, worn, so long ago, by pious feet, that Time, stealing on the pilgrims' steps, had trodden out their track, and left but crumbling stones. Here were the rotten beam, the sinking arch, the sapped and mouldering wall, the lowly trench of earth, the stately tomb on which no epitaph remained,—all,—marble, stone, iron, wood, and dust, one common monument of ruin. The best work and the worst, the plainest and the richest, the stateliest and the least imposing—both of Heaven's work and Man's— all found one common level here, and told one common tale.

Some part of the edifice had been a baronial chapel, and here were effigies of warriors stretched upon their beds of stone with folded hands—cross-legged, those who had fought in the

Holy Wars—girded with their swords, and cased in armour as they had lived. Some of these knights had their own weapons, helmets, coats of mail, hanging upon the walls hard by, and dangling from rusty hooks. Broken and dilapidated as they were, they yet retained their ancient form, and something of their ancient aspect. Thus violent deeds live after men upon the earth, and traces of war and bloodshed will survive in mournful shapes long after those who worked the desolation are but atoms of earth themselves.

The child sat down, in this old, silent place, among the stark figures on the tombs—they made it more quiet there, than elsewhere, to her fancy—and gazing round with a feeling of awe, tempered with a calm delight, felt that now she was happy, and at rest. She took a Bible from the shelf, and read; then, laying it down, thought of the summer days and the bright springtime that would come—of the rays of sun that would fall in aslant, upon the sleeping forms—of the leaves that would flutter at the window, and play in glistening shadows on the pavement—of the songs of birds, and growth of buds and blossoms out of doors—of the sweet air, that would steal in, and gently wave the tattered banners overhead. What if the spot awakened thoughts of death! Die who would, it would still remain the same; these sights and sounds would still go on, as happily as ever. It would be no pain to sleep amidst them.

She left the chapel—very slowly and often turning back to gaze again—and coming to a low door, which plainly led into the tower, opened it, and climbed the winding stair in darkness; save where she looked down, through narrow loop-holes, on the place she had left, or caught a glimmering vision of the dusty bells. At length she gained the end of the ascent and stood upon the turret top.

Oh! the glory of the sudden burst of light; the freshness of the fields and woods, stretching away on every side, and meeting the bright blue sky; the cattle grazing in the pasturage; the smoke, that, coming from among the trees, seemed to rise upward from the green earth; the children yet at their gambols down below—all, everything, so beautiful and happy! It was like passing from death to life; it was drawing nearer Heaven.

The children were gone, when she emerged into the porch, and locked the door. As she passed the school-house she could hear the busy hum of voices. Her friend had begun his labours only on that day. The noise grew louder, and, looking back,

she saw the boys come trooping out and disperse themselves
with merry shouts and play. 'It's a good thing,' thought the
child, 'I am very glad they pass the church.' And then she
stopped, to fancy how the noise would sound inside, and how
gently it would seem to die away upon the ear.

Again that day, yes, twice again, she stole back to the old
chapel, and in her former seat read from the same book, or
indulged the same quiet train of thought. Even when it had
grown dusk, and the shadows of coming night made it more
solemn still, the child remained, like one rooted to the spot,
and had no fear or thought of stirring.

They found her there, at last, and took her home. She
looked pale but very happy, until they separated for the night;
and then, as the poor schoolmaster stooped down to kiss her
cheek, he thought he felt a tear upon his face.

CHAPTER LIV

THE bachelor, among his various occupations, found in the old church a constant source of interest and amusement. Taking that pride in it which men conceive for the wonders of their own little world, he had made its history his study; and many a summer day within its walls, and many a winter's night beside the parsonage fire, had found the bachelor still poring over, and adding to, his goodly store of tale and legend.

As he was not one of those rough spirits who would strip fair Truth of every little shadowy vestment in which time and teeming fancies love to array her—and some of which become her pleasantly enough, serving, like the waters of her well, to add new graces to the charms they half conceal and half suggest, and to awaken interest and pursuit rather than languor and indifference—as, unlike this stern and obdurate class, he loved to see the goddess crowned with those garlands of wild flowers which tradition wreathes for her gentle wearing, and which are often freshest in their homeliest shapes,—he trod with a light step and bore with a light hand upon the dust of centuries, unwilling to demolish any of the airy shrines that had been raised above it, if any good feeling or affection of the human heart were hiding thereabouts. Thus, in the case of an ancient coffin of rough stone, supposed, for many generations, to contain the bones of a certain baron, who, after ravaging, with cut, and thrust, and plunder, in foreign lands, came back with a penitent and sorrowing heart to die at home, but which had been lately shown by learned antiquaries to be no such thing, as the baron in question (so they contended) had died hard in battle, gnashing his teeth and cursing with his latest breath,—the bachelor stoutly maintained that the old tale was the true one; that the baron, repenting him of the evil, had done great charities and meekly given up the ghost; and that, if ever baron went to heaven, that baron was then at peace. In like manner, when the aforesaid antiquaries did argue and contend that a certain secret vault was not the tomb of a grey-haired lady who had been hanged and drawn and quartered by glorious Queen Bess for succouring a wretched priest who fainted of thirst and hunger at her door, the bachelor did solemnly maintain, against all comers, that the church was hallowed by the said poor lady's ashes; that her remains had

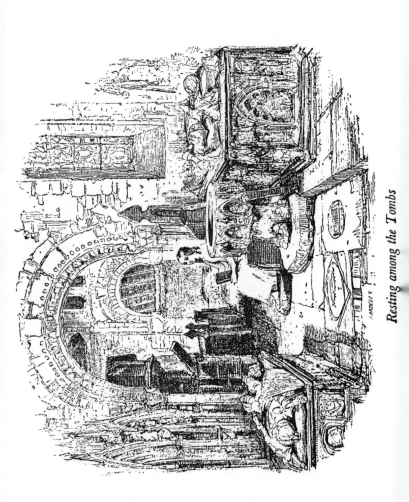

Resting among the Tombs

been collected in the night from four of the city's gates, and thither in secret brought, and there deposited; and the bachelor did further (being highly excited at such times) deny the glory of Queen Bess, and assert the immeasurably greater glory of the meanest woman in her realm, who had a merciful and tender heart. As to the assertion that the flat stone near the door was not the grave of the miser who had disowned his only child and left a sum of money to the church to buy a peal of bells, the bachelor did readily admit the same, and that the place had given birth to no such man. In a word, he would have had every stone, and plate of brass, the monument only of deeds whose memory should survive. All others he was willing to forget. They might be buried in consecrated ground, but he would have had them buried deep, and never brought to light again.

It was from the lips of such a tutor, that the child learnt her easy task. Already impressed, beyond all telling, by the silent building and the peaceful beauty of the spot in which it stood—majestic age surrounded by perpetual youth—it seemed to her, when she heard these things, sacred to all goodness and virtue. It was another world, where sin and sorrow never came; a tranquil place of rest, where nothing evil entered.

When the bachelor had given her in connection with almost every tomb and flat gravestone some history of its own, he took her down into the old crypt, now a mere dull vault, and showed her how it had been lighted up in the time of the monks, and how, amid lamps depending from the roof, and swinging censers exhaling scented odours, and habits glittering with gold and silver, and pictures, and precious stuffs, and jewels all flashing and glistening through the low arches, the chaunt of aged voices had been many a time heard there, at midnight, in old days, while hooded figures knelt and prayed around, and told their rosaries of beads. Thence, he took her above-ground again, and showed her, high up in the old walls, small galleries, where the nuns had been wont to glide along—dimly seen in their dark dresses so far off—or to pause like gloomy shadows, listening to the prayers. He showed her too, how the warriors, whose figures rested on the tombs, had worn those rotting scraps of armour up above—how this had been a helmet, and that a shield, and that a gauntlet—and how they had wielded the great two-handed swords, and beaten men down with yonder iron mace. All that he told the child she treasured in her mind; and sometimes, when she awoke at night from dreams of those old times, and rising from her bed looked out at the dark church, she almost hoped to see the windows lighted up, and hear the organ's swell, and sound of voices, on the rushing wind.

The old sexton soon got better, and was about again. From him the child learnt many other things, though of a different kind. He was not able to work, but one day there was a grave to be made, and he came to overlook the man who dug it. He was in a talkative mood; and the child, at first standing by his side, and afterwards sitting on the grass at his feet, with her thoughtful face raised towards his, began to converse with him.

Now, the man who did the sexton's duty was a little older than he, though much more active. But he was deaf; and when the sexton (who peradventure, on a pinch, might have walked a mile with great difficulty in half-a-dozen hours) exchanged a remark with him about his work, the child could not help noticing that he did so with an impatient kind of pity for his infirmity, as if he were himself the strongest and heartiest man alive.

'I'm sorry to see there is this to do,' said the child when she approached. 'I heard of no one having died.'

'She lived in another hamlet, my dear,' returned the sexton. 'Three mile away.'

'Was she young?'

'Ye—yes,' said the sexton; 'not more than sixty-four, I think. David, was she more than sixty-four?'

David, who was digging hard, heard nothing of the question. The sexton, as he could not reach to touch him with his crutch, and was too infirm to rise without assistance, called his attention by throwing a little mould upon his red nightcap.

'What's the matter now?' said David, looking up.

'How old was Becky Morgan?' asked the sexton.

'Becky Morgan?' repeated David.

'Yes,' replied the sexton; adding in a half compassionate, half irritable tone, which the old man couldn't hear, 'you're getting very deaf, Davy, very deaf to be sure!'

The old man stopped in his work, and cleansing his spade with a piece of slate he had by him for the purpose—and scraping off, in the process, the essence of Heaven knows how many Becky Morgans—set himself to consider the subject.

'Let me think,' quoth he. 'I saw last night what they had put upon the coffin—was it seventy-nine?'

'No, no,' said the sexton.

'Ah yes, it was though,' returned the old man with a sigh. 'For I remember thinking she was very near our age. Yes, it was seventy-nine.'

'Are you sure you did'nt mistake a figure, Davy?' asked the sexton, with signs of some emotion.

'What?' said the old man. 'Say that again.'

'He's very deaf. He's very deaf indeed,' cried the sexton petulantly; 'are you sure you're right about the figures?'

'Oh quite,' replied the old man. 'Why not?'

'He's exceedingly deaf,' muttered the sexton to himself. 'I think he's getting foolish.'

The child rather wondered what had led him to this belief, as, to say the truth, the old man seemed quite as sharp as he, and was infinitely more robust. As the sexton said nothing more just then, however, she forgot it for the time, and spoke again.

'You were telling me,' she said, 'about your gardening. Do you ever plant things here?'

'In the churchyard?' returned the sexton. 'Not I.'

'I have seen some flowers and little shrubs about,' the child rejoined; 'there are some over there, you see. I thought they were of your rearing, though indeed they grow but poorly.'

'They grow as Heaven wills,' said the old man; 'and it kindly ordains that they shall never flourish here.'

'I do not understand you.'

'Why, this is,' said the sexton. 'They mark the graves of those who had very tender, loving friends.'

'I was sure they did!' the child exclaimed. 'I am very glad to know they do!'

'Aye,' returned the old man, 'but stay. Look at them. See how they hang their heads, and droop, and wither. Do you guess the reason?'

'No,' the child replied.

'Because the memory of those who lie below, passes away so soon. At first they tend them, morning, noon, and night; they soon begin to come less frequently; from once a day to once a week; from once a week to once a month; then, at long and uncertain intervals; then, not at all. Such tokens seldom flourish long. I have known the briefest summer flowers outlive them.'

'I grieve to hear it,' said the child.

'Ah! so say the gentlefolks who come down here to look about them,' returned the old man, shaking his head, 'but I say otherwise. 'It's a pretty custom you have in this part of the country,' they say to me sometimes, 'to plant the graves, but it's melancholy to see these things all withering or dead.' I crave their pardon and tell them that, as I take it, 'tis a good sign for the happiness of the living. And so it is. It's nature.'

'Perhaps the mourners learn to look to the blue sky by day, and to the stars by night, and to think that the dead are there, and not in graves,' said the child in an earnest voice.

'Perhaps so,' replied the old man doubtfully. 'It may be.'

'Whether it be as I believe it is, or no,' thought the child within herself, 'I'll make this place *my* garden. It will be no harm at least to work here day by day, and pleasant thoughts will come of it, I am sure.'

Her glowing cheek and moistened eye passed unnoticed by the sexton, who turned towards old David, and called him by his name. It was plain that Becky Morgan's age still troubled him; though why, the child could scarcely understand.

The second or third repetition of his name attracted the old man's attention. Pausing from his work, he leant on his spade, and put his hand to his dull ear.

'Did you call?' he said.

'I have been thinking, Davy,' replied the sexton, 'that she,' he pointed to the grave, 'must have been a deal older than you or me.'

'Seventy-nine,' answered the old man with a shake of the head, 'I tell you that I saw it.'

'Saw it?' replied the sexton; 'aye, but, Davy, women don't always tell the truth about their age.'

'That's true indeed,' said the other old man, with a sudden sparkle in his eye. 'She might have been older.'

'I'm sure she must have been. Why, only think how old she looked. You and I seemed but boys to her.'

'She did look old,' rejoined David. 'You're right. She did look old.'

'Call to mind how old she looked for many a long, long year, and say if she could be but seventy-nine at last—only our age,' said the sexton.

'Five year older at the very least!' cried the other.

'Five!' retorted the sexton. 'Ten. Good eighty-nine. I

call to mind the time her daughter died. She was eighty-nine if she was a day, and tries to pass upon us now, for ten year younger. Oh! human vanity!'

The other old man was not behindhand with some moral reflections on this fruitful theme, and both adduced a mass of evidence, of such weight as to render it doubtful—not whether the deceased was of the age suggested, but whether she had not almost reached the patriarchal term of a hundred. When they had settled this question to their mutual satisfaction, the sexton, with his friend's assistance, rose to go.

'It's chilly, sitting here, and I must be careful—till the summer,' he said, as he prepared to limp away.

'What?' asked old David.

'He's very deaf, poor fellow!' cried the sexton. 'Good-bye!'

'Ah!' said old David, looking after him. 'He's failing very fast. He ages every day.'

And so they parted; each persuaded that the other had less life in him than himself; and both greatly consoled and comforted by the little fiction they had agreed upon, respecting Becky Morgan, whose decease was no longer a precedent of uncomfortable application, and would be no business of theirs for half a score of years to come.

The child remained, for some minutes, watching the deaf old man as he threw out the earth with his shovel, and, often stopping to cough and fetch his breath, still muttered to himself, with a kind of sober chuckle, that the sexton was wearing fast. At length she turned away, and walking thoughtfully through the churchyard, came unexpectedly upon the school-master, who was sitting on a green grave in the sun, reading.

'Nell here?' he said cheerfully, as he closed his book. 'It does me good to see you in the air and light. I feared you were again in the church, where you so often are.'

'Feared!' replied the child, sitting down beside him. 'Is it not a good place?'

'Yes, yes,' said the schoolmaster. 'But you must be gay sometimes—nay, don't shake your head and smile so sadly.'

'Not sadly, if you knew my heart. Do not look at me as if you thought me sorrowful. There is not a happier creature on earth, than I am now.'

Full of grateful tenderness, the child took his hand, and folded it between her own. 'It's God's will!' she said, when they had been silent for some time.

'What?'

'All this,' she rejoined; 'all this about us. But which of us is sad now? You see that *I* am smiling.'

'And so am I,' said the schoolmaster; 'smiling to think how often we shall laugh in this same place. Were you not talking yonder?'

'Yes,' the child rejoined.

'Of something that has made you sorrowful?'

There was a long pause.

'What was it?' said the schoolmaster, tenderly. 'Come. Tell me what it was.'

'I rather grieve—I *do* rather grieve to think,' said the child, bursting into tears, 'that those who die about us, are so soon forgotten.'

'And do you think,' said the schoolmaster, marking the glance she had thrown around, 'that an unvisited grave, a withered tree, a faded flower or two, are tokens of forgetfulness or cold neglect? Do you think there are no deeds, far away from here, in which these dead may be best remembered? Nell, Nell, there may be people busy in the world, at this instant, in whose good actions and good thoughts these very graves—neglected as they look to us—are the chief instruments.'

'Tell me no more,' said the child quickly. 'Tell me no more. I feel, I know it. How could *I* be unmindful of it, when I thought of you?'

'There is nothing,' cried her friend, 'no, nothing innocent or good, that dies, and is forgotten. Let us hold to that faith, or none. An infant, a prattling child, dying in its cradle, will live again in the better thoughts of those who loved it, and will play its part, through them, in the redeeming actions of the world, though its body be burnt to ashes or drowned in the deepest sea. There is not an angel added to the Host of Heaven but does its blessed work on earth in those that loved it here. Forgotten! oh, if the good deeds of human creatures could be traced to their source, how beautiful would even death appear; for how much charity, mercy, and purified affection, would be seen to have their growth in dusty graves!'

'Yes,' said the child, 'it is the truth; I know it is. Who should feel its force so much as I, in whom your little scholar lives again? Dear, dear, good friend, if you knew the comfort you have given me!'

The poor schoolmaster made her no answer, but bent over her in silence; for his heart was full.

They were yet seated in the same place, when the grandfather approached. Before they had spoken many words together, the church clock struck the hour of school, and their friend withdrew.

'A good man,' said the grandfather, looking after him; 'a kind man. Surely *he* will never harm us, Nell. We are safe here, at last, eh? We will never go away from here?'

The child shook her head and smiled.

'She needs rest,' said the old man, patting her cheek; 'too pale—too pale. She is not like what she was.'

'When?' asked the child.

'Ha!' said the old man, 'to be sure—when? How many weeks ago? Could I count them on my fingers? Let them rest though; they're better gone.'

'Much better, dear,' replied the child. 'We will forget them; or, if we ever call them to mind, it shall be only as some uneasy dream that has passed away.'

'Hush!' said the old man, motioning hastily to her with his hand and looking over his shoulder; 'no more talk of the dream, and all the miseries it brought. There are no dreams here. 'Tis a quiet place, and they keep away. Let us never think about them, lest they should pursue us again. Sunken eyes and hollow cheeks—wet, cold, and famine—and horrors before them all, that were even worse—we must forget such things, if we would be tranquil here.'

'Thank Heaven!' inwardly exclaimed the child, 'for this most happy change!'

'I will be patient,' said the old man, 'humble, very thankful, and obedient, if you will let me stay. But do not hide from me; do not steal away alone; let me keep beside you. Indeed, I will be very true and faithful, Nell.'

'I steal away alone! why that,' replied the child, with assumed gaiety, 'would be a pleasant jest indeed. See here, dear grandfather, we'll make this place our garden—why not! It is a very good one—and to-morrow we'll begin, and work together, side by side.'

'It is a brave thought!' cried her grandfather. 'Mind, darling—we begin to-morrow!'

Who so delighted as the old man, when they next day began their labour! Who so unconscious of all associations connected

with the spot, as he! They plucked the long grass and nettles
from the tombs, thinned the poor shrubs and roots, made
the turf smooth, and cleared it of the leaves and weeds.
They were yet in the ardour of their work, when the child,
raising her head from the ground over which she bent,
observed that the bachelor was sitting on the stile close by,
watching them in silence.

'A kind office,' said the little gentleman, nodding to Nell as
she curtseyed to him. 'Have you done all that, this morning?'

'It is very little, sir,' returned the child, with downcast eyes,
'to what we mean to do.'

'Good work, good work,' said the bachelor. 'But do you
only labour at the graves of children, and young people?'

'We shall come to the others in good time, sir,' replied Nell,
turning her head aside, and speaking softly.

It was a slight incident, and might have been design or
accident, or the child's unconscious sympathy with youth.
But it seemed to strike upon her grandfather, though he had
not noticed it before. He looked in a hurried manner at the
graves, then anxiously at the child, then pressed her to his side,
and bade her stop to rest. Something he had long forgotten,
appeared to struggle faintly in his mind. It did not pass away,
as weightier things had done; but came uppermost again, and
yet again, and many times that day, and often afterwards.
Once, while they were yet at work, the child, seeing that he
often turned and looked uneasily at her, as though he were
trying to resolve some painful doubts or collect some scattered thoughts, urged him to tell the reason. But he said it
was nothing—nothing—and, laying her head upon his arm,
patted her fair cheek with his hand, and muttered that she
grew stronger every day, and would be a woman, soon.

Nell's Garden
(p. 408)

CHAPTER LV

FROM that time, there sprung up in the old man's mind, a solicitude about the child which never slept or left him. There are chords in the human heart—strange, varying strings—which are only struck by accident; which will remain mute and senseless to appeals the most passionate and earnest, and respond at last to the slightest casual touch. In the most insensible or childish minds, there is some train of reflection which art can seldom lead, or skill assist, but which will reveal itself, as great truths have done, by chance, and when the discoverer has the plainest end in view. From that time, the old man never, for a moment, forgot the weakness and devotion of the child; from the time of that slight incident, he who had seen her toiling by his side through so much difficulty and suffering, and had scarcely thought of her otherwise than as the partner of miseries which he felt severely in his own person, and deplored for his own sake at least as much as hers, awoke to a sense of what he owed her, and what those miseries had made her. Never, no, never once, in one unguarded moment from that time to the end, did any care for himself, any thought of his own comfort, any selfish consideration or regard distract his thoughts from the gentle object of his love.

He would follow her up and down, waiting till she should tire and lean upon his arm—he would sit opposite to her in the chimney-corner, content to watch, and look, until she raised her head and smiled upon him as of old—he would discharge by stealth, those household duties which tasked her powers too heavily—he would rise, in the cold dark nights, to listen to her breathing in her sleep, and sometimes crouch for hours by her bedside only to touch her hand. He who knows all, can only know what hopes, and fears, and thoughts of deep affection, were in that one disordered brain, and what a change had fallen on the poor old man.

Sometimes—weeks had crept on, then—the child, exhausted, though with little fatigue, would pass whole evenings on a couch beside the fire. At such times, the schoolmaster would bring in books, and read to her aloud; and seldom an evening passed, but the bachelor came in, and took his turn of reading. The old man sat and listened,—with little understanding for the words, but with his eyes fixed upon the child,

—and if she smiled or brightened with the story, he would say it was a good one, and conceive a fondness for the very book. When, in their evening talk, the bachelor told some tale that pleased her (as his tales were sure to do), the old man would painfully try to store it in his mind; nay, when the bachelor left them, he would sometimes slip out after him, and humbly beg that he would tell him such a part again, that he might learn to win a smile from Nell.

But these were rare occasions, happily; for the child yearned to be out of doors, and walking in her solemn garden. Parties, too, would come to see the church; and those who came, speaking to others of the child, sent more; so even at that season of the year they had visitors almost daily. The old man would follow them at a little distance through the building, listening to the voice he loved so well; and when the strangers left, and parted from Nell, he would mingle with them to catch up fragments of their conversation; or he would stand for the same purpose, with his grey head uncovered, at the gate as they passed through.

They always praised the child, her sense and beauty, and he was proud to hear them! But what was that, so often added, which wrung his heart, and made him sob and weep alone, in some dull corner? Alas! even careless strangers—they who had no feeling for her, but the interest of the moment—they who would go away and forget next week that such a being lived—even they saw it—even they pitied her—even they bade him good day compassionately, and whispered as they passed.

The people of the village, too, of whom there was not one but grew to have a fondness for poor Nell; even among them, there was the same feeling; a tenderness towards her—a compassionate regard for her, increasing every day. The very schoolboys, light-hearted and thoughtless as they were, even they cared for her. The roughest among them was sorry if he missed her in the usual place upon his way to school, and would turn out of the path to ask for her at the latticed window. If she were sitting in the church, they perhaps might peep in softly at the open door; but they never spoke to her, unless she rose and went to speak to them. Some feeling was abroad which raised the child above them all.

So, when Sunday came. They were all poor country people in the church, for the castle in which the old family had lived, was an empty ruin, and there were none but humble folks for seven miles around. There, as elsewhere, they had an interest in Nell. They would gather round her in the porch, before and after service; young children would cluster at her skirts; and aged men and women forsake their gossips, to give her kindly greeting. None of them, young or old, thought of passing the child without a friendly word. Many who came from three or four miles distant, brought her little presents; the humblest and rudest had good wishes to bestow.

She had sought out the young children whom she first saw playing in the churchyard. One of these—he who had spoken of his brother—was her little favourite and friend, and often sat by her side in the church, or climbed with her to the tower-top. It was his delight to help her, or to fancy that he did so, and they soon became close companions.

It happened, that, as she was reading in the old spot by herself one day, this child came running in with his eyes full of tears, and after holding her from him, and looking at her eagerly for a moment, clasped his little arms passionately about her neck.

'What now?' said Nell, soothing him. 'What is the matter?'

'She is not one yet!' cried the boy, embracing her still more closely. 'No, no. Not yet.'

She looked at him wonderingly, and putting his hair back from his face, and kissing him, asked what he meant.

'You must not be one, dear Nell,' cried the boy. 'We can't see them. They never come to play with us, or talk to us. Be what you are. You are better so.'

'I do not understand you,' said the child. 'Tell me what you mean.'

'Why, they say,' replied the boy, looking up into her face, 'that you will be an Angel, before the birds sing again. But you won't be, will you? Don't leave us, Nell, though the sky *is* bright. Do not leave us!'

The child dropped her head, and put her hands before her face.

'She cannot bear the thought!' cried the boy, exulting through his tears. 'You will not go. You know how sorry we should be. Dear Nell, tell me that you'll stay amongst us. Oh! Pray, pray, tell me that you will.'

The little creature folded his hands, and knelt down at her feet.

'Only look at me, Nell,' said the boy, 'and tell me that you'll stop, and then I shall know that they are wrong, and will cry no more. Won't you say yes, Nell?'

Still the drooping head and hidden face, and the child quite silent—save for her sobs.

'After a time,' pursued the boy, trying to draw away her hand, 'the kind angels will be glad to think that you are not among them, and that you stayed here to be with us. Willy went away, to join them; but if he had known how I should miss him in our little bed at night, he never would have left me, I am sure.'

Yet the child could make him no answer, and sobbed as though her heart were bursting.

'Why would you go, dear Nell? I know you would not be happy when you heard that we were crying for your loss. They say that Willy is in Heaven now, and that it's always summer there, and yet I'm sure he grieves when I lie down upon his garden bed, and he cannot turn to kiss me. But if you do go, Nell,' said the boy, caressing her, and pressing his face to hers, 'be fond of him for my sake. Tell him how I love him still, and how much I loved you; and when I think that you two are together, and are happy, I'll try to bear it, and never give you pain by doing wrong—indeed I never will!'

The child suffered him to move her hands, and put them round his neck. There was a tearful silence, but it was not long before she looked upon him with a smile, and promised him, in a very gentle, quiet voice, that she would stay, and be his friend, as long as Heaven would let her. He clapped his hands for joy, and thanked her many times; and being charged to tell no person what had passed between them, gave her an earnest promise that he never would.

Nor did he, so far as the child could learn; but was her quiet companion in all her walks and musings, and never again adverted to the theme, which he felt had given her pain, although he was unconscious of its cause. Something of distrust lingered about him still; for he would often come, even in the dark evenings, and call in a timid voice outside the door to know if she were safe within; and being answered yes, and bade to enter, would take his station on a low stool at her feet, and sit there patiently until they came to seek, and take him home. Sure as the morning came, it found him lingering near the house to ask if she were well; and, morning, noon, or night, go where she would, he would forsake his playmates and his sports to bear her company.

'And a good little friend he is, too,' said the old sexton to her once. 'When his elder brother died—elder seems a strange word, for he was only seven years old—I remember this one took it sorely to heart.'

The child thought of what the schoolmaster had told her, and felt how its truth was shadowed out even in this infant.

'It has given him something of a quiet way, I think,' said the old man, 'though for that he is merry enough at times. I'd wager now that you and he have been listening by the old well.'

'Indeed we have not,' the child replied. 'I have been afraid to go near it; for I am not often down in that part of the church, and do not know the ground.'

'Come down with me,' said the old man. 'I have known it from a boy. Come!'

They descended the narrow steps which led into the crypt, and paused among the gloomy arches, in a dim and murky spot.

'This is the place,' said the old man. 'Give me your hand while you throw back the cover, lest you should stumble and fall in. I am too old—I mean rheumatic—to stoop, myself.'

'A black and dreadful place!' exclaimed the child.

'Look in,' said the old man, pointing downward with his finger.

The child complied, and gazed down into the pit.

'It looks like a grave itself,' said the old man.

'It does,' replied the child.

'I have often had the fancy,' said the sexton, 'that it might have been dug at first to make the old place more gloomy, and the old monks more religious. It's to be closed up, and built over.'

The child still stood, looking thoughtfully into the vault.

'We shall see,' said the sexton, 'on what gay heads other earth will have closed, when the light is shut out from here. God knows! They'll close it up, next spring.'

'The birds sing again in spring,' thought the child, as she leaned at her casement window, and gazed at the declining sun. 'Spring! a beautiful and happy time!'

CHAPTER LVI

A DAY or two after the Quilp tea-party at the Wilderness, Mr. Swiveller walked into Sampson Brass's office at the usual hour, and being alone in that Temple of Probity, placed his hat upon the desk, and taking from his pocket a small parcel of black crape, applied himself to folding and pinning the same upon it, after the manner of a hatband. Having completed the construction of this appendage, he surveyed his work with great complacency, and put his hat on again—very much over one eye, to increase the mournfulness of the effect. These arrangements perfected to his entire satisfaction, he thrust his hands into his pockets, and walked up and down the office with measured steps.

'It has always been the same with me,' said Mr. Swiveller, always. ''Twas ever thus, from childhood's hour I've seen my fondest hopes decay, I never loved a tree or flower but 'twas the first to fade away; I never nursed a dear Gazelle, to glad me with its soft black eye, but when it came to know me well, and love me, it was sure to marry a market-gardener.'

Overpowered by these reflections, Mr. Swiveller stopped short at the clients' chair, and flung himself into its open arms.

'And this,' said Mr. Swiveller, with a kind of bantering composure, 'is life, I believe. Oh, certainly. Why not? I'm quite satisfied. I shall wear,' added Richard, taking off his hat again and looking hard at it, as if he were only deterred by pecuniary considerations from spurning it with his foot, 'I shall wear this emblem of woman's perfidy, in remembrance of her with whom I shall never again thread the windings of the mazy; whom I shall never more pledge in the rosy; who, during the short remainder of my existence, will murder the balmy. Ha, ha, ha!'

It may be necessary to observe, lest there should appear any incongruity in the close of this soliloquy, that Mr. Swiveller did not wind up with a cheerful hilarious laugh, which would have been undoubtedly at variance with his solemn reflections, but that, being in a theatrical mood, he merely achieved that performance which is designated in melodramas 'laughing like a fiend,'—for it seems that your fiends always laugh in syllables, and always in three syllables, never more nor less, which is a remarkable property in such gentry, and one worthy of remembrance.

The baleful sounds had hardly died away, and Mr. Swiveller was still sitting in a very grim state in the clients' chair, when there came a ring—or, if we may adapt the sound to his then humour, a knell—at the office bell. Opening the door with all speed, he beheld the expressive countenance of Mr. Chuckster, between whom and himself a fraternal greeting ensued.

'You're devilish early at this pestiferous old slaughter-house,' said that gentleman, poising himself on one leg, and shaking the other in an easy manner.

'Rather,' returned Dick.

'Rather!' retorted Mr. Chuckster, with that air of graceful trifling which so well became him. '*I* should think so. Why, my good feller, do you know what o'clock it is—half-past nine a.m. in the morning?'

'Won't you come in?' said Dick. 'All alone. Swiveller solus. "'Tis now the witching—"'

'"Hour of night!"'

'"When churchyards yawn,"'

'"And graves give up their dead."'

At the end of this quotation in dialogue, each gentleman struck an attitude, and immediately subsiding into prose walked into the office. Such morsels of enthusiasm are common among the Glorious Apollos, and were indeed the links that bound them together, and raised them above the cold dull earth.

'Well, and how are you, my buck?' said Mr. Chuckster, taking a stool. 'I was forced to come into the City upon some little private matters of my own, and couldn't pass the corner of the street without looking in, but upon my soul I didn't expect to find you. It is so everlastingly early.'

Mr. Swiveller expressed his acknowledgments; and it appearing on further conversation that he was in good health, and that Mr. Chuckster was in the like enviable condition, both gentlemen, in compliance with a solemn custom of the ancient Brotherhood to which they belonged, joined in a fragment of the popular duet of 'All's Well,' with a long shake at the end.

'And what's the news?' said Richard.

'The town's as flat, my dear feller,' replied Mr. Chuckster, 'as the surface of a Dutch oven. There's no news. By-the-bye, that lodger of yours is a most extraordinary person. He quite eludes the most vigorous comprehension, you know. Never was such a feller!'

'What has he been doing now?' said Dick.

'By Jove, sir,' returned Mr. Chuckster, taking out an oblong snuff-box, the lid whereof was ornamented with a fox's head curiously carved in brass, 'that man is an unfathomable. Sir, that man has made friends with our articled clerk. There's no harm in him, but he is so amazingly slow and soft. Now, if he wanted a friend, why couldn't he have one that knew a thing or two, and could do him some good by his manners and conversation? I have my faults, sir,' said Mr. Chuckster.

'No, no,' interposed Mr. Swiveller.

'Oh yes I have, I have my faults, no man knows his faults better than I know mine. But,' said Mr. Chuckster, 'I'm not meek. My worst enemies—every man has his enemies, sir, and I have mine—never accused me of being meek. And I tell you what, sir, if I hadn't more of these qualities that commonly endear man to man, than our articled clerk has, I'd steal a Cheshire cheese, tie it round my neck, and drown myself. I'd die degraded, as I had lived. I would upon my honour.'

Mr. Chuckster paused, rapped the fox's head exactly on the nose with the knuckle of the forefinger, took a pinch of snuff, and looked steadily at Mr. Swiveller, as much as to say that if he thought he was going to sneeze, he would find himself mistaken.

'Not contented, sir,' said Mr. Chuckster, 'with making friends with Abel, he has cultivated the acquaintance of his father and mother. Since he came home from that wild-goose chase, he has been there—actually been there. He patronises young Snobby besides; you'll find, sir, that he'll be constantly coming backwards and forwards to this place: yet I don't suppose that beyond the common forms of civility, he has ever exchanged half-a-dozen words with *me*. Now, upon my soul, you know,' said Mr. Chuckster, shaking his head gravely, as men are wont to do when they consider things are going a little too far, 'this is altogether such a low-minded affair, that if I didn't feel for the governor, and know that he could never get on without me, I should be obliged to cut the connection. I should have no alternative.'

Mr. Swiveller, who sat on another stool opposite to his friend, stirred the fire in an excess of sympathy, but said nothing.

A Black and Dreadful Place

(*p. 413*)

'As to young Snob, sir,' pursued Mr. Chuckster with a prophetic look, 'you'll find he'll turn out bad. In our profession we know something of human nature, and take my word for it, that the feller that came back to work out that shilling, will show himself one of these days in his true colours. He's a low thief, sir. He must be.'

Mr. Chuckster being roused, would probably have pursued this subject further, and in more emphatic language, but for a tap at the door, which seeming to announce the arrival of somebody on business, caused him to assume a greater appearance of meekness than was perhaps quite consistent with his late declaration. Mr. Swiveller, hearing the same sound, caused his stool to revolve rapidly on one leg until it brought him to his desk, into which, having forgotten in the sudden flurry of his spirits to part with the poker, he thrust it as he cried 'Come in!'

Who should present himself but that very Kit who had been the theme of Mr. Chuckster's wrath! Never did man pluck up his courage so quickly, or look so fierce, as Mr. Chuckster when he found it was he. Mr. Swiveller stared at him for a moment, and then leaping from his stool, and drawing out the poker from its place of concealment, performed the broadsword exercise with all the cuts and guards complete, in a species of frenzy.

'Is the gentleman at home?' said Kit, rather astonished by this uncommon reception.

Before Mr. Swiveller could make any reply, Mr. Chuckster took occasion to enter his indignant protest against this form of inquiry; which he held to be of a disrespectful and snobbish tendency, inasmuch as the inquirer, seeing two gentlemen then and there present, should have spoken of the other gentleman; or rather (for it was not impossible that the object of his search might be of inferior quality) should have mentioned his name, leaving it to his hearers to determine his degree as they thought proper. Mr. Chuckster likewise remarked, that he had some reason to believe this form of address was personal to himself, and that he was not a man to be trifled with—as certain snobs (whom he did not more particularly mention or describe) might find to their cost.

'I mean the gentleman up-stairs,' said Kit, turning to Richard Swiveller. 'Is he at home?'

'Why?' rejoined Dick.

'Because if he is, I have a letter for him.'

'From whom?' said Dick.

'From Mr. Garland.'

'Oh!' said Dick, with extreme politeness. 'Then you may hand it over, sir. And if you're to wait for an answer, sir, you may wait in the passage, sir, which is an airy and well-ventilated apartment, sir.'

'Thank you,' returned Kit. 'But I am to give it to himself, if you please.'

The excessive audacity of this retort so overpowered Mr. Chuckster, and so moved his tender regard for his friend's honour, that he declared, if he were not restrained by official considerations, he must certainly have annihilated Kit upon the spot; a resentment of the affront which he did consider, under the extraordinary circumstances of aggravation attending it, could but have met with the proper sanction and approval of a jury of Englishmen, who, he had no doubt, would have returned a verdict of Justifiable Homicide, coupled with a high testimony to the morals and character of the Avenger. Mr. Swiveller, without being quite so hot upon the matter, was rather shamed by his friend's excitement, and not a little puzzled how to act (Kit being quite cool and good-humoured), when the single gentleman was heard to call violently down the stairs.

'Didn't I see somebody for me, come in?' cried the lodger.

'Yes, sir,' replied Dick. 'Certainly, sir.'

'Then where is he?' roared the single gentleman.

'He's here, sir,' rejoined Mr. Swiveller. 'Now, young man, don't you hear you're to go up-stairs? Are you deaf?'

Kit did not appear to think it worth his while to enter into any altercation, but hurried off and left the Glorious Apollos gazing at each other in silence.

'Didn't I tell you so?' said Mr. Chuckster. 'What do you think of that?'

Mr. Swiveller being in the main a good-natured fellow, and not perceiving in the conduct of Kit any villany of enormous magnitude, scarcely knew what answer to return. He was relieved from his perplexity, however, by the entrance of Mr. Sampson and his sister Sally, at sight of whom Mr. Chuckster precipitately retired.

Mr. Brass and his lovely companion appeared to have been holding a consultation over their temperate breakfast, upon some matter of great interest and importance. On the occasion of such conferences, they generally appeared in the office some half an hour after their usual time, and in a very smiling state, as though their late plots and designs had tranquillised their minds and shed a light upon their toilsome way. In the present instance, they seemed particularly gay; Miss Sally's aspect being of a most oily kind, and Mr. Brass rubbing his hands in an exceedingly jocose and light-hearted manner.

'Well, Mr. Richard,' said Brass. 'How are we this morning? Are we pretty fresh and cheerful sir—eh, Mr. Richard?'

'Pretty well sir,' replied Dick.

'That's well,' said Brass. 'Ha ha! We should be as gay as larks Mr. Richard—why not? It's a pleasant world we live in sir, a very pleasant world. There are bad people in it Mr. Richard, but if there were no bad people, there would be no good lawyers. Ha ha! Any letters by the post this morning, Mr. Richard?'

Mr. Swiveller answered in the negative.

'Ha!' said Brass, 'no matter. If there's little business to-day, there'll be more to-morrow. A contented spirit, Mr. Richard, is the sweetness of existence. Anybody been here, sir?'

'Only my friend'—replied Dick. '"May we ne'er want a—"'

'"Friend,"' Brass chimed in quickly, '"or a bottle to give him." Ha ha! That's the way the song runs, isn't it? A very good song, Mr. Richard, very good. I like the sentiment of it. Ha ha! Your friend's the young man from Witherden's office I think—yes—"May we ne'er want a—" Nobody else at all been, Mr. Richard?'

'Only somebody to the lodger,' replied Mr. Swiveller.

'Oh indeed!' cried Brass. 'Somebody to the lodger, eh? Ha ha! "May we ne'er want a friend, or a—" Somebody to the lodger, eh, Mr. Richard?'

'Yes,' said Dick, a little disconcerted by the excessive buoyancy of spirits which his employer displayed. 'With him now.'

'With him now!' cried Brass. 'Ha ha! There let 'em be, merry and free, toor rul rol le. Eh, Mr. Richard? Ha ha!'

'Oh certainly,' replied Dick.

'And who,' said Brass, shuffling among his papers, 'who is the lodger's visitor—not a lady visitor, I hope, eh Mr. Richard? The morals of the Marks you know sir—"when lovely woman stoops to folly"—and all that—eh Mr. Richard?'

'Another young man, who belongs to Witherden's too, or half belongs there,' returned Richard. 'Kit, they call him.'

'Kit, eh!' said Brass. 'Strange name—name of a dancing-master's fiddle, eh Mr. Richard? Ha ha! Kit's there, is he? Oh!'

Dick looked at Miss Sally, wondering that she didn't check this uncommon exuberance on the part of Mr. Sampson; but as she made no attempt to do so, and rather appeared to exhibit a tacit acquiescence in it, he concluded that they had just been cheating somebody, and receiving the bill.

'Will you have the goodness, Mr. Richard,' said Brass, taking a letter from his desk, 'just to step over to Peckham Rye with that? There's no answer, but it's rather particular and should go by hand. Charge the office with your coach-hire back, you know; don't spare the office; get as much out of it as you can—clerk's motto—eh Mr. Richard? Ha ha!'

Mr. Swiveller solemnly doffed the aquatic jacket, put on his coat, took down his hat from its peg, pocketed the letter, and departed. As soon as he was gone, up rose Miss Sally Brass, and smiling sweetly at her brother (who nodded and smote his nose in return) withdrew also.

Sampson Brass was no sooner left alone, than he set the office door wide open, and establishing himself at his desk directly opposite, so that he could not fail to see anybody who came down-stairs and passed out at the street door, began to write with extreme cheerfulness and assiduity; humming as he did so, in a voice that was anything but musical, certain vocal snatches which appeared to have reference to the union between Church and State, inasmuch as they were com-pounded of the Evening Hymn and God save the King.

Thus, the attorney of Bevis Marks sat, and wrote, and hummed, for a long time, except when he stopped to listen with a very cunning face, and hearing nothing, went on humming louder, and writing slower than ever. At length, in one of these pauses, he heard his lodger's door opened and shut, and footsteps coming down the stairs. Then, Mr. Brass left off writing entirely, and, with his pen in his hand, hummed his very loudest; shaking his head meanwhile from side to side, like a man whose whole soul was in the music, and smiling in a manner quite seraphic.

It was towards this moving spectacle that the staircase and the sweet sounds guided Kit; on whose arrival before his door

Mr. Brass stopped his singing, but not his smiling, and nodded affably: at the same time beckoning to him with his pen.

'Kit,' said Mr. Brass, in the pleasantest way imaginable, 'how do you do?'

Kit, being rather shy of his friend, made a suitable reply, and had his hand upon the lock of the street door when Mr. Brass called him softly back.

'You are not to go, if you please, Kit,' said the attorney in a mysterious and business-like way. 'You are to step in here, if you please. Dear me, dear me! When I look at you,' said the lawyer, quitting his stool, and standing before the fire with his back towards it, 'I am reminded of the sweetest little face that ever my eyes beheld. I remember your coming there, twice or thrice, when we were in possession. Ah Kit, my dear fellow, gentlemen in my profession have such painful duties to perform sometimes, that you needn't envy us—you needn't indeed!'

'I don't sir,' said Kit, 'though it isn't for the like of me to judge.'

'Our only consolation, Kit,' pursued the lawyer, looking at him in a sort of pensive abstraction, 'is, that although we cannot turn away the wind, we can soften it; we can temper it, if I may say so, to the shorn lambs.'

'Shorn indeed!' thought Kit. 'Pretty close!' But he didn't say so.

'On that occasion, Kit,' said Mr. Brass, 'on that occasion that I have just alluded to, I had a hard battle with Mr. Quilp (for Mr. Quilp is a very hard man) to obtain them the indulgence they had. It might have cost me a client. But suffering virtue inspired me, and I prevailed.'

'He's not so bad after all,' thought honest Kit, as the attorney pursed up his lips, and looked like a man who was struggling with his better feelings.

'I respect *you*, Kit,' said Brass with emotion. 'I saw enough of your conduct, at that time, to respect you, though your station is humble, and your fortune lowly. It isn't the waistcoat that I look at. It is the heart. The checks in the waistcoat are but the wires of the cage. But the heart is the bird. Ah! How many such birds are perpetually moulting, and putting their beaks through the wires to peck at all mankind!'

This poetic figure, which Kit took to be in special allusion to his own checked waistcoat, quite overcame him; Mr. Brass's voice and manner added not a little to its effect, for he discoursed with all the mild austerity of a hermit, and wanted but a cord round the waist of his rusty surtout, and a skull on the chimney-piece, to be completely set up in that line of business.

'Well, well,' said Sampson, smiling as good men smile when they compassionate their own weakness or that of their fellow-creatures, 'this is wide of the bull's-eye. You're to take that, if you please.' As he spoke, he pointed to a couple of half-crowns on the desk.

Kit looked at the coins, and then at Sampson, and hesitated.

'For yourself,' said Brass.

'From——'

'No matter about the person they came from,' replied the lawyer. 'Say me, if you like. We have eccentric friends overhead, Kit, and we mustn't ask questions or talk too much—you understand? You're to take them, that's all; and between you and me, I don't think they'll be the last you'll have to take from the same place. I hope not. Good-bye, Kit. Good-bye!'

With many thanks, and many more self-reproaches for having on such slight grounds suspected one who in their very first conversation turned out such a different man from what he had supposed, Kit took the money and made the best of his way home. Mr. Brass remained airing himself at the fire, and resumed his vocal exercise, and his seraphic smile, simultaneously.

'May I come in?' said Miss Sally, peeping.

'Oh yes, you may come in,' returned her brother.

'Ahem!' coughed Miss Brass interrogatively.

'Why, yes,' returned Sampson, 'I should say as good as done.'

CHAPTER LVII

MR. CHUCKSTER'S indignant apprehensions were not without foundation. Certainly the friendship between the single gentleman and Mr. Garland was not suffered to cool, but had a rapid growth and flourished exceedingly. They were soon in habits of constant intercourse and communication; and the single gentleman labouring at this time under a slight attack of illness—the consequence most probably of his late excited feelings and subsequent disappointment—furnished a reason for their holding yet more frequent correspondence; so, that some one of the inmates of Abel Cottage, Finchley, came backwards and forwards between that place and Bevis Marks, almost every day.

As the pony had now thrown off all disguise, and without any mincing of the matter or beating about the bush, sturdily refused to be driven by anybody but Kit, it generally happened that whether old Mr. Garland came, or Mr. Abel, Kit was of the party. Of all messages and inquiries, Kit was, in right of his position, the bearer; thus it came about that, while the single gentleman remained indisposed, Kit turned into Bevis Marks every morning with nearly as much regularity as the General Postman.

Mr. Sampson Brass, who no doubt had his reasons for looking sharply about him, soon learnt to distinguish the pony's trot and the clatter of the little chaise at the corner of the street. Whenever the sound reached his ears, he would immediately lay down his pen and fall to rubbing his hands and exhibiting the greatest glee.

'Ha ha!' he would cry. 'Here's the pony again! Most remarkable pony, extremely docile, eh Mr. Richard, eh sir?'

Dick would return some matter-of-course reply, and Mr. Brass standing on the bottom rail of his stool, so as to get a view of the street over the top of the window-blind, would take an observation of the visitors.

'The old gentleman again!' he would exclaim, 'a very prepossessing old gentleman, Mr. Richard—charming countenance sir—extremely calm—benevolence in every feature, sir. He quite realises my idea of King Lear, as he appeared when in possession of his kingdom, Mr. Richard—the same good humour, the same white hair and partial baldness, the same liability to be imposed upon. Ah! A sweet subject for contemplation, sir, very sweet!'

Then Mr. Garland having alighted and gone up-stairs, Sampson would nod and smile to Kit from the window, and presently walk out into the street to greet him, when some such conversation as the following would ensue.

'Admirably groomed, Kit'—Mr. Brass is patting the pony—'does you great credit—amazingly sleek and bright to be sure. He literally looks as if he had been varnished all over.'

Kit touches his hat, smiles, pats the pony himself, and expresses his conviction, 'that Mr. Brass will not find many like him.'

'A beautiful animal indeed!' cries Brass. 'Sagacious too?'

'Bless you!' replies Kit, 'he knows what you say to him as well as a Christian does.'

'Does he indeed?' cries Brass, who has heard the same thing in the same place from the same person in the same words a dozen times, but is paralysed with astonishment notwithstanding. 'Dear me!'

'I little thought the first time I saw him, sir,' says Kit, pleased with the attorney's strong interest in his favourite, 'that I should come to be as intimate with him as I am now.'

'Ah!' rejoins Mr. Brass, brim-full of moral precepts and love of virtue. 'A charming subject of reflection for you, very charming. A subject of proper pride and congratulation, Christopher. Honesty is the best policy.—I always find it so myself. I lost forty-seven pound ten by being honest this morning. But it's all gain, it's gain!'

Mr. Brass slyly tickles his nose with his pen, and looks at Kit with the water standing in his eyes. Kit thinks that if ever there was a good man who belied his appearance, that man is Sampson Brass.

'A man,' says Sampson, 'who loses forty-seven pound ten in one morning by his honesty, is a man to be envied. If it had been eighty pound, the luxuriousness of feeling would have been increased. Every pound lost, would have been a hundred-weight of happiness gained. The still small voice, Christopher,' cries Brass, smiling, and tapping himself on the bosom, 'is a-singing comic songs within me, and all is happiness and joy!'

Kit is so improved by the conversation, and finds it go so completely home to his feelings, that he is considering what he

Kit brings a Letter

(p. 417)

shall say, when Mr. Garland appears. The old gentleman is helped into the chaise with great obsequiousness by Mr. Sampson Brass; and the pony, after shaking his head several times, and standing for three or four minutes with all his four legs planted firmly on the ground, as if he had made up his mind never to stir from that spot, but there to live and die, suddenly darts off, without the smallest notice, at the rate of twelve English miles an hour. Then, Mr. Brass and his sister (who has joined him at the door) exchange an odd kind of smile—not at all a pleasant one in its expression—and return to the society of Mr. Richard Swiveller, who, during their absence, has been regaling himself with various feats of pantomime, and is discovered at his desk, in a very flushed and heated condition, violently scratching out nothing with half a penknife.

Whenever Kit came alone, and without the chaise, it always happened that Sampson Brass was reminded of some mission, calling Mr. Swiveller, if not to Peckham Rye again, at all events to some pretty distant place from which he could not be expected to return for two or three hours, or in all probability a much longer period, as that gentleman was not, to say the truth, renowned for using great expedition on such occasions, but rather for protracting and spinning out the time to the very utmost limit of possibility. Mr. Swiveller out of sight, Miss Sally immediately withdrew. Mr. Brass would then set the office door wide open, hum his old tune with great gaiety of heart, and smile seraphically as before. Kit coming down-stairs would be called in; entertained with some moral and agreeable conversation; perhaps entreated to mind the office for an instant while Mr. Brass stepped over the way; and afterwards presented with one or two half-crowns as the case might be. This occurred so often, that Kit, nothing doubting but that they came from the single gentleman who had already rewarded his mother with great liberality, could not enough admire his generosity; and bought so many cheap presents for her, and for little Jacob, and for the baby, and for Barbara to boot, that one or other of them was having some new trifle every day of their lives.

While these acts and deeds were in progress in and out of the office of Sampson Brass, Richard Swiveller, being often left alone therein, began to find the time hang heavy on his hands. For the better preservation of his cheerfulness therefore, and to prevent his faculties from rusting, he provided himself with a cribbage-board and pack of cards, and accustomed himself to play at cribbage with a dummy, for twenty, thirty, or sometimes even fifty thousand pounds a side, besides many hazardous bets to a considerable amount.

As these games were very silently conducted, notwithstanding the magnitude of the interests involved, Mr. Swiveller began to think that on those evenings when Mr. and Miss Brass were out (and they often went out now) he heard a kind of snorting or hard-breathing sound in the direction of the door, which it occurred to him, after some reflection, must proceed from the small servant, who always had a cold from damp living. Looking intently that way one night, he plainly distinguished an eye gleaming and glistening at the keyhole; and having now no doubt that his suspicions were correct, he stole softly to the door, and pounced upon her before she was aware of his approach.

'Oh! I didn't mean any harm indeed, upon my word I didn't,' cried the small servant, struggling like a much larger one. 'It's so very dull, down-stairs. Please don't you tell upon me, please don't.'

'Tell upon you!' said Dick. 'Do you mean to say you were looking through the keyhole for company?'

'Yes, upon my word I was,' replied the small servant.

'How long have you been cooling your eye there?' said Dick.

'Oh ever since you first began to play them cards, and long before.'

Vague recollections of several fantastic exercises with which he had refreshed himself after the fatigues of business, and to all of which, no doubt, the small servant was a party, rather disconcerted Mr. Swiveller; but he was not very sensitive on such points, and recovered himself speedily.

'Well,—come in'—he said, after a little consideration, 'Here—sit down, and I'll teach you how to play.'

'Oh! I durstn't do it,' rejoined the small servant; 'Miss Sally 'ud kill me, if she know'd I come up here.'

'Have you got a fire down-stairs?' said Dick.

'A very little one,' replied the small servant.

'Miss Sally couldn't kill me if she know'd I went down there, so I'll come,' said Richard, putting the cards into his pocket. 'Why, how thin you are! What do you mean by it?'

'It an't my fault.'

'Could you eat any bread and meat?' said Dick, taking down his hat. 'Yes? Ah! I thought so. Did you ever taste beer?'

'I had a sip of it once,' said the small servant.

'Here's a state of things!' cried Mr. Swiveller, raising his eyes to the ceiling. 'She *never* tasted it—it can't be tasted in a sip! Why, how old are you?'

'I don't know.'

Mr. Swiveller opened his eyes very wide, and appeared thoughtful for a moment; then, bidding the child mind the door until he came back, vanished straightway.

Presently, he returned, followed by the boy from the public-house, who bore in one hand a plate of bread and beef, and in the other a great pot, filled with some very fragrant compound, which sent forth a grateful steam, and was indeed choice purl, made after a particular recipe which Mr. Swiveller had imparted to the landlord, at a period when he was deep in his books and desirous to conciliate his friendship. Relieving the boy of his burden at the door, and charging his little companion to fasten it to prevent surprise, Mr. Swiveller followed her into the kitchen.

'There!' said Richard, putting the plate before her. 'First of all clear that off, and then you'll see what's next.'

The small servant needed no second bidding, and the plate was soon empty.

'Next,' said Dick, handing the purl, 'take a pull at that; but moderate your transports, you know, for you're not used to it. Well, is it good?'

'Oh! isn't it?' said the small servant.

Mr. Swiveller appeared gratified beyond all expression by this reply, and took a long draught himself: steadfastly regarding his companion while he did so. These preliminaries disposed of, he applied himself to teaching her the game, which she soon learnt tolerably well, being both sharp-witted and cunning.

'Now,' said Mr. Swiveller, putting two sixpences into a saucer, and trimming the wretched candle, when the cards had been cut and dealt, 'those are the stakes. If you win, you get 'em all. If I win, I get 'em. To make it seem more real and pleasant, I shall call you the Marchioness, do you hear?'

The small servant nodded.

'Then, Marchioness,' said Mr. Swiveller, 'fire away!'

The Marchioness, holding her cards very tight in both hands, considered which to play, and Mr. Swiveller, assuming the gay and fashionable air which such society required, took another pull at the tankard, and waited for her lead.

The Marchioness at Cards

CHAPTER LVIII

MR. SWIVELLER and his partner played several rubbers with varying success, until the loss of three sixpences, the gradual sinking of the purl, and the striking of ten o'clock, combined to render that gentleman mindful of the flight of Time, and the expediency of withdrawing before Mr. Sampson and Miss Sally Brass returned.

'With which object in view, Marchioness,' said Mr. Swiveller gravely, 'I shall ask your ladyship's permission to put the board in my pocket, and to retire from the presence when I have finished this tankard; merely observing, Marchioness, that since life like a river is flowing, I care not how fast it rolls on, ma'am, on, while such purl on the bank still is growing, and such eyes light the waves as they run. Marchioness, your health. You will excuse my wearing my hat, but the palace is damp, and the marble floor is—if I may be allowed the expression—sloppy.'

As a precaution against this latter inconvenience, Mr. Swiveller had been sitting for some time with his feet on the hob, in which attitude he now gave utterance to these apologetic observations, and slowly sipped the last choice drops of nectar.

'The Baron Sampsono Brasso and his fair sister are (you tell me) at the Play?' said Mr. Swiveller, leaning his left arm heavily upon the table, and raising his voice and his right leg after the manner of a theatrical bandit.

The Marchioness nodded.

'Ha!' said Mr. Swiveller, with a portentous frown. ''Tis well. Marchioness!—but no matter. Some wine there. Ho!' He illustrated these melodramatic morsels, by handing the tankard to himself with great humility, receiving it haughtily, drinking from it thirstily, and smacking his lips fiercely.

The small servant, who was not so well acquainted with theatrical conventionalities as Mr. Swiveller (having indeed never seen a play, or heard one spoken of, except by chance through chinks of doors and in other forbidden places), was rather alarmed by demonstrations so novel in their nature, and showed her concern so plainly in her looks, that Mr. Swiveller felt it necessary to discharge his brigand manner for one more suitable to private life, as he asked,

'Do they often go where glory waits 'em, and leave you here?'

'Oh, yes; I believe you they do,' returned the small servant. 'Miss Sally's such a one-er for that, she is.'

'Such a what?' said Dick.

'Such a one-er,' returned the Marchioness.

After a moment's reflection, Mr. Swiveller determined to forego his responsible duty of setting her right, and to suffer her to talk on; as it was evident that her tongue was loosened by the purl, and her opportunities for conversation were not so frequent as to render a momentary check of little consequence.

'They sometimes go to see Mr. Quilp,' said the small servant with a shrewd look; 'they go to a many places, bless you!'

'Is Mr. Brass a wunner?' said Dick.

'Not half what Miss Sally is, he isn't,' replied the small servant, shaking her head. 'Bless you, he'd never do anything without her.'

'Oh! He wouldn't, wouldn't he?' said Dick.

'Miss Sally keeps him in such order,' said the small servant; 'he always asks her advice, he does; and he catches it sometimes. Bless you, you wouldn't believe how much he catches it.'

'I suppose,' said Dick, 'that they consult together a good deal, and talk about a great many people—about me for instance, sometimes, eh, Marchioness?'

The Marchioness nodded amazingly.

'Complimentary?' said Mr. Swiveller.

The Marchioness changed the motion of her head, which had not yet left off nodding, and suddenly began to shake it from side to side, with a vehemence which threatened to dislocate her neck.

'Humph!' Dick muttered. 'Would it be any breach of confidence, Marchioness, to relate what they say of the humble individual who has now the honour to—?'

'Miss Sally says you're a funny chap,' replied his friend.

'Well, Marchioness,' said Mr. Swiveller, 'that's not uncomplimentary. Merriment, Marchioness, is not a bad or a degrading quality. Old King Cole was himself a merry old soul, if we may put any faith in the pages of history.'

'But she says,' pursued his companion, 'that you ain't to be trusted.'

'Why, really, Marchioness,' said Mr. Swiveller, thoughtfully; 'several ladies and gentlemen—not exactly professional persons, but tradespeople, ma'am, tradespeople—have made the same remark. The obscure citizen who keeps the hotel over the way, inclined strongly to that opinion to-night when I ordered him to prepare the banquet. It's a popular prejudice, Marchioness; and yet I am sure I don't know why, for I have been trusted in my time to a considerable amount, and I can safely say that I never forsook my trust until it deserted me—never. Mr. Brass is of the same opinion, I suppose?'

His friend nodded again, with a cunning look which seemed to hint that Mr. Brass held stronger opinions on the subject than his sister; and seeming to recollect herself, added imploringly, 'But don't you ever tell upon me, or I shall be beat to death.'

'Marchioness,' said Mr. Swiveller, rising, 'the word of a gentleman is as good as his bond—sometimes better, as in the present case, where his bond might prove but a doubtful sort of security. I am your friend, and I hope we shall play many more rubbers together in this same saloon. But, Marchioness,' added Richard, stopping in his way to the door, and wheeling slowly round upon the small servant, who was following with the candle; 'it occurs to me that you must be in the constant habit of airing your eye at keyholes, to know all this.'

'I only wanted,' replied the trembling Marchioness, 'to know where the key of the safe was hid; that was all; and I wouldn't have taken much, if I had found it—only enough to squench my hunger.'

'You didn't find it then?' said Dick. 'But of course you didn't, or you'd be plumper. Good night, Marchioness. Fare thee well, and if for ever, then for ever fare thee well—and put up the chain, Marchioness, in case of accidents.'

With this parting injunction, Mr. Swiveller emerged from the house; and feeling that he had by this time taken quite as much to drink as promised to be good for his constitution (purl being a rather strong and heady compound), wisely resolved to betake himself to his lodgings, and to bed at once. Homeward he went therefore; and his apartments (for he still retained the plural fiction) being at no great distance from the office, he was soon seated in his own bed-chamber, where, having pulled off one boot and forgotten the other, he fell into deep cogitation.

'This Marchioness,' said Mr. Swiveller, folding his arms, 'is a very extraordinary person—surrounded by mysteries, ignorant of the taste of beer, unacquainted with her own name (which is less remarkable), and taking a limited view of society through the keyholes of doors—can these things be her destiny, or has some unknown person started an opposition to the decrees of fate? It is a most inscrutable and unmitigated staggerer!'

When his meditations had attained this satisfactory point, he became aware of his remaining boot, of which, with unimpaired solemnity he proceeded to divest himself; shaking his head with exceeding gravity all the time, and sighing deeply.

'These rubbers,' said Mr. Swiveller, putting on his nightcap in exactly the same style as he wore his hat, 'remind me of the matrimonial fireside. Cheggs's wife plays cribbage; all-fours likewise. She rings the changes on 'em now. From sport to sport they hurry her, to banish her regrets, and when they win a smile from her, they think that she forgets—but she don't. By this time, I should say,' added Richard, getting his left cheek into profile, and looking complacently at the reflection of a very little scrap of whisker in the looking-glass; 'by this time, I should say, the iron has entered into her soul. It serves her right!'

Melting from this stern and obdurate, into the tender and pathetic mood, Mr. Swiveller groaned a little, walked wildly up and down, and even made a show of tearing his hair, which, however, he thought better of, and wrenched the tassel from his nightcap instead. At last, undressing himself with a gloomy resolution, he got into bed.

Some men in his blighted position would have taken to drinking; but as Mr. Swiveller had taken to that before, he only took, on receiving the news that Sophy Wackles was lost to him for ever, to playing the flute; thinking after mature consideration that it was a good, sound, dismal occupation, not only in unison with his own sad thoughts, but calculated to awaken a fellow-feeling in the bosoms of his neighbours. In pursuance of this resolution, he now drew a little table to his bedside, and arranging the light and a small oblong music-book to the best advantage, took his flute from its box, and began to play most mournfully.

The air was 'Away with melancholy'—a composition

Mr. Swiveller playing the Flute

which, when it is played very slowly on the flute, in bed, with the further disadvantage of being performed by a gentleman but imperfectly acquainted with the instrument, who repeats one note a great many times before he can find the next, has not a lively effect. Yet, for half the night, or more, Mr. Swiveller, lying sometimes on his back with his eyes upon the ceiling, and sometimes half out of bed to correct himself by the book, played this unhappy tune over and over again; never leaving off, save for a minute or two at a time to take breath and soliloquise about the Marchioness, and then beginning again with renewed vigour. It was not until he had quite exhausted his several subjects of meditation, and had breathed into the flute the whole sentiment of the purl down to its very dregs, and had nearly maddened the people of the house, and at both the next doors, and over the way,—that he shut up the music-book, extinguished the candle, and finding himself greatly lightened and relieved in his mind, turned round and fell asleep.

He awoke in the morning, much refreshed; and having taken half an hour's exercise at the flute, and graciously received a notice to quit from his landlady, who had been in waiting on the stairs for that purpose since the dawn of day, repaired to Bevis Marks; where the beautiful Sally was already at her post, bearing in her looks a radiance, mild as that which beameth from the virgin moon.

Mr. Swiveller acknowledged her presence by a nod, and exchanged his coat for the aquatic jacket; which usually took some time fitting on, for in consequence of a tightness in the sleeves, it was only to be got into by a series of struggles. This difficulty overcome, he took his seat at the desk.

'I say'—quoth Miss Brass, abruptly breaking silence, 'you haven't seen a silver pencil-case this morning, have you?'

'I didn't meet many in the street,' rejoined Mr. Swiveller. 'I saw one—a stout pencil-case of respectable appearance—but as he was in company with an elderly penknife, and a young toothpick with whom he was in earnest conversation, I felt a delicacy in speaking to him.'

'No, but have you?' returned Miss Brass. 'Seriously, you know.'

'What a dull dog you must be to ask me such a question seriously!' said Mr. Swiveller. 'Haven't I this moment come?'

'Well, all I know is,' replied Miss Sally, 'that it's not to be found, and that it disappeared one day this week, when I left it on the desk.'

'Halloa!' thought Richard, 'I hope the Marchioness hasn't been at work here.'

'There was a knife too,' said Miss Sally, 'of the same pattern. They were given to me by my father, years ago, and are both gone. You haven't missed anything yourself, have you?'

Mr. Swiveller involuntarily clapped his hands to the jacket to be quite sure that it *was* a jacket and not a skirted coat; and having satisfied himself of the safety of this, his only moveable in Bevis Marks, made answer in the negative.

'It's a very unpleasant thing, Dick,' said Miss Brass, pulling out the tin box and refreshing herself with a pinch of snuff; 'but between you and me—between friends, you know, for if Sammy knew it, I should never hear the last of it—some of the office money, too, that has been left about, has gone in the same way. In particular, I have missed three half-crowns at three different times.'

'You don't mean that?' cried Dick. 'Be careful what you say, old boy, for this is a serious matter. Are you quite sure? Is there no mistake?'

'It is so, and there can't be any mistake at all,' rejoined Miss Brass emphatically.

'Then by Jove,' thought Richard, laying down his pen, 'I am afraid the Marchioness is done for!'

The more he discussed the subject in his thoughts, the more probable it appeared to Dick that the miserable little servant was the culprit. When he considered on what a spare allowance of food she lived, how neglected and untaught she was, and how her natural cunning had been sharpened by necessity and privation, he scarcely doubted it. And yet he pitied her so much, and felt so unwilling to have a matter of such gravity disturbing the oddity of their acquaintance, that he thought, and thought truly, that rather than receive fifty pounds down, he would have the Marchioness proved innocent.

While he was plunged in very profound and serious meditation upon this theme, Miss Sally sat shaking her head with an air of great mystery and doubt; when the voice of her brother Sampson, carolling a cheerful strain, was heard in the passage, and that gentleman himself, beaming with virtuous smiles, appeared.

'Mr. Richard sir, good morning! Here we are again, sir,

entering upon another day, with our bodies strengthened by slumber and breakfast, and our spirits fresh and flowing. Here we are, Mr. Richard, rising with the sun to run our little course—our course of duty sir—and, like him, to get through our day's work with credit to ourselves and advantage to our fellow-creatures. A charming reflection, sir, very charming!'

While he addressed his clerk in these words, Mr. Brass was, somewhat ostentatiously, engaged in minutely examining and holding up against the light a five-pound bank-note, which he had brought in, in his hand.

Mr. Richard not receiving his remarks with anything like enthusiasm, his employer turned his eyes to his face, and observed that it wore a troubled expression.

'You're out of spirits sir,' said Brass. 'Mr. Richard sir, we should fall to work cheerfully, and not in a despondent state. It becomes us, Mr. Richard sir, to—'

Here the chaste Sarah heaved a loud sigh.

'Dear me!' said Mr. Sampson, 'you too! Is anything the matter? Mr. Richard sir——'

Dick, glancing at Miss Sally, saw that she was making signals to him, to acquaint her brother with the subject of their recent conversation. As his own position was not a very pleasant one until the matter was set at rest one way or other, he did so; and Miss Brass, plying her snuff-box at a most wasteful rate, corroborated his account.

The countenance of Sampson fell, and anxiety overspread his features. Instead of passionately bewailing the loss of his money, as Miss Sally had expected, he walked on tiptoe to the door, opened it, looked outside, shut it softly, returned on tiptoe, and said in a whisper,

'This is a most extraordinary and painful circumstance— Mr. Richard sir, a most painful circumstance. The fact is, that I myself have missed several small sums from the desk, of late, and have refrained from mentioning it, hoping that accident would discover the offender; but it has not done so —it has not done so. Sally—Mr. Richard sir—this is a particularly distressing affair!'

As Sampson spoke, he laid the bank-note upon the desk among some papers, in an absent manner, and thrust his hands into his pockets. Richard Swiveller pointed to it, and admonished him to take it up.

'No, Mr. Richard sir,' rejoined Brass with emotion, 'I will not take it up. I will let it lie there, sir. To take it up, Mr. Richard sir, would imply a doubt of you; and in you, sir, I have unlimited confidence. We will let it lie there, sir, if you please, and we will not take it up by any means.' With that, Mr. Brass patted him twice or thrice on the shoulder, in a most friendly manner, and entreated him to believe that he had as much faith in his honesty as he had in his own.

Although at another time Mr. Swiveller might have looked upon this as a doubtful compliment, he felt it, under the then-existing circumstances, a great relief to be assured that he was not wrongfully suspected. When he had made a suitable reply, Mr. Brass wrung him by the hand, and fell into a brown study, as did Miss Sally likewise. Richard too remained in a thoughtful state; fearing every moment to hear the Marchioness impeached, and unable to resist the conviction that she must be guilty.

When they had severally remained in this condition for some minutes, Miss Sally all at once gave a loud rap upon the desk with her clenched fist, and cried, 'I've hit it!'—as indeed she had, and chipped a piece out of it too; but that was not her meaning.

'Well,' cried Brass anxiously. 'Go on, will you!'

'Why,' replied his sister with an air of triumph, 'hasn't there been somebody always coming in and out of this office for the last three or four weeks; hasn't that somebody been left alone in it sometimes—thanks to you; and do you mean to tell me that that somebody isn't the thief?'

'What somebody?' blustered Brass.

'Why, what do you call him—Kit.'

'Mr. Garland's young man?'

'To be sure.'

'Never!' cried Brass. 'Never. I'll not hear of it. Don't tell me—' said Sampson, shaking his head, and working with both his hands as if he were clearing away ten thousand cobwebs. 'I'll never believe it of him. Never!'

'I say,' repeated Miss Brass, taking another pinch of snuff, 'that he's the thief.'

'I say,' returned Sampson violently, 'that he is *not*. What do you mean? How dare you? Are characters to be whispered away like this? Do you know that he's the honestest and faithfullest fellow that ever lived, and that he has an irreproachable good name? Come in, come in!'

These last words were not addressed to Miss Sally, though they partook of the tone in which the indignant remonstrances that preceded them had been uttered. They were addressed to some person who had knocked at the office-door; and they had hardly passed the lips of Mr. Brass, when this very Kit himself looked in.

'Is the gentleman up-stairs, sir, if you please?'

'Yes, Kit,' said Brass, still fired with an honest indignation, and frowning with knotted brows upon his sister. 'Yes, Kit, he is. I am glad to see you, Kit, I am rejoiced to see you. Look in again, as you come down-stairs, Kit. *That* lad a robber!' cried Brass when he had withdrawn, 'with that frank and open countenance! I'd trust him with untold gold. Mr. Richard sir, have the goodness to step directly to Wrasp and Co.'s in Broad Street, and inquire if they have had instructions to appear in Carkem and Painter. *That* lad a robber,' sneered Sampson, flushed and heated with his wrath. 'Am I blind, deaf, silly; do I know nothing of human nature when I see it before me? Kit a robber! Bah!'

Flinging this final interjection at Miss Sally with immeasurable scorn and contempt, Sampson Brass thrust his head into his desk, as if to shut the base world from his view, and breathed defiance from under its half-closed lid.

CHAPTER LIX

WHEN Kit, having discharged his errand, came down-stairs from the single gentleman's apartment after the lapse of a quarter of an hour or so, Mr. Sampson Brass was alone in the office. He was not singing as usual, nor was he seated at his desk. The open door showed him standing before the fire with his back towards it, and looking so very strange that Kit supposed he must have been suddenly taken ill.

'Is anything the matter sir?' said Kit.

'Matter!' cried Brass. 'No. Why anything the matter?'

'You are so very pale,' said Kit, 'that I should hardly have known you.'

'Pooh pooh! mere fancy,' cried Brass, stooping to throw up the cinders. 'Never better, Kit, never better in all my life. Merry too. Ha ha! How's our friend above-stairs, eh?'

'A great deal better,' said Kit.

'I'm glad to hear it,' rejoined Brass; 'thankful, I may say. An excellent gentleman—worthy, liberal, generous, gives very little trouble—an admirable lodger. Ha ha! Mr. Garland—he's well I hope, Kit—and the pony—my friend, my particular friend you know. Ha ha!'

Kit gave a satisfactory account of all the little household at Abel Cottage. Mr. Brass, who seemed remarkably inattentive and impatient, mounted on his stool, and beckoning him to come nearer, took him by the button-hole.

'I have been thinking, Kit,' said the lawyer, 'that I could throw some little emoluments in your mother's way—You have a mother, I think? If I recollect right, you told me—'

'Oh yes sir, yes certainly.'

'A widow I think? an industrious widow?'

'A harder-working woman or a better mother never lived, sir.'

'Ah!' cried Brass. 'That's affecting, truly affecting. A poor widow struggling to maintain her orphans in decency and comfort, is a delicious picture of human goodness.—Put down your hat, Kit.'

'Thank you sir, I must be going directly.'

'Put it down while you stay, at any rate,' said Brass, taking it from him and making some confusion among the papers, in finding a place for it on the desk. 'I was thinking, Kit, that we have often houses to let for people we are concerned for, and matters of that sort. Now you know we're obliged to put people into those houses to take care of 'em—very often undeserving people that we can't depend upon. What's to prevent our having a person that we *can* depend upon, and enjoying the delight of doing a good action at the same time? I say, what's to prevent our employing this worthy woman, your mother? What with one job and another, there's lodging—and good lodging too—pretty well all the year round, rent free, and a weekly allowance besides, Kit, that would provide her with a great many comforts she don't at present enjoy. Now what do you think of that? Do you see any objection? My only desire is to serve you, Kit; therefore if you do, say so freely.'

As Brass spoke, he moved the hat twice or thrice, and shuffled among the papers again, as if in search of something.

'How can I see any objection to such a kind offer sir?' replied Kit with his whole heart. 'I don't know how to thank you sir, I don't indeed.'

'Why then,' said Brass, suddenly turning upon him and thrusting his face close to Kit's with such a repulsive smile that the latter, even in the very height of his gratitude, drew back, quite startled. 'Why then, *it's done.*'

Kit looked at him in some confusion.

'Done, I say,' added Sampson, rubbing his hands and veiling himself again in his usual oily manner. 'Ha ha! and so you shall find, Kit, so you shall find. But dear me,' said Brass, 'what a time Mr. Richard is gone! A sad loiterer to be sure! Will you mind the office one minute, while I run up-stairs? Only one minute. I'll not detain you an instant longer, on any account, Kit.'

Talking as he went, Mr. Brass bustled out of the office, and in a very short time, returned. Mr. Swiveller came back, almost at the same instant; and as Kit was leaving the room hastily, to make up for lost time, Miss Brass herself encountered him in the doorway.

'Oh!' sneered Miss Sally, looking after him as she entered. 'There goes your pet, Sammy, eh?'

'Ah! There he goes,' replied Brass. 'My pet, if you please. An honest fellow, Mr. Richard sir—a worthy fellow indeed!'

'Hem!' coughed Miss Brass.

'I tell you, you aggravating vagabond,' said the angry

Sampson, 'that I'd stake my life upon his honesty. Am I never to hear the last of this? Am I always to be baited, and beset, by your mean suspicions? Have you no regard for true merit, you malignant fellow? If you come to that, I'd sooner suspect your honesty than his.'

Miss Sally pulled out the tin snuff-box, and took a long, slow pinch: regarding her brother with a steady gaze all the time.

'She drives me wild, Mr. Richard sir,' said Brass, 'she exasperates me beyond all bearing. I am heated and excited sir, I know I am. These are not business manners, sir, nor business looks, but she carries me out of myself.'

'Why don't you leave him alone?' said Dick.

'Because she can't sir,' retorted Brass; 'because to chafe and vex me is a part of her nature sir, and she will and must do it, or I don't believe she'd have her health. But never mind,' said Brass, 'never mind. I've carried my point. I've shown my confidence in the lad. He has minded the office again. Ha ha! Ugh, you viper!'

The beautiful virgin took another pinch, and put the snuff-box in her pocket; still looking at her brother with perfect composure.

'He has minded the office again,' said Brass triumphantly; 'he has had my confidence, and he shall continue to have it; he—why, where's the—'

'What have you lost?' inquired Mr. Swiveller.

'Dear me!' said Brass, slapping all his pockets, one after another, and looking into his desk, and under it, and upon it, and wildly tossing the papers about, 'the note, Mr. Richard sir, the five-pound note—what can have become of it? I laid it down here—God bless me!'

'What!' cried Miss Sally, starting up, clapping her hands, and scattering the papers on the floor. 'Gone! Now who's right? Now who's got it? Never mind five pounds—what's five pounds? He's honest you know, quite honest. It would be mean to suspect *him*. Don't run after him. No, no, not for the world!'

'Is it really gone though?' said Dick, looking at Brass with a face as pale as his own.

'Upon my word, Mr. Richard sir,' replied the lawyer, feeling in all his pockets with looks of the greatest agitation, 'I fear this is a black business. It's certainly gone, sir. What's to be done?'

'Don't run after him,' said Miss Sally, taking more snuff, 'Don't run after him on any account. Give him time to get rid of it, you know. It would be cruel to find him out!'

Mr. Swiveller and Sampson Brass looked from Miss Sally to each other, in a state of bewilderment, and then, as by one impulse, caught up their hats and rushed out into the street —darting along in the middle of the road, and dashing aside all obstructions, as though they were running for their lives.

It happened that Kit had been running too, though not so fast, and having the start of them by some few minutes, was a good distance ahead. As they were pretty certain of the road he must have taken, however, and kept on at a great pace, they came up with him, at the very moment when he had taken breath, and was breaking into a run again.

'Stop!' cried Sampson, laying his hand on one shoulder, while Mr. Swiveller pounced upon the other. 'Not so fast sir. You're in a hurry?'

'Yes, I am,' said Kit, looking from one to the other in great surprise.

'I—I—can hardly believe it,' panted Sampson, 'but something of value is missing from the office. I hope you don't know what.'

'Know what! good Heaven Mr. Brass!' cried Kit, trembling from head to foot; 'you don't suppose—'

'No, no,' rejoined Brass quickly, 'I don't suppose anything. Don't say *I* said you did. You'll come back quietly, I hope?'

'Of course I will,' returned Kit. 'Why not?'

'To be sure!' said Brass. 'Why not? I hope there may turn out to be no why not. If you knew the trouble I've been in, this morning, through taking your part, Christopher, you'd be sorry for it.'

'And I am sure you'll be sorry for having suspected me sir,' replied Kit. 'Come. Let us make haste back.'

'Certainly!' cried Brass, 'the quicker, the better. Mr. Richard—have the goodness sir to take that arm. I'll take this one. It's not easy walking three abreast, but under these circumstances it must be done sir; there's no help for it.'

Kit did turn from white to red, and from red to white again, when they secured him thus, and for a moment seemed disposed to resist. But, quickly recollecting himself, and remembering that if he made any struggle, he would perhaps be dragged by the collar through the public streets, he only repeated,

T

with great earnestness and with the tears standing in his eyes, that they would be sorry for this—and suffered them to lead him off. While they were on the way back, Mr. Swiveller, upon whom his present functions sat very irksomely, took an opportunity of whispering in his ear that if he would confess his guilt, even by so much as a nod, and promise not to do so any more, he would connive at his kicking Sampson Brass on the shins and escaping up a court; but Kit indignantly rejecting this proposal, Mr. Richard had nothing for it, but to hold him tight until they reached Bevis Marks, and ushered him into the presence of the charming Sarah, who immediately took the precaution of locking the door.

'Now, you know,' said Brass, 'if this is a case of innocence, it is a case of that description, Christopher, where the fullest disclosure is the best satisfaction for everybody. Therefore if you'll consent to an examination,' he demonstrated what kind of examination he meant by turning back the cuffs of his coat, 'it will be a comfortable and pleasant thing for all parties.'

'Search me,' said Kit, proudly holding up his arms. 'But mind sir—I know you'll be sorry for this, to the last day of your life.'

'It is certainly a very painful occurrence,' said Brass with a sigh, as he dived into one of Kit's pockets, and fished up a miscellaneous collection of small articles; 'very painful. Nothing here, Mr. Richard, sir, all perfectly satisfactory. Nor here sir. Nor in the waistcoat, Mr. Richard, nor in the coat tails. So far, I am rejoiced, I am sure.'

Richard Swiveller, holding Kit's hat in his hand, was watching the proceedings with great interest, and bore upon his face the slightest possible indication of a smile, as Brass, shutting one of his eyes, looked with the other up the inside of one of the poor fellow's sleeves as if it were a telescope—when Sampson turning hastily to him, bade him search his hat.

'Here's a handkerchief,' said Dick.

'No harm in that sir,' rejoined Brass, applying his eye to the other sleeve, and speaking in the voice of one who was contemplating an immense extent of prospect. 'No harm in a handkerchief sir, whatever. The faculty don't consider it a healthy custom, I believe, Mr. Richard, to carry one's handkerchief in one's hat—I have heard that it keeps the head too warm—but in every other point of view, its being there, is extremely satisfactory—ex-tremely so.'

An exclamation, at once from Richard Swiveller, Miss Sally, and Kit himself, cut the lawyer short. He turned his head, and saw Dick standing with the bank-note in his hand.

'In the hat?' cried Brass in a sort of shriek.

'Under the handkerchief, and tucked beneath the lining,' said Dick, aghast at the discovery.

Mr. Brass looked at him, at his sister, at the walls, at the ceiling, at the floor—everywhere but at Kit, who stood quite stupefied and motionless.

'And this,' cried Sampson, clasping his hands, 'is the world that turns upon its own axis, and has Lunar influences, and revolutions round Heavenly Bodies, and various games of that sort! This is human natur, is it! Oh natur, natur! This is the miscreant that I was going to benefit with all my little arts, and that, even now, I feel so much for, as to wish to let him go! But,' added Mr. Brass with greater fortitude, 'I am myself a lawyer, and bound to set an example in carrying the laws of my happy country into effect. Sally my dear, forgive me, and catch hold of him on the other side. Mr. Richard sir, have the goodness to run and fetch a constable. The weakness is past and over sir, and moral strength returns. A constable, sir, if *you* please!'

KIT stood as one entranced, with his eyes opened wide and fixed upon the ground, regardless alike of the tremulous hold which Mr. Brass maintained on one side of his cravat, and of the firmer grasp of Miss Sally upon the other; although this latter detention was in itself no small inconvenience, as that fascinating woman, besides screwing her knuckles inconveniently into his throat from time to time, had fastened upon him in the first instance with so tight a grip that even in the disorder and distraction of his thoughts he could not divest himself of an uneasy sense of choking. Between the brother and sister he remained in this posture, quite unresisting and passive, until Mr. Swiveller returned, with a police constable at his heels.

This functionary, being, of course, well used to such scenes; looking upon all kinds of robbery, from petty larceny up to housebreaking or ventures on the highway, as matters in the regular course of business; and regarding the perpetrators in the light of so many customers coming to be served at the whole-sale and retail shop of criminal law where he stood behind the counter; received Mr. Brass's statement of facts with about as much interest and surprise, as an undertaker might evince if required to listen to a circumstantial account of the last illness of a person whom he was called in to wait upon professionally; and took Kit into custody with a decent indifference.

'We had better,' said this subordinate minister of justice, 'get to the office while there's a magistrate sitting. I shall want you to come along with us, Mr. Brass, and the—' he looked at Miss Sally as if in some doubt whether she might not be a griffin or other fabulous monster.

'The lady, eh?' said Sampson.

'Ah!' replied the constable. 'Yes—the lady. Likewise the young man that found the property.'

'Mr. Richard, sir,' said Brass in a mournful voice. 'A sad necessity. But the altar of our country sir—'

'You'll have a hackney-coach, I suppose?' interrupted the constable, holding Kit (whom his other captors had released) carelessly by the arm, a little above the elbow. 'Be so good as send for one, will you?'

'But, hear me speak a word,' cried Kit, raising his eyes and looking imploringly about him. 'Hear me speak a word. I am no more guilty than any one of you. Upon my soul I am not. I a thief! Oh, Mr. Brass, you know me better. I am sure you know me better. This is not right of you, indeed.'

'I give you my word, constable—' said Brass. But here the constable interposed with the constitutional principle 'words be blowed;' observing that words were but spoonmeat for babes and sucklings, and that oaths were the food for strong men.

'Quite true, constable,' assented Brass in the same mournful tone. 'Strictly correct. I give you my oath, constable, that down to a few minutes ago, when this fatal discovery was made, I had such confidence in that lad, that I'd have trusted him with—a hackney-coach, Mr. Richard sir; you're very slow, sir.'

'Who is there that knows me,' cried Kit, 'that would not trust me—that does not? ask anybody whether they have ever doubted me; whether I have ever wronged them of a farthing. Was I ever once dishonest when I was poor and hungry, and is it likely I would begin now? Oh consider what you do. How can I meet the kindest friends that ever human creature had, with this dreadful charge upon me!'

Mr. Brass rejoined that it would have been well for the prisoner if he had thought of that before, and was about to make some other gloomy observations when the voice of the single gentleman was heard, demanding from above-stairs what was the matter, and what was the cause of all that noise and hurry. Kit made an involuntary start towards the door in his anxiety to answer for himself, but being speedily detained by the constable, had the agony of seeing Sampson Brass run out alone to tell the story in his own way.

'And he can hardly believe it, either,' said Sampson, when he returned, 'nor nobody will. I wish I could doubt the evidence of my senses, but their depositions are unimpeachable. It's of no use cross-examining my eyes,' cried Sampson, winking and rubbing them, 'they stick to their first account, and will. Now, Sarah, I hear the coach in the Marks; get on your bonnet, and we'll be off. A sad errand! a moral funeral, quite!'

'Mr. Brass,' said Kit, 'do me one favour. Take me to Mr. Witherden's first.'

Sampson shook his head irresolutely.

'Do,' said Kit. 'My master's there. For Heaven's sake, take me there, first.'

'Well, I don't know,' stammered Brass, who perhaps had his reasons for wishing to show as fair as possible in the eyes of the notary. 'How do we stand in point of time, constable, eh?'

The constable, who had been chewing a straw all this while with great philosophy, replied that if they went away at once they would have time enough, but that if they stood shilly-shallying there, any longer, they must go straight to the Mansion House; and finally expressed his opinion that that was where it was, and that was all about it.

Mr. Richard Swiveller having arrived inside the coach, and still remaining immoveable in the most commodious corner with his face to the horses, Mr. Brass instructed the officer to remove his prisoner, and declared himself quite ready. Therefore, the constable, still holding Kit in the same manner, and pushing him on a little before him, so as to keep him at about three-quarters of an arm's length in advance (which is the professional mode), thrust him into the vehicle and followed himself. Miss Sally entered next; and there being now four inside, Sampson Brass got upon the box, and made the coachman drive on.

Still completely stunned by the sudden and terrible change which had taken place in his affairs, Kit sat gazing out of the coach window, almost hoping to see some monstrous phenomenon in the streets which might give him reason to believe he was in a dream. Alas! Everything was too real and familiar: the same succession of turnings, the same houses, the same streams of people running side by side in different directions upon the pavement, the same bustle of carts and carriages in the road, the same well-remembered objects in the shop-windows: a regularity in the very noise and hurry which no dream ever mirrored. Dreamlike as the story was, it was true. He stood charged with robbery; the note had been found upon him, though he was innocent in thought and deed; and they were carrying him back, a prisoner.

Absorbed in these painful ruminations, thinking with a drooping heart of his mother and little Jacob, feeling as though even the consciousness of innocence would be insufficient to support him in the presence of his friends if they believed him guilty, and sinking in hope and courage more

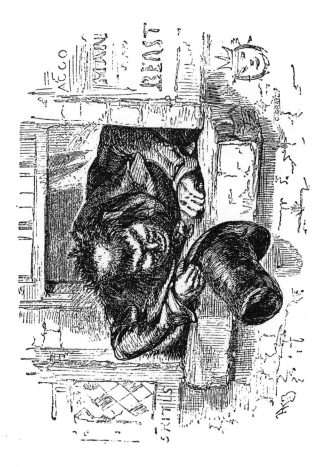

Quilp's Grotesque Politeness

and more as they drew nearer to the notary's, poor Kit was looking earnestly out of the window, observant of nothing,— when all at once, as though it had been conjured up by magic, he became aware of the face of Quilp.

And what a leer there was upon the face! It was from the open window of a tavern that it looked out; and the dwarf had so spread himself over it, with his elbows on the window-sill and his head resting on both his hands, that what between this attitude and his being swollen with suppressed laughter, he looked puffed and bloated into twice his usual breadth. Mr. Brass, on recognising him, immediately stopped the coach. As it came to a halt directly opposite to where he stood, the dwarf pulled off his hat, and saluted the party with a hideous and grotesque politeness.

'Aha!' he cried. 'Where now, Brass? where now? Sally with you too? Sweet Sally! And Dick? Pleasant Dick! And Kit? Honest Kit!'

'He's extremely cheerful!' said Brass to the coachman. 'Very much so! Ah sir—a sad business! Never believe in honesty any more, sir.'

'Why not?' returned the dwarf. 'Why not, you rogue of a lawyer, why not?'

'Bank-note lost in our office sir,' said Brass, shaking his head. 'Found in his hat sir—he previously left alone there— no mistake at all sir—chain of evidence complete—not a link wanting.'

'What!' cried the dwarf, leaning half his body out of window. 'Kit a thief! Kit a thief! Ha ha ha! Why, he's an uglier-looking thief than can be seen anywhere for a penny. Eh Kit—eh? Ha ha ha! Have you taken Kit into custody before he had time and opportunity to beat me! Eh Kit, eh?' And with that, he burst into a yell of laughter, manifestly to the great terror of the coachman, and pointed to a dyer's pole hard by, where a dangling suit of clothes bore some resemblance to a man upon a gibbet.

'Is it coming to that, Kit!' cried the dwarf, rubbing his hands violently. 'Ha ha ha ha! What a disappointment for little Jacob, and for his darling mother! Let him have the Bethel minister to comfort and console him, Brass. Eh Kit, eh? Drive on, coachey, drive on. Bye bye Kit; all good go with you; keep up your spirits; my love to the Garlands—the dear old lady and gentleman. Say I inquired after 'em, will you? Blessings on 'em, on you, and on everybody, Kit. Blessings on all the world!'

With such good wishes and farewells, poured out in a rapid torrent until they were out of hearing, Quilp suffered them to depart; and when he could see the coach no longer, drew in his head, and rolled upon the ground in an ecstasy of enjoyment.

When they reached the notary's, which they were not long in doing, for they had encountered the dwarf in a bye street at a very little distance from the house, Mr. Brass dismounted; and opening the coach door with a melancholy visage, requested his sister to accompany him into the office, with the view of preparing the good people within, for the mournful intelligence that awaited them. Miss Sally complying, he desired Mr. Swiveller to accompany them. So, into the office they went; Mr. Sampson and his sister arm-in-arm; and Mr. Swiveller following, alone.

The notary was standing before the fire in the outer office, talking to Mr. Abel and the elder Mr. Garland, while Mr. Chuckster sat writing at the desk, picking up such crumbs of their conversation as happened to fall in his way. This posture of affairs Mr. Brass observed through the glass-door as he was turning the handle, and seeing that the notary recognised him, he began to shake his head and sigh deeply while that partition yet divided them.

'Sir,' said Sampson, taking off his hat, and kissing the two forefingers of his right-hand beaver glove, 'my name is Brass —Brass of Bevis Marks sir. I have had the honour and pleasure, sir, of being concerned against you in some little testamentary matters. How do you do, sir?'

'My clerk will attend to any business you may have come upon, Mr. Brass,' said the notary, turning away.

'Thank you sir,' said Brass, 'thank you, I am sure. Allow me, sir, to introduce my sister—quite one of us sir, although of the weaker sex—of great use in my business sir, I assure you. Mr. Richard sir, have the goodness to come forward if you please—No really,' said Brass, stepping between the notary and his private office (towards which he had begun to retreat), and speaking in the tone of an injured man, 'really sir, I must, under favour, request a word or two with you, indeed.'

'Mr. Brass,' said the other, in a decided tone, 'I am engaged.

You see that I am occupied with these gentlemen. If you will communicate your business to Mr. Chuckster yonder, you will receive every attention.'

'Gentlemen,' said Brass, laying his right hand on his waist-coat, and looking towards the father and son with a smooth smile —'Gentlemen, I appeal to you—really, gentlemen—consider, I beg of you. I am of the law. I am styled "gentleman" by Act of Parliament. I maintain the title by the annual payment of twelve pound sterling for a certificate. I am not one of your players of music, stage actors, writers of books, or painters of pictures, who assume a station that the laws of their country don't recognise. I am none of your strollers or vagabonds. If any man brings his action against me, he must describe me as a gentleman, or his action is null and void. I appeal to you— is this quite respectful? Really gentlemen—'

'Well, will you have the goodness to state your business then, Mr. Brass?' said the notary.

'Sir,' rejoined Brass, 'I will. Ah Mr. Witherden! you little know the—but I will not be tempted to travel from the point sir. I believe the name of one of these gentlemen is Garland.'

'Of both,' said the notary.

'In-deed!' rejoined Brass, cringing excessively. 'But I might have known that, from the uncommon likeness. Extremely happy, I am sure, to have the honour of an introduction to two such gentlemen, although the occasion is a most painful one. One of you gentlemen has a servant called Kit?'

'Both,' replied the notary.

'Two Kits?' said Brass smiling. 'Dear me!'

'One Kit, sir,' returned Mr. Witherden angrily, 'who is employed by both gentlemen. What of him?'

'This of him sir,' rejoined Brass, dropping his voice impressively. 'That young man, sir, that I have felt un-bounded and unlimited confidence in, and always behaved to as if he was my equal—that young man has this morning committed a robbery in my office, and been taken almost in the fact.'

'This must be some falsehood!' cried the notary.

'It is not possible,' said Mr. Abel.

'I'll not believe one word of it,' exclaimed the old gentle-man.

Mr. Brass looked mildly round upon them, and rejoined,

'Mr. Witherden sir, *your* words are actionable, and if I was a man of low and mean standing, who couldn't afford to be slandered, I should proceed for damages. Hows'ever sir, being what I am, I merely scorn such expressions. The honest warmth of the other gentleman I respect, and I'm truly sorry to be the messenger of such unpleasant news. I shouldn't have put myself in this painful position, I assure you, but that the lad himself desired to be brought here in the first instance, and I yielded to his prayers. Mr. Chuckster sir, will you have the goodness to tap at the window for the constable that's waiting in the coach?'

The three gentlemen looked at each other with blank faces when these words were uttered, and Mr. Chuckster, doing as he was desired, and leaping off his stool with something of the excitement of an inspired prophet whose foretellings had in the fulness of time been realised, held the door open for the entrance of the wretched captive.

Such a scene as there was, when Kit came in, and bursting into the rude eloquence with which Truth at length inspired him, called Heaven to witness that he was innocent, and that how the property came to be found upon him he knew not! Such a confusion of tongues, before the circumstances were related, and the proofs disclosed! Such a dead silence when all was told, and his three friends exchanged looks of doubt and amazement!

'Is it not possible,' said Mr. Witherden, after a long pause, 'that this note may have found its way into the hat by some accident,—such as the removal of papers on the desk, for instance?'

But, this was clearly shown to be quite impossible. Mr. Swiveller, though an unwilling witness, could not help proving to demonstration, from the position in which it was found, that it must have been designedly secreted.

'It's very distressing,' said Brass, 'immensely distressing, I am sure. When he comes to be tried, I shall be very happy to recommend him to mercy on account of his previous good character. I did lose money before, certainly, but it doesn't quite follow that he took it. The presumption's against him—strongly against him—but we're Christians, I hope?'

'I suppose,' said the constable, looking round, 'that no gentleman here, can give evidence as to whether he's been flush of money of late. Do you happen to know, sir?'

'He has had money from time to time, certainly,' returned

Mr. Garland, to whom the man had put the question. 'But that, as he always told me, was given him by Mr. Brass himself.'

'Yes to be sure,' said Kit eagerly. 'You can bear me out in that sir?'

'Eh?' cried Brass, looking from face to face with an expression of stupid amazement.

'The money you know, the half-crowns, that you gave me—from the lodger,' said Kit.

'Oh dear me!' cried Brass, shaking his head and frowning heavily. 'This is a bad case, I find; a very bad case indeed.'

'What! Did you give him no money on account of anybody, sir?' asked Mr. Garland, with great anxiety.

'*I* give him money, sir!' returned Sampson. 'Oh, come you know, this is too barefaced. Constable, my good fellow, we had better be going.'

'What!' shrieked Kit. 'Does he deny that he did? ask him, somebody, pray. Ask him to tell you whether he did or not!'

'Did you, sir?' asked the notary.

'I tell you what, gentlemen,' replied Brass, in a very grave manner, 'he'll not serve his case this way, and really, if you feel any interest in him, you had better advise him to go upon some other tack. Did I, sir? Of course I never did.'

'Gentlemen,' cried Kit, on whom a light broke suddenly, 'Master, Mr. Abel, Mr. Witherden, every one of you—he did it! What I have done to offend him, I don't know, but this is a plot to ruin me. Mind, gentlemen, it's a plot, and whatever comes of it, I will say with my dying breath that he put that note in my hat himself! Look at him, gentlemen! see how he changes colour. Which of us looks the guilty person—he, or I?'

'You hear him, gentlemen?' said Brass, smiling, 'you hear him. Now, does this case strike you as assuming rather a black complexion, or does it not? Is it at all a treacherous case, do you think, or is it one of mere ordinary guilt? Perhaps, gentlemen, if he had not said this in your presence and I had reported it, you'd have held this to be impossible likewise, eh?'

With such pacific and bantering remarks did Mr. Brass refute the foul aspersion on his character; but the virtuous Sarah, moved by stronger feelings, and having at heart, perhaps, a more jealous regard for the honour of her family, flew from her brother's side, without any previous intimation of her design, and darted at the prisoner with the utmost fury. It would undoubtedly have gone hard with Kit's face, but that the wary constable, foreseeing her design, drew him aside at the critical moment, and thus placed Mr. Chuckster in circumstances of some jeopardy; for that gentleman happening to be next the object of Miss Brass's wrath; and rage being, like love and fortune, blind; was pounced upon by the fair enslaver, and had a false collar plucked up by the roots, and his hair very much dishevelled, before the exertions of the company could make her sensible of her mistake.

The constable, taking warning by this desperate attack, and thinking perhaps that it would be more satisfactory to the ends of justice if the prisoner were taken before a magistrate, whole, rather than in small pieces, led him back to the hackney-coach without more ado, and moreover insisted on Miss Brass becoming an outside passenger; to which proposal the charming creature, after a little angry discussion, yielded her consent; and so took her brother Sampson's place upon the box: Mr. Brass with some reluctance agreeing to occupy her seat inside. These arrangements perfected, they drove to the justice-room with all speed, followed by the notary and his two friends in another coach. Mr. Chuckster alone was left behind—greatly to his indignation; for he held the evidence he could have given, relative to Kit's returning to work out the shilling, to be so very material as bearing upon his hypocritical and designing character, that he considered its suppression little better than a compromise of felony.

At the justice-room, they found the single gentleman, who had gone straight there, and was expecting them with desperate impatience. But, not fifty single gentlemen rolled into one could have helped poor Kit, who in half an hour afterwards was committed for trial, and was assured by a friendly officer on his way to prison that there was no occasion to be cast down, for the sessions would soon be on, and he would, in all likelihood, get his little affair disposed of, and be comfortably transported, in less than a fortnight.

CHAPTER LXI

LET moralists and philosophers say what they may, it is very questionable whether a guilty man would have felt half as much misery that night, as Kit did, being innocent. The world, being in the constant commission of vast quantities of injustice, is a little too apt to comfort itself with the idea that if the victim of its falsehood and malice have a clear conscience, he cannot fail to be sustained under his trials, and somehow or other to come right at last; 'in which case,' say they who have hunted him down, '—though we certainly don't expect it—nobody will be better pleased than we.' Whereas, the world would do well to reflect, that injustice is in itself, to every generous and properly constituted mind, an injury, of all others the most insufferable, the most torturing, and the most hard to bear; and that many clear consciences have gone to their account elsewhere, and many sound hearts have broken, because of this very reason; the knowledge of their own deserts only aggravating their sufferings, and rendering them the less endurable.

The world, however, was not in fault in Kit's case. But, Kit was innocent; and knowing this, and feeling that his best friends deemed him guilty—that Mr. and Mrs. Garland would look upon him as a monster of ingratitude—that Barbara would associate him with all that was bad and criminal—that the pony would consider himself forsaken—and that even his own mother might perhaps yield to the strong appearances against him, and believe him to be the wretch he seemed—knowing and feeling all this, he experienced, at first, an agony of mind which no words can describe, and walked up and down the little cell in which he was locked up for the night, almost beside himself with grief.

Even when the violence of these emotions had in some degree subsided, and he was beginning to grow more calm, there came into his mind a new thought, the anguish of which was scarcely less. The child—the bright star of the simple fellow's life—she, who always came back upon him like a beautiful dream,—who had made the poorest part of his existence, the happiest and best—who had ever been so gentle, and considerate, and good—if she were ever to hear of this, what would she think? As this idea occurred to him, the walls of the prison seemed to melt away, and the old place to reveal itself in their stead, as it was wont to be on winter nights—the fireside, the little supper table, the old man's hat, and coat, and stick—the half-opened door, leading to her little room— they were all there. And Nell herself was there, and he—both laughing heartily as they had often done—and when he had got as far as this, Kit could go no farther, but flung himself upon his poor bedstead and wept.

It was a long night, which seemed as though it would have no end; but he slept too, and dreamed—always of being at liberty, and roving about, now with one person and now with another, but ever with a vague dread of being recalled to prison; not that prison, but one which was in itself a dim idea— not of a place, but of a care and sorrow: of something oppressive and always present, and yet impossible to define. At last, the morning dawned, and there was the jail itself—cold, black, and dreary, and very real indeed.

He was left to himself, however, and there was comfort in that. He had liberty to walk in a small paved yard at a certain hour, and learnt from the turnkey, who came to unlock his cell and show him where to wash, that there was a regular time for visiting, every day, and that if any of his friends came to see him, he would be fetched down to the grate. When he had given him this information, and a tin porringer containing his breakfast, the man locked him up again; and went clattering along the stone passage, opening and shutting a great many other doors, and raising numberless loud echoes which resounded through the building for a long time, as if they were in prison too, and unable to get out.

This turnkey had given him to understand that he was lodged, like some few others in the jail, apart from the mass of prisoners; because he was not supposed to be utterly depraved and irreclaimable, and had never occupied apartments in that mansion before. Kit was thankful for this indulgence, and sat reading the church catechism very attentively (though he had known it by heart from a little child), until he heard the key in the lock, and the man entered again.

'Now then,' he said, 'come on!'

'Where to, sir?' asked Kit.

The man contented himself by briefly replying 'Wisitors;' and taking him by the arm in exactly the same manner as the constable had done the day before, led him, through several winding ways and strong gates, into a passage, where he placed him at a grating and turned upon his heel. Beyond this grating, at the distance of about four or five feet, was another exactly like it. In the space between, sat a turnkey reading a newspaper, and outside the further railing, Kit saw, with a palpitating heart, his mother with the baby in her arms; Barbara's mother with her never-failing umbrella; and poor little Jacob, staring in with all his might, as though he were looking for the bird, or the wild beast, and thought the men were mere accidents with whom the bars could have no possible concern.

But, when little Jacob saw his brother, and, thrusting his arms between the rails to hug him, found that he came no nearer, but still stood afar off with his head resting on the arm by which he held to one of the bars, he began to cry most piteously; whereupon, Kit's mother and Barbara's mother, who had restrained themselves as much as possible, burst out sobbing and weeping afresh. Poor Kit could not help joining them, and not one of them could speak a word.

During this melancholy pause, the turnkey read his news-paper with a waggish look (he had evidently got among the facetious paragraphs) until, happening to take his eyes off for an instant, as if to get by dint of contemplation at the very marrow of some joke of a deeper sort than the rest, it appeared to occur to him, for the first time, that somebody was crying.

'Now, ladies, ladies,' he said, looking round with surprise, 'I'd advise you not to waste time like this. It's allowanced here, you know. You mustn't let that child make that noise either. It's against all rules.'

'I'm his poor mother, sir,' sobbed Mrs. Nubbles, curtseying humbly, 'and this is his brother, sir. Oh dear me, dear me!'

'Well!' replied the turnkey, folding his paper on his knee, so as to get with greater convenience at the top of the next column. 'It can't be helped, you know. He ain't the only one in the same fix. You mustn't make a noise about it!'

With that he went on reading. The man was not unnaturally cruel or hard-hearted. He had come to look upon felony as a kind of disorder, like the scarlet fever or erysipelas: some people had it—some hadn't—just as it might be.

'Oh! my darling Kit,' said his mother, whom Barbara's mother had charitably relieved of the baby, 'that I should see my poor boy here!'

'You don't believe that I did what they accuse me of, mother dear?' cried Kit, in a choking voice.

'*I* believe it!' exclaimed the poor woman, '*I* that never knew you tell a lie, or do a bad action from your cradle—that have never had a moment's sorrow on your account, except it was for the poor meals that you have taken with such good humour and content, that I forgot how little there was, when I thought how kind and thoughtful you were, though you were but a child!—I believe it of the son that's been a comfort to me from the hour of his birth until this time, and that I never laid down one night in anger with! I believe it of you, Kit!—'

'Why then, thank God!' said Kit, clutching the bars with an earnestness that shook them, 'and I can bear it, mother! Come what may, I shall always have one drop of happiness in my heart when I think that you said that.'

At this the poor woman fell a-crying again, and Barbara's mother too. And little Jacob, whose disjointed thoughts had by this time resolved themselves into a pretty distinct impression that Kit couldn't go out for a walk if he wanted, and that there were no birds, lions, tigers, or other natural curiosities behind those bars—nothing, indeed, but a caged brother—added his tears to theirs with as little noise as possible.

Kit's mother, drying her eyes (and moistening them, poor soul, more than she dried them), now took from the ground a small basket, and submissively addressed herself to the turnkey, saying, would he please to listen to her for a minute? The turnkey, being in the very crisis and passion of a joke, motioned to her with his hand to keep silent one minute longer, for her life. Nor did he remove his hand into its former posture, but kept it in the same warning attitude until he had finished the paragraph, when he paused for a few seconds, with a smile upon his face, as who should say 'this editor is a comical blade—a funny dog,' and then asked her what she wanted.

'I have brought him a little something to eat,' said the good woman. 'If you please, sir, might he have it?'

'Yes,—he may have it. There's no rule against that. Give it to me when you go, and I'll take care he has it.'

'No, but if you please sir—don't be angry with me sir—I am his mother, and you had a mother once—if I might only see him eat a little bit, I should go away, so much more satisfied that he was all comfortable.'

And again the tears of Kit's mother burst forth, and of

Kit in Jail (p. 456)

Barbara's mother, and of little Jacob. As to the baby, it was crowing and laughing with all its might—under the idea, apparently, that the whole scene had been invented and got up for its particular satisfaction.

The turnkey looked as if he thought the request a strange one and rather out of the common way, but nevertheless he laid down his paper, and coming round to where Kit's mother stood, took the basket from her, and after inspecting its contents, handed it to Kit, and went back to his place. It may be easily conceived that the prisoner had no great appetite, but he sat down on the ground, and ate as hard as he could, while, at every morsel he put into his mouth, his mother sobbed and wept afresh, though with a softened grief that bespoke the satisfaction the sight afforded her.

While he was thus engaged, Kit made some anxious inquiries about his employers, and whether they had expressed any opinion concerning him; but all he could learn was that Mr. Abel had himself broken the intelligence to his mother, with great kindness and delicacy, late on the previous night, but had himself expressed no opinion of his innocence or guilt. Kit was on the point of mustering courage to ask Barbara's mother about Barbara, when the turnkey who had conducted him, reappeared, a second turnkey appeared behind his visitors, and the third turnkey with the newspaper cried 'Time's up!'—adding in the same breath 'Now for the next party!' and then plunging deep into his newspaper again. Kit was taken off in an instant, with a blessing from his mother, and a scream from little Jacob, ringing in his ears. As he was crossing the next yard with the basket in his hand, under the guidance of his former conductor, another officer called to them to stop, and came up with a pint pot of porter in his hand.

'This is Christopher Nubbles, isn't it, that come in last night for felony?' said the man.

His comrade replied that this was the chicken in question.

'Then here's your beer,' said the other man to Christopher. 'What are you looking at? There an't a discharge in it.'

'I beg your pardon,' said Kit. 'Who sent it me?'

'Why, your friend,' replied the man. 'You're to have it every day, he says. And so you will, if he pays for it.'

'My friend!' repeated Kit.

'You're all abroad, seemingly,' returned the other man. 'There's his letter. Take hold!'

Kit took it, and when he was locked up again, read as follows.

'Drink of this cup, you'll find there's a spell in its every drop 'gainst the ills of mortality. Talk of the cordial that sparkled for Helen! *Her* cup was a fiction, but this is reality (Barclay and Co.'s). If they ever send it in a flat state, complain to the Governor. Yours, R. S.'

'R. S.!' said Kit, after some consideration. 'It must be Mr. Richard Swiveller. Well, it's very kind of him, and I thank him heartily.'

CHAPTER LXII

A FAINT light, twinkling from the window of the counting-house on Quilp's wharf, and looking inflamed and red through the night-fog, as though it suffered from it like an eye, forewarned Mr. Sampson Brass, as he approached the wooden cabin with a cautious step, that the excellent proprietor, his esteemed client, was inside, and probably waiting with his accustomed patience and sweetness of temper the fulfilment of the appointment which now brought Mr. Brass within his fair domain.

'A treacherous place to pick one's steps in, of a dark night,' muttered Sampson, as he stumbled for the twentieth time over some stray lumber, and limped in pain. 'I believe that boy strews the ground differently every day, on purpose to bruise and maim one; unless his master does it with his own hands, which is more than likely. I hate to come to this place without Sally. She's more protection than a dozen men.'

As he paid this compliment to the merit of the absent charmer, Mr. Brass came to a halt; looking doubtfully towards the light, and over his shoulder.

'What's he about, I wonder?' murmured the lawyer, standing on tiptoe and endeavouring to obtain a glimpse of what was passing inside, which at that distance was impossible—'drinking, I suppose,—making himself more fiery and furious, and heating his malice and mischievousness till they boil. I'm always afraid to come here by myself, when his account's a pretty large one. I don't believe he'd mind throttling me, and dropping me softly into the river when the tide was at its strongest, any more than he'd mind killing a rat—indeed I don't know whether he wouldn't consider it a pleasant joke. Hark! Now he's singing!'

Mr. Quilp was certainly entertaining himself with vocal exercise, but it was rather a kind of chant than a song; being a monotonous repetition of one sentence in a very rapid manner, with a long stress upon the last word, which he swelled into a dismal roar. Nor did the burden of this performance bear any reference to love, or war, or wine, or loyalty, or any other, the standard topics of song, but to a subject not often set to music or generally known in ballads; the words being these:—'The worthy magistrate, after remarking that the prisoner would find some difficulty in persuading a jury to believe his tale, committed him to take his trial at the approaching sessions; and directed the customary recognisances to be entered into for the pros-e-cu-tion.'

Every time he came to this concluding word, and had exhausted all possible stress upon it, Quilp burst into a shriek of laughter, and began again.

'He's dreadfully imprudent,' muttered Brass, after he had listened to two or three repetitions of the chant. 'Horribly imprudent. I wish he was dumb. I wish he was deaf. I wish he was blind. Hang him,' cried Brass, as the chant began again. 'I wish he was dead!'

Giving utterance to these friendly aspirations in behalf of his client, Mr. Sampson composed his face into its usual state of smoothness, and waiting until the shriek came again and was dying away, went up to the wooden house, and knocked at the door.

'Come in!' cried the dwarf.

'How do you do to-night sir?' said Sampson, peeping in. 'Ha ha ha! How do you do sir? Oh dear me, how very whimsical! Amazingly whimsical to be sure!'

'Come in, you fool!' returned the dwarf, 'and don't stand there shaking your head and showing your teeth. Come in, you false witness, you perjurer, you suborner of evidence, come in!'

'He has the richest humour!' cried Brass, shutting the door behind him; 'the most amazing vein of comicality! But isn't it *rather* injudicious sir—?'

'What?' demanded Quilp. 'What, Judas?'

'Judas!' cried Brass. 'He has such extraordinary spirits! His humour is so extremely playful! Judas! Oh yes—dear me, how very good! Ha ha ha!'

All this time, Sampson was rubbing his hands, and staring, with ludicrous surprise and dismay, at a great, goggle-eyed, blunt-nosed figure-head of some old ship, which was reared up against the wall in a corner near the stove, looking like a goblin or hideous idol whom the dwarf worshipped. A mass of timber on its head, carved into the dim and distant semblance of a cocked hat, together with a representation of a star on the left breast and epaulettes on the shoulders, denoted that it was intended for the effigy of some famous admiral; but, without those helps, any observer might have supposed it the authentic

Revenge is Sweet

portrait of a distinguished merman, or great sea-monster. Being originally much too large for the apartment which it was now employed to decorate, it had been sawn short off at the waist. Even in this state it reached from floor to ceiling; and thrusting itself forward, with that excessively wide-awake aspect, and air of somewhat obtrusive politeness, by which figure-heads are usually characterised, seemed to reduce everything else to mere pigmy proportions.

'Do you know it?' said the dwarf, watching Sampson's eyes. 'Do you see the likeness?'

'Eh?' said Brass, holding his head on one side, and throwing it a little back, as connoisseurs do. 'Now I look at it again, I fancy I see a—yes, there certainly is something in the smile that reminds me of—and yet upon my word I—'

Now, the fact was, that Sampson, having never seen anything in the smallest degree resembling this substantial phantom, was much perplexed; being uncertain whether Mr. Quilp considered it like himself, and had therefore bought it for a family portrait; or whether he was pleased to consider it as the likeness of some enemy. He was not very long in doubt; for, while he was surveying it with that knowing look which people assume when they are contemplating for the first time portraits which they ought to recognise but don't, the dwarf threw down the newspaper from which he had been chanting the words already quoted, and seizing a rusty iron bar, which he used in lieu of poker, dealt the figure such a stroke on the nose that it rocked again.

'Is it like Kit—is it his picture, his image, his very self?' cried the dwarf, aiming a shower of blows at the insensible countenance, and covering it with deep dimples. 'Is it the exact model and counterpart of the dog—is it—is it—is it?' And with every repetition of the question, he battered the great image, until the perspiration streamed down his face with the violence of the exercise.

Although this might have been a very comical thing to look at from a secure gallery, as a bull-fight is found to be a comfortable spectacle by those who are not in the arena, and a house on fire is better than a play to people who don't live near it, there was something in the earnestness of Mr. Quilp's manner which made his legal adviser feel that the counting-house was a little too small, and a deal too lonely, for the complete enjoyment of these humours. Therefore, he stood as

far off as he could, while the dwarf was thus engaged; whimper-
ing out but feeble applause; and when Quilp left off and sat
down again from pure exhaustion, approached with more
obsequiousness than ever.

'Excellent indeed!' cried Brass. 'He he! Oh, very good sir.
You know,' said Sampson, looking round as if in appeal to the
bruised admiral, 'he's quite a remarkable man—quite!'

'Sit down,' said the dwarf. 'I bought the dog yesterday. I've
been screwing gimlets into him, and sticking forks in his eyes,
and cutting my name on him. I mean to burn him at last.'

'Ha ha!' cried Brass. 'Extremely entertaining, indeed!'

'Come here,' said Quilp, beckoning him to draw near.
'What's injudicious, hey?'

'Nothing sir—nothing. Scarcely worth mentioning sir; but
I thought that song—admirably humorous in itself you know
—was perhaps rather—'

'Yes,' said Quilp, 'rather what?'

'Just bordering, or as one may say remotely verging, upon
the confines of injudiciousness perhaps sir,' returned Brass,
looking timidly at the dwarf's cunning eyes, which were
turned towards the fire and reflected its red light.

'Why?' inquired Quilp, without looking up.

'Why, you know sir,' returned Brass, venturing to be more
familiar: '—the fact is sir, that any allusion to these little
combinings together, of friends, for objects in themselves
extremely laudable, but which the law terms conspiracies, are
—you take me sir?—best kept snug and among friends, you
know.'

'Eh!' said Quilp, looking up with a perfectly vacant
countenance. 'What do you mean?'

'Cautious, exceedingly cautious, very right and proper!'
cried Brass, nodding his head. 'Mum sir, even here—my
meaning sir, exactly.'

'*Your* meaning exactly, you brazen scarecrow,—what's your
meaning?' retorted Quilp. 'Why do you talk to me of combining together? Do *I* combine? Do I know anything about
your combinings?'

'No no, sir—certainly not; not by any means,' returned
Brass.

'If you so wink and nod at me,' said the dwarf, looking about
him as if for his poker, 'I'll spoil the expression of your monkey's
face, I will.'

Mr. Swiveller to the Rescue

(p. 472)

'Don't put yourself out of the way I beg sir,' rejoined Brass, checking himself with great alacrity. 'You're quite right sir, quite right. I shouldn't have mentioned the subject sir. It's much better not to. You're quite right sir. Let us change it, if you please. You were asking, sir, Sally told me, about our lodger. He has not returned, Sir.'

'No?' said Quilp, heating some rum in a little saucepan, and watching it to prevent its boiling over. 'Why not?'

'Why sir,' returned Brass, 'he—dear me, Mr. Quilp sir—'

'What's the matter?' said the dwarf, stopping his hand in the act of carrying the saucepan to his mouth.

'You have forgotten the water, sir,' said Brass. 'And— excuse me sir—but it's burning hot.'

Deigning no other than a practical answer to this remon- strance, Mr. Quilp raised the hot saucepan to his lips, and deliberately drank off all the spirit it contained, which might have been in quantity about half a pint, and had been but a moment before, when he took it off the fire, bubbling and hissing fiercely. Having swallowed this gentle stimulant, and shaken his fist at the admiral, he bade Mr. Brass proceed.

'But first,' said Quilp, with his accustomed grin, 'have a drop yourself—a nice drop—a good, warm, fiery drop.'

'Why sir,' replied Brass, 'if there was such a thing as a mouthful of water that could be got without trouble—'

'There's no such thing to be had here,' cried the dwarf. 'Water for lawyers! Melted lead and brimstone, you mean, nice hot blistering pitch and tar—that's the thing for them— eh, Brass, eh?'

'Ha ha ha!' laughed Mr. Brass. 'Oh very biting! and yet it's like being tickled—there's a pleasure in it too, sir!'

'Drink that,' said the dwarf, who had by this time heated some more. 'Toss it off, don't leave any heeltap, scorch your throat and be happy!'

The wretched Sampson took a few short sips of the liquor, which immediately distilled itself into burning tears, and in that form came rolling down his cheeks into the pipkin again, turning the colour of his face and eyelids to a deep red, and giving rise to a violent fit of coughing, in the midst of which he was still heard to declare, with the constancy of a martyr, that it was 'beautiful indeed!' While he was yet in unspeakable agonies, the dwarf renewed their conversation.

'The lodger,' said Quilp,—'what about him?'

'He is still sir,' returned Brass, with intervals of coughing, 'stopping with the Garland family. He has only been home once, sir, since the day of the examination of that culprit. He informed Mr. Richard sir, that he couldn't bear the house after what had taken place; that he was wretched in it; and that he looked upon himself as being in a certain kind of way the cause of the occurrence.—A very excellent lodger sir. I hope we may not lose him.'

'Yah!' cried the dwarf. 'Never thinking of anybody but yourself—why don't you retrench then—scrape up, hoard, economise, eh?'

'Why sir,' replied Brass, 'upon my word I think Sarah's as good an economiser as any going. I do indeed, Mr. Quilp.'

'Moisten your clay, wet the other eye, drink, man!' cried the dwarf. 'You took a clerk to oblige me.'

'Delighted sir, I am sure, at any time,' replied Sampson. 'Yes sir, I did.'

'Then now you may discharge him,' said Quilp. 'There's a means of retrenchment for you at once.'

'Discharge Mr. Richard sir?' cried Brass.

'Have you more than one clerk, you parrot, that you ask the question? Yes.'

'Upon my word sir,' said Brass, 'I wasn't prepared for this—'

'How could you be,' sneered the dwarf, 'when *I* wasn't? How often am I to tell you that I brought him to you that I might always have my eye on him and know where he was—and that I had a plot, a scheme, a little quiet piece of enjoyment afoot, of which the very cream and essence was, that this old man and grandchild (who have sunk underground I think) should be, while he and his precious friend believed them rich, in reality as poor as frozen rats?'

'I quite understood that sir,' rejoined Brass. 'Thoroughly.'

'Well sir,' retorted Quilp, 'and do you understand now, that they're *not* poor—that they can't be, if they have such men as your lodger searching for them, and scouring the country far and wide?'

'Of course I do sir,' said Sampson.

'Of course you do,' retorted the dwarf, viciously snapping at his words. 'Of course do you understand then, that it's no matter what comes of this fellow? of course do you understand that for any other purpose he's no man for me, nor for you?'

'I have frequently said to Sarah sir,' returned Brass, 'that he was of no use at all in the business. You can't put any confidence in him sir. If you'll believe me I've found that fellow, in the commonest little matters of the office that have been trusted to him, blurting out the truth, though expressly cautioned. The aggravation of that chap sir, has exceeded anything you can imagine, it has indeed. Nothing but the respect and obligation I owe to you sir—'

As it was plain that Sampson was bent on a complimentary harangue, unless he received a timely interruption, Mr. Quilp politely tapped him on the crown of his head with the little saucepan, and requested that he would be so obliging as to hold his peace.

'Practical, sir, practical,' said Brass, rubbing the place and smiling; 'but still extremely pleasant—immensely so!'

'Hearken to me, will you?' returned Quilp, 'or I'll be a little more pleasant, presently. There's no chance of his comrade and friend returning. The scamp has been obliged to fly, as I learn, for some knavery, and has found his way abroad. Let him rot there.'

'Certainly sir. Quite proper.—Forcible!' cried Brass, glancing at the admiral again, as if he made a third in company. 'Extremely forcible!'

'I hate him,' said Quilp between his teeth, 'and have always hated him, for family reasons. Besides, he was an intractable ruffian; otherwise *he* would have been of use. This fellow is pigeon-hearted, and light-headed. I don't want him any longer. Let him hang or drown—starve—go to the devil.'

'By all means sir,' returned Brass. 'When would you wish him sir, to—ha, ha!—to make that little excursion?'

'When this trial's over,' said Quilp. 'As soon as that's ended, send him about his business.'

'It shall be done, sir,' returned Brass; 'by all means. It will be rather a blow to Sarah, sir, but she has all her feelings under control. Ah, Mr. Quilp, I often think sir, if it had only pleased Providence to bring you and Sarah together, in earlier life, what blessed results would have flowed from such a union! You never saw our dear father, sir?—A charming gentleman. Sarah was his pride and joy, sir. He would have closed his eyes in bliss, would Foxey, Mr. Quilp, if he could have found her such a partner. You esteem her, sir?'

U

'I love her,' croaked the dwarf.

'You're very good, sir,' returned Brass, 'I am sure. Is there any other order, sir, that I can take a note of, besides this little matter of Mr. Richard?'

'None,' replied the dwarf, seizing the saucepan. 'Let us drink the lovely Sarah.'

'If we could do it in something, sir, that wasn't quite boiling,' suggested Brass humbly, 'perhaps it would be better. I think it will be more agreeable to Sarah's feelings, when she comes to hear from me of the honour you have done her, if she learns it was in liquor rather cooler than the last, sir.'

But to these remonstrances, Mr. Quilp turned a deaf ear. Sampson Brass, who was, by this time, anything but sober, being compelled to take further draughts of the same strong bowl, found that, instead of at all contributing to his recovery, they had the novel effect of making the counting-house spin round and round with extreme velocity, and causing the floor and ceiling to heave in a very distressing manner. After a brief stupor, he awoke to a consciousness of being partly under the table and partly under the grate. This position not being the most comfortable one he could have chosen for himself, he managed to stagger to his feet, and, holding on by the admiral, looked round for his host.

Mr. Brass's first impression was, that his host was gone and had left him there alone—perhaps locked him in for the night. A strong smell of tobacco, however, suggested a new train of ideas, he looked upward, and saw that the dwarf was smoking in his hammock.

'Good-bye, sir,' cried Brass faintly. 'Good-bye, sir.'

'Won't you stop all night?' said the dwarf, peeping out. 'Do stop all night!'

'I couldn't indeed, sir,' replied Brass, who was almost dead from nausea and the closeness of the room. 'If you'd have the goodness to show me a light, so that I may see my way across the yard, sir—'

Quilp was out in an instant; not with his legs first, or his head first, or his arms first, but bodily—altogether.

'To be sure,' he said, taking up a lantern, which was now the only light in the place. 'Be careful how you go, my dear friend. Be sure to pick your way among the timber, for all the rusty nails are upwards. There's a dog in the lane. He bit a man last night, and a woman the night before, and last

Tuesday he killed a child—but that was in play. Don't go too near him.'

'Which side of the road is he, sir?' asked Brass, in great dismay.

'He lives on the right hand,' said Quilp, 'but sometimes he hides on the left, ready for a spring. He's uncertain in that respect. Mind you take care of yourself. I'll never forgive you if you don't. There's the light out—never mind—you know the way—straight on!'

Quilp had slightly shaded the light by holding it against his breast, and now stood chuckling and shaking from head to foot in a rapture of delight, as he heard the lawyer stumbling up the yard, and now and then falling heavily down. At length, however, he got quit of the place, and was out of hearing.

The dwarf shut himself up again, and sprang once more into his hammock.

CHAPTER LXIII

THE professional gentleman who had given Kit that con-
solatory piece of information relative to the settlement of
his trifle of business at the Old Bailey, and the probability of
its being very soon disposed of, turned out to be quite correct in
his prognostications. In eight days' time, the sessions commenced. In one day afterwards, the Grand Jury found a True
Bill against Christopher Nubbles for felony; and in two days
from that finding, the aforesaid Christopher Nubbles was
called upon to plead Guilty or Not Guilty to an Indictment for
that he the said Christopher did feloniously abstract and steal
from the dwelling-place and office of one Sampson Brass,
gentleman, one Bank Note for Five Pounds issued by the
Governor and Company of the Bank of England; in contra-
vention of the Statutes in that case made and provided, and
against the peace of our Sovereign Lord the King, his crown
and dignity.

To this indictment, Christopher Nubbles, in a low and
trembling voice, pleaded Not Guilty: and here, let those who
are in the habit of forming hasty judgments from appearances,
and who would have had Christopher, if innocent, speak out
very strong and loud, observe, that confinement and anxiety
will subdue the stoutest hearts; and that to one who has been
close shut up, though it be only for ten or eleven days, seeing
but stone walls and a very few stony faces, the sudden entrance
into a great hall filled with life, is a rather disconcerting and
startling circumstance. To this, it must be added, that life in
a wig, is, to a large class of people, much more terrifying and
impressive than life with its own head of hair; and if, in
addition to these considerations, there be taken into account
Kit's natural emotion on seeing the two Mr. Garlands and the
little Notary looking on with pale and anxious faces, it will
perhaps seem matter of no very great wonder that he should
have been rather out of sorts, and unable to make himself quite
at home.

Although he had never seen either of the Mr. Garlands, or
Mr. Witherden, since the time of his arrest, he had been given
to understand that they had employed counsel for him.
Therefore, when one of the gentlemen in wigs got up and said
'I am for the prisoner my Lord,' Kit made him a bow; and

when another gentleman in a wig got up and said 'And I'm against him my Lord,' Kit trembled very much, and bowed to him too. And didn't he hope in his own heart that his gentleman was a match for the other gentleman, and would make him ashamed of himself in no time!

The gentleman who was against him had to speak first, and being in dreadfully good spirits (for he had, in the last trial, very nearly procured the acquittal of a young gentleman who had had the misfortune to murder his father) he spoke up, you may be sure; telling the Jury that if they acquitted this prisoner they must expect to suffer no less pangs and agonies than he had told the other Jury they would certainly undergo if they convicted that prisoner. And when he had told them all about the case, and that he had never known a worse case, he stopped a little while, like a man who had something terrible to tell them, and then said that he understood an attempt would be made by his learned friend (and here he looked sideways at Kit's gentleman) to impeach the testimony of those immaculate witnesses whom he should call before them; but he did hope and trust that his learned friend would have a greater respect and veneration for the character of the prosecutor; than whom, as he well knew, there did not exist, and never had existed, a more honourable member of that most honourable profession to which he was attached. And then he said, did the Jury know Bevis Marks? And if they did know Bevis Marks (as he trusted for their own character, they did) did they know the historical and elevating associations connected with that most remarkable spot? Did they believe that a man like Brass could reside in a place like Bevis Marks, and not be a virtuous and most upright character? And when he had said a great deal to them on this point, he remembered that it was an insult to their understandings to make any remarks on what they must have felt so strongly without him, and therefore called Sampson Brass into the witness-box, straightway.

Then up comes Mr. Brass, very brisk and fresh; and, having bowed to the judge, like a man who has had the pleasure of seeing him before, and who hopes he has been pretty well since their last meeting, folds his arms, and looks at his gentleman as much as to say 'Here I am—full of evidence—Tap me!' And the gentleman does tap him presently, and with great discretion too; drawing off the evidence by little and little, and making it run quite clear and bright in the eyes of all present. Then,

Kit's gentleman takes him in hand, but can make nothing of him; and after a great many very long questions and very short answers, Mr. Sampson Brass goes down in glory.

To him succeeds Sarah, who in like manner is easy to be managed by Mr. Brass's gentleman, but very obdurate to Kit's. In short, Kit's gentleman can get nothing out of her but a repetition of what she has said before (only a little stronger this time, as against his client), and therefore lets her go, in some confusion. Then, Mr. Brass's gentleman calls Richard Swiveller, and Richard Swiveller appears accordingly.

Now, Mr. Brass's gentleman has it whispered in his ear that this witness is disposed to be friendly to the prisoner—which, to say the truth, he is rather glad to hear, as his strength is considered to lie in what is familiarly termed badgering. Wherefore, he begins by requesting the officer to be quite sure that this witness kisses the book, and then goes to work at him, tooth and nail.

'Mr. Swiveller,' says this gentleman to Dick, when he had told his tale with evident reluctance and a desire to make the best of it: 'Pray sir, where did you dine yesterday?'—'Where did I dine yesterday?'—'Aye sir, where did you dine yesterday—was it near here sir?'—'Oh to be sure—yes—just over the way'—'To be sure. Yes. Just over the way,' repeats Mr. Brass's gentleman, with a glance at the court—'Alone sir?'— 'I beg your pardon,' says Mr. Swiveller, who has not caught the question—'*Alone* sir?' repeats Mr. Brass's gentleman in a voice of thunder, 'did you dine alone? Did you treat anybody sir? Come!'—'Oh yes to be sure—yes, I did,' says Mr. Swiveller with a smile. 'Have the goodness to banish a levity, sir, which is very ill-suited to the place in which you stand (though perhaps you have reason to be thankful that it's only that place),' says Mr. Brass's gentleman, with a nod of the head, insinuating that the dock is Mr. Swiveller's legitimate sphere of action; 'and attend to me. You were waiting about here, yesterday, in expectation that this trial was coming on. You dined over the way. You treated somebody. Now, was that somebody brother to the prisoner at the bar?'—Mr. Swiveller is proceeding to explain—'Yes or No sir,' cries Mr. Brass's gentleman—'But will you allow me—'—'Yes or No sir'— 'Yes it was, but—'—'Yes it was,' cries the gentleman taking him up short—'And a very pretty witness *you* are!'

Down sits Mr. Brass's gentleman. Kit's gentleman, no

A Quiet Game of Cribbage
(p. 475)

knowing how the matter really stands, is afraid to pursue the subject. Richard Swiveller retires abashed. Judge, jury, and spectators have visions of his lounging about, with an ill-looking, large-whiskered, dissolute young fellow of six feet high. The reality is, little Jacob, with the calves of his legs exposed to the open air, and himself tied up in a shawl. Nobody knows the truth; everybody believes a falsehood; and all because of the ingenuity of Mr. Brass's gentleman.

Then, come the witnesses to character, and here Mr. Brass's gentleman shines again. It turns out that Mr. Garland has had no character with Kit, no recommendation of him but from his own mother, and that he was suddenly dismissed by his former master for unknown reasons. 'Really, Mr. Garland,' says Mr. Brass's gentleman, 'for a person who has arrived at your time of life, you are, to say the least of it, singularly indiscreet, I think.' The Jury think so too, and find Kit guilty. He is taken off, humbly protesting his innocence. The spectators settle themselves in their places with renewed attention, for there are several female witnesses to be examined in the next case, and it has been rumoured that Mr. Brass's gentleman will make great fun in cross-examining them for the prisoner.

Kit's mother, poor woman, is waiting at the grate below stairs, accompanied by Barbara's mother (who, honest soul! never does anything but cry, and hold the baby), and a sad interview ensues. The newspaper-reading turnkey has told them all. He don't think it will be transportation for life, because there's time to prove the good character yet, and that is sure to serve him. He wonders what he did it for. 'He never did it!' cries Kit's mother. 'Well,' says the turnkey, 'I won't contradict you. It's all one, now, whether he did it or not.'

Kit's mother can reach his hand through the bars, and she clasps it—God, and those to whom he has given such tenderness, only know in how much agony. Kit bids her keep a good heart, and, under pretence of having the children lifted up to kiss him, prays Barbara's mother in a whisper to take her home.

'Some friend will rise up for us, mother,' cried Kit, 'I am sure. If not now, before long. My innocence will come out, mother, and I shall be brought back again; I feel confidence in that. You must teach little Jacob and the baby how all this was, for if they thought I had ever been dishonest, when they grew old enough to understand, it would break my heart to know it, if I was thousands of miles away.—Oh! is there no good gentleman here, who will take care of her?'

The hand slips out of his, for the poor creature sinks down upon the earth, insensible. Richard Swiveller comes hastily up, elbows the bystanders out of the way, takes her (after some trouble) in one arm after the manner of theatrical ravishers, and, nodding to Kit, and commanding Barbara's mother to follow, for he has a coach waiting, bears her swiftly off.

Well; Richard took her home. And what astonishing absurdities in the way of quotation from song and poem, he perpetrated on the road, no man knows. He took her home, and stayed till she was recovered; and, having no money to pay the coach, went back in state to Bevis Marks, bidding the driver (for it was Saturday night) wait at the door while he went in for 'change.'

'Mr. Richard sir,' said Brass cheerfully, 'good evening!'

Monstrous as Kit's tale had appeared, at first, Mr. Richard did, that night, half suspect his affable employer of some deep villany. Perhaps it was but the misery he had just witnessed which gave his careless nature this impulse; but, be that as it may, it was very strong upon him, and he said in as few words as possible, what he wanted.

'Money?' cried Brass, taking out his purse. 'Ha ha! To be sure Mr. Richard, to be sure sir. All men must live. You haven't change for a five-pound note, have you sir?'

'No,' returned Dick, shortly.

'Oh!' said Brass, 'here's the very sum. That saves trouble. You're very welcome I'm sure.—Mr. Richard sir—'

Dick, who had by this time reached the door, turned round.

'You needn't,' said Brass, 'trouble yourself to come back any more sir.'

'Eh?'

'You see, Mr. Richard,' said Brass, thrusting his hands in his pockets, and rocking himself to and fro on his stool, 'the fact is, that a man of your abilities is lost sir, quite lost, in our dry and mouldy line. It's terrible drudgery—shocking. I should say, now, that the stage, or the—or the army Mr. Richard—or something very superior in the licensed victualling way—was the kind of thing that would call out the genius of such a man as you. I hope you'll look in to see us now and then. Sally, sir, will be delighted I'm sure. She's extremely sorry to lose you Mr. Richard, but a sense of her duty to society reconciles her. An amazing creature that, sir! You'll find the money quite correct, I think. There's a cracked window, sir, but I've not made any deduction on that account. Whenever we part with friends, Mr. Richard, let us part liberally. A delightful sentiment sir!'

To all these rambling observations, Mr. Swiveller answered not one word, but, returning for the aquatic jacket, rolled it into a tight round ball: looking steadily at Brass meanwhile as if he had some intention of bowling him down with it. He only took it under his arm, however, and marched out of the office in profound silence. When he had closed the door, he re-opened it, stared in again for a few moments with the same portentous gravity, and nodding his head once, in a slow and ghost-like manner, vanished.

He paid the coachman, and turned his back on Bevis Marks, big with great designs for the comforting of Kit's mother and the aid of Kit himself.

But the lives of gentlemen devoted to such pleasures as Richard Swiveller, are extremely precarious. The spiritual excitement of the last fortnight, working upon a system affected in no slight degree by the spirituous excitement of some years, proved a little too much for him. That very night, Mr. Richard was seized with an alarming illness, and in twenty-four hours was stricken with a raging fever.

CHAPTER LXIV

TOSSING to and fro upon his hot, uneasy bed; tormented by a fierce thirst which nothing could appease; unable to find, in any change of posture, a moment's peace or ease; and rambling, ever, through deserts of thought where there was no resting-place, no sight or sound suggestive of refreshment or repose, nothing but a dull eternal weariness, with no change but the restless shiftings of his miserable body, and the weary wandering of his mind, constant still to one ever-present anxiety—to a sense of something left undone, of some fearful obstacle to be surmounted, of some carking care that would not be driven away, and which haunted the distempered brain, now in this form, now in that, always shadowy and dim, but recognisable for the same phantom in every shape it took: darkening every vision like an evil conscience, and making slumber horrible—in these slow tortures of his dread disease, the unfortunate Richard lay wasting and consuming inch by inch, until, at last, when he seemed to fight and struggle to rise up, and to be held down by devils, he sank into a deep sleep, and dreamed no more.

He awoke. With a sensation of most blissful rest, better than sleep itself, he began gradually to remember something of these sufferings, and to think what a long night it had been, and whether he had not been delirious twice or thrice. Happening, in the midst of these cogitations, to raise his hand, he was astonished to find how heavy it seemed, and yet how thin and light it really was. Still, he felt indifferent and happy; and having no curiosity to pursue the subject, remained in the same waking slumber until his attention was attracted by a cough. This made him doubt, whether he had locked his door last night, and feel a little surprised at having a companion in the room. Still, he lacked energy to follow up this train of thought; and unconsciously fell, in a luxury of repose, to staring at some green stripes on the bed-furniture, and associating them strangely with patches of fresh turf, while the yellow ground between made gravel-walks, and so helped out a long perspective of trim gardens.

He was rambling in imagination on these terraces, and had quite lost himself among them indeed, when he heard the cough once more. The walks shrunk into stripes again at the sound, and raising himself a little in the bed, and holding the curtain open with one hand, he looked out.

The same room certainly, and still by candlelight; but with what unbounded astonishment did he see all those bottles, and basins, and articles of linen airing by the fire, and such-like furniture of a sick chamber—all very clean and neat, but all quite different from anything he had left there, when he went to bed! The atmosphere, too, filled with a cool smell of herbs and vinegar; the floor newly sprinkled; the—the what? The Marchioness?

Yes; playing cribbage with herself at the table. There she sat, intent upon her game, coughing now and then in a subdued manner as if she feared to disturb him—shuffling the cards, cutting, dealing, playing, counting, pegging—going through all the mysteries of cribbage as if she had been in full practice from her cradle!

Mr. Swiveller contemplated these things for a short time, and suffering the curtain to fall into its former position, laid his head on the pillow again.

'I'm dreaming,' thought Richard, 'that's clear. When I went to bed, my hands were not made of egg-shells; and now I can almost see through 'em. If this is not a dream, I have woke up, by mistake, in an Arabian Night, instead of a London one. But I have no doubt I'm asleep. Not the least.'

Here the small servant had another cough.

'Very remarkable!' thought Mr. Swiveller. 'I never dreamt such a real cough as that, before. I don't know, indeed, that I ever dreamt either a cough or a sneeze. Perhaps it's part of the philosophy of dreams that one never does. There's another—and another—I say!—I'm dreaming rather fast!'

For the purpose of testing his real condition, Mr. Swiveller, after some reflection, pinched himself in the arm.

'Queerer still!' he thought. 'I came to bed rather plump than otherwise, and now there's nothing to lay hold of. I'll take another survey.'

The result of this additional inspection was, to convince Mr. Swiveller that the objects by which he was surrounded were real, and that he saw them, beyond all question, with his waking eyes.

'It's an Arabian Night; that's what it is,' said Richard. 'I'm in Damascus or Grand Cairo. The Marchioness is a Genie, and having had a wager with another Genie about who is the handsomest young man alive, and the worthiest to be the husband of the Princess of China, has brought me away, room and all, to compare us together. Perhaps,' said Mr. Swiveller, turning languidly round on his pillow, and looking on that side of his bed which was next the wall, 'the Princess may be still—No, she's gone.'

Not feeling quite satisfied with this explanation, as, even taking it to be the correct one, it still involved a little mystery and doubt, Mr. Swiveller raised the curtain again, determined to take the first favourable opportunity of addressing his companion. An occasion soon presented itself. The Marchioness dealt, turned up a knave, and omitted to take the usual advantage; upon which Mr. Swiveller called out as loud as he could—'Two for his heels!'

The Marchioness jumped up quickly, and clapped her hands. 'Arabian Night, certainly,' thought Mr. Swiveller; 'they always clap their hands instead of ringing the bell. Now for the two thousand black slaves, with jars of jewels on their heads!'

It appeared, however, that she had only clapped her hands for joy; as, directly afterwards she began to laugh, and then to cry; declaring, not in choice Arabic but in familiar English, that she was 'so glad, she didn't know what to do.'

'Marchioness,' said Mr. Swiveller, thoughtfully, 'be pleased to draw nearer. First of all, will you have the goodness to inform me where I shall find my voice; and secondly, what has become of my flesh?'

The Marchioness only shook her head mournfully, and cried again; whereupon Mr. Swiveller (being very weak) felt his own eyes affected likewise.

'I begin to infer, from your manner, and these appearances, Marchioness,' said Richard, after a pause, and smiling with a trembling lip, 'that I have been ill.'

'You just have!' replied the small servant, wiping her eyes. 'And haven't you been a talking nonsense!'

'Oh!' said Dick. 'Very ill, Marchioness, have I been?'

'Dead, all but,' replied the small servant. 'I never thought you'd get better. Thank Heaven you have!'

Mr. Swiveller was silent for a long while. By and bye, he began to talk again: inquiring how long he had been there.

'Three weeks to-morrow,' replied the small servant.

'Three what?' said Dick.

'Weeks,' returned the Marchioness emphatically; 'three long, slow, weeks.'

The bare thought of having been in such extremity, caused Richard to fall into another silence, and to lie flat down again, at his full length. The Marchioness, having arranged the bed-clothes more comfortably, and felt that his hands and forehead were quite cool—a discovery that filled her with delight—cried a little more, and then applied herself to getting tea ready, and making some thin dry toast.

While she was thus engaged, Mr. Swiveller looked on with a grateful heart, very much astonished to see how thoroughly at home she made herself, and attributing this attention, in its origin, to Sally Brass,' whom, in his own mind, he could not thank enough. When the Marchioness had finished her toasting, she spread a clean cloth on a tray, and brought him some crisp slices and a great basin of weak tea, with which (she said) the doctor had left word he might refresh himself when he awoke. She propped him up with pillows, if not as skilfully as if she had been a professional nurse all her life, at least as tenderly; and looked on with unutterable satisfaction while the patient—stopping every now and then to shake her by the hand—took his poor meal with an appetite and relish, which the greatest dainties of the earth, under any other circumstances, would have failed to provoke. Having cleared away, and disposed everything comfortably about him again, she sat down at the table to take her own tea.

'Marchioness,' said Mr. Swiveller, 'how's Sally?'

The small servant screwed her face into an expression of the very uttermost entanglement of slyness, and shook her head.

'What, haven't you seen her lately?' said Dick.

'Seen her!' cried the small servant. 'Bless you, I've run away!'

Mr. Swiveller immediately laid himself down again quite flat, and so remained for about five minutes. By slow degrees he resumed his sitting posture after that lapse of time, and inquired:

'And where do you live, Marchioness?'

'Live!' cried the small servant. 'Here!'

'Oh!' said Mr. Swiveller.

And with that he fell down flat again, as suddenly as if he had been shot. Thus he remained, motionless and bereft of speech, until she had finished her meal, put everything in its place, and swept the hearth; when he motioned her to bring a chair to the bedside, and, being propped up again, opened a farther conversation.

'And so,' said Dick, 'you have run away?'

'Yes,' said the Marchioness, 'and they've been a tizing of me.'

'Been—I beg your pardon,' said Dick—'what have they been doing?'

'Been a tizing of me—tizing you know—in the newspapers,' rejoined the Marchioness.

'Aye, aye,' said Dick, 'advertising?'

The small servant nodded, and winked. Her eyes were so red with waking and crying, that the Tragic Muse might have winked with greater consistency. And so Dick felt.

'Tell me,' said he, 'how it was that you thought of coming here.'

'Why, you see,' returned the Marchioness, 'when you was gone, I hadn't any friend at all, because the lodger he never come back, and I didn't know where either him or you was to be found, you know. But one morning, when I was—'

'Was near a keyhole?' suggested Mr. Swiveller, observing that she faltered.

'Well then,' said the small servant, nodding; 'when I was near the office keyhole—as you see me through, you know—I heard somebody saying that she lived here, and was the lady whose house you lodged at, and that you was took very bad, and wouldn't nobody come and take care of you. Mr. Brass, he says, "It's no business of mine," he says; and Miss Sally, she says, "He's a funny chap, but it's no business of mine;" and the lady went away, and slammed the door to, when she went out, I can tell you. So I run away that night, and come here, and told 'em you was my brother, and they believed me, and I've been here ever since.'

'This poor little Marchioness has been wearing herself to death!' cried Dick.

'No I haven't,' she returned, 'not a bit of it. Don't you mind about me. I like sitting up, and I've often had a sleep, bless you, in one of them chairs. But if you could have seen how you tried to jump out o' winder, and if you could have heard how you used to keep on singing and making speeches, you wouldn't have believed it—I'm so glad you're better, Mr. Liverer.'

'Liverer indeed!' said Dick thoughtfully. 'It's well I *am* a liverer. I strongly suspect I should have died, Marchioness, but for you.'

At this point, Mr. Swiveller took the small servant's hand in his, again, and being, as we have seen, but poorly, might in struggling to express his thanks have made his eyes as red as hers, but that she quickly changed the theme by making him lie down, and urging him to keep very quiet.

'The doctor,' she told him, 'said you was to be kept quite still, and there was to be no noise nor nothing. Now, take a rest, and then we'll talk again. I'll sit by you, you know. If you shut your eyes, perhaps you'll go to sleep. You'll be all the better for it, if you do.'

The Marchioness, in saying these words, brought a little table to the bedside, took her seat at it, and began to work away at the concoction of some cooling drink, with the address of a score of chemists. Richard Swiveller, being indeed fatigued, fell into a slumber, and waking in about half an hour, inquired what time it was.

'Just gone half after six,' replied his small friend, helping him to sit up again.

'Marchioness,' said Richard, passing his hand over his forehead and turning suddenly round, as though the subject but that moment flashed upon him, 'what has become of Kit?'

He had been sentenced to transportation for a great many years, she said.

'Has he gone?' asked Dick—'his mother—how is she,—what has become of her?'

His nurse shook her head, and answered that she knew nothing about them. 'But, if I thought,' said she, very slowly, 'that you'd keep quiet, and not put yourself into another fever, I could tell you—but I won't now.'

'Yes, do,' said Dick. 'It will amuse me.'

'Oh! would it though!' rejoined the small servant, with a horrified look. 'I know better than that. Wait till you're better and then I'll tell you.'

Dick looked very earnestly at his little friend: and his eyes, being large and hollow from illness, assisted the expression so much, that she was quite frightened, and besought him not to think any more about it. What had already fallen from her, however, had not only piqued his curiosity, but seriously alarmed him, wherefore he urged her to tell him the worst at once.

'Oh there's no worst in it,' said the small servant. 'It hasn't anything to do with you.'

'Has it anything to do with—is it anything you heard through chinks or keyholes—and that you were not intended to hear?' asked Dick, in a breathless state.

'Yes,' replied the small servant.

'In—in Bevis Marks?' pursued Dick hastily. 'Conversations between Brass and Sally?'

'Yes,' cried the small servant again.

Richard Swiveller thrust his lank arm out of bed, and, griping her by the wrist and drawing her close to him, bade her out with it, and freely too, or he would not answer for the consequences; being wholly unable to endure that state of excitement and expectation. She, seeing that he was greatly agitated, and that the effects of postponing her revelation might be much more injurious than any that were likely to ensue from its being made at once, promised compliance, on condition that the patient kept himself perfectly quiet, and abstained from starting up or tossing about.

'But if you begin to do that,' said the small servant, 'I'll leave off. And so I tell you.'

'You can't leave off, till you have gone on,' said Dick. 'And do go on, there's a darling. Speak, sister, speak. Pretty Polly, say. Oh tell me when, and tell me where, pray, Marchioness, I beseech you!'

Unable to resist these fervent adjurations, which Richard Swiveller poured out as passionately as if they had been of the most solemn and tremendous nature, his companion spoke thus:

'Well! Before I run away, I used to sleep in the kitchen—where we played cards, you know. Miss Sally used to keep the key of the kitchen door in her pocket, and she always come down at night to take away the candle and rake out the fire. When she had done that, she left me to go to bed in the dark, locked the door on the outside, put the key in her pocket again, and kept me locked up till she come down in the morning—very early I can tell you—and let me out. I was terrible afraid of being kept like this, because if there was a fire, I thought they might forget me and only take care of themselves you know. So, whenever I see an old rusty key anywhere, I picked it up and tried if it would fit the door, and at last I found in the dust cellar a key that *did* fit it.'

Here, Mr. Swiveller made a violent demonstration with his legs. But the small servant immediately pausing in her talk, he subsided again, and pleading a momentary forgetfulness of their compact, entreated her to proceed.

'They kept me very short,' said the small servant. 'Oh! you can't think how short they kept me! So I used to come out at night after they'd gone to bed, and feel about in the dark for bits of biscuit, or sangwitches that you'd left in the office, or even pieces of orange-peel to put into cold water and make believe it was wine. Did you ever taste orange-peel and water?'

Mr. Swiveller replied that he had never tasted that ardent liquor; and once more urged his friend to resume the thread of her narrative.

'If you make believe very much, it's quite nice,' said the small servant, 'but if you don't, you know, it seems as if it would bear a little more seasoning, certainly. Well, sometimes I used to come out after they'd gone to bed, and sometimes before, you know; and one or two nights before there was all that precious noise in the office—when the young man was took, I mean—I come up-stairs while Mr. Brass and Miss Sally was a-sittin' at the office fire; and I'll tell you the truth, that I come to listen again, about the key of the safe.'

Mr. Swiveller gathered up his knees so as to make a great cone of the bed-clothes, and conveyed into his countenance an expression of the utmost concern. But, the small servant pausing, and holding up her finger, the cone gently disappeared, though the look of concern did not.

'There was him and her,' said the small servant, 'a-sittin' by the fire, and talking softly together. Mr. Brass says to Miss Sally, "Upon my word," he says, "it's a dangerous thing, and it might get us into a world of trouble, and I don't half like it." She says—you know her way—she says, "You're the chickenest-hearted, feeblest, faintest man I ever see, and I think," she says, "that I ought to have been the brother, and you the sister. Isn't Quilp," she says, "our principal support?" "He certainly is," says Mr. Brass. "And an't we," she says, "constantly ruining somebody or other in the way of business?" "We certainly are," says Mr. Brass. "Then does it signify," she says, "about ruining this Kit when Quilp desires it?" "It certainly does not signify," says Mr. Brass. Then, they whispered and laughed for a long time about there being no danger if it was well done, and then Mr. Brass pulls out his pocket-book, and says, "Well," he says, "here it is—Quilp's own five-pound note. We'll agree that way, then," he says. 'Kit's coming to-morrow morning, I know. While he's upstairs, you'll get out of the way, and I'll clear off Mr. Richard. Having Kit alone, I'll hold him in conversation, and put this property in his hat. I'll manage so, besides," he says, "that Mr. Richard shall find it there, and be the evidence. And if that don't get Christopher out of Mr. Quilp's way, and satisfy Mr. Quilp's grudges," he says, "the Devil's in it." Miss Sally laughed, and said that was the plan, and as they seemed to be moving away, and I was afraid to stop any longer, I went down-stairs again.— There!'

The small servant had gradually worked herself into as much agitation as Mr. Swiveller, and therefore made no effort to restrain him when he sat up in bed and hastily demanded whether this story had been told to anybody.

'How could it be?' replied his nurse. 'I was almost afraid to think about it, and hoped the young man would be let off. When I heard 'em say they had found him guilty of what he didn't do, you was gone, and so was the lodger—though I think I should have been frightened to tell him, even if he'd been there. Ever since I come here, you've been out of your senses, and what would have been the good of telling you then?'

'Marchioness,' said Mr. Swiveller, plucking off his nightcap and flinging it to the other end of the room; 'if you'll do me the favour to retire for a few minutes and see what sort of a night it is, I'll get up.'

'You mustn't think of such a thing,' cried his nurse.

'I must indeed,' said the patient, looking round the room. 'Whereabouts are my clothes?'

'Oh I'm so glad—you haven't got any,' replied the Marchioness.

'Ma'am!' said Mr. Swiveller, in great astonishment.

'I've been obliged to sell them, every one, to get the things that was ordered for you. But don't take on about that,' urged the Marchioness, as Dick fell back upon his pillow. 'You're too weak to stand, indeed.'

'I am afraid,' said Richard dolefully, 'that you're right What ought I to do? what is to be done?'

It naturally occurred to him on very little reflection, that the first step to take would be to communicate with one of the Mr Garlands instantly. It was very possible that Mr. Abel had no

The Marchioness in the Chaise

(p. 486)

yet left the office. In as little time as it takes to tell it, the small servant had the address in pencil on a piece of paper; a verbal description of father and son, which would enable her to recognise either, without difficulty; and a special caution to be shy of Mr. Chuckster, in consequence of that gentleman's known antipathy to Kit. Armed with these slender powers, she hurried away, commissioned to bring either old Mr. Garland or Mr. Abel, bodily, to that apartment.

'I suppose,' said Dick, as she closed the door slowly, and peeped into the room again, to make sure that he was comfortable, 'I suppose there's nothing left—not so much as a waistcoat even?'

'No, nothing.'

'It's embarrassing,' said Mr. Swiveller, 'in case of fire—even an umbrella would be something—but you did quite right, dear Marchioness. I should have died without you!'

IT was well for the small servant that she was of a sharp, quick nature, or the consequence of sending her out alone, from the very neighbourhood in which it was most dangerous for her to appear, would probably have been the restoration of Miss Sally Brass to the supreme authority over her person. Not unmindful of the risk she ran, however, the Marchioness no sooner left the house than she dived into the first dark by-way that presented itself, and, without any present reference to the point to which her journey tended, made it her first business to put two good miles of brick and mortar between herself and Bevis Marks.

When she had accomplished this object, she began to shape her course for the notary's office, to which—shrewdly inquiring of apple-women and oyster-sellers at street-corners, rather than in lighted shops or of well-dressed people, at the hazard of attracting notice—she easily procured a direction. As carrier-pigeons, on being first let loose in a strange place, beat the air at random for a short time, before darting off towards the spot for which they are designed, so did the Marchioness flutter round and round until she believed herself in safety, and then bear swiftly down upon the port for which she was bound.

She had no bonnet—nothing on her head but a great cap which, in some old time, had been worn by Sally Brass, whose taste in head-dresses was, as we have seen, peculiar—and her speed was rather retarded than assisted by her shoes, which, being extremely large and slipshod, flew off every now and then, and were difficult to find again, among the crowd of passengers. Indeed, the poor little creature experienced so much trouble and delay from having to grope for these articles of dress in mud and kennel, and suffered in these researches so much jostling, pushing, squeezing, and bandying from hand to hand, that by the time she reached the street in which the notary lived, she was fairly worn out and exhausted, and could not refrain from tears.

But to have got there at last, was a great comfort, especially as there were lights still burning in the office window, and therefore some hope that she was not too late. So, the Marchioness dried her eyes with the backs of her hands, and, stealing softly up the steps, peeped in through the glass door.

Mr. Chuckster was standing behind the lid of his desk, making such preparations towards finishing off for the night, as pulling down his wristbands and pulling up his shirt-collar, settling his neck more gracefully in his stock, and secretly arranging his whiskers by the aid of a little triangular bit of looking-glass. Before the ashes of the fire, stood two gentlemen, one of whom she rightly judged to be the notary, and the other (who was buttoning his great-coat and was evidently about to depart immediately) Mr. Abel Garland.

Having made these observations, the small spy took counsel with herself, and resolved to wait in the street until Mr. Abel came out, as there would be then no fear of having to speak before Mr. Chuckster, and less difficulty in delivering her message. With this purpose she slipped out again, and crossing the road, sat down upon a doorstep just opposite.

She had hardly taken this position, when there came dancing up the street, with his legs all wrong, and his head everywhere by turns, a pony. This pony had a little phaeton behind him, and a man in it; but neither man nor phaeton seemed to embarrass him in the least, as he reared up on his hind legs, or stopped, or went on, or stood still again, or backed, or went sideways, without the smallest reference to them,—just as the fancy seized him, and as if he were the freest animal in creation. When they came to the notary's door, the man called out in a very respectful manner, 'Woa then,'—intimating that if he might venture to express a wish, it would be that they stopped there. The pony made a moment's pause; but, as if it occurred to him that to stop when he was required might be to establish an inconvenient and dangerous precedent he immediately started off again, rattled at a fast trot to the street corner, wheeled round, came back, and then stopped of his own accord.

'Oh! you're a precious creatur!' said the man—who didn't venture by the bye to come out in his true colours until he was safe on the pavement. 'I wish I had the rewarding of you,— I do.'

'What has he been doing?' said Mr. Abel, tying a shawl round his neck as he came down the steps.

'He's enough to fret a man's heart out,' replied the hostler. 'He is the most wicious rascal—Woa then, will you?'

'He'll never stand still, if you call him names,' said Mr. Abel, getting in, and taking the reins. 'He's a very good fellow if you know how to manage him. This is the first time he has been out, this long while, for he has lost his old driver and wouldn't stir for anybody else, till this morning. The lamps are right, are they? That's well. Be here to take him to-morrow, if you please. Good night!'

And, after one or two strange plunges, quite of his own invention, the pony yielded to Mr. Abel's mildness, and trotted gently off.

All this time Mr. Chuckster had been standing at the door, and the small servant had been afraid to approach. She had nothing for it now, therefore, but to run after the chaise, and to call to Mr. Abel to stop. Being out of breath when she came up with it, she was unable to make him hear. The case was desperate; for the pony was quickening his pace. The Marchioness hung on behind for a few moments, and, feeling that she could go no farther, and must soon yield, clambered by a vigorous effort into the hinder seat, and in so doing lost one of the shoes for ever.

Mr. Abel being in a thoughtful frame of mind, and having quite enough to do to keep the pony going, went jogging on without looking round: little dreaming of the strange figure that was close behind him, until the Marchioness, having in some degree recovered her breath, and the loss of her shoe, and the novelty of her position, uttered close into his ear, the words—

'I say, sir—'

He turned his head quickly enough then, and stopping the pony, cried, with some trepidation, 'God bless me, what is this?'

'Don't be frightened, sir,' replied the still panting messenger. 'Oh I've run such a way after you!'

'What do you want with me?' said Mr. Abel. 'How did you come here?'

'I got in behind,' replied the Marchioness. 'Oh please drive on, sir—don't stop—and go towards the City, will you? And oh do please make haste, because it's of consequence. There's somebody wants to see you there. He sent me to say would you come directly, and that he knowed all about Kit, and could save him yet, and prove his innocence.'

'What do you tell me, child?'

'The truth, upon my word and honour I do. But please to drive on—quick, please! I've been such a time gone, he'll think I'm lost.'

Mr. Abel involuntarily urged the pony forward. The pony, impelled by some secret sympathy or some new caprice, burst into a great pace, and neither slackened it, nor indulged in any eccentric performances, until they arrived at the door of Mr. Swiveller's lodging, where, marvellous to relate, he consented to stop when Mr. Abel checked him.

'See! It's that room up there,' said the Marchioness, pointing to one where there was a faint light. 'Come!'

Mr. Abel, who was one of the simplest and most retiring creatures in existence, and naturally timid withal, hesitated; for he had heard of people being decoyed into strange places to be robbed and murdered, under circumstances very like the present, and, for anything he knew to the contrary, by guides very like the Marchioness. His regard for Kit, however, overcame every other consideration. So, entrusting Whisker to the charge of a man who was lingering hard by in expectation of the job, he suffered his companion to take his hand, and to lead him up the dark and narrow stairs.

He was not a little surprised to find himself conducted into a dimly-lighted sick chamber, where a man was sleeping tranquilly in bed.

'An't it nice to see him lying there so quiet?' said his guide, in an earnest whisper. 'Oh! you'd say it was, if you had only seen him two or three days ago.'

Mr. Abel made no answer, and, to say the truth, kept a long way from the bed and very near the door. His guide, who appeared to understand his reluctance, trimmed the candle, and taking it in her hand, approached the bed. As she did so, the sleeper started up, and he recognised in the wasted face the features of Richard Swiveller.

'Why, how is this?' said Mr. Abel kindly, as he hurried towards him. 'You have been ill?'

'Very,' replied Dick. 'Nearly dead. You might have chanced to hear of your Richard on his bier, but for the friend I sent to fetch you. Another shake of the hand, Marchioness, if you please. Sit down, sir.'

Mr. Abel seemed rather astonished to hear of the quality of his guide, and took a chair by the bedside.

'I have sent for you, sir,' said Dick—'but she told you on what account?'

'She did. I am quite bewildered by all this. I really don't know what to say or think,' replied Mr. Abel.

'You'll say that presently,' retorted Dick. 'Marchioness, take a seat on the bed, will you? Now, tell this gentleman all that you told me; and be particular. Don't you speak another word, sir.'

The story was repeated; it was, in effect, exactly the same as before, without any deviation or omission. Richard Swiveller kept his eyes fixed on his visitor during its narration, and directly it was concluded, took the word again.

'You have heard it all, and you'll not forget it. I'm too giddy and too queer to suggest anything; but you and your friends will know what to do. After this long delay, every minute is an age. If ever you went home fast in your life, go home fast to-night. Don't stop to say one word to me, but go. She will be found here, whenever she's wanted; and as to me, you're pretty sure to find me at home, for a week or two. There are more reasons than one for that. Marchioness, a light! If you lose another minute looking at me, sir, I'll never forgive you!'

Mr. Abel needed no more remonstrance or persuasion. He was gone in an instant; and the Marchioness, returning from lighting him down-stairs, reported that the pony, without any preliminary objection whatever, had dashed away at full gallop.

'That's right!' said Dick; 'and hearty of him; and I honour him from this time. But get some supper and a mug of beer, for I am sure you must be tired. Do have a mug of beer. It will do me as much good to see you take it as if I might drink it myself.'

Nothing but this assurance could have prevailed upon the small nurse to indulge in such a luxury. Having eaten and drunk to Mr. Swiveller's extreme contentment, given him his drink, and put everything in neat order, she wrapped herself in an old coverlet and lay down upon the rug before the fire.

Mr. Swiveller was by that time murmuring in his sleep, 'Strew then, oh strew, a bed of rushes. Here will we stay, till morning blushes. Good night, Marchioness!'

CHAPTER LXVI

ON awaking in the morning, Richard Swiveller became conscious, by slow degrees, of whispering voices in his room. Looking out between the curtains, he espied Mr. Garland, Mr. Abel, the notary, and the single gentleman, gathered round the Marchioness, and talking to her with great earnestness but in very subdued tones—fearing, no doubt, to disturb him. He lost no time in letting them know that this precaution was unnecessary, and all four gentlemen directly approached his bedside. Old Mr. Garland was the first to stretch out his hand, and inquire how he felt.

Dick was about to answer that he felt much better, though still as weak as need be, when his little nurse, pushing the visitors aside and pressing up to his pillow as if in jealousy of their interference, set his breakfast before him, and insisted on his taking it before he underwent the fatigue of speaking or of being spoken to. Mr. Swiveller, who was perfectly ravenous, and had had, all night, amazingly distinct and consistent dreams of mutton chops, double stout, and similar delicacies, felt even the weak tea and dry toast such irresistible temptations, that he consented to eat and drink on one condition.

'And that is,' said Dick, returning the pressure of Mr. Garland's hand, 'that you answer me this question truly, before I take a bit or drop. Is it too late?'

'For completing the work you began so well last night?' returned the old gentleman. 'No. Set your mind at rest on that point. It is not, I assure you.'

Comforted by this intelligence, the patient applied himself to his food with a keen appetite, though evidently not with a greater zest in the eating than his nurse appeared to have in seeing him eat. The manner of his meal was this:—Mr. Swiveller, holding the slice of toast or cup of tea in his left hand, and taking a bite or drink, as the case might be, constantly kept, in his right, one palm of the Marchioness tight locked; and to shake, or even to kiss this imprisoned hand, he would stop every now and then, in the very act of swallowing, with perfect seriousness of intention, and the utmost gravity. As often as he put anything into his mouth, whether for eating or drinking, the face of the Marchioness lighted up beyond all description; but, whenever he gave her one or other of these tokens of recognition, her countenance became overshadowed, and she began to sob. Now, whether she was in her laughing joy, or in her crying one, the Marchioness could not help turning to the visitors with an appealing look, which seemed to say, 'You see this fellow—can I help this?'—and they, being thus made, as it were, parties to the scene, as regularly answered by another look, 'No. Certainly not.' This dumb-show, taking place during the whole time of the invalid's breakfast, and the invalid himself, pale and emaciated, per-forming no small part in the same, it may be fairly questioned whether at any meal, where no word, good or bad, was spoken from beginning to end, so much was expressed by gestures in themselves so slight and unimportant.

At length—and to say the truth before very long—Mr. Swiveller had despatched as much toast and tea as in that stage of his recovery it was discreet to let him have. But, the cares of the Marchioness did not stop here; for, disappearing for an instant and presently returning with a basin of fair water, she laved his face and hands, brushed his hair, and in short made him as spruce and smart as anybody under such circumstances could be made; and all this, in as brisk and business-like a manner, as if he were a very little boy, and she his grown-up nurse. To these various attentions, Mr. Swiveller submitted in a kind of grateful astonishment beyond the reach of language. When they were at last brought to an end, and the Marchioness had withdrawn into a distant corner to take her own poor breakfast (cold enough by that time), he turned his face away for some few moments, and shook hands heartily with the air.

'Gentlemen,' said Dick, rousing himself from this pause, and turning round again, 'you'll excuse me. Men who have been brought so low as I have been, are easily fatigued. I am fresh again now, and fit for talking. We're short of chairs here, among other trifles, but if you'll do me the favour to sit upon the bed—'

'What can we do for you?' said Mr. Garland, kindly.

'If you could make the Marchioness yonder, a Marchioness, in real, sober earnest,' returned Dick, 'I'd thank you to get it done off-hand. But as you can't, and as the question is not what you will do for me, but what you will do for somebody else who has a better claim upon you, pray sir let me know what you intend doing.'

Delicacies for Mr. Swiveller

(*p. 493*)

'It's chiefly on that account that we have come just now,' said the single gentleman, 'for you will have another visitor presently. We feared you would be anxious unless you knew from ourselves what steps we intended to take, and therefore came to you before we stirred in the matter.'

'Gentlemen,' returned Dick, 'I thank you. Anybody in the helpless state that you see me in, is naturally anxious. Don't let me interrupt you, sir.'

'Then, you see, my good fellow,' said the single gentleman, 'that while we have no doubt whatever of the truth of this disclosure, which has so providentially come to light—'

'Meaning hers?' said Dick, pointing towards the Marchioness.

'—Meaning hers, of course. While we have no doubt of that, or that a proper use of it would procure the poor lad's immediate pardon and liberation, we have a great doubt whether it would, by itself, enable us to reach Quilp, the chief agent in this villany. I should tell you that this doubt has been confirmed into something very nearly approaching certainty by the best opinions we have been enabled, in this short space of time, to take upon the subject. You'll agree with us, that to give him even the most distant chance of escape, if we could help it, would be monstrous. You say with us, no doubt, if somebody must escape, let it be any one but he.'

'Yes,' returned Dick, 'certainly. That is if somebody *must*— but upon my word, I'm unwilling that anybody should. Since laws were made for every degree, to curb vice in others as well as in me—and so forth you know—doesn't it strike you in that light?'

The single gentleman smiled as if the light in which Mr. Swiveller had put the question were not the clearest in the world, and proceeded to explain that they contemplated proceeding by stratagem in the first instance; and that their design was to endeavour to extort a confession from the gentle Sarah.

'When she finds how much we know, and how we know it,' he said, 'and that she is clearly compromised already, we are not without strong hopes that we may be enabled through her means to punish the other two effectually. If we could do that, she might go scot-free for aught I cared.'

Dick received this project in anything but a gracious manner, representing with as much warmth as he was then capable of

X

showing, that they would find the old buck (meaning Sarah)
more difficult to manage than Quilp himself—that, for any
tampering, terrifying, or cajolery, she was a very unpromising
and unyielding subject—that, she was of a kind of brass not
easily melted or moulded into shape—in short, that they were
no match for her, and would be signally defeated. But, it was
in vain to urge them to adopt some other course. The single
gentleman has been described as explaining their joint intentions, but it should have been written that they all spoke
together; that if any one of them by chance held his peace for
a moment, he stood gasping and panting for an opportunity to
strike in again: in a word, that they had reached that pitch of
impatience and anxiety where men can neither be persuaded
nor reasoned with; and that it would have been as easy to turn
the most impetuous wind that ever blew, as to prevail on them
to reconsider their determination. So, after telling Mr.
Swiveller how they had not lost sight of Kit's mother and the
children; how they had never once even lost sight of Kit
himself, but had been unremitting in their endeavours to procure a mitigation of his sentence; how they had been perfectly
distracted between the strong proofs of his guilt, and their own
fading hopes of his innocence; and how he, Richard Swiveller,
might keep his mind at rest, for everything should be happily
adjusted between that time and night;—after telling him all
this, and adding a great many kind and cordial expressions,
personal to himself, which it is unnecessary to recite, Mr.
Garland, the notary, and the single gentleman, took their
leaves at a very critical time, or Richard Swiveller must
assuredly have been driven into another fever, whereof the
results might have been fatal.

Mr. Abel remained behind, very often looking at his watch
and at the room door, until Mr. Swiveller was roused from a
short nap, by the setting-down on the landing-place outside,
as from the shoulders of a porter, of some giant load, which
seemed to shake the house, and made the little physic-bottles
on the mantel-shelf ring again. Directly this sound reached
his ears, Mr. Abel started up, and hobbled to the door, and
opened it; and behold! there stood a strong man, with a
mighty hamper, which, being hauled into the room and
presently unpacked, disgorged such treasures of tea, and coffee,
and wine, and rusks, and oranges, and grapes, and fowls ready
trussed for boiling, and calves'-foot jelly, and arrow-root, and

sago, and other delicate restoratives, that the small servant, who had never thought it possible that such things could be, except in shops, stood rooted to the spot in her one shoe, with her mouth and eyes watering in unison, and her power of speech quite gone. But, not so Mr. Abel; or the strong man who emptied the hamper, big as it was, in a twinkling; and not so the nice old lady, who appeared so suddenly that she might have come out of the hamper too (it was quite large enough), and who, bustling about on tiptoe and without noise—now here, now there, now everywhere at once—began to fill out the jelly in teacups, and to make chicken broth in small saucepans, and to peel oranges for the sick man and to cut them up in little pieces, and to ply the small servant with glasses of wine and choice bits of everything until more substantial meat could be prepared for her refreshment. The whole of which appearances were so unexpected and bewildering, that Mr. Swiveller, when he had taken two oranges and a little jelly, and had seen the strong man walk off with the empty basket, plainly leaving all that abundance for his use and benefit, was fain to lie down and fall asleep again, from sheer inability to entertain such wonders in his mind.

Meanwhile, the single gentleman, the Notary, and Mr. Garland, repaired to a certain coffee-house, and from that place indited and sent a letter to Miss Sally Brass, requesting her, in terms mysterious and brief, to favour an unknown friend who wished to consult her, with her company there, as speedily as possible. The communication performed its errand so well, that within ten minutes of the messenger's return and report of its delivery, Miss Brass herself was announced.

'Pray, ma'am,' said the single gentleman, whom she found alone in the room, 'take a chair.'

Miss Brass sat herself down, in a very stiff and frigid state, and seemed—as indeed she was—not a little astonished to find that the lodger and her mysterious correspondent were one and the same person.

'You did not expect to see me?' said the single gentleman.

'I didn't think much about it,' returned the beauty. 'I supposed it was business of some kind or other. If it's about the apartments, of course you'll give my brother regular notice, you know—or money. That's very easily settled. You're a responsible party, and in such a case lawful money and lawful notice are pretty much the same.'

'I am obliged to you for your good opinion,' retorted the single gentleman, 'and quite concur in these sentiments. But, that is not the subject on which I wish to speak with you.'

'Oh!' said Sally. 'Then just state the particulars, will you? I suppose it's professional business?'

'Why, it *is* connected with the law, certainly.'

'Very well,' returned Miss Brass. 'My brother and I are just the same. I can take any instructions, or give you any advice.'

'As there are other parties interested beside myself,' said the single gentleman, rising and opening the door of an inner room, 'we had better confer together. Miss Brass is here, gentlemen.'

Mr. Garland and the Notary walked in, looking very grave: and, drawing up two chairs, one on each side of the single gentleman, formed a kind of fence round the gentle Sarah, and penned her into a corner. Her brother Sampson under such circumstances would certainly have evinced some confusion or anxiety, but she—all composure—pulled out the tin box, and calmly took a pinch of snuff.

'Miss Brass,' said the Notary, taking the word at this crisis, 'we professional people understand each other, and, when we choose, can say what we have to say, in very few words. You advertised a runaway servant, the other day?'

'Well,' returned Miss Sally, with a sudden flush overspreading her features, 'what of that?'

'She is found, ma'am,' said the Notary, pulling out his pocket-handkerchief with a flourish. 'She is found.'

'Who found her?' demanded Sarah hastily.

'We did, ma'am—we three. Only last night, or you would have heard from us before.'

'And now I *have* heard from you,' said Miss Brass, folding her arms, as though she were about to deny something to the death, 'what have you got to say? Something you have got into your heads about her, of course. Prove it, will you—that's all. Prove it. You have found her, you say. I can tell you (if you don't know it) that you have found the most artful, lying, pilfering, devilish little minx that was ever born.—Have you got her here?' she added, looking sharply round.

'No, she is not here at present,' returned the Notary. 'But she is quite safe.'

'Ha!' cried Sally, twitching a pinch of snuff out of her box, as spitefully as if she were in the very act of wrenching off the small servant's nose; 'she shall be safe enough from this time, I warrant you.'

'I hope so,' replied the Notary.—'Did it occur to you for the first time, when you found she had run away, that there were two keys to your kitchen door?'

Miss Sally took another pinch, and putting her head on one side, looked at her questioner, with a curious kind of spasm about her mouth, but with a cunning aspect of immense expression.

'Two keys,' repeated the Notary; 'one of which gave her the opportunities of roaming through the house at nights when you supposed her fast locked up, and of overhearing confidential consultations—among others, that particular conference, to be described to-day before a justice, which you will have an opportunity of hearing her relate; that conference which you and Mr. Brass held together, on the night before that most unfortunate and innocent young man was accused of robbery, by a horrible device of which I will only say that it may be characterised by the epithets which you have applied to this wretched little witness, and by a few stronger ones besides.'

Sally took another pinch. Although her face was wonderfully composed, it was apparent that she was wholly taken by surprise, and that what she had expected to be taxed with, in connection with her small servant, was something very different from this.

'Come, come, Miss Brass,' said the Notary, 'you have great command of feature, but you feel, I see, that by a chance which never entered your imagination, this base design is revealed, and two of its plotters must be brought to justice. Now, you know the pains and penalties you are liable to, and so I need not dilate upon them, but I have a proposal to make to you. You have the honour of being sister to one of the greatest scoundrels unhung; and, if I may venture to say so to a lady, you are in every respect quite worthy of him. But, connected with you two is a third party, a villain of the name of Quilp, the prime mover of the whole diabolical device, who I believe to be worse than either. For his sake, Miss Brass, do us the favour to reveal the whole history of this affair. Let me remind you that your doing so, at our instance, will place you in a safe and comfortable position—your present one is not desirable—and cannot injure your brother; for against him and

you we have quite sufficient evidence (as you hear) already. I
will not say to you that we suggest this course in mercy (for, to
tell you the truth, we do not entertain any regard for you), but
it is a necessity to which we are reduced, and I recommend it
to you as a matter of the very best policy. Time,' said Mr.
Witherden, pulling out his watch, 'in a business like this, is
exceedingly precious. Favour us with your decision as speedily
as possible, ma'am.'

With a smile upon her face, and looking at each of the three
by turns, Miss Brass took two or three more pinches of snuff,
and having by this time very little left, travelled round and
round the box with her forefinger and thumb, scraping up
another. Having disposed of this likewise and put the box
carefully in her pocket, she said,—

'I am to accept or reject at once, am I?'

'Yes,' said Mr. Witherden.

The charming creature was opening her lips to speak in reply,
when the door was hastily opened too, and the head of Sampson
Brass was thrust into the room.

'Excuse me,' said that gentleman hastily. 'Wait a bit!'

So saying, and quite indifferent to the astonishment his
presence occasioned, he crept in, shut the door, kissed his
greasy glove as servilely as if it were the dust, and made a most
abject bow.

'Sarah,' said Brass, 'hold your tongue if you please, and let
me speak. Gentlemen, if I could express the pleasure it gives
me to see three such men in a happy unity of feeling and
concord of sentiment, I think you would hardly believe me.
But though I am unfortunate—nay, gentlemen, criminal, if we
are to use harsh expressions in a company like this—still, I have
my feelings like other men. I have heard of a poet, who remarked
that feelings were the common lot of all. If he could have been
a pig, gentlemen, and have uttered that sentiment, he would
still have been immortal.'

'If you're not an idiot,' said Miss Brass harshly, 'hold your
peace.'

'Sarah, my dear,' returned her brother, 'thank you. But I
know what I am about, my love, and will take the liberty of
expressing myself accordingly. Mr. Witherden, sir, your
handkerchief is hanging out of your pocket—would you allow
me to—'

As Mr. Brass advanced to remedy this accident, the Notary

Mr. Brass unexpectedly appears

shrunk from him with an air of disgust. Brass, who over and above his usual prepossessing qualities, had a scratched face, a green shade over one eye, and a hat grievously crushed, stopped short, and looked round with a pitiful smile.

'He shuns me,' said Sampson, 'even when I would, as I may say, heap coals of fire upon his head. Well! Ah! But I am a falling house, and the rats (if I may be allowed the expression in reference to a gentleman I respect and love beyond everything) fly from me! Gentlemen—regarding your conversation just now, I happened to see my sister on her way here, and, wondering where she could be going to, and being—may I venture to say?—naturally of a suspicious turn, followed her. Since then, I have been listening.'

'If you're not mad,' interposed Miss Sally, 'stop there, and say no more.'

'Sarah, my dear,' rejoined Brass with undiminished politeness, 'I thank you kindly, but will still proceed. Mr. Witherden, sir, as we have the honour to be members of the same profession—to say nothing of that other gentleman having been my lodger, and having partaken, as one may say, of the hospitality of my roof—I think you might have given me the refusal of this offer in the first instance. I do indeed. Now, my dear sir,' cried Brass, seeing that the Notary was about to interrupt him, 'suffer me to speak, I beg.'

Mr. Witherden was silent, and Brass went on.

'If you will do me the favour,' he said, holding up the green shade, and revealing an eye most horribly discoloured, 'to look at this, you will naturally inquire, in your own minds, how did I get it. If you look from that, to my face, you will wonder what could have been the cause of all these scratches. And if from them to my hat, how it came into the state in which you see it. Gentlemen,' said Brass, striking the hat fiercely with his clenched hand, 'to all these questions I answer—Quilp!'

The three gentlemen looked at each other, but said nothing.

'I say,' pursued Brass, glancing aside at his sister, as though he were talking for her information, and speaking with a snarling malignity, in violent contrast to his usual smoothness, 'that I answer to all these questions,—Quilp—Quilp, who deludes me into his infernal den, and takes a delight in looking on and chuckling while I scorch, and burn, and bruise, and maim myself—Quilp, who never once, no, never once, in all our communications together, has treated me otherwise than as a dog—Quilp, whom I have always hated with my whole heart, but never so much as lately. He gives me the cold shoulder on this very matter as if he had had nothing to do with it, instead of being the first to propose it. I can't trust him. In one of his howling, raving, blazing humours, I believe he'd let it out, if it was murder, and never think of himself so long as he could terrify me. Now,' said Brass, picking up his hat again and replacing the shade over his eye, and actually crouching down, in the excess of his servility, 'what does all this lead to?—what should you say it led me to, gentlemen?—could you guess at all near the mark?'

Nobody spoke. Brass stood smirking for a little while, as if he had propounded some choice conundrum; and then said:

'To be short with you, then, it leads me to this. If the truth has come out, as it plainly has in a manner that there's no standing up against—and a very sublime and grand thing is Truth, gentlemen, in its way, though like other sublime and grand things, such as thunder-storms and that, we're not always over and above glad to see it—I had better turn upon this man than let this man turn upon me. It's clear to me that I am done for. Therefore, if anybody is to split, I had better be the person and have the advantage of it. Sarah, my dear, comparatively speaking you're safe. I relate these circumstances for my own profit.'

With that, Mr. Brass, in a great hurry, revealed the whole story; bearing as heavily as possible on his amiable employer, and making himself out to be rather a saint-like and holy character, though subject—he acknowledged—to human weaknesses. He concluded thus:

'Now, gentlemen, I am not a man who does things by halves. Being in for a penny, I am ready, as the saying is, to be in for a pound. You must do with me what you please, and take me where you please. If you wish to have this in writing, we'll reduce it into manuscript immediately. You will be tender with me, I am sure. I am quite confident you will be tender with me. You are men of honour, and have feeling hearts. I yielded from necessity to Quilp, for though necessity has no law, she has her lawyers. I yield to you from necessity too; from policy besides; and because of feelings that have been a pretty long time working within me. Punish Quilp, gentlemen.

Weigh heavily upon him. Grind him down. Tread him under
foot. He has done as much by me, for many and many a day.'

Having now arrived at the conclusion of his discourse,
Sampson checked the current of his wrath, kissed his glove
again, and smiled as only parasites and cowards can.

'And this,' said Miss Brass, raising her head, with which she
had hitherto sat resting on her hands, and surveying him from
head to foot with a bitter sneer, 'this is my brother, is it? This
is my brother, that I have worked and toiled for, and believed
to have had something of the man in him!'

'Sarah, my dear,' returned Sampson, rubbing his hands
feebly; 'you disturb our friends. Besides you—you're disappointed, Sarah, and, not knowing what you say, expose
yourself.'

'Yes, you pitiful dastard,' retorted the lovely damsel, 'I
understand you. You feared that I should be beforehand with
you. But do you think that *I* would have been enticed to say a
word? I'd have scorned it, if they had tried and tempted me
for twenty years!'

'He he!' simpered Brass, who, in his deep debasement, really
seemed to have changed sexes with his sister, and to have made
over to her any spark of manliness he might have possessed.
'You think so, Sarah, you think so perhaps; but you would have
acted quite different, my good fellow. You will not have forgotten that it was a maxim with Foxey—our revered father,
gentlemen—"Always suspect everybody." That's the maxim
to go through life with! If you were not actually about to
purchase your own safety when I showed myself, I suspect
you'd have done it by this time. And therefore I've done it
myself, and spared you the trouble as well as the shame. The
shame, gentlemen,' added Brass, allowing himself to be slightly
overcome, 'if there is any, is mine. It's better that a female
should be spared it.'

With deference to the better opinion of Mr. Brass, and more
particularly to the authority of his Great Ancestor, it may be
doubted, with humility, whether the elevating principle laid
down by the latter gentleman, and acted upon by his descen-
dant, is always a prudent one, or attended in practice with the
desired results. This is, beyond question, a bold and presumptuous doubt, inasmuch as many distinguished characters,
called men of the world, long-headed customers, knowing dogs,
shrewd fellows, capital hands at business, and the like, have

made, and do daily make, this axiom their polar star and compass. Still, the doubt may be gently insinuated. And in illustration it may be observed, that if Mr. Brass, not being over-suspicious, had, without prying and listening, left his sister to manage the conference on their joint behalf, or prying and listening, had not been in such a mighty hurry to anticipate her (which he would not have been, but for his distrust and jealousy), he would probably have found himself much better off in the end. Thus, it will always happen that these men of the world, who go through it in armour, defend themselves from quite as much good as evil; to say nothing of the inconvenience and absurdity of mounting guard with a microscope at all times, and of wearing a coat of mail on the most innocent occasions.

The three gentlemen spoke together apart, for a few moments. At the end of their consultation, which was very brief, the Notary pointed to the writing materials on the table, and informed Mr. Brass that if he wished to make any statement in writing, he had the opportunity of doing so. At the same time he felt bound to tell him that they would require his attendance, presently, before a justice of the peace, and that in what he did or said, he was guided entirely by his own discretion.

'Gentlemen,' said Brass, drawing off his gloves, and crawling in spirit upon the ground before them, 'I will justify the tenderness with which I know I shall be treated; and as, without tenderness, I should, now that this discovery has been made, stand in the worst position of the three, you may depend upon it I will make a clean breast. Mr. Witherden, sir, a kind of faintness is upon my spirits—if you would do me the favour to ring the bell and order up a glass of something warm and spicy, I shall, notwithstanding what has passed, have a melancholy pleasure in drinking your good health. I had hoped,' said Brass, looking round with a mournful smile, 'to have seen you three gentlemen, one day or another, with your legs under the mahogany in my humble parlour in the Marks. But hopes are fleeting. Dear me!'

Mr. Brass found himself so exceedingly affected, at this point, that he could say or do nothing more until some refreshment arrived. Having partaken of it, pretty freely for one in his agitated state, he sat down to write.

The lovely Sarah, now with her arms folded, and now with

her hands clasped behind her, paced the room with manly strides while her brother was thus employed, and sometimes stopped to pull out her snuff-box and bite the lid. She continued to pace up and down until she was quite tired, and then fell asleep on a chair near the door.

It has been since supposed, with some reason, that this slumber was a sham or feint, as she contrived to slip away unobserved in the dusk of the afternoon. Whether this was an intentional and waking departure, or a somnambulistic leave-taking and walking in her sleep, may remain a subject of contention; but, on one point (and indeed the main one) all parties are agreed. In whatever state she walked away, she certainly did not walk back again.

Mention having been made of the dusk of the afternoon, it will be inferred that Mr. Brass's task occupied some time in the completion. It was not finished until evening; but, being done at last, that worthy person and the three friends adjourned in a hackney-coach to the private office of a Justice, who, giving Mr. Brass a warm reception and detaining him in a secure place that he might insure to himself the pleasure of seeing him on the morrow, dismissed the others with the cheering assurance that a warrant could not fail to be granted next day for the apprehension of Mr. Quilp, and that a proper application and statement of all the circumstances to the secretary of state (who was fortunately in town), would no doubt procure Kit's free pardon and liberation without delay.

And now, indeed, it seemed that Quilp's malignant career was drawing to a close, and that retribution, which often travels slowly—especially when heaviest—had tracked his footsteps with a sure and certain scent and was gaining on him fast. Unmindful of her stealthy tread, her victim holds his course in fancied triumph. Still at his heels she comes, and once afoot, is never turned aside!

Their business ended, the three gentlemen hastened back to the lodgings of Mr. Swiveller, whom they found progressing so favourably in his recovery as to have been able to sit up for half an hour, and to have conversed with cheerfulness. Mrs. Garland had gone home some time since, but Mr. Abel was still sitting with him. After telling him all they had done, the two Mr. Garlands and the single gentleman, as if by some previous understanding, took their leaves for the night, leaving the invalid alone with the notary and the small servant.

'As you are so much better,' said Mr. Witherden, sitting down at the bedside, 'I may venture to communicate to you a piece of news which has come to me professionally.'

The idea of any professional intelligence from a gentleman connected with legal matters, appeared to afford Richard anything but a pleasing anticipation. Perhaps he connected it in his own mind with one or two outstanding accounts, in reference to which he had already received divers threatening letters. His countenance fell as he replied,

'Certainly, sir. I hope it's not anything of a very disagreeable nature, though?'

'If I thought it so, I should choose some better time for communicating it,' replied the notary. 'Let me tell you, first, that my friends who have been here to-day, know nothing of it, and that their kindness to you has been quite spontaneous and with no hope of return. It may do a thoughtless, careless man, good, to know that.'

Dick thanked him, and said he hoped it would.

'I have been making some inquiries about you,' said Mr. Witherden, 'little thinking that I should find you under such circumstances as those which have brought us together. You are the nephew of Rebecca Swiveller, spinster, deceased, of Cheselbourne in Dorsetshire.'

'Deceased!' cried Dick.

'Deceased. If you had been another sort of nephew, you would have come into possession (so says the will, and I see no reason to doubt it) of five-and-twenty thousand pounds. As it is, you have fallen into an annuity of one hundred and fifty pounds a year; but I think I may congratulate you even upon that.'

'Sir,' said Dick, sobbing and laughing together, 'you may. For, please God, we'll make a scholar of the poor Marchioness yet! And she shall walk in silk attire, and siller have to spare, or may I never rise from this bed again!'

The End of Quilp

(p. 510)

CHAPTER LXVII

UNCONSCIOUS of the proceedings faithfully narrated in the last chapter, and little dreaming of the mine which had been sprung beneath him (for, to the end that he should have no warning of the business afoot, the profoundest secrecy was observed in the whole transaction), Mr. Quilp remained shut up in his hermitage, undisturbed by any suspicion, and extremely well satisfied with the result of his machinations. Being engaged in the adjustment of some accounts—an occupation to which the silence and solitude of his retreat were very favourable—he had not strayed from his den for two whole days. The third day of his devotion to this pursuit found him still hard at work, and little disposed to stir abroad.

It was the day next after Mr. Brass's confession, and, consequently, that which threatened the restriction of Mr. Quilp's liberty, and the abrupt communication to him of some very unpleasant and unwelcome facts. Having no intuitive perception of the cloud which lowered upon his house, the dwarf was in his ordinary state of cheerfulness; and, when he found he was becoming too much engrossed by business with a due regard to his health and spirits, he varied its monotonous routine with a little screeching, or howling, or some other innocent relaxation of that nature.

He was attended, as usual, by Tom Scott, who sat crouching over the fire after the manner of a toad, and, from time to time, when his master's back was turned, imitating his grimaces with a fearful exactness. The figure-head had not yet disappeared, but remained in its old place. The face, horribly seared by the frequent application of the red-hot poker, and further ornamented by the insertion, in the tip of the nose, of a tenpenny nail, yet smiled blandly in its less lacerated parts, and seemed, like a sturdy martyr, to provoke its tormentor to the commission of new outrages and insults.

The day, in the highest and brightest quarters of the town, was damp, dark, cold, and gloomy. In that low and marshy spot, the fog filled every nook and corner with a thick dense cloud. Every object was obscure at one or two yards' distance. The warning lights and fires upon the river were powerless beneath this pall, and, but for a raw and piercing chillness in the air, and now and then the cry of some bewildered boatman as he rested on his oars and tried to make out where he was, the river itself might have been miles away.

The mist, though sluggish and slow to move, was of a keenly searching kind. No muffling up in furs and broadcloth kept it out. It seemed to penetrate into the very bones of the shrinking wayfarers, and to rack them with cold and pains. Everything was wet and clammy to the touch. The warm blaze alone defied it, and leaped and sparkled merrily. It was a day to be at home, crowding about the fire, telling stories of travellers who had lost their way in such weather on heaths and moors; and to love a warm hearth more than ever.

The dwarf's humour, as we know, was to have a fireside to himself; and when he was disposed to be convivial, to enjoy himself alone. By no means insensible to the comfort of being within doors, he ordered Tom Scott to pile the little stove with coals, and, dismissing his work for that day, determined to be jovial.

To this end, he lighted up fresh candles and heaped more fuel on the fire; and having dined off a beefsteak, which he cooked himself in somewhat of a savage and cannibal-like manner, brewed a great bowl of hot punch, lighted his pipe, and sat down to spend the evening.

At this moment, a low knocking at the cabin-door arrested his attention. When it had been twice or thrice repeated, he softly opened the little window, and thrusting his head out, demanded who was there.

'Only me, Quilp,' replied a woman's voice.

'Only you!' cried the dwarf, stretching his neck to obtain a better view of his visitor. 'And what brings you here, you jade? How dare you approach the ogre's castle, eh?'

'I have come with some news,' rejoined his spouse. 'Don't be angry with me.'

'Is it good news, pleasant news, news to make a man skip and snap his fingers?' said the dwarf. 'Is the dear old lady dead?'

'I don't know what news it is, or whether it's good or bad,' rejoined his wife.

'Then she's alive,' said Quilp, 'and there's nothing the matter with her. Go home again, you bird of evil note, go home!'

'I have brought a letter,' cried the meek little woman.

'Toss it in at the window here, and go your ways,' said Quilp, interrupting her, 'or I'll come out and scratch you.'

'No, but please, Quilp—do hear me speak,' urged his submissive wife, in tears. 'Please do!'

'Speak then,' growled the dwarf with a malicious grin. 'Be quick and short about it. Speak, will you?'

'It was left at our house this afternoon,' said Mrs. Quilp, trembling, 'by a boy who said he didn't know from whom it came, but that it was given to him to leave, and that he was told to say it must be brought on to you directly, for it was of the very greatest consequence.—But please,' she added, as her husband stretched out his hand for it, 'please let me in. You don't know how wet and cold I am, or how many times I have lost my way in coming here through this thick fog. Let me dry myself at the fire for five minutes. I'll go away directly you tell me to, Quilp. Upon my word I will.'

Her amiable husband hesitated for a few moments; but, bethinking himself that the letter might require some answer, of which she could be the bearer, closed the window, opened the door, and bade her enter. Mrs. Quilp obeyed right willingly, and, kneeling down before the fire to warm her hands, delivered into his, a little packet.

'I'm glad you're wet,' said Quilp, snatching it, and squinting at her. 'I'm glad you're cold. I'm glad you lost your way. I'm glad your eyes are red with crying. It does my heart good to see your little nose so pinched and frosty.'

'Oh, Quilp!' sobbed his wife. 'How cruel it is of you!'

'Did she think I was dead?' said Quilp, wrinkling his face into a most extraordinary series of grimaces. 'Did she think she was going to have all the money, and to marry somebody she liked? Ha ha ha! Did she?'

These taunts elicited no reply from the poor little woman, who remained on her knees, warming her hands, and sobbing, to Mr. Quilp's great delight. But, just as he was contemplating her, and chuckling excessively, he happened to observe that Tom Scott was delighted too; wherefore, that he might have no presumptuous partner in his glee, the dwarf instantly collared him, dragged him to the door, and after a short scuffle, kicked him into the yard. In return for this mark of attention, Tom immediately walked upon his hands to the window, and—if the expression be allowable—looked in with his shoes: besides rattling his feet upon the glass like a Banshee upside down. As a matter of course, Mr. Quilp lost no time in resorting to the infallible poker, with which, after some dodging and lying in ambush, he paid his young friend one or two such unequivocal compliments that he vanished precipitately, and left him in quiet possession of the field.

'So! That little job being disposed of,' said the dwarf, coolly, 'I'll read my letter. Humph!' he muttered, looking at the direction. 'I ought to know this writing. Beautiful Sally!'

Opening it, he read, in a fair, round, legal hand, as follows:

'Sammy has been practised upon, and has broken confidence. It has all come out. You had better not be in the way, for strangers are going to call upon you. They have been very quiet as yet, because they mean to surprise you. Don't lose time. I didn't. I am not to be found anywhere. If I was you, I wouldn't be, either. S. B., late of B. M.'

To describe the changes that passed over Quilp's face, as he read this letter half-a-dozen times, would require some new language: such, for power of expression, as was never written, read, or spoken. For a long time he did not utter one word; but, after a considerable interval, during which Mrs. Quilp was almost paralysed with the alarm his looks engendered, he contrived to gasp out,

'If I had him here. If I only had him here——'

'Oh, Quilp!' said his wife, 'what's the matter? Who are you angry with?'

'—I should drown him,' said the dwarf, not heeding her. 'Too easy a death, too short, too quick—but the river runs close at hand. Oh! if I had him here! Just to take him to the brink coaxingly and pleasantly,—holding him by the button-hole—joking with him,—and, with a sudden push, to send him splashing down! Drowning men come to the surface three times they say. Ah! To see him those three times, and mock him as his face came bobbing up,—oh, what a rich treat that would be!'

'Quilp!' stammered his wife, venturing at the same time to touch him on the shoulder: 'what has gone wrong?'

She was so terrified by the relish with which he pictured this pleasure to himself, that she could scarcely make herself intelligible.

'Such a bloodless cur!' said Quilp, rubbing his hands very slowly, and pressing them tight together. 'I thought his cowardice and servility were the best guarantee for his keeping silence. Oh Brass, Brass—my dear, good, affectionate, faithful, complimentary, charming friend—if I only had you here!'

His wife, who had retreated lest she should seem to listen to these mutterings, ventured to approach him again, and was about to speak, when he hurried to the door, and called Tom Scott, who, remembering his late gentle admonition, deemed it prudent to appear immediately.

'There!' said the dwarf, pulling him in. 'Take her home. Don't come here to-morrow, for this place will be shut up. Come back no more till you hear from me or see me. Do you mind?'

Tom nodded sulkily, and beckoned Mrs. Quilp to lead the way.

'As for you,' said the dwarf, addressing himself to her, 'ask no questions about me, make no search for me, say nothing concerning me. I shall not be dead, mistress, and that'll comfort you. He'll take care of you.'

'But, Quilp? What is the matter? Where are you going? Do say something more?'

'I'll say that,' said the dwarf, seizing her by the arm, 'and do that too, which undone and unsaid would be best for you, unless you go directly.'

'Has anything happened?' cried his wife. 'Oh! Do tell me that?'

'Yes,' snarled the dwarf. 'No. What matter which? I have told you what to do. Woe betide you if you fail to do it, or disobey me by a hair's breadth. Will you go?'

'I am going, I'll go directly; but,' faltered his wife, 'answer me one question first. Has this letter any connexion with dear little Nell? I must ask you that—I must indeed, Quilp. You cannot think what days and nights of sorrow I have had through having once deceived that child. I don't know what harm I may have brought about, but, great or little, I did it for you, Quilp. My conscience misgave me when I did it. Do answer me this question, if you please?'

The exasperated dwarf returned no answer, but turned round and caught up his usual weapon with such vehemence, that Tom Scott dragged his charge away, by main force, and as swiftly as he could. It was well he did so, for Quilp, who was nearly mad with rage, pursued them to the neighbouring lane, and might have prolonged the chase, but for the dense mist which obscured them from his view, and appeared to thicken every moment.

'It will be a good night for travelling anonymously,' he

said, as he returned slowly: being pretty well breathed with his run. 'Stay. We may look better here. This is too hospitable and free.'

By a great exertion of strength, he closed the two old gates, which were deeply sunken in the mud, and barred them with a heavy beam. That done, he shook his matted hair from about his eyes, and tried them.—Strong and fast.

'The fence between this wharf and the next is easily climbed,' said the dwarf, when he had taken these precautions.

'There's a back lane, too, from there. That shall be my way out. A man need know his road well, to find it in this lovely place to-night. I need fear no unwelcome visitors while this lasts, I think.'

Almost reduced to the necessity of groping his way with his hands (it had grown so dark and the fog had so much increased), he returned to his lair; and, after musing for some time over the fire, busied himself in preparations for a speedy departure.

While he was collecting a few necessaries and cramming them into his pockets, he never once ceased communing with himself in a low voice, or unclenched his teeth: which he had ground together on finishing Miss Brass's note.

'Oh Sampson!' he muttered, 'good worthy creature—if I could but hug you! If I could only fold you in my arms, and squeeze your ribs, as I *could* squeeze them if I once had you tight—what a meeting there would be between us! If we ever do cross each other again, Sampson, we'll have a greeting not easily to be forgotten, trust me. This time, Sampson, this moment when all had gone on so well, was so nicely chosen! It was so thoughtful of you, so penitent, so good. Oh, if we were face to face in this room again, my white-livered man of law, how well contented one of us would be!'

There he stopped; and raising the bowl of punch to his lips, drank a long deep draught, as if it were fair water and cooling to his parched mouth. Setting it down abruptly, and resuming his preparations, he went on with his soliloquy.

'There's Sally,' he said, with flashing eyes; 'the woman has spirit, determination, purpose—was she asleep, or petrified? She could have stabbed him—poisoned him safely. She might have seen this coming on. Why does she give me notice when it's too late? When he sat there,—yonder there, over there,—with his white face, and red head, and sickly smile, why didn'

I know what was passing in his heart? It should have stopped beating, that night, if I had been in his secret, or there are no drugs to lull a man to sleep, or no fire to burn him!'

Another draught from the bowl; and, cowering over the fire with a ferocious aspect, he muttered to himself again.

'And this, like every other trouble and anxiety I have had of late times, springs from that old dotard and his darling child—two wretched feeble wanderers! I'll be their evil genius yet. And you, sweet Kit, honest Kit, virtuous, innocent Kit, look to yourself. Where I hate, I bite. I hate you, my darling fellow, with good cause, and proud as you are to-night, I'll have my turn.—What's that?'

A knocking at the gate he had closed. A loud and violent knocking. Then, a pause; as if those who knocked had stopped to listen. Then, the noise again, more clamorous and importunate than before.

'So soon!' said the dwarf. 'And so eager! I am afraid I shall disappoint you. It's well I'm quite prepared. Sally, I thank you!'

As he spoke, he extinguished the candle. In his impetuous attempts to subdue the brightness of the fire, he overset the stove, which came tumbling forward, and fell with a crash upon the burning embers it had shot forth in its descent, leaving the room in pitchy darkness. The noise at the gate still continuing, he felt his way to the door, and stepped into the open air.

At that moment the knocking ceased. It was about eight o'clock; but the dead of the darkest night would have been as noon-day in comparison with the thick cloud which then rested upon the earth, and shrouded everything from view. He darted forward for a few paces, as if into the mouth of some dim, yawning cavern; then, thinking he had gone wrong, changed the direction of his steps; then, stood still, not knowing where to turn.

'If they would knock again,' said Quilp, trying to peer into the gloom by which he was surrounded, 'the sound might guide me! Come! Batter the gate once more!'

He stood listening intently, but the noise was not renewed. Nothing was to be heard in that deserted place, but, at intervals, the distant barkings of dogs. The sound was far away—now in one quarter, now answered in another—nor was it any guide, for it often came from shipboard, as he knew.

'If I could find a wall or fence,' said the dwarf, stretching out his arms, and walking slowly on, 'I should know which way to turn. A good, black, devil's night this, to have my dear friend here! If I had but that wish, it might, for anything I cared, never be day again.'

As the word passed his lips, he staggered and fell—and next moment was fighting with the cold dark water!

For all its bubbling up and rushing in his ears, he could hear the knocking at the gate again—could hear a shout that followed it—could recognise the voice. For all his struggling and plashing, he could understand that they had lost their way, and had wandered back to the point from which they started; that they were all but looking on, while he was drowning; that they were close at hand, but could not make an effort to save him; that he himself had shut and barred them out. He answered the shout—with a yell, which seemed to make the hundred fires that danced before his eyes tremble and flicker, as if a gust of wind had stirred them. It was of no avail. The strong tide filled his throat, and bore him on, upon its rapid current.

Another mortal struggle, and he was up again, beating the water with his hands, and looking out, with wild and glaring eyes that showed him some black object he was drifting close upon. The hull of a ship! He could touch its smooth and slippery surface with his hand. One loud cry now—but the resistless water bore him down before he could give it utterance, and, driving him under it, carried away a corpse.

It toyed and sported with its ghastly freight, now bruising it against the slimy piles, now hiding it in mud or long rank grass, now dragging it heavily over rough stones and gravel, now feigning to yield it to its own element, and in the same action luring it away, until, tired of the ugly plaything, it flung it on a swamp—a dismal place where pirates had swung in chains, through many a wintry night—and left it there to bleach.

And there it lay, alone. The sky was red with flame, and the water that bore it there had been tinged with the sullen light as it flowed along. The place the deserted carcass had left so recently, a living man, was now a blazing ruin. There was something of the glare upon its face. The hair, stirred by the damp breeze, played in a kind of mockery of death—such a mockery as the dead man himself would have delighted in when alive—about its head, and its dress fluttered idly in the night wind.

CHAPTER LXVIII

LIGHTED rooms, bright fires, cheerful faces, the music of glad voices, words of love and welcome, warm hearts, and tears of happiness—what a change is this! But it is to such delights that Kit is hastening. They are awaiting him, he knows. He fears he will die of joy, before he gets among them.

They have prepared him for this, all day. He is not to be carried off to-morrow with the rest, they tell him first. By degrees they let him know that doubts have arisen, that inquiries are to be made, and perhaps he may be pardoned after all. At last, the evening being come, they bring him to a room where some gentlemen are assembled. Foremost among them is his good old master, who comes and takes him by the hand. He hears that his innocence is established, and that he is pardoned. He cannot see the speaker, but he turns towards the voice, and in trying to answer, falls down insensible.

They recover him again, and tell him he must be composed, and bear this like a man. Somebody says he must think of his poor mother. It is because he does think of her so much, that the happy news has overpowered him. They crowd about him, and tell him that the truth has gone abroad, and that all the town and country ring with sympathy for his misfortunes. He has no ears for this. His thoughts, as yet, have no wider range than home. Does *she* know it? what did she say? who told her? He can speak of nothing else.

They make him drink a little wine, and talk kindly to him for a while, until he is more collected, and can listen, and thank them. He is free to go. Mr. Garland thinks, if he feels better, it is time they went away. The gentlemen cluster round him, and shake hands with him. He feels very grateful to them for the interest they have in him, and for the kind promises they make; but the power of speech is gone again, and he has much ado to keep his feet, even though leaning on his master's arm.

As they come through the dismal passages, some officers of the jail who are in waiting there, congratulate him, in their rough way, on his release. The newsmonger is of the number, but his manner is not quite hearty—there is something of surliness in his compliments. He looks upon Kit as an intruder, as one who has obtained admission to that place on false pretences, who has enjoyed a privilege without being duly qualified. He may be a very good sort of young man, he thinks, but he has no business there, and the sooner he is gone, the better.

The last door shuts behind them. They have passed the outer wall, and stand in the open air—in the street he has so often pictured to himself when hemmed in by the gloomy stones, and which has been in all his dreams. It seems wider and more busy than it used to be. The night is bad, and yet how cheerful and gay in his eyes! One of the gentlemen, in taking leave of him, pressed some money into his hand. He has not counted it; but when they have gone a few paces beyond the box for poor Prisoners, he hastily returns and drops it in.

Mr. Garland has a coach waiting in a neighbouring street, and, taking Kit inside with him, bids the man drive home. At first, they can only travel at a foot-pace, and then with torches going on before, because of the heavy fog. But, as they get farther from the river, and leave the closer portions of the town behind, they are able to dispense with this precaution and to proceed at a brisker rate. On the road, hard galloping would be too slow for Kit; but, when they are drawing near their journey's end, he begs they may go more slowly, and, when the house appears in sight, that they may stop—only for a minute or two, to give him time to breathe.

But there is no stopping then, for the old gentleman speaks stoutly to him, the horses mend their pace, and they are already at the garden-gate. Next minute, they are at the door. There is a noise of tongues, and tread of feet, inside. It opens. Kit rushes in, and finds his mother clinging round his neck.

And there, too, is the ever-faithful Barbara's mother, still holding the baby as if she had never put it down since that sad day when they little hoped to have such joy as this—there she is, Heaven bless her, crying her eyes out, and sobbing as never woman sobbed before; and there is little Barbara—poor little Barbara, so much thinner and so much paler, and yet so very pretty—trembling like a leaf and supporting herself against the wall; and there is Mrs. Garland, neater and nicer than ever, fainting away stone dead with nobody to help her; and there is Mr. Abel, violently blowing his nose, and wanting to embrace everybody; and there is the single gentleman hovering round them all, and constant to nothing for an instant;

and there is that good, dear, thoughtful little Jacob, sitting all alone by himself on the bottom stair, with his hands on his knees like an old man, roaring fearfully without giving any trouble to anybody; and each and all of them are for the time clean out of their wits, and do jointly and severally commit all manner of follies.

And even when the rest have in some measure come to themselves again, and can find words and smiles, Barbara—that soft-hearted, gentle, foolish little Barbara—is suddenly missed, and found to be in a swoon by herself in the back parlour, from which swoon she falls into hysterics, and from which hysterics into a swoon again, and is, indeed, so bad, that despite a mortal quantity of vinegar and cold water she is hardly a bit better at last than she was at first. Then, Kit's mother comes in and says, will he come and speak to her; and Kit says 'Yes,' and goes; and he says in a kind voice 'Barbara!' and Barbara's mother tells her that 'it's only Kit;' and Barbara says (with her eyes closed all the time) 'Oh! but is it him indeed?' and Barbara's mother says 'To be sure it is, my dear; there's nothing the matter now.' And in further assurance that he's safe and sound, Kit speaks to her again; and then Barbara goes off into another fit of laughter, and then into another fit of crying; and then Barbara's mother and Kit's mother nod to each other and pretend to scold her—but only to bring her to herself the faster, bless you!—and being experienced matrons, and acute at perceiving the first dawning symptoms of recovery, they comfort Kit with the assurance that 'she'll do now,' and so dismiss him to the place from whence he came.

Well! In that place (which is the next room) there are decanters of wine, and all that sort of thing, set out as grand as if Kit and his friends were first-rate company; and there is little Jacob, walking, as the popular phrase is, into a home-made plum-cake, at a most surprising pace, and keeping his eye on the figs and oranges which are to follow, and making the best use of his time, you may believe. Kit no sooner comes in, than that single gentleman (never was such a busy gentleman) charges all the glasses—bumpers—and drinks his health, and tells him he shall never want a friend while *he* lives; and so does Mr. Garland, and so does Mrs. Garland, and so does Mr. Abel. But, even this honour and distinction is not all, for the single gentleman forthwith pulls out of his pocket a massive silver watch—going hard, and right to half a second—and upon the back of this watch is engraved Kit's name, with flourishes all over; and in short it is Kit's watch, bought expressly for him, and presented to him on the spot. You may rest assured that Mr. and Mrs. Garland can't help hinting about their present, in store, and that Mr. Abel tells outright that he has his; and that Kit is the happiest of the happy.

There is one friend he has not seen yet, and as he cannot be conveniently introduced into the family circle, by reason of his being an iron-shod quadruped, Kit takes the first opportunity of slipping away and hurrying to the stable. The moment he lays his hand upon the latch, the pony neighs the loudest pony's greeting; before he has crossed the threshold, the pony is capering about his loose box (for he brooks not the indignity of a halter), mad to give him welcome; and when Kit goes up to caress and pat him, the pony rubs his nose against his coat, and fondles him more lovingly than ever pony fondled man. It is the crowning circumstance of his earnest, heartfelt reception; and Kit fairly puts his arm round Whisker's neck and hugs him.

But how comes Barbara to trip in there? and how smart she is again! she has been at her glass since she recovered. How comes Barbara in the stable, of all places in the world? Why, since Kit has been away, the pony would take his food from nobody but her, and Barbara, you see, not dreaming that Christopher was there, and just looking in, to see that everything was right, has come upon him unawares. Blushing little Barbara!

It may be that Kit has caressed the pony enough; it may be that there are even better things to caress than ponies. He leaves him for Barbara at any rate, and hopes she is better. Yes. Barbara is a great deal better. She is afraid—and here Barbara looks down and blushes more—that he must have thought her very foolish. 'Not at all,' says Kit. Barbara is glad of that, and coughs—Hem!—just the slightest cough possible—not more than that.

What a discreet pony when he chooses! He is as quiet now as if he were of marble. He has a very knowing look, but that he always has. 'We have hardly had time to shake hands, Barbara,' says Kit. Barbara gives him hers. Why, she is trembling now! Foolish, fluttering Barbara!

Kit's Visit to the Stable

Arm's length? The length of an arm is not much. Barbara's was not a long arm, by any means, and besides, she didn't hold it out straight, but bent a little. Kit was so near her when they shook hands, that he could see a small tiny tear, yet trembling on an eyelash. It was natural that he should look at it, unknown to Barbara. It was natural that Barbara should raise her eyes unconsciously, and find him out. Was it natural that at that instant, without any previous impulse or design, Kit should kiss Barbara? He did it, whether or no. Barbara said 'for shame,' but let him do it too—twice. He might have done it thrice, but the pony kicked up his heels and shook his head, as if he were suddenly taken with convulsions of delight, and Barbara being frightened, ran away—not straight to where her mother and Kit's mother were, though, lest they should see how red her cheeks were, and should ask her why. Sly little Barbara!

When the first transports of the whole party had subsided, and Kit and his mother, and Barbara and her mother, with little Jacob and the baby to boot, had had their suppers together—which there was no hurrying over, for they were going to stop there all night—Mr. Garland called Kit to him, and taking him into a room where they could be alone, told him that he had something yet to say, which would surprise him greatly. Kit looked so anxious and turned so pale on hearing this, that the old gentleman hastened to add, he would be agreeably surprised; and asked him if he would be ready next morning for a journey.

'For a journey, sir!' cried Kit.

'In company with me and my friend in the next room. Can you guess its purpose?'

Kit turned paler yet, and shook his head.

'Oh yes. I think you do already,' said his master. 'Try.'

Kit murmured something rather rambling and unintelligible, but he plainly pronounced the words 'Miss Nell,' three or four times—shaking his head while he did so, as if he would add that there was no hope of that.

But Mr. Garland, instead of saying 'Try again,' as Kit had made sure he would, told him very seriously, that he had guessed right.

'The place of their retreat is indeed discovered,' he said, 'at last. And that is our journey's end.'

Kit faltered out such questions as, where was it, and how had it been found, and how long since, and was she well and happy?

'Happy she is, beyond all doubt,' said Mr. Garland. 'And well, I—I trust she will be soon. She has been weak and ailing, as I learn, but she was better when I heard this morning, and they were full of hope. Sit you down, and you shall hear the rest.'

Scarcely venturing to draw his breath, Kit did as he was told. Mr. Garland then related to him, how he had a brother (of whom he would remember to have heard him speak, and whose picture, taken when he was a young man, hung in the best room), and how this brother lived a long way off, in a country-place, with an old clergyman who had been his early friend. How, although they loved each other as brothers should, they had not met for many years, but had communicated by letter from time to time, always looking forward to some period when they would take each other by the hand once more, and still letting the Present time steal on, as it was the habit for men to do, and suffering the Future to melt into the Past. How this brother, whose temper was very mild and quiet and retiring—such as Mr. Abel's—was greatly beloved by the simple people among whom he dwelt, who quite revered the Bachelor (for so they called him), and had every one experienced his charity and benevolence. How even those slight circumstances had come to his knowledge, very slowly and in course of years, for the Bachelor was one of those whose goodness shuns the light, and who have more pleasure in discovering and extolling the good deeds of others, than in trumpeting their own, be they never so commendable. How, for that reason, he seldom told them of his village friends; but how, for all that, his mind had become so full of two among them—a child and an old man, to whom he had been very kind—that, in a letter received a few days before, he had dwelt upon them from first to last, and had told such a tale of their wandering, and mutual love, that few could read it without being moved to tears. How he, the recipient of that letter, was directly led to the belief that these must be the very wanderers for whom so much search had been made, and whom Heaven had directed to his brother's care. How he had written for such further information as would put the fact beyond all doubt; how it had that morning arrived; had confirmed his first impression into a certainty; and was the immediate cause of that journey being planned, which they were to take to-morrow.

'In the meantime,' said the old gentleman, rising, and laying his hand on Kit's shoulder, 'you have a great need of rest; for such a day as this would wear out the strongest man. Good night, and Heaven send our journey may have a prosperous ending!'

KIT was no sluggard next morning, but, springing from his bed some time before day, began to prepare for his welcome expedition. The hurry of spirits consequent upon the events of yesterday, and the unexpected intelligence he had heard at night, had troubled his sleep through the long dark hours, and summoned such uneasy dreams about his pillow that it was rest to rise.

But, had it been the beginning of some great labour with the same end in view—had it been the commencement of a long journey, to be performed on foot in that inclement season of the year, to be pursued under every privation and difficulty, and to be achieved only with great distress, fatigue, and suffering—had it been the dawn of some painful enterprise, certain to task his utmost powers of resolution and endurance, and to need his utmost fortitude, but only likely to end, if happily achieved, in good fortune and delight to Nell—Kit's cheerful zeal would have been as highly roused: Kit's ardour and impatience would have been, at least, the same.

Nor was he alone excited and eager. Before he had been up a quarter of an hour the whole house were astir and busy. Everybody hurried to do something towards facilitating the preparations. The single gentleman, it is true, could do nothing himself, but he overlooked everybody else and was more locomotive than anybody. The work of packing and making ready went briskly on, and by daybreak every preparation for the journey was completed. Then, Kit began to wish they had not been quite so nimble; for the travelling-carriage which had been hired for the occasion was not to arrive until nine o'clock, and there was nothing but breakfast to fill up the intervening blank of one hour and a half.

Yes there was, though. There was Barbara. Barbara was busy, to be sure, but so much the better—Kit could help her, and that would pass away the time better than any means that could be devised. Barbara had no objection to this arrangement, and Kit, tracking out the idea which had come upon him so suddenly overnight, began to think that surely Barbara was fond of him, and surely he was fond of Barbara.

Now, Barbara, if the truth must be told—as it must and ought to be—Barbara seemed, of all the little household, to

take least pleasure in the bustle of the occasion; and when
Kit, in the openness of his heart, told her how glad and overjoyed it made him, Barbara became more downcast still, and
seemed to have even less pleasure in it than before!

'You have not been home so long, Christopher,' said Barbara—and it is impossible to tell how carelessly she said it—
'You have not been home so long, that you need be glad to go
away again, I should think.'

'But for such a purpose,' returned Kit. 'To bring back Miss
Nell! To see her again! Only think of that! I am so pleased
too, to think that *you* will see her, Barbara, at last.'

Barbara did not absolutely say that she felt no gratification
on this point, but she expressed the sentiment so plainly by
one little toss of her head, that Kit was quite disconcerted,
and wondered, in his simplicity, why she was so cool about
it.

'You'll say she has the sweetest and beautifullest face you
ever saw, I know,' said Kit, rubbing his hands. 'I'm sure
you'll say that.'

Barbara tossed her head again.

'What's the matter, Barbara?' said Kit.

'Nothing,' cried Barbara. And Barbara pouted—not sulkily,
or in an ugly manner, but just enough to make her look
more cherry-lipped than ever.

There is no school in which a pupil gets on so fast, as that
in which Kit became a scholar when he gave Barbara the kiss.
He saw what Barbara meant now—he had his lesson by heart
all at once—she was the book—there it was before him, as
plain as print.

'Barbara,' said Kit, 'you're not cross with me?'

Oh dear no! Why should Barbara be cross? And what
right had she to be cross? And what did it matter whether
she was cross or not? Who minded *her!*

'Why, *I* do,' said Kit. 'Of course I do.'

Barbara didn't see why it was of course, at all.

Kit was sure she must. Would she think again?

Certainly, Barbara would think again. No, she didn't see
why it was of course. She didn't understand what Christopher
meant. And besides she was sure they wanted her up stairs by
this time, and she must go, indeed——

'No, but, Barbara,' said Kit, detaining her gently, 'let us
part friends. I was always thinking of you, in my troubles. I

should have been a great deal more miserable than I was, if it hadn't been for you.'

Goodness gracious, how pretty Barbara was when she coloured—and when she trembled, like a little shrinking bird!

'I am telling you the truth, Barbara, upon my word, but not half so strong as I could wish,' said Kit. 'When I want you to be pleased to see Miss Nell, it's only because I like you to be pleased with what pleases me—that's all. As to her, Barbara, I think I could almost die to do her service, but you would think so too, if you knew her as I do. I am sure you would.'

Barbara was touched, and sorry to have appeared indifferent.

'I have been used, you see,' said Kit, 'to talk and think of her, almost as if she was an angel. When I look forward to meeting her again, I think of her smiling as she used to do, and being glad to see me, and putting out her hand and saying, 'It's my own old Kit,' or some such words as those—like what she used to say. I think of seeing her happy, and with friends about her, and brought up as she deserves, and as she ought to be. When I think of myself, it's as her old servant, and one that loved her dearly, as his kind, good, gentle mistress; and who would have gone—yes, and still would go—through any harm to serve her. Once, I couldn't help being afraid that if she came back with friends about her she might forget, or be ashamed of having known, a humble lad like me, and so might speak coldly, which would have cut me, Barbara, deeper than I can tell. But when I came to think again, I felt sure that I was doing her wrong in this; and so I went on, as I did at first, hoping to see her once more, just as she used to be. Hoping this, and remembering what she was, has made me feel as if I would always try to please her, and always be what I should like to seem to her if I was still her servant. If I'm the better for that—and I don't think I'm the worse—I am grateful to her ·for it, and love and honour her the more. That's the plain honest truth, dear Barbara, upon my word it is!'

Little Barbara was not of a wayward or capricious nature and, being full of remorse, melted into tears. To what more conversation this might have led, we need not stop to inquire for the wheels of the carriage were heard at that moment, and being followed by a smart ring at the garden gate, caused th

Farewell to the Travellers

bustle in the house, which had lain dormant for a short time, to burst again into tenfold life and vigour.

Simultaneously with the travelling equipage, arrived Mr. Chuckster in a hackney cab, with certain papers and supplies of money for the single gentleman, into whose hands he delivered them. This duty discharged, he subsided into the bosom of the family; and, entertaining himself with a strolling or peripatetic breakfast, watched, with genteel indifference, the process of loading the carriage.

'Snobby's in this, I see, sir?' he said to Mr. Abel Garland. 'I thought he wasn't in the last trip because it was expected that his presence wouldn't be acceptable to the ancient buffalo.'

'To whom, sir,' demanded Mr. Abel.

'To the old gentleman,' returned Mr. Chuckster, slightly abashed.

'Our client prefers to take him now,' said Mr. Abel, drily. 'There is no longer any need for that precaution, as my father's relationship to a gentleman in whom the objects of his search have full confidence, will be a sufficient guarantee for the friendly nature of their errand.'

'Ah!' thought Mr. Chuckster, looking out of window, 'anybody but me! Snobby before me, of course. He didn't happen to take that particular five-pound note, but I have not the smallest doubt that he's always up to something of that sort. I always said it, long before this came out. Devilish pretty girl that! 'Pon my soul, an amazing little creature!'

Barbara was the subject of Mr. Chuckster's commendations; and as she was lingering near the carriage (all being now ready for its departure), that gentleman was suddenly seized with a strong interest in the proceedings, which impelled him to swagger down the garden, and take up his position at a convenient ogling distance. Having had great experience of the sex, and being perfectly acquainted with all those little artifices which find the readiest road to their hearts, Mr. Chuckster, on taking his ground, planted one hand on his hip, and with the other adjusted his flowing hair. This is a favourite attitude in the polite circles, and, accompanied with a graceful whistling, has been known to do immense execution.

Such, however, is the difference between town and country, that nobody took the smallest notice of this insinuating figure; the wretches being wholly engaged in bidding the travellers farewell, in kissing hands to each other, waving handkerchiefs, and the like tame and vulgar practices. For, now, the single gentleman and Mr. Garland were in the carriage, and the postboy was in the saddle, and Kit, well wrapped and muffled up, was in the rumble behind; and Mrs. Garland was there, and Mr. Abel was there, and Kit's mother was there, and little Jacob was there, and Barbara's mother was visible in remote perspective, nursing the ever-wakeful baby; and all were nodding, beckoning, curtseying, or crying out 'Good-bye!' with all the energy they could express. In another minute, the carriage was out of sight; and Mr. Chuckster remained alone on the spot where it had lately been, with a vision of Kit standing up in the rumble waving his hand to Barbara, and of Barbara in the full light and lustre of his eyes—*his* eyes—Chuckster's—Chuckster the successful—on whom ladies of quality had looked with favour from phaetons in the parks on Sundays—waving hers to Kit!

How Mr. Chuckster, entranced by this monstrous fact, stood for some time rooted to the earth, protesting within himself that Kit was the Prince of felonious characters, and very Emperor or Great Mogul of Snobs, and how he clearly traced this revolting circumstance back to that old villany of the shilling, are matters foreign to our purpose; which is to track the rolling wheels, and bear the travellers company on their cold, bleak journey.

It was a bitter day. A keen wind was blowing, and rushed against them fiercely: bleaching the hard ground, shaking the white frost from the trees and hedges, and whirling it away like dust. But, little cared Kit for weather. There was a freedom and freshness in the wind, as it came howling by, which, let it cut never so sharp, was welcome. As it swept on with its cloud of frost, bearing down the dry twigs and boughs and withered leaves, and carrying them away pell-mell, it seemed as though some general sympathy had got abroad, and everything was in a hurry, like themselves. The harder the gusts, the better progress they appeared to make. It was a good thing to go struggling and fighting forward, vanquishing them one by one; to watch them driving up, gathering strength and fury as they came along; to bend for a moment, as they whistled past; and then, to look back and see them speed away, their hoarse noise dying in the distance, and the stout trees cowering down before them.

All day long, it blew without cessation. The night was clear and starlight, but the wind had not fallen, and the cold was piercing. Sometimes—towards the end of a long stage—Kit could not help wishing it were a little warmer; but when they stopped to change horses, and he had had a good run, and what with that, and the bustle of paying the old postillion, and rousing the new one, and running to and fro again until the horses were put to, he was so warm that the blood tingled and smarted in his fingers' ends—then he felt as if to have it one degree less cold would be to lose half the delight and glory of the journey: and up he jumped again, right cheerily, singing to the merry music of the wheels as they rolled away, and, leaving the townspeople in their warm beds, pursued their course along the lonely road.

Meantime the two gentlemen inside, who were little disposed to sleep, beguiled the time with conversation. As both were anxious and expectant, it naturally turned upon the subject of their expedition, on the manner in which it had been brought about, and on the hopes and fears they entertained respecting it. Of the former they had many, of the latter few—none perhaps beyond that indefinable uneasiness which is inseparable from suddenly awakened hope, and protracted expectation.

In one of the pauses of their discourse, and when half the night had worn away, the single gentleman, who had gradually become more and more silent and thoughtful, turned to his companion and said abruptly:

'Are you a good listener?'

'Like most other men, I suppose,' returned Mr. Garland, smiling. 'I can be, if I am interested; and if not interested, I should still try to appear so. Why do you ask?'

'I have a short narrative on my lips,' rejoined his friend, 'and will try you with it. It is very brief.'

Pausing for no reply, he laid his hand on the old gentleman's sleeve, and proceeded thus:

'There were once two brothers, who loved each other dearly. There was a disparity in their ages—some twelve years. I am not sure but they may insensibly have loved each other the better for that reason. Wide as the interval between them was, however, they became rivals too soon. The deepest and strongest affection of both their hearts settled upon one object.

'The youngest—there were reasons for *his* being sensitive

and watchful—was the first to find this out. I will not tell you what misery he underwent, what agony of soul he knew, how great his mental struggle was. He had been a sickly child. His brother, patient and considerate in the midst of his own high health and strength, had many and many a day denied himself the sports he loved, to sit beside his couch, telling him old stories till his pale face lighted up with an unwonted glow; to carry him in his arms to some green spot, where he could tend the poor pensive boy as he looked upon the bright summer day, and saw all nature healthy but himself; to be, in any way, his fond and faithful nurse. I may not dwell on all he did, to make the poor, weak creature love him, or my tale would have no end. But when the time of trial came, the younger brother's heart was full of those old days. Heaven strengthened it to repay the sacrifices of inconsiderate youth by one of thoughtful manhood. He left his brother to be happy. The truth never passed his lips, and he quitted the country, hoping to die abroad.

'The elder brother married her. She was in Heaven before long, and left him with an infant daughter.

'If you have seen the picture-gallery of any one old family, you will remember how the same face and figure—often the fairest and slightest of them all—come upon you in different generations; and how you trace the same sweet girl through a long line of portraits—never growing old or changing—the Good Angel of the race—abiding by them in all reverses—redeeming all their sins—

'In this daughter the mother lived again. You may judge with what devotion he who lost that mother almost in the winning, clung to this girl, her breathing image. She grew to womanhood, and gave her heart to one who could not know its worth. Well! Her fond father could not see her pine and droop. He might be more deserving than he thought him. He surely might become so, with a wife like her. He joined their hands, and they were married.

'Through all the misery that followed this union; through all the cold neglect and undeserved reproach; through all the poverty he brought upon her; through all the struggles of their daily life, too mean and pitiful to tell, but dreadful to endure; she toiled on, in the deep devotion of her spirit, and in her better nature, as only women can. Her means and substance wasted; her father nearly beggared by her husband's hand,

and the hourly witness (for they lived now under one roof) of her ill-usage and unhappiness,—she never, but for him, bewailed her fate. Patient, and upheld by strong affection to the last, she died a widow of some three weeks' date, leaving to her father's care two orphans; one a son of ten or twelve years old; the other a girl—such another infant child—the same in helplessness, in age, in form, in feature—as she had been herself when her young mother died.

'The elder brother, grandfather to these two children, was now a broken man; crushed and borne down, less by the weight of years than by the heavy hand of sorrow. With the wreck of his possessions, he began to trade—in pictures first, and then in curious ancient things. He had entertained a fondness for such matters from a boy, and the tastes he had cultivated were now to yield him an anxious and precarious subsistence.

'The boy grew like his father in mind and person; the girl so like her mother, that when the old man had her on his knee, and looked into her mild blue eyes, he felt as if awakening from a wretched dream, and his daughter were a little child again. The wayward boy soon spurned the shelter of his roof, and sought associates more congenial to his taste. The old man and the child dwelt alone together.

'It was then, when the love of two dead people who had been nearest and dearest to his heart, was all transferred to this slight creature; when her face, constantly before him, reminded him, from hour to hour, of the too early change he had seen in such another—of all the sufferings he had watched and known, and all his child had undergone; when the young man's profligate and hardened course drained him of money as his father's had, and even sometimes occasioned them temporary privation and distress; it was then that there began to beset him, and to be ever in his mind, a gloomy dread of poverty and want. He had no thought for himself in this. His fear was for the child. It was a spectre in his house, and haunted him night and day.

'The younger brother had been a traveller in many countries, and had made his pilgrimage through life alone. His voluntary banishment had been misconstrued, and he had borne (not without pain) reproach and slight for doing that which had wrung his heart, and cast a mournful shadow on his path. Apart from this, communication between him and the elder was difficult, and uncertain, and often failed; still, it was not so wholly broken off but that he learnt—with long blanks and gaps between each interval of information—all that I have told you now.

'Then, dreams of their young, happy life—happy to him though laden with pain and early care—visited his pillow yet oftener than before; and every night, a boy again, he was at his brother's side. With the utmost speed he could exert, he settled his affairs; converted into money all the goods he had; and, with honourable wealth enough for both, with open heart and hand, with limbs that trembled as they bore him on, with emotion such as men can hardly bear and live, arrived one evening at his brother's door!'

The narrator, whose voice had faltered lately, stopped. 'The rest,' said Mr. Garland, pressing his hand after a pause, 'I know.'

'Yes,' rejoined his friend, 'we may spare ourselves the sequel. You know the poor result of all my search. Even when by dint of such inquiries as the utmost vigilance and sagacity could set on foot, we found they had been seen with two poor travelling showmen—and in time discovered the men themselves—and in time, the actual place of their retreat; even then, we were too late. Pray God we are not too late again!'

'We cannot be,' said Mr. Garland. 'This time we must succeed.'

'I have believed and hoped so,' returned the other. 'I try to believe and hope so still. But a heavy weight has fallen on my spirits, my good friend, and the sadness that gathers over me, will yield to neither hope nor reason.'

'That does not surprise me,' said Mr. Garland; 'it is a natural consequence of the events you have recalled; of this dreary time and place; and above all, of this wild and dismal night. A dismal night, indeed! Hark! how the wind is howling!'

CHAPTER LXX

DAY broke, and found them still upon their way. Since leaving home, they had halted here and there for necessary refreshment, and had frequently been delayed, especially in the night-time, by waiting for fresh horses. They had made no other stoppages, but the weather continued rough, and the roads were often steep and heavy. It would be night again before they reached their place of destination.

Kit, all bluff and hardened with the cold, went on manfully; and, having enough to do to keep his blood circulating, to picture to himself the happy end of this adventurous journey, and to look about him and be amazed at everything, had little spare time for thinking of discomforts. Though his impatience, and that of his fellow-travellers, rapidly increased as the day waned, the hours did not stand still. The short daylight of winter soon faded away, and it was dark again when they had yet many miles to travel.

As it grew dusk, the wind fell; its distant moanings were more low and mournful; and, as it came creeping up the road, and rattling covertly among the dry brambles on either hand, it seemed like some great phantom for whom the way was narrow, whose garments rustled as it stalked along. By degrees it lulled and died away, and then it came on to snow.

The flakes fell fast and thick, soon covering the ground some inches deep, and spreading abroad a solemn stillness. The rolling wheels were noiseless, and the sharp ring and clatter of the horses' hoofs, became a dull, muffled tramp. The life of their progress seemed to be slowly hushed, and something death-like to usurp its place.

Shading his eyes from the falling snow, which froze upon their lashes and obscured his sight, Kit often tried to catch the earliest glimpse of twinkling lights denoting their approach to some not distant town. He could descry objects enough at such times, but none correctly. Now, a tall church spire appeared in view, which presently became a tree, a barn, a shadow on the ground, thrown on it by their own bright lamps. Now, there were horsemen, foot-passengers, carriages, going on before, or meeting them in narrow ways; which, when they were close upon them. turned to shadows too. A wall, a ruin, a sturdy gable end, would rise up in the road; and, when they were plunging headlong at it, would be the road itself. Strange turnings too, bridges, and sheets of water, appeared to start up here and there, making the way doubtful and uncertain; and yet they were on the same bare road, and these things, like the others, as they were passed, turned into dim allusions.

He descended slowly from his seat—for his limbs were numbed—when they arrived at a lone posting-house, and inquired how far they had to go to reach their journey's end. It was a late hour in such by-places, and the people were abed; but a voice answered from an upper window, Ten miles. The ten minutes that ensued appeared an hour; but at the end of that time, a shivering figure led out the horses they required, and after another brief delay they were again in motion.

It was a cross-country road, full, after the first three or four miles, of holes and cart-ruts, which, being covered by the snow, were so many pitfalls to the trembling horses, and obliged them to keep a foot-pace. As it was next to impossible for men so much agitated as they were by this time, to sit still and move so slowly, all three got out and plodded on behind the carriage. The distance seemed interminable, and the walk was most laborious. As each was thinking within himself that the driver must have lost his way, a church bell, close at hand, struck the hour of midnight, and the carriage stopped. It had moved softly enough, but when it ceased to crunch the snow, the silence was as startling as if some great noise had been replaced by perfect stillness.

'This is the place, gentlemen,' said the driver, dismounting from his horse, and knocking at the door of a little inn. 'Halloa! Past twelve o'clock is the dead of night here.'

The knocking was loud and long, but it failed to rouse the drowsy inmates. All continued dark and silent as before. They fell back a little, and looked up at the windows, which were mere black patches in the whitened house-front. No light appeared. The house might have been deserted, or the sleepers dead, for any air of life it had about it.

They spoke together with a strange inconsistency, in whispers; unwilling to disturb again the dreary echoes they had just now raised.

'Let us go on,' said the younger brother, 'and leave this

good fellow to wake them, if he can. I cannot rest until I know that we are not too late. Let us go on, in the name of Heaven!'

They did so, leaving the postillion to order such accommodation as the house afforded, and to renew his knocking. Kit accompanied them with a little bundle, which he had hung in the carriage when they left home, and had not forgotten since —the bird in his old cage—just as she had left him. She would be glad to see her bird, he knew.

The road wound gently downward. As they proceeded, they lost sight of the church whose clock they had heard, and of the small village clustering round it. The knocking, which was now renewed, and which in that stillness they could plainly hear, troubled them. They wished the man would forbear, or that they had told him not to break the silence until they returned.

The old church tower, clad in a ghostly garb of pure cold white, again rose up before them, and a few moments brought them close beside it. A venerable building—grey, even in the midst of the hoary landscape. An ancient sun-dial on the belfry wall was nearly hidden by the snow-drift, and scarcely to be known for what it was. Time itself seemed to have grown dull and old, as if no day were ever to displace the melancholy night.

A wicket gate was close at hand, but there was more than one path across the churchyard to which it led, and, uncertain which to take, they came to a stand again.

The village street—if street that could be called which was an irregular cluster of poor cottages of many heights and ages, some with their fronts, some with their backs, and some with gable ends towards the road, with here and there a sign-post, or a shed encroaching on the path—was close at hand. There was a faint light in a chamber window not far off, and Kit ran towards that house to ask their way.

His first shout was answered by an old man within, who presently appeared at the casement, wrapping some garment round his throat as a protection from the cold, and demanded who was abroad at that unseasonable hour, wanting him.

''Tis hard weather this,' he grumbled, 'and not a night to call me up in. My trade is not of that kind that I need be roused from bed. The business on which folks want me, will keep cold, especially at this season. What do you want?'

'I would not have roused you, if I had known you were old and ill,' said Kit.

'Old!' repeated the other peevishly. 'How do you know I am old? Not so old as you think, friend, perhaps. As to being ill, you will find many young people in worse case than I am. More's the pity that it should be so—not that I should be strong and hearty for my years, I mean, but that they should be weak and tender. I ask your pardon though,' said the old man, 'if I spoke rather rough at first. My eyes are not good at night—that's neither age nor illness; they never were—and I didn't see you were a stranger.'

'I am sorry to call you from your bed,' said Kit, 'but those gentlemen you may see by the churchyard gate, are strangers too, who have just arrived from a long journey, and seek the parsonage-house. You can direct us?'

'I should be able to,' answered the old man, in a trembling voice, 'for, come next summer, I have been sexton here, good fifty years. The right-hand path, friend, is the road.—There is no ill news for our good gentleman, I hope?'

Kit thanked him, and made him a hasty answer in the negative; he was turning back, when his attention was caught by the voice of a child. Looking up, he saw a very little creature at a neighbouring window.

'What is that?' cried the child, earnestly. 'Has my dream come true? Pray speak to me, whoever that is, awake and up.'

'Poor boy!' said the sexton, before Kit could answer, 'how goes it, darling?'

'Has my dream come true?' exclaimed the child again, in a voice so fervent that it might have thrilled to the heart of any listener. 'But no, that can never be! How could it be— Oh! how could it!'

'I guess his meaning,' said the sexton. 'To bed again, poor boy!'

'Ay!' cried the child, in a burst of despair. 'I knew it could never be, I felt too sure of that, before I asked! But, all to-night, and last night too, it was the same. I never fall asleep, but that cruel dream comes back.'

'Try to sleep again,' said the old man, soothingly. 'It will go in time.'

'No, no, I would rather that it stayed—cruel as it is, I would rather that it stayed,' rejoined the child. 'I am not afraid to have it in my sleep, but I am so sad—so very, very sad.'

The old man blessed him, the child in tears replied Good night, and Kit was again alone.

He hurried back, moved by what he had heard, though more by the child's manner than by anything he had said, as his meaning was hidden from him. They took the path indicated by the sexton, and soon arrived before the parsonage wall. Turning round to look about them when they had got thus far, they saw, among some ruined buildings at a distance, one single solitary light.

It shone from what appeared to be an old oriel window, and being surrounded by the deep shadows of overhanging walls, sparkled like a star. Bright and glimmering as the stars above their heads, lonely and motionless as they, it seemed to claim some kindred with the eternal lamps of Heaven, and to burn in fellowship with them.

'What light is that?' said the younger brother.

'It is surely,' said Mr. Garland, 'in the ruin where they live. I see no other ruin hereabouts.'

'They cannot,' returned the brother hastily, 'be waking at this late hour—'

Kit interposed directly, and begged that, while they rang and waited at the gate, they would let him make his way to where this light was shining, and try to ascertain if any people were about. Obtaining the permission he desired, he darted off with breathless eagerness, and, still carrying the birdcage in his hand, made straight towards the spot.

It was not easy to hold that pace among the graves, and at another time he might have gone more slowly, or round by the path. Unmindful of all obstacles, however, he pressed forward without slackening his speed, and soon arrived within a few yards of the window.

He approached as softly as he could, and advancing so near the wall as to brush the whitened ivy with his dress, listened. There was no sound inside. The church itself was not more quiet. Touching the glass with his cheek, he listened again. No. And yet there was such a silence all around, that he felt sure he could have heard even the breathing of a sleeper, if there had been one there.

A strange circumstance, a light in such a place at that time of night, with no one near it.

A curtain was drawn across the lower portion of the window, and he could not see into the room. But there was no shadow

z

thrown upon it from within. To have gained a footing on the wall and tried to look in from above, would have been attended with some danger—certainly with some noise, and the chance of terrifying the child, if that really were her habitation. Again and again he listened; again and again the same wearisome blank.

Leaving the spot with slow and cautious steps, and skirting the ruin for a few paces, he came at length to a door. He knocked. No answer. But there was a curious noise inside. It was difficult to determine what it was. It bore a resemblance to the low moaning of one in pain, but it was not that, being far too regular and constant. Now it seemed a kind of song, now a wail—seemed, that is, to his changing fancy, for the sound itself was never changed or checked. It was unlike anything he had ever heard; and in its tone there was something fearful, chilling, and unearthly.

The listener's blood ran colder now, than ever it had done in frost and snow, but he knocked again. There was no answer, and the sound went on without any interruption. He laid his hand softly upon the latch, and put his knee against the door. It was secured on the inside, but yielded to the pressure, and turned upon its hinges. He saw the glimmering of a fire upon the old walls, and entered.

CHAPTER LXXI

THE dull, red glow of a wood fire—for no lamp or candle burnt within the room—showed him a figure, seated on the hearth with its back towards him, bending over the fitful light. The attitude was that of one who sought the heat. It was, and yet was not. The stooping posture and the cowering form were there, but no hands were stretched out to meet the grateful warmth, no shrug or shiver compared its luxury with the piercing cold outside. With limbs huddled together, head bowed down, arms crossed upon the breast, and fingers tightly clenched, it rocked to and fro upon its seat without a moment's pause, accompanying the action with the mournful sound he had heard.

The heavy door had closed behind him on his entrance, with a crash that made him start. The figure neither spoke, nor turned to look, nor gave in any other way the faintest sign of having heard the noise. The form was that of an old man, his white head akin in colour to the mouldering embers upon which he gazed. He, and the failing light and dying fire, the time-worn room, the solitude, the wasted life, and gloom, were all in fellowship. Ashes, and dust, and ruin!

Kit tried to speak, and did pronounce some words, though what they were he scarcely knew. Still the same terrible low cry went on—still the same rocking in the chair—the same stricken figure was there, unchanged and heedless of his presence.

He had his hand upon the latch, when something in the form—distinctly seen as one log broke and fell, and, as it fell, blazed up—arrested it. He returned to where he had stood before—advanced a pace—another—another still. Another, and he saw the face. Yes! Changed as it was, he knew it well.

'Master!' he cried, stooping on one knee and catching at his hand. 'Dear master. Speak to me!'

The old man turned slowly towards him; and muttered in a hollow voice,

'This is another!—How many of these spirits there have been to-night!'

'No spirit, master. No one but your old servant. You know me now, I am sure? Miss Nell—where is she—where is she?'

'They all say that!' cried the old man. 'They all ask the same question. A spirit!'

'Where is she?' demanded Kit. 'Oh tell me but that,—but that, dear master!'

'She is asleep—yonder—in there.'

'Thank God!'

'Aye! Thank God!' returned the old man. 'I have prayed to Him, many, and many, and many a livelong night, when she has been asleep, He knows. Hark! Did she call?'

'I heard no voice.'

'You did. You hear her now. Do you tell me that you don't hear *that?*'

He started up, and listened again.

'Nor that?' he cried, with a triumphant smile. 'Can anybody know that voice so well as I? Hush! hush!'

Motioning to him to be silent, he stole away into another chamber. After a short absence (during which he could be heard to speak in a softened soothing tone) he returned, bearing in his hand a lamp.

'She is still asleep,' he whispered. 'You were right. She did not call—unless she did so in her slumber. She has called to me in her sleep before now, sir; as I have sat by, watching, I have seen her lips move, and have known, though no sound came from them, that she spoke of me. I feared the light might dazzle her eyes and wake her, so I brought it here.'

He spoke rather to himself than to the visitor, but when he had put the lamp upon the table, he took it up, as if impelled by some momentary recollection or curiosity, and held it near his face. Then, as if forgetting his motive in the very action, he turned away and put it down again.

'She is sleeping soundly,' he said; 'but no wonder. Angel hands have strewn the ground deep with snow, that the lightest footstep may be lighter yet; and the very birds are dead, that they may not wake her. She used to feed them, sir. Though never so cold and hungry, the timid things would fly from us. They never flew from her!'

Again he stopped to listen, and scarcely drawing breath listened for a long, long time. That fancy past, he opened an old chest, took out some clothes as fondly as if they had been living things, and began to smooth and brush them with his hand.

'Why dost thou lie so idle there, dear Nell,' he murmured

The Journey's End

(*p. 531*)

'when there are bright red berries out of doors waiting for thee to pluck them? Why dost thou lie so idle there, when thy little friends come creeping to the door, crying "Where is Nell— sweet Nell?"—and sob, and weep, because they do not see thee! She was always gentle with children. The wildest would do her bidding—she had a tender way with them, indeed she had!'

Kit had no power to speak. His eyes were filled with tears.

'Her little homely dress,—her favourite!' cried the old man, pressing it to his breast, and patting it with his shrivelled hand. 'She will miss it when she wakes. They have hid it here in sport, but she shall have it—she shall have it. I would not vex my darling, for the wide world's riches. See here—these shoes —how worn they are—she kept them to remind her of our last long journey. You see where the little feet went bare upon the ground. They told me, afterwards, that the stones had cut and bruised them. *She* never told me that. No, no, God bless her! and, I have remembered since, she walked behind me, sir, that I might not see how lame she was—but yet she had my hand in hers, and seemed to lead me still.'

He pressed them to his lips, and having carefully put them back again, went on communing with himself—looking wistfully from time to time towards the chamber he had lately visited.

'She was not wont to be a lie-abed; but she was well then. We must have patience. When she is well again, she will rise early, as she used to do, and ramble abroad in the healthy morning time. I often tried to track the way she had gone, but her small footstep left no print upon the dewy ground, to guide me. Who is that? Shut the door. Quick!—Have we not enough to do to drive away that marble cold, and keep her warm?'

The door was indeed opened, for the entrance of Mr. Garland and his friend, accompanied by two other persons. These were the schoolmaster, and the bachelor. The former held a light in his hand. He had, it seemed, but gone to his own cottage to replenish the exhausted lamp, at the moment when Kit came up and found the old man alone.

He softened again at sight of these two friends, and, laying aside the angry manner—if to anything so feeble and so sad the term can be applied—in which he had spoken when the door opened, resumed his former seat, and subsided, by little and little, into the old action, and the old, dull, wandering sound.

Of the strangers, he took no heed whatever. He had seen them, but appeared quite incapable of interest or curiosity. The younger brother stood apart. The bachelor drew a chair towards the old man, and sat down close beside him. After a long silence, he ventured to speak.

'Another night, and not in bed!' he said softly; 'I hoped you would be more mindful of your promise to me. Why do you not take some rest?'

'Sleep has left me,' returned the old man. 'It is all with her!'

'It would pain her very much to know that you were watching thus,' said the bachelor. 'You would not give her pain?'

'I am not so sure of that, if it would only rouse her. She has slept so very long. And yet I am rash to say so. It is a good and happy sleep—eh?'

'Indeed it is,' returned the bachelor. 'Indeed, indeed, it is!'

'That's well!—and the waking'—faltered the old man.

'Happy too. Happier than tongue can tell, or heart of man conceive.'

They watched him as he rose and stole on tiptoe to the other chamber where the lamp had been replaced. They listened as he spoke again within its silent walls. They looked into the faces of each other, and no man's cheek was free from tears. He came back, whispering that she was still asleep, but that he thought she had moved. It was her hand, he said—a little—a very, very little—but he was pretty sure she had moved it—perhaps in seeking his. He had known her do that, before now, though in the deepest sleep the while. And when he had said this, he dropped into his chair again, and clasping his hands above his head, uttered a cry never to be forgotten.

The poor schoolmaster motioned to the bachelor that he would come on the other side, and speak to him. They gently unlocked his fingers, which he had twisted in his grey hair, and pressed them in their own.

'He will hear me,' said the schoolmaster, 'I am sure. He will hear either me or you if we beseech him. She would, at all times.'

'I will hear any voice she liked to hear,' cried the old man. 'I love all she loved!'

'I know you do,' returned the schoolmaster. 'I am certain of it. Think of her; think of all the sorrows and afflictions you have shared together; of all the trials, and all the peaceful pleasures, you have jointly known.'

'I do. I do. I think of nothing else.'

'I would have you think of nothing else to-night—of nothing but those things which will soften your heart, dear friend, and open it to old affections and old times. It is so that she would speak to you herself, and in her name it is that I speak now.'

'You do well to speak softly,' said the old man. 'We will not wake her. I should be glad to see her eyes again, and to see her smile. There is a smile upon her young face now, but it is fixed and changeless. I would have it come and go. That shall be in Heaven's good time. We will not wake her.'

'Let us not talk of her in her sleep, but as she used to be when you were journeying together, far away—as she was at home, in the old house from which you fled together—as she was, in the old cheerful time,' said the schoolmaster.

'She was always cheerful—very cheerful,' cried the old man, looking steadfastly at him. 'There was ever something mild and quiet about her, I remember, from the first; but she was of a happy nature.'

'We have heard you say,' pursued the schoolmaster, 'that in this and in all goodness, she was like her mother. You can think of, and remember her?'

He maintained his steadfast look, but gave no answer.

'Or even one before her,' said the bachelor. 'It is many years ago, and affliction makes the time longer, but you have not forgotten her whose death contributed to make this child so dear to you, even before you knew her worth or could read her heart? Say, that you could carry back your thoughts to very distant days—to the time of your early life—when, unlike this fair flower, you did not pass your youth alone. Say, that you could remember, long ago, another child who loved you dearly, you being but a child yourself. Say, that you had a brother, long forgotten, long unseen, long separated from you, who now, at last, in your utmost need came back to comfort and console you—'

'To be to you what you were once to him,' cried the younger, falling on his knee before him; 'to repay your old affection, brother dear, by constant care, solicitude, and love; to be, at your right hand, what he has never ceased to be when oceans rolled between us; to call to witness his unchanging truth and mindfulness of bygone days, whole years of desolation. Give me but one word of recognition, brother—and never—no, never, in the brightest moment of our youngest days, when, poor silly boys, we thought to pass our lives together—have we been half as dear and precious to each other as we shall be from this time hence!'

The old man looked from face to face, and his lips moved; but no sound came from them in reply.

'If we were knit together then,' pursued the younger brother, 'what will be the bond between us now? Our love and fellowship began in childhood, when life was all before us, and will be resumed when we have proved it, and are but children at the last. As many restless spirits, who have hunted fortune, fame, or pleasure through the world, retire in their decline to where they first drew breath, vainly seeking to be children once again before they die, so we, less fortunate than they in early life, but happier in its closing scenes, will set up our rest again among our boyish haunts, and going home with no hope realised, that had its growth in manhood—carrying back nothing that we brought away, but our old yearnings to each other—saving no fragment from the wreck of life, but that which first endeared it—may be, indeed, but children as at first. And even,' he added in an altered voice, 'even if what I dread to name has come to pass—even if that be so, or is to be (which Heaven forbid and spare us!)—still, dear brother, we are not apart, and have that comfort in our great affliction.'

By little and little, the old man had drawn back towards the inner chamber, while these words were spoken. He pointed there, as he replied, with trembling lips,

'You plot among you to wean my heart from her. You never will do that—never while I have life. I have no relative or friend but her—I never had—I never will have. She is all in all to me. It is too late to part us now.'

Waving them off with his hand, and calling softly to her as he went, he stole into the room. They who were left behind, drew close together, and after a few whispered words—not unbroken by emotion, or easily uttered—followed him. They moved so gently, that their footsteps made no noise; but there were sobs from among the group, and sounds of grief and mourning.

For she was dead. There, upon her little bed, she lay at rest. The solemn stillness was no marvel now.

She was dead. No sleep so beautiful and calm, so free from

At Rest

trace of pain, so fair to look upon. She seemed a creature fresh from the hand of God, and waiting for the breath of life; not one who had lived and suffered death.

Her couch was dressed with here and there some winter berries and green leaves, gathered in a spot she had been used to favour. 'When I die, put near me something that has loved the light, and had the sky above it always.' Those were her words.

She was dead. Dear, gentle, patient, noble Nell was dead. Her little bird—a poor slight thing the pressure of a finger would have crushed—was stirring nimbly in its cage; and the strong heart of its child-mistress was mute and motionless for ever.

Where were the traces of her early cares, her sufferings, and fatigues? All gone. Sorrow was dead indeed in her, but peace and perfect happiness were born; imaged in her tranquil beauty and profound repose.

And still her former self lay there, unaltered in this change. Yes. The old fireside had smiled upon that same sweet face; it had passed, like a dream, through haunts of misery and care; at the door of the poor schoolmaster on the summer evening, before the furnace fire upon the cold wet night, at the still bedside of the dying boy, there had been the same mild lovely look. So shall we know the angels in their majesty, after death.

The old man held one languid arm in his, and had the small hand tight folded to his breast, for warmth. It was the hand she had stretched out to him with her last smile—the hand that had led him on, through all their wanderings. Ever and anon he pressed it to his lips; then hugged it to his breast again, murmuring that it was warmer now; and, as he said it, he looked, in agony, to those who stood around, as if imploring them to help her.

She was dead, and past all help, or need of it. The ancient rooms she had seemed to fill with life, even while her own was waning fast—the garden she had tended—the eyes she had gladdened—the noiseless haunts of many a thoughtful hour—the paths she had trodden as it were but yesterday—could know her never more.

'It is not,' said the schoolmaster, as he bent down to kiss her on the cheek, and gave his tears free vent, 'it is not on earth that Heaven's justice ends. Think what earth is, compared with the World to which her young spirit has winged its early flight; and say, if one deliberate wish expressed in solemn terms above this bed could call her back to life, which of us would utter it!'

CHAPTER LXXII

WHEN morning came, and they could speak more calmly on the subject of their grief, they heard how her life had closed.

She had been dead two days. They were all about her at the time, knowing that the end was drawing on. She died soon after daybreak. They had read and talked to her in the earlier portion of the night, but as the hours crept on, she sunk to sleep. They could tell, by what she faintly uttered in her dreams, that they were of her journeyings with the old man; they were of no painful scenes, but of people who had helped and used them kindly, for she often said 'God bless you!' with great fervour. Waking, she never wandered in her mind but once, and that was of beautiful music which she said was in the air. God knows. It may have been.

Opening her eyes at last, from a very quiet sleep, she begged that they would kiss her once again. That done, she turned to the old man with a lovely smile upon her face—such, they said, as they had never seen, and never could forget—and clung with both her arms about his neck. They did not know that she was dead, at first.

She had spoken very often of the two sisters, who, she said, were like dear friends to her. She wished they could be told how much she thought about them, and how she had watched them as they walked together, by the river side at night. She would like to see poor Kit, she had often said of late. She wished there was somebody to take her love to Kit. And, even then, she never thought or spoke about him, but with something of her old, clear, merry laugh.

For the rest, she had never murmured or complained; but with a quiet mind, and manner quite unaltered—save that she every day became more earnest and more grateful to them—faded like the light upon a summer's evening.

The child who had been her little friend came there, almost as soon as it was day, with an offering of dried flowers which he begged them to lay upon her breast. It was he who had come to the window overnight and spoken to the sexton, and they saw in the snow traces of small feet, where he had been lingering near the room in which she lay, before he went to bed. He had a fancy, it seemed, that they had left her there alone; and could not bear the thought.

He told them of his dream again, and that it was of her being restored to them, just as she used to be. He begged hard to see her, saying that he would be very quiet, and that they need not fear his being alarmed, for he had sat alone by his young brother all day long when *he* was dead, and had felt glad to be so near him. They let him have his wish; and indeed he kept his word, and was, in his childish way, a lesson to them all.

Up to that time, the old man had not spoken once—except to her—or stirred from the bedside. But, when he saw her little favourite, he was moved as they had not seen him yet, and made as though he would have him come nearer. Then, pointing to the bed, he burst into tears for the first time, and they who stood by, knowing that the sight of this child had done him good, left them alone together.

Soothing him with his artless talk of her, the child persuaded him to take some rest, to walk abroad, to do almost as he desired him. And when the day came on, which must remove her in her earthly shape from earthly eyes for ever, he led him away, that he might not know when she was taken from him.

They were to gather fresh leaves and berries for her bed. It was Sunday—a bright, clear, wintry afternoon—and as they traversed the village street, those who were walking in their path drew back to make way for them, and gave them a softened greeting. Some shook the old man kindly by the hand, some stood uncovered while he tottered by, and many cried 'God help him!' as he passed along.

'Neighbour!' said the old man, stopping at the cottage where his young guide's mother dwelt, 'how is it that the folks are nearly all in black to-day? I have seen a mourning ribbon or a piece of crape on almost every one.'

She could not tell, the woman said.

'Why, you yourself—you wear the colour too?' he said. 'Windows are closed that never used to be by day. What does this mean?'

Again the woman said she could not tell.

'We must go back,' said the old man, hurriedly. 'We must see what this is.'

'No, no,' cried the child, detaining him. 'Remember what

you promised. Our way is to the old green lane, where she and I so often were, and where you found us, more than once, making those garlands for her garden. Do not turn back!'

'Where is she now?' said the old man. 'Tell me that.'

'Do you not know?' returned the child. 'Did we not leave her, but just now?'

'True. True. It *was* her we left—was it?'

He pressed his hand upon his brow, looked vacantly round. and as if impelled by a sudden thought, crossed the road, and entered the sexton's house. He and his deaf assistant were sitting before the fire. Both rose up, on seeing who it was.

The child made a hasty sign to them with his hand. It was the action of an instant, but that, and the old man's look, were quite enough.

'Do you—do you bury any one to-day?' he said, eagerly.

'No, no! Who should we bury, sir?' returned the sexton.

'Aye, who indeed? I say with you, who indeed?'

'It is a holiday with us, good sir,' returned the sexton mildly. 'We have no work to do to-day.'

'Why then, I'll go where you will,' said the old man, turning to the child. 'You're sure of what you tell me? You would not deceive me? I am changed, even in the little time since you last saw me.'

'Go thy ways with him, sir,' cried the sexton, 'and Heaven be with ye both!'

'I am quite ready,' said the old man, meekly. 'Come, boy, come—' and so submitted to be led away.

And now the bell—the bell she had so often heard, by night and day, and listened to with solemn pleasure almost as a living voice—rung its remorseless toll, for her, so young, so beautiful, so good. Decrepit age, and vigorous life, and blooming youth, and helpless infancy, poured forth—on crutches, in the pride of strength and health, in the full blush of promise, in the mere dawn of life—to gather round her tomb. Old men were there, whose eyes were dim and senses failing—grandmothers, who might have died ten years ago, and still been old—the deaf, the blind, the lame, the palsied, the living dead in many shapes and forms, to see the closing of that early grave. What was the death it would shut in, to that which still could crawl and creep above it!

Along the crowded path they bore her now; pure as the newly-fallen snow that covered it; whose day on earth had been as fleeting. Under the porch, where she had sat when Heaven in its mercy brought her to that peaceful spot, she passed again; and the old church received her in its quiet shade.

They carried her to one old nook, where she had many and many a time sat musing, and laid their burden softly on the pavement. The light streamed on it through the coloured window—a window, where the boughs of trees were ever rustling in the summer, and where the birds sang sweetly all day long. With every breath of air that stirred among those branches in the sunshine, some trembling, changing light, would fall upon her grave.

Earth to earth, ashes to ashes, dust to dust! Many a young hand dropped in its little wreath, many a stifled sob was heard. Some—and they were not a few—knelt down. All were sincere and truthful in their sorrow.

The service done, the mourners stood apart, and the villagers closed round to look into the grave before the pavement-stone should be replaced. One, called to mind how he had seen her sitting on that very spot, and how her book had fallen on her lap, and she was gazing with a pensive face upon the sky. Another, told how he had wondered much that one so delicate as she, should be so bold; how she had never feared to enter the church alone at night, but had loved to linger there when all was quiet, and even to climb the tower stair, with no more light than that of the moon rays stealing through the loopholes in the thick old wall. A whisper went about among the oldest, that she had seen and talked with angels; and when they called to mind how she had looked, and spoken, and her early death, some thought it might be so, indeed. Thus, coming to the grave in little knots, and glancing down, and giving place to others, and falling off in whispering groups of three or four, the church was cleared in time, of all but the sexton and the mourning friends.

They saw the vault covered, and the stone fixed down. Then, when the dusk of evening had come on, and not a sound disturbed the sacred stillness of the place—when the bright moon poured in her light on tomb and monument, on pillar, wall, and arch, and most of all (it seemed to them) upon her quiet grave—in that calm time, when outward things and inward thoughts teem with assurances of immortality, and worldly hopes and fears are humbled in the dust before them—

then, with tranquil and submissive hearts they turned away, and left the child with God.

Oh! it is hard to take to heart the lesson that such deaths will teach, but let no man reject it, for it is one that all must learn, and is a mighty, universal Truth. When Death strikes down the innocent and young, for every fragile form from which he lets the panting spirit free, a hundred virtues rise, in shapes of mercy, charity, and love, to walk the world, and bless it. Of every tear that sorrowing mortals shed on such green graves, some good is born, some gentler nature comes. In the Destroyer's steps there spring up bright creations that defy his power, and his dark path becomes a way of light to Heaven.

It was late when the old man came home. The boy had led him to his own dwelling, under some pretence, on their way back; and, rendered drowsy by his long ramble and late want of rest, he had sunk into a deep sleep by the fireside. He was perfectly exhausted, and they were careful not to rouse him. The slumber held him a long time, and when he at length awoke the moon was shining.

The younger brother, uneasy at his protracted absence, was watching at the door for his coming, when he appeared in the pathway with his little guide. He advanced to meet them, and tenderly obliging the old man to lean upon his arm, conducted him with slow and trembling steps towards the house.

He repaired to her chamber, straight. Not finding what he had left there, he returned with distracted looks to the room in which they were assembled. From that, he rushed into the schoolmaster's cottage, calling her name. They followed close upon him, and when he had vainly searched it, brought him home.

With such persuasive words as pity and affection could suggest, they prevailed upon him to sit among them and hear what they should tell him. Then endeavouring by every little artifice to prepare his mind for what must come, and dwelling with many fervent words upon the happy lot to which she had been removed, they told him, at last, the truth. The moment it had passed their lips, he fell down among them like a murdered man.

For many hours, they had little hope of his surviving; but grief is strong, and he recovered.

If there be any who have never known the blank that follows death—the weary void—the sense of desolation that will come upon the strongest minds, when something familiar and beloved is missed at every turn—the connection between inanimate and senseless things, and the object of recollection, when every household god becomes a monument and every room a grave—if there be any who have not known this, and proved it by their own experience, they can never faintly guess how, for many days, the old man pined and moped away the time, and wandered here and there as seeking something, and had no comfort.

Whatever power of thought or memory he retained, was all bound up in her. He never understood, or seemed to care to understand, about his brother. To every endearment and attention he continued listless. If they spoke to him on this or any other theme—save one—he would hear them patiently for awhile, then turn away, and go on seeking as before.

On that one theme, which was in his and all their minds, it was impossible to touch. Dead! He could not hear or bear the word. The slightest hint of it would throw him into a paroxysm, like that he had had when it was first spoken. In what hope he lived, no man could tell; but, that he had some hope of finding her again—some faint and shadowy hope, deferred from day to day, and making him from day to day more sick and sore at heart—was plain to all.

They bethought them of a removal from the scene of this last sorrow; of trying whether change of place would rouse or cheer him. His brother sought the advice of those who were accounted skilful in such matters, and they came and saw him. Some of the number stayed upon the spot, conversed with him when he would converse, and watched him as he wandered up and down, alone and silent. Move him where they might, they said, he would ever seek to get back there. His mind would run upon that spot. If they confined him closely, and kept a strict guard upon him, they might hold him prisoner, but if he could by any means escape, he would surely wander back to that place, or die upon the road.

The boy, to whom he had submitted at first, had no longer any influence with him. At times he would suffer the child to walk by his side, or would even take such notice of his presence as giving him his hand, or would stop to kiss his cheek, or pat him on the head. At other times, he would entreat him

—not unkindly—to be gone, and would not brook him near. But, whether alone, or with this pliant friend, or with those who would have given him, at any cost or sacrifice, some consolation or some peace of mind, if happily the means could have been devised; he was at all times the same—with no love or care for anything in life—a broken-hearted man.

At length, they found, one day, that he had risen early, and, with his knapsack on his back, his staff in hand, her own straw hat, and little basket full of such things as she had been used to carry, was gone. As they were making ready to pursue him far and wide, a frightened schoolboy came who had seen him, but a moment before, sitting in the church—upon her grave, he said.

They hastened there, and going softly to the door, espied him in the attitude of one who waited patiently. They did not disturb him then, but kept a watch upon him all that day. When it grew quite dark, he rose and returned home, and went to bed, murmuring to himself, 'She will come to-morrow!'

Upon the morrow he was there again from sunrise until night; and still at night he laid him down to rest, and murmured, 'She will come to-morrow!'

And thenceforth, every day, and all day long, he waited at her grave, for her. How many pictures of new journeys over pleasant country, of resting-places under the free broad sky, of rambles in the fields and woods, and paths not often trodden —how many tones of that one well-remembered voice, how many glimpses of the form, the fluttering dress, the hair that waved so gaily in the wind—how many visions of what had been, and what he hoped was yet to be—rose up before him, in the old, dull, silent church! He never told them what he thought, or where he went. He would sit with them at night, pondering with a secret satisfaction, they could see, upon the flight that he and she would take before night came again; and still they would hear him whisper in his prayers, 'Lord! Let her come to-morrow!'

The last time was on a genial day in spring. He did not return at the usual hour, and they went to seek him. He was lying dead upon the stone.

They laid him by the side of her whom he had loved so well; and, in the church where they had often prayed, and mused, and lingered hand in hand, the child and the old man slept together.

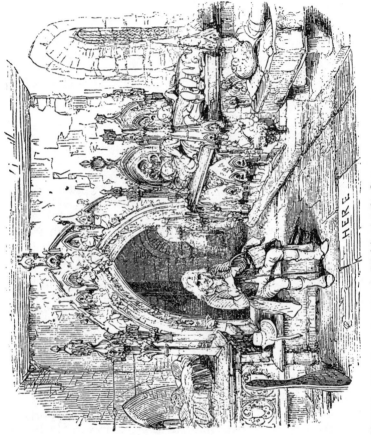

Waiting at the Grave

THE magic reel, which, rolling on before, has led the chronicler thus far, now slackens in its pace, and stops. It lies before the goal; the pursuit is at an end.

It remains but to dismiss the leaders of the little crowd who have borne us company upon the road, and so to close the journey.

Foremost among them, smooth Sampson Brass and Sally, arm in arm, claim our polite attention.

Mr. Sampson, then, being detained, as already has been shown, by the justice upon whom he called, and being so strongly pressed to protract his stay that he could by no means refuse, remained under his protection for a considerable time, during which the great attention of his entertainer kept him so extremely close, that he was quite lost to society, and never even went abroad for exercise saving into a small paved yard. So well, indeed, was his modest and retiring temper understood by those with whom he had to deal, and so jealous were they of his absence, that they required a kind of friendly bond to be entered into by two substantial housekeepers, in the sum of fifteen hundred pounds a-piece, before they would suffer him to quit their hospitable roof—doubting, it appeared, that he would return, if once let loose, on any other terms. Mr. Brass, struck with the humour of this jest, and carrying out its spirit to the utmost, sought from his wide connection a pair of friends whose joint possessions fell some halfpence short of fifteen pence, and proffered them as bail—for that was the merry word agreed upon on both sides. These gentlemen being rejected after twenty-four hours' pleasantry, Mr. Brass consented to remain, and did remain, until a club of choice spirits called a Grand Jury (who were in the joke) summoned him to trial before twelve other wags for perjury and fraud, who in their turn found him guilty with a most facetious joy,—nay, the very populace entered into the whim, and when Mr. Brass was moving in a hackney-coach towards the building where these wags assembled, saluted him with rotten eggs and carcases of kittens, and feigned to wish to tear him into shreds, which greatly increased the comicality of the thing, and made him relish it the more, no doubt.

To work this sportive vein still further, Mr. Brass, by his

counsel, moved in arrest of judgment that he had been led to criminate himself, by assurances of safety and promises of pardon, and claimed the leniency which the law extends to such confiding natures as are thus deluded. After solemn argument, this point (with others of a technical nature, whose humorous extravagance it would be difficult to exaggerate) was referred to the judges for their decision, Sampson being meantime removed to his former quarters. Finally, some of the points were given in Sampson's favour, and some against him; and the upshot was, that, instead of being desired to travel for a time in foreign parts, he was permitted to grace the mother country under certain insignificant restrictions.

These were, that he should, for a term of years, reside in a spacious mansion where several other gentlemen were lodged and boarded at the public charge, who went clad in a sober uniform of grey turned up with yellow, had their hair cut extremely short, and chiefly lived on gruel and light soup. It was also required of him that he should partake of their exercise of constantly ascending an endless flight of stairs; and lest his legs, unused to such exertion, should be weakened by it, that he should wear upon one ankle an amulet or charm of iron. These conditions being arranged, he was removed one evening to his new abode, and enjoyed, in common with nine other gentlemen, and two ladies, the privilege of being taken to his place of retirement in one of Royalty's own carriages.

Over and above these trifling penalties, his name was erased and blotted out from the roll of attorneys; which erasure has been always held in these latter times to be a great degradation and reproach, and to imply the commission of some amazing villany—as indeed it would seem to be the case, when so many worthless names remain among its better records, unmolested.

Of Sally Brass, conflicting rumours went abroad. Some said with confidence that she had gone down to the docks in male attire, and had become a female sailor; others darkly whispered that she had enlisted as a private in the second regiment of Foot Guards, and had been seen in uniform, and on duty, to wit, leaning on her musket and looking out of a sentry-box in St. James's Park, one evening. There were many such whispers as these in circulation; but the truth appears to be that, after the lapse of some five years (during which there is no direct evidence of her having been seen at all), two wretched people were more than once observed to crawl at dusk from the inmost recesses of St. Giles's, and to take their way along the streets, with shuffling steps and cowering shivering forms, looking into the roads and kennels as they went in search of refuse food or disregarded offal. These forms were never beheld but in those nights of cold and gloom, when the terrible spectres, who lie at all other times in the obscene hiding-places of London, in archways, dark vaults and cellars, venture to creep into the streets; the embodied spirits of Disease, and Vice, and Famine. It was whispered by those who should have known, that these were Sampson and his sister Sally; and to this day, it is said, they sometimes pass, on bad nights, in the same loathsome guise, close at the elbow of the shrinking passenger.

The body of Quilp being found—though not until some days had elapsed—an inquest was held on it near the spot where it had been washed ashore. The general supposition was that he had committed suicide, and, this appearing to be favoured by all the circumstances of his death, the verdict was to that effect. He was left to be buried with a stake through his heart in the centre of four lonely roads.

It was rumoured afterwards that this horrible and barbarous ceremony had been dispensed with, and that the remains had been secretly given up to Tom Scott. But even here, opinion was divided; for some said Tom dug them up at midnight, and carried them to a place indicated to him by the widow. It is probable that both these stories may have had their origin in the simple fact of Tom's shedding tears upon the inquest—which he certainly did, extraordinary as it may appear. He manifested, besides, a strong desire to assault the jury; and being restrained and conducted out of court, darkened its only window by standing on his head upon the sill, until he was dexterously tilted upon his feet again by a cautious beadle.

Being cast upon the world by his master's death, he determined to go through it upon his head and hands, and accordingly began to tumble for his bread. Finding, however, his English birth an insurmountable obstacle to his advancement in this pursuit (notwithstanding that his art was in high repute and favour), he assumed the name of an Italian image lad, with whom he had become acquainted; and afterwards tumbled with extraordinary success, and to overflowing audiences.

Little Mrs. Quilp never quite forgave herself the one deceit that lay so heavy on her conscience, and never spoke or thought of it but with bitter tears. Her husband had no relations, and she was rich. He had made no will, or she would probably have been poor. Having married the first time at her mother's instigation, she consulted in her second choice nobody but herself. It fell upon a smart young fellow enough; and as he made it a preliminary condition that Mrs. Jiniwin should be thenceforth an out-pensioner, they lived together after marriage with no more than the average amount of quarrelling, and led a merry life upon the dead dwarf's money.

Mr. and Mrs. Garland, and Mr. Abel, went out as usual (except that there was a change in their household, as will be seen presently), and in due time the latter went into partnership with his friend the notary, on which occasion there was a dinner, and a ball, and great extent of dissipation. Unto this ball there happened to be invited the most bashful young lady that was ever seen, with whom Mr. Abel happened to fall in love. *How* it happened, or how they found it out, or which of them first communicated the discovery to the other, nobody knows. But, certain it is that in course of time they were married; and equally certain it is that they were the happiest of the happy; and no less certain it is that they deserved to be so. And it is pleasant to write down that they reared a family; because any propagation of goodness and benevolence is no small addition to the aristocracy of nature, and no small subject of rejoicing for mankind at large.

The pony preserved his character for independence and principle down to the last moment of his life; which was an unusually long one, and caused him to be looked upon, indeed, as the very Old Parr of ponies. He often went to and fro with the little phaeton between Mr. Garland's and his son's, and, as the old people and the young were frequently together, had a stable of his own at the new establishment, into which he would walk of himself with surprising dignity. He condescended to play with the children, as they grew old enough to cultivate his friendship, and would run up and down the little paddock with them like a dog; but though he relaxed so far, and allowed them such small freedoms as caresses, or even to look at his shoes or hang on by his tail, he never permitted any one among them to mount his back or drive him; thus showing that even their familiarity must have its limits, and that there were points between them far too serious for trifling.

He was not unsusceptible of warm attachments in his later life, for when the good bachelor came to live with Mr. Garland upon the clergyman's decease, he conceived a great friendship for him, and amiably submitted to be driven by his hands without the least resistance. He did no work for two or three years before he died, but lived in clover; and his last act (like a choleric old gentleman) was to kick his doctor.

Mr. Swiveller, recovering very slowly from his illness, and entering into the receipt of his annuity, bought for the Marchioness a handsome stock of clothes, and put her to school forthwith, in redemption of the vow he had made upon his fevered bed. After casting about for some time for a name which should be worthy of her, he decided in favour of Sophronia Sphynx, as being euphonious and genteel, and furthermore indicative of mystery. Under this title the Marchioness repaired, in tears, to the school of his selection, from which, as she soon distanced all competitors, she was removed before the lapse of many quarters to one of a higher grade. It is but bare justice to Mr. Swiveller to say, that, although the expenses of her education kept him in straitened circumstances for half-a-dozen years, he never slackened in his zeal, and always held himself sufficiently repaid by the accounts he heard (with great gravity) of her advancement, on his monthly visits to the governess, who looked upon him as a literary gentleman of eccentric habits, and of a most prodigious talent in quotation.

In a word, Mr. Swiveller kept the Marchioness at this establishment until she was, at a moderate guess, full nineteen years of age—good-looking, clever, and good-humoured; when he began to consider seriously what was to be done next. On one of his periodical visits, while he was revolving this question in his mind, the Marchioness came down to him, alone, looking more smiling and more fresh than ever. Then, it occurred to him, but not for the first time, that if she would marry him, how comfortable they might be! So Richard asked her; whatever she said, it wasn't No; and they were married in good earnest that day week. Which gave Mr. Swiveller frequent occasion to remark at divers subsequent periods that there had been a young lady saving up for him after all.

A little cottage at Hampstead being to let, which had in its garden a smoking-box, the envy of the civilised world, they agreed to become its tenants, and, when the honeymoon was

over, entered upon its occupation. To this retreat Mr.
Chuckster repaired regularly every Sunday to spend the day—
usually beginning with breakfast—and here he was the great
purveyor of general news and fashionable intelligence. For
some years he continued a deadly foe to Kit, protesting that he
had a better opinion of him when he was supposed to have
stolen the five-pound note, than when he was shown to be
perfectly free of the crime; inasmuch as his guilt would have
had in it something daring and bold, whereas his innocence was
but another proof of a sneaking and crafty disposition. By slow
degrees, however, he was reconciled to him in the end; and
even went so far as to honour him with his patronage, as one
who had in some measure reformed, and was therefore to be
forgiven. But he never forgot or pardoned that circumstance
of the shilling; holding that if he had come back to get another
he would have done well enough, but that his returning to work
out the former gift was a stain upon his moral character which
no penitence or contrition could ever wash away.

Mr. Swiveller, having always been in some measure of a
philosophic and reflective turn, grew immensely contemplative,
at times, in the smoking-box, and was accustomed at such
periods to debate in his own mind the mysterious question of
Sophronia's parentage. Sophronia herself supposed she was an
orphan; but Mr. Swiveller, putting various slight circumstances
together, often thought Miss Brass must know better than that;
and, having heard from his wife of her strange interview with
Quilp, entertained sundry misgivings whether that person, in
his lifetime, might not also have been able to solve the riddle,
had he chosen. These speculations, however, gave him no
uneasiness; for Sophronia was ever a most cheerful, affectionate,
and provident wife to him; and Dick (excepting for an
occasional outbreak with Mr. Chuckster, which she had the
good sense rather to encourage than oppose) was to her an
attached and domesticated husband. And they played many
hundred thousand games of cribbage together. And let it be
added, to Dick's honour, that, though we have called her
Sophronia, he called her the Marchioness from first to last; and
that upon every anniversary of the day on which he found her
in his sick-room, Mr. Chuckster came to dinner, and there was
great glorification.

The gamblers, Isaac List and Jowl, with their trusty con-
federate Mr. James Groves of unimpeachable memory,

pursued their course with varying success, until the failure of a spirited enterprise in the way of their profession, dispersed them in various directions, and caused their career to receive a sudden check from the long and strong arm of the law. This defeat had its origin in the untoward detection of a new associate—young Frederick Trent—who thus became the unconscious instrument of their punishment and his own.

For the young man himself he rioted abroad for a brief term, living by his wits—which means by the abuse of every faculty that worthily employed raises man above the beasts, and so degraded, sinks him far below them. It was not long before his body was recognised by a stranger, who chanced to visit that hospital in Paris where the drowned are laid out to be owned; despite the bruises and disfigurements which were said to have been occasioned by some previous scuffle. But the stranger kept his own counsel until he returned home, and it was never claimed or cared for.

The young brother, or the single gentleman, for that designation is more familiar, would have drawn the poor schoolmaster from his lone retreat, and made him his companion and friend. But the humble village teacher was timid of venturing into the noisy world, and had become fond of his dwelling in the old churchyard. Calmly happy in his school, and in the spot, and in the attachment of Her little mourner, he pursued his quiet course in peace; and was, through the righteous gratitude of his friend—let this brief mention suffice for that—a *poor* schoolmaster no more.

That friend—single gentleman, or younger brother, which you will—had at his heart a heavy sorrow; but it bred in him no misanthropy or monastic gloom. He went forth into the world, a lover of his kind. For a long, long time, it was his chief delight to travel in the steps of the old man and the child (so far as he could trace them from her last narrative), to halt where they had halted, sympathise where they had suffered, and rejoice where they had been made glad. Those who had been kind to them, did not escape his search. The sisters at the school—they who were her friends, because themselves so friendless—Mrs. Jarley of the wax-work, Codlin, Short—he found them all; and trust me, the man who fed the furnace fire was not forgotten.

Kit's story having got abroad, raised him up a host of friends, and many offers of provision for his future life. He had no idea at first of ever quitting Mr. Garland's service; but, after serious remonstrance and advice from that gentleman, began to contemplate the possibility of such a change being brought about in time. A good post was procured for him, with a rapidity which took away his breath, by some of the gentlemen who had believed him guilty of the offence laid to his charge, and who had acted upon that belief. Through the same kind agency, his mother was secured from want, and made quite happy. Thus, as Kit often said, his great misfortune turned out to be the source of all his subsequent prosperity.

Did Kit live a single man all his days, or did he marry? Of course he married, and who should be his wife but Barbara? And the best of it was, he married so soon that little Jacob was an uncle, before the calves of his legs, already mentioned in this history, had ever been encased in broadcloth pantaloons,—though that was not quite the best either, for of necessity the baby was an uncle too. The delight of Kit's mother and of Barbara's mother upon the great occasion is past all telling; finding they agreed so well on that, and on all other subjects, they took up their abode together, and were a most harmonious pair of friends from that time forth. And hadn't Astley's cause to bless itself for their all going together once a quarter—to the pit—and didn't Kit's mother always say, when they painted the outside, that Kit's last treat had helped to that, and wonder what the manager would feel if he but knew it as they passed his house!

When Kit had children six and seven years old, there was a Barbara among them, and a pretty Barbara she was. Nor was there wanting an exact fac-simile and copy of little Jacob, as he appeared in those remote times when they taught him what oysters meant. Of course there was an Abel, own godson to the Mr. Garland of that name; and there was a Dick, whom Mr. Swiveller did especially favour. The little group would often gather round him of a night and beg him to tell again that story of good Miss Nell who died. This, Kit would do; and when they cried to hear it, wishing it longer too, he would teach them how she had gone to Heaven, as all good people did; and how, if they were good, like her, they might hope to be there too, one day, and to see and know her as he had done when he was quite a boy. Then, he would relate to them how needy he used to be, and how she had taught him what he was otherwise too poor to learn, and how the old man had been used to say 'she always laughs at Kit;' at which they would brush away their tears, and laugh themselves to think that she had done so, and be again quite merry.

He sometimes took them to the street where she had lived; but new improvements had altered it so much, it was not like the same. The old house had been long ago pulled down, and a fine broad road was in its place. At first he would draw with his stick a square upon the ground to show them where it used to stand. But, he soon became uncertain of the spot, and could only say it was thereabouts, he thought, and these alterations were confusing.

Such are the changes which a few years bring about, and so do things pass away, like a tale that is told!